The
Life
and
Major
Writings
of

THOMAS PAINE

The
Life
and
Major
Writings
of

THOMAS PAINE

Includes
Common Sense,
The American Crisis,
Rights of Man,
The Age of Reason
and
Agrarian Justice

◆———————◆

Collected,
edited
and annotated
by
PHILIP S.
FONER

A Citadel Press Book
Published by Carol Publishing Group

CONTENTS

INTRODUCTION
THOMAS PAINE—WORLD CITIZEN AND DEMOCRAT

"HIS name is Paine, a gentleman about two years from England —a man who, General Lee says, has genius in his eyes." So John Adams described the author of the widely-discussed pamphlet, *Common Sense,* published anonymously early in 1776.

Thomas Paine, the man with "genius in his eyes," was born January 29, 1737, at Thetford in Norfolk, England, of a Quaker father and an Anglican mother. His father was a poor corset-maker who could barely afford to send his son to a free school where he was taught just enough to master reading, writing and arithmetic. At thirteen young Paine began to work with his father as a staymaker; three years later he ran away from home, went to sea and served as a sailor on a privateer in the Seven Years' War. He returned to London after two eventful voyages which included a terrific sea-battle and lived by finding such occupations as he could. He worked for a while as a staymaker; then became a government worker, holding a minor job in the collection of the excise, and, after he was dismissed from this post, was employed in 1767 in a school at Kensington. A year later he was working for the government again as an excise officer at Lewes, Sussex. He had married in 1759, but the marriage was cut short by the death of his wife a year later. His second marriage in 1771 was cut short by a legal separation.

During these years Paine took steps to supplement the meagre education he had received at the Thetford Grammar School. From his pitiful earnings as a staymaker and exciseman, he purchased books and scientific apparatus such as a pair of globes. When he lived in London during the period 1757–59, he attended in his spare time the lectures on Newtonian astronomy given by Benjamin Martin, James Ferguson, and Dr. Bevis. He continued his process of self-education throughout his life, convinced that "every person of learning is finally his own teacher." "I seldom passed five minutes of my life however circumstanced," he once observed, "in which I did not acquire some knowledge." No one who traces his lifelong pursuit of education and notes the authors he cites in his writings, will lightly accept the conventional sneer that Paine displayed an "immense ignorance" throughout his career.

Both his Quaker background and his study of Newtonian science influenced his thinking along progressive lines, though neither probably had the effect that some writers have stressed.[1] Unquestionably Paine was influenced to some degree by his acquaintance with the religion of his father, for the Quakers were pioneers in many humanitarian enterprises, including anti-slavery, women's rights and prison reform. Undoubtedly, too, by revealing to Paine a harmonious and universal order guided by divinely-created law, Newtonian science greatly influenced his political and religious thinking. But life itself was an extremely important teacher. During the first thirty-seven years of his life he saw enough misery in England, enough of the contrast between the affluence of the upper classes and the poverty and suffering of the masses to influence his thinking for the remainder of his days.

In the England of his youth and manhood Paine saw the vicious effects of the enclosure system which threw thousands of small, independent farmers into the cities and transformed them from independent yeomanry to landless factory workers and agricultural laborers. All about him he saw thousands struggling in the midst of misery and degradation to eke out an existence, and daily passed "ragged and hungry children, and persons of seventy and eighty years of age, begging in the streets." He knew too from his own intolerably inadequate salary how difficult it was to secure even a subsistence living standard at a time when commodity prices were soaring and wages remained practically stationary. He also noticed the vicious operations of the poor laws which almost reduced workers to serfs, witnessed the brutality of the savage criminal code and observed how it was directed chiefly against the lower classes. Nor could he help noticing the burdens imposed upon the poor by the Anglican Church with its tithes and privileges, the role that family influence played in English politics, the

[1] Moncure Daniel Conway, Paine's indefatigable biographer, contended that the most important source for his religious and many of his political ideas was Quakerism. It is generally conceded today by Paine scholars that Conway greatly exaggerated this influence.

Professor Harry Hayden Clark, the most important student of Paine since Conway, argues that Paine's religious concepts and even many of his economic and social ideas had their source in the Newtonian concept of the universe. Although Professor Clark had made a great contribution to the study of Paine in revealing the Newtonian influence on his thought, it is the opinion of the present writer that he has erred in the same manner that Conway did by overemphasizing this influence. Certainly Professor Clark succeeds only in turning Paine upside down when he argues that his political ideas grew out of his religious ideas. See his important article, "Toward a Reinterpretation of Thomas Paine," *American Literature*, vol. V, May, 1933, pp. 133–145, and his valuable introduction to *Thomas Paine: Representative Selections*, New York, 1944.

inequalities of the rotten-borough system (in Thetford alone thirty-one persons elected two members of the House of Commons), and the corruption that characterized government administration.

These experiences left their mark upon Paine. Himself a working man, he was to use his pen, time and again, in an effort to improve the status of the laboring classes. Indeed, his earliest known prose composition and his first important pamphlet, *The Case of the Officers of Excise,* was written to achieve this purpose. In 1772 he was chosen by excisemen to address Parliament in their behalf requesting higher wages. After the pamphlet was written, Paine spent the winter of 1772–73 trying to influence members of Parliament to grant the underpaid excisemen an increase of wages. Regarded as a trouble-maker by the authorities for attempting to organize his fellow excisemen, he was dismissed from the service.

Paine lost his government job on April 8, 1774. A week later he was forced to sell his shop and possessions to escape imprisonment for debt. Having tasted the bitter dregs of British tyranny long enough, Paine decided to begin life all over again in the New World. He left England in October, 1774, and on November 30 landed in America bearing a letter of introduction from Benjamin Franklin whom he had approached in London. Franklin's letter to his son-in-law, Richard Bache, recommended Paine as "an ingenious worthy young man," who might make good in Philadelphia as "a clerk, or assistant tutor in a school, or assistant surveyor."

Arriving in America armed with Franklin's letter, Paine speedily obtained employment with Robert Aitken, a Philadelphia printer. Soon he became the editor of the *Pennsylvania Magazine* which Aitken had started with very little success to publish. On March 4, 1775, the man who had left England branded as a ne'er-do-well wrote a joyful letter to his benefactor. "Your countenancing me," he informed Franklin, "has obtained for me many friends and much reputation . . . I have been applied to by several gentlemen to instruct their sons . . . and a printer and bookseller here, a man of reputation and property, Robert Aitken, . . . has applied to me for assistance. He had not above six hundred subscribers when I first assisted him. We now have upwards of fifteen hundred and daily increasing . . ."

For eighteen months, beginning with the second number in February, 1775, Paine served as editor of the *Pennsylvania Magazine,* and during this time he published enough important articles in this and other journals to be remembered as a significant figure in American history, even if he had never written anything else. A few weeks after his arrival in America, Paine wrote an article entitled, "African Slavery in America," which ranks as the best of the early attacks upon slavery in this country. Paine put the enslavement of the Negro people on a level with "murder, robbery,. lewdness, and barbarity," and called upon Americans immediately to "discontinue and renounce it, with grief and abhorrence." When the article was printed on March 8, 1775, Paine gained a wide reputation for his liberal views, and won for himself the friendship of Dr. Benjamin Rush and other important figures in literary and philosophical circles.

The time was ripe for the activity of a lover of liberty when Paine arrived in America. The struggle between England and her colonies had been raging since 1763, and the very atmosphere breathed revolutionary slogans. In his early articles for the *Pennsylvania Magazine,* however, Paine did not deal with any of the pressing political problems confronting the colonists in their quarrel with the mother country. In part this was due to the insistence of his timid publisher, for Aitken was determined not to antagonize any wealthy subscribers who viewed the revolutionary movement with alarm. But it was also due to Paine's belief that it was still possible to reconcile the differences between England and her colonies. Soon a rush of events showed him the futility of this outlook. On April 19, 1775, the battle of Lexington and Concord was fought, an event which convinced Paine that "all plans, proposals, etc.," to settle the conflict by compromise were "like the almanacks of the last year; which though proper then, are superceded and useless now." And on June 15 Washington was appointed commander-in-chief of the Continental army. A day later the battle of Bunker Hill occurred.

Moved by these and other events of a similar nature, Paine started to use his pen to aid the revolutionary movement. On September 16, 1775, he published a poem in the *Pennsylvania Evening Post* entitled, "The Liberty Tree," the last stanza of which attacked the king as well as Parliament and issued a call

> From the East to the West blow the trumpet to arms,
>   Thro' the land let the sound of it flee:
> Let the far and the near all unite with a cheer,
>   In defense of our Liberty Tree.

But Paine was already forming the outlines of a much more important call to arms, for he discovered that poetry was not enough to convince men in high circles that it was time to open a "new system" in America. He was determined to change "the sentiments of the people from dependence to Independence and from the monarchial to the republican form of government . . ." This was no simple task to accomplish. While the mass of the artisans, mechanics and day-laborers in the urban centres and many small farmers in the rural districts were prepared for such a step, many of the members of the colonial aristocracy were by no means ready to follow Paine down the road leading to Independence and Republicanism. Independence, they feared, would bring to an end the rule of the upper classes in America, and Republicanism signified nothing less than anarchy and mob-rule. Better to tolerate the tyranny of the British government, they reasoned, than to chance the dangers of a democratic upheaval in America.

Paine moved quickly to meet and overcome these fears and hesitations. In a short article, "A Serious Thought," published in the *Pennsylvania Journal* on October 18, 1775, he sharply projected the idea of independence. Discussing the barbaric conduct of the British in India and criticizing England for her treatment of the Indians in America and for having "employed herself in the most horrid of all traffics, that of human flesh . . . [and] ravaged the hapless shore of Africa, robbing it of its unoffending inhabitants to cultivate her stolen dominions in the West," he went on to say: "When I reflect on these, I hesitate not for a moment to believe that the Almighty will finally separate America from Britain. Call it Independence or what you will, if it is the cause of God and humanity it will go on."

In December, 1775, Paine showed the manuscript of a pamphlet he had finished to David Rittenhouse and Dr. Benjamin Rush, and the latter, according to his own account, suggested to him the title for the work and found a publisher, Robert Bell, with sufficient courage to print it. The work came off the press on January 10, 1776. It was entitled *Common Sense*.

Paine was not the first person to advocate independence in America; John Adams had done so, for example, even before *Common Sense* was published. Nevertheless, the influence and power of this fifty-page pamphlet can hardly be exaggerated. "With the publication of *Common Sense* in January 1776," writes John C. Miller in his *Origins of the American Revolution* (p. 468), "Tom Paine broke the ice that was slowly congealing the revolutionary movement." And Evarts B. Greene, the distinguished historian of the Revolutionary era, observes in his recently-published study, *The Revolutionary Generation* (p. 209), "Thomas Paine's *Common Sense,* more than any other single piece of writing, set Americans to thinking of the possibility and desirability of an independent place among the nations."

Written in simple, plain, and direct language easily read and understood by all, *Common Sense* became overnight a best-seller; shortly after its publication almost a half a million copies were sold, and many of its most trenchant paragraphs were reprinted in newspapers all over the country. Soon the common people were quoting sections from the booklet which hammered home the need for separation, held up hereditary monarchy to contempt, denounced the British ruling classes for exploiting the lower classes in America and in England, and urged the colonies to declare themselves free and independent states so that they might establish in America a haven of refuge for the oppressed peoples of Europe. More cautious and conservative Americans quoted other sections, particularly the arguments Paine advanced in support of a declaration of independence: the prospect that by independence America could remain aloof from the European conflicts into which she was constantly being drawn by her connection with the British Empire; the possibilities of enormous markets in all of Europe for merchants and farmers once the restrictions imposed by the British on American economic life were broken, and the great certainty of obtaining foreign aid in the war for independence.[2] Shortly after reading the booklet many upper class Americans who had hesitated to support independence for fear of meeting the power of the British singlehanded and did not yet clearly see the advantages of separation, declared with Washington that they were ready "to shake off all connections with a state so unjust and unnatural."

Terrified by the influence of Paine's booklet, the Tories sought frantically to nullify its effects upon the people. Several answers to Paine's

[2] Paine argued that France would aid America if she declared herself independent. *Common Sense* was itself an important factor in helping mobilize French support for the American cause. It was translated promptly into French, with the expurgation of anti-monarchist passages, and published in Paris on May 4, 1776. Silas Deane, American Commissioner to France, wrote home on August 18, 1776, that the booklet "has a greater run, if possible here than in America." Professor Aulard, historian of the French Revolution, has observed that "the bold phrases of Thomas Paine's republican pamphlet, *Common Sense,* resounded throughout France." See "The Deane Papers . . . ," *New York Historical Society Collections,* vol. I, p. 214, and A. Aulard, *The French Revolution: A Political History,* London, 1910, vol. I, p. 112.

"artful, insidious, and pernicious" work were published, the most important attack consisting of a series of letters signed "Cato," which were first printed in the *Philadelphia Gazette* beginning in April, 1776. Paine immediately wrote four letters in reply, known as *The Forester's Letters,* in which he expanded and amplified many of the arguments he had first advanced in favor of independence in *Common Sense.* Widely reprinted in contemporary newspapers, these articles strengthened the popular demand for immediate independence. This demand in turn influenced the appointment on June 28 by the Continental Congress of a committee of five to draft a declaration of independence.

Although primarily absorbed during these exciting months with the battle against tyranny abroad, Paine did not entirely ignore the struggle for democracy in America. Together with Benjamin Franklin and other progressive leaders in Pennsylvania, he assisted in mobilizing the popular forces for the enactment of a liberal state constitution. Supported by the Philadelphia artisans and the western farmers, these men gradually swept away all vestiges of aristocratic rule in the state. Drawn up by Paine and Franklin, the Pennsylvania constitution, adopted late in 1776, provided for universal suffrage, democratic representation, complete religious freedom, and a unicameral legislature, elected annually. It was by far the most advanced state constitution adopted during the American Revolution, and Paine took pride in his part in shaping the document, although he later questioned the wisdom of a unicameral legislature.[3]

But Paine was doing more than writing Constitutions. In August, 1776, he joined the Pennsylvania Associators as voluntary secretary to General Roberdeau and, on September 19 was appointed aide-de-camp to General Greene who was at Fort Lee in New Jersey. By this time Washington's army, badly defeated in the battle of Long Island, was retreating toward New Jersey and, in November and December streamed across the state in disorderly fashion toward Philadelphia. It was a dark hour for the American cause. Morale in the army and on the home front was at its lowest ebb; a feeling prevailed that the enemy was invincible and that the war might as well end now. Naturally, the Tory speakers and newspapers emphasized that there was no hope for America other than in capitulation, and the flight of Congress from Philadelphia to Baltimore made these arguments seem plausible.

[3] For an excellent analysis of the Pennsylvania Constitution, see J. Paul Selsam, *The Pennsylvania Constitution of 1776,* Philadelphia, 1936.

Seated by a campfire near Newark, New Jersey, Paine started work on an appeal to the people in this hour of crisis. When he was finished, he rushed to Philadelphia and published in the *Pennsylvania Journal* of December 19, 1776, his *Crisis I,* and almost immediately it was issued in three pamphlet editions. His opening words in these days of adversity, "These are the times that try men's souls," rang out like a bugle and heartened the little band of patriots left with Washington. The soldiers who heard the words of Paine's great document—Washington ordered it read to his men—were inspired to face the floes, a blizzard and the swift current of the Delaware River on Christmas Eve and achieve the victory at Trenton which gave the Americans new courage.

Between 1776 and 1783 Paine published thirteen numbered essays and three extra numbers of *The Crisis* papers, each one signed "Common Sense." All were perfectly timed and perfectly adapted to the needs of the time. Did Lord Howe issue a proclamation urging Americans to negotiate a peace? Paine immediately answered him, exposed his proposal and attacked his Tory sympathizers in America. Did the Conway Cabal seek to oust Washington? Paine rushed to press to counteract this conspiracy. Did England send over a Commission for the purpose of winning the Americans away from the French? Paine issued a *Crisis* pamphlet which thoroughly ridiculed the negotiated peace overtures and was influential in compelling the Commission to return to England empty-handed. Was there a danger that the war would be lost because of financial difficulties? Paine published his *Crisis Extraordinary* to prove that it would cost more to submit than to support the war financially. "Can it then be a question," he concluded after estimating the costs of defending the country and governing it after the war as two and three-quarters millions sterling, "whether it is better to raise two millions to defend the country, and govern it ourselves, and only three quarters of a million afterwards, or pay six millions to have it conquered and let the enemy govern it?" Finally, did it appear that the American victory would be rendered valueless by the absence of a strong union? Paine reminded the people that they could not help but "be strongly impressed with the advantage, as well as the necessity of strengthening that happy union which has been our salvation."

Reprinted in most of the northern papers and in some of those in the South, the *Crisis* enormously aided the American cause and contributed to no small extent to ultimate victory. George Washington, Robert Morris, and Robert R. Livingston wrote early in 1782 that Paine had been "of considerable utility to the common cause by several of his Publications," and secured from Congress a salary of $800 a year to enable him to continue to use his "abilities" in "informing the People and rousing them into action."

In addition to "informing the people and rousing them into action," Paine held various posts in the national and state governments during the war. In 1777 Congress appointed him secretary to the Committee on Foreign Affairs, in which capacity he did much to obtain supplies, a large loan and military assistance from France. The fact that his services were appreciated moved him deeply. In a letter recently discovered, he wrote Franklin in Paris, on October 24, 1778: "I have the pleasure of being respected and I feel a little of that satisfactory kind of pride that tells me I have some right to it." [4]

A month after this letter was written Paine became involved in a controversy with Silas Deane that abruptly brought his pleasure to an end, caused a torrent of abuse and defamation to be heaped on his head, and ultimately cost him his job as secretary to the Committee on Foreign Affairs.

The crux of the debate between Paine and Silas Deane centred on the question whether the supplies furnished the United States by France before the Franco-American alliance of 1778, through Caron de Beaumarchais, adventurer and playwright, were a gift from the king of France or comprised a loan to the United States. Deane, attempting to profit personally from French aid to the United States and, as it was established later, had conspired with the British (for a considerable sum) against the American Revolution, maintained that the transactions were of a purely commercial nature and demanded payment of a five percent commission on purchases made for the American government. Paine supporting the position of Arthur Lee, also American Commissioner to France, charged that Deane was simply conspiring to defraud Congress of money. On December 14, 1778, in a letter *To Silas Deane, Esq're,* in the *Pennsylvania Packet,* Paine launched his public attack upon Deane. Answers from Deane's supporters followed, and Paine was compelled to continue the controversy. As he did so, however, he was also forced, to prove his contentions, to quote from secret documents to which he had access as secretary of the Committee on Foreign Affairs. Soon afterwards he had to resign his post owing to the opposi-

[4] Dixon Wecter, "Thomas Paine and the Franklins," *American Literature,* vol. XII, November, 1940, p. 313.

tion of those in Congress, who feared that his revelations jeopardized the alliance with France, as well as of those who considered Paine entirely too radical and believed he should never have been appointed in the first place. Gouverneur Morris, archconservative, told Congress that it was unseemly that the office of Secretary of Foreign Affairs should be held by "a mere adventurer *from England,* without fortune, without family or connexions, ignorant even of grammar."

Paine's resignation did not end the controversy over Silas Deane. For many months articles on the subject appeared daily in the Philadelphia press. Most of them were printed over pseudonyms, but it is known that Paine, Arthur Lee, Richard Henry Lee, and Timothy Matlock penned those denouncing Deane, while Deane, Robert Morris, Matthew Clarkson, William Duer, and Gouverneur Morris spoke for the opposition. As the war of words continued other issues emerged, though in many ways they were related to the general question at issue. Paine had entered the controversy over Deane not merely because he wished to save Congress money, but also because he felt that the type of profiteering disclosed by Deane's conduct was too general in the country and endangered the revolutionary cause. He developed this theme in articles to the press after his resignation, pointing particularly to Robert Morris whose firm held important public contracts while he was conducting congressional business, and who was associated with Silas Deane in personal as well as governmental transactions.[5] Paine publicly attacked Morris for his business associations with Deane, suggested that the State legislatures investigate such activities by all former and present delegates to Congress, and expressed the hope that the Pennsylvania legislature would take the lead.

It is clear, therefore, that what started out as a debate over the role of an American Commissioner to France had become a struggle between radicals and conservatives in Pennsylvania. Here the wealthy merchants and professional aristocrats had been organizing since early in 1777 to overthrow the democratic State Constitution which committed the cardinal sin of allowing the common people according to their number a voice in their government. But the friends of the Constitution—mechanics and small farmers—also were organized to defend their charter

---

[5] On one occasion Morris wrote to Deane, then in France: "It seems to me that the present oppert'y of improving our fortunes ought not to be lost, especially as the very means of doing it will contribute to the service of our country at the same time." See Thomas P. Abernathy, "Commercial Activities of Silas Deane in France," *American Historical Review,* vol. XXXIX, pp. 477–485.

of liberty. Paine, spokesman for the city artisans and mechanics, took his stand with the friends of the constitution he had helped to write. In articles to the press he defended the document and attacked those who sought to deprive the people of their democratic rights.[6]

Paine also spoke for the people, especially the artisans, in his articles denouncing monopolizing practices which caused the cost of living to soar and were responsible for reducing the morale of workers who found it difficult to secure wage-increases. He was present at a mass meeting held on the 27th of May in the State House yard where a series of resolutions were adopted denouncing combinations "for raising the prices of goods and provisions." He also served on a Committee of Inspection before which leading merchants suspected of unscrupulous business methods were forced to appear.

In the State elections which took place on October 12, 1779, the Constitutionalists won a resounding victory and, as a reward for his part in arousing popular support for the Constitution, the new Assembly elected Paine its Clerk. Actually, his position was more important than the name implies, for he was the close friend and advisor of Assembly leaders and influenced important legislation.

In his new position Paine soon had an opportunity to see one of his dreams realized. Late in 1775, in his short article entitled "A Serious Thought," he had looked forward to the day when God "shall have blest us, and made us a people *dependent only upon Him,* then may our gratitude be shown by an act of continental legislation, which shall put a stop to the importation of Negroes for sale, soften the hard fate of those already here, and in time procure their freedom." Five years later, as Clerk of the Pennsylvania Assembly, Paine wrote the "Preamble to the Act Passed by the Pennsylvania Assembly March 1, 1780," which provided for the gradual emancipation of Negro slaves in the state. It was the first legislative measure passed in America for the emancipation of slaves.

While serving as Clerk, Paine was called upon to read to the Assembly Washington's appeal, dated May 28, 1780, for assistance to pay, feed and clothe his troops. "I assure you," Washington wrote in this letter, "every idea you can form of our distresses will fall short of the reality. There is such a combination of circumstances to exhaust the patience

[6] All of Paine's letters and articles on the Deane controversy appear in the second volume of the present edition of his writings. For excellent background material see Robert L. Brunhouse, *The Counter-Revolution in Pennsylvania,* Philadelphia, 1942.

of the soldiery that it begins at length to be worn out, and we see in every line of the army the most serious features of mutiny and sedition." Paine did not forget this appeal after he finished reading. Leaving the assembly hall he drew out one thousand dollars due him on salary, sent five hundred dollars to Blair McClenaghan, a prominent merchant, and included a plea for the men of wealth to rally to aid the cause. "I feel the utmost concern," Paine wrote, "that the fairest cause that men ever engaged in, and with the fairest prospect of success should now be sunk so low, and that not from any new ability in the enemy but from a wilful neglect and decay of every species of public spirit in ourselves." He went on to point out that much financial assistance could not be expected from the artisans and small farmers, since it was "now hard time with many poor people." It remained, therefore, for the wealthy to fill the gap, which they should rush to do for "as it is the rich that will suffer most by the ravages of an Enemy it is not only duty but true policy to do something spirited." He hoped his five hundred dollars— "and if that is not sufficient I will add 500 more"—would inaugurate a movement to rescue the cause in this dark hour. He was willing to bury all past political differences and cooperate with any patriotic society "no matter who may complete it." [7] Acting upon Paine's suggestion, several wealthy merchants and bankers in Philadelphia, with Robert Morris at their head, started the Bank of Pennsylvania to supply the army with provisions.

Undoubtedly Paine's action in this crisis marked a change in his attitude toward men like Morris whom he had publicly denounced only a few months before. It does not, however, mark, as some writers have asserted, the beginning of a conservative trend in Paine's thinking. The simple fact is that the author of *Common Sense* had enough common sense to realize that the American Revolution could not be successful unless all classes willing to support the war were united, and he did not exclude men of wealth from this unity. Paine fully appreciated what Washington had meant when he wrote that everything had to give way to the primary task of winning the war—factional disputes, class antagonisms, even personal quarrels. "The present situation of our public affairs," the commander-in-chief once observed, "affords abundant causes of distress, we should be very careful how we aggravate or multiply them, by private bickerings. . . . All little differences and animosities, calculated to increase the unavoidable evils of the times, should be for-

[7] Thomas Paine *Mss.*, New York Historical Society.

gotten, or at least postponed." [8] Paine was not merely willing to forget or postpone but even to cooperate with his former enemies to rescue "the fairest cause that Men ever engaged in."

National unity meant unity among the states as well as among different classes. Paine, therefore, turned his attention late in 1780 to the problem of eliminating state antagonisms and rivalries in the hope that he could convince them to cooperate for the well-being of the entire nation. The immediate issue that aroused his attention was the delay in the ratification of the Articles of Confederation because of a conflict over claims to land in the west. Congress had adopted the Articles on November 17, 1777, and submitted them to the several states for ratification. Maryland, having definite western limits, refused to ratify the new frame of government until Virginia ceded her claims to western land to the national government.

Paine's pamphlet, *Public Good,* published in Philadelphia on December 30, 1780, demolished Virginia's claims to land in the west, contended that the land should belong not to the individual states but to the United States because they had been secured by the united effort of all the states during the war, and concluded by calling for a stronger central government. He urged the convening of "a continental convention, for the purpose of forming a continental constitution, defining and describing the powers and authority of Congress."

Two years later, in 1782–83, Paine spoke out again for a stronger central government and once again emphasized the need to adhere to "the principle of union," which he correctly regarded as "our magna charta—our anchor in the world of empires." In an effort to obtain a revenue to carry on the war Congress proposed a five-per-cent duty on imported articles, the money to be used to pay the interest on loans to be made in Holland. Unanimous consent of the states was necessary to grant Congress the power to levy this duty, and, when Rhode Island refused her assent an *impasse* was created. In this situation Paine once again demonstrated his grasp of the needs of the time by publishing a series of letters addressed to the people of Rhode Island urging them to consent to the five-per-cent impost plan. Signing himself "A Friend to Rhode Island and the Union," he reminded his readers that all the embarrassments faced by the new Republic "are ascribable to the loose and almost disjointed condition of the Union. . . ." We need "to talk

[8] Philip S. Foner, editor, *George Washington: Selections from His Writings,* New York, 1944, pp. 22–23.

less about our independence," he argued, "and more about our union." Independence without a strong union would be meaningless, for "the union of America is the foundation-stone of her independence; the rock on which it is built." It was "the great Palladium of our liberty and safety." [9]

To bring this message to the people of Rhode Island, Paine even went to the trouble to visit the state at his own expense. He made the trip in the dead of winter on a horse he borrowed from a friend in New Jersey. Unfortunately neither his presence nor his letters to the *Providence Gazette* produced any effect and he was forced to leave the state without accomplishing anything.

It is clear that Paine was among the first to point out, even before the American Revolution was over, the need for a stronger central government to replace the weak Articles of Confederation. Little wonder, therefore, that in later years he was enraged to discover the Federalists claiming for themselves the sole distinction of having favored a stronger central government to take the place of the Articles of Confederation. He observed in 1802 that if "by *Federalist* is to be understood one who was for cementing the Union by a general government operating equally over all the States, in all matters that embraced the common interest, . . . *I ought to stand first on the list of Federalist.*" For had he not as early as 1780 and 1782 recognized that "the continental belt was too loosely buckled"?

At the end of the Revolution Paine found himself poverty-stricken. In a moving memorial to Congress, endorsed by Washington, he set forth his services to America and begged for financial assistance. His revolutionary writings had circulated widely, but he had not profited from their sale. Indeed, he had contributed from his own pocket to make them available to as wide a reading public as possible. Referring to the phenomenal distribution of *Common Sense,* Paine wrote in his memorial:

> "As my wish was to serve an oppressed people, and assist in a just and good cause, I conceived that the honor of it would be promoted by my declining to make even the usual profits of an author, by the publication, and therefore I gave up the profits of the first edition into the hands of Col. Joseph Deane and Mr.

[9] Paine's letters to the people of Rhode Island appear in the second volume of the present edition of his writings. See also Harry Hayden Clark, editor, *Six New Letters of Thomas Paine,* Madison, Wisconsin, 1939.

Thomas Pryor both of the city of Philadelphia to be disposed of by them in any public service or private charity. After this I printed six thousand at my own expense and directed Mr. Bradford to sell them at the price of the printing and paper. It may, perhaps, be said, that as I had made a dangerous step, it was my interest to make it as little so as possible by promoting by every means, the success of the principle on which my own safety rested, but this would be an uncandid way of accounting for public spirit and conduct." [10]

Yet for all his public spirit and conduct he faced a desperate future. "I cannot help viewing my situation as singularly inconvenient," he frankly informed Congress. "Trade I do not understand. Land I have none, or what is equal to none. I have exiled myself from one country without making a home of another; and I cannot help sometimes asking myself, what am I better off than a refugee, and that of the most extraordinary kind, a refugee from the country I have obliged and served, to that which can owe me no good will."

Paine's enemies in Congress were still too powerful and the memorial was buried. Fortunately, two states came to his aid. Pennsylvania gave him £500 in cash, and New York presented him with a confiscated Loyalist farm at New Rochelle, the last grant being recommended because "his literary works, and those especially under the signature of Common Sense, and the Crisis, inspired the citizens of this state with unanimity, confirmed their confidence in the rectitude of their cause, and have ultimately contributed to the freedom, sovereignty, and independence of the United States." He remained on his farm and in the village of Bordentown, New Jersey until 1787, devoting most of his time to inventions such as an iron bridge without piers, and a smokeless candle. These were years when he could truly say, "the natural bent of my mind was to science."

Yet he could not remain entirely aloof from the political scene. Independence did not overnight usher in the era of national prosperity Paine had predicted in *Common Sense*. A few men, to be sure, made money through speculation and investments, but the mass of the small farmers and city mechanics found it difficult to make ends meet. The dumping of British goods on the American market caused a serious

[10] "A Representation of the Services of Thomas Paine, 1783," *Mss.*, New York Historical Society. The entire memorial appears in the second volume of the present edition of Paine's writings.

amount of unemployment in urban areas. In the rural districts the farmers faced foreclosures and imprisonment for debt.

In every state the small farmers organized a campaign to obtain paper money and stay laws. Pennsylvania was no exception. Here, however, the battle for paper money legislation merged into a movement to revoke the charter of the Bank of North America which had grown out of the Bank of Pennsylvania founded by Paine, Robert Morris and a group of merchants in 1780. The back-country farmers feared that it would be valueless to obtain paper money legislation if the bank was still in existence, for if the institution refused to accept paper money on the same terms as specie, the public would have no faith in the bills. Accordingly, a bill to repeal the bank's charter was introduced in the Pennsylvania legislature and by April 4, 1786, passed its second reading.

The pro-bank forces now rallied to defeat the repeal bill. James Wilson wrote a pamphlet supporting the bank, but the material was so heavy and couched in such complicated legal terminology that it had little popular appeal. This was the situation when Paine's *Dissertations on Government, The Affairs of the Bank, and Paper Money* came off the press in February, 1786.

Paine was reluctant to enter the controversy over the bank. "It was my intention," he wrote to his "Old Friend," Daniel Clymer, in September, 1786, "at the conclusion of the war to have laid down the pen and satisfied myself with silently beholding the prosperity of my country, in whose difficulties I had done my share, and in the raising of which, to an independent Empire, I had added my mite . . ." [11]

Paine did not join in the popular agitation conducted by the back-country farmers in favor of paper money legislation and in opposition to the bank, because he believed that these measures were unwise and harmful to the general well-being of the country. He felt that the bank was essential for commercial development in Pennsylvania and that its services were indispensable for the growth of the state. To destroy a financial institution did not seem to him to be either progressive or necessary. "The whole community," he wrote in his *Dissertations,* "derives benefit from the operation of the bank . . ." As for paper money, it was nothing more than an unjust balm for those debtors who were determined to steal by depreciation "the widow's dowry and children's portion." In any event, neither a legislature nor the people had the right

[11] Paine to Daniel Clymer, September, 1786, Paine *Mss.,* Historical Society of Pennsylvania.

to revoke certain kinds of economic contracts agreed to by a preceding legislature and another party. This, however, did not mean that a contract could last forever. A legislature could not grant a contract forever, for the simple reason that the present generation could no more bind its children to economic contracts than it could set up a government for posterity.

Paine knew that by joining the pro-bank forces he would invite the charge that he had sold out the people. Such charges were made. A representative from the West referred to him as "an unprincipled author, who let his pen out for hire," and a writer who called himself "Atticus" attacked him as a turn-coat, adding: "I cannot conceive in the wide extent of creation, a being more deserving of our abhorrence and contempt, than a writer, who having formerly vindicated the principles of freedom, abandons them to abet the cause of a faction, who exerts the little talent which Heaven has alloted him, . . . to vilify measures which it is his duty to respect, and . . . [devotes] his pen to the ruin of his country."

These attacks did not halt Paine in his determination to fight the battle to the bitter end, and his will was strengthened by the realization that if the farmers had turned against him the city mechanics and artisans as well as merchants and bankers supported him. The urban workers also opposed paper money legislation fearing the effects of inflation on their living standards and favored the continued existence of the bank as essential for business expansion which meant employment opportunities. In a series of letters to the Philadelphia papers Paine attacked the repeal of the bank's charter and called for its restoration.[12]

[12] Paine's letters to the press during the controversy over the bank appear in the second volume of the present edition of his writings. For an interesting discussion of the conflict in Pennsylvania over the bank, see Janet Wilson, "The Bank of North America and Pennsylvania Politics, 1781–1787," *Pennsylvania Magazine of History and Biography,* vol. LXVI, January, 1942, pp. 3–28.

Paine's role in supporting the bank and in calling for a stronger Union has been cited by several recent students as proof of his conservatism before he left America in 1787, and it is argued that during this period he tended to align himself with men like Hamilton, John Adams, Robert Morris and others who were known as conservatives (see Harry Hayden Clark's introduction to *Six New Letters of Thomas Paine* and J. Dorfman, "The Economic Philosophy of Thomas Paine," *Political Science Quarterly,* vol. LIII, September, 1938, pp. 372–386). Neither of these writers take into account the fact that Paine's views were supported by the urban artisans for whom he was a spokesman. Moreover, to argue that Paine's economic objectives were much the same as Hamilton's is entirely to ignore the fact that Paine, even in the bank controversy, wanted property to serve the welfare of all classes in society, while Hamilton always spoke out for protection only for the

In the fall elections of 1786 Paine's position was upheld by a majority of the voters. A few months later the bank's charter was restored.

In April, 1787, Paine left for Europe to promote his plan to build a single-arch bridge across the Schuylkill river in Philadelphia. He expected to remain abroad no more than a year and to spend most of his time in France where engineering was best understood. He met Jefferson in France, was hailed as a friend of Franklin and a distinguished writer and became acquainted with leading scientists and political liberals. The Academy of Science appointed a committee to study the plans for his bridge and, after an investigation this body reported that "Mr. Paine's Plan of an Iron Bridge is ingeniously imagined, that the construction of it is simple, solid, and proper to give it the necessary strength for resisting the effects resulting from its burden, and that it is deserving of a trial . . ." The report was presented on August 29th. The next day Paine left for England.

In the land of his birth Paine visited his aged mother at Thetford, met and was enthusiastically received by Charles Fox, Lord Landsdowne, Lord Shelburne and Edmund Burke, and began to make plans for the construction of his bridge. But soon he was thinking less and less about his bridge and more and more about the exciting events in France.[13] Science, after all, could not flourish without democracy.

The news of the French Revolution filled Paine with joy. But he was not surprised. He had never regarded the American Revolution as a local affair, "but universal, and through which the principles of all

"rich and well-born." See the excellent refutation of J. Dorfman's contention by Howard Penniman in the *American Political Science Review*, vol. XXXVII, April, 1943, pp. 244–262.

Although Paine and Hamilton both supported a stronger central government at this time, it must be remembered that the former, like Jefferson, did so because he believed that it was necessary to preserve Republicanism in America. He certainly would never have favored the type of central government proposed by Hamilton in the Federal Convention. Evidently the Hamiltonians thought so too, for they were not anxious to have Paine attend the Convention. Unlike some present-day writers they did not regard him as a conservative.

[13] Paine's bridge was eventually constructed in England, but he himself received no credit for it and made no profits. When Sir Robert Smyth, Paine's friend, attempted to secure some reward for the original inventor, he received a letter from a subscriber to the construction company admitting that "the first idea was taken from Mr. Paine's bridge exhibited at Paddington." Nothing, however, could be done to compensate Mr. Paine. Thomas Paine to Thomas Jefferson, October 1, 1800, Jefferson Papers, Library of Congress.

lovers of mankind are affected." In his celebrated *Letter to the Abbé Raynal*, published in 1782, Paine had predicted that the American Revolution would influence England and France until "every corner of the mind is swept of its cobwebs, poison and dust, and made fit for the reception of generous happiness."

Paine spent four months in France at the invitation of Lafayette and Condorcet. He gave advice on the formation of a constitution, aided in drawing up the Declaration of the Rights of Man and of the Citizen, and witnessed the uprisings to overthrow despotism and feudal privileges. His heart "leaped with joy" when he received from Lafayette the key of the Bastille for presentation to Washington. "That the principles of America opened the Bastille," he wrote in his letter forwarding the key, "is not to be doubted, and therefore the Key comes to the right place."

Even when he returned to England, Paine's mind was still riveted on events across the channel. He continued to send Lafayette suggestions to be incorporated in the new government, and reported on reactions in England to developments in France. "Here is a courtly and an aristocratical hatred against the principles of the French Revolution . . . ," he wrote to William Short, American representative in France, from London early in June, 1790.[14]

In the fall of 1790 Paine returned to Paris where he mingled again with Brissot, Condorcet, Lafayette and other leaders of the Revolution. A business crisis sent him back again to England. In November he began work on his greatest pamphlet, *The Rights of Man,* in answer to Edmund Burke's *Reflections on the French Revolution* which appeared on November 1, 1790.

Burke's speech "On Reconciliation with America" in 1775 had aroused Paine's admiration for the man who was considered America's greatest English friend. His personal contacts with Burke in England after the American Revolution increased this feeling, and he considered him "a friend to mankind." But he was both terribly shocked and speedily disillusioned after he read Burke's vicious denunciation of the French Revolution in his parliamentary speech on February 9, 1790. Soon after this Paine saw an advertisement of the forthcoming publication of

---

[14] Paine to William Short June 1, 1790, Short Papers, Library of Congress. See also Harold W. Landin, editor, "Some Letters of Thomas Paine and William Short on the Nootka Sound Crisis," *Journal of Modern History,* vol. XIII, September, 1941, pp. 357–374.

Burke's pamphlet, and promised his friends in France that whenever it appeared he would answer it.[15]

Paine finished the pamphlet in February, 1791, and turned it over to a friend, Johnson, to have it published. After a few copies were issued, this publisher became frightened. Paine then gave the pamphlet to a committee consisting of William Godwin, Thomas Holcroft, and Thomas Hollis, and left for France. From Paris he forwarded a preface for the English edition, and the work appeared on March 13, 1791. The pamphlet sold for three shillings, the same price as Burke's *Reflections,* and it was believed in Tory circles that this expensive format would give it a limited circulation.

The pamphlet immediately gained a wide circulation. Within a few weeks the book sold fifty thousand copies, and on April 5th, Sir Samuel Romilly wrote to a friend in France that "in the course of a fortnight it has gone through three editions; and, what I own has a good deal surprised me, has made converts of many persons who were before enemies to the revolution." The Society for Constitutional Information and other popular societies in England, to whose support Paine gave the large income from the sale, distributed the book all over the British Isles. Soon Englishmen were quoting passages from the *Rights of Man* with as much fervor as Americans had once recited sections from *Common Sense.* Workers, small farmers and liberal members of the middle and upper class used Paine's words to deny Burke's contention of the right of the Parliament of 1688 to bind posterity forever to their settlement, to defend the French Revolution, and many even quoted him to urge Englishmen to follow the example set by their brothers across the channel.

While popular societies in England sang Paine's praises, toasted his name and adopted resolutions thanking him for his "most masterly book," the author himself was busy in France fighting for Republicanism. Louis XVI had been intercepted in his flight to join the royalist émigrés and had been brought back to Paris. On July 1, 1791, Paine and Achille Duchâtelet placarded the streets of Paris with a manifesto

---

[15] Burke's impassioned *Reflections on the French Revolution* also called forth replies from writers like Mary Wollstonecraft, James Mackintosh, Joel Barlow and William Godwin. All of them like Paine argued that governmental institutions were not sacred and unalterable. For a discussion of these booklets, see Walter P. Hall, *British Radicalism, 1791–97,* New York, 1912 and C. H. Lockett, *The Relations of French and English Society, 1763–1793,* London, 1920. See also Frederick Sheldon, "Thomas Paine in England and France," *Atlantic Monthly,* vol. IV, December, 1859, pp. 690–709.

which denounced the king and monarchy and boldly proclaimed that the time had come to establish a republic. A few days later Paine published in *Lé Republicain,* which he and Condorcet had founded, an attack on the monarchy. He elaborated his attack on the monarchy in a public letter to the Abbé Sieyès, who had replied to Paine's article and had advocated the retention of the king.

Paine returned to England on July 13, 1791. A month later he issued his *Address and Declaration of the Friends of Universal Peace and Liberty* in which he again defended the French Revolution. "We have nothing to apprehend from the poor; for we are pleading their cause," he wrote. "And we fear not proud oppression, for we have truth on our side. We say, and we repeat it, that the French Revolution opens to the world an opportunity in which all good citizens must rejoice—that of promoting the general happiness of man."

After the appearance of Burke's reply to the first part of *Rights of Man,* entitled *An Appeal from the New to the Old Whigs,* Paine started work on Part II of his great book. It was more of an exposition of Paine's principles of government and society than a reply to Burke and, as Vernon L. Parrington has pointed out, was "the maturest elaboration of Paine's political philosophy. . . ." In this work Paine analyzed the basic reasons for discontent in contemporary society and offered his remedy for the misery he saw all about him.

"When in countries that we call civilized," he writes, "we see age going to the workhouse and youth to the gallows, something must be wrong in the system of government." "Why is it," he asks, "that scarcely any are executed but the poor"? Poverty and an evil environment— "lack of education for the young and a decent livelihood for the old" —were the reasons for this unfortunate state of affairs, and these conditions prevailed because the government failed to provide for the happiness of the people. In England, of course, one could not expect the government to act otherwise, for it consisted only of representatives of special privileges and special interests. "No better reason can be given," he declares, "why the house of legislature should be composed entirely of men whose occupations is in letting landed property than why it should be composed of those who hire, or brewers, or bakers, or of any other separate class of men."

Paine did not confine himself to advocating a reform in the composition of the government. He outlined a plan for popular education, for the relief of the poor, for pensions for aged people, for donations, or premiums, to be given for births and marriages, together with an allowance for funeral expenses of people dying out of work and away from their friends, and for State employment and lodging-houses to aid unemployed workingmen.

To raise a revenue for the operation of his plan, Paine proposed the levying of a progressive income tax. Not only would this secure the funds necessary for the proper functioning of the government, but it would bring about the abolition of primogeniture which was both "unnatural and unjust" and a great waste of the national wealth.

In Part II of the *Rights of Man* Paine also outlined his suggestions for peaceful and harmonious relations among nations to render wars unnecessary. He advocated the signing of a treaty between England, France, the United States and Holland under which no new ships were to be built by any of the signers, while their existing naval establishments were to be reduced one-half of their existing strength. "If men will permit themselves," he wrote, "to think as rational beings ought to think, nothing can appear more ridiculous and absurd . . . than to be at the expense of building navies, filling them with men, and then hauling them out into the ocean to see which can sink each other the fastest." Thus though not the first Paine was one of the earliest advocates of an international association of nations to outlaw war.[16] He was also one of the first to prophesy, as he does in Part II of *Rights of Man,* "the independence of South America, and the opening of those countries of immense extent and wealth to the general commerce of the world."

Part Two had a phenomenal circulation. Thirty thousand copies were distributed by the political clubs at their own expense among the poor. Although living in poverty Paine turned over to the London Constitutional Society the thousand pounds which he had received from royalties, enabling it to distribute the book even more widely. Not only did he arrange for the printing of a cheap edition because the original cost too much, thereby preventing it from reaching the common people, but he even gave up the copyright to the public. At least one hundred thousand copies of the cheap edition were sold in England, Ireland and Scotland.

[16] Paine first presented his views on the value of an international association of nations to preserve peace in his *Letter to the Abbé Raynal.* This work may be said to mark an important transition in Paine's thinking in the sense that after it he began to think more and more in internationalist terms. See Darrel Abel, "The Significance of the 'Letter to the Abbé Raynal' in the Progress of Thomas Paine's Thought," *Pennsylvania Magazine of History and Biography,* vol. LXVI, April, 1942, pp. 176–190.

The influence of *Rights of Man* was by no means confined to England. In America, for example, it became the book of the hour, greatly influenced the rise of the Democratic-Republican Societies, and in turn was scattered broadcast throughout the country by these popular clubs.[17] Thomas Jefferson welcomed the book as an antidote to the "political heresies" of the reactionary Federalists and, when attacked for upholding Paine's principles, wrote that he merited the same censure visited upon the author of *Rights of Man*, "for I profess the same principles." Philip Freneau, editor and poet of the Jeffersonian movement, ran excerpts from Paine's work in his *National Gazette*, and proudly announced on May 31, 1792, as his reason that "there is no American newspaper but might, with credit to itself, now and then occupy part of a column with extracts from a work that so forcibly inculcates the genuine principles of natural and equal liberty." Freneau even wrote a poem entitled "Lines Occasioned by Reading Mr. Paine's Rights of Man," in which he assured the author that America would "Remain the guardian of the Rights of Man."

In the meantime in England a storm was breaking over Paine's head. As Paine himself pointed out later, the first part of *Rights of Man* was met by the government with "profound silence," because they "beheld it as an unexpected gale that would soon blow over." When the Second Part appeared, they tried at first to follow the same course, but their silence had no "influence in stifling the progress of the work." As long, however, that it was published in an expensive edition they were not too worried. But when it began to be distributed in cheap editions at cost, the attitude changed. From "that moment," wrote Paine, "and not before, I expected a prosecution, and the event has proved that I was not mistaken."

There is more to the story. At first Premier Pitt tried to prevent the publication of Part II by bribing the publisher. When this failed, the government sponsored and paid for the publication of a slanderous biography of Paine. Then the press began to raise the false bogey of Jacobinism and instituted a cry against seditious doctrines said to be circulated by emissaries from France who were bribed by "Paris Gold" to overthrow British institutions. Mobs were inspired to burn Paine in effigy; individuals were instructed to wear boots whose hobnails were

---

[17] In his excellent study of these popular societies Eugene P. Link says that it was "the internationalist Thomas Paine who deserves the credit for fathering the democratic societies." See his *Democratic-Republican Societies, 1790–1800*, New York, 1942, p. 104.

marked "T.P.," so that they could trample upon Paine and his principles, and a great outcry was organized against "the notorious Tom Paine." A Royal Proclamation against seditious writings was issued on May 21, 1792, and on June 8 Paine himself was charged with sedition and his trial was set for December 18.

While British royalty was persecuting Paine, the French nation hailed him as their champion and claimed him for herself. During the first week of September he was elected to represent Calais, Oise, Somme, and Puy de Dome in the National Assembly. "Come, friend of the people," they wrote him, "to swell the number of patriots in an assembly which will decide the destiny of the human race. The happy period you have predicted for the nation has arrived. Come! do not deceive their hopes."

On September 12 Paine made a revolutionary speech to the society of the "Friends of Liberty." The next day, warned by the poet William Blake to flee at once to avoid arrest, Paine went to Dover. There he was able to get by the customs officials and depart for France by showing a letter from Washington. Twenty minutes after he got out to sea the authorities arrived to arrest him. He left behind in the hands of a customs officer at Dover "a printed proof copy" of his *Letter to the Addressers* which he wrote in the summer of 1792 in reply to the charges of seditious libel. In this pamphlet he boldly proceeded to inform his persecutors:

"If to expose the fraud and imposition of monarchy and every species of hereditary government—to lessen the oppression of taxes—to propose plans for the education of helpless infancy, and the comfortable support of the aged and distressed—to endeavor to conciliate nations to each other—to extirpate the horrid practice of war—to promote universal peace, civilization, and commerce—and to break the chains of political superstition, and raise degraded man to his proper rank;—if these things be libellous, let me live the life of a libeller, and let the name of *libeller* be engraven on my tomb!"

On December 18 Paine's *Rights of Man* was prosecuted in England. The author was found guilty of seditious libel before a pensioned judge and a packed jury in London. Since the defendant was absent, the English ruling classes had to content themselves with outlawing him.

The defendant at this very time was receiving a rousing reception in France. Soon after his arrival at Calais, Paine took his seat in the Convention. He speedily discovered that much had happened in France since his last visit to the country, and much of what had happened he could not understand.

In England Paine was associated with the extreme Left, but in France his associates were already becoming the Right. The Girondists, with whom Paine was associated, represented the bourgeoisie of France who viewed the Revolution as their property to be used for their profit and interests. They did not believe in a truly democratic government, and were mainly concerned with keeping the Revolution in check so that the common people would not have too much of a voice in affairs of state. Meanwhile, they were not averse to lining their own pockets through speculation, profiteering and sheer corruption. They frequently mouthed revolutionary slogans, but their conduct indicated that these were merely words. They used Paine and his reputation as a spokesman for the common man for their own purposes, and on more than one occasion pushed him forward to defend a program that they did not dare to advocate openly.[18]

Paine does not appear to have understood much of what was taking place behind the scenes in France. For one thing, he knew nothing of the language; for another, he had never experienced a movement as advanced as that represented by the Jacobins, led by men like Marat, Robespierre, and Saint-Just. Nor for that matter did he fully grasp the changing character of the revolution after 1792. He did not, for example, see that a dictatorship of the people was necessary to save France at a time when the reactionary forces in Europe were uniting with counter-revolutionary elements inside France to destroy the revolution. Nor did he fully grasp the fact that the French Revolution was not and could not be merely a duplication of the American Revolution, for the simple reason that the French masses were fighting to overthrow the burden of centuries of oppression and tyranny, and were compelled to meet the power of reaction throughout Europe in their efforts to achieve their goal.

Paine's difficulties in France came quickly. He arrived in Paris on September 19, 1792, just after the September massacres during which many of the Royalist conspirators in Paris had been executed. Three days later the Convention, responding to the demand of the Parisian masses led by the Jacobins, proclaimed the Republic. On September

[18] For an excellent analysis of the role of the Girondists together with several penetrating comments on Paine, see Albert Mathiez, *The French Revolution*, New York, 1928.

25, in an "Address to the People of France," Paine congratulated the Convention "on the abolition of Royalty," but revealed the influence of his Girondist associations by deploring the terror which had been directed against the Royalists.

The Convention had been convened primarily to draft a new constitution and to dispose of the case of Louis XVI. Paine was one of the nine members of the committee for drawing up a Constitution for France. He worked with Danton, Brissot, Condorcet, Sieyès and four others in writing the document, but it was not adopted. Soon afterwards he invited the enmity of the Jacobins by his opposition to the execution of Louis XVI.

After it was revealed during his trial that the king had been conspiring with the French émigrés and the courts of Europe to wage war upon the people of France, the Jacobins demanded the death of the king as a traitor to the country. Having failed to avoid the trial, and having been defeated in their maneuvers to adjourn it, the Girondists sought to soften the verdict on the king. The Girondist leaders themselves did not dare to oppose the death penalty directly, but left it to less important speakers to propose banishment or internment.

In taking his stand in opposition to the execution of the king, Paine was unconsciously doing just what the Girondist leaders wanted him to do. But he had his own reasons for taking his stand. Nor did he share the Girondist attitude on every aspect of the problem. In his letter to the President of the Convention, November 20, 1792, Paine had urged that "Louis Capet" be tried for his role in the conspiracy of the "crowned brigands" against liberty. This was hardly in keeping with the Girondist position at this time. On January 14, 1793, when voting took place on the Girondist proposal that the question of the king's fate be referred to the people, Paine voted with the Mountain (Jacobins) against his own party. When he arose in the Convention to make his plea against the execution of the king (it was read for him in French to the delegates), he made it clear that he did not do so out of any deference to Royalty but because he feared that the execution would give England a useful pretext for declaring war against France, and because he still could not forget that the king had once aided America to gain her independence. He pleaded with the delegates that they should not give "the tyrant of England the triumph of seeing the man perish on the scaffold who had aided my much-beloved America to break his chains."

On January 19, 1793, the Convention heard an address in opposition to the execution delivered for Paine by a delegate who had translated it from the original. Marat interrupted the speaker to charge that the translation was incorrect and that the sentiments could not be those of Paine. The incident revealed that troubled times were in store for Paine.

When the Girondists were overthrown by the Mountain, Paine attended fewer and fewer meetings of the Convention, and after June 2 ceased altogether to appear in the legislative body. Not understanding that the party with which he had been allied had brought misery and hardship upon the people of France, he could not be expected to grasp the necessity for the new radical measures introduced by the Jacobins to cope with enemies of the revolution at home and abroad.

Although Robespierre and his associates took action against most of Paine's former friends directly after the Girondists were overthrown, they did not arrest him until December 28, 1793. And then it is more than likely that had not Gouverneur Morris, the American minister to France from 1792 to 1794, conspired to keep Paine imprisoned, he would have been speedily released. After his arrest Paine appealed to his rights as an American citizen,[19] but Morris, who hated both Paine and his writings and the French Revolution, turned a deaf ear. As one of Morris's biographers puts it: "But the American minister was too clever to let such a fish escape. He told Robespierre that he did not acknowledge Mr. Paine's right to pass as an American." [20] He had also intimated to the Jacobins, who were anxious to gain the support of America against England, that Paine was thoroughly disliked in America and that the United States would not be disturbed if Paine were kept in prison. Meanwhile, Morris let his own government believe that he had done everything possible to help Paine. Not realizing the role the American minister was playing with respect to the government of the United States, Paine later placed the blame for his prolonged stay in prison on Washington and in his *Letter* to the President launched a bitter attack charging him with having deserted both his former friend and supporter and the cause of freedom.

Paine remained in the Luxembourg prison until November 4, 1794. He expected every day would be his last on earth, and it is probable that he was once saved from the guillotine by the mistake of a guard in marking his door. He nearly died because of an ulcer in his side and

19 Paine had been arrested under a law directed against aliens of hostile nations.
20 Daniel Walther, *Gouverneur Morris*, New York, 1934, pp. 247–248.

was more dead than alive when rescued from prison by James Monroe who replaced Morris as American minister to France. Even ten months after his release Monroe, who nursed Paine at his own home, did not believe he would live long. "The symptoms have become worse," Monroe wrote on September 15, 1795, "and the prospect now is that he will not be able to hold out more than a month or two at the farthest. I shall certainly pay the utmost attention to this gentleman, as he is one of those whose merits in our Revolution were most distinguished."

Paine eventually recovered, was readmitted to the convention in 1795, offered a pension which he refused, and remained in France until September 1, 1802, when he sailed for the United States.

On his way to prison, December 28, 1793, Paine delivered into the hands of his friend Joel Barlow a manuscript which when published in English in 1794 brought upon him a barrage of vituperation that has lasted until the present day. The work was the first part of *The Age of Reason*. Part II was written during his stay in Monroe's home after his release from prison.

Written when Paine was in his fifty-seventh year, *The Age of Reason* represented the results of years of study and reflection by its author on the place of religion in society. When, at the age of twenty, he attended lectures in London on Newtonian astronomy, he must have been influenced by the thought that as Newton found the laws which govern the world of physics so man could find the laws which govern society by observing nature. Again, he probably reached the conclusion some time later that since the clergy in many countries were on the side of oppression and served the vested interests in the interest of reaction, it was essential for the future of progress that their influence be destroyed. As early as *Common Sense* in 1776, he writes that he "saw the exceeding probability that a revolution in the system of government would be followed by a revolution in the system of religion." Although he says nothing in *Rights of Man* about the need for this "revolution in the system of religion," he makes it clear that the idea was still with him. He states that he has avoided the subject "because I am inclined to believe that what is called the present ministry wish to see contention about religion kept up to prevent the nation turning its attention to subjects of government."

During his stay in France, Paine became convinced that it was no longer possible to avoid the subject. As he noticed the reactionary activities of the clergy as plotters against the Revolution, he became even more convinced that to preserve republican principles it was necessary to destroy the priesthood. He was also worried by the fact that in their hatred of the counter-revolutionary role played by the clergy the people of France "were running headlong into Atheism . . ." At one stroke he might save the true religion, Deism, from atheism and republicanism from despotism. With this in mind he wrote his famous theological treatise.

Thomas Paine was no Atheist, Theodore Roosevelt to the contrary. Together with the foremost liberals and intellectuals in America and Europe, he believed in Deism.[21] And like many of these thinkers, Franklin, Jefferson, Wollaston, etc., he was influenced by the intellectual revolution achieved by Newton and Locke in their discovery of a systematic and harmonious universe whose laws could be ascertained by human reason. After seeing the application of the light of rationalism in the political revolutions in America and in France, it seemed to him that the next step was to apply this same rationalism in religion. In his *Letter to Erskine,* Paine wrote: "Of all the tyrannies that effect mankind, tyranny in religion is the worst; every other species of tyranny is limited to the world we live in; but this attempts to stride beyond the grave, and seeks to pursue us into eternity."

Paine's views about the Bible and religion were in no sense original for every one of them had been expressed by Deists before him. But these men had written heavy treatises for scholars. Paine wrote in his usual simple and clear language for the common man. He took Deism out of the sphere of academic discussions and made it a living creed for the average man. By doing so, of course, he threatened the hold of the clergy upon the people. As long as Deism was confined to intellectuals in the upper middle class and liberal sections of the nobility there was no danger to the vested interests of the priesthood. But once it became, as it did after the publication of *The Age of Reason,* a subject for discussion among the common people, the outlook was entirely different. Men, who had said many times before the same things Paine set down in his work, had been ignored. Paine was forced to endure a barrage of calumny and vituperation such as has been visited upon few men in our history.

In one other respect Paine was different from others who had written

[21] The evolution of Paine's religious opinions toward deism has been recently discussed by Robert P. Falk in the article "Thomas Paine: Deist or Quaker," *Pennsylvania Magazine of History and Biography,* vol. LXII, January, 1938, pp. 52–63.

on the subject. He did not bother to use diplomatic language in expressing the things he did not believe and the reasons for his disbelief in them. As he himself said, he went "marching through the Christian forest with an axe." And as he marched through the Christian forest he destroyed with his axe the stories of creation, the garden of Eden, the Resurrection, Mysteries and Miracles, prophecies and Prophets, and everything else through to Revelation, basing all his arguments on science and reason. After completing his journey through the forest, he concludes: "Of all the systems of religion that ever were invented, there is none more *derogatory to the Almighty,* more unedifying to man, more repugnant to reason, and more contradictory to itself than this thing called Christianity." All this does not mean, however, that Paine denies the greatness of Jesus as a man. "Nothing that is said here can apply," he writes, "even with the most distant disrespect, to the real character of Jesus Christ. He was a virtuous and amiable man. The morality that he preached and practised was of the most benevolent kind . . ."

Paine's entire religious creed is put quite simply. By unaided reason man could know that there is a God, that he has certain duties toward Him and his fellow-man, and that the performance of these duties made for his welfare in the present life and hereafter. He ends his work on a note of hope: "Certain . . . I am that when opinions are free, either in matters of government or religion, truth will finally and powerfully prevail." He could not foresee that there were those who were not interested in allowing opinions to be free and, because he transformed Deism from an aristocratic into a popular movement, would make life miserable for him.

In the winter of 1795–96, shortly after he completed the second part of *The Age of Reason,* and while he was still at the home of Monroe in Paris, Paine wrote his last great pamphlet, *Agrarian Justice.* The work resulted from two separate motivating factors. Paine wished, in the first place, to answer a sermon printed by the Bishop of Llandaff, on "The wisdom and goodness of God in having made both rich and poor." He dismissed this remark with the statement that God "made only male and female, and gave them the earth for their inheritance." He was also moved to write his pamphlet by the struggle in France over the confiscation of *émigré* property. After the local communes had initiated a campaign to enforce the laws calling for the confiscation of such property, the Directory, representing the bourgeoisie who had engineered the overthrow of Robespierre, put a stop to this procedure. At the same time a movement was initiated by the Directory to crush the remnants of the radical forces among the masses to pave the way for the unchal lenged rule of the upper classes. In an effort to overthrow the counter-revolution and to seize power to wield it against the upper classes, the radical forces, led by Babeuf, made preparations for a *coup d'état*. Included in the program of the Babouvists were the demands for the abolition of inheritance and the confiscation of the properties of counter-revolutionists, of those who had accumulated wealth from public office, of persons who neglected to cultivate their lands, and of individuals who lived without working. The conspiracy was discovered and crushed in May, 1796.

This was the situation when Paine's *Agrarian Justice* was published. He did not go as far as Babeuf, although he approved of the objective of the insurrection in aiming to remove social inequalities in property. Paine held that there were two kinds of property: natural property (the earth in its uncultivated stage), and "improved" property. He had no intention of taking away "improved" property, but argued that the "earth, in its natural uncultivated state was, and ever would have continued to be, *the common property of the human race*." The introduction of private property added, through cultivation, a "tenfold" value to created earth. At the same time, however, it "dispossessed more than half the inhabitants of every nation of their natural inheritance, without providing . . . an indemnification for that loss, and has thereby created a species of poverty and wretchedness that did not exist before." To remedy this situation and assist the persons thus dispossessed, Paine maintained that every proprietor "of cultivated land" owed to the community a ground-rent for the land which he held. With this sum Paine aimed to set up a National Fund, out of which there would be paid to every person, "when arrived at the age of twenty-one years, the sum of fifteen pounds sterling, as a compensation in part, for the loss of his or her natural inheritance, by the system of landed property," and "the sum of ten pounds per annum, during life, to every person now living, of the age of fifty years, and to all others as they shall arrive at that age."

The system he proposed, Paine maintained, would so organize civilization "that the whole weight of misery can be removed." It would aid the blind, the lame and the aged poor, and at the same time guarantee that the new generation would never become poor. And all this would not be achieved through charity. "It is not charity, but a right," he cried, "not bounty but justice, that I am pleading for." [22] In a burst of indignation over the exploitation of workingmen by employers, he wrote: ". . . if we examine the case minutely it will be found that the accumulation of personal property is, in many instances, the effect of paying too little for the labour that produced it; the consequence of which is, that the working hand perishes in old age, and that the employer abounds in affluence."

Paine remained in France despite his dislike for the reaction that set in with the Directory and continued during Napoleon's Consulate. He felt that France deserved enthusiastic support for seeking to end feudalism and autocracy, and was convinced that even though democracy was not developing as completely as he had hoped, the basic advances of the Revolution in destroying feudal privileges would remain. France was still to him, therefore, the revolutionary republic of Europe and as such merited the assistance of all true democrats, especially in its efforts to defeat England which Paine regarded as the bulwark of reaction in the western world. Britain's defeat in war, he was convinced, would end the rule of the English aristocracy, and pave the way for a democratic republic in England which, in alliance with the United States and France, would guarantee the spread of republicanism throughout the world and international peace. "There will be no lasting peace for France, nor for the world," wrote Paine, "until the tyranny and corruption of the English government be abolished, and England, like Italy, become a sister republic."

Paine submitted a plan to the French Directory for a military expedition against England, whose purpose would be to overthrow the monarchy and assist the people to proclaim a democratic republic. Napoleon, who had not yet revealed his plans of becoming a military dictator, received Paine's proposal enthusiastically and even visited the writer to discuss the possibilities. Paine himself contributed funds he could hardly spare toward the expedition, but it never materialized.

Eventually Paine realized that his usefulness in France was over. He was not molested under the Consulate, but his democratic views such as his support of the Haitian revolution led by Touissant L'Ouverture

[22] Dorfman (*op. cit.*, p. 380), argues that in *Agrarian Justice* Paine was primarily concerned with the protection of property from the dangerous masses and sought to convince the property-holders to give up some of their holdings in order that they might be able to save the rest. This rather than the improvement of the condition of the poor was his aim, he concludes. A mere reading of the book reveals how unjustified is this conclusion. See, however, Penniman, *op. cit.*, p. 251, for an able refutation of this contention.

and his agitation against the slave trade, were looked upon unfavorably. He waited to return to the country which had made him an author.

The fifteen years Paine had spent in Europe since his departure from America had been crowded with world-shaking events, and in most of them he had been an active participant. He had seen the French Revolution uproot hallowed traditions, sweep away feudal remnants and revolutionize class and property relations. He had witnessed the upsurge of the revolutionary movement in England and saw how it was pulverized after Pitt's repressive laws of 1796. He had not fully understood the need for stern measures adopted by the people in meeting and defeating counter-revolution, and his prediction of an easy triumph for republican principles had not been realized. But his faith in the people and the cause of democracy was still unshaken. The measures adopted by the people in their striving for freedom had caused many liberals to blanch and revise their ideas. But they had left his convictions undisturbed. He returned to America convinced that in the end freedom would triumph all over the world.

Soon after his inauguration as President in 1801, Jefferson wrote Paine a cordial letter inviting him to return to the United States on the American warship, *Maryland,* the honored guest of the nation he had helped to found. He assured Paine that the attitude of his presidential predecessors towards him had not been a true reflection of the sentiment of a grateful nation. "I am in hopes you will find us returned generally to sentiments worthy of former times," wrote Jefferson. "In these it will be your glory steadily to have laboured, and with as much effect as any man living. That you may long live to continue your useful labours, and to reap their reward in the thankfulness of nations, is my sincere prayer. Accept assurances of my high esteem and affectionate attachment."

Paine sailed from France on September 1 and landed at Baltimore on October 30, 1802. He was hailed by the Jeffersonians and especially by the advocates of Deism, the "Republican Religion." But the Federalists, the reactionary clergy and others in the anti-democratic camp began the vile attack upon him that was to follow him to his grave. Every paper, Paine wrote to a friend in London, was "filled with applause or abuse."

The abuse, however, soon drowned out the applause. The Federalists hated everything Paine stood for, and they did not forget that he had vigorously denounced Washington and condemned the Alien and Sedition laws of the Adams administration. But primarily they considered his return as a useful stick with which to beat and possibly defeat the Jeffersonians. Hence the Federalist press began a campaign of vilification that probably has no equal in our history. As one student has put it, "the reactionary press exhausted the resources of the dictionary to express the unutterable, only to sink back at last with impotent rage." These newspapers called Paine "the scavenger of faction," "lilly-livered sinical rogue," "loathsome reptile," "demi-human archbeast," "an object of disgust, of abhorrence, of absolute loathing to every decent man except the President of the United States." "What! invite to the United States that lying, drunken, brutal infidel," cried the *New England Palladium* of Boston, "who rejoices in the opportunity of basking and wallowing in the confusion, devastation, bloodshed, rapine and murder, in which his soul delights?" The Philadelphia *Portfolio* urged "every honest and insulted man of dignity . . . to shake off the very dust of his feet and to abandon America" the moment "the loathsome Thomas Paine" started to express his views in this country.[28]

Even Paine's former friends in America began to avoid him. Samuel Adams broke off his friendship and Benjamin Rush refused to have anything to do with him, both giving as their reason that the principles set forth in *The Age of Reason* were too "offensive." For a time Paine even thought that Jefferson had turned against him. When the President postponed their meeting after his arrival in Washington, Paine wrote to Jefferson asking him to return his models. He had hoped, he added, to discuss his scientific plans with the President: "But you have not only shown no disposition towards it, but have, in some measure, by a sort of shyness, as if you stood in fear of federal observation, precluded it. I am not the only one, who makes observations of this kind."

Jefferson replied immediately assuring Paine that he was mistaken and only the fact that he had been busy had prevented their meeting. Praising his models, the President went on: "You have certainly misunderstood what you deem shyness. Of that I have not a thought towards you, but on the contrary have openly maintained in conversation the duty of showing our respect to you and of defying federal calumny in this as in other cases by doing what is Right. As to fearing it, if I ever

[28] For interesting accounts of Paine's return to the United States, see G. Adolph Koch, *Republican Religion*, New York, 1933, pp. 130–146; Frederick Sheldon, "Thomas Paine's Second Appearance in the United States," *Atlantic Monthly*, vol. IV, July, 1859, pp. 1–17, and Dixon Wecter, "Hero in Reverse," *Virginia Quarterly Review*, vol. XVIII, Spring, 1942, pp. 243–259.

could have been weak enough for that, they have taken care to cure me of it thoroughly." [24]

Paine visited Jefferson and discussed political and scientific issues. He refused to accept any public office, but continued to advise the President through correspondence on many important political issues of the day as well as to supply him with ideas on the European situation based on his rich experience abroad. Most of his time, however, was devoted to activity in aiding Elihu Palmer promote the religion of Deism in New York. He contributed articles and letters to the *Prospect* expanding some of the themes he had touched upon in *The Age of Reason*. It was unfortunate in one sense that he concentrated so largely upon religious issues, for it rendered his political activities less useful. But he was forced to elaborate his position to clear himself of unjustified charges, and he believed that the struggle against the reactionary clergy was essential for the further progress of the Jeffersonian cause in America.

But the campaign of slander increased the more he ventured to attack the strong-hold of reaction. On one occasion, when he tried to engage passage from New York to Trenton, the stagedriver refused him a seat. "My stage and horses were once struck by lightning, and I don't want him to suffer again," he told Paine to the amusement of his well-to-do passengers. Later a singer in a New York Presbyterian church was suspended for having visited him. His moderate appetite for brandy was distorted into drunkenness by cartoonists and writers. In 1806 came the greatest effrontery of all when he was denied the right to vote by Federalist officials in New Rochelle on the charge that he was not an American citizen.

Although he led an increasingly harried life, Paine enjoyed the company of "the laboring class of emigrants," and spent many enjoyable days with Robert Fulton, who shared his democratic views, observing his steamboat experiments on the Hudson. For several months in the winter of 1807 he lived with John Wesley Jarvis. The painter wrote to a friend on May 2nd, "I have had Tom Paine living with me for these five months. He is one of the most pleasant companions I have met with for an old man." [25]

[24] Thomas Jefferson to Thomas Paine, January 13, 1803, Jefferson Papers, Library of Congress.
[25] H. E. Dickson, "Day vs. Jarvis," *Pennsylvania Magazine of History and Biography*, vol. lxiii, April, 1939, p. 187.

Paine spent his last years in poverty. Broken in health and reduced in finances, he was forced to move to a miserable lodging house on Fulton Street in New York City. Just before he died on June 8, 1809, two clergymen gained access to his room hoping to hear him recant his heresies. To their question concerning his religious opinions, Paine simply said: "Let me alone; good morning."

Paine was buried on his farm in New Rochelle. But even in the grave it was not considered fitting that the great, militant democrat, Thomas Paine, should enjoy peace and dignity. Curiosity-seekers desecrated his tombstone, and twenty years after his death, William Cobbett, the English reformer who had once joined in the campaign of vilification, stole Paine's bones and shipped them to England. Sometime later the remains disappeared. "As to his bones," wrote Moncure Daniel Conway, "no man knows the place of their rest to this day. His principles rest not. His thoughts, untraceable like his dust, are blown about the world which he held in his heart." [26]

Three years before his death, in a letter to the mayor of Philadelphia, Paine summarized these principles:

"My motive and object in all my political works, beginning with Common Sense, the first work I ever published, have been to rescue man from tyranny and false systems and false principles of government, and enable him to be free, and establish government for himself; and I have borne my share of danger in Europe and in America in every attempt I have made for this

[26] Freneau predicted as much in his poem, *Stanzas, At the Decease of Thomas Paine* . . . :

"Princes and kings decay and die
    And, instant rise again:
But this is not the case, trust me
    With men like THOMAS PAINE.

"To tyrants and the tyrant crew,
    Indeed, he was the bane:
He writ, and gave them all their due,
    And signed it—THOMAS PAINE.

"Oh! how we loved to see him write
    And curb the race of Cain!
They hope and wish that Thomas P——
    May never rise again.

"What idle hopes!—yes—such a man
    May yet appear again.—
When they are dead, they die for aye:
    Not so with THOMAS PAINE."

purpose. And my motive and object in all my publications on religious subjects, beginning with the first part of the Age of Reason, have been to bring man to a right reason that God has him; to impress on him the great principles of divine morality, justice, mercy, and a benevolent disposition to all men and to all creatures; and to excite in him a spirit of trust, confidence and consolation in his creator, unshackled by the fable and fiction of books, by whatever invented name they may be called. I am happy in the continual contemplation of what I have done, and I thank God that he gave me talents for the purpose and fortitude to do it. It will make the continual consolation of my departing hours, whenever they finally arrive."

For years following his death Paine remained forgotten by so-called respectability. But in working class circles he was remembered. Paine's birthday was celebrated annually by the early American labor movement, and toasts were regularly offered in honor of "The author of *Common Sense* and the *Crisis:* His *Rights of Man* effective artillery for tearing down rotten Despotisms; his *Agrarian Justice* excellent material for building up democratic and social republics." [27] The workingmen who attended the annual celebration of Paine's birthday could recite his works from memory, and in their homes copies of these books and pamphlets were handed down from generation to generation. They loved this hard-hitting pamphleteer who had fought the people's fight against tyranny, and they understood what he had meant when he had said, "My country is the world: to do good, my religion."

Today Thomas Paine is just beginning to receive the homage due him. The studies of the late Professor Parrington, whose essay on Paine in his *The Colonial Mind, 1620–1800* is one of the best, and of Professor Harry Hayden Clark, whose extensive examinations of Paine's economic religious and political theories are replete with meaning, have contributed vastly to break down the tradition of the religious infidel and the ignoramus who was merely a flowery demagogue. This is as it should be, for Paine merits a lasting place in the democratic tradition. Like Jefferson he believed in the dignity of the common man, and with Jefferson urged that all men should have an equal opportunity to shape their own destinies and the destiny of the world in which they lived. Those who honor Jefferson as the Father of Democracy would do well to remember that he professed "the same principles" as those expounded by Paine in the *Rights of Man*.

[27] *Working Man's Advocate*, February 5, 1828; *National Laborer*, February 4, 1836; *Young America*, February 5, 1846; *Boston Investigator*, February 13, 1850.

"No writer," Jefferson observed in 1821, "has exceeded Paine in ease and familiarity of style, in perspicuity of expression, happiness of elucidation, and in simple and unassuming language." Paine's writings inspired men of his day in America, in England and in France to live and die for freedom, and left behind in these countries a vision of a world of men free in body and mind. At a time when men and women are fighting to realize that type of world it would be well to read again the words of Thomas Paine who wrote so much and so well to build the heritage of freedom we are battling to preserve and extend.

Philip S. Foner

CHRONOLOGICAL TABLE
OF THOMAS PAINE'S WRITINGS

This edition of Paine's writings has not been arranged in strictly chronological order, although within each section a chronological arrangement has been followed. To enable the reader to follow Paine's career as a writer according to the time when his essays, articles, dissertations, poems and letters were written or published, the following table has been arranged by the editor. The dates usually refer to the time when Paine wrote the particular material referred to, but in cases where it was not possible to ascertain this fact the date of publication has been used. In the right hand columns are references to the volume and page in this collection of Paine's writings in which the text is to be found.

SELECTED BIBLIOGRAPHY

Abel, Darrel, "The Significance of the 'Letter to the Abbé Raynal,' in the Progress of Thomas Paine's Thought," *Pennsylvania Magazine of History and Biography*, vol. LXVI, April, 1942, pp. 176–190.

Birley, R., *English Jacobinism*, Oxford, 1924.

Brailsford, Henry N., *Shelley, Godwin, and Their Circle*, London, 1913.

Brinton, Crane, "Thomas Paine," *Dictionary of American Biography*, vol. XIV, New York, 1934, pp. 159–166.

Brown, Gilbert Patten, "The author-hero of two hemispheres," *Torch of Israel*, July, 1941, pp. 1–3.

Brown, P. A., *The French Revolution in England*, London, 1918.

Brunhouse, Robert L., *The Counter-Revolution in Pennsylvania, 1776–1790*, Philadelphia, 1942.

Clark, Harry H., "Thomas Paine's Relation to Voltaire and Rousseau," *Revue Anglo-Américaine*, vol. IX, Avril et Juin, 1932, pp. 305–318, 393–405.

Clark, Harry H., "Toward a Reinterpretation of Thomas Paine," *American Literature*, vol. V, May, 1933, pp. 133–145.

Clark, Harry H., "Thomas Paine's Theories of Rhetoric," *Transactions of the Wisconsin Academy of Sciences, Arts and Letters*, vol. XXVIII, 1933, pp. 307–339.

Clark, Harry H., "An Historical Interpretation of Thomas Paine's Religion," *University of California Chronicle*, vol. XXXV, January, 1933, pp. 56–87.

Clark, Harry H., ed., *Six New Letters of Thomas Paine*, Madison, Wis., 1939.

Clark, Harry H., ed., *Thomas Paine: Representative Selections*, New York, 1944.

Conway, Moncure D., *The Life of Thomas Paine*, New York, 1892, 2 vols.

Davidson, Philip, *Propaganda and the American Revolution, 1763–1783*, Chapel Hill, N. C., 1941.

Dorfman, J., "The Economic Philosophy of Thomas Paine," *Political Science Quarterly*, vol. LIII, September, 1938, pp. 372–386.

Falk, Robert P., "Thomas Paine and the Attitude of the Quakers to the American Revolution," *Pennsylvania Magazine of History and Biography*, vol. LXIII, July, 1939, pp. 302–310.

SELECTED BIBLIOGRAPHY

Falk, R. B., "Thomas Paine: Deist or Quaker?" *Pennsylvania Magazine of History and Biography*, vol. LXII, January, 1938, pp. 52–63.

Foner, Philip S., *Morale Education in the American Army*, New York, 1944.

Gibbens, V. E., "Tom Paine and the idea of Progress," *Pennsylvania Magazine of History and Biography*, vol. LXVI, April, 1942, pp. 191–204.

Jourdain, M., "Thomas Paine," *Open Court*, vol. XXXV, October, 1921, pp. 577–583.

Koch, G. A., *Republican Religion*, New York, 1933.

Link, Eugene P., *Democratic-Republican Societies, 1790–1800*, New York, 1942.

Lockett, C. H., *The Relations of French and English Society, 1763–1793*, London, 1920.

Matthews, Albert, "Thomas Paine and the Declaration of Independence," *Massachusetts Historical Society Proceedings*, vol. XLIII, 1910, pp. 241–253.

Merriam, C. E. Jr., "The Political Theories of Thomas Paine," *Political Science Quarterly*, vol. XIV, pp. 389–404.

Morais, Herbert M., *Deism in Eighteenth Century America*, New York, 1934.

Muzzey, David, "Thomas Paine and American Independence," *American Review*, Vol. IV, May–June, 1926, pp. 529–541.

Nicolson, Marjorie, "Thomas Paine, Edward Nares, and Mrs. Piozzi's Marginalia," *Huntington Library Bulletin*, No. X, October, 1936, pp. 103–133.

Palmer, R. R., "Tom Paine, victim of the rights of man," *Pennsylvania Magazine of History and Biography*, vol. LXVI, April, 1942, pp. 161–175.

Parrington, Vernon L., "Thomas Paine: Republican Pamphleteer," in *Main Currents in American Thought*, New York, 1927, pp. 327–341.

Penniman, Howard, "Thomas Paine—Democrat," *American Political Science Review*, vol. XXXVII, April, 1943, pp. 244–262.

Persinger, C. E., "The Political Philosophy of Thomas Paine," in The University of Nebraska's *Graduate Bulletin*, vol. C, Series VI, No. 3, July, 1901, pp. 54–74.

Roper, R. C., "Thomas Paine—First to urge the League of Nations," *Public*, vol. XXII, May 10, 1919, pp. 488–489.

Roper, R. C., "Citizen of the World," *Public*, vol. XXII, November 15, 1919, pp. 259–260.

Roper, R. C., "Thomas Paine: Scientist-Religionist," *Scientific Monthly*, vol. LVIII, 1944, pp. 101–111.

Seibel, George, "Thomas Paine in Germany," *Open Court*, vol. XXXIV, January, 1920, pp. 7–14.

Seitz, D. C., "Thomas Paine the Bridge Builder," *Virginia Quarterly Review*, vol. III, October, 1927, pp. 570–584.

Selsam, J. P., *The Pennsylvania Constitution of 1776*, Philadelphia, 1936.

Sheldon, Frederick, "Thomas Paine's Second Appearance in the United States," *Atlantic Monthly*, vol. IV, July, 1859, pp. 1–17.

Sheldon, Frederick, "Thomas Paine's First Appearance in America," *Atlantic Monthly*, vol. IV, November, 1859, pp. 565–575.

Sheldon, Frederick, "Thomas Paine in England and France," *Atlantic Monthly*, vol. IV, December, 1859, pp. 690–709.

Smith, Frank, "The Authorship of 'An Occasional Letter on the Female Sex,'" *American Literature*, vol. II, November, 1930, pp. 277–280.

Smith, Frank, *Thomas Paine, Liberator*, New York, 1938.

Stephen, Leslie, "Thomas Paine," in *Dictionary of National Biography*, vol. XLIII, pp. 69–79.

Sykes, Rev. Norman, "Thomas Paine," in Hearnshaw, F. J. C., ed., *Social and Political Ideas of the Revolutionary Era*, London, 1931, pp. 100–140.

Tyler, M. C., "Thomas Paine and the Outbreak of the Doctrine of Independence," and "Thomas Paine as Literary Freelance in the War for Independence," in *Literary History of the American Revolution, 1763–1783*, vol. I, pp. 451–474, vol. II, pp. 35–49.

Van der Weyde, William, *Thomas Paine's last days in New York*, New York, 1910.

Van Doren, Carl, "Thomas Paine," in Macy, John, ed., *American Writers on American Literature*, New York, 1931.

Washburne, E. B., "Thomas Paine and the French Revolution," *Scribner's Monthly*, vol. XX, September, 1880, pp. 771–786.

Wecter, Dixon, "Thomas Paine and the Franklins," *American Literature*, vol. XII, 1940, pp. 306–317.

Wecter, Dixon, "Hero in Reverse," *Virginia Quarterly Review*, vol. XVIII, Spring, 1942, pp. 243–259.

Woodward, W. E., *Tom Paine: America's Godfather*, New York, 1945.

Wyatt, Edith F., "Our First Internationalist," *New Republic*, vol. XLVIII, September 15, 1926, pp. 90–92.

Zunder, T. A., "Notes on the Friendship of Joel Barlow and Tom Paine," *American Book Collector*, vol. VI, pp. 96–99.

The
Life
and
Major
Writings
of

THOMAS
PAINE

COMMON SENSE

EDITOR'S NOTE

Common Sense, published anonymously, was issued at Philadelphia on January 10, 1776, and immediately became a best seller reaching an extraordinary circulation. This fifty-page pamphlet became the war-cry of the Revolutionary movement as tens of thousands of copies circulated through the country. It called boldly for a declaration of independence; denounced the King of England as a "hardened, sullen-tempered Pharaoh," "the Royal Brute of Great Britain"; vigorously attacked all forms of monarchy and the very principle of monarchism; made the first appeal for an American Republic, and urged the colonies to establish in North America a haven of refuge for the oppressed peoples of the world.

More than any other factor Paine's pamphlet fixed the idea of independence firmly in the public mind. "This animated piece," observed one contemporary, "dispels . . . the prejudice of the mind against the doctrine of independence and pours upon it . . . an inundation of light and truth. . . . The ineffable delight with which it is perused, and its doctrines imbibed, is a demonstration that the seeds of independence, though imported with the troops from Britain, will grow surprisingly with proper cultivation in the fields of America." (Quoted in Frank Moore, editor, *Diary of the American Revolution,* 2 volumes, New York, 1859–60, vol. I, p. 209.) In a letter to Colonel Joseph Reed, January 31, 1776, George Washington wrote: "A few more of such flaming arguments as were exhibited at Falmouth and Norfolk [two towns burned by the British], added to the sound doctrine and unanswerable reasoning of 'Common Sense', will not leave numbers at a loss to decide upon the propriety of a separation." Two months later he wrote again to Colonel Reed: "By private letters which I have lately received from Virginia, I find that 'Common Sense' is working a powerful change there in the minds of many men." (Jared Sparks, editor, *The Writings of George Washington,* twelve volumes, New York, 1848, vol. III, p. 347; Benson J. Lossing, *Washington and the American Republic,* 3 volumes, New York, vol. II, p. 12.)

THOMAS PAINE'S INTRODUCTION TO
COMMON SENSE

PERHAPS the sentiments contained in the following pages, are not
yet sufficiently fashionable to procure them general favor; a long
habit of not thinking a thing *wrong,* gives it a superficial appearance of
being *right,* and raises at first a formidable outcry in defence of custom.
But the tumult soon subsides. Time makes more converts than reason.

As a long and violent abuse of power is generally the means of calling the right of it in question, (and in matters too which might never
have been thought of, had not the sufferers been aggravated into the
inquiry,) and as the king of England hath undertaken in his *own right,*
to support the Parliament in what he calls *theirs,* and as the good people
of this country are grievously oppressed by the combination, they have
an undoubted privilege to inquire into the pretensions of both, and
equally to reject the usurpation of *either.*

In the following sheets, the author has studiously avoided every
thing which is personal among ourselves. Compliments as well as censure to individuals make no part thereof. The wise and the worthy need
not the triumph of a pamphlet; and those whose sentiments are injudicious or unfriendly will cease of themselves, unless too much pains
is bestowed upon their conversions.

The cause of America is in a great measure the cause of all mankind.
Many circumstances have, and will arise, which are not local, but universal, and through which the principles of all lovers of mankind are
affected, and in the event of which their affections are interested. The
laying a country desolate with fire and sword, declaring war against
the natural rights of all mankind, and extirpating the defenders thereof

from the face of the earth, is the concern of every man to whom nature hath given the power of feeling; of which class, regardless of party censure, is

THE AUTHOR.

AUTHOR'S POSTSCRIPT TO PREFACE IN THE THIRD EDITION

P. S. The publication of this new edition hath been delayed, with a view of taking notice (had it been necessary) of any attempt to refute the Doctrine of Independence. As no answer hath yet appeared, it is now presumed that none will, the time needful for getting such a performance ready for the public being considerably past.

Who the author of this production is, is wholly unnecessary to the public, as the object for attention is the *doctrine itself,* not the *man.* Yet it may not be unnecessary to say that he is unconnected with any party, and under no sort of influence, public or private, but the influence of reason and principle.

PHILADELPHIA, February 14, 1776.

COMMON SENSE

ON THE ORIGIN AND DESIGN OF GOVERNMENT IN GENERAL, WITH CONCISE REMARKS ON THE ENGLISH CONSTITUTION

SOME writers have so confounded society with government, as to leave little or no distinction between them; whereas they are not only different, but have different origins. Society is produced by our wants and government by our wickedness; the former promotes our happiness *positively* by uniting our affections, the latter *negatively* by restraining our vices. The one encourages intercourse, the other creates distinctions. The first is a patron, the last a punisher.

Society in every state is a blessing, but government, even in its best state, is but a necessary evil; in its worst state an intolerable one: for when we suffer, or are exposed to the same miseries *by a government,* which we might expect in a country *without government,* our calamity is heightened by reflecting that we furnish the means by which we suffer. Government, like dress, is the badge of lost innocence; the palaces of kings are built upon the ruins of the bowers of paradise. For were the impulses of conscience clear, uniform and irresistibly obeyed, man would need no other law-giver; but that not being the case, he finds it necessary to surrender up a part of his property to furnish means for the protection of the rest; and this he is induced to do by the same prudence which in every other case advises him, out of two evils to choose the least. Wherefore, security being the true design and end of government, it unanswerably follows that whatever form thereof appears most likely to ensure it to us, with the least expence and greatest benefit, is preferable to all others.

In order to gain a clear and just idea of the design and end of government, let us suppose a small number of persons settled in some sequestered part of the earth, unconnected with the rest; they will then represent the first peopling of any country, or of the world. In this state of natural liberty, society will be their first thought. A thousand motives will excite them thereto; the strength of one man is so unequal to his wants, and his mind so unfitted for perpetual solitude, that he is soon obliged to seek assistance and relief of another, who in his turn requires the same. Four or five united would be able to raise a tolerable dwelling in the midst of a wilderness, but one man might labor out the common period of life without accomplishing any thing; when he had felled his timber he could not remove it, nor erect it after it was removed; hunger in the mean time would urge him to quit his work, and every different want would call him a different way. Disease, nay even misfortune, would be death; for though neither might be mortal, yet either would disable him from living, and reduce him to a state in which he might rather be said to perish than to die.

Thus necessity, like a gravitating power, would soon form our newly arrived emigrants into society, the reciprocal blessings of which would supercede, and render the obligations of law and government unnecessary while they remained perfectly just to each other; but as nothing but Heaven is impregnable to vice, it will unavoidably happen that in proportion as they surmount the first difficulties of emigration, which bound them together in a common cause, they will begin to relax in their duty and attachment to each other: and this remissness will point out the necessity of establishing some form of government to supply the defect of moral virtue.

Some convenient tree will afford them a State House, under the branches of which the whole colony may assemble to deliberate on public matters. It is more than probable that their first laws will have the title only of regulations and be enforced by no other penalty than public disesteem. In this first parliament every man by natural right will have a seat.

But as the colony increases, the public concerns will increase likewise, and the distance at which the members may be separated, will render it too inconvenient for all of them to meet on every occasion as at first, when their number was small, their habitations near, and the public concerns few and trifling. This will point out the convenience of their consenting to leave the legislative part to be managed by a select number chosen from the whole body, who are supposed to have the same concerns at stake which those have who appointed them, and who will act in the same manner as the whole body would act were they present. If the colony continue increasing, it will become necessary to augment the number of representatives, and that the interest of every part of the colony may be attended to, it will be found best to divide the whole into convenient parts, each part sending its proper number: and that the *elected* might never form to themselves an interest separate from the *electors,* prudence will point out the propriety of having elections often: because as the *elected* might by that means return and mix again with the general body of the *electors* in a few months, their fidelity to the public will be secured by the prudent reflection of not making a rod for themselves. And as this frequent interchange will establish a common interest with every part of the community, they will mutually and naturally support each other, and on this, (not on the unmeaning name of king,) depends the *strength of government, and the happiness of the governed.*

Here then is the origin and rise of government; namely, a mode rendered necessary by the inability of moral virtue to govern the world; here too is the design and end of government, viz. freedom and security. And however our eyes may be dazzled with show, or our ears deceived by sound; however prejudice may warp our wills, or interest darken our understanding, the simple voice of nature and reason will say, 'tis right.

I draw my idea of the form of government from a principle in nature which no art can overturn, viz. that the more simple any thing is, the less liable it is to be disordered, and the easier repaired when disordered; and with this maxim in view I offer a few remarks on the so much boasted Constitution of England. That it was noble for the dark and slavish times in which it was erected, is granted. When the world was overrun with tyranny the least remove therefrom was a glorious rescue. But that it is imperfect, subject to convulsions, and incapable of producing what it seems to promise, is easily demonstrated.

Absolute governments, (though the disgrace of human nature) have this advantage with them, they are simple; if the people suffer, they know the head from which their suffering springs; know likewise the remedy; and are not bewildered by a variety of causes and cures. But the Constitution of England is so exceedingly complex, that the nation may suffer for years together without being able to discover in which part the fault lies; some will say in one and some in another, and every political physician will advise a different medicine.

I know it is difficult to get over local or long standing prejudices, yet if we will suffer ourselves to examine the component parts of the English Constitution, we shall find them to be the base remains of two ancient tyrannies, compounded with some new Republican materials.

First.—The remains of monarchical tyranny in the person of the king.

Secondly.—The remains of aristocratical tyranny in the persons of the peers.

Thirdly.—The new Republican materials, in the persons of the Commons, on whose virtue depends the freedom of England.

The two first, by being hereditary, are independent of the people; wherefore in a *constitutional sense* they contribute nothing towards the freedom of the State.

To say that the Constitution of England is an *union* of three powers, reciprocally *checking* each other, is farcical; either the words have no meaning, or they are flat contradictions.

To say that the Commons is a check upon the king, presupposes two things.

First.—That the king is not to be trusted without being looked after; or in other words, that a thirst for absolute power is the natural disease of monarchy.

Secondly.—That the Commons, by being appointed for that purpose, are either wiser or more worthy of confidence than the crown.

But as the same constitution which gives the Commons a power to check the king by withholding the supplies, gives afterwards the king a power to check the Commons, by empowering him to reject their other bills; it again supposes that the king is wiser than those whom it has already supposed to be wiser than him. A mere absurdity!

There is something exceedingly ridiculous in the composition of monarchy; it first excludes a man from the means of information, yet empowers him to act in cases where the highest judgment is required. The state of a king shuts him from the world, yet the business of a king requires him to know it thoroughly; wherefore the different parts, by unnaturally opposing and destroying each other, prove the whole character to be absurd and useless.

Some writers have explained the English Constitution thus: the king, say they, is one, the people another; the peers are a house in behalf of the king, the Commons in behalf of the people; but this hath all the distinctions of a house divided against itself; and though the expressions be pleasantly arranged, yet when examined they appear idle and ambiguous; and it will always happen, that the nicest construction that words are capable of, when applied to the description of something which either cannot exist, or is too incomprehensible to be within the compass of description, will be words of sound only, and though they may amuse the ear, they cannot inform the mind: for this explanation includes a previous question, viz. *how came the king by a power which the people are afraid to trust, and always obliged to check?* Such a power could not be the gift of a wise people, neither can any power, *which needs checking,* be from God; yet the provision which the Constitution makes supposes such a power to exist.

But the provision is unequal to the task; the means either cannot or will not accomplish the end, and the whole affair is a *Felo de se:* for as the greater weight will always carry up the less, and as all the wheels of a machine are put in motion by one, it only remains to know which power in the constitution has the most weight, for that will govern: and though the others, or a part of them, may clog, or, as the phrase is, check the rapidity of its motion, yet so long as they cannot stop it, their endeavours will be ineffectual: The first moving power will at last have its way, and what it wants in speed is supplied by time.

That the crown is this overbearing part in the English Constitution needs not be mentioned, and that it derives its whole consequence merely from being the giver of places and pensions is self-evident; wherefore, though we have been wise enough to shut and lock a door against absolute Monarchy, we at the same time have been foolish enough to put the crown in possession of the key.

The prejudice of Englishmen, in favor of their own government, by king, lords and Commons, arises as much or more from national pride than reason. Individuals are undoubtedly safer in England than in some other countries: but the will of the king is as much the law of the land in Britain as in France, with this difference, that instead of proceeding directly from his mouth, it is handed to the people under the formidable shape of an act of Parliament. For the fate of Charles the First hath only made kings more subtle—not more just.

Wherefore, laying aside all national pride and prejudice in favor of modes and forms, the plain truth is that *it is wholly owing to the constitution of the people, and not to the constitution of the government* that the crown is not as oppressive in England as in Turkey.

An inquiry into the *constitutional errors* in the English form of government, is at this time highly necessary; for as we are never in a proper condition of doing justice to others, while we continue under the influence of some leading partiality, so neither are we capable of doing it to ourselves while we remain fettered by any obstinate prejudice. And as a man who is attached to a prostitute is unfitted to choose or judge of a wife, so any prepossession in favor of a rotten constitution of government will disable us from discerning a good one.

Of Monarchy and Hereditary Succession

Mankind being originally equals in the order of creation, the equality could only be destroyed by some subsequent circumstance: the distinctions of rich and poor may in a great measure be accounted for, and that without having recourse to the harsh ill-sounding names of oppression and avarice. Oppression is often the *consequence,* but seldom or never the *means* of riches; and though avarice will preserve a man from being necessitously poor, it generally makes him too timorous to be wealthy.

But there is another and greater distinction for which no truly natural or religious reason can be assigned, and that is the distinction of men into KINGS and SUBJECTS. Male and female are the distinctions of nature, good and bad the distinctions of heaven; but how a race of men came into the world so exalted above the rest, and distinguished like some new species, is worth inquiring into, and whether they are the means of happiness or of misery to mankind.

In the early ages of the world, according to the scripture chronology there were no kings; the consequence of which was, there were no wars; it is the pride of kings which throws mankind into confusion.

Holland, without a king hath enjoyed more peace for this last century than any of the monarchical governments in Europe. Antiquity favors the same remark; for the quiet and rural lives of the first Patriarchs have a happy something in them, which vanishes when we come to the history of Jewish royalty.

Government by kings was first introduced into the world by the heathens, from whom the children of Israel copied the custom. It was the most prosperous invention the devil ever set on foot for the promotion of idolatry. The heathens paid divine honors to their deceased kings, and the Christian world has improved on the plan by doing the same to their living ones. How impious is the title of sacred majesty applied to a worm, who in the midst of his splendor is crumbling into dust!

As the exalting one man so greatly above the rest cannot be justified on the equal rights of nature, so neither can it be defended on the authority of scripture; for the will of the Almighty as declared by Gideon, and the prophet Samuel, expressly disapproves of government by kings. All anti-monarchical parts of scripture, have been very smoothly glossed over in monarchical governments, but they undoubtedly merit the attention of countries which have their governments yet to form. *Render unto Cesar the things which are Cesar's,* is the scripture doctrine of courts, yet it is no support of monarchical government, for the Jews at that time were without a king, and in a state of vassalage to the Romans.

Near three thousand years passed away, from the Mosaic account of the creation, till the Jews under a national delusion requested a king. Till then their form of government (except in extraordinary cases where the Almighty interposed) was a kind of Republic, administered by a judge and the elders of the tribes. Kings they had none, and it was held sinful to acknowledge any being under that title but the Lord of Hosts. And when a man seriously reflects on the idolatrous homage which is paid to the persons of kings, he need not wonder that the Almighty, ever jealous of his honor, should disapprove a form of government which so impiously invades the prerogative of heaven.

Monarchy is ranked in scripture as one of the sins of the Jews, for which a curse in reserve is denounced against them. The history of that transaction is worth attending to.

The children of Israel being oppressed by the Midianites, Gideon marched against them with a small army, and victory through the divine

interposition decided in his favor. The Jews, elate with success, and attributing it to the generalship of Gideon, proposed making him a king,
saying, *Rule thou over us, thou and thy son, and thy son's son.* Here was
temptation in its fullest extent; not a kingdom only, but an hereditary
one; but Gideon in the piety of his soul replied, *I will not rule over you,
neither shall my son rule over you.* THE LORD SHALL RULE OVER YOU.
Words need not be more explicit; Gideon doth not decline the honor,
but denieth their right to give it; neither doth he compliment them with
invented declarations of his thanks, but in the positive style of a prophet
charges them with disaffection to their proper Sovereign, the King of
Heaven.

About one hundred and thirty years after this, they fell again into the
same error. The hankering which the Jews had for the idolatrous customs of the heathens, is something exceedingly unaccountable; but so it
was, that laying hold of the misconduct of Samuel's two sons, who were
intrusted with some secular concerns, they came in an abrupt and clamorous manner to Samuel, saying, *Behold thou art old, and thy sons walk
not in thy ways, now make us a king to judge us like all the other
nations.* And here we cannot but observe that their motives were bad,
viz. that they might be *like* unto other nations, i. e. the heathens, whereas
their true glory lay in being as much *unlike* them as possible. *But the
thing displeased Samuel when they said, give us a king to judge us;
and Samuel prayed unto the Lord, and the Lord said unto Samuel,
hearken unto the voice of the people in all that they say unto thee, for
they have not rejected thee, but they have rejected me,* THAT I SHOULD NOT
REIGN OVER THEM. *According to all the works which they have done since
the day that I brought them up out of Egypt even unto this day, wherewith they have forsaken me, and served other Gods: so do they also unto
thee. Now therefore hearken unto their voice, howbeit, protest solemnly
unto them and show them the manner of the king that shall reign over
them,* i. e. not of any particular king, but the general manner of the kings
of the earth whom Israel was so eagerly copying after. And notwithstanding the great distance of time and difference of manners, the character is still in fashion. *And Samuel told all the words of the Lord unto
the people, that asked of him a king. And he said, This shall be the
manner of the king that shall reign over you. He will take your sons
and appoint them for himself for his chariots and to be his horsemen,
and some shall run before his chariots* (this description agrees with the
present mode of impressing men) *and he will appoint him captains over*

thousands and captains over fifties, will set them to ear his ground and to reap his harvest, and to make his instruments of war, and instruments of his chariots. And he will take your daughters to be confectionaries, and to be cooks, and to be bakers (this describes the expense and luxury as well as the oppression of kings) *and he will take your fields and your vineyards, and your olive yards, even the best of them, and give them to his servants. And he will take the tenth of your seed, and of your vine-yards, and give them to his officers and to his servants* (by which we see that bribery, corruption, and favouritism, are the standing vices of kings) *and he will take the tenth of your men servants, and your maid servants, and your goodliest young men, and your asses, and put them to his work: and he will take the tenth of your sheep, and ye shall be his servants, and ye shall cry out in that day because of your king which ye shall have chosen,* AND THE LORD WILL NOT HEAR YOU IN THAT DAY. This accounts for the continuation of monarchy; neither do the characters of the few good kings which have lived since, either sanctify the title, or blot out the sinfulness of the origin; the high encomium given of David takes no notice of him *officially as a king,* but only as a *man* after God's own heart. *Nevertheless the people refused to obey the voice of Samuel, and they said, Nay but we will have a king over us, that we may be like all the nations, and that our king may judge us, and go out before us and fight our battles.* Samuel continued to reason with them but to no pur-pose; he set before them their ingratitude, but all would not avail; and seeing them fully bent on their folly, he cried out, *I will call unto the Lord, and he shall send thunder and rain* (which was then a punish-ment, being in the time of wheat harvest) *that ye may perceive and see that your wickedness is great which ye have done in the sight of the Lord,* IN ASKING YOU A KING. *So Samuel called unto the Lord, and the Lord sent thunder and rain that day, and all the people greatly feared the Lord and Samuel. And all the people said unto Samuel, Pray for thy servants unto the Lord thy God that we die not, for* WE HAVE ADDED UNTO OUR SINS THIS EVIL, TO ASK A KING. These portions of scripture are direct and positive. They admit of no equivocal construction. That the Almighty hath here entered his protest against monarchical govern-ment is true, or the scripture is false. And a man hath good reason to believe that there is as much of kingcraft as priestcraft in withholding the scripture from the public in popish countries. For monarchy in every instance is the popery of government.

To the evil of monarchy we have added that of hereditary succession; and as the first is a degradation and lessening of ourselves, so the second, claimed as a matter of right, is an insult and imposition on posterity. For all men being originally equals, no one by birth could have a right to set up his own family in perpetual preference to all others for ever, and though himself might deserve some decent degree of honors of his cotemporaries, yet his descendants might be far too unworthy to inherit them. One of the strongest natural proofs of the folly of hereditary right in kings, is that nature disapproves it, otherwise she would not so frequently turn it into ridicule, by giving mankind an *ass for a lion*.

Secondly, as no man at first could possess any other public honors than were bestowed upon him, so the givers of those honors could have no power to give away the right of posterity, and though they might say "We choose you for our head," they could not without manifest injustice to their children say "that your children and your children's children shall reign over ours forever." Because such an unwise, unjust, unnatural compact might (perhaps) in the next succession put them under the government of a rogue or a fool. Most wise men in their private sentiments have ever treated hereditary right with contempt; yet it is one of those evils which when once established is not easily removed: many submit from fear, others from superstition, and the more powerful part shares with the king the plunder of the rest.

This is supposing the present race of kings in the world to have had an honorable origin: whereas it is more than probable, that, could we take off the dark covering of antiquity and trace them to their first rise, we should find the first of them nothing better than the principal ruffian of some restless gang; whose savage manners or pre-eminence in subtilty obtained him the title of chief among plunderers: and who by increasing in power and extending his depredations, overawed the quiet and defenceless to purchase their safety by frequent contributions. Yet his electors could have no idea of giving hereditary right to his descendants, because such a perpetual exclusion of themselves was incompatible with the free and unrestrained principles they professed to live by. Wherefore, hereditary succession in the early ages of monarchy could not take place as a matter of claim, but as something casual or complemental; but as few or no records were extant in those days, and traditionary history stuff'd with fables, it was very easy, after the lapse of a few generations, to trump up some superstitious tale conveniently timed, Mahomet-like, to cram hereditary right down the throats of the vulgar. Perhaps the disorders which threatened, or seemed to threaten, on the decease of a leader and the choice of a new one (for elections among ruffians could not be very orderly) induced many at first to favor hereditary pretensions; by which means it happened, as it hath happened since, that what at first was submitted to as a convenience was afterwards claimed as a right.

England since the conquest hath known some few good monarchs, but groaned beneath a much larger number of bad ones; yet no man in his senses can say that their claim under William the Conqueror is a very honorable one. A French bastard landing with an armed banditti and establishing himself king of England against the consent of the natives, is in plain terms a very paltry rascally original. It certainly hath no divinity in it. However it is needless to spend much time in exposing the folly of hereditary right; if there are any so weak as to believe it, let them promiscuously worship the ass and the lion, and welcome. I shall neither copy their humility, nor disturb their devotion.

Yet I should be glad to ask how they suppose kings came at first? The question admits but of three answers, viz. either by lot, by election, or by usurpation. If the first king was taken by lot, it establishes a precedent for the next, which excludes hereditary succession. Saul was by lot, yet the succession was not hereditary, neither does it appear from that transaction that there was any intention it ever should. If the first king of any country was by election, that likewise establishes a precedent for the next; for to say, that the right of all future generations is taken away, by the act of the first electors, in their choice not only of a king but of a family of kings for ever, hath no parallel in or out of scripture but the doctrine of original sin, which supposes the free will of all men lost in Adam; and from such comparison, and it will admit of no other, hereditary succession can derive no glory. For as in Adam all sinned, and as in the first electors all men obeyed; as in the one all mankind were subjected to Satan, and in the other to sovereignty; as our innocence was lost in the first, and our authority in the last; and as both disable us from reassuming some former state and privilege, it unanswerably follows that original sin and hereditary succession are parallels. Dishonorable rank! inglorious connection! yet the most subtle sophist cannot produce a juster simile.

As to usurpation, no man will be so hardy as to defend it; and that William the Conqueror was an usurper is a fact not to be contradicted.

The plain truth is, that the antiquity of English monarchy will not bear looking into.

But it is not so much the absurdity as the evil of hereditary succession which concerns mankind. Did it insure a race of good and wise men it would have the seal of divine authority, but as it opens a door to the *foolish*, the *wicked*, and the *improper*, it has in it the nature of oppression. Men who look upon themselves born to reign, and others to obey, soon grow insolent. Selected from the rest of mankind, their minds are early poisoned by importance; and the world they act in differs so materially from the world at large, that they have but little opportunity of knowing its true interests, and when they succeed to the government are frequently the most ignorant and unfit of any throughout the dominions.

Another evil which attends hereditary succession is, that the throne is subject to be possessed by a minor at any age; all which time the regency acting under the cover of a king have every opportunity and inducement to betray their trust. The same national misfortune happens when a king worn out with age and infirmity enters the last stage of human weakness. In both these cases the public becomes a prey to every miscreant who can tamper successfully with the follies either of age or infancy.

The most plausible plea which hath ever been offered in favor of hereditary succession is, that it preserves a nation from civil wars; and were this true, it would be weighty; whereas it is the most bare-faced falsity ever imposed upon mankind. The whole history of England disowns the fact. Thirty kings and two minors have reigned in that distracted kingdom since the conquest, in which time there has been (including the revolution) no less than eight civil wars and nineteen rebellions. Wherefore instead of making for peace, it makes against it, and destroys the very foundation it seems to stand upon.

The contest for monarchy and succession, between the houses of York and Lancaster, laid England in a scene of blood for many years. Twelve pitched battles besides skirmishes and sieges were fought between Henry and Edward. Twice was Henry prisoner to Edward, who in his turn was prisoner to Henry. And so uncertain is the fate of war and the temper of a nation, when nothing but personal matters are the ground of a quarrel, that Henry was taken in triumph from a prison to a palace, and Edward obliged to fly from a palace to a foreign land; yet, as sudden transitions of temper are seldom lasting, Henry in his turn was driven from the throne, and Edward re-called to succeed him. The Parliament always following the strongest side.

This contest began in the reign of Henry the Sixth, and was not entirely extinguished till Henry the Seventh, in whom the families were united. Including a period of 67 years, viz. from 1422 to 1489.

In short, monarchy and succession have laid (not this or that kingdom only) but the world in blood and ashes. 'Tis a form of government which the word of God bears testimony against, and blood will attend it.

If we inquire into the business of a king, we shall find that in some countries they may have none; and after sauntering away their lives without pleasure to themselves or advantage to the nation, withdraw from the scene, and leave their successors to tread the same idle round. In absolute monarchies the whole weight of business civil and military lies on the king; the children of Israel in their request for a king urged this plea, "that he may judge us, and go out before us and fight our battles." But in countries where he is neither a judge nor a general, as in England, a man would be puzzled to know what *is* his business.

The nearer any government approaches to a Republic, the less business there is for a king. It is somewhat difficult to find a proper name for the government of England. Sir William Meredith calls it a Republic; but in its present state it is unworthy of the name, because the corrupt influence of the crown, by having all the places in its disposal, hath so effectually swallowed up the power, and eaten out the virtue of the House of Commons (the republican part in the Constitution) that the government of England is nearly as monarchical as that of France or Spain. Men fall out with names without understanding them. For 'tis the republican and not the monarchical part of the Constitution of England which Englishmen glory in, viz. the liberty of choosing an House of Commons from out of their own body—and it is easy to see that when republican virtues fail, slavery ensues. Why is the Constitution of England sickly, but because monarchy hath poisoned the Republic; the crown has engrossed the Commons.

In England a king hath little more to do than to make war and give away places; which, in plain terms, is to empoverish the nation and set it together by the ears. A pretty business indeed for a man to be allowed eight hundred thousand sterling a year for, and worshipped into the bargain! Of more worth is one honest man to society, and in the sight of God, than all the crowned ruffians that ever lived.

Thoughts on the Present State of American Affairs

In the following pages I offer nothing more than simple facts, plain arguments, and common sense: and have no other preliminaries to settle with the reader, than that he will divest himself of prejudice and prepossession, and suffer his reason and his feelings to determine for themselves: that he will put on, or rather that he will not put off, the true character of a man, and generously enlarge his views beyond the present day.

Volumes have been written on the subject of the struggle between England and America. Men of all ranks have embarked in the controversy, from different motives, and with various designs; but all have been ineffectual, and the period of debate is closed. Arms as the last resource decide the contest; the appeal was the choice of the king, and the continent has accepted the challenge.

It hath been reported of the late Mr. Pelham (who though an able minister was not without his faults) that on his being attacked in the House of Commons on the score that his measures were only of a temporary kind, replied, *"they will last my time."* Should a thought so fatal and unmanly possess the colonies in the present contest, the name of ancestors will be remembered by future generations with detestation.

The sun never shone on a cause of greater worth. 'Tis not the affair of a city, a county, a province, or a kingdom; but of a continent—of at least one eighth part of the habitable globe. 'Tis not the concern of a day, a year, or an age; posterity are virtually involved in the contest, and will be more or less affected even to the end of time, by the proceedings now. Now is the seed-time of continental union, faith and honor. The least fracture now will be like a name engraved with the point of a pin on the tender rind of a young oak; the wound would enlarge with the tree, and posterity read it in full grown characters.

By referring the matter from argument to arms, a new era for politics is struck—a new method of thinkings has arisen. All plans, proposals, &c. prior to the nineteenth of April, *i. e.* to the commencement of hostilities,[1] are like the almanacks of the last year; which though proper

---

[1] On the night of April 18, 1775, the British troops moved out of Boston to capture the military supplies stored by the American patriots at Concord and to arrest Sam Adams and John Hancock who were known to be near Lexington. Roused by Paul Revere and William Dawes, armed citizens met the British troops and on April 19 the battle of Lexington and Concord was fought. Taking positions behind trees, barns, and rocks, the American minute

then, are superceded and useless now. Whatever was advanced by the advocates on either side of the question then, terminated in one and the same point, viz. a union with Great Britain; the only difference between the parties was the method of effecting it; the one proposing force, the other friendship; but it has so far happened that the first has failed, and the second has withdrawn her influence.

As much has been said of the advantages of reconciliation, which, like an agreeable dream, has passed away and left us as we were, it is but right that we should examine the contrary side of the argument, and inquire into some of the many material injuries which these colonies sustain, and always will sustain, by being connected with and dependant on Great Britain. To examine that connection and dependance, on the principles of nature and common sense, to see what we have to trust to, if separated, and what we are to expect, if dependant.

I have heard it asserted by some, that as America has flourished under her former connection with Great Britain, the same connection is necessary towards her future happiness, and will always have the same effect. Nothing can be more fallacious than this kind of argument. We may as well assert that because a child has thrived upon milk, that it is never to have meat, or that the first twenty years of our lives is to become a precedent for the next twenty. But even this is admitting more than is true; for I answer roundly, that America would have flourished as much, and probably much more, had no European power taken any notice of her. The commerce by which she hath enriched herself are the necessaries of life, and will always have a market while eating is the custom of Europe.

But she has protected us, say some. That she hath engrossed us is true, and defended the continent at our expense as well as her own, is admitted; and she would have defended Turkey from the same motive, *viz.* for the sake of trade and dominion.

Alas! we have been long led away by ancient prejudices and made large sacrifices to superstition. We have boasted the protection of Great Britain, without considering, that her motive was *interest* not *attachment;* and that she did not protect us from *our enemies* on *our account;* but from *her enemies* on *her own account,* from those who had no quarrel with us on any *other account,* and who will always be our

---

men cut the British troops to pieces. Only about two-thirds of the original enemy force managed to return to Boston alive. The shot heard round the world convinced Thomas Paine that reconciliation with Great Britain was no longer possible.—*Editor.*

enemies on the *same account*. Let Britain waive her pretensions to the continent, or the continent throw off the dependance, and we should be at peace with France and Spain, were they at war with Britain. The miseries of Hanover's last war ought to warn us against connections.

It hath lately been asserted in Parliament, that the colonies have no relation to each other but through the parent country, *i. e.* that Pennsylvania and the Jerseys, and so on for the rest, are sister colonies by the way of England; this is certainly a very roundabout way of proving relationship, but it is the nearest and only true way of proving enmity (or enemyship, if I may so call it.) France and Spain never were, nor perhaps ever will be, our enemies as *Americans,* but as our being the *subjects of Great Britain.*

But Britain is the parent country, say some. Then the more shame upon her conduct. Even brutes do not devour their young, nor savages make war upon their families; wherefore, the assertion, if true, turns to her reproach; but it happens not to be true, or only partly so, and the phrase *parent* or *mother country* hath been jesuitically adopted by the king and his parasites, with a low papistical design of gaining an unfair bias on the credulous weakness of our minds. Europe, and not England, is the parent country of America. This new world hath been the asylum for the persecuted lovers of civil and religious liberty from *every part* of Europe. Hither have they fled, not from the tender embraces of the mother, but from the cruelty of the monster; and it is so far true of England, that the same tyranny which drove the first emigrants from home, pursues their descendants still.

In this extensive quarter of the globe, we forget the narrow limits of three hundred and sixty miles (the extent of England) and carry our friendship on a larger scale; we claim brotherhood with every European Christian, and triumph in the generosity of the sentiment.

It is pleasant to observe by what regular gradations we surmount the force of local prejudices, as we enlarge our acquaintance with the world. A man born in any town in England divided into parishes, will naturally associate most with his fellow parishioners (because their interests in many cases will be common) and distinguish him by the name of *neighbor;* if he meet him but a few miles from home, he drops the narrow idea of a street, and salutes him by the name of *townsman;* if he travel out of the county and meet him in any other, he forgets the minor divisions of street and town, and calls him *countryman, i. e. countyman;* but if in their foreign excursions they should associate in

France, or any other part of *Europe,* their local remembrance would be enlarged into that of *Englishman.* And by a just parity of reasoning, all Europeans meeting in America, or any other quarter of the globe, are *countrymen;* for England, Holland, Germany, or Sweden, when compared with the whole, stand in the same places on the larger scale, which the divisions of street, town, and county do on the smaller ones; distinctions too limited for continental minds. Not one third of the inhabitants, even of this province, [Pennsylvania], are of English descent. Wherefore, I reprobate the phrase of parent or mother country applied to England only, as being false, selfish, narrow and ungenerous.

But, admitting that we were all of English descent, what does it amount to? Nothing. Britain, being now an open enemy, extinguishes every other name and title: and to say that reconciliation is our duty, is truly farcical. The first king of England, of the present line (William the Conqueror) was a Frenchman, and half the peers of England are descendants from the same country; wherefore, by the same method of reasoning, England ought to be governed by France.

Much hath been said of the united strength of Britain and the colonies, that in conjunction they might bid defiance to the world. But this is mere presumption; the fate of war is uncertain, neither do the expressions mean any thing; for this continent would never suffer itself to be drained of inhabitants, to support the British arms in either Asia, Africa or Europe.

Besides, what have we to do with setting the world at defiance? Our plan is commerce, and that, well attended to, will secure us the peace and friendship of all Europe; because it is the interest of all Europe to have America a free port. Her trade will always be a protection, and her barrenness of gold and silver secure her from invaders.

I challenge the warmest advocate for reconciliation to show a single advantage that this continent can reap by being connected with Great Britain. I repeat the challenge; not a single advantage is derived. Our corn will fetch its price in any market in Europe, and our imported goods must be paid for, buy them where we will.

But the injuries and disadvantages which we sustain by that connection, are without number; and our duty to mankind at large, as well as to ourselves, instruct us to renounce the alliance: because, any submission to, or dependence on, Great Britain, tends directly to involve this continent in European wars and quarrels, and set us at variance with nations who would otherwise seek our friendship, and against whom we have neither anger nor complaint. As Europe is our market for trade, we ought to form no partial connection with any part of it. It is the true interest of America to steer clear of European contentions, which she never can do, while, by her dependence on Britain, she is made the make-weight in the scale of British politics.

Europe is too thickly planted with kingdoms to be long at peace, and whenever a war breaks out between England and any foreign power, the trade of America goes to ruin, *because of her connection with Britain.* The next war may not turn out like the last, and should it not, the advocates for reconciliation now will be wishing for separation then, because neutrality in that case would be a safer convoy than a man of war. Every thing that is right or reasonable pleads for separation. The blood of the slain, the weeping voice of nature cries, 'TIS TIME TO PART. Even the distance at which the Almighty hath placed England and America is a strong and natural proof that the authority of the one over the other, was never the design of heaven. The time likewise at which the continent was discovered, adds weight to the argument, and the manner in which it was peopled, encreases the force of it. The Reformation was preceded by the discovery of America: As if the Almighty graciously meant to open a sanctuary to the persecuted in future years, when home should afford neither friendship nor safety.

The authority of Great Britain over this continent, is a form of government, which sooner or later must have an end. And a serious mind can draw no true pleasure by looking forward, under the painful and positive conviction that what he calls "the present constitution" is merely temporary. As parents, we can have no joy, knowing that this government is not sufficiently lasting to insure any thing which we may bequeath to posterity. And by a plain method of argument, as we are running the next generation into debt, we ought to do the work of it, otherwise we use them meanly and pitifully. In order to discover the line of our duty rightly, we should take our children in our hand, and fix our station a few years farther into life; that eminence will present a prospect which a few present fears and prejudices conceal from our sight.

Though I would carefully avoid giving unnecessary offence, yet I am inclined to believe, that all those who espouse the doctrine of reconciliation, may be included within the following descriptions.

Interested men, who are not to be trusted, weak men who *cannot* see, prejudiced men who will not see, and a certain set of moderate men who think better of the European world than it deserves; and this last class, by an ill-judged deliberation, will be the cause of more calamities to this continent than all the other three.

It is the good fortune of many to live distant from the scene of present sorrow; the evil is not sufficiently brought to their doors to make them feel the precariousness with which all American property is possessed. But let our imaginations transport us a few moments to Boston; that seat of wretchedness will teach us wisdom, and instruct us for ever to renounce a power in whom we can have no trust. The inhabitants of that unfortunate city who but a few months ago were in ease and affluence, have now no other alternative than to stay and starve, or turn out to beg.[2] Endangered by the fire of their friends if they continue within the city, and plundered by the soldiery if they leave it, in their present situation they are prisoners without the hope of redemption, and in a general attack for their relief they would be exposed to the fury of both armies.

Men of passive tempers look somewhat lightly over the offences of Great Britain, and, still hoping for the best, are apt to call out, *Come, come, we shall be friends again for all this.* But examine the passions and feelings of mankind: bring the doctrine of reconciliation to the touchstone of nature, and then tell me whether you can hereafter love, honor, and faithfully serve the power that hath carried fire and sword into your land? If you cannot do all these, then are you only deceiving yourselves, and by your delay bringing ruin upon posterity. Your future connection with Britain, whom you can neither love nor honor, will be forced and unnatural, and being formed only on the plan of present convenience, will in a little time fall into a relapse more wretched than the first. But if you say, you can still pass the violations over, then I ask, hath your house been burnt? Hath your property been destroyed before your face? Are your wife and children destitute of a bed to lie on, or bread to live on? Have you lost a parent or a child by their hands, and yourself the ruined and wretched survivor? If you have not, then are

[2] To punish the inhabitants of Boston for the dumping into Boston harbor of 342 chests of teas worth 18,000 sterling, Parliament passed a series of measures known as the Coercive Acts. The Boston Port Bill, effective June 1, 1774, closed the town's harbor to all shipping until the East India Company was reimbursed. The second act provided that Crown agents charged with offenses while performing their duty might be tried in other colonies or in England. The third provided for the quartering of British troops in Boston, and the fourth gave the governor power to appoint members of the provincial Council, restrict the holding of town meetings, and provide for the appointment of jurors.

Paine's reference to the plight of the citizens of Boston was not an exaggeration. According to one contemporary estimate some 15,000 people in Boston were on the verge of starvation by the end of May, 1775.—*Editor.*

you not a judge of those who have. But if you have, and can still shake hands with the murderers, then are you unworthy the name of husband, father, friend, or lover, and whatever may be your rank or title in life, you have the heart of a coward, and the spirit of a sycophant.

This is not inflaming or exaggerating matters, but trying them by those feelings and affections which nature justifies, and without which we should be incapable of discharging the social duties of life, or enjoying the felicities of it. I mean not to exhibit horror for the purpose of provoking revenge, but to awaken us from fatal and unmanly slumbers, that we may pursue determinately some fixed object. 'Tis not in the power of Britain or of Europe to conquer America, if she doth not conquer herself by delay and timidity. The present winter is worth an age if rightly employed, but if lost or neglected the whole continent will partake of the misfortune; and there is no punishment which that man doth not deserve, be he who, or what, or where he will, that may be the means of sacrificing a season so precious and useful.

'Tis repugnant to reason, to the universal order of things, to all examples from former ages, to suppose that this continent can long remain subject to any external power. The most sanguine in Britain doth not think so. The utmost stretch of human wisdom cannot, at this time, compass a plan, short of separation, which can promise the continent even a year's security. Reconciliation is *now* a fallacious dream. Nature has deserted the connection, and art cannot supply her place. For, as Milton wisely expresses, "never can true reconcilement grow where wounds of deadly hate have pierced so deep."

Every quiet method for peace hath been ineffectual. Our prayers have been rejected with disdain; and hath tended to convince us that nothing flatters vanity or confirms obstinacy in kings more than repeated petitioning—and nothing hath contributed more than that very measure to make the kings of Europe absolute. Witness Denmark and Sweden. Wherefore, since nothing but blows will do, for God's sake let us come to a final separation, and not leave the next generation to be cutting throats under the violated unmeaning names of parent and child.

To say they will never attempt it again is idle and visionary; we thought so at the repeal of the Stamp Act, yet a year or two undeceived us; as well may we suppose that nations which have been once defeated will never renew the quarrel.

As to government matters, 'tis not in the power of Britain to do this continent justice: the business of it will soon be too weighty and intricate to be managed with any tolerable degree of convenience, by a power so distant from us, and so very ignorant of us; for if they cannot conquer us, they cannot govern us. To be always running three or four thousand miles with a tale or a petition, waiting four or five months for an answer, which, when obtained, requires five or six more to explain it in, will in a few years be looked upon as folly and childishness. There was a time when it was proper, and there is a proper time for it to cease.

Small islands not capable of protecting themselves are the proper objects for government [3] to take under their care; but there is something absurd, in supposing a Continent to be perpetually governed by an island. In no instance hath nature made the satellite larger than its primary planet; and as England and America, with respect to each other, reverse the common order of nature, it is evident that they belong to different systems. England to Europe: America to itself.

I am not induced by motives of pride, party or resentment to espouse the doctrine of separation and independence; I am clearly, positively, and conscientiously persuaded that it is the true interest of this continent to be so; that everything short of *that* is mere patchwork, that it can afford no lasting felicity,—that it is leaving the sword to our children, and shrinking back at a time when a little more, a little further, would have rendered this continent the glory of the earth.

As Britain hath not manifested the least inclination towards a compromise, we may be assured that no terms can be obtained worthy the acceptance of the continent, or any ways equal to the expence of blood and treasure we have been already put to.

The object contended for, ought always to bear some just proportion to the expense. The removal of North, or the whole detestable junto, is a matter unworthy the millions we have expended. A temporary stoppage of trade was an inconvenience, which would have sufficiently balanced the repeal of all the acts complained of, had such repeals been obtained; but if the whole continent must take up arms, if every man must be a soldier, 'tis scarcely worth our while to fight against a contemptible ministry only. Dearly, dearly do we pay for the repeal of the acts, if that is all we fight for; for, in a just estimation 'tis as great a folly to pay a Bunker Hill price for law as for land. As I have always considered the independency of this continent, as an event which sooner or later must arrive, so from the late rapid progress of the continent to

---

[3] In several later editions the word "kingdoms" was substituted for "government."— *Editor.*

maturity, the event cannot be far off. Wherefore, on the breaking out of hostilities, it was not worth the while to have disputed a matter which time would have finally redressed, unless we meant to be in earnest: otherwise it is like wasting an estate on a suit at law, to regulate the trespasses of a tenant whose lease is just expiring. No man was a warmer wisher for a reconciliation than myself, before the fatal nineteenth of April, 1775, but the moment the event of that day was made known, I rejected the hardened, sullen-tempered Pharaoh of England for ever; and disdain the wretch, that with the pretended title of FATHER OF HIS PEOPLE can unfeelingly hear of their slaughter, and composedly sleep with their blood upon his soul.

But admitting that matters were now made up, what would be the event? I answer, the ruin of the continent. And that for several reasons.

First. The powers of governing still remaining in the hands of the king, he will have a negative over the whole legislation of this continent. And as he hath shown himself such an inveterate enemy to liberty, and discovered such a thirst for arbitrary power, is he, or is he not, a proper person to say to these colonies, *You shall make no laws but what I please!?* And is there any inhabitant of America so ignorant as not to know, that according to what is called the *present Constitution,* this continent can make no laws but what the king gives leave to; and is there any man so unwise as not to see, that (considering what has happened) he will suffer no law to be made here but such as suits *his* purpose? We may be as effectually enslaved by the want of laws in America, as by submitting to laws made for us in England. After matters are made up (as it is called) can there be any doubt, but the whole power of the crown will be exerted to keep this continent as low and humble as possible? Instead of going forward we shall go backward, or be perpetually quarrelling, or ridiculously petitioning. We are already greater than the king wishes us to be, and will he not hereafter endeavor to make us less? To bring the matter to one point, Is the power who is jealous of our prosperity, a proper power to govern us? Whoever says *No,* to this question, is an independent for independency means no more than this, whether we shall make our own laws, or, whether the king, the greatest enemy this continent hath, or can have, shall tell us *there shall be no laws but such as I like.*

But the king, you will say, has a negative in England; the people there can make no laws without his consent. In point of right and good order, it is something very ridiculous that a youth of twenty-one (which hath often happened) shall say to several millions of people older and wiser than himself, "I forbid this or that act of yours to be law." But in this place I decline this sort of reply, though I will never cease to expose the absurdity of it, and only answer that England being the king's residence, and America not so, makes quite another case. The king's negative here is ten times more dangerous and fatal than it can be in England; for there he will scarcely refuse his consent to a bill for putting England into as strong a state of defense as possible, and in America he would never suffer such a bill to be passed.

America is only a secondary object in the system of British politics. England consults the good of this country no further than it answers her own purpose. Wherefore, her own interest leads her to suppress the growth of ours in every case which doth not promote her advantage, or in the least interferes with it. A pretty state we should soon be in under such a second hand government, considering what has happened! Men do not change from enemies to friends by the alteration of a name: And in order to show that reconciliation now is a dangerous doctrine, I affirm, *that it would be policy in the king at this time to repeal the acts, for the sake of reinstating himself in the government of the provinces;* In order that HE MAY ACCOMPLISH BY CRAFT AND SUBTLETY, IN THE LONG RUN, WHAT HE CANNOT DO BY FORCE AND VIOLENCE IN THE SHORT ONE. Reconciliation and ruin are nearly related.

Secondly. That as even the best terms which we can expect to obtain can amount to no more than a temporary expedient, or a kind of government by guardianship, which can last no longer than till the colonies come of age, so the general face and state of things in the interim will be unsettled and unpromising. Emigrants of property will not choose to come to a country whose form of government hangs but by a thread, and who is every day tottering on the brink of commotion and disturbance; and numbers of the present inhabitants would lay hold of the interval to dispose of their effects, and quit the continent.

But the most powerful of all arguments is, that nothing but independence, *i. e.* a continental form of government, can keep the peace of the continent and preserve it inviolate from civil wars. I dread the event of a reconciliation with Britain now, as it is more than probable that it will be followed by a revolt some where or other, the consequences of which may be far more fatal than all the malice of Britain.

Thousands are already ruined by British barbarity; (thousands more will probably suffer the same fate). Those men have other feelings than us who have nothing suffered. All they now possess is liberty; what they before enjoyed is sacrificed to its service, and having nothing more to lose they disdain submission. Besides, the general temper of the colonies, towards a British government will be like that of a youth who is nearly out of his time; they will care very little about her: And a government which cannot preserve the peace is no government at all, and in that case we pay our money for nothing; and pray what is it that Britain can do, whose power will be wholly on paper, should a civil tumult break out the very day after reconciliation? I have heard some men say, many of whom I believe spoke without thinking, that they dreaded an independence, fearing that it would produce civil wars: It is but seldom that our first thoughts are truly correct, and that is the case here; for there is ten times more to dread from a patched up connection than from independence. I make the sufferer's case my own, and I protest, that were I driven from house and home, my property destroyed, and my circumstances ruined, that as a man, sensible of injuries, I could never relish the doctrine of reconciliation, or consider myself bound thereby.

The colonies have manifested such a spirit of good order and obedience to continental government, as is sufficient to make every reasonable person easy and happy on that head. No man can assign the least pretence for his fears, on any other grounds, than such as are truly childish and ridiculous, viz., that one colony will be striving for superiority over another.

Where there are no distinctions there can be no superiority; perfect equality affords no temptation. The Republics of Europe are all (and we may say always) in peace. Holland and Switzerland are without wars, foreign or domestic: Monarchical governments, it is true, are never long at rest: the crown itself is a temptation to enterprising ruffians at home; and that degree of pride and insolence ever attendant on regal authority, swells into a rupture with foreign powers in instances where a republican government, by being formed on more natural principles, would negociate the mistake.

If there is any true cause of fear respecting independence, it is because no plan is yet laid down. Men do not see their way out. Wherefore, as an opening into that business I offer the following hints; at the same time modestly affirming, that I have no other opinion of them myself, than that they may be the means of giving rise to something better.

Could the straggling thoughts of individuals be collected, they would frequently form materials for wise and able men to improve into useful matter.

Let the assemblies be annual, with a president only. The representation more equal, their business wholly domestic, and subject to the authority of a Continental Congress.

Let each colony be divided into six, eight, or ten, convenient districts, each district to send a proper number of delegates to Congress, so that each colony send at least thirty. The whole number in Congress will be at least 390. Each Congress to sit and to choose a President by the following method. When the delegates are met, let a colony be taken from the whole thirteen colonies by lot, after which let the Congress choose (by ballot) a President from out of the delegates of that province. In the next Congress, let a colony be taken by lot from twelve only, omitting that colony from which the president was taken in the former Congress, and so proceeding on till the whole thirteen shall have had their proper rotation. And in order that nothing may pass into a law but what is satisfactorily just, not less than three-fifths of the Congress to be called a majority. He that will promote discord, under a government so equally formed as this, would have joined Lucifer in his revolt.

But as there is a peculiar delicacy from whom, or in what manner, this business must first arise, and as it seems most agreeable and consistent that it should come from some intermediate body between the governed and the governors, that is, between the Congress and the people, let a continental conference be held in the following manner, and for the following purpose,

A committee of twenty-six members of Congress, *viz.* Two for each colony. Two members from each House of Assembly, or Provincial Convention; and five representatives of the people at large, to be chosen in the capital city or town of each province, for, and in behalf of the whole province, by as many qualified voters as shall think proper to attend from all parts of the province for that purpose; or, if more convenient, the representatives may be chosen in two or three of the most populous parts thereof. In this conference, thus assembled, will be united the two grand principles of business, *knowledge* and *power*. The Members of Congress, Assemblies, or Conventions, by having had experience in national concerns, will be able and useful counsellors, and the whole, being impowered by the people, will have a truly legal authority.

The conferring members being met, let their business be to frame a

Continental Charter, or Charter of the United Colonies; (answering to what is called the Magna Charta of England) fixing the number and manner of choosing Members of Congress, Members of Assembly, with their date of sitting; and drawing the line of business and jurisdiction between them: Always remembering, that our strength is continental, not provincial. Securing freedom and property to all men, and above all things, the free exercise of religion, according to the dictates of conscience; with such other matter as it is necessary for a charter to contain. Immediately after which, the said conference to dissolve, and the bodies which shall be chosen conformable to the said charter, to be the legislators and governors of this continent for the time being: Whose peace and happiness, may GOD preserve. AMEN.

Should any body of men be hereafter delegated for this or some similar purpose, I offer them the following extracts from that wise observer on governments, Dragonetti. "The science," says he, "of the politician consists in fixing the true point of happiness and freedom. Those men would deserve the gratitude of ages, who should discover a mode of government that contained the greatest sum of individual happiness, with the least national expense." (Dragonetti on "Virtues and Reward.")

But where, say some, is the king of America? I'll tell you, friend, he reigns above, and doth not make havoc of mankind like the royal brute of Great Britain. Yet that we may not appear to be defective even in earthly honors, let a day be solemnly set apart for proclaiming the charter; let it be brought forth placed on the divine law, the Word of God; let a crown be placed thereon, by which the world may know, that so far as we approve of monarchy, that in America the law is king. For as in absolute governments the king is law, so in free countries the law ought to be king; and there ought to be no other. But lest any ill use should afterwards arise, let the crown at the conclusion of the ceremony be demolished, and scattered among the people whose right it is.

A government of our own is our natural right: and when a man seriously reflects on the precariousness of human affairs, he will become convinced, that it is infinitely wiser and safer, to form a Constitution of our own in a cool deliberate manner, while we have it in our power, than to trust such an interesting event to time and chance. If we omit it now, some Massanello [4] may hereafter arise, who, laying hold of popular dis-

---

[4] Thomas Anello, otherwise Massanello, a fisherman of Naples, who after spiriting up his countrymen in the public market place, against the oppression of the Spaniards, to whom the place was then subject, prompted them to revolt, and in the space of a day became king.—*Author.*

quietudes, may collect together the desperate and the discontented, and by assuming to themselves the powers of government, finally sweep away the liberties of the continent like a deluge. Should the government of America return again into the hands of Britain, the tottering situation of things will be a temptation for some desperate adventurer to try his fortune; and in such a case, what relief can Britain give? Ere she could hear the news, the fatal business might be done; and ourselves suffering like the wretched Britons under the oppression of the conqueror. Ye that oppose independence now, ye know not what ye do: ye are opening a door to eternal tyranny, by keeping vacant the seat of government. There are thousands and tens of thousands, who would think it glorious to expel from the continent, that barbarous and hellish power, which hath stirred up the Indians and the Negroes to destroy us; the cruelty hath a double guilt, it is dealing brutally by us, and treacherously by them.

To talk of friendship with those in whom our reason forbids us to have faith, and our affections wounded through a thousand pores instruct us to detest, is madness and folly. Every day wears out the little remains of kindred between us and them; and can there be any reason to hope, that as the relationship expires, the affection will increase, or that we shall agree better when we have ten times more and greater concerns to quarrel over than ever?

Ye that tell us of harmony and reconciliation, can ye restore to us the time that is past? Can ye give to prostitution its former innocence? neither can ye reconcile Britain and America. The last cord now is broken, the people of England are presenting addresses against us. There are injuries which nature cannot forgive; she would cease to be nature if she did. As well can the lover forgive the ravisher of his mistress, as the continent forgive the murders of Britain. The Almighty hath implanted in us these unextinguishable feelings for good and wise purposes. They are the guardians of his image in our hearts. They distinguish us from the herd of common animals. The social compact would dissolve, and justice be extirpated from the earth, or have only a casual existence were we callous to the touches of affection. The robber and the murderer would often escape unpunished, did not the injuries which our tempers sustain, provoke us into justice.

O! ye that love mankind! Ye that dare oppose not only the tyranny but the tyrant, stand forth! Every spot of the old world is overrun with oppression. Freedom hath been hunted round the globe. Asia and Africa have long expelled her. Europe regards her like a stranger, and England hath given her warning to depart. O! receive the fugitive, and prepare in time an asylum for mankind.

OF THE PRESENT ABILITY OF AMERICA;

WITH SOME MISCELLANEOUS REFLECTIONS

I have never met with a man, either in England or America, who hath not confessed his opinion, that a separation between the countries would take place one time or other. And there is no instance in which we have shown less judgment, than in endeavoring to describe, what we call, the ripeness or fitness of the continent for independence.

As all men allow the measure, and vary only in their opinion of the time, let us, in order to remove mistakes, take a general survey of things, and endeavor if possible to find out the *very* time. But I need not go far, the inquiry ceases at once, for the *time hath found us.* The general concurrence, the glorious union of all things, proves the fact.

'Tis not in numbers but in unity that our great strength lies; yet our present numbers are sufficient to repel the force of all the world. The continent has at this time the largest body of armed and disciplined men of any power under heaven: and is just arrived at that pitch of strength, in which no single colony is able to support itself, and the whole, when united, is able to do any thing. Our land force is more than sufficient, and as to naval affairs, we cannot be insensible that Britain would never suffer an American man of war to be built, while the continent remained in her hands. Wherefore, we should be no forwarder a hundred years hence in that branch than we are now; but the truth is, we should be less so, because the timber of the country is every day diminishing, and that which will remain at last, will be far off or difficult to procure.

Were the continent crowded with inhabitants, her sufferings under the present circumstances would be intolerable. The more seaport-towns we had, the more should we have both to defend and to lose. Our present numbers are so happily proportioned to our wants, that no man need be idle. The diminution of trade affords an army, and the necessities of an army create a new trade.

Debts we have none: and whatever we may contract on this account will serve as a glorious memento of our virtue. Can we but leave posterity with a settled form of government, an independent constitution of its own, the purchase at any price will be cheap. But to expend millions for the sake of getting a few vile acts repealed, and routing the present ministry only, is unworthy the charge, and is using posterity with the utmost cruelty; because it is leaving them the great work to do, and a debt upon their backs from which they derive no advantage. Such a thought's unworthy a man of honor, and is the true characteristic of a narrow heart and a piddling politician.

The debt we may contract doth not deserve our regard if the work be but accomplished. No nation ought to be without a debt. A national debt is a national bond; and when it bears no interest, is in no case a grievance. Britain is oppressed with a debt of upwards of one hundred and forty millions sterling, for which she pays upwards of four millions interest. And as a compensation for her debt, she has a large navy. America is without a debt, and without a navy; yet for the twentieth part of the English national debt, could have a navy as large again. The navy of England is not worth at this time more than three millions and a half sterling.

The first and second editions of this pamphlet were published without the following calculations, which are now given as a proof that the above estimation of the navy is a just one. See Entic's "Naval History," Intro., p. 56.

The charge of building a ship of each rate, and furnishing her with masts, yards, sails, and rigging, together with a proportion of eight months boatswain's and carpenter's sea-stores, as calculated by Mr. Burchett, Secretary to the navy.

For a ship of 100 guns,	35,553 *l.*
90	29,886
80	23,638
70	17,785
60	14,197
50	10,606
40	7,558
30	5,846
20	3,710

And hence it is easy to sum up the value, or cost, rather, of the whole British navy, which, in the year 1757, when it was at its greatest glory, consisted of the following ships and guns.

Ships.	Guns.	Cost of one.	Cost of all.
6	100	55,553 *l.*	213,318 *l.*
12	90	29,886	358,632
12	80	23,638	283,656
43	70	17,785	764,755
35	60	14,197	496,895
40	50	10,605	424,240
45	40	7,558	340,110
58	20	3,710	215,180
85 Sloops, bombs, and fireships, one with another, at		2,000	170,000
		Cost,	3,266,786 *l.*
		Remains for guns,	233,214
		Total,	3,500,000 *l.*

No country on the globe is so happily situated, or so internally capable of raising a fleet as America. Tar, timber, iron and cordage are her natural produce. We need go abroad for nothing. Whereas the Dutch, who make large profits by hiring out their ships of war to the Spaniards and Portuguese, are obliged to import most of the materials they use. We ought to view the building a fleet as an article of commerce, it being the natural manufactory of this country. 'Tis the best money we can lay out. A navy when finished is worth more than it cost: And is that nice point in national policy, in which commerce and protection are united. Let us build; if we want them not, we can sell; and by that means replace our paper currency with ready gold and silver.

In point of manning a fleet, people in general run into great errors; it is not necessary that one fourth part should be sailors. The terrible privateer, Captain Death, stood the hottest engagement of any ship last war, yet had not twenty sailors on board, though her complement of men was upwards of two hundred. A few able and social sailors will soon instruct a sufficient number of active landsmen in the common work of a ship. Wherefore we never can be more capable of beginning on maritime matters than now, while our timber is standing, our fisheries blocked up, and our sailors and shipwrights out of employ. Men of war, of seventy and eighty guns, were built forty years ago in New England,

and why not the same now? Ship building is America's greatest pride, and in which she will, in time, excel the whole world. The great empires of the east are mostly inland, and consequently excluded from the possibility of rivalling her. Africa is in a state of barbarism; and no power in Europe, hath either such an extent of coast, or such an internal supply of materials. Where nature hath given the one, she hath withheld the other; to America only hath she been liberal to both. The vast empire of Russia is almost shut out from the sea; wherefore her boundless forests, her tar, iron, and cordage are only articles of commerce.

In point of safety, ought we to be without a fleet? We are not the little people now, which we were sixty years ago; at that time we might have trusted our property in the streets, or fields rather, and slept securely without locks or bolts to our doors and windows. The case is now altered, and our methods of defence ought to improve with our increase of property. A common pirate, twelve months ago, might have come up the Delaware, and laid the city of Philadelphia under contribution for what sum he pleased; and the same might have happened to other places. Nay, any daring fellow, in a brig of fourteen or sixteen guns, might have robbed the whole continent, and carried off half a million of money. These are circumstances which demand our attention, and point out the necessity of naval protection.

Some perhaps will say, that after we have made it up with Britain, she will protect us. Can they be so unwise as to mean, that she will keep a navy in our harbors for that purpose? Common sense will tell us, that the power which hath endeavored to subdue us, is of all others, the most improper to defend us. Conquest may be effected under the pretence of friendship; and ourselves, after a long and brave resistance, be at last cheated into slavery. And if her ships are not to be admitted into our harbors, I would ask, how is she to protect us? A navy three or four thousand miles off can be of little use, and on sudden emergencies, none at all. Wherefore if we must hereafter protect ourselves, why not do it for ourselves? Why do it for another?

The English list of ships of war, is long and formidable, but not a tenth part of them are at any one time fit for service, numbers of them are not in being; yet their names are pompously continued in the list, if only a plank be left of the ship: and not a fifth part of such as are fit for service, can be spared on any one station at one time. The East and West Indies, Mediterranean, Africa, and other parts, over which Britain extends her claim, make large demands upon her navy. From a mixture of prejudice and inattention, we have contracted a false notion respecting the navy of England, and have talked as if we should have the whole of it to encounter at once, and, for that reason, supposed that we must have one as large; which not being instantly practicable, has been made use of by a set of disguised Tories to discourage our beginning thereon. Nothing can be further from truth than this; for if America had only a twentieth part of the naval force of Britain, she would be by far an over-match for her; because, as we neither have, nor claim any foreign dominion, our whole force would be employed on our own coast, where we should, in the long run, have two to one the advantage of those who had three or four thousand miles to sail over, before they could attack us, and the same distance to return in order to refit and recruit. And although Britain, by her fleet, hath a check over our trade to Europe, we have as large a one over her trade to the West Indies, which, by laying in the neighborhood of the continent, lies entirely at its mercy.

Some method might be fallen on to keep up a naval force in time of peace, if we should not judge it necessary to support a constant navy. If premiums were to be given to merchants to build and employ in their service, ships mounted with twenty, thirty, forty, or fifty guns, (the premiums to be in proportion to the loss of bulk to the merchant,) fifty or sixty of those ships, with a few guardships on constant duty, would keep up a sufficient navy, and that without burdening ourselves with the evil so loudly complained of in England, of suffering their fleet in time of peace to lie rotting in the docks. To unite the sinews of commerce and defence is sound policy; for when our strength and our riches play into each other's hand, we need fear no external enemy.

In almost every article of defence we abound. Hemp flourishes even to rankness, so that we need not want cordage. Our iron is superior to that of other countries. Our small arms equal to any in the world. Cannon we can cast at pleasure. Saltpeter and gunpowder we are every day producing. Our knowledge is hourly improving. Resolution is our inherent character, and courage has never yet forsaken us. Wherefore, what is it that we want? Why is it that we hesitate? From Britain we can expect nothing but ruin. If she is once admitted to the government of America again, this continent will not be worth living in. Jealousies will be always arising; insurrections will be constantly happening; and who will go forth to quell them? Who will venture his life to reduce his own countrymen to a foreign obedience? The difference between Pennsylvania and Connecticut, respecting some unlocated lands, shows the insignificance of a British government, and fully proves that nothing but continental authority can regulate continental matters.

Another reason why the present time is preferable to all others, is, that the fewer our numbers are, the more land there is yet unoccupied, which, instead of being lavished by the king on his worthless dependants, may be hereafter applied, not only to the discharge of the present debt, but to the constant support of government. No nation under heaven hath such an advantage as this.

The infant state of the colonies, as it is called, so far from being against, is an argument in favor of independence. We are sufficiently numerous, and were we more so we might be less united. 'Tis a matter worthy of observation, that the more a country is peopled, the smaller their armies are. In military numbers, the ancients far exceeded the moderns: and the reason is evident, for trade being the consequence of population, men became too much absorbed thereby to attend to any thing else. Commerce diminishes the spirit both of patriotism and military defence. And history sufficiently informs us, that the bravest achievements were always accomplished in the non-age of a nation. With the increase of commerce England hath lost its spirit. The city of London, notwithstanding its numbers, submits to continued insults with the patience of a coward. The more men have to lose, the less willing are they to venture. The rich are in general slaves to fear, and submit to courtly power with the trembling duplicity of a spaniel.

Youth is the seed-time of good habits as well in nations as in individuals. It might be difficult, if not impossible, to form the continent into one government half a century hence. The vast variety of interests, occasioned by an increase of trade and population, would create confusion. Colony would be against colony. Each being able would scorn each other's assistance: and while the proud and foolish gloried in their little distinctions, the wise would lament that the union had not been formed before. Wherefore the present time is the true time for establishing it. The intimacy which is contracted in infancy, and the friendship which is formed in misfortune, are of all others the most lasting and unalterable. Our present union is marked with both these characters: we are young, and we have been distressed; but our concord hath withstood our troubles, and fixes a memorable era for posterity to glory in.

The present time, likewise, is that peculiar time which never happens to a nation but once, viz. the time of forming itself into a government. Most nations have let slip the opportunity, and by that means have been compelled to receive laws from their conquerors, instead of making laws for themselves. First, they had a king, and then a form of government; whereas the articles or charter of government should be formed first, and men delegated to execute them afterwards: but from the errors of other nations let us learn wisdom, and lay hold of the present opportunity—*to begin government at the right end.*

When William the Conqueror subdued England, he gave them law at the point of the sword; and, until we consent that the seat of government in America be legally and authoritatively occupied, we shall be in danger of having it filled by some fortunate ruffian, who may treat us in the same manner, and then, where will be our freedom? where our property?

As to religion, I hold it to be the indispensable duty of government to protect all conscientious professors thereof, and I know of no other business which government has to do therewith. Let a man throw aside that narrowness of soul, that selfishness of principle, which the niggards of all professions are so unwilling to part with, and he will be at once delivered of his fears on that head. Suspicion is the companion of mean souls, and the bane of all good society. For myself, I fully and conscientiously believe, that it is the will of the Almighty that there should be a diversity of religious opinions among us. It affords a larger field for our Christian kindness: were we all of one way of thinking, our religious dispositions would want matter for probation; and on this liberal principle I look on the various denominations among us, to be like children of the same family, differing only in what is called their Christian names.

In pages [28–29] I threw out a few thoughts on the propriety of a Continental Charter (for I only presume to offer hints, not plans) and in this place, I take the liberty of re-mentioning the subject, by observing, that a charter is to be understood as a bond of solemn obligation, which the whole enters into, to support the right of every separate part, whether of religion, professional freedom, or property. A firm bargain and a right reckoning make long friends.

I have heretofore likewise mentioned the necessity of a large and equal representation; and there is no political matter which more deserves our attention. A small number of electors, or a small number of representatives, are equally dangerous. But if the number of the representatives be not only small, but unequal, the danger is encreased. As an instance of this, I mention the following; when the petition of the associators was before the House of Assembly of Pennsylvania, twenty-eight members only were present; all the Bucks county members, being eight, voted against it, and had seven of the Chester members done the same, this whole province had been governed by two counties only; and this danger it is always exposed to. The unwarrantable stretch likewise, which that house made in their last sitting, to gain an undue authority over the delegates of that province, ought to warn the people at large, how they trust power out of their own hands. A set of instructions for their delegates were put together, which in point of sense and business would have dishonoured a school-boy, and after being approved by a few, a very few, without doors, were carried into the house, and there passed *in behalf of the whole colony;* whereas, did the whole colony know with what ill will that house had entered on some necessary public measures, they would not hesitate a moment to think them unworthy of such a trust.

Immediate necessity makes many things convenient, which if continued would grow into oppressions. Expedience and right are different things. When the calamities of America required a consultation, there was no method so ready, or at that time so proper, as to appoint persons from the several houses of Assembly for that purpose; and the wisdom with which they have proceeded hath preserved this continent from ruin. But as it is more than probable that we shall never be without a Congress, every well wisher to good order must own that the mode for choosing members of that body, deserves consideration. And I put it as a question to those who make a study of mankind, whether representation and election is not too great a power for one and the same body of men to possess? When we are planning for posterity, we ought to remember that virtue is not hereditary.

It is from our enemies that we often gain excellent maxims, and are frequently surprised into reason by their mistakes. Mr. Cornwall (one of the Lords of the Treasury) treated the petition of the New York Assembly with contempt, because *that* house, he said, consisted but of twenty-six members, which trifling number, he argued, could not with decency be put for the whole. We thank him for his involuntary honesty.[5]

To CONCLUDE, however strange it may appear to some, or however unwilling they may be to think so, matters not, but many strong and striking reasons may be given to show, that nothing can settle our affairs

---

[5] Those who would fully understand of what great consequence a large and equal representation is to a state, should read Burgh's *Political Disquisitions.—Author.*

so expeditiously as an open and determined DECLARATION FOR INDEPEND-
ENCE. Some of which are,

Firstly—It is the custom of nations, when any two are at war, for some
other powers, not engaged in the quarrel, to step in as mediators, and
bring about the preliminaries of a peace: But while America calls herself the subject of Great Britain, no power, however well disposed she
may be, can offer her mediation. Wherefore, in our present state we may
quarrel on for ever.

Secondly—It is unreasonable to suppose, that France or Spain will give
us any kind of assistance, if we mean only to make use of that assistance
for the purpose of repairing the breach, and strengthening the connection between Britain and America; because, those powers would be sufferers by the consequences.

Thirdly—While we profess ourselves the subjects of Britain, we must,
in the eyes of foreign nations, be considered as Rebels. The precedent is
somewhat dangerous to their peace, for men to be in arms under the
name of subjects: we, on the spot, can solve the paradox; but to unite
resistance and subjection, requires an idea much too refined for common understanding.

Fourthly—Were a manifesto to be published, and despatched to foreign courts, setting forth the miseries we have endured, and the peaceful
methods which we have ineffectually used for redress; declaring at the
same time, that not being able any longer to live happily or safely under
the cruel disposition of the British court, we had been driven to the
necessity of breaking off all connections with her; at the same time,
assuring all such courts of our peaceable disposition towards them, and
of our desire of entering into trade with them: such a memorial would
produce more good effects to this continent, than if a ship were freighted
with petitions to Britain.

Under our present denominations of British subjects, we can neither
be received nor heard abroad: the custom of all courts is against us, and
will be so, until by an independence we take rank with other nations.

These proceedings may at first seem strange and difficult, but like all
other steps which we have already passed over, will in a little time become familiar and agreeable: and until an independence is declared,
the continent will feel itself like a man who continues putting off some
unpleasant business from day to day, yet knows it must be done, hates to
set about it, wishes it over, and is continually haunted with the thoughts
of its necessity.

Appendix to "Common Sense"

Since the publication of the first edition of this pamphlet, or rather, on the same day on which it came out, the king's speech made its appearance in this city [Philadelphia]. Had the spirit of prophecy directed the birth of this production, it could not have brought it forth at a more seasonable juncture, or at a more necessary time. The bloody-mindedness of the one, shows the necessity of pursuing the doctrine of the other. Men read by way of revenge. And the speech, instead of terrifying, prepared a way for the manly principles of independence.

Ceremony, and even silence, from whatever motives they may arise, have a hurtful tendency when they give the least degree of countenance to base and wicked performances; wherefore, if this maxim be admitted, it naturally follows, that the king's speech, as being a piece of finished villainy, deserved and still deserves, a general execration, both by the Congress and the people. Yet, as the domestic tranquillity of a nation, depends greatly on the *chastity* of what might properly be called NA-TIONAL MANNERS, it is often better to pass some things over in silent disdain, than to make use of such new methods of dislike, as might introduce the least innovation on that guardian of our peace and safety. And, perhaps, it is chiefly owing to this prudent delicacy, that the king's speech hath not before now suffered a public execution. The speech, if it may be called one, is nothing better than a wilful audacious libel against the truth, the common good, and the existence of mankind; and is a formal and pompous method of offering up human sacrifices to the pride of tyrants. But this general massacre of mankind, is one of the privileges and the certain consequences of kings; for as nature knows them *not,* they know *not her,* and although they are beings of our *own* creating, they know not *us,* and are become the gods of their creators. The speech hath one good quality, which is, that it is not calculated to deceive, neither can we, even if we would, be deceived by it. Brutality and tyranny appear on the face of it. It leaves us at no loss: And every line convinces, even in the moment of reading, that he who hunts the woods for prey, the naked and untutored Indian, is less savage than the king of Britain.

Sir John Dalrymple, the putative father of a whining jesuitical piece, fallaciously called, *"The address of the people of England to the inhabitants of America,"* hath perhaps from a vain supposition that the people *here* were to be frightened at the pomp and description of a king, given (though very unwisely on his part) the real character of the present one: "But," says this writer, "if you are inclined to pay compliments to an administration, which we do not complain of (meaning the Marquis of Rockingham's at the repeal of the Stamp Act) it is very unfair in you to withhold them from that prince, *by whose* NOD *?* LONE *they were permitted to do any thing."* This is toryism with a witness! Here is idolatry even without a mask: And he who can calmly hear and digest such doctrine, hath forfeited his claim to rationality—an apostate from the order of manhood—and ought to be considered as one who hath not only given up the proper dignity of man, but sunk himself beneath the rank of animals, and contemptibly crawls through the world like a worm.

However, it matters very little now what the king of England either says or does; he hath wickedly broken through every moral and human obligation, trampled nature and conscience beneath his feet, and by a steady and constitutional spirit of insolence and cruelty procured for himself an universal hatred. It is *now* the interest of America to provide for herself. She hath already a large and young family, whom it is more her duty to take care of, than to be granting away her property to support a power who is become a reproach to the names of men and christians—YE, whose office it is to watch the morals of a nation, of whatsoever sect or denomination ye are of, as well as ye who are more immediately the guardians of the public liberty, if ye wish to preserve your native country uncontaminated by European corruption, ye must in secret wish a separation. But leaving the moral part to private reflection, I shall chiefly confine my further remarks to the following heads:

First, That it is the interest of America to be separated from Britain.

Secondly, Which is the easiest and most practicable plan, RECONCILIA-TION or INDEPENDENCE? with some occasional remarks.

In support of the first, I could, if I judged it proper, produce the opinion of some of the ablest and most experienced men on this continent: and whose sentiments on that head, are not yet publicly known. It is in reality a self-evident position: for no nation in a state of foreign dependence, limited in its commerce, and cramped and fettered in its legislative powers, can ever arrive at any material eminence. America doth not yet know what opulence is; and although the progress which she hath made stands unparalleled in the history of other nations, it is but childhood compared with what she would be capable of arriving at, had she, as she ought to have, the legislative powers in her own hands.

England is at this time proudly coveting what would do her no good were she to accomplish it; and the continent hesitating on a matter which will be her final ruin if neglected. It is the commerce and not the conquest of America by which England is to be benefited, and that would in a great measure continue, were the countries as independent of each other as France and Spain; because in many articles neither can go to a better market. But it is the independence of this country of Britain, or any other, which is now the main and only object worthy of contention, and which, like all other truths discovered by necessity, will appear clear and stronger every day.

First, Because it will come to that one time or other.

Secondly, Because the longer it is delayed, the harder it will be to accomplish.

I have frequently amused myself both in public and private companies, with silently remarking the specious errors of those who speak without reflecting. And among the many which I have heard, the following seems the most general, viz. that had this rupture happened forty or fifty years hence, instead of now, the continent would have been more able to have shaken off the dependence. To which I reply, that our military ability, *at this time,* arises from the experience gained in the last war, and which in forty or fifty years' time, would be totally extinct. The continent would not, by that time, have a general, or even a military officer left; and we, or those who may succeed us, would be as ignorant of martial matters as the ancient Indians: and this single position, closely attended to, will unanswerably prove that the present time is preferable to all others. The argument turns thus: At the conclusion of the last war,[6] we had experience, but wanted numbers; and forty or fifty years hence, we shall have numbers, without experience; wherefore, the proper point of time, must be some particular point between the two extremes, in which a sufficiency of the former remains, and a proper increase of the latter is obtained: And that point of time is the present time.

The reader will pardon this digression, as it does not properly come under the head I first set out with, and to which I again return by the following position, viz.:

Should affairs be patched up with Britain, and she to remain the governing and sovereign power of America, (which, as matters are now circumstanced, is giving up the point entirely) we shall deprive

[6] The reference is to the French and Indian war.—*Editor.*

ourselves of the very means of sinking the debt we have, or may contract. The value of the back lands, which some of the provinces are
clandestinely deprived of, by the unjust extension of the limits of Canada,[7] valued only at five pounds sterling per hundred acres, amount to
upwards of twenty-five millions, Pennsylvania currency; and the quit-
rents, at one penny sterling per acre, to two millions yearly.

It is by the sale of those lands that the debt may be sunk, without bur-
then to any, and the quit-rent reserved thereon will always lessen, and
in time will wholly support, the yearly expense of government. It matters not how long the debt is in paying, so that the lands when sold be
applied to the discharge of it, and for the execution of which the Congress for the time being will be the continental trustees.

I proceed now to the second head, viz. Which is the easiest and most
practicable plan, reconciliation or independence; with some occasional
remarks.

He who takes nature for his guide, is not easily beaten out of his
argument, and on that ground, I answer generally—*That* independence
being a single simple line, *contained within ourselves; and reconciliation, a matter exceedingly perplexed and complicated, and in which a
treacherous capricious court is to interfere, gives the answer without
a doubt.*

The present state of America is truly alarming to every man who is
capable of reflection. Without law, without government, without any
other mode of power than what is founded on, and granted by, courtesy.
Held together by an unexampled occurrence of sentiment, which is nevertheless subject to change, and which every secret enemy is endeavoring
to dissolve. Our present condition is, Legislation without law; wisdom
without a plan; a constitution without a name; and, what is strangely
astonishing, perfect independence contending for dependence. The instance is without a precedent, the case never existed before, and who can
tell what may be the event? The property of no man is secure in the
present unbraced system of things. The mind of the multitude is left at
random, and seeing no fixed object before them, they pursue such as
fancy or opinion presents. Nothing is criminal; there is no such thing as
treason; wherefore, every one thinks himself at liberty to act as he
pleases. The Tories would not have dared to assemble offensively, had
they known that their lives, by that act, were forfeited to the laws of

[7] The Quebec Act of 1774 extended the boundaries of the province of Quebec to the
Ohio and the Mississippi.—*Editor.*

the state. A line of distinction should be drawn between English soldiers taken in battle, and inhabitants of America taken in arms. The first are prisoners, but the latter traitors. The one forfeits his liberty, the other his head.

Notwithstanding our wisdom, there is a visible feebleness in some of our proceedings which gives encouragement to dissensions. The continental belt is too loosely buckled: And if something is not done in time, it will be too late to do any thing, and we shall fall into a state, in which neither reconciliation nor independence will be practicable. The king and his worthless adherents are got at their old game of dividing the continent, and there are not wanting among us printers who will be busy in spreading specious falsehoods. The artful and hypocritical letter which appeared a few months ago in two of the New York papers, and likewise in two others, is an evidence that there are men who want both judgment and honesty.

It is easy getting into holes and corners, and talking of reconciliation: But do such men seriously consider how difficult the task is, and how dangerous it may prove, should the continent divide thereon? Do they take within their view all the various orders of men whose situation and circumstances, as well as their own, are to be considered therein? Do they put themselves in the place of the sufferer whose *all* is *already* gone, and of the soldier, who hath quitted *all* for the defence of his country? If their ill-judged moderation be suited to their own private situations *only,* regardless of others, the event will convince them that "they are reckoning without their host."

Put us, say some, on the footing we were in the year 1763: To which I answer, the request is not now in the power of Britain to comply with, neither will she propose it; but if it were, and even should be granted, I ask, as a reasonable question, By what means is such a corrupt and faithless court to be kept to its engagements? Another parliament, nay, even the present, may hereafter repeal the obligation, on the pretence of its being violently obtained, or unwisely granted; and, in that case, Where is our redress? No going to law with nations; cannon are the barristers of crowns; and the sword, not of justice, but of war, decides the suit. To be on the footing of 1763, it is not sufficient, that the laws only be put in the same state, but, that our circumstances likewise be put in the same state; our burnt and destroyed towns repaired or built up, our private losses made good, our public debts (contracted for defence) discharged; otherwise we shall be millions worse than we were at that enviable period. Such a request, had it been complied with a year ago, would have won the heart and soul of the continent, but now it is too late. "The Rubicon is passed."

Besides, the taking up arms, merely to enforce the repeal of a pecuniary law, seems as unwarrantable by the divine law, and as repugnant to human feelings, as the taking up arms to enforce obedience thereto. The object, on either side, doth not justify the means; for the lives of men are too valuable to be cast away on such trifles. It is the violence which is done and threatened to our persons; the destruction of our property by an armed force; the invasion of our country by fire and sword, which conscientiously qualifies the use of arms: and the instant in which such mode of defence became necessary, all subjection to Britain ought to have ceased; and the independence of America should have been considered as dating its era from, and published by, *the first musket that was fired against her*. This line is a line of consistency; neither drawn by caprice, nor extended by ambition; but produced by a chain of events, of which the colonies were not the authors.

I shall conclude these remarks, with the following timely and wellintended hints. We ought to reflect, that there are three different ways by which an independency may hereafter be effected; and that *one* of those *three,* will, one day or other, be the fate of America, viz. By the legal voice of the people in Congress; by a military power; or by a mob: It may not always happen that our soldiers are citizens, and the multitude a body of reasonable men; virtue, as I have already remarked, is not hereditary, neither is it perpetual. Should an independency be brought about by the first of those means, we have every opportunity and every encouragement before us, to form the noblest, purest constitution on the face of the earth. We have it in our power to begin the world over again. A situation, similar to the present, hath not happened since the days of Noah until now. The birthday of a new world is at hand, and a race of men, perhaps as numerous as all Europe contains, are to receive their portion of freedom from the events of a few months. The reflection is awful, and in this point of view, how trifling, how ridiculous, do the little paltry cavilings of a few weak or interested men appear, when weighed against the business of a world.

Should we neglect the present favorable and inviting period, and independence be hereafter effected by any other means, we must charge the consequence to ourselves, or to those rather whose narrow and prejudiced souls are habitually opposing the measure, without either inquiring or reflecting. There are reasons to be given in support of independence which men should rather privately think of, than be publicly told of. We ought not now to be debating whether we shall be independent or not, but anxious to accomplish it on a firm, secure, and honorable basis, and uneasy rather that it is not yet began upon. Every day convinces us of its necessity. Even the Tories (if such beings yet remain among us) should, of all men, be the most solicitous to promote it; for as the appointment of committees at first protected them from popular rage, so, a wise and well established form of government will be the only certain means of continuing it securely to them. Wherefore, if they have not virtue enough to be WHIGS, they ought to have prudence enough to wish for independence.

In short, independence is the only bond that tie and keep us together. We shall then see our object, and our ears will be legally shut against the schemes of an intriguing, as well as cruel, enemy. We shall then, too, be on a proper footing to treat with Britain; for there is reason to conclude, that the pride of that court will be less hurt by treating with the American States for terms of peace, than with those, whom she denominates "rebellious subjects," for terms of accommodation. It is our delaying in that, encourages her to hope for conquest, and our backwardness tends only to prolong the war. As we have, without any good effect therefrom, withheld our trade to obtain a redress of our grievances, let us now try the alternative, by independently redressing them ourselves, and then offering to open the trade. The mercantile and reasonable part of England, will be still with us; because, peace, with trade, is preferable to war without it. And if this offer be not accepted, other courts may be applied to.

On these grounds I rest the matter. And as no offer hath yet been made to refute the doctrine contained in the former editions of this pamphlet, it is a negative proof, that either the doctrine cannot be refuted, or, that the party in favor of it are too numerous to be opposed. WHEREFORE, instead of gazing at each other with suspicious or doubtful curiosity, let each of us hold out to his neighbor the hearty hand of friendship, and unite in drawing a line, which, like an act of oblivion, shall bury in forgetfulness every former dissension. Let the names of Whig and Tory be extinct; and let none other be heard among us, than those of *a good citizen; an open and resolute friend;* and *a virtuous supporter of the* RIGHTS *of* MANKIND, *and of the* FREE AND INDEPENDENT STATES OF AMERICA.

AMERICAN CRISIS

EDITOR'S NOTE

TO THE *CRISIS* PAPERS

During the long and difficult struggle against England, Paine bore his full share as soldier and public official. But it was through his powerful pen that he best served the Revolutionary cause. At every critical point during the war, a new article came from his pen, written in language the plain people in the Continental Army and on the home front could understand, to bolster the Patriot forces, to explain the reasons for defeat and to rally the Americans for the next battle with the enemy with such ringing phrases as, " 'The United States of America' will sound as pompously in the world or in history, as the 'Kingdom of Great Britain' "; "We have crowded the business of an age into the compass of a few months"; and "We fight not to enslave, but to set a country free, and to make room upon earth for honest men to live in." For the significance of these articles in bolstering the morale of the fighting men, see Philip S. Foner, *Morale Education in the American Army: War for Independence, War of 1812, and Civil War*, New York, 1944.

Paine wrote sixteen pamphlets in the series which he entitled *The American Crisis* and signed them *Common Sense*. The papers were issued in thirteen numbered pamphlets with three additional numbers between 1776 and 1783. He ridiculed British officers, denounced the Tories, clarified the issues at stake in the war, appealed to the people of England to abandon making war on their former colonies, flayed the advocates of negotiated peace, drew up schemes for taxation and proposed plans for the strengthening of the American Union. These pamphlets, printed on many types and scraps of paper, were distributed widely, but Paine with his customary devotion to the Revolutionary cause refused to accept a penny for his work, even going into debt to cover the cost of publication.

THE AMERICAN CRISIS

I

Crisis I was written on a drum-head by campfire while Paine was accompanying General Washington's forces during the heartbreaking days of the retreat across New Jersey. The Revolution seemed to be lost; the enemy appeared to be invincible, and the morale of soldiers and civilians alike was at its lowest ebb. Something had to be done quickly, Colonel Joseph Reed wrote to Washington about this time, "or we must give up the cause."

Washington shared Reed's opinion. He was planning a surprise attack which would give to American affairs "a more pleasing aspect than they now have." On Christmas eve, 1776, Washington and his decimated forces were rowed across the Delaware to launch a surprise attack upon the slumbering Hessians who were stationed below Trenton. Before the soldiers embarked to battle the floes, a blizzard, and the swift current of the river, they listened, at Washington's command, to a reading of Paine's new pamphlet. The opening words alone—"These are the times that try men's souls: The summer soldier and the sunshine patriot will, in this crisis, shrink from the service of his country; but he that stands it NOW, deserves the love and thanks of man and woman"—inspired the ragged Continentals and played a crucial role in the gaining of the much-needed victory against overwhelming the enemy forces at Trenton. The pamphlet roused the entire continent. Even Paine's bitter enemy, Cheetham admitted that it had a dynamic effect on the Revolutionary cause. "The number," he writes, "was read in the camp, to every corporal's guard, and in the army and out of it had more than the intended effect. The convention of New York, reduced by dispersion, occasioned by alarm, to nine members, was rallied and reanimated. Militiamen who, already tired of the war, were straggling from the army, returned. Hope succeeded to despair, cheerfulness to gloom, and firmness to irresolution. . . ."—*Editor*.

THESE are the times that try men's souls. The summer soldier and the sunshine patriot will, in this crisis, shrink from the service of their country; but he that stands it *now,* deserves the love and thanks of man and woman. Tyranny, like hell, is not easily conquered; yet we have this consolation with us, that the harder the conflict, the more glorious the triumph. What we obtain too cheap, we esteem too lightly: it is dearness only that gives every thing its value. Heaven knows how to put a proper price upon its goods; and it would be strange indeed if so celestial an article as FREEDOM should not be highly rated. Britain, with an army to enforce her tyranny, has declared that she has a right (*not only to* TAX) but "TO BIND *us in* ALL CASES WHATSOEVER," [1] and if being *bound in that manner,* is not slavery, then is there not such a thing as slavery upon earth. Even the expression is impious; for so unlimited a power can belong only to God.

Whether the independence of the continent was declared too soon, or delayed too long, I will not now enter into as an argument; my own simple opinion is, that had it been eight months earlier, it would have been much better. We did not make a proper use of last winter, neither could we, while we were in a dependent state. However, the fault, if it were one, was all our own; [2] we have none to blame but ourselves. But no great deal is lost yet. All that Howe [3] has been doing for this month past, is rather a ravage than a conquest, which the spirit of the Jerseys, a year ago, would have quickly repulsed, and which time and a little resolution will soon recover.

I have as little superstition in me as any man living, but my secret opinion has ever been, and still is, that God Almighty will not give up a people to military destruction, or leave them unsupportedly to perish, who have so earnestly and so repeatedly sought to avoid the calamities of war, by every decent method which wisdom could invent. Neither

[1] Paine is quoting from the first paragraph of the Declaratory Act repealing the Stamp Act, February 24, 1766, which stated: "That the King's Majesty, by and with the consent of the lords, spiritual and temporal, and Commons of Great Britain in Parliament assembled, had, hath, and of right ought to have full power and authority to make laws and statutes of sufficient force and validity to bind the colonies and people of America, subjects of the crown of Great Britain, in all cases whatsoever."—*Editor.*

[2] The present winter is worth an age, if rightly employed; but, if lost or neglected, the whole continent will partake of the evil; and there is no punishment that man does not deserve, be he who, or what, or where he will, that may be the means of sacrificing a season so precious and useful.—*Author's* note,—a citation from his "Common Sense."

[3] Sir William Howe, the British commander-in-chief in America from 1775 to 1778.— *Editor.*

have I so much of the infidel in me, as to suppose that He has relinquished the government of the world, and given us up to the care of devils; and as I do not, I cannot see on what grounds the king of Britain can look up to heaven for help against us: a common murderer, a highwayman, or a house-breaker, has as good a pretence as he.

'Tis surprising to see how rapidly a panic will sometimes run through a country. All nations and ages have been subject to them. Britain has trembled like an ague at the report of a French fleet of flat-bottomed boats; and in the fourteenth [fifteenth] century the whole English army, after ravaging the kingdom of France, was driven back like men petrified with fear; and this brave exploit was performed by a few broken forces collected and headed by a woman, Joan of Arc. Would that heaven might inspire some Jersey maid to spirit up her countrymen, and save her fair fellow sufferers from ravage and ravishment! Yet panics, in some cases, have their uses; they produce as much good as hurt. Their duration is always short; the mind soon grows through them, and acquires a firmer habit than before. But their peculiar advantage is, that they are the touchstones of sincerity and hypocrisy, and bring things and men to light, which might otherwise have lain forever undiscovered. In fact, they have the same effect on secret traitors, which an imaginary apparition would have upon a private murderer. They sift out the hidden thoughts of man, and hold them up in public to the world. Many a disguised Tory has lately shown his head, that shall penitentially solemnize with curses the day on which Howe arrived upon the Delaware.

As I was with the troops at Fort Lee,[4] and marched with them to the edge of Pennsylvania, I am well acquainted with many circumstances, which those who live at a distance know but little or nothing of. Our situation there was exceedingly cramped, the place being a narrow neck of land between the North River and the Hackensack. Our force was inconsiderable, being not one-fourth so great as Howe could bring against us. We had no army at hand to have relieved the garrison, had we shut ourselves up and stood on our defence. Our ammunition, light artillery, and the best part of our stores, had been removed, on the apprehension that Howe would endeavor to penetrate the Jerseys, in which case Fort Lee could be of no use to us; for it must occur to every

[4] Paine enlisted August, 1776, in the Pennsylvania division of the Flying Camp, under General Roberdeau, a body of troops that could be sent to any part of the country. He was stationed at Fort Lee in September, 1776, where General Nathanael Greene appointed him aide-de-camp.—*Editor.*

thinking man, whether in the army or not, that these kind of field forts are only for temporary purposes, and last in use no longer than the enemy directs his force against the particular object which such forts are raised to defend. Such was our situation and condition at Fort Lee on the morning of the 20th of November, when an officer arrived with information that the enemy with 200 boats had landed about seven miles above; Major General [Nathanael] Greene, who commanded the garrison, immediately ordered them under arms, and sent express to General Washington at the town of Hackensack, distant by the way of the ferry = six miles. Our first object was to secure the bridge over the Hackensack, which laid up the river between the enemy and us, about six miles from us, and three from them. General Washington arrived in about three-quarters of an hour, and marched at the head of the troops towards the bridge, which place I expected we should have a brush for; however, they did not choose to dispute it with us, and the greatest part of our troops went over the bridge, the rest over the ferry, except some which passed at a mill on a small creek, between the bridge and the ferry, and made their way through some marshy grounds up to the town of Hackensack, and there passed the river. We brought off as much baggage as the wagons could contain, the rest was lost. The simple object was to bring off the garrison, and march them on till they could be strengthened by the Jersey or Pennsylvania militia, so as to be enabled to make a stand. We staid four days at Newark, collected our out-posts with some of the Jersey militia, and marched out twice to meet the enemy, on being informed that they were advancing, though our numbers were greatly inferior to theirs. Howe, in my little opinion, committed a great error in generalship in not throwing a body of forces off from Staten Island through Amboy, by which means he might have seized all our stores at Brunswick, and intercepted our march into Pennsylvania; but if we believe the power of hell to be limited, we must likewise believe that their agents are under some providential control.[5]

I shall not now attempt to give all the particulars of our retreat to the Delaware; suffice it for the present to say, that both officers and men, though greatly harassed and fatigued, frequently without rest, covering, or provision, the inevitable consequences of a long retreat,

[5] Howe's failure to follow up initial successes may have been due to his belief that it would be better for the British empire to conciliate rather than to coerce the colonies. For an excellent discussion of his strategy, see Leonard Lundin, *Cockpit of the Revolution: The War for Independence in New Jersey* (Princeton, N.J., 1940), pp. 148–157.—*Editor.*

bore it with a manly and martial spirit. All their wishes centred in one, which was, that the country would turn out and help them to drive the enemy back. Voltaire has remarked that King William never appeared to full advantage but in difficulties and in action; the same remark may be made on General Washington, for the character fits him. There is a natural firmness in some minds which cannot be unlocked by trifles, but which, when unlocked, discovers a cabinet of fortitude; and I reckon it among those kind of public blessings, which we do not immediately see, that God hath blessed him with uninterrupted health, and given him a mind that can even flourish upon care.

I shall conclude this paper with some miscellaneous remarks on the state of our affairs; and shall begin with asking the following question, Why is it that the enemy have left the New England provinces, and made these middle ones the seat of war? The answer is easy: New England is not infested with Tories, and we are. I have been tender in raising the cry against these men, and used numberless arguments to show them their danger, but it will not do to sacrifice a world either to their folly or their baseness. The period is now arrived, in which either they or we must change our sentiments, or one or both must fall. And what is a Tory? Good God! what is he? I should not be afraid to go with a hundred Whigs against a thousand Tories, were they to attempt to get into arms. Every Tory is a coward; for servile, slavish, self-interested fear is the foundation of Toryism; and a man under such influence, though he may be cruel, never can be brave.

But, before the line of irrecoverable separation be drawn between us, let us reason the matter together: Your conduct is an invitation to the enemy, yet not one in a thousand of you has heart enough to join him. Howe is as much deceived by you as the American cause is injured by you. He expects you will all take up arms, and flock to his standard, with muskets on your shoulders. Your opinions are of no use to him, unless you support him personally, for 'tis soldiers, and not Tories, that he wants.

I once felt all that kind of anger, which a man ought to feel, against the mean principles that are held by the Tories: a noted one, who kept a tavern at Amboy, was standing at his door, with as pretty a child in his hand, about eight or nine years old, as I ever saw, and after speaking his mind as freely as he thought was prudent, finished with this unfatherly expression, *"Well! give me peace in my day."* Not a man lives on the continent but fully believes that a separation must some time or other finally take place, and a generous parent should have said, *"If there must be trouble, let it be in my day, that my child may have peace;"* and this single reflection, well applied, is sufficient to awaken every man to duty. Not a place upon earth might be so happy as America. Her situation is remote from all the wrangling world, and she has nothing to do but to trade with them. A man can distinguish himself between temper and principle, and I am as confident, as I am that God governs the world, that America will never be happy till she gets clear of foreign dominion. Wars, without ceasing, will break out till that period arrives, and the continent must in the end be conqueror; for though the flame of liberty may sometimes cease to shine, the coal can never expire.

America did not, nor does not want force; but she wanted a proper application of that force. Wisdom is not the purchase of a day, and it is no wonder that we should err at the first setting off. From an excess of tenderness, we were unwilling to raise an army, and trusted our cause to the temporary defence of a well-meaning militia.[6] A summer's experience has now taught us better; yet with those troops, while they were collected, we were able to set bounds to the progress of the enemy, and, thank God! they are again assembling. I always considered militia as the best troops in the world for a sudden exertion, but they will not do for a long campaign. Howe, it is probable, will make an attempt on this city;[7] should he fail on this side the Delaware, he is ruined. If he succeeds, our cause is not ruined. He stakes all on his side against a part on ours; admitting he succeeds, the consequence will be, that armies from both ends of the continent will march to assist their suffering friends in the middle states; for he cannot go everywhere, it is impossible. I consider Howe as the greatest enemy the Tories have; he is bringing a war into their country, which, had it not been for him and partly for themselves, they had been clear of. Should he now be expelled, I wish with all the devotion of a Christian, that the names of Whig and Tory may never more be mentioned; but should the Tories give him encouragement to come, or assistance if he come, I as sincerely wish that our next year's arms may expel them from the continent, and the Congress

---

[6] Paine shared Washington's opinion that a permanent army raised for the duration of the war was essential for an American victory. For Washington's views on this subject, see John C. Fitzpatrick, editor, *George Washington: Writings from the Original Manuscript Sources, 1775-1799* (Washington, 1931-1940), vol. VI, pp. 331-333; vol. VII, p. 43.—*Editor.*

[7] The reference is to Philadelphia, to which city Paine had gone to arrange for the publication of the *Crisis No. I.*—*Editor.*

appropriate their possessions to the relief of those who have suffered in well-doing. A single successful battle next year will settle the whole. America could carry on a two years' war by the confiscation of the property of disaffected persons, and be made happy by their expulsion. Say not that this is revenge, call it rather the soft resentment of a suffering people, who, having no object in view but the *good* of *all,* have staked their *own all* upon a seemingly doubtful event. Yet it is folly to argue against determined hardness; eloquence may strike the ear, and the language of sorrow draw forth the tear of compassion, but nothing can reach the heart that is steeled with prejudice.

Quitting this class of men, I turn with the warm ardor of a friend to those who have nobly stood, and are yet determined to stand the matter out: I call not upon a few, but upon all: not on *this* state or *that* state, but on *every* state: up and help us; lay your shoulders to the wheel; better have too much force than too little, when so great an object is at stake. Let it be told to the future world, that in the depth of winter, when nothing but hope and virtue could survive, that the city and the country, alarmed at one common danger, came forth to meet and to repulse it. Say not that thousands are gone, turn out your tens of thousands; throw not the burden of the day upon Providence, but *"show your faith by your works,"* that God may bless you. It matters not where you live, or what rank of life you hold, the evil or the blessing will reach you all. The far and the near, the home counties and the back, the rich and the poor, will suffer or rejoice alike. The heart that feels not now is dead; the blood of his children will curse his cowardice, who shrinks back at a time when a little might have saved the whole, and made *them* happy. I love the man that can smile in trouble, that can gather strength from distress, and grow brave by reflection. 'Tis the business of little minds to shrink; but he whose heart is firm, and whose conscience approves his conduct, will pursue his principles unto death. My own line of reasoning is to myself as straight and clear as a ray of light. Not all the treasures of the world, so far as I believe, could have induced me to support an offensive war, for I think it murder; but if a thief breaks into my house, burns and destroys my property, and kills or threatens to kill me, or those that are in it, and to *"bind me in all cases whatsoever"* [8] to his absolute will, am I to suffer it? What signifies it to me, whether he who does it is a king or a common man; my countryman or not my countryman; whether it be done by an individual vil-

---

[8] Paine is again quoting from the Declaratory Act of Parliament, February, 1766.—*Editor.*

lain, or an army of them? If we reason to the root of things we shall find no difference; neither can any just cause be assigned why we should punish in the one case and pardon in the other. Let them call me rebel and welcome, I feel no concern from it; but I should suffer the misery of devils, were I to make a whore of my soul by swearing allegiance to one whose character is that of a sottish, stupid, stubborn, worthless, brutish man. I conceive likewise a horrid idea in receiving mercy from a being, who at the last day shall be shrieking to the rocks and mountains to cover him, and fleeing with terror from the orphan, the widow, and the slain of America.

There are cases which cannot be overdone by language, and this is one. There are persons, too, who see not the full extent of the evil which threatens them; they solace themselves with hopes that the enemy, if he succeed, will be merciful. It is the madness of folly, to expect mercy from those who have refused to do justice; and even mercy, where conquest is the object, is only a trick of war; the cunning of the fox is as murderous as the violence of the wolf, and we ought to guard equally against both. Howe's first object is, partly by threats and partly by promises, to terrify or seduce the people to deliver up their arms and receive mercy. The ministry recommended the same plan to Gage, and this is what the tories call making their peace, *"a peace which passeth all understanding"* indeed! A peace which would be the immediate forerunner of a worse ruin than any we have yet thought of. Ye men of Pennsylvania, do reason upon these things! Were the back counties to give up their arms, they would fall an easy prey to the Indians, who are all armed: this perhaps is what some Tories would not be sorry for. Were the home counties to deliver up their arms, they would be exposed to the resentment of the back counties, who would then have it in their power to chastise their defection at pleasure. And were any one state to give up its arms, *that* state must be garrisoned by all Howe's army of Britons and Hessians to preserve it from the anger of the rest. Mutual fear is the principal link in the chain of mutual love, and woe be to that state that breaks the compact. Howe is mercifully inviting you to barbarous destruction, and men must be either rogues or fools that will not see it. I dwell not upon the vapors of imagination; I bring reason to your ears, and, in language as plain as A, B, C, hold up truth to your eyes.

I thank God, that I fear not. I see no real cause for fear. I know our situation well, and can see the way out of it. While our army was collected, Howe dared not risk a battle; and it is no credit to him that he decamped from the White Plains, and waited a mean opportunity to ravage the defenceless Jerseys; but it is great credit to us, that, with a handful of men, we sustained an orderly retreat for near an hundred miles, brought off our ammunition, all our field pieces, the greatest part of our stores, and had four rivers to pass. None can say that our retreat was precipitate, for we were near three weeks in performing it, that the country might have time to come in. Twice we marched back to meet the enemy, and remained out till dark. The sign of fear was not seen in our camp, and had not some of the cowardly and disaffected inhabitants spread false alarms through the country, the Jerseys had never been ravaged. Once more we are again collected and collecting; our new army at both ends of the continent is recruiting fast, and we shall be able to open the next campaign with sixty thousand men, well armed and clothed. This is our situation, and who will may know it. By perseverance and fortitude we have the prospect of a glorious issue; by cowardice and submission, the sad choice of a variety of evils—a ravaged country— a depopulated city—habitations without safety, and slavery without hope—our homes turned into barracks **and** bawdy-houses for Hessians, and a future race to provide for, whose fathers we shall doubt of. Look on this picture and weep over it! and if there yet remains one thoughtless wretch who believes it not, let him suffer it unlamented.

COMMON SENSE.

December 23, 1776.[9]

[9] This is the date for the publication of the pamphlet. The essay had already appeared in the *Pennsylvania Journal* of December, 19, 1776.—*Editor*.

THE AMERICAN CRISIS

II

The second number of *The American Crisis* was addressed to Richard Viscount Howe, brother of William Howe, the British commander-in-chief in America. Lord Howe was sent over by the British ministry to bring an offer to the Americans that all persons who should desist from rebellion and lend their "aid in restoring tranquillity" would receive full and free pardon from the King. Lord Howe arrived in America on July 12, 1776 and thereafter issued several proclamations to the American people in an effort to effect a reconciliation between Great Britain and America.—*Editor*.

To Lord Howe

"What's in the name of *lord*, that I should fear
To bring my grievance to the public ear?"

CHURCHILL.

UNIVERSAL empire is the prerogative of a writer. His concerns are with all mankind, and though he cannot command their obedience, he can assign them their duty. The Republic of Letters is more ancient than monarchy, and of far higher character in the world than the vassal court of Britain; he that rebels against reason is a real rebel, but he that in defence of reason rebels against tyranny has a better title to *"Defender of the Faith,"* than George the Third.

As a military man your lordship may hold out the sword of war, and call it the *"ultima ratio regum": the last reason of kings;* we in return can show you the sword of justice, and call it "the best scourge of tyrants." The first of these two may threaten, or even frighten for a

58

while, and cast a sickly languor over an insulted people, but reason will soon recover the debauch, and restore them again to tranquil fortitude. Your lordship, I find, has now commenced author, and published a proclamation; I have published a *Crisis*. As they stand, they are the antipodes of each other; both cannot rise at once, and one of them must descend; and so quick is the revolution of things, that your lordship's performance, I see, has already fallen many degrees from its first place, and is now just visible on the edge of the political horizon.

It is surprising to what a pitch of infatuation, blind folly and obstinacy will carry mankind, and your lordship's drowsy proclamation is a proof that it does not even quit them in their sleep. Perhaps you thought America too was taking a nap, and therefore chose, like Satan to Eve, to whisper the delusion softly, lest you should awaken her. This continent, sir, is too extensive to sleep all at once, and too watchful, even in its slumbers, not to startle at the unhallowed foot of an invader. You may issue your proclamations, and welcome, for we have learned to "reverence ourselves," and scorn the insulting ruffian that employs you. America, for your deceased brother's sake, would gladly have shown you respect and it is a new aggravation to her feelings, that Howe should be forgetful, and raise his sword against those, who at their own charge raised a monument to his brother.[1] But your master has commanded, and you have not enough of nature left to refuse. Surely there must be something strangely degenerating in the love of monarchy, that can so completely wear a man down to an ingrate, and make him proud to lick the dust that kings have trod upon. A few more years, should you survive them, will bestow on you the title of "an old man": and in some hour of future reflection you may probably find the fitness of Wolsey's despairing penitence—"had I served my God as faithfully as I have served my king, he would not thus have forsaken me in my old age."

The character you appear to us in, is truly ridiculous. Your friends, the Tories, announced your coming, with high descriptions of your unlimited powers; but your proclamation has given them the lie, by showing you to be a commissioner without authority. Had your powers been ever so great they were nothing to us, further than we pleased; because we had the same right which other nations had, to do what we thought was best. *"The* UNITED STATES *of* AMERICA," will sound as pompously in

---

[1] The reference is to George Augustus Howe who was killed at Ticonderoga on July 8, 1758. The General Court of Massachusetts appropriated £250 for a monument in his honor in Westminster Abbey.—*Editor*.

the world or in history, as "the kingdom of Great Britain"; [2] the character of *General Washington* will fill a page with as much lustre as that of *Lord Howe:* and the *Congress* have as much right to command the *king and Parliament* in London to desist from legislation, as *they* or *you* have to command Congress. Only suppose how laughable such an edict would appear from us, and then, in that merry mood, do but turn the tables upon yourself, and you will see how your proclamation is received here. Having thus placed you in a proper position in which you may have a full view of your folly, and learn to despise it, I hold up to you, for that purpose, the following quotation from your own lunarian proclamation.—"And we (Lord Howe and General Howe) do command (and in his majesty's name forsooth) all such persons as are assembled together, under the name of general or provincial congresses, committees, conventions or other associations, by whatever name or names known and distinguished, to desist and cease from all such treasonable actings and doings."

You introduce your proclamation by referring to your declarations of the 14th of July and 19th of September. In the last of these you sunk yourself below the character of a private gentleman. That I may not seem to accuse you unjustly, I shall state the circumstance: by a verbal invitation of yours, communicated to Congress by General Sullivan, then a prisoner on his parole, you signified your desire of conferring with some members of that body as private gentlemen.[3] It was beneath the dignity of the American Congress to pay any regard to a message that at best was but a genteel affront, and had too much of the ministerial complexion of tampering with private persons; and which might probably have been the case, had the gentlemen who were deputed on the business possessed that kind of easy virtue which an English courtier is so truly distinguished by. Your request, however, was complied with,

[2] Paine used this ringing phrase frequently to rally the American people after a defeat at arms.—*Editor.*

[3] General John Sullivan, captured in the battle of Long Island, was sent by Lord Howe to Congress to inform the members that he (Lord Howe) would use his influence to get all the obnoxious acts of Parliament repealed, but that he would first like to confer with some of the members of Congress informally. A committee, consisting of Benjamin Franklin, John Rutledge, and John Adams was appointed by Congress to confer with Lord Howe and met with him in conference at Staten Island on September 11, 1776. The committee demanded a recognition of the independence of the United States as a condition which had to precede all negotiation. This brought the conference to an end. A little while later Lord Howe issued another proclamation announcing the intention of the British government to reconsider the various measures resented by the American people, and urging all Americans to rely on this promise and give up the struggle.—*Editor.*

for honest men are naturally more tender of their civil than their political fame. The interview ended as every sensible man thought it would; for your lordship knows, as well as the writer of the *Crisis,* that it is impossible for the King of England to promise the repeal, or even the revisal of any acts of parliament; wherefore, on your part, you had nothing to say, more than to request, in the room of demanding, the entire surrender of the continent; and then, if that was complied with, to promise that the inhabitants should escape with their lives. This was the upshot of the conference. You informed the conferees that you were two months in soliciting these powers. We ask, what powers? for as commissioner you have none. If you mean the power of pardoning, it is an oblique proof that your master was determined to sacrifice all before him; and that you were two months in dissuading him from his purpose. Another evidence of his savage obstinacy! From your own account of the matter we may justly draw these two conclusions: 1st, That you serve a monster; and 2d, That never was a messenger sent on a more foolish errand than yourself. This plain language may perhaps sound uncouthly to an ear vitiated by courtly refinements, but words were made for use, and the fault lies in deserving them, or the abuse in applying them unfairly.

Soon after your return to New York, you published a very illiberal and unmanly handbill against the Congress; for it was certainly stepping out of the line of common civility, first to screen your national pride by soliciting an interview with them as private gentlemen, and in the conclusion to endeavor to deceive the multitude by making a handbill attack on the whole body of the Congress; you got them together under one name, and abused them under another. But the king you serve, and the cause you support, afford you so few instances of acting the gentleman, that out of pity to your situation the Congress pardoned the insult by taking no notice of it.

You say in that handbill, "that they, the Congress, disavowed every purpose for reconciliation not consonant with their extravagant and inadmissible claim of independence." Why, God bless me! what have you to do with our independence? We ask no leave of yours to set it up; we ask no money of yours to support it; we can do better without your fleets and armies than with them; you may soon have enough to do to protect yourselves without being burdened with us. We are very willing to be at peace with you, to buy of you and sell to you, and, like young beginners in the world, to work for our living; therefore, why do you put yourselves out of cash, when we know you cannot spare it, and we do not desire you to run into debt? I am willing, sir, that you should see your folly in every point of view I can place it in, and for that reason descend sometimes to tell you in jest what I wish you to see in earnest. But to be more serious with you, why do you say, "their independence?" To set you right, sir, we tell you, that the independency is ours, not theirs. The Congress were authorized by every state on the continent to publish it to all the world, and in so doing are not to be considered as the inventors, but only as the heralds that proclaimed it, or the office from which the sense of the people received a legal form; and it was as much as any or all their heads were worth, to have treated with you on the subject of submission under any name whatever. But we know the men in whom we have trusted; can England say the same of her Parliament?

I come now more particularly to your proclamation of the 30th of November last. Had you gained an entire conquest over all the armies of America, and then put forth a proclamation, offering (what you call) mercy, your conduct would have had some specious show of humanity; but to creep by surprise into a province, and there endeavor to terrify and seduce the inhabitants from their just allegiance to the rest by promises, which you neither meant nor were able to fulfil, is both cruel and unmanly: cruel in its effects; because, unless you can keep all the ground you have marched over, how are you, in the words of your proclamation, to secure to your proselytes "the enjoyment of their property?" What is to become either of your new adopted subjects, or your old friends, the Tories, in Burlington, Bordentown, Trenton, Mount Holly, and many other places, where you proudly lorded it for a few days, and then fled with the precipitation of a pursued thief? What, I say, is to become of those wretches? What is to become of those who went over to you from this city and State? What more can you say to them than "shift for yourselves"? Or what more can they hope for than to wander like vagabonds over the face of the earth? You may now tell them to take their leave of America, and all that once was theirs. Recommend them, for consolation, to your master's court; there perhaps they may make a shift to live on the scraps of some dangling parasite, and choose companions among thousands like themselves. A traitor is the foulest fiend on earth.

In a political sense we ought to thank you for thus bequeathing estates to the continent; we shall soon, at this rate, be able to carry on a war without expense, and grow rich by the ill policy of Lord Howe, and the generous defection of the Tories. Had you set your foot into this city, you would have bestowed estates upon us which we never thought of, by bringing forth traitors we were unwilling to suspect. But these men, you'll say, "are his majesty's most faithful subjects"; let that honor, then, be all their fortune, and let his majesty take them to himself.

I am now thoroughly disgusted with them; they live in ungrateful ease, and bend their whole minds to mischief. It seems as if God had given them over to a spirit of infidelity, and that they are open to conviction in no other line but that of punishment. It is time to have done with tarring, feathering, carting, and taking securities for their future good behavior; every sensible man must feel a conscious shame at seeing a poor fellow hawked for a show about the streets, when it is known he is only the tool of some principal villain, biassed into his offence by the force of false reasoning, or bribed thereto, through sad necessity. We dishonor ourselves by attacking such trifling characters while greater ones are suffered to escape; 'tis our duty to find *them* out, and their proper punishment would be to exile them from the continent for ever. The circle of them is not so great as some imagine; the influence of a few have tainted many who are not naturally corrupt. A continual circulation of lies among those who are not much in the way of hearing them contradicted, will in time pass for truth; and the crime lies not in the believer but the inventor. I am not for declaring war with every man that appears not so warm as myself: difference of constitution, temper, habit of speaking, and many other things, will go a great way in fixing the outward character of a man, yet simple honesty may remain at bottom. Some men have naturally a military turn, and can brave hardships and the risk of life with a cheerful face; others have not; no slavery appears to them so great as the fatigue of arms, and no terror so powerful as that of personal danger. What can we say? We cannot alter nature, neither ought we to punish the son because the father begot him in a cowardly mood. However, I believe most men have more courage than they know of, and that a little at first is enough to begin with. I knew the time when I thought that the whistling of a cannon ball would have frightened me almost to death; but I have since tried it, and find that I can stand it with as little discomposure, and, I believe, with a much easier conscience than your lordship. The same dread would return to me again were I in your situation, for my solemn belief of your cause is, that it is hellish and damnable, and, under that conviction, every thinking man's heart *must* fail him.

From a concern that a good cause should be dishonored by the least disunion among us, I said in my former paper, No. I. "That should the enemy now be expelled, I wish, with all the sincerity of a Christian, that the names of Whig and Tory might never more be mentioned"; but there is a knot of men among us of such a venomous cast, that they will not admit even one's good wishes to act in their favor. Instead of rejoicing that heaven had, as it were, providentially preserved this city from plunder and destruction, by delivering so great a part of the enemy into our hands with so little effusion of blood, they stubbornly affected to disbelieve it till within an hour, nay, half an hour, of the prisoners arriving; and the Quakers put forth a testimony, dated the 20th of December, signed "John Pemberton," declaring their attachment to the British government.[4] These men are continually harping on the great sin of *our* bearing arms, but the king of Britain may lay waste the world in blood and famine, and they, poor fallen souls, have nothing to say.

In some future paper I intend to distinguish between the different kind of persons who have been denominated Tories; for this I am clear in, that all are not so who have been called so, nor all men Whigs who were once thought so; and as I mean not to conceal the name of any true friend when there shall be occasion to mention him, neither will I that of an enemy, who ought to be known, let his rank, station or religion be what it may. Much pains have been taken by some to set your lordship's private character in an amiable light, but as it has chiefly been done by men who know nothing about you, and who are no ways remarkable for their attachment to us, we have no just authority for believing it. George the Third has imposed upon us by the same arts, but *time,* at length, has done him justice, and the same fate may probably attend your lordship. Your avowed purpose here is to kill, conquer, plunder, pardon, and enslave: and the ravages of your army through the Jerseys have been marked with as much barbarism as if you had openly professed yourself the prince of ruffians; not even the appearance of humanity has been preserved either on the march or the retreat of your troops;

---

[4] I have ever been careful of charging offences upon whole societies of men, but as the paper referred to is put forth by an unknown set of men, who claim to themselves the right of representing the whole: and while the whole Society of Quakers admit its validity by a silent acknowledgment, it is impossible that any distinction can be made by the public: and the more so, because the New York paper of the 30th of December, printed by permission of our enemies, says that "the Quakers begin to speak openly of their attachment to the British Constitution." We are certain that we have many friends among them, and wish to know them.—*Author.*

no general order that I could ever learn, has ever been issued to prevent or even forbid your troops from robbery, wherever they came, and the only instance of justice, if it can be called such, which has distinguished you for impartiality, is, that you treated and plundered all alike; what could not be carried away has been destroyed, and mahogany furniture has been deliberately laid on fire for fuel, rather than the men should be fatigued with cutting wood.[5] There was a time when the Whigs confided much in your supposed candor, and the Tories rested themselves in your favor; the experiments have now been made, and failed; in every town, nay, every cottage, in the Jerseys, where your arms have been, is a testimony against you. How you may rest under this sacrifice of character I know not; but this I know, that you sleep and rise with the daily curses of thousands upon you; perhaps the misery which the Tories have suffered by your proffered mercy may give them some claim to their country's pity, and be in the end the best favor you could show them.

In a folio general-order book belonging to Col. Rhal's battalion, taken at Trenton, and now in the possession of the council of safety for this state, the following barbarous order is frequently repeated, "His excellency the *Commander-in-Chief* orders, that all inhabitants who shall be found with arms, not having an officer with them, shall be immediately taken and hung up." [6] How many you may thus have privately sacrificed, we know not, and the account can only be settled in another world. Your treatment of prisoners, in order to distress them to enlist in your infernal service, is not to be equalled by any instance in Europe. Yet this is the humane Lord Howe and his brother, whom the Tories and their three-quarter kindred, the Quakers, or some of them at least, have been holding up for patterns of justice and mercy!

A bad cause will ever be supported by bad means and bad men; and whoever will be at the pains of examining strictly into things, will find that one and the same spirit of oppression and impiety, more or less, governs through your whole party in both countries: not many days

[5] As some people may doubt the truth of such wanton destruction, I think it necessary to inform them that one of the people called Quakers, who lives at Trenton, gave me this information at the house of Mr. Michael Hutchinson, (one of the same profession,) who lives near Trenton ferry on the Pennsylvania side, Mr. Hutchinson being present.—*Author.*

[6] Colonel Johann Gottlieb Rahl, or Rall as his name is written today, was a Hessian officer who had distinguished himself by forcing the Americans to evacuate Forts Washington and Lee, and also by leading the pursuit of Washington to the Delaware. As a reward he was placed in chief command at Trenton, where he was slain by Washington's men on December 26, 1776.—*Editor.*

ago, I accidentally fell in company with a person of this city noted for espousing your cause, and on my remarking to him, "that it appeared clear to me, by the late providential turn of affairs, that God Almighty was visibly on our side," he replied, "We care nothing for that, you may have Him, and welcome; if we have but enough of the devil on our side, we shall do." However carelessly this might be spoken, matters not, 'tis still the insensible principle that directs all your conduct and will at last most assuredly deceive and ruin you.

If ever a nation was mad and foolish, blind to its own interest and bent on its own destruction, it is Britain. There are such things as national sins, and though the punishment of individuals may be reserved to *another* world, national punishment can only be inflicted in *this* world. Britain, as a nation, is, in my inmost belief, the greatest and most ungrateful offender against God on the face of the whole earth. Blessed with all the commerce she could wish for, and furnished, by a vast extension of dominion, with the means of civilizing both the eastern and western world, she has made no other use of both than proudly to idolize her own "thunder," and rip up the bowels of whole countries for what she could get. Like Alexander, she has made war her sport, and inflicted misery for prodigality's sake. The blood of India is not yet repaid, nor the wretchedness of Africa yet requited. Of late she has enlarged her list of national cruelties by her butcherly destruction of the Caribbs of St. Vincent's, and returning an answer by the sword to the meek prayer for *"Peace, liberty and safety."* These are serious things, and whatever a foolish tyrant, a debauched court, a trafficking legislature, or a blinded people may think, the national account with heaven must some day or other be settled: all countries have sooner or later been called to their reckoning; the proudest empires have sunk when the balance was struck; and Britain, like an individual penitent, must undergo her day of sorrow, and the sooner it happens to her the better. As I wish it over, I wish it to come, but withal wish that it may be as light as possible.

Perhaps your lordship has no taste for serious things; by your connections in England I should suppose not; therefore I shall drop this part of the subject, and take it up in a line in which you will better understand me.

By what means, may I ask, do you expect to conquer America? If you could not effect it in the summer, when our army was less than yours, nor in the winter, when we had none, how are you to do it? In point of generalship you have been outwitted, and in point of fortitude out-done; your advantages turn out to your loss, and show us that it is in our power to ruin you by gifts: like a game of drafts, we can move out of *one* square to let you come in, in order that we may afterwards take two or three for one; and as we can always keep a double corner for ourselves, we can always prevent a total defeat. You cannot be so insensible as not to see that we have two to one the advantage of you, because we con-quer by a drawn game, and you lose by it. Burgoyne might have taught your lordship this knowledge; he has been long a student in the doctrine of chances.

I have no other idea of conquering countries than by subduing the armies which defend them: have you done this, or can you do it? If you have not, it would be civil in you to let your proclamations alone for the present; otherwise, you will ruin more Tories by your grace and favor, than you will Whigs by your arms.

Were you to obtain possession of this city, you would not know what to do with it more than to plunder it. To hold it in the manner you hold New York, would be an additional dead weight upon your hands; and if a general conquest is your object, you had better be without the city than with it. When you have defeated all our armies, the cities will fall into your hands of themselves; but to creep into them in the manner you got into Princeton, Trenton, &c. is like robbing an orchard in the night before the fruit be ripe, and running away in the morning. Your experiment in the Jerseys is sufficient to teach you that you have some-thing more to do than barely to get into other people's houses; and your new converts, to whom you promised all manner of protection, and seduced into new guilt by pardoning them from their former vir-tues, must begin to have a very contemptible opinion both of your power and your policy. Your authority in the Jerseys is now reduced to the small circle which your army occupies, and your proclamation is no where else seen unless it be to be laughed at. The mighty subduers of the continent have retreated into a nutshell, and the proud forgivers of our sins are fled from those they came to pardon; and all this at a time when they were despatching vessel after vessel to England with the great news of every day. In short, you have managed your Jersey expedition so very dexterously, that the dead only are conquerors, because none will dispute the ground with them.

In all the wars which you have formerly been concerned in you had only armies to contend with; in this case you have both an army and a country to combat with. In former wars, the countries followed the fate of their capitals; Canada fell with Quebec, and Minorca with Port Mahon or St. Phillips; by subduing those, the conquerors opened a way into, and became masters of the country: here it is otherwise; if you get possession of a city here, you are obliged to shut yourselves up in it, and can make no other use of it, than to spend your country's money in. This is all the advantage you have drawn from New York; and you would draw less from Philadelphia, because it requires more force to keep it, and is much further from the sea. A pretty figure you and the Tories would cut in this city, with a river full of ice, and a town full of fire; for the immediate consequence of your getting here would be, that you would be cannonaded out again, and the Tories be obliged to make good the damage; and this sooner or later will be the fate of New York.

I wish to see the city saved, not so much from military as from natural motives. 'Tis the hiding place of women and children, and Lord Howe's proper business is with our armies. When I put all the circumstances together which ought to be taken, I laugh at your notion of conquering America. Because you lived in a little country, where an army might run over the whole in a few days, and where a single company of soldiers might put a multitude to the rout, you expected to find it the same here. It is plain that you brought over with you all the narrow notions you were bred up with, and imagined that a proclamation in the king's name was to do great things; but Englishmen always travel for knowledge, and your lordship, I hope, will return, if you return at all, much wiser than you came.

We may be surprised by events we did not expect, and in that interval of recollection you may gain some temporary advantage: such was the case a few weeks ago, but we soon ripen again into reason, collect our strength, and while you are preparing for a triumph, we come upon you with a defeat. Such it has been, and such it would be were you to try it a hundred times over. Were you to garrison the places you might march over, in order to secure their subjection, (for remember you can do it by no other means,) your army would be like a stream of water running to nothing. By the time you extended from New York to Virginia, you would be reduced to a string of drops not capable of hanging together; while we, by retreating from State to State, like a river turning back upon itself, would acquire strength in the same proportion as you lost it, and in the end be capable of overwhelming you. The country, in the meantime, would suffer, but it is a day of suffering, and we ought to expect it. What we contend for is worthy the affliction we may go through. If we get but bread to eat, and any kind of raiment to put on, we ought not only to be contented, but thankful. More than *that* we ought not to look for, and less than *that* heaven has not yet suffered us to want. He that would sell his birthright for a little *salt,* is as worthless as he who sold it for pottage without salt; and he that would part with it for a gay coat, or a plain coat, ought for ever to be a slave in buff. What are salt, sugar and finery, to the inestimable blessings of "Liberty and Safety!" Or what are the inconveniences of a few months to the tributary bondage of ages? The meanest peasant in America, blessed with these sentiments, is a happy man compared with a New York Tory; he can eat his morsel without repining, and when he has done, can sweeten it with a repast of wholesome air; he can take his child by the hand and bless it, without feeling the conscious shame of neglecting a parent's duty.

In publishing these remarks I have several objects in view.

On your part they are to expose the folly of your pretended authority as a commissioner; the wickedness of your cause in general; and the impossibility of your conquering us at any rate. On the part of the public, my intention is, to show them their true and sold interest; to encourage them to their own good, to remove the fears and falsities which bad men have spread, and weak men have encouraged; and to excite in all men a love for union, and a cheerfulness for duty.

I shall submit one more case to you respecting your conquest of this country, and then proceed to new observations.

Suppose our armies in every part of this continent were immediately to disperse, every man to his home, or where else he might be safe, and engage to reassemble again on a certain future day; it is clear that you would then have no army to contend with, yet you would be as much at a loss in that case as you are now; you would be afraid to send your troops in parties over to the continent, either to disarm or prevent us from assembling, lest they should not return; and while you kept them together, having no arms of ours to dispute with, you could not call it a conquest; you might furnish out a pompous page in the London *Gazette* or a New York paper, but when we returned at the appointed time, you would have the same work to do that you had at first.

It has been the folly of Britain to suppose herself more powerful than she really is, and by that means has arrogated to herself a rank in the world she is not entitled to: for more than this century past she has not been able to carry on a war without foreign assistance. In Marlborough's campaigns, and from that day to this, the number of German troops and officers assisting her have been about equal with her own; ten thousand Hessians were sent to England last war to protect her from a French invasion; and she would have cut but a poor figure in her Canadian and West Indian expeditions, had not America been lavish both of her money and men to help her along. The only instance in which she was engaged singly, that I can recollect, was against the rebellion in Scotland, in the years 1745 and 1746, and in that, out of three battles, she was twice beaten, till by thus reducing their numbers, (as we shall yours) and taking a supply ship that was coming to Scotland with clothes, arms and money, (as we have often done,) she was at last enabled to defeat them. England was never famous by land; her officers have generally been suspected of cowardice, have more of the air of a dancing-master than a soldier, and by the samples which we have taken prisoners, we give the preference to ourselves. Her strength, of late, has lain in her extravagance; but as her finances and credit are now low, her sinews in that line begin to fail fast. As a nation she is the poorest in Europe; for were the whole kingdom, and all that is in it, to be put up for sale like the estate of a bankrupt, it would not fetch as much as she owes; yet this thoughtless wretch must go to war, and with the avowed design, too, of making us beasts of burden, to support her in riot and debauchery, and to assist her afterwards in distressing those nations who are now our best friends. This ingratitude may suit a Tory, or the unchristian peevishness of a fallen Quaker, but none else.

'Tis the unhappy temper of the English to be pleased with any war, right or wrong, be it but successful; but they soon grow discontented with ill fortune, and it is an even chance that they are as clamorous for peace next summer, as the king and his ministers were for war last winter. In this natural view of things, your lordship stands in a very critical situation: your whole character is now staked upon your laurels; if they wither, you wither with them; if they flourish, you cannot live long to look at them; and at any rate, the black account hereafter is not far off. What lately appeared to us misfortunes, were only blessings in disguise; and the seeming advantages on your side have turned out to our profit. Even our loss of this city, as far as we can see, might be a principal gain to us: the more surface you spread over, the thinner you will be, and the easier wiped away; and our consolation under that apparent disaster would be, that the estates of the Tories would become securities for the repairs. In short, there is no old ground we can fail upon, but some new foundation rises again to support us. "We have put, sir, our hands to the plough, and cursed be he that looketh back."

Your king, in his speech to parliament last spring, declared, "That he had no doubt but the great force they had enabled him to send to America, would effectually reduce the rebellious colonies." It has not, neither can it; but it has done just enough to lay the foundation of its own next year's ruin. You are sensible that you left England in a divided, distracted state of politics, and, by the command you had here, you became a principal prop in the court party; their fortunes rest on yours; by a single express you can fix their value with the public, and the degree to which their spirits shall rise or fall; they are in your hands as stock, and you have the secret of the *alley* with you. Thus situated and connected, you become the unintentional mechanical instrument of your own and their overthrow. The king and his ministers put conquest out of doubt, and the credit of both depended on the proof. To support them in the interim, it was necessary that you should make the most of every thing, and we can tell by Hugh Gaine's New York paper [7] what the complexion of the London *Gazette* is. With such a list of victories the nation cannot expect you will ask new supplies; and to confess your want of them would give the lie to your triumphs, and impeach the king and his ministers of treasonable deception. If you make the necessary demand at home, your party sinks; if you make it not, you sink yourself; to ask it now is too late, and to ask it before was too soon, and unless it arrive quickly will be of no use. In short, the part you have to act, cannot be acted; and I am fully persuaded that all you have to trust to is, to do the best you can with what force you have got, or little more. Though we have greatly exceeded you in point of generalship and bravery of men, yet, as a people, we have not entered into the full soul of enterprise; for I, who know England and the disposition of the people well, am confident, that it is easier for us to effect a revolution there, than you a conquest here; a few thousand men landed in England with the declared design of deposing the present king, bringing his ministers to trial, and setting up the Duke of Gloucester in his stead, would assuredly carry their point, while you are grovelling here, ignorant of the matter. As I send all my papers to England, this, like *Common Sense,* will find its way there; and though it may put one party on their guard, it will in-

[7] The paper referred to was the New York *Mercury*, a Tory sheet published by Hugh Gaine. The printer was a Whig who turned Tory early in the War.—*Editor.*

form the other, and the nation in general, of our design to help them.

Thus far, sir, I have endeavored to give you a picture of present affairs: you may draw from it what conclusions you please. I wish as well to the true prosperity of England as you can, but I consider INDEPENDENCE *as America's natural right and interest,* and never could see any real disservice it would be to Britain. If an English merchant receives an order, and is paid for it, it signifies nothing to him who governs the country. This is my creed of politics. If I have any where expressed myself overwarmly, 'tis from a fixed, immovable hatred I have, and ever had, to cruel men and cruel measures. I have likewise an aversion to monarchy, as being too debasing to the dignity of man; but I never troubled others with my notions till very lately, nor ever published a syllable in England in my life.[8] What I write is pure nature, and my pen and my soul have ever gone together. My writings I have always given away, reserving only the expense of printing and paper, and sometimes not even that. I never courted either fame or interest, and my manner of life, to those who know it, will justify what I say. My study is to be useful, and if your lordship loves mankind as well as I do, you would, seeing you cannot conquer us, cast about and lend your hand towards accomplishing a peace. Our independence with God's blessing we will maintain against all the world; but as we wish to avoid evil ourselves, we wish not to inflict it on others. I am never over-inquisitive into the secrets of the cabinet, but I have some notion that, if you neglect the present opportunity, it will not be in our power to make a separate peace with you afterwards; for whatever treaties or alliances we form, we shall most faithfully abide by; wherefore you may be deceived if you think you can make it with us at any time. A lasting independent peace is my wish, end and aim; and to accomplish that, *I pray God the* Americans *may never be defeated, and I trust while they have good officers, and are well commanded,* and willing to be commanded, *that they* NEVER WILL BE.

COMMON SENSE

PHILADELPHIA, Jan. 13, 1777.

[8] It has sometimes been charged that Paine was not consistent in making this statement on the ground that he had written *The Case of the Officers of Excise* in 1772 while he was still in England. But this petition to Parliament for the Excisemen was not published until 1793.—*Editor.*

THE AMERICAN CRISIS

III

The third *Crisis* was dated April 19, 1777, the second anniversary of the Battle of Lexington and Concord. It was aimed primarily at the internal enemies of the Revolution. With those who still vacillated Paine had no patience. "Here is the touchstone to try men by," the revolutionary pamphleteer wrote. "He that is not a supporter of the independent State of America . . . is, in the American sense of the word, a TORY; and the instant that he endeavors to bring his toryism into practice, he becomes a TRAITOR." Tories endeavoring to secure their property by supporting the enemy, he suggests, should be made to fear more losing it in the event of an American victory. Paine proposes an "oath or affirmation" renouncing allegiance to the King, and pledging support to the United States. He also suggests that a tax of ten, fifteen, or twenty percent be levied on all property. All who took the oath could exempt their property by declaring ready to aid the Revolutionary cause whenever they were called upon. Those who refused to take the oath would be paying a tax on their insurance with the enemy. "It would not only be good policy," Paine points out, "but strict justice to raise fifty or one hundred thousand pounds, or more, if it is necessary, out of the estates and property of the King of England's votaries, resident in Philadelphia, to be distributed as a reward to those inhabitants of the city and State who should turn out and repulse the enemy should they attempt to march this way." Paine's proposal was followed in part on June 13, 1777, when Pennsylvania required an oath of allegiance to the State from all over eighteen years of age.

Two days before the *Crisis III* was published (April 17, 1777), Paine had been appointed by Congress Secretary of the Committee on Foreign Affairs. —*Editor.*

IN THE progress of politics, as in the common occurrences of life, we are not only apt to forget the ground we have travelled over, but frequently neglect to gather up experience as we go. We expend, if I may so say, the knowledge of every day on the circumstances that produce it, and journey on in search of new matter and new refinements: but as it is pleasant and sometimes useful to look back, even to the first periods of infancy, and trace the turns and windings through which we have passed, so we may likewise derive many advantages by halting a while in our political career, and taking a review of the wondrous complicated labyrinth of little more than yesterday.

Truly may we say, that never did men grow old in so short a time! We have crowded the business of an age into the compass of a few months, and have been driven through such a rapid succession of things, that for the want of leisure to think, we unavoidably wasted knowledge as we came, and have left nearly as much behind us as we brought with us: but the road is yet rich with the fragments, and, before we finally lose sight of them, will repay us for the trouble of stopping to pick them up.

Were a man to be totally deprived of memory, he would be incapable of forming any just opinion; every thing about him would seem a chaos: he would have even his own history to ask from every one; and by not knowing how the world went in his absence, he would be at a loss to know how it *ought* to go on when he recovered, or rather, returned to it again. In like manner, though in a less degree, a too great inattention to past occurrences retards and bewilders our judgment in everything; while, on the contrary, by comparing what is past with what is present, we frequently hit on the true character of both, and become wise with very little trouble. It is a kind of counter-march, by which we get into the rear of time, and mark the movements and meanings of things as we make our return. There are certain circumstances, which, at the time of their happening, are a kind of riddles, and as every riddle is to be followed by its answer, so those kind of circumstances will be followed by their events, and those events are always the true solution. A considerable space of time may lapse between, and unless we continue our observations from the one to the other, the harmony of them will pass away unnoticed: but the misfortune is, that partly from the pressing necessity of some instant things, and partly from the impatience of our own tempers, we are frequently in such a hurry to make out the meaning of everything as fast as it happens, that we thereby never truly understand it; and not only start new difficulties to ourselves by so doing, but, as it were, embarrass Providence in her good designs.

I have been civil in stating this fault on a large scale, for, as it now stands, it does not appear to be levelled against any particular set of men; but were it to be refined a little further, it might afterwards be applied to the Tories with a degree of striking propriety: those men have been remarkable for drawing sudden conclusions from single facts. The least apparent mishap on our side, or the least seeming advantage on the part of the enemy, have determined with them the fate of a whole campaign. By this hasty judgment they have converted a retreat into a defeat; mistook generalship for error; while every little advantage purposely given the enemy, either to weaken their strength by dividing it, embarrass their councils by multiplying their objects, or to secure a greater post by the surrender of a less, has been instantly magnified into a conquest. Thus, by quartering ill policy upon ill principles, they have frequently promoted the cause they designed to injure, and injured that which they intended to promote.

It is probable the campaign may open before this number comes from the press. The enemy have long lain idle, and amused themselves with carrying on the war by proclamations only. While they continue their delay our strength increases, and were they to move to action now, it is a circumstantial proof that they have no reinforcement coming; wherefore, in either case, the comparative advantage will be ours. Like a wounded, disabled whale, they want only time and room to die in; and though in the agony of their exit, it may be unsafe to live within the flapping of their tail, yet every hour shortens their date, and lessens their power of mischief. If any thing happens while this number is in the press, it will afford me a subject for the last pages of it. At present I am tired of waiting; and as neither the enemy, nor the state of politics have yet produced any thing new, I am thereby left in the field of general matter, undirected by any striking or particular object. This *Crisis,* therefore, will be made up rather of variety than novelty, and consist more of things useful than things wonderful.

The success of the cause, the union of the people, and the means of supporting and securing both, are points which cannot be too much attended to. He who doubts of the former is a desponding coward, and he who wilfully disturbs the latter is a traitor. Their characters are easily fixed, and under these short descriptions I leave them for the present.

One of the greatest degrees of sentimental union which America ever knew, was in denying the right of the British parliament *"to bind the colonies in all cases whatsoever."* [1] The Declaration is, in its form, an almighty one, and is the loftiest stretch of arbitrary power that ever one set of men or one country claimed over another. Taxation was nothing more than the putting the declared right into practice; and this failing, recourse was had to arms, as a means to establish both the right *and* the practice, or to answer a worse purpose, which will be mentioned in the course of this number. And in order to repay themselves the expense of an army, and to profit by their own injustice, the colonies were, by another law, declared to be in a state of actual rebellion, and of consequence all property therein would fall to the conquerors.

The colonies, on their part, *first,* denied the right; *secondly,* they suspended the use of taxable articles, and petitioned against the practice of taxation: and these failing, they, *thirdly,* defended their property by force, as soon as it was forcibly invaded, and, in answer to the declaration of rebellion and non-protection, published their Declaration of Independence and right of self-protection.

These, in a few words, are the different stages of the quarrel; and the parts are so intimately and necessarily connected with each other as to admit of no separation. A person, to use a trite phrase, must be a Whig or a Tory in a lump. His feelings, as a man, may be wounded; his charity, as a Christian, may be moved; but his political principles must go through all the cases on one side or the other. He cannot be a Whig in *this* stage, and a Tory in *that.* If he says he is against the united independence of the continent, he is to all intents and purposes against her in all the rest; because *this last* comprehends the whole. And he may just as well say, that Britain was right in declaring us rebels; right in taxing us; and right in declaring her *"right to bind the colonies in all cases whatsoever."* It signifies nothing what neutral ground, of his own creating, he may skulk upon for shelter, for the quarrel in no stage of it hath afforded any such ground; and either we or Britain are absolutely right or absolutely wrong through the whole.

Britain, like a gamester nearly ruined, has now put all her losses into one bet, and is playing a desperate game for the total. If she wins it, she wins from me my life; she wins the continent as the forfeited property of rebels; the right of taxing those that are left as reduced subjects; and

---

[1] Here Paine again quotes from the first paragraph of the Declaratory Act passed by Parliament in February, 1766.—*Editor.*

the power of binding them slaves: and the single die which determines this unparalleled event is, whether we support our independence or she overturn it. This is coming to the point at once. Here is the touchstone to try men by. *He that is not a supporter of the independent States of America in the same degree that his religious and political principles would suffer him to support the government of any other country, of which he called himself a subject, is, in the American sense of the word,* A TORY; *and the instant that he endeavors to bring his toryism into practice, he becomes* A TRAITOR. The first can only be detected by a general test, and the law hath already provided for the latter.

It is unnatural and impolitic to admit men who would root up our independence to have any share in our legislation, either as electors or representatives; because the support of our independence rests, in a great measure, on the vigor and purity of our public bodies. Would Britain, even in time of peace, much less in war, suffer an election to be carried by men who professed themselves to be not her subjects, or allow such to sit in Parliament? Certainly not.

But there are a certain species of Tories with whom conscience or principle has nothing to do, and who are so from avarice only. Some of the first fortunes on the continent, on the part of the Whigs, are staked on the issue of our present measures. And shall disaffection only be rewarded with security? Can any thing be a greater inducement to a miserly man, than the hope of making his Mammon safe? And though the scheme be fraught with every character of folly, yet, so long as he supposes, that by doing nothing materially criminal against America on one part, and by expressing his private disapprobation against independence, as palliative with the enemy, on the other part, he stands in a safe line between both; while, I say, this ground he suffered to remain, craft, and the spirit of avarice, will point it out, and men will not be wanting to fill up this most contemptible of all characters.

These men, ashamed to own the sordid cause from whence their disaffection springs, add thereby meanness to meanness, by endeavoring to shelter themselves under the mask of hypocrisy; that is, they had rather be thought to be Tories from *some kind of principle,* than Tories by having *no principle at all.* But till such time as they can show some real reason, natural, political, or conscientious, on which their objections to independence are founded, we are not obliged to give them credit for being Tories of the first stamp, but must set them down as Tories of the last.

In the second number of the *Crisis,* I endeavored to show the impossibility of the enemy's making any conquest of America, that nothing was wanting on our part but patience and perseverance, and that, with these virtues, our success, as far as human speculation could discern, seemed as certain as fate. But as there are many among us, who, influenced by others, have regularly gone back from the principles they once held, in proportion as we have gone forward; and as it is the unfortunate lot of many a good man to live within the neighborhood of disaffected ones; I shall, therefore, for the sake of confirming the one and recovering the other, endeavor, in the space of a page or two, to go over some of the leading principles in support of independence. It is a much pleasanter task to prevent vice than to punish it, and, however our tempers may be gratified by resentment, or our national expenses eased by forfeited estates, harmony and friendship is, nevertheless, the happiest condition a country can be blessed with.

The principal arguments in support of independence may be comprehended under the four following heads.

1st, The natural right of the continent to independence.

2d, Her interest in being independent.

3d, The necessity,—and

4th, The moral advantages arising therefrom.

I. The natural right of the continent to independence, is a point which never yet was called in question. It will not even admit of a debate. To deny such a right, would be a kind of atheism against nature: and the best answer to such an objection would be, *"The fool hath said in his heart there is no God."*

II. The interest of the continent in being independent is a point as clearly right as the former. America, by her own internal industry, and unknown to all the powers of Europe, was, at the beginning of the dispute, arrived at a pitch of greatness, trade and population, beyond which it was the interest of Britain not to suffer her to pass, lest she should grow too powerful to be kept subordinate. She began to view this country with the same uneasy malicious eye, with which a covetous guardian would view his ward, whose estate he had been enriching himself by for twenty years, and saw him just arriving at manhood. And America owes no more to Britain for her present maturity, than the ward would to the guardian for being twenty-one years of age. That America hath flourished *at the time* she was under the government of Britain, is true;

but there is every natural reason to believe, that had she been an independent country from the first settlement thereof, uncontrolled by any foreign power, free to make her own laws, regulate and encourage her own commerce, she had by this time been of much greater worth than now. The case is simply this: the first settlers in the different colonies were left to shift for themselves, unnoticed and unsupported by any European government; but as the tyranny and persecution of the old world daily drove numbers to the new, and as, by the favor of heaven on their industry and perseverance, they grew into importance, so, in a like degree, they became an object of profit to the greedy eyes of Europe. It was impossible, in this state of infancy, however thriving and promising, that they could resist the power of any armed invader that should seek to bring them under his authority. In this situation, Britain thought it worth her while to claim them, and the continent received and acknowledged the claimer. It was, in reality, of no very great importance who was her master, seeing, that from the force and ambition of the different powers of Europe, she must, till she acquired strength enough to assert her own right, acknowledge some one. As well, perhaps, Britain as another; and it might have been as well to have been under the states of Holland as any. The same hopes of engrossing and profiting by her trade, by not oppressing it too much, would have operated alike with any master, and produced to the colonies the same effects. The clamor of protection, likewise, was all a farce; because, in order to make that protection necessary, she must first, by her own quarrels, create us enemies. Hard terms indeed!

To know whether it be the interest of the continent to be independent, we need only ask this easy, simple question: Is it the interest of a man to be a boy all his life? The answer to one will be the answer to both. America hath been one continued scene of legislative contention from the first king's representative to the last; and this was unavoidably founded in the natural opposition of interest between the old country and the new. A governor sent from England, or receiving his authority therefrom, ought never to have been considered in any other light than that of a genteel commissioned spy, whose private business was information, and his public business a kind of civilized oppression. In the first of these characters he was to watch the tempers, sentiments and disposition of the people, the growth of trade, and the increase of private fortunes; and, in the latter, to suppress all such acts of the assemblies, however beneficial to the people, which did not directly or indirectly throw some increase of power or profit into the hands of those that sent him.

America, till now, could never be called a *free country,* because her legislation depended on the will of a man three thousand miles distant, whose interest was in opposition to ours, and who, by a single "no," could forbid what law he pleased.

The freedom of trade, likewise, is, to a trading country, an article of such importance, that the principal source of wealth depends upon it; and it is impossible that any country can flourish, as it otherwise might do, whose commerce is engrossed, cramped and fettered by the laws and mandates of another—yet these evils, and more than I can here enumerate, the continent has suffered by being under the government of England. By an independence we clear the whole at once—put an end to the business of unanswered petitions and fruitless remonstrances—exchange Britain for Europe—shake hands with the world—live at peace with the world—and trade to any market where we can buy and sell.

III. The necessity, likewise, of being independent, even before it was declared, became so evident and important, that the continent ran the risk of being ruined every day that she delayed it. There was reason to believe that Britain would endeavor to make an European matter of it, and, rather than lose the whole, would dismember it, like Poland, and dispose of her several claims to the highest bidder. Genoa, failing in her attempts to reduce Corsica, made a sale of it to the French, and such trafficks have been common in the old world. We had at that time no ambassador in any part of Europe, to counteract her negotiations, and by that means she had the range of every foreign court uncontradicted on our part. We even knew nothing of the treaty for the Hessians till it was concluded, and the troops ready to embark.[2] Had we been

---

[2] The reference is to the treaty concluded by the British ministry with several German rulers in the fall of 1775. By that agreement the Duke of Brunswick was to furnish four thousand eighty-four men; the landgrave of Hesse Cassel (who married George III's aunt), twelve thousand one hundred and four; the prince of Hesse, six hundred and eighty-eight, and the prince of Waldeck, six hundred and seventy; making a total of seventeen thousand five hundred and twenty-six soldiers, including officers. These German mercenaries were hired—the German princes were to receive thirty-six dollars a year for each man and large annual subsidies—to subdue the American people. "Of all the acts of 'transcendent folly and wickedness' perpetrated by the British Ministry," writes John C. Miller, "none did more to convince the Americans of the necessity of an immediate declaration of independence than the hiring of foreign mercenaries to help suppress the rebellion in the colonies." (*Origins of the American Revolution* [Boston, 1943], p. 476).— *Editor.*

independent before, we had probably prevented her obtaining them. We had no credit abroad, because of our rebellious dependency. Our ships could claim no protection in foreign ports, because we afforded them no justifiable reason for granting it to us. The calling ourselves subjects, and at the same time fighting against the power which we acknowledged, was a dangerous precedent to all Europe. If the grievances justified the taking up arms, they justified our separation; if they did not justify our separation, neither could they justify our taking up arms. All Europe was interested in reducing us as rebels, and all Europe (or the greatest part at least) is interested in supporting us as independent States. At home our condition was still worse; our currency had no foundation, and the fall of it would have ruined Whig and Tory alike. We had no other law than a kind of moderated passion; no other civil power than an honest mob; and no other protection than the temporary attachment of one man to another. Had independence been delayed a few months longer, this continent would have been plunged into irrecoverable confusion: some violent for it, some against it, till, in the general cabal, the rich would have been ruined, and the poor destroyed. It is to independence that every Tory owes the present safety which he lives in; for by that, and that only, we emerged from a state of dangerous suspense, and became a regular people.

The necessity, likewise, of being independent, had there been no rupture between Britain and America, would, in a little time, have brought one on. The increasing importance of commerce, the weight and perplexity of legislation, and the entangled state of European politics, would daily have shown to the continent the impossibility of continuing subordinate; for, after the coolest reflections on the matter, this must be allowed, that Britain was too jealous of America to govern it justly; too ignorant of it to govern it well; and too far distant from it to govern it at all.

IV. But what weigh most with all men of serious reflection are, the *moral advantages* arising from independence: war and desolation have become the trade of the old world; and America neither could nor can be under the government of Britain without becoming a sharer of her guilt, and a partner in all the dismal commerce of death. The spirit of duelling, extended on a national scale, is a proper character for European wars. They have seldom any other motive than pride, or any other object than fame. The conquerors and the conquered are generally ruined alike, and the chief difference at last is, that the one marches home with his honors, and the other without them. 'Tis the natural temper of the English to fight for a feather, if they suppose that feather to be an affront; and America, without the right of asking why, must have abetted in every quarrel, and abided by its fate. It is a shocking situation to live in, that one country must be brought into all the wars of another, whether the measure be right or wrong, or whether she will or not; yet this, in the fullest extent, was, and ever would be, the unavoidable consequence of the connection. Surely the Quakers forgot their own principles when, in their late Testimony, they called *this connection,* with these military and miserable appendages hanging to it— *"the happy constitution."*

Britain, for centuries past, has been nearly fifty years out of every hundred at war with some power or other. It certainly ought to be a conscientious as well as political consideration with America, not to dip her hands in the bloody work of Europe. Our situation affords us a retreat from their cabals, and the present happy union of the states bids fair for extirpating the future use of arms from one quarter of the world; yet such have been the irreligious politics of the present leaders of the Quakers, that, for the sake of they scarce know what, they would cut off every hope of such a blessing by tying this continent to Britain, like Hector to the chariot wheel of Achilles, to be dragged through all the miseries of endless European wars.

The connection, viewed from this ground, is distressing to every man who has the feelings of humanity. By having Britain for our master, we became enemies to the greatest part of Europe, and they to us: and the consequence was war inevitable. By being our own masters, independent of any foreign one, we have Europe for our friends, and the prospect of an endless peace among ourselves. Those who were advocates for the British government over these colonies, were obliged to limit both their arguments and their ideas to the period of an European peace only; the moment Britain became plunged in war, every supposed convenience to us vanished, and all we could hope for was not to be ruined. Could this be a desirable condition for a young country to be in?

Had the French pursued their fortune immediately after the defeat of Braddock [in the] last war,[3] this city and province had then experienced the woful calamities of being a British subject. A scene of the same kind might happen again; for America, considered as a subject to the

---

[3] In the summer of 1755 General Edward Braddock and his men were surprised and routed by 900 French and Indians seven miles from Fort Duquesne.—*Editor.*

crown of Britain, would ever have been the seat of war, and the bone of contention between the two powers.

On the whole, if the future expulsion of arms from one quarter of the world would be a desirable object to a peaceable man; if the freedom of trade to every part of it can engage the attention of a man of business; if the support or fall of millions of currency can affect our interests; if the entire possession of estates, by cutting off the lordly claims of Britain over the soil, deserves the regard of landed property; and if the right of making our own laws, uncontrolled by royal or ministerial spies or mandates, be worthy our care as freemen;—then are all men interested in the support of independence; and may he that supports it not, be driven from the blessing, and live unpitied beneath the servile sufferings of scandalous subjection!

We have been amused with the tales of ancient wonders; we have read, and wept over the histories of other nations: applauded, censured, or pitied, as their cases affected us. The fortitude and patience of the sufferers—the justness of their cause—the weight of their oppressions and oppressors—the object to be saved or lost—with all the consequences of a defeat or a conquest—have, in the hour of sympathy, bewitched our hearts, and chained it to their fate: but where is the power that ever made war upon petitioners? Or where is the war on which a world was staked till now?

We may not, perhaps, be wise enough to make all the advantages we ought of our independence; but they are, nevertheless, marked and presented to us with every character of *great* and *good,* and worthy the hand of him who sent them. I look through the present trouble to a time of tranquillity, when we shall have it in our power to set an example of peace to all the world. Were the Quakers really impressed and influenced by the quiet principles they profess to hold, they would, however they might disapprove the means, be the first of all men to approve of *independence,* because, by separating ourselves from the cities of Sodom and Gomorrah, it affords an opportunity never given to man before of carrying their favourite principle of peace into general practice, by establishing governments that shall hereafter exist without wars. O! ye fallen, cringing, priest-and-Pemberton-ridden people! What more can we say of ye than that a religious Quaker is a valuable character, and a political Quaker a real Jesuit.

Having thus gone over some of the principal points in support of independence, I must now request the reader to return back with me to the period when it first began to be a public doctrine, and to examine the progress it has made among the various classes of men. The area I mean to begin at, is the breaking out of hostilities, April 19th, 1775. Until this event happened, the continent seemed to view the dispute as a kin of law-suit for a matter of right, litigating between the old country and the new; and she felt the same kind and degree of horror, as if she had seen an oppressive plaintiff, at the head of a band of ruffians, enter the court, while the cause was before it, and put the judge, the jury, the defendant and his counsel, to the sword. Perhaps a more heart-felt convulsion never reached a country with the same degree of power and rapidity before, and never may again. Pity for the sufferers, mixed with indignation at the violence, and heightened with apprehensions of undergoing the same fate, made the affair of Lexington the affair of the continent. Every part of it felt the shock, and all vibrated together. A general promotion of sentiment took place: those who had drank deeply into Whiggish principles, that is, the right and necessity not only of opposing, but wholly setting aside the power of the crown as soon as it became practically dangerous (for in theory it was always so), stepped into the first stage of independence; while another class of Whigs, equally sound in principle, but not so sanguine in enterprise, attached themselves the stronger to the cause, and fell close in with the rear of the former; their partition was a mere point. Numbers of the moderate men, whose chief fault, at that time, arose from entertaining a better opinion of Britain than she deserved, convinced now of their mistake, gave her up, and publicly declared themselves good Whigs. While the Tories, seeing it was no longer a laughing matter, either sank into silent obscurity, or contented themselves with coming forth and abusing General Gage: not a single advocate appeared to justify the action of that day; it seemed to appear to every one with the same magnitude, struck every one with the same force, and created in every one the same abhorrence. From this period we may date the growth of independence.

If the many circumstances which happened at this memorable time, be taken in one view, and compared with each other, they will justify a conclusion which seems not to have been attended to, I mean a fixed design in the king and ministry of driving America into arms, in order that they might be furnished with a pretence for seizing the whole continent, as the immediate property of the crown. A noble plunder for hungry courtiers!

It ought to be remembered, that the first petition from the Congress was at this time unanswered on the part of the British king.[4] That the motion, called Lord North's motion, of the 20th of February, 1775, arrived in America the latter end of March.[5] This motion was to be laid, by the several governors then in being, before the assembly of each province; and the first assembly before which it was laid, was the assembly of Pennsylvania, in May following. This being a just state of the case, I then ask, why were hostilities commenced between the time of passing the resolve in the House of Commons, of the 20th of February, and the time of the assemblies meeting to deliberate upon it? Degrading and famous as that motion was, there is nevertheless reason to believe that the king and his adherents were afraid the colonies would agree to it, and lest they should, took effectual care they should not, by provoking them with hostilities in the interim. They had not the least doubt at that time of conquering America at one blow; and what they expected to get by a conquest being infinitely greater than any thing they could hope to get either by taxation or accommodation, they seemed determined to prevent even the possibility of hearing each other, lest America should disappoint their greedy hopes of the whole, by listening even to their own terms. On the one hand they refused to hear the petition of the continent, and on the other hand took effectual care the continent should not hear them.

That the motion of the 20th February and the orders for commencing hostilities were both concerted by the same person or persons, and not the latter by General Gage, as was falsely imagined at first, is evident from an extract of a letter of his to the administration, read among other papers in the House of Commons; in which he informs his masters, *"That though their idea of his disarming certain counties was a right one, yet it required him to be master of the country, in order to enable him to execute it."* This was prior to the commencement of hostilities,

[4] In July, 1775, the Continental Congress adopted a humble address to the king known as the Olive Branch petition. This was a victory for the more conservative elements in Congress, led by John Dickinson, who favored a conciliatory program which would permit the colonies to remain within the empire. In August, 1775, the king refused to accept the Olive Branch petition. With its refusal by the Crown, the radicals in the Continental Congress gained the upper hand.—*Editor.*

[5] Instead of direct parliamentary taxation Lord North proposed the adoption of a requisition system in which Parliament, instead of the king, would present its demands to the colonial legislatures. As long as the colonists taxed themselves to Parliament's satisfaction, Parliament would not tax them. The proposal, Lord North made clear, did not wipe out the principles set forth in the Declaratory Act. Parliament would simply refrain from exercising its rights. In August, 1775, Congress rejected Lord North's conciliatory plan.—*Editor.*

and consequently before the motion of the 20th February could be deliberated on by the several assemblies.

Perhaps it may be asked, why was the motion passed, if there was at
the same time a plan to aggravate the Americans not to listen to it? Lord
North assigned one reason himself, which was *a hope of dividing them.*
This was publicly tempting them to reject it; that if, in case the injury
of arms should fail in provoking them sufficiently, the insult of such a
declaration might fill it up. But by passing the motion and getting it
afterwards rejected in America, it enabled them, in their wicked idea of
politics, among other things, to hold up the colonies to foreign powers,
with every possible mark of disobedience and rebellion. They had applied to those powers not to supply the continent with arms, ammunition, etc., and it was necessary they should incense them against us, by
assigning on their own part some seeming reputable reason why. By
dividing, it had a tendency to weaken the States, and likewise to perplex the adherents of America in England. But the principal scheme,
and that which has marked their character in every part of their conduct, was a design of precipitating the colonies into a state which they
might afterwards deem rebellion, and, under that pretence, put an end to
all future complaints, petitions and remonstrances, by seizing the whole
at once. They had ravaged one part of the globe, till it could glut them
no longer; their prodigality required new plunder, and through the
East Indian article *tea* they hoped to transfer their rapine from that
quarter of the world to this.[6] Every designed quarrel had its pretence;
and the same barbarian avarice accompanied the *plant* to America, which
ruined the country that produced it.

That men never turn rogues without turning fools is a maxim, sooner
or later, universally true. The commencement of hostilities, being in
the beginning of April, was, of all times the worst chosen: the Congress
were to meet the tenth of May following, and the distress the continent
felt at this unparalleled outrage gave a stability to that body which no
other circumstance could have done. It suppressed too all inferior debates, and bound them together by a necessitous affection, without giving them time to differ upon trifles. The suffering likewise softened the
whole body of the people into a degree of pliability, which laid the principal foundation-stone of union, order, and government; and which, at

[6] In 1773 Parliament passed a law which practically gave the East India Company, which
was on the brink of bankruptcy, a monopoly of the colonial tea trade. This measure led
to the Boston Tea Party, December 16, 1773.—*Editor.*

any other time, might only have fretted and then faded away unnoticed and unimproved. But Providence, who best knows how to time her misfortunes as well as her immediate favors, chose this to be the time, and who dare dispute it?

It did not seem the disposition of the people, at this crisis, to heap petition upon petition, while the former remained unanswered. The measure however was carried in Congress, and a second petition was sent; of which I shall only remark that it was submissive even to a dangerous fault, because the prayer of it appealed solely to what it called the prerogative of the crown, while the matter in dispute was confessedly constitutional. But even this petition, flattering as it was, was still not so harmonious as the chink of cash, and consequently not sufficiently grateful to the tyrant and his ministry. From every circumstance it is evident, that it was the determination of the British court to have nothing to do with America but to conquer her fully and absolutely. They were certain of success, and the field of battle was the only place of treaty. I am confident there are thousands and tens of thousands in America who wonder *now* that they should ever have thought otherwise; but the sin of that day was the sin of civility; yet it operated against our present good in the same manner that a civil opinion of the devil would against our future peace.

Independence was a doctrine scarce and rare, even towards the conclusion of the year 1775; all our politics had been founded on the hope of expectation of making the matter up—a hope, which, though general on the side of America, had never entered the head or heart of the British court. Their hope was conquest and confiscation. Good heavens! what volumes of thanks does America owe to Britain? What infinite obligation to the tool that fills, with paradoxical vacancy, the throne! Nothing but the sharpest essence of villainy, compounded with the strongest distillation of folly, could have produced a menstruum that would have effected a separation. The Congress in 1774 administered an abortive medicine to independence, by prohibiting the importation of goods, and the succeeding Congress rendered the dose still more dangerous by continuing it. Had independence been a settled system with America, (as Britain has advanced,) she ought to have *doubled* her importation, and prohibited in some degree her exportation. And this single circumstance is sufficient to acquit America before any jury of nations, of having a continental plan of independence in view; a charge which, had it been true, would have been honorable, but is so grossly false, that either the amazing ignorance or the wilful dishonesty of the British court is effectually proved by it.

The second petition, like the first, produced no answer; it was scarcely acknowledged to have been received; the British court were too determined in their villainy even to act it artfully, and in their rage for conquest neglected the necessary subtleties for obtaining it. They might have divided, distracted and played a thousand tricks with us, had they been as cunning as they were cruel.

This last indignity gave a new spring to independence. Those who knew the savage obstinacy of the king, and the jobbing, gambling spirit of the court, predicted the fate of the petition, as soon as it was sent from America; for the men being known, their measures were easily foreseen. As politicians we ought not so much to ground our hopes on the reasonableness of the thing we ask, as on the reasonableness of the person of whom we ask it: who would expect discretion from a fool, candor from a tyrant, or justice from a villain?

As every prospect of accommodation seemed now to fail fast, men began to think seriously on the matter; and their reason being thus stripped of the false hope which had long encompassed it, became approachable by fair debate: yet still the bulk of the people hesitated; they startled at the novelty of independence, without once considering that our getting into arms at first was a more extraordinary novelty, and that all other nations had gone through the work of independence before us. They doubted likewise the ability of the continent to support it, without reflecting that it required the same force to obtain an accommodation by arms as an independence. If the one was acquirable, the other was the same; because, to accomplish either, it was necessary that our strength should be too great for Britain to subdue; and it was too unreasonable to suppose, that with the power of being masters, we should submit to be servants.[7] Their caution at this time was exceedingly misplaced; for if they were able to defend their property and maintain their rights by

---

[7] In this state of political suspense the pamphlet *Common Sense* made its appearance, and the success it met with does not become me to mention. Dr. Franklin, Mr. Samuel and John Adams, were severally spoken of as the supposed author. I had not, at that time, the pleasure either of personally knowing or being known to the two last gentlemen. The favor of Dr. Franklin's friendship I possessed in England, and my introduction to this part of the world was through his patronage. I happened, when a school-boy, to pick up a pleasing natural history of Virginia, and my inclination from that day of seeing the western side of the Atlantic never left me. In October, 1775, Dr. Franklin proposed giving me such materials as were in his hands, towards completing a history of the present transactions, and seemed desirous of having the first volume out the next Spring. I had

arms, they, consequently, were able to defend and support their independence; and in proportion as these men saw the necessity and correct-
ness of the measure, they honestly and openly declared and adopted it,
and the part that they had acted since has done them honor and fully
established their characters. Error in opinion has this peculiar advantage
with it, that the foremost point of the contrary ground may at any time
be reached by the sudden exertion of a thought; and it frequently happens in sentimental differences, that some striking circumstance, or some
forcible reason quickly conceived, will effect in an instant what neither
argument nor example could produce in an age.

I find it impossible in the small compass I am limited to, to trace out
the progress which independence has made on the minds of the different
classes of men, and the several reasons by which they were moved. With
some, it was a passionate abhorrence against the king of England and
his ministry, as a set of savages and brutes; and these men, governed
by the agony of a wounded mind, were for trusting every thing to hope
and heaven, and bidding defiance at once. With others, it was a growing
conviction that the scheme of the British court was to create, ferment
and drive on a quarrel, for the sake of confiscated plunder: and men of
this class ripened into independence in proportion as the evidence increased. While a third class conceived it was the true interest of America,
internally and externally, to be her own master, and gave their support
to independence, step by step, as they saw her abilities to maintain it
enlarge. With many, it was a compound of all these reasons; while those
who were too callous to be reached by either, remained, and still remain
Tories.

The *legal necessity* of being independent, with several collateral reasons, is pointed out in an elegant masterly manner, in a charge to the
grand jury for the district of Charleston, by the Hon. William Henry
Drayton, chief justice of South Carolina, [April 23, 1776]. This performance, and the address of the convention of New York, are pieces, in my
humble opinion, of the first rank in America.

The principal causes why independence has not been so universally
supported as it ought, are *fear* and *indolence,* and the causes why it has

---

then formed the outlines of *Common Sense,* and finished nearly the first part; and as I
supposed the doctor's design in getting out a history, was to open the new year with a
new system, I expected to surprise him with a production on that subject, much earlier
than he thought of; and without informing him what I was doing, got it ready for the
press as fast as I conveniently could, and sent him the first pamphlet that was printed off.
—*Author.*

been opposed, are, *avarice, down-right villainy,* and *lust of personal power.* There is not such a being in America as a Tory from conscience; some secret defect or other is interwoven in the character of all those, be they men or women, who can look with patience on the brutality, luxury and debauchery of the British court, and the violations of their army here. A woman's virtue must sit very lightly on her who can even hint a favorable sentiment in their behalf. It is remarkable that the whole race of prostitutes in New York were tories; and the schemes for supporting the Tory cause in this city, for which several are now in jail, and one hanged, were concerted and carried on in common bawdy-houses, assisted by those who kept them.

The connection between vice and meanness is a fit subject for satire, but when the satire is a fact, it cuts with the irresistible power of a diamond. If a Quaker, in defence of his just rights, his property, and the chastity of his house, takes up a musket, he is expelled the meeting; but the present king of England, who seduced and took into keeping a sister of their society, is reverenced and supported by repeated Testimonies, while the friendly noodle from whom she was taken (and who is now in this city) continues a drudge in the service of his rival, as if proud of being cuckolded by a creature called a king.[8]

Our support and success depend on such a variety of men and circumstances, that every one who does but wish well, is of some use: there are men who have a strange aversion to arms, yet have hearts to risk every shilling in the cause, or in support of those who have better talents for defending it. Nature, in the arrangement of mankind, has fitted some for every service in life: were all soldiers, all would starve and go naked, and were none soldiers, all would be slaves. As *disaffection* to independence is the badge of a Tory, so *affection* to it is the mark of a Whig; and the different services of the Whigs, down from those who nobly contribute every thing, to those who have nothing to render but their wishes, tend all to the same center, though with different degrees of merit and ability. The larger we make the circle, the more we shall harmonize, and the stronger we shall be. All we want to shut out is disaffection, and, *that excluded,* we must accept from each other such duties as we are best fitted to bestow. A narrow system of politics, like a narrow system of religion, is calculated only to sour the temper, and be at variance with mankind.

[8] The Quaker "sister" referred to was Hannah Lightfoot. The man to whom she was said to have been married—Axford—was probably in Philadelphia.—*Editor.*

All we want to know in America is simply this, who is for independence, and who is not? Those who are for it, will support it, and the remainder will undoubtedly see the reasonableness of paying the charges; while those who oppose or seek to betray it, must expect the more rigid fate of the jail and the gibbet. There is a bastard kind of generosity, which being extended to all men, is as fatal to society, on one hand, as the want of true generosity is on the other. A lax manner of administering justice, falsely termed moderation, has a tendency both to dispirit public virtue, and promote the growth of public evils. Had the late committee of safety taken cognizance of the last Testimony of the Quakers and proceeded against such delinquents as were concerned therein, they had, probably, prevented the treasonable plans which have been concerted since. When one villain is suffered to escape, it encourages another to proceed, either from a hope of escaping likewise, or an apprehension that we dare not punish. It has been a matter of general surprise, that no notice was taken of the incendiary publication of the Quakers, of the 20th of November last; a publication evidently intended to promote sedition and treason, and encourage the enemy, who were then within a day's march of this city, to proceed on and possess it. I here present the reader with a memorial which was laid before the board of safety a few days after the Testimony appeared. Not a member of that board, that I conversed with, but expressed the highest detestation of the perverted principles and conduct of the Quaker junto, and a wish that the board would take the matter up; notwithstanding which, it was suffered to pass away unnoticed, to the encouragement of new acts of treason, the general danger of the cause, and the disgrace of the state.

To the honorable the Council of Safety of the State of Pennsylvania.

At a meeting of a reputable number of the inhabitants of the city of Philadelphia, impressed with a proper sense of the justice of the cause which this continent is engaged in, and animated with a generous fervor for supporting the same, it was resolved, that the following be laid before the board of safety:

"We profess liberality of sentiment to all men; with this distinction *only,* that those who do not deserve it would become wise and *seek* to deserve it. We hold the pure doctrines of universal liberty of conscience, and conceive it our duty to endeavor to secure that sacred right to others, as well as to defend it for ourselves; for we undertake not to judge of the religious rectitude of tenets, but leave the whole matter to Him who made us.

"We persecute no man, neither will we abet in the persecution of any man for religion's sake; our common relation to others being that of fellow-citizens and fellow-subjects of one single community; and in this line of connection we hold out the right hand of fellowship to all men. But we should conceive ourselves to be unworthy members of the *free and independent States of America,* were we unconcernedly to see or to suffer any treasonable wound, public or private, directly or indirectly, to be given against the peace and safety of the same. We inquire not into the rank of the offenders, nor into their religious persuasion; we have no business with either, our part being only to find them out and exhibit them to justice.

"A printed paper, dated the 20th of November, and signed *'John Pemberton,'* [9] whom we suppose to be an inhabitant of this city, has lately been dispersed abroad, a copy of which accompanies this. Had the framers and publishers of that paper conceived it their duty to exhort the youth and others of their society, to a patient submission under the present trying visitations, and humbly to wait the event of heaven towards them, they had therein shown a Christian temper, and we had been silent; but the anger and political virulence with which their instructions are given, and the abuse with which they stigmatize all ranks of men not thinking like themselves, leave no doubt on our minds from what spirit their publication proceeded: and it is disgraceful to the pure cause of truth, that men can dally with words of the most sacred import, and play them off as mechanically as if religion consisted only in contrivance. We know of no instance in which the Quakers have been compelled to bear arms, or to do any thing which might strain their conscience; wherefore their advice, 'to withstand and refuse to submit to the arbitrary instructions and ordinances of men,' appear to us a false alarm, and could only be treasonably calculated to gain favor with our enemies, when they are seemingly on the brink of invading this State, or, what is still worse, to weaken the hands of our defence, that their entrance into this city might be made practicable and easy.

"We disclaim all tumult and disorder in the punishment of offenders; and wish to be governed, not by temper but by reason, in the manner of treating them. We are sensible that our cause has suffered by the two following errors: first, by ill-judged lenity to traitorous persons in some cases; and, secondly, by only a passionate treatment of them in others. For the future we disown both, and wish to be steady in our proceedings, and serious in our punishments.

"Every State in America has, by the repeated voice of its inhabitants, directed and authorized the Continental Congress to publish a formal Declara-

[9] John Pemberton was a prominent Quaker and founder of the Antislavery Society, April 14, 1775. He became a Tory and, together with about twenty others, was sent to Virginia and imprisoned for several months.—*Editor.*

tion of Independence of, and separation from, the oppressive king and Parliament of Great Britain; and we look on every man as an enemy, who does not in some line or other, give his assistance towards supporting the same; at the same time we consider the offence to be heightened to a degree of unpardonable guilt, when such persons, under the show of religion, endeavor, either by writing, speaking, or otherwise, to subvert, overturn, or bring reproach upon the independence of this continent as declared by Congress.

"The publishers of the paper signed '*John Pemberton,*' have called in a loud manner to their friends and connections, 'to withstand or refuse' obedience to whatever 'instructions or ordinances' may be published, not warranted by (what they call) 'that happy Constitution under which they and others long enjoyed tranquillity and peace.' If this be not treason, we know not what may properly be called by that name.

"To us it is a matter of surprise and astonishment, that men with the word '*peace, peace,*' continually on their lips, should be so fond of living under and supporting a government, and at the same time calling it '*happy,*' which is never better pleased than when a war—that has filled India with carnage and famine, Africa with slavery, and tampered with Indians and negroes to cut the throats of the freemen of America. We conceive it a disgrace to this State, to harbor or wink at such palpable hypocrisy. But as we seek not to hurt the hair of any man's head, when we can make ourselves safe without, we wish such persons to restore peace to themselves and us, by removing themselves to some part of the king of Great Britain's dominions, as by that means they may live unmolested by us and we by them; for our fixed opinion is, that those who do not deserve a place among us, ought not to have one.

"We conclude with requesting the Council of Safety to take into consideration the paper signed '*John Pemberton,*' and if it shall appear to them to be of a dangerous tendency, or of a treasonable nature, that they would commit the signer, together with such other persons as they can discover were concerned therein, into custody, until such time as some mode of trial shall ascertain the full degree of their guilt and punishment; in the doing of which, we wish their judges, whoever they may be, to disregard the man, his connections, interest, riches, poverty, or principles of religion, and to attend to the nature of his offence only."

The most cavilling sectarian cannot accuse the foregoing with containing the least ingredient of persecution. The free spirit on which the American cause is founded, disdains to mix with such an impurity, and leaves it as rubbish fit only for narrow and suspicious minds to grovel in. Suspicion and persecution are weeds of the same dunghill, and flourish together. Had the Quakers minded their religion and their business, they might have lived through this dispute in enviable ease, and none would have molested them. The common phrase with these people is, *'Our principles are peace.'* To which may be replied, *and your practices are the reverse;* for never did the conduct of men oppose their own doctrine more notoriously than the present race of the Quakers. They have artfully changed themselves into a different sort of people to what they used to be, and yet have the address to persuade each other that they are not altered; like antiquated virgins, they see not the havoc deformity has made upon them, but pleasantly mistaking wrinkles for dimples, conceive themselves yet lovely and wonder at the stupid world for not admiring them.

Did no injury arise to the public by this apostasy of the Quakers from themselves, the public would have nothing to do with it; but as both the design and consequences are pointed against a cause in which the whole community are interested, it is therefore no longer a subject confined to the cognizance of the meeting only, but comes, as a matter of criminality, before the authority either of the particular State in which it is acted, or of the continent against which it operates. Every attempt, now, to support the authority of the king and Parliament of Great Britain over America, is treason against *every* State; therefore it is impossible that any *one* can pardon or screen from punishment an offender against *all*.

But to proceed: while the infatuated Tories of this and other States were last spring talking of commissioners, accommodation, making the matter up, and the Lord knows what stuff and nonsense, their *good* king and ministry were glutting themselves with the revenge of reducing America to *unconditional submission,* and solacing each other with the certainty of conquering it in *one campaign.* The following quotations are from the parliamentary register of the debates of the House of Lords, March 5th, 1776:

"The Americans," says Lord Talbot,[10] "have been obstinate, undutiful, and ungovernable from the very beginning, from their first early and infant settlements; and I am every day more and more convinced that this people never will be brought back to their duty, and the subordinate relation they stand in to this country, *till reduced to unconditional, effectual submission; no concession on our part, no lenity, no endurance,* will have any other effect but that of increasing their insolence."

[10] Steward of the king's household.—*Author.*

"The stuggle," says Lord Townsend,[11] "is now a struggle for power; the die is cast, and the *only point* which now remains to be determined is, in what manner the war can be most effectually prosecuted and speedily finished, in order to procure that *unconditional submission,* which has been so ably stated by the noble Earl with the white staff" (meaning Lord Talbot;) "and I have no reason to doubt that the measures now pursuing will put an end to the war in the course of a *single campaign.* Should it linger longer, we shall then have reason to expect that some foreign power will interfere, and take advantage of our domestic troubles and civil distractions."

Lord Littleton. "My sentiments are pretty well known. I shall only observe now that lenient measures have had no other effect than to produce insult after insult; that the more we conceded, the higher America rose in her demands, and the more insolent she has grown. It is for this reason that I am now for the most effective and decisive measures; and am of opinion that no alternative is left us, but to relinquish America for ever, or finally determine to compel her to acknowledge the legislative authority of this country; and it is the principle of an *unconditional submission* I would be for maintaining."

Can words be more expressive than these? Surely the Tories will believe the Tory lords! The truth is, they *do believe them* and know as fully as any Whig on the continent knows, that the king and ministry never had the least design of an accommodation with America, but an absolute, unconditional conquest. And the part which the Tories were to act, was, by downright lying, to endeavor to put the continent off its guard, and to divide and sow discontent in the minds of such Whigs as they might gain an influence over. In short, to keep up a distraction here, that the force sent from England might be able to conquer in *"one campaign."* They and the ministry were, by a different game, playing into each other's hands. The cry of the Tories in England was, *"No reconciliation, no accommodation,"* in order to obtain the greater military force; while those in America were crying nothing but *"reconciliation and accommodation,"* that the force sent might conquer with the less resistance.

But this *"single campaign"* is over, and America not conquered. The whole work is yet to do, and the force much less to do it with. Their condition is both despicable and deplorable: out of cash—out of heart, and out of hope. A country furnished with arms and ammunition as America now is, with three millions of inhabitants, and three thousand miles

[11] Formerly General Townsend, at Quebec, and late lord-lieutenant of Ireland.—*Author.*

distant from the nearest enemy that can approach her, is able to look and laugh them in the face.

Howe appears to have two objects in view, either to go up the North River, or come to Philadelphia.

By going up the North River, he secures a retreat for his army through Canada, but the ships must return if they return at all, the same way they went; as our army would be in the rear, the safety of their passage down is a doubtful matter. By such a motion he shuts himself from all supplies from Europe, but through Canada, and exposes his army and navy to the danger of perishing. The idea of his cutting off the communication between the eastern and southern states, by means of the North River, is merely visionary. He cannot do it by his shipping; because no ship can lay long at anchor in any river within reach of the shore; a single gun would drive a first rate from such a station. This was fully proved last October at Forts Washington and Lee, where one gun only, on each side of the river, obliged two frigates to cut and be towed off in an hour's time. Neither can he cut it off by his army; because the several posts they must occupy would divide them almost to nothing, and expose them to be picked up by ours like pebbles on a river's bank; but admitting that he could, where is the injury? Because, while his whole force is cantoned out, as sentries over the water, they will be very innocently employed, and the moment they march into the country the communication opens.

The most probable object is Philadelphia, and the reasons are many. Howe's business is to conquer it, and in proportion as he finds himself unable to the task, he will employ his strength to distress women and weak minds, in order to accomplish through *their* fears what he cannot accomplish by his *own* force. His coming or attempting to come to Philadelphia is a circumstance that proves his weakness: for no general that felt himself able to take the field and attack his antagonist would think of bringing his army into a city in the summer time; and this mere shifting the scene from place to place, without effecting any thing, has feebleness and cowardice on the face of it, and holds him up in a contemptible light to all who can reason justly and firmly. By several informations from New York, it appears that their army in general, both officers and men, have given up the expectation of conquering America; their eye now is fixed upon the spoil. They suppose Philadelphia to be rich with stores, and as they think to get more by robbing a town than by attacking an army, their movement towards the city is probable. We are not now contending against an army of soldiers, but against a band of thieves, who had rather plunder than fight, and have no other hope of conquest than by cruelty.

They expect to get a mighty booty, and strike another general panic, by making a sudden movement and getting possession of this city; but unless they can march *out* as well as *in,* or get the entire command of the river, to remove off their plunder, they may probably be stopped with the stolen goods upon them. They have never yet succeeded wherever they have been opposed, but at Fort Washington. At Charleston their defeat was effectual.[12] At Ticonderoga they ran away.[13] In every skirmish at Kingsbridge and the White Plains they were obliged to retreat,[14] and the instant that our arms were turned upon them in the Jerseys, they turned likewise, and those that turned not were taken.

The necessity of always fitting our internal police to the circumstances of the times we live in, is something so strikingly obvious, that no sufficient objection can be made against it. The safety of all societies depends upon it; and where this point is not attended to, the consequences will either be a general languor or a tumult. The encouragement and protection of the good subjects of any state, and the suppression and punishment of bad ones, are the principal objects for which all authority is instituted, and the line in which it ought to operate. We have in this city a strange variety of men and characters, and the circumstances of the times require that they should be publicly known; it is not the number of Tories that hurt us, so much as the not finding out who they are; men must now take one side or the other, and abide by the consequences: the Quakers, trusting to their short-sighted sagacity, have, most unluckily for them, made their declaration in their last Testimony, and we ought *now* to take them at their word. They have involuntarily read themselves out of the continental meeting, and cannot hope to be restored to it again but by payment and penitence. Men whose political principles are founded on avarice, are beyond the reach of reason, and the only cure of Toryism of this cast is to tax it. A substantial good drawn from

[12] The reference is to the battle on Sullivan Island, an outpost of Charleston, on June 28, 1776. The British loss in killed and wounded was two hundred and five, the American loss in killed and wounded was thirty-seven. The American victory saved Charleston and freed the southern states from the invader for more than two years.—*Editor.*

[13] The reference is to the capture of Ticonderoga by Ethan Allen and his Green Mountain Boys on May 10, 1775.—*Editor.*

[14] In the battle of White Plains, October 12, 1776, the British lost 229 men and the Americans 140.—*Editor.*

a real evil, is of the same benefit to society, as if drawn from a virtue; and where men have not public spirit to render themselves serviceable, it ought to be the study of government to draw the best use possible from their vices. When the governing passion of any man, or set of men, is once known, the method of managing them is easy; for even misers, whom no public virtue can impress, would become generous, could a heavy tax be laid upon covetousness.

The Tories have endeavored to insure their property with the enemy, by forfeiting their reputation with us; from which may be justly inferred, that their governing passion is avarice. Make them as much afraid of losing on one side as on the other, and you stagger their Toryism; make them more so, and you reclaim them; for their principle is to worship the power which they are most afraid of.

This method of considering men and things together, opens into a large field for speculation, and affords me an opportunity of offering some observations on the state of our currency, so as to make the support of it go hand in hand with the suppression of disaffection and the encouragement of public spirit.

The thing which first presents itself in inspecting the state of the currency, is, that we have too much of it, and that there is a necessity of reducing the quantity, in order to increase the value. Men are daily growing poor by the very means that they take to get rich; for in the same proportion that the prices of all goods on hand are raised, the value of all money laid by is reduced. A simple case will make this clear; let a man have 100*l*. in cash, and as many goods on hand as will to-day sell for 20*l*.; but not content with the present market price, he raises them to 40*l*. and by so doing obliges others, in their own defence, to raise cent. per cent. likewise; in this case it is evident that his hundred pounds laid by, is reduced fifty pounds in value; whereas, had the market lowered cent. per cent., his goods would have sold but for ten, but his hundred pounds would have risen in value to two hundred; because it would then purchase as many goods again, or support his family as long again as before. And, strange as it may seem, he is one hundred and fifty pounds the poorer for raising his goods, to what he would have been had he lowered them; because the forty pounds which his goods sold for, is, by the general raise of the market cent. per cent., rendered of no more value than the ten pounds would be had the market fallen in the same proportion; and, consequently, the whole difference of gain or loss is on the difference in value of the hundred pounds laid by, *viz.* from fifty to two hundred. This rage for raising goods is for several reasons much more the fault of the Tories than the Whigs; and yet the Tories (to their shame and confusion ought they to be told of it) are by far the most noisy and discontented. The greatest part of the Whigs, by being now either in the army or employed in some public service, are *buyers* only and not *sellers,* and as this evil has its origin in trade, it cannot be charged on those who are out of it.

But the grievance has now become too general to be remedied by partial methods, and the only effectual cure is to reduce the quantity of money: with half the quantity we should be richer than we are now, because the value of it would be doubled, and consequently our attachment to it increased; for it is not the number of dollars that a man has, but how far they will go, that makes him either rich or poor.

These two points being admitted, *viz.* that the quantity of money is too great, and that the prices of goods can only be effectually reduced by reducing the quantity of the money, the next point to be considered is, the method how to reduce it.

The circumstances of the times, as before observed, require that the public characters of all men should *now* be fully understood, and the only general method of ascertaining it is by an oath or affirmation, renouncing all allegiance to the king of Great Britain, and to support the independence of the United States, as declared by Congress. Let, at the same time, a tax of ten, fifteen, or twenty per cent. per annum, to be collected quarterly, be levied on all property. These alternatives, by being perfectly voluntary, will take in all sorts of people. Here is the test; here is the tax. He who takes the former, conscientiously proves his affection to the cause, and binds himself to pay his quota by the best *services* in his power, and is thereby justly exempt from the latter; and those who choose the latter, pay their quota in money, to be excused from the former, or rather, it is the price paid to us for their supposed, though mistaken, insurance with the enemy.

But this is only a part of the advantage which would arise by knowing the different characters of men. The Whigs stake everything on the issue of their arms, while the Tories, by their disaffection, are sapping and undermining their strength; and, of consequence, the property of the Whigs is the more exposed thereby; and whatever injury their estates may sustain by the movements of the enemy, must either be borne by themselves, who have done everything which has *yet* been done, or by the Tories, who have not only done nothing, but have, by their disaffection, invited the enemy on.

In the present crisis we ought to know, square by square and house by house, who are in real allegiance with the United Independent States, and who are not. Let but the line be made clear and distinct, and all men will then know what they are to trust to. It would not only be good policy but strict justice, to raise fifty or one hundred thousand pounds, or more, if it is necessary, out of the estates and property of the king of England's votaries, resident in Philadelphia, to be distributed, as a reward to those inhabitants of the city and State, who should turn out and repulse the enemy, should they attempt to march this way; and likewise, to bind the property of all such persons to make good the damages which that of the Whigs might sustain. In the undistinguishable mode of conducting a war, we frequently make reprisals at sea, on the vessels of persons in England, who are friends to our cause compared with the resident Tories among us.

In every former publication of mine, from *Common Sense* down to the last *Crisis,* I have generally gone on the charitable supposition, that the Tories were rather a mistaken than a criminal people, and have applied argument after argument, with all the candor and temper which I was capable of, in order to set every part of the case clearly and fairly before them, and if possible to reclaim them from ruin to reason. I have done my duty by them and have now done with that doctrine, taking it for granted, that those who yet hold their disaffection are either a set of avaricious miscreants, who would sacrifice the continent to save themselves, or a banditti of hungry traitors, who are hoping for a division of the spoil. To which may be added, a list of crown or proprietary dependents, who, rather than go without a portion of power, would be content to share it with the devil. Of such men there is no hope; and their obedience will only be according to the danger set before them, and the power that is exercised over them.

A time will shortly arrive, in which, by ascertaining the characters of persons now, we shall be guarded against their mischiefs then; for in proportion as the enemy despair of conquest, they will be trying the arts of seduction and the force of fear by all the mischiefs which they can inflict. But in war we may be certain of these two things, *viz.* that cruelty in an enemy, and motions made with more than usual parade, are always signs of weakness. He that can conquer, finds his mind too free and pleasant to be brutish; and he that intends to conquer, never makes too much show of his strength.

We now know the enemy we have to do with. While drunk with the certainy of victory, they disdained to be civil; and in proportion as disappointment makes them sober, and their apprehensions of an European war alarm them, they will become cringing and artful; honest they cannot be. But our answer to them, in either condition they may be in, is short and full—"As free and independent States we are willing to make peace with you to-morrow, but we neither can hear nor reply in any other character."

If Britain cannot conquer us, it proves that she is neither able to govern nor protect us, and our particular situation now is such, that any connection with her would be unwisely exchanging a half-defeated enemy for two powerful ones. Europe, by every appearance, is now on the eve, nay, on the morning twilight of a war, and any alliance with George the Third brings France and Spain upon our backs; a separation from him attaches them to our side; therefore, the only road to peace, honor and commerce is *Independence*.

Written this fourth year of the UNION,[15] *which God preserve.*

COMMON SENSE.

PHILADELPHIA, April 19, 1777.

[15] Paine dated from the organization of the intercolonial committee, in 1773.—*Editor.*

THE AMERICAN CRISIS

IV

The fourth number of the *Crisis* was written on the day following the Battle of Brandywine, September 11, 1777. The British won the battle but at a considerable price losing many more men than the Americans. When the news reached Philadelphia that the American army had retreated to Chester, people began to flee from the city and Congress itself left for Lancaster. Paine was convinced that "unless something was done the City [Philadelphia] would be lost." (Letter to Benjamin Franklin, May 16, 1778.) To arouse the citizens to a sense of their duty, and to stimulate Washington's weary and ill-clad soldiers, he penned the *Crisis IV*. Howe, Paine assured the fighting men, was weaker than before the battle, and the Americans could not lose, "unless we sit down and suffer them to do it." He ends his paper with one of his most famous utterances: "We fight not to enslave, but to set a country free, and to make room upon the earth for honest men to live in."—*Editor*.

THOSE who expect to reap the blessings of freedom, must, like men, undergo the fatigues of supporting it. The event of yesterday was one of those kind of alarms which is just sufficient to rouse us to duty, without being of consequence enough to depress our fortitude. It is not a field of a few acres of ground, but a cause, that we are defending, and whether we defeat the enemy in one battle, or by degrees, the consequences will be the same.

Look back at the events of last winter and the present year, there you will find that the enemy's successes always contributed to reduce them. What they have gained in ground, they paid so dearly for in numbers, that their victories have in the end amounted to defeats. We have always been masters at the last push, and always shall be while we do our duty. Howe has been once on the banks of the Delaware, and from thence driven back with loss and disgrace: and why not be again driven from the Schuylkill? His condition and ours are very different. He has everybody to fight, we have only his *one* army to cope with, and which wastes away at every engagement: we can not only reinforce, but can redouble our numbers; he is cut off from all supplies, and must sooner or later inevitably fall into our hands.

Shall a band of ten or twelve thousand robbers, who are this day fifteen hundred or two thousand men less in strength than they were yesterday, conquer America, or subdue even a single state? The thing cannot be, unless we sit down and suffer them to do it. Another such a brush, notwithstanding we lost the ground, would, by still reducing the enemy, put them in a condition to be afterwards totally defeated.

Could our whole army have come up to the attack at one time, the consequences had probably been otherwise; but our having different parts of the Brandywine creek to guard, and the uncertainty which road to Philadelphia the enemy would attempt to take, naturally afforded them an opportunity of passing with their main body at a place where only a part of ours could be posted; for it must strike every thinking man with conviction, that it requires a much greater force to oppose an enemy in several places, than is sufficient to defeat him in any one place.

Men who are sincere in defending their freedom, will always feel concern at every circumstance which seems to make against them; it is the natural and honest consequence of all affectionate attachments, and the want of it is a vice. But the dejection lasts only for a moment; they soon rise out of it with additional vigor; the glow of hope, courage and fortitude, will, in a little time, supply the place of every inferior passion, and kindle the whole heart into heroism.

There is a mystery in the countenance of some causes, which we have not always present judgment enough to explain. It is distressing to see an enemy advancing into a country, but it is the only place in which we can beat them, and in which we have always beaten them, whenever they made the attempt. The nearer any disease approaches to a crisis, the nearer it is to a cure. Danger and deliverance make their advances together, and it is only the last push, in which one or the other takes the lead.

There are many men who will do their duty when it is not wanted; but a genuine public spirit always appears most when there is most occasion for it. Thank God! our army, though fatigued, is yet entire. The attack made by us yesterday, was under many disadvantages, naturally arising from the uncertainty of knowing which route the enemy would take; and, from that circumstance, the whole of our force could not be brought up together time enough to engage all at once. Our strength is yet reserved; and it is evident that Howe does not think himself a gainer by the affair, otherwise he would this morning have moved down and attacked General Washington.

Gentlemen of the city and country, it is in your power, by a spirited improvement of the present circumstance, to turn it to a real advantage. Howe is now weaker than before, and every shot will contribute to reduce him. You are more immediately interested than any other part of the continent: your all is at stake; it is not so with the general cause; you are devoted by the enemy to plunder and destruction: it is the encouragement which Howe, the chief of plunderers, has promised his army. Thus circumstanced, you may save yourselves by a manly resistance, but you can have no hope in any other conduct. I never yet knew our brave general, or any part of the army, officers or men, out of heart, and I have seen them in circumstances a thousand times more trying than the present. It is only those that are not in action, that feel languor and heaviness, and the best way to rub it off is to turn out, and make sure work of it.

Our army must undoubtedly feel fatigue, and want a reinforcement of rest though not of valor. Our own interest and happiness call upon us to give them every support in our power, and make the burden of the day, on which the safety of this city depends, as light as possible. Remember, gentlemen, that we have forces both to the northward and southward of Philadelphia, and if the enemy be but stopped till those can arrive, this city will be saved, and the enemy finally routed. You have too much at stake to hesitate. You ought not to think an hour upon the matter, but to spring to action at once. Other states have been invaded, have likewise driven off the invaders. Now our time and turn is come, and perhaps the finishing stroke is reserved for us. When we look back on the dangers we have been saved from, and reflect on the success we have been blessed with, it would be sinful either to be idle or to despair.

I close this paper with a short address to General Howe. You, sir, are only lingering out the period that shall bring with it your defeat. You have yet scarce began upon the war, and the further you enter, the faster will your troubles thicken. What you now enjoy is only a respite from ruin; an invitation to destruction; something that will lead on to our deliverance at your expense. We know the cause which we are engaged in, and though a passionate fondness for it may make us grieve at every injury which threatens it, yet, when the moment of concern is over, the determination to duty returns. We are not moved by the gloomy smile of a worthless king, but by the ardent glow of generous patriotism. We fight not to enslave, but to set a country free, and to make room upon the earth for honest men to live in. In such a case we are sure that we are right; and we leave to you the despairing reflection of being the tool of a miserable tyrant.

COMMON SENSE.

PHILADELPHIA, Sept. 12, 1777.

THE AMERICAN CRISIS

V

The fifth *Crisis* was dated at Lancaster, Pennsylvania, March 21, 1778, and was written at a very critical period of the war. Internal dissensions among the officers of the Continental Army threatened to split apart the armed forces of the nation. And the sharp contrast between the luxurious life of the Tories who remained with Howe in Philadelphia after he had possessed the city on September 26, 1777, and the wretched conditions facing the soldiers with Washington at Valley Forge was demoralizing the entire country.

The first part of this *Crisis,* addressed "to General Sir William Howe" reminded the wrangling patriots who the common enemy was; the second, addressed "to the inhabitants of America" pointed to the great opportunities facing the nation if the people acted promptly and decisively. "The only way to finish a war," cried Paine, "with the least possible bloodshed, or perhaps without any, is to collect an army against the power of which the enemy shall have no chance." This note of courage did much to lift the sagging morale of soldiers and civilians alike.—*Editor.*

To General Sir William Howe

TO ARGUE with a man who has renounced the use and authority of reason, and whose philosophy consists in holding humanity in contempt, is like administering medicine to the dead, or endeavoring to convert an atheist by scripture. Enjoy, sir, your insensibility of feeling and reflecting. It is the prerogative of animals. And no man will envy you these honors, in which a savage only can be your rival and a bear your master.

As the generosity of this country rewarded your brother's services in the last war, with an elegant monument in Westminster Abbey, it is consistent that she should bestow some mark of distinction upon you. You certainly deserve her notice, and a conspicuous place in the catalogue of extraordinary persons. Yet it would be a pity to pass you from the world in state, and consign you to magnificent oblivion among the tombs, without telling the future beholder why. Judas is as much known as John, yet history ascribes their fame to very different actions.

Sir William has undoubtedly merited a monument; but of what kind, or with what inscription, where placed or how embellished, is a question that would puzzle all the heralds of St. James's in the profoundest mood of historical deliberation. We are at no loss, sir, to ascertain your real character, but somewhat perplexed how to perpetuate its identity, and preserve it uninjured from the transformations of time or mistake. A statuary may give a false expression to your bust, or decorate it with some equivocal emblems, by which you may happen to steal into reputation and impose upon the hereafter traditionary world. Ill nature or ridicule may conspire, or a variety of accidents combine to lessen, enlarge, or change Sir William's fame; and no doubt but he who has taken so much pains to be singular in his conduct, would choose to be just as singular in his exit, his monument and his epitaph.

The usual honors of the dead, to be sure, are not sufficiently sublime to escort a character like you to the republic of dust and ashes; for however men may differ in their ideas of grandeur or of government here, the grave is nevertheless a perfect republic. Death is not the monarch of the dead, but of the dying. The moment he obtains a conquest he loses a subject, and, like the foolish king you serve, will, in the end, war himself out of all his dominions.

As a proper preliminary towards the arrangement of your funeral honors, we readily admit of your new rank of *knighthood*. The title is perfectly in character, and is your own, more by merit than creation. There are knights of various orders, from the knight of the windmill to the knight of the post. The former is your patron for exploits, and the latter will assist you in settling your accounts. No honorary title could be more happily applied! The ingenuity is sublime! And your royal master has discovered more genius in fitting you therewith, than in generating the most finished figure for a button, or descanting on the properties of a button mould.

But how, sir, shall we dispose of you? The invention of a statuary is exhausted, and Sir William is yet unprovided with a monument. America is anxious to bestow her funeral favors upon you, and wishes to do it in a manner that shall distinguish you from all the deceased heroes of the last war. The Egyptian method of embalming is not known to the present age, and hieroglyphical pageantry hath outlived the science of deciphering it. Some other method, therefore, must be thought of to immortalize the new knight of the windmill and post. Sir William, thanks to his stars, is not oppressed with very delicate ideas. He has no ambition of being wrapped up and handed about in myrrh, aloes and cassia. Less expensive odors will suffice; and it fortunately happens that the simple genius of America has discovered the art of preserving bodies, and embellishing them too, with much greater frugality than the ancients. In balmage, sir, of humble tar, you will be as secure as Pharaoh, and in a hieroglyphic of feathers, rival in finery all the mummies of Egypt.

As you have already made your exit from the moral world, and by numberless acts both of passionate and deliberate injustice engraved an *"here lieth"* on your deceased honor, it must be mere affectation in you to pretend concern at the humors or opinions of mankind respecting you. What remains of you may expire at any time. The sooner the better. For he who survives his reputation, lives out of despite of himself, like a man listening to his own reproach.

Thus entombed and ornamented, I leave you to the inspection of the curious, and return to the history of your yet surviving actions. The character of Sir William has undergone some extraordinary revolutions since his arrival in America. It is now fixed and known; and we have nothing to hope from your candor or to fear from your capacity. Indolence and inability have too large a share in your composition, ever to suffer you to be anything more than the hero of little villainies and unfinished adventures. That, which to some persons appeared moderation in you at first, was not produced by any real virtue of your own, but by a contrast of passions, dividing and holding you in perpetual irresolution. One vice will frequently expel another, without the least merit in the man; as powers in contrary directions reduce each other to rest.

It became you to have supported a dignified solemnity of character; to have shown a superior liberality of soul; to have won respect by an obstinate perseverance in maintaining order, and to have exhibited on all occasions such an unchangeable graciousness of conduct, that while we beheld in you the resolution of an enemy, we might admire in you the sincerity of a man. You came to America under the high sounding titles of commander and commissioner; not only to suppress what you call rebellion, by arms, but to shame it out of countenance by the excellence of your example. Instead of which, you have been the patron of low and vulgar frauds, the encourager of Indian cruelties; and have imported a cargo of vices blacker than those which you pretend to suppress.

Mankind are not universally agreed in their determination of right and wrong; but there are certain actions which the consent of all nations and individuals has branded with the unchangeable name of *meanness*. In the list of human vices we find some of such a refined constitution, they cannot be carried into practice without seducing some virtue to their assistance; but *meanness* has neither alliance nor apology. It is generated in the dust and sweepings of other vices, and is of such a hateful figure that all the rest conspire to disown it. Sir William, the commissioner of George the Third, has at last vouchsafed to give it rank and pedigree. He has placed the fugitive at the council board, and dubbed it companion of the order of knighthood.

The particular act of meanness which I allude to in this description, is forgery. You, sir, have abetted and patronized the forging and uttering counterfeit continental bills. In the same New York newspapers in which your own proclamation under your master's authority was published, offering, or pretending to offer, pardon and protection to these states, there were repeated advertisements of counterfeit money for sale, and persons who have come officially from you, and under the sanction of your flag, have been taken up in attempting to put them off.

A conduct so basely mean in a public character is without precedent or pretence. Every nation on earth, whether friends or enemies, will unite in despising you. 'Tis an incendiary war upon society, which nothing can excuse or palliate,—an improvement upon beggarly villainy —and shows an inbred wretchedness of heart made up between the venomous malignity of a serpent and the spiteful imbecility of an inferior reptile.

The laws of any civilized country would condemn you to the gibbet without regard to your rank or titles, because it is an action foreign to the usage and custom of war; and should you fall into our hands, which pray God you may, it will be a doubtful matter whether we are to consider you as a military prisoner or a prisoner for felony.

Besides, it is exceedingly unwise and impolitic in you, or any other persons in the English service, to promote or even encourage, or wink at the crime of forgery, in any case whatever. Because, as the riches of England, as a nation, are chiefly in paper, and the far greater part of trade among individuals is carried on by the same medium, that is, by notes and drafts on one another, they, therefore, of all people in the world, ought to endeavor to keep forgery out of sight, and, if possible, not to revive the idea of it. It is dangerous to make men familiar with a crime which they may afterwards practise to much greater advantage against those who first taught them. Several officers in the English army have made their exit at the gallows for forgery on their agents; for we all know, who know any thing of England, that there is not a more necessitous body of men, taking them generally, than what the English officers are. They contrive to make a show at the expense of the tailors, and appear clean at the charge of the washer-women.

England, has at this time, nearly two hundred million pounds sterling of public money in paper, for which she has no real property: besides a large circulation of bank notes, bank post bills, and promissory notes and drafts of private bankers, merchants and tradesmen. She has the greatest quantity of paper currency and the least quantity of gold and silver of any nation in Europe; the real specie, which is about sixteen millions sterling, serves only as change in large sums, which are always made in paper, or for payment in small ones. Thus circumstanced, the nation is put to its wit's end, and obliged to be severe almost to criminality, to prevent the practice and growth of forgery. Scarcely a session passes at the Old Bailey, or an execution at Tyburn, but witnesses this truth, yet you, sir, regardless of the policy which her necessity obliges her to adopt, have made your whole army intimate with the crime. And as all armies at the conclusion of a war, are too apt to carry into practice the vices of the campaign, it will probably happen, that England will hereafter abound in forgeries, to which art the practitioners were first initiated under your authority in America. You, sir, have the honor of adding a new vice to the military catalogue; and the reason, perhaps, why the invention was reserved for you, is, because no general before was mean enough even to think of it.

That a man whose soul is absorbed in the low traffic of vulgar vice, is incapable of moving in any superior region, is clearly shown in you by the event of every campaign. Your military exploits have been without plan, object or decision. Can it be possible that you or your employers suppose that the possession of Philadelphia will be any ways equal to the expense or expectation of the nation which supports you? What advantages does England derive from any achievements of yours? To *her* it is perfectly indifferent what place you are in, so long as the business of conquest is unperformed and the charge of maintaining you remains the same.

If the principal events of the three campaigns be attended to, the balance will appear against you at the close of each; but the last, in point of importance to us, has exceeded the former two. It is pleasant to look back on dangers past, and equally as pleasant to meditate on present ones when the way out begins to appear. That period is now arrived, and the long doubtful winter of war is changing to the sweeter prospects of victory and joy. At the close of the campaign, in 1775, you were obliged to retreat from Boston. In the summer of 1776, you appeared with a numerous fleet and army in the harbor of New York. By what miracle the continent was preserved in that season of danger is a subject of admiration! If instead of wasting your time against Long Island you had run up the North River, and landed any where above New York, the consequence must have been, that either you would have compelled General Washington to fight you with very unequal numbers, or he must have suddenly evacuated the city with the loss of nearly all the stores of his army, or have surrendered for want of provisions; the situation of the place naturally producing one or the other of these events.

The preparations made to defend New York were, nevertheless, wise and military; because your forces were then at sea, their numbers uncertain; storms, sickness, or a variety of accidents might have disabled their coming, or so diminished them on their passage, that those which survived would have been incapable of opening the campaign with any prospect of success; in which case the defence would have been sufficient and the place preserved; for cities that have been raised from nothing with an infinitude of labor and expense, are not to be thrown away on the bare probability of their being taken. On these grounds the preparations made to maintain New York were as judicious as the retreat afterwards. While you, in the interim, let slip the *very* opportunity which seemed to put conquest in your power.

Through the whole of that campaign you had nearly double the forces which General Washington immediately commanded. The principal plan at that time, on our part, was to wear away the season with as little loss as possible, and to raise the army for the next year. Long Island, New York, Forts Washington and Lee were not defended after your superior force was known under any expectation of their being finally maintained, but as a range of outworks, in the attacking of which your time might be wasted, your numbers reduced, and your vanity amused by possessing them on our retreat. It was intended to have withdrawn the garrison from Fort Washington after it had answered the former of those purposes, but the fate of that day put a prize into your hands without much honor to yourselves.

Your progress through the Jerseys was accidental; you had it not even in contemplation, or you would not have sent a principal part of your forces to Rhode Island beforehand. The utmost hope of America in the year 1776, reached no higher than that she might not then be conquered. She had no expectation of defeating you in that campaign. Even the most cowardly Tory allowed, that, could she withstand the shock of *that* summer, her independence would be past a doubt. You had *then* greatly the advantage of her. You were formidable. Your military knowledge was supposed to be complete. Your fleets and forces arrived without an accident. You had neither experience nor reinforcements to wait for. You had nothing to do but to begin, and your chance lay in the first vigorous onset.

America was young and unskilled. She was obliged to trust her defence to time and practice; and has, by mere dint of perseverance, maintained her cause, and brought the enemy to a condition, in which she is now capable of meeting him on any grounds.

It is remarkable that in the campaign of 1776 you gained no more, notwithstanding your great force, than what was given you by consent of evacuation, except Fort Washington; while every advantage obtained by us was by fair and hard fighting. The defeat of Sir Peter Parker was complete.[1] The conquest of the Hessians at Trenton, by the remains of a retreating army, which but a few days before you affected to despise, is an instance of their heroic perseverance very seldom to be met with. And the victory over the British troops at Princeton, by a harassed and wearied party, who had been engaged the day before and marched all night without refreshment, is attended with such a scene of circumstances and superiority of generalship, as will ever give it a place in the first rank in the history of great actions.

When I look back on the gloomy days of last winter, and see America

[1] Sir Peter Parker came from Ireland to assist Sir Henry Clinton conquer the Carolinas. His fleet suffered a defeat at Cape Fear in April, 1776, and at Charleston on June 28, 1776.—*Editor.*

suspended by a thread, I feel a triumph of joy at the recollection of her delivery, and a reverence for the characters which snatched her from destruction. To doubt *now* would be a species of infidelity, and to forget the instruments which saved us *then* would be ingratitude.

The close of that campaign left us with the spirit of conquerors. The northern districts were relieved by the retreat of General Carleton over the lakes. The army under your command were hunted back and had their bounds prescribed. The continent began to feel its military importance, and the winter passed pleasantly away in preparations for the next campaign.

However confident you might be on your first arrival, the result of the year 1776 gave you some idea of the difficulty, if not impossibility of conquest. To this reason I ascribe your delay in opening the campaign of 1777. The face of matters, on the close of the former year, gave you no encouragement to pursue a discretionary war as soon as the spring admitted the taking the field; for though conquest, in that case, would have given you a double portion of fame, yet the experiment was too hazardous. The ministry, had you failed, would have shifted the whole blame upon you, charged you with having acted without orders, and condemned at once both your plan and execution.

To avoid the misfortunes, which might have involved you and your money accounts in perplexity and suspicion, you prudently waited the arrival of a plan of operations from England, which was that you should proceed for Philadelphia by way of the Chesapeake, and that Burgoyne, after reducing Ticonderoga, should take his route by Albany, and, if necessary, join you.

The splendid laurels of the last campaign have flourished in the north. In that quarter America has surprised the world, and laid the foundation of this year's glory. The conquest of Ticonderoga, (if it may be called a conquest) has, like all your other victories, led on to ruin. Even the provisions taken in that fortress (which by General Burgoyne's return was sufficient in bread and flour for nearly 5000 men for ten weeks, and in beef and pork for the same number of men for one month) served only to hasten his overthrow, by enabling him to proceed to Saratoga, the place of his destruction. A short review of the operations of the last campaign will show the condition of affairs on both sides.

You have taken Ticonderoga and marched into Philadelphia. These are all the events which the year has produced on your part. A trifling campaign indeed, compared with the expenses of England and the conquest of the continent. On the other side, a considerable part of your northern force has been routed by the New York militia under General Herkemer. Fort Stanwix has bravely survived a compound attack of soldiers and savages, and the besiegers have fled. The Battle of Bennington has put a thousand prisoners into our hands, with all their arms, stores, artillery and baggage. General Burgoyne, in two engagements, has been defeated; himself, his army, and all that were his and theirs are now ours. Ticonderoga and Independence [forts] are retaken, and not the shadow of an enemy remains in all the northern districts. At this instant we have upwards of eleven thousand prisoners, between sixty and seventy [captured] pieces of brass ordnance, besides small arms, tents, stores, etc.

In order to know the real value of those advantages, we must reverse the scene, and suppose General Gates and the force he commanded to be at your mercy as prisoners, and General Burgoyne, with his army of soldiers and savages, to be already joined to you in Pennsylvania. So dismal a picture can scarcely be looked at. It has all the tracings and colorings of horror and despair; and excites the most swelling emotions of gratitude by exhibiting the miseries we are so graciously preserved from.

I admire the distribution of laurels around the continent. It is the earnest of future union. South Carolina has had her day of sufferings and of fame; and the other southern States have exerted themselves in proportion to the force that invaded or insulted them. Towards the close of the campaign, in 1776, these middle States were called upon and did their duty nobly. They were witnesses to the almost expiring flame of human freedom. It was the close struggle of life and death, the line of invisible division; and on which the unabated fortitude of a Washington prevailed, and saved the spark that has since blazed in the north with unrivalled lustre.

Let me ask, sir, what great exploits have you performed? Through all the variety of changes and opportunities which the war has produced, I know no one action of yours that can be styled masterly. You have moved in and out, backward and forward, round and round, as if valor consisted in a military jig. The history and figure of your movements would be truly ridiculous could they be justly delineated. They resemble the labors of a puppy pursuing his tail; the end is still at the same distance, and all the turnings round must be done over again.

The first appearance of affairs at Ticonderoga wore such an unpromising aspect, that it was necessary, in July, to detach a part of the forces to the support of that quarter, which were otherwise destined or intended to act against you; and this, perhaps, has been the means of postponing your downfall to another campaign. The destruction of one army at a time is work enough. We know, sir, what we are about, what we have to do, and how to do it.

Your progress from the Chesapeake, was marked by no capital stroke of policy or heroism. Your principal aim was to get General Washington between the Delaware and Schuylkill, and between Philadelphia and your army. In that situation, with a river on each of his flanks, which united about five miles below the city, and your army above him, you could have intercepted his reinforcements and supplies, cut off all his communication with the country, and, if necessary, have despatched assistance to open a passage for General Burgoyne. This scheme was too visible to succeed: for had General Washington suffered you to command the open country above him, I think it a very reasonable conjecture that the conquest of Burgoyne would not have taken place, because you could, in that case, have relieved him. It was therefore necessary, while that important victory was in suspense, to trepan *you* into a situation in which you could only be on the defensive, without the power of affording him assistance. The manœuvre had its effect, and Burgoyne was conquered.

There had been something unmilitary and passive in you from the time of your passing the Schuylkill and getting possession of Philadelphia, to the close of the campaign. You mistook a trap for a conquest, the probability of which had been made known to Europe, and the edge of your triumph taken off by our own information long before.

Having got you into this situation, a scheme for a general attack upon you at Germantown was carried into execution on the 4th of October, and though the success was not equal to the excellence of the plan, yet the attempting it proved the genius of America to be on the rise, and her power approaching to superiority. The obscurity of the morning was your best friend, for a fog is always favorable to a hunted enemy. Some weeks after this you likewise planned an attack on General Washington while at Whitemarsh. You marched out with infinite parade, but on finding him preparing to attack you next morning, you prudently turned about, and retreated to Philadelphia with all the precipitation of a man conquered in imagination.

Immediately after the battle of Germantown, the probability of Burgoyne's defeat gave a new policy to affairs in Pennsylvania, and it was judged most consistent with the general safety of America, to wait the issue of the northern campaign. Slow and sure is sound work. The news of that victory arrived in our camp on the 18th of October, and no sooner did that shout of joy, and the report of the thirteen cannon reach your ears, than you resolved upon a retreat, and the next day, that is, on the 19th you withdrew your drooping army into Philadelphia. This movement was evidently dictated by fear; and carried with it a positive confession that you dreaded a second attack. It was hiding yourself among women and children, and sleeping away the choicest part of the campaign in expensive inactivity. An army in a city can never be a conquering army. The situation admits only of defence. It is mere shelter: and every military power in Europe will conclude you to be eventually defeated.

The time when you made this retreat was the very time you ought to have fought a battle, in order to put yourself in condition of recovering in Pennsylvania what you had lost in Saratoga. And the reason why you did not, must be either prudence or cowardice; the former supposes your inability, and the latter needs no explanation. I draw no conclusions, sir, but such as are naturally deduced from known and visible facts, and such as will always have a being while the facts which produced them remain unaltered.

After this retreat a new difficulty arose which exhibited the power of Britain in a very contemptible light; which was the attack and defence of Mud Island. For several weeks did that little unfinished fortress stand out against all the attempts of Admiral and General Howe. It was the fable of Bender realized on the Delaware. Scheme after scheme, and force upon force were tried and defeated. The garrison, with scarce anything to cover them but their bravery, survived in the midst of mud, shot and shells, and were at last obliged to give it up more to the powers of time and gunpowder than to military superiority of the besiegers.[2]

It is my sincere opinion that matters are in much worse condition with you than what is generally known. Your master's speech at the opening of Parliament, is like a soliloquy on ill luck. It shows him to be coming a little to his reason, for sense of pain is the first symptom of recovery, in

---

[2] Paine himself participated in the Mud Island battle. In his letter to Benjamin Franklin, May 16, 1778, he writes: "At noon I went with Col. [Christopher] Greene, who commanded at Red Bank [fort] over to fort Mifflin(Mud Island). Then enemy opened that day 2 two-gun Batteries, and a Mortar Battery, on the fort. . . . I came away in the evening."—*Editor*.

profound stupefaction. His condition is deplorable. He is obliged to submit to all the insults of France and Spain, without daring to know or resent them; and thankful for the most trivial evasions to the most humble remonstrances. The time *was* when he could not deign an answer to a petition from America, and the time now *is* when he dare not give an answer to an affront from France. The capture of Burgoyne's army will sink his consequence as much in Europe as in America. In his speech he expresses his suspicions at the warlike preparations of France and Spain, and as he has only the one army which you command to support his character in the world with, it remains very uncertain when, or in what quarter it will be most wanted, or can be best employed; and this will partly account for the great care you take to keep it from action and attacks, for should Burgoyne's fate be yours, which it probably will, England may take her endless farewell not only of all America but of all the West Indies.

Never did a nation invite destruction upon itself with the eagerness and the ignorance with which Britain has done. Bent upon the ruin of a young and unoffending country, she has drawn the sword that has wounded herself to the heart, and in the agony of her resentment has applied a poison for a cure. Her conduct towards America is a compound of rage and lunacy; she aims at the government of it, yet preserves neither dignity nor character in her methods to obtain it. Were government a mere manufacture or article of commerce, immaterial by whom it should be made or sold, we might as well employ her as another, but when we consider it as the fountain from whence the general manners and morality of a country take their rise, that the persons entrusted with the execution thereof are by their serious example an authority to support these principles, how abominably absurd is the idea of being hereafter governed by a set of men who have been guilty of forgery, perjury, treachery, theft and every species of villainy which the lowest wretches on earth could practise or invent. What greater public curse can befall any country than to be under such authority, and what greater blessing than to be delivered therefrom. The soul of any man of sentiment would rise in brave rebellion against them, and spurn them from the earth.

The malignant and venomous tempered General Vaughan [3] has

[3] General Vaughan was with Cornwallis at Cape Fear and later commanded the British land army which captured the Dutch Island of St. Eustatius, February 3, 1781.— *Editor.*

amused his savage fancy in burning the whole town of Kingston, in York government, and the late governor of that state, Mr. Tryon,[4] in his letter to General Parsons, has endeavored to justify it and declared his wish to burn the houses of every committeeman in the country. Such a confession from one who was once intrusted with the powers of civil government, is a reproach to the character. But it is the wish and the declaration of a man whom anguish and disappointment have driven to despair, and who is daily decaying into the grave with constitutional rottenness.

There is not in the compass of language a sufficiency of words to express the baseness of your king, his ministry and his army. They have refined upon villainy till it wants a name. To the fiercer vices of former ages they have added the dregs and scummings of the most finished rascality, and are so completely sunk in serpentine deceit, that there is not left among them *one* generous enemy.

From such men and such masters, may the gracious hand of Heaven preserve America! And though the sufferings she now endures are heavy, and severe, they are like straws in the wind compared to the weight of evils she would feel under the government of your king, and his pensioned Parliament.

There is something in meanness which excites a species of resentment that never subsides, and something in cruelty which stirs up the heart to the highest agony of human hatred; Britain has filled up both these characters till no addition can be made, and has not reputation left with us to obtain credit for the slightest promise. The will of God has parted us, and the deed is registered for eternity. When she shall be a spot scarcely visible among the nations, America shall flourish the favorite of heaven, and the friend of mankind.

For the domestic happiness of Britain and the peace of the world, I wish she had not a foot of land but what is circumscribed within her own island. Extent of dominion has been her ruin, and instead of civilizing others has brutalized herself. Her late reduction of India, under

[4] Tryon was Governor of North Carolina when the War for Independence started. He had earned a reputation for tyranny and cruelty in that colony for the brutal manner in which he had suppressed the Carolina backwoods' movement to redress abuses in the government of the colony. The Regulators, as the frontiersmen who rose in revolt in 1770 were known, were routed and a number of their leaders were executed at Governor Tryon's orders. After the war began, Tryon was transferred to New York where he maintained his reputation for cruelty.—*Editor.*

Clive and his successors,[5] was not so properly a conquest as an extermi-
nation of mankind. She is the only power who could practise the
prodigal barbarity of tying men to mouths of loaded cannon and blow-
ing them away. It happens that General Burgoyne, who made the report of that horrid transaction, in the House of Commons, is now a
prisoner with us, and though an enemy, I can appeal to him for the
truth of it, being confident that he neither can nor will deny it. Yet
Clive received the approbation of the last Parliament.

When we take a survey of mankind, we cannot help cursing the
wretch, who, to the unavoidable misfortunes of nature, shall wilfully
add the calamities of war. One would think there were evils enough in
the world without studying to increase them, and that life is sufficiently
short without shaking the sand that measures it. The histories of
Alexander, and Charles of Sweden, are the histories of human devils;
a good man cannot think of their actions without abhorrence, nor of
their deaths without rejoicing. To see the bounties of heaven destroyed,
the beautiful face of nature laid waste, and the choicest works of creation and art tumbled into ruin, would fetch a curse from the soul of
piety itself. But in this country the aggravation is heightened by a new
combination of affecting circumstances. America was young, and, compared with other countries, was virtuous. None but a Herod of uncommon malice would have made war upon infancy and innocence: and
none but a people of the most finished fortitude, dared under those
circumstances, have resisted the tyranny. The natives, or their ancestors,
had fled from the former oppressions of England, and with the industry
of bees had changed a wilderness into a habitable world. To Britain
they were indebted for nothing. The country was the gift of heaven,
and God alone is their Lord and Sovereign.

The time, sir, will come when you, in a melancholy hour, shall
reckon up your miseries by your murders in America. Life, with you,
begins to wear a clouded aspect. The vision of pleasurable delusion is

[5] Paine is referring to the Battle of Plassey in 1757 which resulted in a British victory
and gave them control of the fertile province of Bengal. The reference to the barbarities
practiced by the British in India was in no sense an exaggeration.

Clive was brought to trial before Parliament on the charge of misgovernment, gave
a long, impassioned speech in his defense, and was acquitted.

Paine's interest in the problem of India at this early date and his understanding of the
relation of this problem to that of the American struggle reveal how advanced a thinker
he was.—*Editor*.

wearing away, and changing to the barren wild of age and sorrow. The poor reflection of having served your king will yield you no consolation in your parting moments. He will crumble to the same undistinguished ashes with yourself, and have sins enough of his own to answer for. It is not the farcical benedictions of a bishop, nor the cringing hypocrisy of a court of chaplains, nor the formality of an act of Parliament, that can change guilt into innocence, or make the punishment one pang the less. You may, perhaps, be unwilling to be serious, but this destruction of the goods of Providence, this havoc of the human race, and this sowing the world with mischief, must be accounted for to him who made and governs it. To us they are only present sufferings, but to him they are deep rebellions.

If there is a sin superior to every other, it is that of wilful and offensive war. Most other sins are circumscribed within narrow limits, that is, the power of *one* man cannot give them a very general extension, and many kinds of sins have only a mental existence from which no infection arises; but he who is the author of a war, lets loose the whole contagion of hell, and opens a vein that bleeds a nation to death. We leave it to England and Indians to boast of these honors; we feel no thirst for such savage glory; a nobler flame, a purer spirit animates America. She has taken up the sword of virtuous defence; she has bravely put herself between Tyranny and Freedom, between a curse and a blessing, determined to expel the one and protect the other.

It is the object only of war that makes it honorable. And if there was ever a *just* war since the world began, it is this in which America is now engaged. She invaded no land of yours. She hired no mercenaries to burn your towns, nor Indians to massacre their inhabitants. She wanted nothing from you, and was indebted for nothing to you: and thus circumstanced, her defence is honorable and her prosperity is certain.

Yet it is not on the *justice* only, but likewise on the *importance* of this cause that I ground my seeming enthusiastical confidence of our success. The vast extension of America makes her of too much value in the scale of Providence, to be cast like a pearl before swine, at the feet of an European island; and of much less consequence would it be that Britain were sunk in the sea than that America should miscarry. There has been such a chain of extraordinary events in the discovery of this country at first, in the peopling and planting it afterwards, in the rearing and nursing it to its present state, and in the protection of it through the present war, that no man can doubt, but Providence has some nobler end to accomplish than the gratification of the petty elector of Hanover, or the ignorant and insignificant king of Britain.

As the blood of the martyrs has been the seed of the Christian church, so the political persecutions of England will and have already enriched America with industry, experience, union and importance. Before the present era she was a mere chaos of uncemented colonies, individually exposed to the ravages of the Indians and the invasion of any power that Britain should be at war with. She had nothing that she could call her own. Her felicity depended upon accident. The convulsions of Europe might have thrown her from one conqueror to another, till she had been the slave of all, and ruined by every one; for until she had spirit enough to become her own master, there was no knowing to which master she should belong. That period, thank God, is past, and she is no longer the dependent, disunited colonies of Britain, but the independent and United States of America, knowing no master but heaven and herself. You, or your king, may call this "delusion," "rebellion," or what name you please. To us it is perfectly indifferent. The issue will determine the character, and time will give it a name as lasting as his own.

You have now, sir, tried the fate of three campaigns, and can fully declare to England, that nothing is to be got on your part, but blows and broken bones, and nothing on hers but waste of trade and credit, and an increase of poverty and taxes. You are now only where you might have been two years ago, without the loss of a single ship, and yet not a step more forward towards the conquest of the continent; because, as I have already hinted, "an army in a city can never be a conquering army." The full amount of your losses, since the beginning of the war, exceeds twenty thousand men, besides millions of treasure, for which you have nothing in exchange. Our expenses, though great, are circulated within ourselves. Yours is a direct sinking of money, and that from both ends at once; first, in hiring troops out of the nation, and in paying them afterwards, because the money in neither case can return to Britain. We are already in possession of the prize, you only in pursuit of it. To us it is a real treasure, to you it would be only an empty triumph. Our expenses will repay themselves with tenfold interest, while yours entail upon you everlasting poverty.

Take a review, sir, of the ground which you have gone over, and let it teach you policy, if it cannot honesty. You stand but on a very tottering foundation. A change of the ministry in England may probably bring your measures into question, and your head to the block. Clive, with all his successes, had some difficulty in escaping, and yours being all a war of losses, will afford you less pretensions, and your enemies more grounds for impeachment.[6]

Go home, sir, and endeavor to save the remains of your ruined country, by a just representation of the madness of her measures. A few moments, well applied, may yet preserve her from political destruction. I am not one of those who wish to see Europe in a flame, because I am persuaded that such an event will not shorten the war. The rupture, at present, is confined between the two powers of America and England. England finds that she cannot conquer America, and America has no wish to conquer England. You are fighting for what you can never obtain, and we defending what we never mean to part with. A few words, therefore, settle the bargain. Let England mind her own business and we will mind ours. Govern yourselves, and we will govern ourselves. You may then trade where you please unmolested by us, and we will trade where we please unmolested by you; and such articles as we can purchase of each other better than elsewhere may be mutually done. If it were possible that you could carry on the war for twenty years you must still come to this point at last, or worse, and the sooner you think of it the better it will be for you.

My official situation enables me to know the repeated insults which Britain is obliged to put up with from foreign powers, and the wretched shifts that she is driven to, to gloss them over.[7] Her reduced strength and exhausted coffers in a three years' war with America, has given a powerful superiority to France and Spain. She is not now a match for them. But if neither councils can prevail on her to think, nor sufferings awaken her to reason, she must e'en go on, till the honor of England becomes a proverb of contempt, and Europe dub her the Land of Fools.

I am, Sir, with every wish for an honorable peace,
    Your friend, enemy, and countryman,

COMMON SENSE.

[6] Sir William .Howe resigned his command of the British Army in May, 1778 and returned to England to defend himself in Parliament. His military conduct was vigorously criticized in Parliament, but the final vote virtually exonerated him. He was succeeded by Sir Henry Clinton who became the commander-in-chief of the British armies in America. —*Editor*.

[7] Paine is referring to his post of Secretary of the Committee of Foreign Affairs in the Continental Congress. He was elected to the post by Congress on April 17, 1777.—*Editor*.

To the Inhabitants of America

With all the pleasure with which a man exchanges bad company for good, I take my leave of Sir William and return to you. It is now nearly three years since the tyranny of Britain received its first repulse by the arms of America. A period which has given birth to a new world, and erected a monument to the folly of the old.

I cannot help being sometimes surprised at the complimentary references which I have seen and heard made to ancient histories and transactions. The wisdom, civil governments, and sense of honor of the states of Greece and Rome, are frequently held up as objects of excellence and imitation. Mankind have lived to very little purpose, if, at this period of the world, they must go two or three thousand years back for lessons and examples. We do great injustice to ourselves by placing them in such a superior line. We have no just authority for it, neither can we tell why it is that we should suppose ourselves inferior.

Could the mist of antiquity be cleared away, and men and things be viewed as they really were, it is more than probable that they would admire us, rather than we them. America has surmounted a greater variety and combination of difficulties, than, I believe, ever fell to the share of any one people, in the same space of time, and has replenished the world with more useful knowledge and sounder maxims of civil government than were ever produced in any age before. Had it not been for America, there had been no such thing as freedom left throughout the whole universe. England has lost hers in a long chain of right reasoning from wrong principles, and it is from this country, now, that she must learn the resolution to redress herself, and the wisdom how to accomplish it.

The Grecians and Romans were strongly possessed of the *spirit* of liberty but *not the principle,* for at the time that they were determined not to be slaves themselves, they employed their power to enslave the rest of mankind. But this distinguished era is blotted by no one misanthropical vice. In short, if the principle on which the cause is founded, the universal blessings that are to arise from it, the difficulties that accompanied it, the wisdom with which it has been debated, the fortitude by which it has been supported, the strength of the power which we had to oppose, and the condition in which we undertook it, be all taken in one view, we may justly style it the most virtuous and illustrious revolution that ever graced the history of mankind.

A good opinion of ourselves is exceedingly necessary in private life, but absolutely necessary in public life, and of the utmost importance in supporting national character. I have no notion of yielding the palm of the United States to any Grecians or Romans that were ever born. We have equalled the bravest in times of danger, and excelled the wisest in construction of civil governments.

From this agreeable eminence let us take a review of present affairs. The spirit of corruption is so inseparably interwoven with British politics, that their ministry suppose all mankind are governed by the same motives. They have no idea of a people submitting even to temporary inconvenience from an attachment to rights and privileges. Their plans of business are calculated *by* the hour and *for* the hour, and are uniform in nothing but the corruption which gives them birth. They never had, neither have they at this time, any regular plan for the conquest of America by arms. They know not how to go about it, neither have they power to effect it if they did know. The thing is not within the compass of human practicability, for America is too extensive either to be fully conquered or *passively* defended. But she may be *actively* defended by defeating or making prisoners of the army that invades her. And this is the only system of defence that can be effectual in a large country.

There is something in a war carried on by invasion which makes it differ in circumstances from any other mode of war, because he who conducts it cannot tell whether the ground he gains be for him, or against him, when he first obtains it. In the winter of 1776, General Howe marched with an air of victory through the Jerseys, the consequence of which was his defeat; and General Burgoyne at Saratoga experienced the same fate from the same cause. The Spaniards, about two years ago, were defeated by the Algerines in the same manner, that is, their first triumphs became a trap in which they were totally routed. And whoever will attend to the circumstances and events of a war carried on by invasion, will find, that any invader, in order to be finally conquered must first begin to conquer.

I confess myself one of those who believe the loss of Philadelphia to be attended with more advantages than injuries. The case stood thus: The enemy imagined Philadelphia to be of more importance to us than it really was; for we all know that it had long ceased to be a port: not a cargo of goods had been brought into it for near a twelvemonth, nor any fixed manufactories, nor even ship-building, carried on in it; yet as the enemy believed the conquest of it to be practicable, and to that belief added the absurd idea that the soul of all America was centred there, and would be conquered there, it naturally follows that their possession of it, by not answering the end proposed, must break up the plans they had so foolishly gone upon, and either oblige them to form a new one, for which their present strength is not sufficient, or to give over the attempt.

We never had so small an army to fight against, nor so fair an opportunity of final success as *now*. The death wound is already given. The day is ours if we follow it up. The enemy, by his situation, is within our reach, and by his reduced strength is within our power. The ministers of Britain may rage as they please, but our part is to conquer their armies. Let them wrangle and welcome, but let it not draw our attention from the *one* thing needful. *Here, in this spot* is our own business to be accomplished, our felicity secured. What we have now to do is as clear as light, and the way to do it is as straight as a line. It needs not to be commented upon, yet, in order to be perfectly understood I will put a case that cannot admit of a mistake.

Had the armies under Generals Howe and Burgoyne been united, and taken post at Germantown, and had the northern army under General Gates been joined to that under General Washington, at Whitemarsh, the consequence would have been a general action; and if in that action we had killed and taken the same number of officers and men, that is, between nine and ten thousand, with the same quantity of artillery, arms, stores, etc. as have been taken at the northward, and obliged General Howe with the remains of his army, that is, with the same number he now commands, to take shelter in Philadelphia, we should certainly have thought ourselves the greatest heroes in the world; and should, as soon as the season permitted, have collected together all the force of the continent and laid siege to the city, for it requires a much greater force to besiege an enemy in a town than to defeat him in the field. The case *now* is just the same as if it had been produced by the means I have here supposed. Between nine and ten thousand have been killed and taken, all their stores are in our possession, and General Howe, in consequence of that victory, has thrown himself for shelter into Philadelphia. He, or his trifling friend Galloway,[8] may form what pretences they please, yet no just reason can be given for their going into winter quarters so early as the 19th of October, but their apprehensions of a de-

---

[8] Joseph Galloway was a leading Tory in Philadelphia. He fled to General Howe and aided him in the Philadelphia campaign.—*Editor.*

feat if they continued out, or their conscious inability of keeping the field with safety. I see no advantage which can arise to America by hunting the enemy from state to state. It is a triumph without a prize, and wholly unworthy the attention of a people determined to conquer. Neither can any state promise itself security while the enemy remains in a condition to transport themselves from one part of the continent to another. Howe, likewise, cannot conquer where we have no army to oppose, therefore any such removals in him are mean and cowardly, and reduces Britain to a common pilferer. If he retreats from Philadelphia, he will be despised; if he stays, he may be shut up and starved out, and the country, if he advances into it, may become his Saratoga. He has his choice of evils and we of opportunities. If he moves early, it is not only a sign but a proof that he expects no reinforcement, and his delay will prove that he either waits for the arrival of a plan to go upon, or force to execute it, or both; in *which* case our strength will increase more than his, therefore in *any* case we cannot be wrong if we do but proceed.

The particular condition of Pennsylvania deserves the attention of all the other States. Her military strength must not be estimated by the number of inhabitants. Here are men of all nations, characters, professions and interests. Here are the firmest Whigs, surviving, like sparks in the ocean, unquenched and uncooled in the midst of discouragement and disaffection. Here are men losing their all with cheerfulness, and collecting fire and fortitude from the flames of their own estates. Here are others skulking in secret, many making a market of the times, and numbers who are changing to Whig or Tory with the circumstances of every day.

It is by a mere dint of fortitude and perseverance that the Whigs of this State have been able to maintain so good a countenance, and do even what they have done. We want help, and the sooner it can arrive the more effectual it will be. The invaded State, be it which it may, will always feel an additional burden upon its back, and be hard set to support its civil power with sufficient authority; and this difficulty will rise or fall, in proportion as the other states throw in their assistance to the common cause.

The enemy will most probably make many manœuvres at the opening of this campaign, to amuse and draw off the attention of the several States from the *one thing needful*. We may expect to hear of alarms and pretended expeditions to *this* place and *that* place, to the southward, the eastward, and the northward, all intended to prevent our forming into one formidable body. The less the enemy's strength is, the more subtleties of this kind will they make use of. Their existence depends upon it, because the force of America, when collected, is sufficient to swallow their present army up. It is therefore our business to make short work of it, by bending our whole attention to *this one principal point,* for the instant that the main body under General Howe is defeated, all the inferior alarms throughout the continent, like so many shadows, will follow his downfall.

The only way to finish a war with the least possible bloodshed, or perhaps without any, is to collect an army, against the power of which the enemy shall have no chance. By not doing this, we prolong the war, and double both the calamities and expenses of it. What a rich and happy country would America be, were she, by a vigorous exertion, to reduce Howe as she has reduced Burgoyne. Her currency would rise to millions beyond its present value. Every man would be rich, and every man would have it in his power to be happy. And why not do these things? What is there to hinder? America is her own mistress and can do what she pleases.

If we had not at this time a man in the field, we could, nevertheless, raise an army in a few weeks sufficient to overwhelm all the force which General Howe at present commands. Vigor and determination will do anything and everything. We began the war with this kind of spirit, why not end it with the same? Here, gentlemen, is the enemy. Here is the army. The interest, the happiness of all America, is centred in this half ruined spot. Come and help us. Here are laurels, come and share them. Here are Tories, come and help us to expel them. Here are Whigs that will make you welcome, and enemies that dread your coming.

The worst of all policies is that of doing things by halves. Penny-wise and pound-foolish, has been the ruin of thousands. The present spring, if rightly improved, will free us from our troubles, and save us the expense of millions. We have now only one army to cope with. No opportunity can be fairer; no prospect more promising. I shall conclude this paper with a few outlines of a plan, either for filling up the battalions with expedition, or for raising an additional force, for any limited time, on any sudden emergency.

That in which every man is interested, is every man's duty to support. And any burden which falls equally on all men, and from which every man is to receive an equal benefit, is consistent with the most perfect ideas of liberty. I would wish to revive something of that virtuous ambition which first called America into the field. Then every man was eager to do his part, and perhaps the principal reason why we have in any degree fallen therefrom, is because we did not set a right value by it at first, but left it to blaze out of itself, instead of regulating and preserving it by just proportions of rest and service.

Suppose any State whose number of effective inhabitants was 80,000, should be required to furnish 3,200 men towards the defence of the continent on any sudden emergency.

1st, Let the whole number of effective inhabitants be divided into hundreds; then if each of those hundreds turn out four men, the whole number of 3,200 will be had.

2d, Let the name of each hundred men be entered in a book, and let four dollars be collected from each man, with as much more as any of the gentlemen, whose abilities can afford it, shall please to throw in, which gifts likewise shall be entered against the names of the donors.

3d, Let the sums so collected be offered as a present, over and above the bounty of twenty dollars, to any four who may be inclined to propose themselves as volunteers: if more than four offer, the majority of the subscribers present shall determine which; if none offer, then four out of the hundred shall be taken by lot, who shall be entitled to the said sums, and shall either go, or provide others that will, in the space of six days.

4th, As it will always happen that in the space of ground on which a hundred men shall live, there will be always a number of persons who, by age and infirmity, are incapable of doing personal service, and as such persons are generally possessed of the greatest part of property in any country, their portion of service, therefore, will be to furnish each man with a blanket, which will make a regimental coat, jacket, and breeches, or clothes in lieu thereof, and another for a watch cloak, and two pair of shoes; for however choice people may be of these things matters not in cases of this kind; those who live always in houses can find many ways to keep themselves warm, but it is a shame and a sin to suffer a soldier in the field to want a blanket while there is one in the country.

Should the clothing not be wanted, the superannuated or infirm persons possessing property, may, in lieu thereof, throw in their money subscriptions towards increasing the bounty; for though age will naturally exempt a person from personal service, it cannot exempt him from his share of the charge, because the men are raised for the defence of property and liberty jointly.

There never was a scheme against which objections might not be raised. But this alone is not a sufficient reason for rejection. The only line to judge truly upon is to draw out and admit all the objections which can fairly be made, and place against them all the contrary qualities, conveniences and advantages, then by striking a balance you come at the true character of any scheme, principle or position.

The most material advantages of the plan here proposed are, ease, expedition, and cheapness; yet the men so raised get a much larger bounty than is any where at present given; because all the expenses, extravagance, and consequent idleness of recruiting are saved or prevented. The country incurs no new debt nor interest thereon; the whole matter being all settled at once and entirely done with. It is a subscription answering all the purposes of a tax, without either the charge or trouble of collecting. The men are ready for the field with the greatest possible expedition, because it becomes the duty of the inhabitants themselves, in every part of the country, to find their proportion of men instead of leaving it to a recruiting sergeant, who, be he ever so industrious, cannot know always where to apply.

I do not propose this as a regular digested plan, neither will the limits of this paper admit of any further remarks upon it. I believe it to be a hint capable of much improvement, and as such submit it to the public.

COMMON SENSE.[9]

LANCASTER, March 21, 1778.

[9] In November, 1802, Paine said that he wrote *Crisis* V to defeat the Conway Cabal which sought to oust Washington as Commander-in-Chief of the Continental Army. Washington's defeat in the battle of Germantown together with Gates' victory at Saratoga in October, 1777, had strengthened the Cabal.—*Editor*.

THE AMERICAN CRISIS

VI

On February 17, 1778, Lord North, prime minister of England, proposed, and Parliament approved, a measure granting the Americans everything but independence. No revenue taxes were to be levied; the coercive measures and the tea duty were to be repealed; full pardon was to be granted, and all acts of Parliament relating to the colonies adopted after February, 1763, were to be suspended. Five commissioners were sent from England to America to present these terms and "to treat, consult and agree upon means of quieting the disorders in the colonies of North America." George Johnstone, a member of the commission, was forced to withdraw after it became known that he had attempted to bribe Joseph Reed of Pennsylvania, offering him "£10,000 sterling and any office in the colonies in his Majesty's gift." The peace commission was finally composed of the persons to whom Paine addressed his *Crisis VI*.

On June 6, 1778, Congress informed the commissioners that it would only accept "such terms of peace as may consist with the honor of independent nations." As a last resort, on October 3, the commissioners issued a Manifesto and Proclamation over the head of Congress to the American people. They called upon the people to rise up against Congress and accept the terms offered by Parliament. They told all soldiers in the American armies that they might either return to peaceful pursuits or, "if the honours of a military life are become their object," fight for the king in the battles of the "United British Empire against our late mutual and natural enemy" [France]. ". . . It is both our wish and duty," the commissioners asserted bluntly, "to encourage and support any men or bodies of men in their return of loyalty to our sovereign and of affection to our fellow-subjects."

To overcome any influence this Manifesto and Proclamation might exert among the soldiers and civilians, Paine wrote his sixth *Crisis*. This pamphlet explains in large part why the commissioners' Proclamation "ran against a wall of American unity as hard as Congress." (Carl Van Doren, *Secret History of the American Revolution* [New York, 1941], p. 114.) On November 27, 1778, the commissioners sailed from America bringing home to England the news that their mission had failed and that the Americans were determined to fight until independence was achieved.—*Editor*.

To the Earl of Carlisle, General Clinton, and William Eden, Esq., British Commissioners at New York

THERE is a dignity in the warm passions of a Whig, which is never to be found in the cold malice of a Tory. In the one nature is only heated—in the other she is poisoned. The instant the former has it in his power to punish, he feels a disposition to forgive; but the canine venom of the latter knows no relief but revenge. This general distinction will, I believe, apply in all cases, and suits as well the meridian of England as America.

As I presume your last proclamation will undergo the strictures of other pens, I shall confine my remarks to only a few parts thereof. All that you have said might have been comprised in half the compass. It is tedious and unmeaning, and only a repetition of your former follies, with here and there an offensive aggravation. Your cargo of pardons will have no market. It is unfashionable to look at them—even speculation is at an end. They have become a perfect drug, and no way calculated for the climate.

In the course of your proclamation you say, "The policy as well as the *benevolence of Great Britain* have thus far checked the extremes of war, when they tended to distress a people still considered as their fellow subjects, and to desolate a country shortly to become again a source of mutual advantage." What you mean by "the *benevolence* of Great Britain" is to me inconceivable. To put a plain question; do you consider yourselves men or devils? For until this point is settled, no determinate sense can be put upon the expression. You have already equalled and in many cases excelled, the savages of either Indies; and if you have yet a cruelty in store you must have imported it, unmixed with every human material, from the original warehouse of hell.

To the interposition of Providence, and her blessings on our endeavors, and not to British benevolence are we indebted for the short chain that limits your ravages. Remember you do not, at this time, command a foot of land on the continent of America. Staten Island, York Island, a small part of Long Island, and Rhode Island, circumscribe your power; and even those you hold at the expense of the West Indies. To avoid a defeat, or prevent a desertion of your troops, you have taken up your quarters in holes and corners of inaccessible security; and in order to conceal what every one can perceive, you now endeavor to impose your weakness upon us for an act of mercy. If you think to succeed by such shadowy devices, you are but infants in the political world; you have the A, B, C, of stratagem yet to learn, and are wholly ignorant of the people you have to contend with. Like men in a state of intoxication, you forget that the rest of the world have eyes, and that the same stupidity which conceals you from yourselves exposes you to their satire and contempt.

The paragraph which I have quoted, stands as an introduction to the following: "But when that country [America] professes the unnatural design, not only of estranging herself from us, but of mortgaging herself and her resources to our enemies, the whole contest is changed: and the question is how far Great Britain may, by every means in her power, destroy or render useless, a connection contrived for her ruin, and the aggrandizement of France. Under such circumstances, the laws of self-preservation must direct the conduct of Britain, and, if the British colonies are to become an accession to France, will direct her to render that accession of as little avail as possible to her enemy."

I consider you in this declaration, like madmen biting in the hour of death. It contains likewise a fraudulent meanness; for, in order to justify a barbarous conclusion, you have advanced a false position. The treaty we have formed with France is open, noble, and generous. It is true policy, founded on sound philosophy, and neither a surrender or mortgage, as you would scandalously insinuate. I have seen every article, and speak from positive knowledge. In France, we have found an affectionate friend and faithful ally; [1] in Britain, we have found nothing but tyranny, cruelty, and infidelity.

But the happiness is, that the mischief you threaten, is not in your power to execute; and if it were, the punishment would return upon you in a ten-fold degree. The humanity of America has hitherto re-

[1] The reference is to the Treaty of Alliance between France and the United States signed in February, 1778. The treaty provided for the recognition of American independence, promised military aid to the young republic and pledged each country not to make peace with Britain unless the other approved.—Editor.

strained her from acts of retaliation, and the affection she retains for many individuals in England, who have fed, clothed and comforted her prisoners, has, to the present day, warded off her resentment, and operated as a screen to the whole. But even these considerations must cease, when national objects interfere and oppose them. Repeated aggravations will provoke a retort, and policy justify the measure. We mean now to take you seriously up upon your own ground and principle, and as you do, so shall you be done by.

You ought to know, gentlemen, that England and Scotland, are far more exposed to incendiary desolation than America, in her present state, can possibly be. We occupy a country, with but few towns, and whose riches consist in land and annual produce. The two last can suffer but little, and that only within a very limited compass. In Britain it is otherwise. Her wealth lies chiefly in cities and large towns, the depositories of manufactures and fleets of merchantmen. There is not a nobleman's country seat but may be laid in ashes by a single person. Your own may probably contribute to the proof: in short, there is no evil which cannot be returned when you come to incendiary mischief. The ships in the Thames, may certainly be as easily set on fire, as the temporary bridge was a few years ago; yet of that affair no discovery was ever made; and the loss you would sustain by such an event, executed at a proper season, is infinitely greater than any you can inflict. The East India House and the Bank, neither are nor can be secure from this sort of destruction, and, as Dr. Price justly observes, a fire at the latter would bankrupt the nation.[2] It has never been the custom of France and England when at war, to make those havocs on each other, because the ease with which they could retaliate rendered it as impolitic as if each had destroyed his own.

But think not, gentlemen, that our distance secures you, or our invention fails us. We can much easier accomplish such a point than any nation in Europe. We talk the same language, dress in the same habit, and appear with the same manners as yourselves. We can pass from one

[2] The reference is to Dr. Richard Price, an English radical who defended the Americans and their conduct. His *Observations on the Nature of Civil Liberty* published in London in 1776 was widely read in America, and many Americans appreciated his complaint that "the meanest persons among us [in England] is disposed to look upon himself as having a body of subjects in *America;* and to be offended at the denial of his right to make laws for them, though perhaps he does not know what colour they are, or what language they talk. . . . We have been so used to speak of the Colonies as *our* Colonies and to think of them as in a state of subordination to us, and as holding their existence in *America* only for our use." pp. 31-32.—*Editor.*

part of England to another unsuspected; many of us are as well acquainted with the country as you are, and should you impolitically provoke us, you will most assuredly lament the effects of it. Mischiefs of
this kind require no army to execute them. The means are obvious, and
the opportunities unguardable. I hold up a warning to your senses, if
you have any left, and "to the unhappy people likewise, whose affairs
are committed to you." [3] I call not with the rancor of an enemy, but the
earnestness of a friend, on the deluded people of England, lest, between
your blunders and theirs, they sink beneath the evils contrived for us.

"He who lives in a glass house," says a Spanish proverb, "should never
begin throwing stones." This, gentlemen, is exactly your case, and you
must be the most ignorant of mankind, or suppose us so, not to see on
which side the balance of accounts will fall. There are many other modes
of retaliation, which, for several reasons, I choose not to mention. But
be assured of this, that the instant you put your threat into execution, a
counter-blow will follow it. If you openly profess yourselves savages, it
is high time we should treat you as such, and if nothing but distress can
recover you to reason, to punish will become an office of charity.

While your fleet lay last winter in the Delaware, I offered my service
to the Pennsylvania Navy Board then at Trenton, as one who would
make a party with them, or any four or five gentlemen, on an expedition
down the river to set fire to it, and though it was not then accepted, nor
the thing personally attempted, it is more than probable that your own
folly will provoke a much more ruinous act. Say not when mischief is
done, that you had not warning, and remember that we do not begin it,
but mean to repay it. Thus much for your savage and impolitic threat.

In another part of your proclamation you say, "But if the honors of a
military life are become the object of the Americans, let them seek those
honors under the banners of their rightful sovereign, and in fighting
the battles of the united British Empire, against our late mutual and
natural enemies." Surely! the union of absurdity with madness was
never marked in more distinguishable lines than these. Your rightful
sovereign, as you call him, may do well enough for you, who dare not
inquire into the humble capacities of the man; but we, who estimate
persons and things by their real worth, cannot suffer our judgments to
be so imposed upon; and unless it is your wish to see him exposed, it
ought to be your endeavor to keep him out of sight. The less you have
to say about him the better. We have done with him, and that ought

---

[3] General [Sir H.] Clinton's letter to Congress.—*Author.*

to be answer enough. You have been often told so. Strange! that the answer must be so often repeated. You go a-begging with your king as with a brat, or with some unsaleable commodity you were tired of; and though every body tells you no, no, still you keep hawking him about. But there is one that will have him in a little time, and as we have no inclination to disappoint you of a customer, we bid nothing for him.

The impertinent folly of the paragraph that I have just quoted, deserves no other notice than to be laughed at and thrown by, but the principle on which it is founded is detestable. We are invited to submit to a man who has attempted by every cruelty to destroy us, and to join him in making war against France, who is already at war against him for our support.

Can Bedlam, in concert with Lucifer, form a more mad and devilish request? Were it possible a people could sink into such apostasy they would deserve to be swept from the earth like the inhabitants of Sodom and Gomorrah. The proposition is an universal affront to the rank which man holds in the creation, and an indignity to him who placed him there. It supposes him made up without a spark of honor, and under no obligation to God or man.

What sort of men or Christians must you suppose the Americans to be, who, after seeing their most humble petitions insultingly rejected; the most grievous laws passed to distress them in every quarter; an undeclared war let loose upon them, and Indians and Negroes invited to the slaughter; who, after seeing their kinsmen murdered, their fellow citizens starved to death in prisons, and their houses and property destroyed and burned; who, after the most serious appeals to heaven, the most solemn abjuration by oath of all government connected with you, and the most heart-felt pledges and protestations of faith to each other; and who, after soliciting the friendship, and entering into alliances with other nations, should at last break through all these obligations, civil and divine, by complying with your horrid and infernal proposal. Ought we ever after to be considered as a part of the human race? Or ought we not rather to be blotted from the society of mankind, and become a spectacle of misery to the world? But there is something in corruption, which, like a jaundiced eye, transfers the color of itself to the object it looks upon, and sees every thing stained and impure; for unless you were capable of such conduct yourselves, you would never have supposed such a character in us. The offer fixes your infamy. It exhibits you as a nation without faith; with whom oaths and treaties are considered as trifles, and the breaking them as the breaking of a bubble. Regard to decency, or to rank, might have taught you better; or pride inspired you, though virtue could not. There is not left a step in the degradation of character to which you can now descend; you have put your foot on the ground floor, and the key of the dungeon is turned upon you.

That the invitation may want nothing of being a complete monster, you have thought proper to finish it with an assertion which has no foundation, either in fact or philosophy; and as Mr. Ferguson, your secretary, is a man of letters, and has made civil society his study, and published a treatise on that subject, I address this part to him.[4]

In the close of the paragraph which I last quoted, France is styled the "natural enemy" of England, and by way of lugging us into some strange idea, she is styled "the late mutual and natural enemy" of both countries. I deny that she ever was the natural enemy of either; and that there does not exist in nature such a principle. The expression is an unmeaning barbarism, and wholly unphilosophical, when applied to beings of the same species, let their station in the creation be what it may. We have a perfect idea of a natural enemy when we think of the devil, because the enmity is perpetual, unalterable and unabateable. It admits, neither of peace, truce, or treaty; consequently the warfare is eternal, and therefore it is natural. But man with man cannot arrange in the same opposition. Their quarrels are accidental and equivocally created. They become friends or enemies as the change of temper, or the cast of interest inclines them. The Creator of man did not constitute them the natural enemy of each other. He has not made any one order of beings so. Even wolves may quarrel, still they herd together. If any two nations are so, then must all nations be so, otherwise it is not nature but custom, and the offence frequently originates with the accuser. England is as truly the natural enemy of France, as France is of England, and perhaps more so. Separated from the rest of Europe, she has contracted an unsocial habit of manners, and imagines in others the jealousy she creates in herself. Never long satisfied with peace, she supposes the discontent universal, and buoyed up with her own importance, conceives herself the only object pointed at. The expression has been often used, and always with a fraudulent design; for when the idea of a natural enemy is conceived, it pre-

---

[4] Adam Ferguson, who served as secretary of the peace commission, was the renowned professor of moral philosophy at the University of Edinburgh. He was the author of an *Essay on the History of Civil Society* published in 1767, and *Institutes of Moral Philosophy* published in 1769.—*Editor*.

vents all other inquiries, and the real cause of the quarrel is hidden in the universality of the conceit. Men start at the notion of a natural enemy, and ask no other question. The cry obtains credit like the alarm of a mad dog, and is one of those kind of tricks, which, by operating on the common passions, secures their interest through their folly.

But we, sir, are not to be thus imposed upon. We live in a large world, and have extended our ideas beyond the limits and prejudices of an island. We hold out the right hand of friendship to all the universe, and we conceive that there is a sociality in the manners of France, which is much better disposed to peace and negotiation than that of England, and until the latter becomes more civilized, she cannot expect to live long at peace with any power. Her common language is vulgar and offensive, and children suck in with their milk the rudiments of insult—"The arm of Britain! The mighty arm of Britain! Britain that shakes the earth to its center and its poles! The scourge of France! The terror of the world! That governs with a nod, and pours down vengeance like a God." This language neither makes a nation great or little; but it shows a savageness of manners, and has a tendency to keep national animosity alive. The entertainments of the stage are calculated to the same end, and almost every public exhibition is tinctured with insult. Yet England is always in dread of France,—terrified at the apprehension of an invasion, suspicious of being outwitted in a treaty, and privately cringing though she is publicly offending. Let her, therefore, reform her manners and do justice, and she will find the idea of a natural enemy to be only a phantom of her own imagination.

Little did I think, at this period of the war, to see a proclamation which could promise you no one useful purpose whatever, and tend only to expose you. One would think that you were just awakened from a four years' dream, and knew nothing of what had passed in the interval. Is this a time to be offering pardons, or renewing the long forgotten subjects of charters and taxation? Is it worth your while, after every force has failed you, to retreat under the shelter of argument and persuasion? Or can you think that we, with nearly half your army prisoners, and in alliance with France, are to be begged or threatened into submission by a piece of paper? But as commissioners at a hundred pounds sterling a week each, you conceive yourselves bound to do something, and the genius of ill-fortune told you, that you must write.

For my own part, I have not put pen to paper these several months. Convinced of our superiority by the issue of every campaign, I was inclined to hope, that that which all the rest of the world now see, would become visible to you, and therefore felt unwilling to ruffle your temper by fretting you with repetitions and discoveries. There have been intervals of hesitation in your conduct, from which it seemed a pity to disturb you, and a charity to leave you to yourselves. You have often stopped, as if you intended to think, but your thoughts have ever been too early or too late.

There was a time when Britain disdained to answer, or even hear a petition from America. That time is past and she in her turn is petitioning our acceptance. We now stand on higher ground, and offer her peace; and the time will come when she, perhaps in vain, will ask it from us. The latter case is as probable as the former ever was. She cannot refuse to acknowledge our independence with greater obstinacy than she before refused to repeal her laws; and if America alone could bring her to the one, united with France she will reduce her to the other. There is something in obstinacy which differs from every other passion; whenever it fails it never recovers, but either breaks like iron, or crumbles sulkily away like a fractured arch. Most other passions have their periods of fatigue and rest; their suffering and their cure; but obstinacy has no resource, and the first wound is mortal. You have already begun to give it up, and you will, from the natural construction of the vice, find yourselves both obliged and inclined to do so.

If you look back you see nothing but loss and disgrace. If you look forward the same scene continues, and the close is an impenetrable gloom. You may plan and execute little mischiefs, but are they worth the expense they cost you, or will such partial evils have any effect on the general cause? Your expedition to Egg Harbor, will be felt at a distance like an attack upon a hen-roost, and expose you in Europe, with a sort of childish frenzy. Is it worth while to keep an army to protect you in writing proclamations, or to get once a year into winter quarters? Possessing yourselves of towns is not conquest, but convenience, and in which you will one day or other be trepanned. Your retreat from Philadelphia, was only a timely escape, and your next expedition may be less fortunate.

It would puzzle all the politicians in the universe to conceive what you stay for, or why you should have stayed so long. You are prosecuting a war in which you confess you have neither object nor hope, and that conquest, could it be effected, would not repay the charges: in the mean while the rest of your affairs are running to ruin, and a European war kindling against you. In such a situation, there is neither doubt nor difficulty; the first rudiments of reason will determine the choice, for if peace can be procured with more advantages than even a conquest can be obtained, he must be an idiot indeed that hesitates.

But you are probably buoyed up by a set of wretched mortals, who, having deceived themselves, are cringing, with the duplicity of a spaniel, for a little temporary bread. Those men will tell you just what you please. It is their interest to amuse, in order to lengthen out their protection. They study to keep you amongst them for that very purpose; and in proportion as you disregard their advice, and grow callous to their complaints, they will stretch into improbability, and season their flattery the higher. Characters like these are to be found in every country, and every country will despise them.

COMMON SENSE.

PHILADELPHIA, Oct. 20, 1778.

THE AMERICAN CRISIS

VII

Several of the articles in the *Crisis* series were addressed to the English people; indeed, as Paine points out in the seventh *Crisis* it had always been his "design to dedicate a *Crisis*" to them. In these articles Paine explained the issues at stake in the war, indicated how they were related to the struggle of the English progressives against despotism, at home, showed how impossible it was for England ever to defeat the Americans, and called upon the English people to follow the example of the United States by starting their own revolution and convening a Congress.—*Editor*.

To the People of England

THERE are stages in the business of serious life in which to amuse is cruel, but to deceive is to destroy; and it is of little consequence, in the conclusion, whether men deceive themselves, or submit, by a kind of mutual consent, to the impositions of each other. That England has long been under the influence of delusion or mistake, needs no other proof than the unexpected and wretched situation that she is now involved in: and so powerful has been the influence, that no provision was ever made or thought of against the misfortune, because the possibility of its happening was never conceived.

The general and successful resistance of America, the conquest of Burgoyne,[1] and a war in France, were treated in parliament as the

---

[1] General John ("Gentleman Johnny") Burgoyne surrendered at Saratoga on October 14, 1777. His army of about 5,000 was permitted to return to Britain on condition that it promised not to fight again. The victory was extremely important since it brought an end of all British efforts to seize the Hudson Valley, and paved the way for France's entrance into the war as an ally of the United States.—*Editor*.

dreams of a discontented opposition, or a distempered imagination. They were beheld as objects unworthy of a serious thought, and the bare intimation of them afforded the ministry a triumph of laughter. Short triumph indeed! For everything which has been predicted has happened, and all that was promised has failed. A long series of politics so remarkably distinguished by a succession of misfortunes, without one alleviating turn, must certainly have something in it systematically wrong. It is sufficient to awaken the most credulous into suspicion, and the most obstinate into thought. Either the means in your power are insufficient, or the measures ill planned; either the execution has been bad, or the thing attempted impracticable; or, to speak more emphatically, either you are not able or heaven is not willing. For, why is it that you have not conquered us? Who, or what has prevented you? You have had every opportunity that you could desire, and succeeded to your utmost wish in every preparatory means. Your fleets and armies have arrived in America without an accident. No uncommon fortune has intervened. No foreign nation has interfered until the time which you had allotted for victory was passed. The opposition, either in or out of parliament, neither disconcerted your measures, retarded or diminished your force. They only foretold your fate. Every ministerial scheme was carried with as high a hand as if the whole nation had been unanimous. Every thing wanted was asked for, and every thing asked for was granted.

A greater force was not within the compass of your abilities to send, and the time you sent it was of all others the most favorable. You were then at rest with the whole world beside. You had the range of every court in Europe uncontradicted by us. You amused us with a tale of commissioners of peace, and under that disguise collected a numerous army and came almost unexpectedly upon us. The force was much greater than we looked for; and that which we had to oppose it with, was unequal in numbers, badly armed, and poorly disciplined; beside which, it was embodied only for a short time, and expired within a few months after your arrival. We had governments to form; measures to concert; an army to train, and every necessary article to import or to create. Our non-importation scheme had exhausted our stores, and your command by sea intercepted our supplies. We were a people unknown, and unconnected with the political world, and strangers to the disposition of foreign powers. Could you possibly wish for a more favorable conjunction of circumstances? Yet all these have happened and passed away, and, as it were, left you with a laugh. There are likewise events of such an original nativity as can never happen again, unless a new world should arise from the ocean.

If any thing can be a lesson to presumption, surely the circumstances of this war will have their effect. Had Britain been defeated by any European power, her pride would have drawn consolation from the importance of her conquerors; but in the present case, she is excelled by those that she affected to despise, and her own opinions retorting upon herself, become an aggravation of her disgrace. Misfortune and experience are lost upon mankind, when they produce neither reflection nor reformation. Evils, like poisons, have their uses, and there are diseases which no other remedy can reach. It has been the crime and folly of England to suppose herself invincible, and that, without acknowledging or perceiving that a full third of her strength was drawn from the country she is now at war with. The arm of Britain has been spoken of as the arm of the Almighty, and she has lived of late as if she thought the whole world created for her diversion. Her politics, instead of civilizing, has tended to brutalize mankind, and under the vain, unmeaning title of "Defender of the Faith," [2] she has made war like an Indian against the religion of humanity.[3] Her cruelties in the East Indies will *never* be forgotten, and it is somewhat remarkable that the produce of that ruined country, transported to America, should there kindle up a war to punish the destroyer. The chain is continued, though with a mysterious kind of uniformity both in the crime and the punishment. The latter runs parallel with the former, and time and fate will give it a perfect illustration.

When information is withheld, ignorance becomes a reasonable excuse; and one would charitably hope that the people of England do not encourage cruelty from choice but from mistake. Their recluse situation, surrounded by the sea, preserves them from the calamities of war, and keeps them in the dark as to the conduct of their own armies. They see not, therefore they feel not. They tell the tale that is told them and believe it, and accustomed to no other news than their own, they receive it, stripped of its horrors and prepared for the palate of the nation, through the channel of the London Gazette. They are made to believe that their generals and armies differ from those of other nations, and have nothing of rudeness or barbarity in them. They suppose them what

[2] One of the titles of the King of England.—*Editor.*

[3] This is probably the first time the phrase, "the religion of humanity," was used. The reference to "Indian" is to the tribes in America.—*Editor.*

they wish them to be. They feel a disgrace in thinking otherwise, and naturally encourage the belief from a partiality to themselves. There was a time when I felt the same prejudices, and reasoned from the same errors; but experience, sad and painful experience, has taught me better. What the conduct of former armies was, I know not, but what the conduct of the present is, I well know. It is low, cruel, indolent and profligate; and had the people of America no other cause for separation than what the army has occasioned, that alone is cause sufficient.

The field of politics in England is far more extensive than that of news. Men have a right to reason for themselves, and though they cannot contradict the intelligence in the London Gazette, they may frame upon it what sentiments they please. But the misfortune is, that a general ignorance has prevailed over the whole nation respecting America. The ministry and the minority have both been wrong. The former was always so, the latter only lately so. Politics, to be executively right, must have a unity of means and time, and a defect in either overthrows the whole. The ministry rejected the plans of the minority while they were practicable, and joined in them when they became impracticable. From wrong measures they got into wrong time, and have now completed the circle of absurdity by closing it upon themselves.

I happened to come to America a few months before the breaking out of hostilities.[4] I found the disposition of the people such, that they might have been led by a thread and governed by a reed. Their suspicion was quick and penetrating, but their attachment to Britain was obstinate, and it was at that time a kind of treason to speak against it. They disliked the ministry, but they esteemed the nation. Their idea of grievance operated without resentment, and their single object was reconciliation. Bad as I believed the ministry to be, I never conceived them capable of a measure so rash and wicked as the commencing of hostilities; much less did I imagine the nation would encourage it. I viewed the dispute as a kind of law-suit, in which I supposed the parties would find a way either to decide or settle it. I had no thoughts of independence or of arms. The world could not then have persuaded me that I should be either a soldier or an author. If I had any talents for either, they were buried in me, and might ever have continued so, had not the necessity of the times dragged and driven them into action. I had formed my plan of life, and conceiving myself happy, wished every body else so. But when the country, into which I had just set my foot, was set on fire about my ears,

---

[4] Paine arrived in America on November 30, 1774.—*Editor.*

it was time to stir. It was time for every man to stir. Those who had been long settled had something to defend; those who had just come had something to pursue; and the call and the concern was equal and universal. For in a country where all men were once adventurers, the difference of a few years in their arrival could make none in their right.

The breaking out of hostilities opened a new suspicion in the politics of America, which, though at that time very rare, has since been proved to be very right. What I allude to is, "a secret and fixed determination in the British Cabinet to annex America to the crown of England as a conquered country." If this be taken as the object, then the whole line of conduct pursued by the ministry, though rash in its origin and ruinous in its consequences, is nevertheless uniform and consistent in its parts. It applies to every case and resolves every difficulty. But if taxation, or any thing else, be taken in its room, there is no proportion between the object and the charge. Nothing but the whole soil and property of the country can be placed as a possible equivalent against the millions which the ministry expended. No taxes raised in America could possibly repay it. A revenue of two millions sterling a year would not discharge the sum and interest accumulated thereon, in twenty years.

Reconciliation never appears to have been the wish or the object of the administration; they looked on conquest as certain and infallible, and, under that persuasion, sought to drive the Americans into what they might style a general rebellion, and then, crushing them with arms in their hands, reap the rich harvest of a general confiscation, and silence them for ever. The dependents at court were too numerous to be provided for in England. The market for plunder in the East Indies was over; and the profligacy of government required that a new mine should be opened, and that mine could be no other than America, conquered and forfeited. They had no where else to go. Every other channel was drained; and extravagance, with the thirst of a drunkard, was gaping for supplies.

If the ministry deny this to have been their plan, it becomes them to explain what was their plan. For either they have abused us in coveting property they never labored for, or they have abused you in expending an amazing sum upon an incompetent object. Taxation, as I mentioned before, could never be worth the charge of obtaining it by arms; and any kind of formal obedience which America could have made, would have weighed with the lightness of a laugh against such a load of expense. It is therefore most probable that the ministry will at last justify their policy by their dishonesty, and openly declare, that their original design was conquest: and, in this case, it well becomes the people of England to consider how far the nation would have been benefited by the success.

In a general view, there are few conquests that repay the charge of making them, and mankind are pretty well convinced that it can never be worth their while to go to war for profit's sake. If they are made war upon, their country invaded, or their existence at stake, it is their duty to defend and preserve themselves, but in every other light, and from every other cause, is war inglorious and detestable. But to return to the case in question—

When conquests are made of foreign countries, it is supposed that the *commerce* and *dominion* of the country which made them are extended. But this could neither be the object nor the consequence of the present war. You enjoyed the whole commerce before. It could receive no possible addition by a conquest, but on the contrary, must diminish as the inhabitants were reduced in numbers and wealth. You had the same *dominion* over the country which you used to have, and had no complaint to make against her for breach of any part of the contract between you or her, or contending against any established custom, commercial, political or territorial. The country and commerce were both your own when you *began* to conquer, in the same manner and form as they had been your own a hundred years before. Nations have sometimes been induced to make conquests for the sake of reducing the power of their enemies, or bringing it to a balance with their own. But this could be no part of your plan. No foreign authority was claimed here, neither was any such authority suspected by you, or acknowledged or imagined by us. What then, in the name of heaven, could you go to war for? Or what chance could you possibly have in the event, but either to hold the same country which you held before, and that in a much worse condition, or to lose, with an amazing expense, what you might have retained without a farthing of charges?

War never can be the interest of a trading nation, any more than quarrelling can be profitable to a man in business. But to make war with those who trade with us, is like setting a bull-dog upon a customer at the shop-door. The least degree of common sense shows the madness of the latter, and it will apply with the same force of conviction to the former. Piratical nations, having neither commerce or commodities of their own to lose, may make war upon all the world, and lucratively find their account in it; but it is quite otherwise with Britain: for, besides the stoppage of trade in time of war, she exposes more of her own property to be lost, than she has the chance of taking from others. Some ministerial gentlemen in parliament have mentioned the greatness of her trade as an apology for the greatness of her loss. This is miserable politics indeed! Because it ought to have been given as a reason for her not engaging in a war at first. The coast of America commands the West India trade almost as effectually as the coast of Africa does that of the Straits; and England can no more carry on the former without the consent of America, than she can the latter without a Mediterranean pass.

In whatever light the war with America is considered upon commercial principles, it is evidently the interest of the people of England not to support it; and why it has been supported so long, against the clearest demonstrations of truth and national advantage, is, to me, and must be to all the reasonable world, a matter of astonishment. Perhaps it may be said that I live in America, and write this from interest. To this I reply, that my principle is universal. My attachment is to all the world, and not to any particular part, and if what I advance is right, no matter where or who it comes from. We have given the proclamation of your commissioners a currency in our newspapers, and I have no doubt you will give this a place in yours. To oblige and be obliged is fair.

Before I dismiss this part of my address, I shall mention one more circumstance in which I think the people of England have been equally mistaken: and then proceed to other matters.

There is such an idea existing in the world, as that of *national honor,* and this, falsely understood, is oftentimes the cause of war. In a Christian and philosophical sense, mankind seem to have stood still at individual civilization, and to retain as nations all the original rudeness of nature. Peace by treaty is only a cessation of violence for a reformation of sentiment. It is a substitute for a principle that is wanting and ever will be wanting till the idea of *national honor* be rightly understood. As individuals we profess ourselves Christians, but as nations we are heathens, Romans, and what not. I remember the late Admiral Saunders declaring in the House of Commons, and that in the time of peace, "That the city of Madrid laid in ashes was not a sufficient atonement for the Spaniards taking off the rudder of an English sloop of war." I do not ask whether this is Christianity or morality, I ask whether it is decency? whether it is proper language for a nation to use? In private life we call it by the plain name of bullying, and the elevation of rank cannot alter its character. It is, I think, exceedingly easy to define what ought to be understood by national honor; for that which is the best character for an individual is the best character for a nation; and wherever the latter exceeds or falls beneath the former, there is a departure from the line of true greatness.

I have thrown out this observation with a design of applying it to Great Britain. Her ideas of national honor seem devoid of that benevolence of heart, that universal expansion of philanthropy, and that triumph over the rage of vulgar prejudice, without which man is inferior to himself, and a companion of common animals. To know who she shall regard or dislike, she asks what country they are of, what religion they profess, and what property they enjoy. Her idea of national honor seems to consist in national insult, and that to be a great people, is to be neither a Christian, a philosopher, or a gentleman, but to threaten with the rudeness of a bear, and to devour with the ferocity of a lion. This perhaps may sound harsh and uncourtly, but it is too true, and the more is the pity.

I mention this only as her general character. But towards America she has observed no character at all; and destroyed by her conduct what she assumed in her title. She set out with the title of parent, or mother country. The association of ideas which naturally accompany this expression, are filled with everything that is fond, tender and forbearing. They have an energy peculiar to themselves, and, overlooking the accidental attachment of common affections, apply with infinite softness to the first feelings of the heart. It is a political term which every mother can feel the force of, and every child can judge of. It needs no painting of mine to set it off, for nature only can do it justice.

But has any part of your conduct to America corresponded with the title you set up? If in your general national character you are unpolished and severe, in this you are inconsistent and unnatural, and you must have exceeding false notions of national honor to suppose that the world can admire a want of humanity or that national honor depends on the violence of resentment, the inflexibility of temper, or the vengeance of execution.

I would willingly convince you, and that with as much temper as the times will suffer me to do, that as you opposed your own interest by quarrelling with us, so likewise your national honor, rightly conceived and understood, was no ways called upon to enter into a war with America; had you studied true greatness of heart, the first and fairest ornament of mankind, you would have acted directly contrary to all that you have done, and the world would have ascribed it to a generous cause. Besides which, you had (though with the assistance of this country) secured a powerful name by the last war. You were known and dreaded abroad; and it would have been wise in you to have suffered the world to have slept undisturbed under that idea. It was to you a force existing without expense. It produced to you all the advantages of real power; and you were stronger through the universality of that charm, than any future fleets and armies may probably make you. Your greatness was so secured and interwoven with your silence that you ought never to have awakened mankind, and had nothing to do but to be quiet. Had you been true politicians you would have seen all this, and continued to draw from the magic of a name, the force and authority of a nation.

Unwise as you were in breaking the charm, you were still more unwise in the manner of doing it. Samson only told the secret, but you have performed the operation; you have shaven your own head, and wantonly thrown away the locks. America was the hair from which the charm was drawn that infatuated the world. You ought to have quarrelled with no power; but with her upon no account. You had nothing to fear from any condescension you might make. You might have humored her, even if there had been no justice in her claims, without any risk to your reputation; for Europe, fascinated by your fame, would have ascribed it to your benevolence, and America, intoxicated by the grant, would have slumbered in her fetters.

But this method of studying the progress of the passions, in order to ascertain the probable conduct of mankind, is a philosophy in politics which those who preside at St. James's have no conception of. They know no other influence than corruption and reckon all their probabilities from precedent. A new case is to them a new world, and while they are seeking for a parallel they get lost. The talents of Lord Mansfield [5] can be estimated at best no higher than those of a sophist. He understands the subtleties but not the elegance of nature; and by continually viewing mankind through the cold medium of the law, never thinks of penetrating into the warmer region of the mind. As for Lord North, it is his happiness to have in him more philosophy than sentiment, for he bears flogging like a top, and sleeps the better for it. His punishment becomes his support, for while he suffers the lash for his

[5] The reference is to Lord Mansfield, Chief Justice of England.—*Editor.*

sins, he keeps himself up by twirling about. In politics, he is a good arithmetician, and in every thing else nothing at all.

There is one circumstance which comes so much within Lord North's province as a financier, that I am surprised it should escape him, which is, the different abilities of the two countries in supporting the expense; for, strange as it may seem, England is not a match for America in this particular. By a curious kind of revolution in accounts, the people of England seem to mistake their poverty for their riches; that is, they reckon their national debt as a part of their national wealth. They make the same kind of error which a man would do, who after mortgaging his estate, should add the money borrowed, to the full value of the estate, in order to count up his worth, and in this case he would conceive that he got rich by running into debt. Just thus it is with England. The government owed at the beginning of this war one hundred and thirty-five millions sterling, and though the individuals to whom it was due had a right to reckon their shares as so much private property, yet to the nation collectively it was so much poverty. There are as effectual limits to public debts as to private ones, for when once the money borrowed is so great as to require the whole yearly revenue to discharge the interest thereon, there is an end to further borrowing; in the same manner as when the interest of a man's debts amounts to the yearly income of his estate, there is an end to his credit. This is nearly the case with England, the interest of her present debt being at least equal to one half of her yearly revenue, so that out of ten millions annually collected by taxes, she has but five that she can call her own.

The very reverse of this was the case with America; she began the war without any debt upon her, and in order to carry it on, she neither raised money by taxes, nor borrowed it upon interest, but created it; and her situation at this time continues so much the reverse of yours that taxing would make her rich, whereas it would make you poor. When we shall have sunk the sum which we have created, we shall then be out of debt, be just as rich as when we began, and all the while we are doing it shall feel no difference, because the value will rise as the quantity decreases.

There was not a country in the world so capable of bearing the expense of a war as America; not only because she was not in debt when she began, but because the country is young and capable of infinite improvement, and has an almost boundless tract of new lands in store; whereas England has got to her extent of age and growth, and has not unoccupied land or property in reserve. The one is like a young heir coming to a large improvable estate; the other like an old man whose chances are over, and his estate mortgaged for half its worth.

In the second number of the Crisis, which I find has been republished in England, I endeavored to set forth the impracticability of conquering America. I stated every case, that I conceived could possibly happen, and ventured to predict its consequences. As my conclusions were drawn not artfully, but naturally, they have all proved to be true. I was upon the spot; knew the politics of America, her strength and resources, and by a train of services, the best in my power to render, was honored with the friendship of the congress, the army and the people. I considered the cause a just one. I know and feel it a just one, and under that confidence never made my own profit or loss an object. My endeavor was to have the matter well understood on both sides, and I conceived myself tendering a general service, by setting forth to the one the impossibility of being conquered, and to the other the impossibility of conquering. Most of the arguments made use of by the ministry for supporting the war, are the very arguments that ought to have been used against supporting it; and the plans, by which they thought to conquer, are the very plans in which they were sure to be defeated. They have taken every thing up at the wrong end. Their ignorance is astonishing, and were you in my situation you would see it. They may, perhaps, have your confidence, but I am persuaded that they would make very indifferent members of Congress. I know what England is, and what America is, and from the compound of knowledge, am better enabled to judge of the issue than what the king or any of his ministers can be.

In this number I have endeavored to show the ill policy and disadvantages of the war. I believe many of my remarks are new. Those which are not so, I have studied to improve and place in a manner that may be clear and striking. Your failure is, I am persuaded, as certain as fate. America is above your reach. She is at least your equal in the world, and her independence neither rests upon your consent, nor can it be prevented by your arms. In short, you spend your substance in vain, and impoverish yourselves without a hope.

But suppose you had conquered America, what advantages, collectively or individually, as merchants, manufacturers, or conquerors, could you have looked for? This is an object you seemed never to have attended to. Listening for the sound of victory, and led away by the frenzy of arms, you neglected to reckon either the cost or the consequences. You must all pay towards the expense; the poorest among you must bear his share, and it is both your right and your duty to weigh seriously the matter. Had America been conquered, she might have been parcelled out in grants to the favorites at court, but no share of it would have fallen to you. Your taxes would not have been lessened, because she would have been in no condition to have paid any towards your relief. We are rich by contrivance of our own, which would have ceased as soon as you became masters. Our paper money will be of no use in England, and silver and gold we have none. In the last war you made many conquests, but were any of your taxes lessened thereby? On the contrary, were you not taxed to pay for the charge of making them, and has not the same been the case in every war?

To the Parliament I wish to address myself in a more particular manner. They appear to have supposed themselves partners in the chase, and to have hunted with the lion from an expectation of a right in the booty; but in this it is most probable they would, as legislators, have been disappointed. The case is quite a new one, and many unforeseen difficulties would have arisen thereon. The Parliament claimed a legislative right over America, and the war originated from that pretence. But the army is supposed to belong to the crown, and if America had been conquered through their means, the claim of the legislature would have been suffocated in the conquest. Ceded, or conquered, countries are supposed to be out of the authority of Parliament. Taxation is exercised over them by prerogative and not by law. It was attempted to be done in the Grenadas a few years ago, and the only reason why it was not done was because the crown had made a prior relinquishment of its claim. Therefore, Parliament have been all this while supporting measures for the establishment of their authority, in the issue of which, they would have been triumphed over by the prerogative. This might have opened a new and interesting opposition between the Parliament and the crown. The crown would have said that it conquered for itself, and that to conquer for Parliament was an unknown case. The Parliament might have replied, that America not being a foreign country, but a country in rebellion, could not be said to be conquered, but reduced; and thus continued their claim by disowning the term. The crown might have rejoined, that however America might be considered at first, she became foreign at last by a declaration of independence, and a treaty with France; and that her case being, by that treaty, put within the law of nations, was out of the law of Parliament, who might have maintained, that as their claim over America had never been surrendered, so neither could it be taken away. The crown might have insisted, that though the claim of Parliament could not be taken away, yet, being an inferior, it might be superseded; and that, whether the claim was withdrawn from the object, or the object taken from the claim, the same separation ensued; and that America being subdued after a treaty with France, was to all intents and purposes a regal conquest, and of course the sole property of the king. The Parliament, as the legal delegates of the people, might have contended against the term "inferior," and rested the case upon the antiquity of power, and this would have brought on a set of very interesting and rational questions.

1st, What is the original fountain of power and honor in any country?

2d, Whether the prerogative does not belong to the people?

3d, Whether there is any such thing as the English constitution?

4th, Of what use is the crown to the people?

5th, Whether he who invented a crown was not an enemy to mankind?

6th, Whether it is not a shame for a man to spend a million a year and do no good for it, and whether the money might not be better applied?

7th, Whether such a man is not better dead than alive?

8th, Whether a Congress, constituted like that of America, is not the most happy and consistent form of government in the world?—With a number of others of the same import.

In short, the contention about the dividend might have distracted the nation; for nothing is more common than to agree in the conquest and quarrel for the prize; therefore it is, perhaps, a happy circumstance, that our successes have prevented the dispute.

If the Parliament had been thrown out in their claim, which it is most probable they would, the nation likewise would have been thrown out in their expectation; for as the taxes would have been laid on by the crown without the Parliament, the revenue arising therefrom, if any could have arisen, would not have gone into the exchequer, but into the privy purse, and so far from lessening the taxes, would not even have been added to them, but served only as pocket money to the crown. The more I reflect on this matter, the more I am satisfied at the blindness and ill policy of my countrymen, whose wisdom seems to operate without discernment, and their strength without an object.

To the great bulwark of the nation, I mean the mercantile and manufacturing part thereof, I likewise present my address. It is your interest to see America an independent, and not a conquered country. If conquered, she is ruined; and if ruined, poor; consequently the trade will be a trifle, and her credit doubtful. If independent, she flourishes, and from her flourishing must your profits arise. It matters nothing to you who governs America, if your manufactures find a consumption there. Some articles will consequently be obtained from other places, and it is right that they should; but the demand for others will increase, by the great influx of inhabitants which a state of independence and peace will occasion, and in the final event you may be enriched. The commerce of America is perfectly free, and ever will be so. She will consign away no part of it to any nation. She has not to her friends, and certainly will not to her enemies; though it is probable that your narrow-minded politicians, thinking to please you thereby, may some time or other unnecessarily make such a proposal. Trade flourishes best when it is free, and it is weak policy to attempt to fetter it. Her treaty with France is on the most liberal and generous principles, and the French, in their conduct towards her, have proved themselves to be philosophers, politicians, and gentlemen.

To the ministry I likewise address myself. You, gentlemen, have studied the ruin of your country, from which it is not within your abilities to rescue her. Your attempts to recover her are as ridiculous as your plans which involved her are detestable. The commissioners, being about to depart, will probably bring you this, and with it my sixth number, addressed to them; and in so doing they carry back more *Common Sense* than they brought, and you likewise will have more than when you sent them.

Having thus addressed you severally, I conclude by addressing you collectively. It is a long lane that has no turning. A period of sixteen years of misconduct and misfortune, is certainly long enough for any one nation to suffer under; and upon a supposition that war is not declared between France and you, I beg to place a line of conduct before you that will easily lead you out of all your troubles. It has been hinted before, and cannot be too much attended to.

Suppose America had remained unknown to Europe till the present year, and that Mr. Banks and Dr. Solander, in another voyage round the world, had made the first discovery of her, in the same condition that she is now in, of arts, arms, numbers, and civilization. What, I ask, in that case, would have been your conduct towards her? For *that* will point out what it ought to be now. The problems and their solutions are equal, and the right line of the one is the parallel of the other. The question takes in every circumstance that can possibly arise. It reduces politics to a simple thought, and is moreover a mode of investigation, in which, while you are studying your interest the simplicity of the case will cheat you into good temper. You have nothing to do but to suppose that you have found America, and she appears found to your hand, and while in the joy of your heart you stand still to admire her, the path of politics rises straight before you.

Were I disposed to paint a contrast, I could easily set off what you have done in the present case, against what you would have done in *that* case, and by justly opposing them, conclude a picture that would make you blush. But, as, when any of the prouder passions are hurt, it is much better philosophy to let a man slip into a good temper than to attack him in a bad one, for that reason, therefore, I only state the case, and leave you to reflect upon it.

To go a little back into politics, it will be found that the true interest of Britain lay in proposing and promoting the independence of America immediately after the last peace; for the expense which Britain had then incurred by defending America as her own dominions, ought to have shown her the policy and necessity of changing the *style* of the country, as the best probable method of preventing future wars and expense, and the only method by which she could hold the commerce without the charge of sovereignty. Besides which, the title which she assumed, of parent country, led to, and pointed out the propriety, wisdom and advantage of a separation; for, as in private life, children grow into men, and by setting up for themselves, extend and secure the interest of the whole family, so in the settlement of colonies large enough to admit of maturity, the same policy should be pursued, and the same consequences would follow. Nothing hurts the affections both of parents and children so much, as living too closely connected, and keeping up the distinction too long. Domineering will not do over those, who, by a progress in life, have become equal in rank to their parents, that is, when they have families of their own; and though they may conceive themselves the subjects of their advice, will not suppose them the objects of their government. I do not, by drawing this parallel, mean to admit the title of *parent country,* because, if it is due any where, it is due to Europe collectively, and the first settlers from England were driven here by persecution. I mean only to introduce the term for the sake of policy and to show from your title the line of your interest.

When you saw the state of strength and opulence, and that by her own industry, which America arrived at, you ought to have advised her to set up for herself, and proposed an alliance of interest with her, and in so doing you would have drawn, and that at her own expense, more real advantage, and more military supplies and assistance, both of ships and men, than from any weak and wrangling government that you could exercise over her. In short, had you studied only the domestic politics of a family, you would have learned how to govern the state; but, instead of this easy and natural line, you flew out into every thing which was wild and outrageous, till, by following the passion and stupidity of the pilot, you wrecked the vessel within sight of the shore.

Having shown what you ought to have done, I now proceed to show why it was not done. The caterpillar circle of the court had an interest to pursue, distinct from, and opposed to yours; for though by the independence of America and an alliance therewith, the trade would have continued, if not increased, as in many articles neither country can go to a better market, and though by defending and protecting herself, she would have been no expense to you, and consequently your national charges would have decreased, and your taxes might have been proportionably lessened thereby; yet the striking off so many places from the court calendar was put in opposition to the interest of the nation. The loss of thirteen government ships, with their appendages, here and in England, is a shocking sound in the ear of a hungry courtier. Your present king and ministry will be the ruin of you; and you had better risk a revolution and call a Congress, than be thus led on from madness to despair, and from despair to ruin. America has set you the example, and you may follow it and be free.

I now come to the last part, a war with France. This is what no man in his senses will advise you to, and all good men would wish to prevent. Whether France will declare war against you, is not for me in this place to mention, or to hint, even if I knew it; but it must be madness in you to do it first. The matter is come now to a full crisis, and peace is easy if willingly set about. Whatever you may think, France has behaved handsomely to you. She would have been unjust to herself to have acted otherwise than she did; and having accepted our offer of alliance she gave you genteel notice of it. There was nothing in her conduct reserved or indelicate, and while she announced her determination to support her treaty, she left you to give the first offence. America, on her part, has exhibited a character of firmness to the world. Unprepared and unarmed, without form or government, she singly opposed a nation that domineered over half the globe. The greatness of the deed demands respect; and though you may feel resentment, you are compelled both to wonder and admire.

Here I rest my arguments and finish my address. Such as it is, it is a gift, and you are welcome. It was always my design to dedicate a *Crisis* to you, when the time should come that would properly *make it a Crisis;* and when, likewise, I should catch myself in a temper to write it, and suppose you in a condition to read it. *That* time has now arrived, and with it the opportunity for conveyance. For the commissioners—*poor commissioners!* having proclaimed, that *"yet forty days and Nineveh shall be overthrown,"* have waited out the date, and, discontented with their God, are returning to their gourd.[6] And all the harm I wish them is, that it may not *wither* about their ears, and that they may not make their exit in the belly of a whale.

COMMON SENSE.

PHILADELPHIA, Nov. 21, 1778.

P. S.—Though in the tranquillity of my mind I have concluded with a laugh, yet I have something to mention to the *commissioners,* which, to them, is serious and worthy their attention. Their authority is derived from an Act of Parliament, which likewise describes and *limits* their *official* powers. Their commission, therefore, is only a recital, and personal investiture, of those powers, or a nomination and description of the persons who are to execute them. Had it contained any thing contrary to, or gone beyond the line of, the written law from which it is derived, and by which it is bound, it would, by the English constitution, have been treason in the crown, and the king been subject to an impeachment. He dared not, therefore, put in his commission what you have put in your proclamation, that is, he dared not have authorised you in that commission to burn and destroy any thing in America. You are both in the *act* and in the *commission* styled *commissioners for restoring peace,* and the methods for doing it are there pointed out. Your last proclamation is signed by you as commissioners *under that act.* You make Parliament the patron of its contents. Yet, in the body of it, you insert matters contrary both to the spirit and letter of the act, and what likewise your king dared not have put in his commission to you. The state of things in England, gentlemen, is too ticklish for you to run hazards. You are *accountable to Parliament for the execution of that act according*

---

[6] The reference, of course, is to the peace commissioners.—*Editor.*

to the letter of it. Your heads may pay for breaking it, for you certainly have broke it by exceeding it. And as a friend, who would wish you to escape the paw of the lion, as well as the belly of the whale, I civilly hint to you, *to keep within compass.*

Sir Harry Clinton,[7] strictly speaking, is as accountable as the rest; for though a general, he is likewise a commissioner, acting under a superior authority. His first obedience is due to the act; and his plea of being a general, will not and cannot clear him as a commissioner, for that would suppose the crown, in its single capacity, to have a power of dispensing with an Act of Parliament. Your situation, gentlemen, is nice and critical, and the more so because England is unsettled. Take heed! Remember the times of Charles the First! For Laud and St[r]afford fell by trusting to a hope like yours.[8]

Having thus shown you the danger of your proclamation, I now show you the folly of it. The means contradict your design: you threaten to lay waste, in order to render America a useless acquisition of alliance to France. I reply, that the more destruction you commit (if you could do it) the more valuable to France you make that alliance. You can destroy only houses and goods; and by so doing you increase our demand upon her for materials and merchandise; for the wants of one nation, provided it has *freedom* and *credit,* naturally produce riches to the other; and, as you can neither ruin the land nor prevent the vegetation, you would increase the exportation of our produce in payment, which would be to her a new fund of wealth. In short, had you cast about for a plan on purpose to enrich your enemies, you could not have hit upon a better.

C. S.

[7] Sir Henry Clinton succeeded Sir William Howe as commander-in-chief of the British army in America.—*Editor.*

[8] Archbishop Laud and the Earl of Strafford (Sir Thomas Wentworth), ministers to Charles the First, were arrested by order of Parliament in November 1640, tried for treason and executed.—*Editor.*

THE AMERICAN CRISIS

VIII

Address to the People of England

"TRUSTING (says the king of England in his speech of November last,) in the divine providence, and in the justice of my cause, I am firmly resolved to prosecute the war with vigor, and to make every exertion in order to compel our enemies to equitable terms of peace and accommodation." To this declaration the United States of America, and the confederated powers of Europe will reply, *if Britain will have war, she shall have enough of it.*

Five years have nearly elapsed since the commencement of hostilities, and every campaign, by a gradual decay, has lessened your ability to conquer, without producing a serious thought on your condition or your fate. Like a prodigal lingering in an habitual consumption, you feel the relics of life, and mistake them for recovery. New schemes, like new medicines, have administered fresh hopes, and prolonged the disease instead of curing it. A change of generals, like a change of physicians, served only to keep the flattery alive, and furnish new pretences for new extravagance.

"Can Britain fail?" [1] has been proudly asked at the undertaking of every enterprise; and that *"whatever she wills is fate,"* [2] has been given with the solemnity of prophetic confidence; and though the question has been constantly replied to by disappointment, and the prediction falsified by misfortune, yet still the insult continued, and your catalogue

---

[1] Whitehead's New Year's ode for 1776.—*Author.*

[2] Ode at the installation of Lord North, for Chancellor of the University of Oxford.—*Author.*

of national evils increased therewith. Eager to persuade the world of her power, she considered destruction as the minister of greatness, and conceived that the glory of a nation like that of an [American] Indian, lay in the number of its scalps and the miseries which it inflicts.

Fire, sword and want, as far as the arms of Britain could extend them, have been spread with wanton cruelty along the coast of America; and while you, remote from the scene of suffering, had nothing to lose and as little to dread, the information reached you like a tale of antiquity, in which the distance of time defaces the conception, and changes the severest sorrows into conversable amusement.

This makes the second paper, addressed perhaps in vain, to the people of England. That advice should be taken wherever example has failed, or precept be regarded where warning is ridiculed, is like a picture of hope resting on despair: but when time shall stamp with universal currency the facts you have long encountered with a laugh, and the irresistible evidence of accumulated losses, like the handwriting on the wall, shall add terror to distress, you will then, in a conflict of suffering, learn to sympathize with others by feeling for yourselves.

The triumphant appearance of the combined fleets in the channel and at your harbor's mouth, and the expedition of Captain Paul Jones, on the western and eastern coasts of England and Scotland,[3] will, by placing you in the condition of an endangered country, read to you a stronger lecture on the calamities of invasion, and bring to your minds a truer picture of promiscuous distress, than the most finished rhetoric can describe or the keenest imagination conceive.

Hitherto you have experienced the expenses, but nothing of the miseries of war. Your disappointments have been accompanied with no immediate suffering, and your losses came to you only by intelligence. Like fire at a distance you heard not even the cry; you felt not the danger, you saw not the confusion. To you every thing has been foreign but the taxes to support it. You knew not what it was to be alarmed at midnight with an armed enemy in the streets. You were strangers to the

---

[3] In the summer of 1779 John Paul Jones commanded an expedition upon the coasts of Great Britain in order to bring the war home to the enemy. A terrific naval battle took place on September 23, 1779 between the British ship *Serapis* and the American vessel the *Bon Homme Richard* commanded by Paul Jones. The Americans emerged victorious and the moral effect of the victory was enormous. The King of France made Paul Jones a knight of the order of merit and the Empress of Russia bestowed upon him the ribbon of St. Anne. Jones was a very close friend of Paine and the writer gained great satisfaction from the reference to the American naval victory.—*Editor.*

distressing scene of a family in flight, and to the thousand restless cares and tender sorrows that incessantly arose. To see women and children wandering in the severity of winter, with the broken remains of a well furnished house, and seeking shelter in every crib and hut, were matters that you had no conception of. You knew not what it was to stand by and see your goods chopped for fuel, and your beds ripped to pieces to make packages for plunder. The misery of others, like a tempestuous night, added to the pleasures of your own security. You even enjoyed the storm, by contemplating the difference of conditions, and that which carried sorrow into the breasts of thousands served but to heighten in you a species of tranquil pride. Yet these are but the fainter sufferings of war, when compared with carnage and slaughter, the miseries of a military hospital, or a town in flames.

The people of America, by anticipating distress, had fortified their minds against every species you could inflict. They had resolved to abandon their homes, to resign them to destruction, and to seek new settlements rather than submit. Thus familiarized to misfortune, before it arrived, they bore their portion with the less regret: the justness of their cause was a continual source of consolation, and the hope of final victory, which never left them, served to lighten the load and sweeten the cup allotted them to drink.

But when their troubles shall become yours, and invasion be transferred upon the invaders, you will have neither their extended wilderness to fly to, their cause to comfort you, nor their hope to rest upon. Distress with them was sharpened by no self-reflection. They had not brought it on themselves. On the contrary, they had by every proceeding endeavored to avoid it, and had descended even below the mark of congressional character, to prevent a war. The national honor or the advantages of independence were matters which, at the commencement of the dispute, they had never studied, and it was only at the last moment that the measure was resolved on. Thus circumstanced, they naturally and conscientiously felt a dependence upon providence. They had a clear pretension to it, and had they failed therein, infidelity had gained a triumph.

But your condition is the reverse of theirs. Every thing you suffer you have sought: nay, had you created mischiefs on purpose to inherit them, you could not have secured your title by a firmer deed. The world awakens with no pity at your complaints. You felt none for others; you deserve none for yourselves. Nature does not interest herself in cases like yours, but, on the contrary, turns from them with dislike, and abandons them to punishment. You may now present memorials to what court you please, but so far as America is the object, none will listen. The policy of Europe, and the propensity there in every mind to curb insulting ambition, and bring cruelty to judgment, are unitedly against you; and where nature and interest reinforce with each other, the compact is too intimate to be dissolved.

Make but the case of others your own, and your own theirs, and you will then have a clear idea of the whole. Had France acted towards her colonies as you have done, you would have branded her with every epithet of abhorrence; and had you, like her, stepped in to succor a struggling people, all Europe must have echoed with your own applauses. But entangled in the passion of dispute you see it not as you ought, and form opinions thereon which suit with no interest but your own. You wonder that America does not rise in union with you to impose on herself a portion of your taxes and reduce herself to unconditional submission. You are amazed that the southern powers of Europe do not assist you in conquering a country which is afterwards to be turned against themselves; and that the northern ones do not contribute to reinstate you in America who already enjoy the market for naval stores by the separation. You seem surprised that Holland does not pour in her succors to maintain you mistress of the seas, when her own commerce is suffering by your act of navigation; or that any country should study her own interest while yours is on the carpet.

Such excesses of passionate folly, and unjust as well as unwise resentment, have driven you on, like Pharaoh, to unpitied miseries, and while the importance of the quarrel shall perpetuate your disgrace, the flag of America will carry it round the world. The natural feelings of every rational being will be against you, and wherever the story shall be told, you will have neither excuse nor consolation left. With an unsparing hand, and an insatiable mind, you have desolated the world, to gain dominion and to lose it; and while, in a frenzy of avarice and ambition, the east and the west are doomed to tributary bondage, you rapidly earned destruction as the wages of a nation.

At the thoughts of a war at home, every man amongst you ought to tremble. The prospect is far more dreadful there than in America. Here the party that was against the measures of the continent were in general composed of a kind of neutrals, who added strength to neither army. There does not exist a being so devoid of sense and sentiment as to covet *"unconditional submission,"* and therefore no man in America could be with you in principle. Several might from a cowardice of mind, prefer it to the hardships and dangers of opposing it; but the same disposition that gave them such a choice, unfitted them to act either for or against us. But England is rent into parties, with equal shares of resolution. The principle which produced the war divides the nation. Their animosities are in the highest state of fermentation, and both sides, by a call of the militia, are in arms. No human foresight can discern, no conclusion can be formed, what turn a war might take, if once set on foot by an invasion. She is not now in a fit disposition to make a common cause of her own affairs, and having no conquests to hope for abroad, and nothing but expenses arising at home, her everything is staked upon a defensive combat, and the further she goes the worse she is off.

There are situations that a nation may be in, in which peace or war, abstracted from every other consideration, may be politically right or wrong. When nothing can be lost by a war, but what must be lost without it, war is then the policy of that country; and such was the situation of America at the commencement of hostilities: but when no security can be gained by a war, but what may be accomplished by a peace, the case becomes reversed, and such now is the situation of England.

That America is beyond the reach of conquest, is a fact which experience has shown and time confirmed, and this admitted, what, I ask, is now the object of contention? If there be any honor in pursuing self-destruction with inflexible passion—if national suicide be the perfection of national glory, you may, with all the pride of criminal happiness, expire unenvied and unrivalled. But when the tumult of war shall cease, and the tempest of present passions be succeeded by calm reflection, or when those, who, surviving its fury, shall inherit from you a legacy of debts and misfortunes, when the yearly revenue shall scarcely be able to discharge the interest of the one, and no possible remedy be left for the other, ideas far different from the present will arise, and embitter the remembrance of former follies. A mind disarmed of its rage feels no pleasure in contemplating a frantic quarrel. Sickness of thought, the sure consequence of conduct like yours, leaves no ability for enjoyment, no relish for resentment; and though, like a man in a fit, you feel not the injury of the struggle, nor distinguish between strength and disease, the weakness will nevertheless be proportioned to the violence, and the sense of pain increase with the recovery.

To what persons or to whose system of politics you owe your present

state of wretchedness, is a matter of total indifference to America. They
have contributed, however unwillingly, to set her above themselves, and
she, in the tranquillity of conquest, resigns the inquiry. The case now is
not so properly who began the war, as who continues it. That there are
men in all countries to whom a state of war is a mine of wealth, is a fact
never to be doubted. Characters like these naturally breed in the putre-
faction of distempered times, and after fattening on the disease, they
perish with, or, impregnated with the stench, retreat into obscurity.

But there are several erroneous notions to which you likewise owe a
share of your misfortunes, and which, if continued, will only increase
your trouble and your losses. An opinion hangs about the gentlemen of
the minority, that America would relish measures under *their* administration, which she would not from the present cabinet. On this rock Lord
Chatham [4] would have split had he gained the helm, and several of his
survivors are steering the same course. Such distinctions in the infancy
of the argument had some degree of foundation, but they now serve no
other purpose than to lengthen out a war, in which the limits of a
dispute, being fixed by the fate of arms, and guaranteed by treaties, are
not to be changed or altered by trivial circumstances.

The ministry, and many of the minority, sacrifice their time in disputing on a question with which they have nothing to do, namely,
whether America shall be independent or not. Whereas the only question that can come under their determination is, whether they will
accede to it or not. They confound a military question with a political
one, and undertake to supply by a vote what they lost by a battle. Say
she shall not be independent, and it will signify as much as if they voted
against a decree of fate, or say that she shall, and she will be no more
independent than before. Questions which, when determined, cannot
be executed, serve only to show the folly of dispute and the weakness of
disputants.

From a long habit of calling America your own, you suppose her
governed by the same prejudices and conceits which govern yourselves.
Because you have set up a particular denomination of religion to the
exclusion of all others, you imagine she must do the same, and because
you, with an unsociable narrowness of mind, have cherished enmity

[4] William Pitt, soon to assume the title of Lord Chatham, became Prime Minister of
England in 1766. The "great Colossus Pitt" fell from power in 1767. Pitt was extremely
popular in America for a time because of his conviction that Parliament could not tax the
colonies. He lost some of his popularity, however, when he agreed to the acceptance of a
peerage.—*Editor*.

against France and Spain, you suppose her alliance must be defective in friendship. Copying her notions of the world from you, she formerly thought as you instructed, but now feeling herself free, and the prejudice removed, she thinks and acts upon a different system. It frequently happens that in proportion as we are taught to dislike persons and countries, not knowing why, we feel an ardor of esteem upon the removal of the mistake: it seems as if something was to be made amends for, and we eagerly give in to every office of friendship, to atone for the injury of the error.

But, perhaps, there is something in the extent of countries, which, among the generality of people, insensibly communicates extension of the mind. The soul of an islander, in its native state, seems bounded by the foggy confines of the water's edge, and all beyond affords to him matters only for profit or curiosity, not for friendship. His island is to him his world, and fixed to that, his every thing centers in it; while those who are inhabitants of a continent, by casting their eye over a larger field, take in likewise a larger intellectual circuit, and thus approaching nearer to an acquaintance with the universe, their atmosphere of thought is extended, and their liberality fills a wider space. In short, our minds seem to be measured by countries when we are men, as they are by places when we are children, and until something happens to disentangle us from the prejudice, we serve under it without perceiving it.

In addition to this, it may be remarked, that men who study any universal science, the principles of which are universally known, or admitted, and applied without distinction to the common benefit of all countries, obtain thereby a larger share of philanthropy than those who only study national arts and improvements. Natural philosophy, mathematics and astronomy, carry the mind from the country to the creation, and give it a fitness suited to the extent. It was not Newton's honor, neither could it be his pride, that he was an Englishman, but that he was a philosopher: the heavens had liberated him from the prejudices of an island, and science had expanded his soul as boundless as his studies.

COMMON SENSE.

PHILADELPHIA, March, 1780.[5]

[5] A year and a half had passed since the last *Crisis* paper had been issued.

THE AMERICAN CRISIS

IX

The Ninth *Crisis* was written during an extremely gloomy period of the War. On May 28, 1780, Washington's letter to Joseph Reed of Pennsylvania describing the desperate situation of the American Army was read to the Pennsylvania Assembly by Thomas Paine, the Clerk. "I assure you," Paine read from Washington's letter, "every idea you can form of our distresses will fall short of the reality. There is such a combination of circumstances to exhaust the patience of the soldiery that it begins at length to be worn out, and we see in every line of the army the most serious features of mutiny and sedition."

Paine immediately proposed that a fund of money be raised to aid the patriot cause and headed the subscription with five hundred dollars. The idea rapidly spread, and resulted in the raising of £300,000 which was used to supply the Army through the campaign.

On May 12, 1780, Charleston, South Carolina, besieged by the British for forty days, surrendered and General Lincoln and his whole army of 3,000 Continental soldiers became prisoners of war. His spirit and confidence not at all dashed by this discouraging news, Paine declared in this *Crisis,* which is dated June 9, 1780, that the reported fate of Charleston, "afflicting as it may be . . . will renew in us the spirit of former days, and will produce in us an advantage more important than its loss." Such piecemeal work, he points out, was not conquering the continent. In a postscript he adds: "Charleston is gone, and I believe for the want of a sufficient supply of provisions. The man that does not now feel for the honor of the best and noblest cause that ever a country engaged in, and exert himself accordingly, is no longer worthy of a peaceable residence among a people determined to be free."—*Editor*.

HAD America pursued her advantages with half the spirit that she resisted her misfortunes, she would, before now, have been a conquering and a peaceful people; but lulled in the lap of soft tranquillity, she rested on her hopes, and adversity only has convulsed her into action. Whether subtlety or sincerity at the close of the last year induced the enemy to an appearance for peace, is a point not material to know; it is sufficient that we see the effects it has had on our politics, and that we sternly rise to resent the delusion.

The war, on the part of America, has been a war of natural feelings. Brave in distress; serene in conquest; drowsy while at rest; and in every situation generously disposed to peace; a dangerous calm, and a most heightened zeal have, as circumstances varied, succeeded each other. Every passion but that of despair has been called to a tour of duty; and so mistaken has been the enemy, of our abilities and disposition, that when she supposed us conquered, we rose the conquerors. The extensiveness of the United States, and the variety of their resources; the universality of their cause, the quick operation of their feelings, and the similarity of their sentiments, have, in every trying situation, produced a *something,* which, favored by providence, and pursued with ardor, has accomplished in an instant the business of a campaign. We have never deliberately sought victory, but snatched it; and bravely undone in an hour the blotted operations of a season.

The reported fate of Charleston, like the misfortunes of 1776, has at last called forth a spirit, and kindled up a flame, which perhaps no other event could have produced. If the enemy has circulated a falsehood, they have unwisely aggravated us into life, and if they have told us the truth, they have unintentionally done us a service. We were returning with folded arms from the fatigues of war, and thinking and sitting leisurely down to enjoy repose. The dependence that has been put upon Charleston threw a drowsiness over America. We looked on the business done—the conflict over—the matter settled—or that all which remained unfinished would follow of itself. In this state of dangerous relaxation, exposed to the poisonous infusions of the enemy, and having no common danger to attract our attention, we were extinguishing, by stages, the ardor we began with, and surrendering by piece-meal the virtue that defended us.

Afflicting as the loss of Charleston may be, yet if it universally rouse us from the slumber of twelve months past, and renew in us the spirit of former days, it will produce an advantage more important than its loss. America ever *is* what she *thinks* herself to be. Governed by sentiment, and acting her own mind, she becomes, as she pleases, the victor or the victim.

It is not the conquest of towns, nor the accidental capture of garrisons, than can reduce a country so extensive as this. The sufferings of one part can never be relieved by the exertions of another, and there is no situation the enemy can be placed in that does not afford to us the same advantages which he seeks himself. By dividing his force, he leaves every post attackable. It is a mode of war that carries with it a confession of weakness, and goes on the principle of distress rather than conquest.

The decline of the enemy is visible, not only in their operations, but in their plans; Charleston originally made but a secondary object in the system of attack, and it is now become their principal one, because they have not been able to succeed elsewhere. It would have carried a cowardly appearance in Europe had they formed their grand expedition, in 1776, against a part of the continent where there was no army, or not a sufficient one to oppose them; but failing year after year in their impressions here, and to the eastward and northward, they deserted their capital design, and prudently contenting themselves with what they can get, give a flourish of honor to conceal disgrace.

But this piece-meal work is not conquering the continent. It is a discredit in them to attempt it, and in us to suffer it. It is now full time to put an end to a war of aggravations, which, on one side, has no possible object, and on the other has every inducement which honor, interest, safety and happiness can inspire. If we suffer them much longer to remain among us, we shall become as bad as themselves. An association of vice will reduce us more than the sword. A nation hardened in the practice of iniquity knows better how to profit by it, than a young country newly corrupted. We are not a match for them in the line of advantageous guilt, nor they for us on the principles which we bravely set out with. Our first days were our days of honor. They have marked the character of America wherever the story of her wars are told; and convinced of this, we have nothing to do but wisely and unitedly to tread the well known track. The progress of a war is often as ruinous to individuals, as the issue of it is to a nation; and it is not only necessary that our forces be such that we be conquerors in the end, but that by timely exertions we be secure in the interim. The present campaign will afford an opportunity which has never presented itself before, and the preparations for it are equally necessary, whether Charleston stand or fall. Suppose the first, it is in that case only a failure of the enemy, not a defeat. All the conquest that a besieged town can hope for, is, not to be conquered; and compelling an enemy to raise the siege, is to the besieged a victory. But there must be a probability amounting almost to a certainty, that would justify a garrison marching out to attack a retreat. Therefore should Charleston not be taken, and the enemy abandon the siege, every other part of the continent should prepare to meet them; and, on the contrary, should it be taken, the same preparations are necessary to balance the loss, and put ourselves in a position to co-operate with our allies, immediately on their arrival.

We are not now fighting our battles alone, as we were in 1776; England, from a malicious disposition to America, has not only not declared war against France and Spain, but, the better to prosecute her passions here, has afforded those powers no military object, and avoids them, to distress us. She will suffer her West India islands to be overrun by France, and her southern settlements to be taken by Spain, rather than quit the object that gratifies her revenge. This conduct, on the part of Britain, has pointed out the propriety of France sending a naval and land force to co-operate with America on the spot. Their arrival cannot be very distant, nor the ravages of the enemy long. The recruiting the army, and procuring the supplies, are the two things most necessary to be accomplished, and a capture of either of the enemy's divisions will restore to America peace and plenty.

At a crisis, big, like the present, with expectation and events, the whole country is called to unanimity and exertion. Not an ability ought now to sleep, that can produce but a mite to the general good, nor even a whisper to pass that militates against it. The necessity of the case, and the importance of the consequences, admit no delay from a friend, no apology from an enemy. To spare now, would be the height of extravagance, and to consult present ease, would be to sacrifice it perhaps forever.

America, rich in patriotism and produce, can want neither men nor supplies, when a serious necessity calls them forth. The slow operation of taxes, owing to the extensiveness of collection, and their depreciated value before they arrived in the treasury, have, in many instances, thrown a burden upon government, which has been artfully interpreted by the enemy into a general decline throughout the country. Yet this, inconvenient as it may at first appear, is not only remediable, but may be turned to an immediate advantage; for it makes no real difference, whether a certain number of men, or company of militia (and in this country every man is a militia-man), are directed by law to send a recruit at their own expense, or whether a tax is laid on them for that purpose, and the man hired by government afterwards. The first, if there is any difference, is both cheapest and best, because it saves the expense which would attend collecting it as a tax, and brings the man sooner into the field than the modes of recruiting formerly used; and, on this principle, a law has been passed in this state, for recruiting two men from each company of militia, which will add upwards of a thousand to the force of the country.

But the flame which has broken forth in this city since the report from New York, of the loss of Charleston, not only does honor to the place, but, like the blaze of 1776, will kindle into action the scattered sparks throughout America. The valor of a country may be learned by the bravery of its soldiery, and the general cast of its inhabitants, but confidence of success is best discovered by the active measures pursued by men of property; and when the spirit of enterprise becomes so universal as to act at once on all ranks of men, a war may then, and not till then, be styled truly popular.

In 1776, the ardor of the enterprising part was considerably checked by the real revolt of some, and the coolness of others. But in the present case, there is a firmness in the substance and property of the country to the public cause. An association has been entered into by the merchants, tradesmen, and principal inhabitants of the city [Philadelphia], to receive and support the new state money at the value of gold and silver; a measure which, while it does them honor, will likewise contribute to their interest, by rendering the operations of the campaign convenient and effectual.[1]

Nor has the spirit of exertion stopped here. A voluntary subscription is likewise begun, to raise a fund of hard money, to be given as bounties, to fill up the full quota of the Pennsylvania line. It has been the remark of the enemy, that every thing in America has been done by the force of government; but when she sees individuals throwing in their voluntary aid, and facilitating the public measures in concert with the established

---

[1] Paine forgets to mention the fact that it was he, clerk of the Pennsylvania Assembly, who proposed the subscription and headed it with a contribution of five hundred dollars.— Editor.

powers of the country, it will convince her that the cause of America stands not on the will of a few but on the broad foundation of property and popularity.[2]

Thus aided and thus supported, disaffection will decline, and the withered head of tyranny expire in America. The ravages of the enemy will be short and limited, and like all their former ones, will produce a victory over themselves.

COMMON SENSE.

PHILADELPHIA, June 9, 1780.

P. S. At the time of writing this number of the Crisis, the loss of Charleston, though believed by some, was more confidently disbelieved by others. But there ought to be no longer a doubt upon the matter. Charleston is gone, and I believe for the want of a sufficient supply of provisions. The man that does not now feel for the honor of the best and noblest cause that ever a country engaged in, and exert himself accordingly, is no longer worthy of a peaceable residence among a people determined to be free.

C. S.

[2] The linking of "property" with "popularity" indicates Paine's interest in cementing the greatest unity of all classes to achieve victory. By "property" he meant the action of several wealthy merchants in Philadelphia in aiding Paine in forming what became the Bank of North America to finance the supplies needed by the Continental Army.— *Editor*.

THE CRISIS EXTRAORDINARY

The particular crisis which led Paine to write this supplementary number of *The American Crisis* was financial in character. Congress was almost entirely without power to levy taxes. "One State," wrote Washington on May 31, 1780, "will comply with a requisition of Congress; another neglects to do it; a third executes it by halves; and all differ either in the manner, the matter, or so much in point of time, that we are always working up hill, and ever shall be; and, while such a system as the present one or rather want of one prevails, we shall ever be unable to apply our strength or resources to any advantage." "The crisis, in every point of view, is extraordinary," Washington observed, and it is this sentence that probably inspired Paine to entitle his article *The Crisis Extraordinary*. In the article Paine presents a plan for raising revenue, and indicates the necessity for such a plan as well as the advantages to be derived from it. He compares the English system of taxation to the American and points out that we can defend "the country for one eighth of what Britain would levy on us."

At the end of *Crisis Extraordinary,* Paine adds in the form of a postscript the story of Benedict Arnold's treason as indicated in his attempt to turn over to the British, through Major André, the vital stronghold, West Point.

In order to sell his work as cheaply as possible and provide for it the widest possible distribution, Paine paid for the printing himself.—*Editor.*

On the Subject of Taxation

IT IS impossible to sit down and think seriously on the affairs of America, but the original principles upon which she resisted, and the glow and ardor which they inspired, will occur like the undefaced remembrance of a lovely scene. To trace over in imagination the purity of the cause, the voluntary sacrifices that were made to support it, and all the various turnings of the war in its defence, is at once both paying and receiving respect. The principles deserve to be remembered, and to remember them rightly is repossessing them. In this indulgence of generous recollection, we become gainers by what we seem to give, and the more we bestow the richer we become.

So extensively right was the ground on which America proceeded, that it not only took in every just and liberal sentiment which could impress the heart, but made it the direct interest of every class and order of men to defend the country. The war, on the part of Britain, was originally a war of covetousness. The sordid and not the splendid passions gave it being. The fertile fields and prosperous infancy of America appeared to her as mines for tributary wealth. She viewed the hive, and disregarding the industry that had enriched it, thirsted for the honey. But in the present stage of her affairs, the violence of temper is added to the rage of avarice; and therefore, that which at the first setting out proceeded from purity of principle and public interest, is now heightened by all the obligations of necessity; for it requires but little knowledge of human nature to discern what would be the consequence, were America again reduced to the subjection of Britain. Uncontrolled power, in the hands of an incensed, imperious, and rapacious conqueror, is an engine of dreadful execution, and woe be to that country over which it can be exercised. The names of Whig and Tory would then be sunk in the general term of rebel, and the oppression, whatever it might be, would, with very few instances of exception, light equally on all.

Britain did not go to war with America for the sake of dominion, because she was then in possession; neither was it for the extension of trade and commerce, because she had monopolized the whole, and the country had yielded to it; neither was it to extinguish what *she* might call rebellion, because before she began no resistance existed. It could then be from no other motive than avarice, or a design of establishing, in the first instance, the same taxes in America as are paid in England (which, as I shall presently show, are above eleven times heavier than the taxes we now pay for the present year, 1780) or, in the second instance, to confiscate the whole property of America, in case of resistance and conquest of the latter, of which she had then no doubt.

I shall now proceed to show what the taxes in England are, and what the yearly expense of the present war is to her—what the taxes of this country amount to, and what the annual expense of defending it effectually will be to us; and shall endeavor concisely to point out the cause of our difficulties, and the advantages on one side, and the consequences on the other, in case we do, or do not, put ourselves in an effectual state of defence. I mean to be open, candid, and sincere. I see a universal wish to expel the enemy from the country, a murmuring because the war is not carried on with more vigor, and my intention is to show, as shortly as possible, both the reason and the remedy.

The number of souls in England (exclusive of Scotland and Ireland) is seven millions,[1] and the number of souls in America is three millions.

The amount of taxes in England (exclusive of Scotland and Ireland) was, before the present war commenced, eleven millions six hundred and forty-two thousand six hundred and fifty-three pounds sterling; which, on an average, is no less a sum than one pound thirteen shillings and three-pence sterling per head per annum, men, women, and children; besides county taxes, taxes for the support of the poor, and a tenth of all the produce of the earth for the support of the bishops and clergy.[2] Nearly five millions of this sum went annually to pay the interest of the national debt, contracted by former wars, and the remaining sum of six millions six hundred and forty-two thousand six hundred pounds was

[1] This is taking the highest number that the people of England have been, or can be rated at.—*Author.*

[2] The following is taken from Dr. Price's state of the taxes of England, pp. 96, 97, 98.
An account of the money drawn from the public by taxes, annually, being the medium of three years before the year 1776.

Amount of customs in England	2,528,275 *l.*
Amount of the excise in England	4,649,892
Land tax at 3*s.*	1,300,000
Land tax at 1*s.* in the pound	450,000
Salt duties	218,739
Duties on stamps, cards, dice, advertisements, bonds, leases, indentures, newspapers, almanacks, etc.	280,788
Duties on houses and windows	385,369
Post office, seizures, wine licences, hackney coaches, etc.	250,000
Annual profits from lotteries	150,000
Expense of collecting the excise in England	297,887
Expense of collecting the customs in England	468,703
Interest of loans on the land tax at 4*s.* expenses of collection, militia, etc.	250,000
Perquisites, etc. to custom-house officers, &c. supposed	250,000
Expense of collecting the salt duties in England 10½ per cent	27,000
Bounties on fish exported	18,000
Expense of collecting the duties on stamps, cards, advertisements, etc. at 5 and ¼ per cent.	18,000

Total   11,642,653 *l.*
Author.

applied to defray the yearly expense of government, the peace establishment of the army and navy, placemen, pensioners, etc.; consequently the whole of the enormous taxes being thus appropriated, she had nothing to spare out of them towards defraying the expenses of the present war or any other. Yet had she not been in debt at the beginning of the war, as we were not, and, like us, had only a land and not a naval war to carry on, her then revenue of eleven millions and a half pounds sterling would have defrayed all her annual expenses of war and government within each year.

But this not being the case with her, she is obliged to borrow about ten millions pounds sterling, yearly, to prosecute the war that she is now engaged in, (this year she borrowed twelve) and lay on new taxes to discharge the interest; allowing that the present war has cost her only fifty millions sterling, the interest thereon, at five per cent., will be two millions and an half; therefore the amount of her taxes now must be fourteen millions, which on an average is no less than forty shillings sterling, per head, men, women and children, throughout the nation. Now as this expense of fifty millions was borrowed on the hopes of conquering America, and as it was avarice which first induced her to commence the war, how truly wretched and deplorable would the condition of this country be, were she, by her own remissness, to suffer an enemy of such a disposition, and so circumstanced, to reduce her to subjection.

I now proceed to the revenues of America.

I have already stated the number of souls in America to be three millions, and by a calculation that I have made, which I have every reason to believe is sufficiently correct, the whole expense of the war, and the support of the several governments, may be defrayed for two million pounds sterling annually; which, on an average, is thirteen shillings and four pence per head, men, women, and children, and the peace establishment at the end of the war will be but three quarters of a million, or five shillings sterling per head. Now, throwing out of the question everything of honor, principle, happiness, freedom, and reputation in the world, and taking it up on the simple ground of interest, I put the following case:

Suppose Britain was to conquer America, and, as a conqueror, was to lay her under no other conditions than to pay the same proportion towards her annual revenue which the people of England pay: our share, in that case, would be six million pounds sterling yearly. Can it then be a question, whether it is best to raise two millions to defend the country, and govern it ourselves, and only three quarters of a million afterwards, or pay six millions to have it conquered, and let the enemy govern it?

Can it be supposed that conquerors would choose to put themselves in a worse condition than what they granted to the conquered? In England, the tax on rum is five shillings and one penny sterling per gallon, which is one silver dollar and fourteen coppers. Now would it not be laughable to imagine, that after the expense they have been at, they would let either Whig or Tory drink it cheaper than themselves? Coffee, which is so inconsiderable an article of consumption and support here, is there loaded with a duty which makes the price between five and six shillings per pound, and a penalty of fifty pounds sterling on any person detected in roasting it in his own house. There is scarcely a necessary of life that you can eat, drink, wear, or enjoy, that is not there loaded with a tax; even the light from heaven is only permitted to shine into their dwellings by paying eighteen pence sterling per window annually; and the humblest drink of life, small beer, cannot there be purchased without a tax of nearly two coppers per gallon, besides a heavy tax upon the malt, and another on the hops before it is brewed, exclusive of a land-tax on the earth which produces them. In short, the condition of that country, in point of taxation, is so oppressive, the number of her poor so great, and the extravagance and rapaciousness of the court so enormous, that, were they to effect a conquest of America, it is then only that the distresses of America would begin. Neither would it signify anything to a man whether he be Whig or Tory. The people of England, and the ministry of that country, know us by no such distinctions. What they want is clear, solid revenue, and the modes which they would take to procure it, would operate alike on all. Their manner of reasoning would be short, because they would naturally infer, that if we were able to carry on a war of five or six years against them, we were able to pay the same taxes which they do.

I have already stated that the expense of conducting the present war, and the government of the several states, may be done for two millions sterling, and the establishment in the time of peace, for three quarters of a million.[3]

[3] I have made the calculations in sterling, because it is a rate generally known in all the states, and because, likewise, it admits of an easy comparison between our expenses to support the war, and those of the enemy. Four silver dollars and a half is one pound sterling, and three pence over.—*Author.*

As to navy matters, they flourish so well, and are so well attended to by individuals, that I think it consistent on every principle of real use and economy, to turn the navy into hard money (keeping only three or four packets) and apply it to the service of the army. We shall not have a ship the less; the use of them, and the benefit from them, will be greatly increased, and their expense saved. We are now allied with a formidable naval power,[4] from whom we derive the assistance of a navy. And the line in which we can prosecute the war, so as to reduce the common enemy and benefit the alliance most effectually, will be by attending closely to the land service.

I estimate the charge of keeping up and maintaining an army, officering them, and all expenses included, sufficient for the defence of the country, to be equal to the expense of forty thousand men at thirty pounds sterling per head, which is one million two hundred thousand pounds.

I likewise allow four hundred thousand pounds for continental expenses at home and abroad.

And four hundred thousand pounds for the support of the several state governments—the amount will then be:

For the army	1,200,000 *l.*
Continental expenses at home and abroad	400,000
Government of the several states	400,000
Total	2,000,000 *l.*

I take the proportion of this state, Pennsylvania, to be an eighth part of the thirteen United States; the quota then for us to raise will be two hundred and fifty thousand pounds sterling; two hundred thousand of which will be our share for the support and pay of the army, and continental expenses at home and abroad, and fifty thousand pounds for the support of the state government.

In order to gain an idea of the proportion in which the raising such a sum will fall, I make the following calculation:

Pennsylvania contains three hundred and seventy-five thousand inhabitants, men, women and children; which is likewise an eighth of the number of inhabitants of the whole United States: therefore, two hundred and fifty thousand pounds sterling to be raised among three hundred and seventy-five thousand persons, is, on an average, thirteen shillings and four pence per head, per annum, or something more than one

---

[4] The reference is to France.—*Editor.*

shilling sterling per month. And our proportion of three quarters of a million for the government of the country, in time of peace, will be ninety-three thousand seven hundred and fifty pounds sterling; fifty thousand of which will be for the government expenses of the state, and forty-three thousand seven hundred and fifty pounds for continental expenses at home and abroad.

The peace establishment then will, on an average, be five shillings sterling per head. Whereas, was England now to stop, and the war cease, her peace establishment would continue the same as it is now, viz. forty shillings per head; therefore was our taxes necessary for carrying on the war, as much per head as hers now is, and the difference to be only whether we should, at the end of the war, pay at the rate of five shillings per head, or forty shillings per head, the case needs no thinking of. But as we can securely defend and keep the country for one third less than what our burden would be if it was conquered, and support the governments afterwards for one eighth of what Britain would levy on us, and could I find a miser whose heart never felt the emotion of a spark of principle, even that man, uninfluenced by every love but the love of money, and capable of no attachment but to his interest, would and must, from the frugality which governs him, contribute to the defence of the country, or he ceases to be a miser and becomes an idiot. But when we take in with it every thing that can ornament mankind; when the line of our interest becomes the line of our happiness; when all that can cheer and animate the heart, when a sense of honor, fame, character, at home and abroad, are interwoven not only with the security but the increase of property, there exists not a man in America, unless he be an hired emissary, who does not see that his good is connected with keeping up a sufficient defence.

I do not imagine that an instance can be produced in the world, of a country putting herself to such an amazing charge to conquer and enslave another, as Britain has done. The sum is too great for her to think of with any tolerable degree of temper; and when we consider the burden she sustains, as well as the disposition she has shown, it would be the height of folly in us to suppose that she would not reimburse herself by the most rapid means, had she America once more within her power. With such an oppression of expense, what would an empty conquest be to her! What relief under such circumstances could she derive from a victory without a prize? It was money, it was revenue she first went to war for, and nothing but *that* would satisfy her. It is not the nature of avarice to be satisfied with any thing else. Every passion that acts upon mankind has a peculiar mode of operation. Many of them are temporary and fluctuating; they admit of cessation and variety. But avarice is a fixed, uniform passion. It neither abates of its vigor nor changes its object; and the reason why it does not, is founded in the nature of things, for wealth has not a rival where avarice is a ruling passion. One beauty may excel another, and extinguish from the mind of man the pictured remembrance of a former one: but wealth is the phœnix of avarice, and therefore it cannot seek a new object, because there is not another in the world.

I now pass on to show the value of the present taxes, and compare them with the annual expense; but this I shall preface with a few explanatory remarks.

There are two distinct things which make the payment of taxes difficult; the one is the large and real value of the sum to be paid, and the other is the scarcity of the thing in which the payment is to be made; and although these appear to be one and the same, they are in several instances not only different, but the difficulty springs from different causes.

Suppose a tax to be laid equal to one half of what a man's yearly income is, such a tax could not be paid, because the property could not be spared; and on the other hand, suppose a very trifling tax was laid, to be collected in *pearls,* such a tax likewise could not be paid, because they could not be had. Now any person may see that these are distinct cases, and the latter of them is a representation of our own.

That the difficulty cannot proceed from the former, that is, from the real value or weight of the tax, is evident at the first view to any person who will consider it.

The amount of the quota of taxes for this State for the year, 1780, (and so in proportion for every other State,) is twenty millions of dollars, which at seventy for one,[5] is but sixty-four thousand two hundred and eighty pounds three shillings sterling, and on an average, is no more than three shillings and five pence sterling per head, per annum, per man, woman and child, or threepence two-fifths per head per month. Now here is a clear, positive fact, that cannot be contradicted, and which proves that the difficulty cannot be in the weight of the tax, for in itself it is a trifle, and far from being adequate to our quota of the expense of

[5] This was the rate of depreciation of Pennsylvania currency.—*Editor.*

the war. The quit-rents [6] of one penny sterling per acre on only one half of the state, come to upwards of fifty thousand pounds, which is almost as much as all the taxes of the present year, and as those quit-rents made no part of the taxes then paid, and are now discontinued, the quantity of money drawn for public service this year, exclusive of the militia fines, which I shall take notice of in the process of this work, is less than what was paid and payable in any year preceding the revolution, and since the last war; what I mean is, that the quit-rents and taxes taken together came to a larger sum then, than the present taxes without the quit-rents do now.

My intention by these arguments and calculations is to place the difficulty to the right cause, and show that it does not proceed from the weight or worth of the tax, but from the scarcity of the medium in which it is paid; and to illustrate this point still further, I shall now show, that if the tax of twenty millions of dollars was of four times the real value it now is, or nearly so, which would be about two hundred and fifty thousand pounds sterling, and would be our full quota, this sum would have been raised with more ease, and have been less felt, than the present sum of only sixty-four thousand two hundred and eighty pounds.

The convenience or inconvenience of paying a tax in money arises from the quantity of money that can be spared out of trade.

When the emissions stopped, the continent was left in possession of two hundred millions of dollars, perhaps as equally dispersed as it was possible for trade to do it. And as no more was to be issued, the rise or fall of prices could neither increase nor diminish the quantity. It therefore remained the same through all the fluctuations of trade and exchange.

Now had the exchange stood at twenty for one, which was the rate Congress calculated upon when they arranged the quota of the several states, the latter end of last year, trade would have been carried on for nearly four times less money than it is now, and consequently the twenty millions would have been spared with much greater ease, and when collected would have been of almost four times the value that they now are. And on the other hand, was the depreciation to be ninety or one hundred for one, the quantity required for trade would be more than at sixty or seventy for one, and though the value of them would be less, the difficulty of sparing the money out of trade would be greater. And on these facts and arguments I rest the matter, to prove that it is not the want of property, but the scarcity of the medium by which the proportion of property for taxation is to be measured out, that makes the embarrassment which we live under. There is not money enough, and, what is equally as true, the people will not let there be money enough.

While I am on the subject of the currency, I shall offer one remark which will appear true to everybody, and can be accounted for by nobody, which is, that the better the times were, the worse the money grew; and the worse the times were, the better the money stood. It never depreciated by any advantage obtained by the enemy. The troubles of 1776, and the loss of Philadelphia in 1777, made no sensible impression on it, and every one knows that the surrender of Charleston did not produce the least alteration in the rate of exchange, which, for long before, and for more than three months after, stood at sixty for one. It seems as if the certainty of its being our own, made us careless of its value, and that the most distant thoughts of losing it made us hug it the closer, like something we were loth to part with; or that we depreciate it for our pastime, which, when called to seriousness by the enemy, we leave off to renew again at our leisure. In short, our good luck seems to break us, and our bad makes us whole.

Passing on from this digression, I shall now endeavor to bring into one view the several parts which I have already stated, and form thereon some propositions, and conclude.

I have placed before the reader, the average tax per head, paid by the people of England; which is forty shillings sterling.

And I have shown the rate on an average per head, which will defray all the expenses of the war to us, and support the several governments without running the country into debt, which is thirteen shillings and four pence.

I have shown what the peace establishment may be conducted for, viz. an eighth part of what it would be, if under the government of Britain.

And I have likewise shown what the average per head of the present taxes is, namely, three shillings and fivepence sterling, or threepence two-fifths per month; and that their whole yearly value, in sterling, is only sixty-four thousand two hundred and eighty pounds. Whereas our quota, to keep the payments equal with the expenses, is two hundred and fifty thousand pounds. Consequently, there is a deficiency of one hundred and eighty-five thousand seven hundred and twenty pounds, and the same proportion of defect, according to the several quotas, happens in every other state. And this defect is the cause why the army has been so indifferently fed, clothed and paid. It is the cause, likewise, of the nerveless state of the campaign, and the insecurity of the country. Now, if a tax equal to thirteen and fourpence per head, will remove all these difficulties, and make people secure in their homes, leave them to follow the business of their stores and farms unmolested, and not only drive out but keep out the enemy from the country; and if the neglect of raising this sum will let them in, and produce the evils which might be prevented—on which side, I ask, does the wisdom, interest and policy lie? Or, rather, would it not be an insult to reason, to put the question? The sum, when proportioned out according to the several abilities of the people, can hurt no one, but an inroad from the enemy ruins hundreds of families.

Look at the destruction done in this city [Philadelphia]. The many houses totally destroyed, and others damaged; the waste of fences in the country round it, besides the plunder of furniture, forage, and provisions. I do not suppose that half a million sterling would reinstate the sufferers; and, does this, I ask, bear any proportion to the expense that would make us secure? The damage, on an average, is at least ten pounds sterling per head, which is as much as thirteen shillings and fourpence per head comes to for fifteen years. The same has happened on the frontiers, and in the Jerseys, New York, and other places where the enemy has been—Carolina and Georgia are likewise suffering the same fate.

That the people generally do not understand the insufficiency of the taxes to carry on the war, is evident, not only from common observation, but from the construction of several petitions which were presented to the Assembly of this state, against the recommendation of Congress of the 18th of March last, for taking up and funding the present currency at forty to one, and issuing new money in its stead. The prayer of the petition was, *that the currency might be appreciated by taxes* (meaning the present taxes) *and that part of the taxes be applied to the support of the army, if the army could not be otherwise supported.* Now it could not have been possible for such a petition to have been presented, had the petitioners known, that so far from *part* of the taxes being sufficient for the support of the army, the *whole* of them falls three-fourths short of the year's expenses.

Before I proceed to propose methods by which a sufficiency of money may be raised, I shall take a short view of the general state of the country.

Notwithstanding the weight of the war, the ravages of the enemy, and the obstructions she has thrown in the way of trade and commerce, so soon does a young country outgrow misfortune, that America has already surmounted many that heavily oppressed her. For the first year or two of the war, we were shut up within our ports, scarce venturing to look towards the ocean. Now our rivers are beautified with large and valuable vessels, our stores filled with merchandise, and the produce of the country has a ready market, and an advantageous price. Gold and silver, that for a while seemed to have retreated again within the bowels of the earth, have once more risen into circulation, and every day adds new strength to trade, commerce and agriculture. In a pamphlet, written by Sir John Dalrymple,[7] and dispersed in America in the year 1775, he asserted that *two twenty-gun ships, nay, says he, tenders of those ships, stationed between Albermarle sound and Chesapeake bay, would shut up the trade of America for 600 miles.* How little did Sir John Dalrymple know of the abilities of America!

While under the government of Britain, the trade of this country was loaded with restrictions. It was only a few foreign ports which we were allowed to sail to. Now it is otherwise; and allowing that the quantity of trade is but half what it was before the war, the case must show the vast advantage of an open trade, because the present quantity under her restrictions could not support itself; from which I infer, that if half the quantity without the restrictions can bear itself up nearly, if not quite, as well as the whole when subject to them, how prosperous must the condition of America be when the whole shall return open with all the world. By the trade I do not mean the employment of a merchant only, but the whole interest and business of the country taken collectively.

It is not so much my intention, by this publication, to propose particular plans for raising money, as it is to show the necessity and the advantages to be derived from it. My principal design is to form the disposition of the people to the measures which I am fully persuaded it is their interest and duty to adopt, and which need no other force to accomplish them than the force of being felt. But as every hint may be useful, I shall throw out a sketch, and leave others to make such improvements upon it as to them may appear reasonable.

[7] Dalrymple was also the commander of the British troops in Boston during the Boston Massacre, March 5, 1770.—*Editor.*

The annual sum wanted is two millions, and the average rate in which it falls, is thirteen shillings and fourpence per head.

Suppose, then, that we raise half the sum and sixty thousand pounds over. The average rate thereof will be seven shillings per head.

In this case we shall have half the supply that we want, and an annual fund of sixty thousand pounds whereon to borrow the other million; because sixty thousand pounds is the interest of a million at six per cent.; and if at the end of another year we should be obliged, by the continuance of the war, to borrow another million, the taxes will be increased to seven shillings and sixpence; and thus for every million borrowed, an additional tax, equal to sixpence per head, must be levied.

The sum to be raised next year will be one million and sixty thousand pounds: one half of which I would propose should be raised by duties on imported goods, and prize goods, and the other half by a tax on landed property and houses, or such other means as each state may devise.

But as the duties on imports and prize goods must be the same in all the states, therefore the rate per cent., or what other form the duty shall be laid, must be ascertained and regulated by Congress, and ingrafted in that form into the law of each state; and the monies arising therefrom carried into the treasury of each state. The duties to be paid in gold or silver.

There are many reasons why a duty on imports is the most convenient duty or tax that can be collected; one of which is, because the whole is payable in a few places in a country, and it likewise operates with the greatest ease and equality, because as every one pays in proportion to what he consumes, so people in general consume in proportion to what they can afford; and therefore the tax is regulated by the abilities which every man supposes himself to have, or in other words, every man becomes his own assessor, and pays by a little at a time, when it suits him to buy. Besides, it is a tax which people may pay or let alone by not consuming the articles; and though the alternative may have no influence on their conduct, the power of choosing is an agreeable thing to the mind. For my own part, it would be a satisfaction to me was there a duty on all sorts of liquors during the war, as in my idea of things it would be an addition to the pleasures of society to know, that when the health of the army goes round, a few drops from every glass becomes theirs. How often have I heard an emphatical wish, almost accompanied by a tear,

"Oh, that our poor fellows in the field had some of this!" Why then need we suffer under a fruitless sympathy, when there is a way to enjoy both the wish and the entertainment at once.

But the great national policy of putting a duty upon imports is, that it either keeps the foreign trade in our own hands, or draws something for the defence of the country from every foreigner who participates in it with us.

Thus much for the first half of the taxes, and as each state will best devise means to raise the other half, I shall confine my remarks to the resources of this state.

The quota, then, of this state, of one million and sixty thousand pounds, will be one hundred and thirty-three thousand two hundred and fifty pounds, the half of which is sixty-six thousand six hundred and twenty-five pounds; and supposing one fourth part of Pennsylvania inhabited, then a tax of one bushel of wheat on every twenty acres of land, one with another, would produce the sum, and all the present taxes to cease. Whereas, the tithes of the bishops and clergy in England, exclusive of the taxes, are upwards of half a bushel of wheat on *every single* acre of land, good and bad, throughout the nation.

In the former part of this paper, I mentioned the militia fines, but reserved speaking of the matter, which I shall now do. The ground I shall put it upon is, that two millions sterling a year will support a sufficient army, and all the expenses of war and government, without having recourse to the inconvenient method of continually calling men from their employments, which, of all others, is the most expensive and the least substantial. I consider the revenues created by taxes as the first and principal thing, and fines only as secondary and accidental things. It was not the intention of the militia law to apply the fines to anything else but the support of the militia, neither do they produce any revenue to the state, yet these fines amount to more than all the taxes: for taking the muster-roll to be sixty thousand men, the fine on forty thousand who may not attend, will be sixty thousand pounds sterling, and those who muster, will give up a portion of time equal to half that sum, and if the eight classes should be called within the year, and one third turn out, the fine on the remaining forty thousand would amount to seventy-two millions of dollars, besides the fifteen shillings on every hundred pounds of property, and the charge of seven and a half per cent. for collecting, in certain instances which, on the whole, would be upwards of two hundred and fifty thousand pounds sterling.

Now if those very fines disable the country from raising a sufficient revenue without producing an equivalent advantage, would it not be for the ease and interest of all parties to increase the revenue, in the manner I have proposed, or any better, if a better can be devised, and cease the operation of the fines? I would still keep the militia as an organized body of men, and should there be a real necessity to call them forth, pay them out of the proper revenues of the state, and increase the taxes a third or fourth per cent. on those who do not attend. My limits will not allow me to go further into this matter, which I shall therefore close with this remark; that fines are, of all modes of revenue, the most unsuited to the minds of a free country. When a man pays a tax, he knows that the public necessity requires it, and therefore feels a pride in discharging his duty; but a fine seems an atonement for neglect of duty, and of consequence is paid with discredit, and frequently levied with severity.

I have now only one subject more to speak of, with which I shall conclude, which is, the resolve of Congress of the 18th of March last, for taking up and funding the present currency at forty for one, and issuing new money in its stead.

Every one knows that I am not the flatterer of Congress, but in this instance *they are right;* and if that measure is supported, the currency will acquire a value, which, without it, it will not. But this is not all: it will give relief to the finances until such time as they can be properly arranged, and save the country from being immediately doubled taxed under the present mode. In short, support that measure, and it will support you.

I have now waded through a tedious course of difficult business, and over an untrodden path. The subject, on every point in which it could be viewed, was entangled with perplexities, and enveloped in obscurity, yet such are the resources of America, that she wants nothing but system to secure success.

COMMON SENSE.

PHILADELPHIA, Oct. 4, 1780.

P. S. While this paper was preparing for the press, the treachery of General Arnold [8] became known, and engrossed the attention and conversation of the public; and that, not so much on account of the traitor

---

[8] For an excellent analysis of Arnold's treachery and the forces that were responsible for his actions, see Carl Van Doren, *Secret History of the American Revolution* (New York, 1942), pp. 143–391.—*Editor.*

as the magnitude of the treason, and the providence evident in the discovery. The matter, as far as it is at present known, is thus briefly related:

General Arnold about six weeks before had obtained the command of the important post of West Point, situated on the North River, about sixty miles above New York, and an hundred below Albany, there being no other defenceable pass between it and the last mentioned place. At what time, or in what manner, he first entered into a negotiation with the enemy for betraying the fort and garrison into their hands, does not yet appear.

While Arnold commanded at West Point, General Washington and the Minister of France went to Hartford in Connecticut, to consult on matters, in concert with Admiral Terney, commander of the French fleet stationed at Rhode Island. In the mean time Arnold held a conference with Major André, Adjutant-General to General Clinton, whom he traitorously furnished with plans of the fort, state of the garrison, minutes of the last council of war, and the manner in which he would post the troops when the enemy should attempt a surprise; and then gave him a pass, by the name of Mr. John Anderson, to go to the lines at the White Plains or lower, if he Mr. Anderson thought proper, he being (the pass said) on public business.

Thus furnished André parted from Arnold, set off for New York, and had nearly arrived at the extent of our lines, when he was stopped by a party of militia, to whom he produced his pass, but they, not being satisfied with his account, insisted on taking him before the commanding officer, Lieut. Col. Jamieson. Finding himself in this situation, and hoping to escape by a bribe, he offered them his purse, watch and a promise of any quantity of goods they would accept, which these honest men nobly and virtuously scorned, and confident with their duty took him to the proper officer. On examination there was found on him the above mentioned papers and several others, all in the handwriting of General Arnold, and finding himself thus detected, he confessed his proper name and character. He was accordingly made a close prisoner, and the papers sent off by express to West Point, at which place General Washington had arrived soon after the arrival of the packet. On this disclosure, he went in quest of Arnold, whom he had not seen that day, but all that could be learned was that Arnold had received a letter some short time before which had much confused him, since which he had disappeared. Colonel Hamilton, one of General Washington's aids, with some others were sent after him, but he, having the start, eluded the pursuit, took boat under pretence of a flag, and got on board the *Vulture* sloop of war lying in the North River; on which it may be truly said, that one vulture was receiving another. From on board this vessel he addressed a letter to General Washington, which, in whatever light it may be viewed, confirms him a finished villain.

The true character of Arnold is that of a desperado. His whole life has been a life of jobs; and where either plunder or profit was the object, no danger deterred, no principle restrained him. In his person he was smart and active, somewhat diminutive, weak in his capacities and trifling in his conversation; and though gallant in the field, was defective in the talents necessary for command. The early convulsion of the times afforded him an introduction into life, to the elegance of which he was before a stranger, and the eagerness of the public to reward and encourage enterprise, procured him at once both applause and promotion. His march to Quebec gave him fame, and the plunder of Montreal put the first stamp to his public character.[9] His behavior, at Danbury and Saratoga once more covered over his crimes, which again broke forth in the plunder of Philadelphia, under pretence of supplying the army. From this time, the true spring of his conduct being known, he became both disregarded and disesteemed, and this last instance of his treachery has proved the public judgment right.

When we take a review of the history of former times it will turn out to the honor of America that, notwithstanding the trying variety of her situation, this is the only instance of defection in a general officer; and even in this case, the unshaken honesty of those who detected him heightens the national character, to which his apostasy serves as a foil. From the nature of his crime, and his disposition to monopolize, it is reasonable to conclude he had few or no *direct* accomplices. His sole object was to make a monied bargain; and to be consistent with himself, he would as readily betray the side he has deserted to, as that he deserted from.

But there is one reflection results from this black business that deserves

[9] The Canadian campaign started with the capture of Fort Ticonderoga by Ethan Allen and of Crown Point by Benedict Arnold. About six months later, November, 1775, Arnold arrived before Quebec after having led his forces across the Maine wilderness. In December he and General Montgomery joined forces and launched an attack against the city on December 31, in which Arnold was wounded and Montgomery killed. After laying siege to the city the Americans were compelled to abandon the campaign and left in disorderly retreat.—*Editor.*

notice, which is that it shows the declining power of the enemy. An attempt to bribe is a sacrifice of military fame, and a confession of inability to conquer; as a proud people they ought to be above it, and as soldiers to despise it; and however they may feel on the occasion, the world at large will despise them for it, and consider America superior to their arms.

C. S.

THE AMERICAN CRISIS

X

On October 19, 1781, Lord Cornwallis, outnumbered three to one on land and cut off from fresh supplies by sea, surrendered his army of 7,000 men at Yorktown. A month later, November 27, 1781, King George the Third delivered a bellicose speech at the opening of Parliament, and Parliament voted to continue the war. In *Crisis X,* March 5, 1782, Paine replied to the King's speech.

In the second part of this article Paine placed great stress upon the need for united national action and centralized government as against the particularism of the separate states, and stressed the supremacy of the Federal Government: "Each State is to the United States what each individual is to the state he lives in. And it is on this grand point, this movement upon one centre, that our existence as a nation, our happiness as a people, and our safety as individuals, depend."—*Editor.*

On the King of England's Speech

O F ALL the innocent passions which actuate the human mind there is none more universally prevalent than curiosity. It reaches all mankind, and in matters which concern us, or concern us not, it alike provokes in us a desire to know them.

Although the situation of America, superior to every effort to enslave her, and daily rising to importance and opulence, has placed her above the region of anxiety, it has still left her within the circle of curiosity; and her fancy to see the speech of a man who had proudly threatened to bring her to his feet, was visibly marked with that tranquil confidence which cared nothing about its contents. It was inquired after with a smile, read with a laugh, and dismissed with disdain.

But, as justice is due, even to an enemy, it is right to say, that the speech is as well managed as the embarrassed condition of their affairs could well admit of; and though hardly a line of it is true, except the mournful story of Cornwallis,[1] it may serve to amuse the deluded commons and people of England, for whom it was calculated.

"The war," says the speech, "is still unhappily prolonged by that restless ambition which first excited our enemies to commence it, and which still continues to disappoint my earnest wishes and diligent exertions to restore the public tranquillity."

How easy it is to abuse truth and language, when men, by habitual wickedness, have learned to set justice at defiance. That the very man who began the war, who with the most sullen insolence refused to answer, and even to hear the humblest of all petitions, who has encouraged his officers and his army in the most savage cruelties, and the most scandalous plunderings, who has stirred up the Indians on one side, and the negroes on the other, and invoked every aid of hell in his behalf, should now, with an affected air of pity, turn the tables from himself, and charge to another the wickedness that is his own, can only be equalled by the baseness of the heart that spoke it.

To be nobly wrong is more manly than to be meanly right, is an expression I once used on a former occasion,[2] and it is equally applicable now. We feel something like respect for consistency even in error. We lament the virtue that is debauched into a vice, but the vice that affects a virtue becomes the more detestable: and amongst the various assumptions of character, which hypocrisy has taught, and men have practised, there is none that raises a higher relish of disgust, than to see disappointed inveteracy twisting itself, by the most visible falsehoods, into an appearance of piety which it has no pretensions to.

"But I should not," continues the speech, "answer the trust committed to the sovereign of a *free people,* nor make a suitable return to my subjects for their constant, zealous, and affectionate attachment to my person, family and government, if I consented to sacrifice, either to my own desire of peace, or to their temporary ease and relief, *those essential rights and permanent interests,* upon the maintenance and preservation of which, the future strength and security of this country must principally depend."

---

[1] Paine is referring to Cornwallis' defeat.—*Editor.*
[2] The reference is to the opening sentence of "The Forester's" first letter to Cato.—*Editor.*

That the man whose ignorance and obstinacy first involved and still continues the nation in the most hopeless and expensive of all wars, should now meanly flatter them with the name of a *free people,* and make a merit of his crime, under the disguise of their essential rights and permanent interests, is something which disgraces even the character of perverseness. Is he afraid they will send him to Hanover,[3] or what does he fear? Why is the sycophant thus added to the hypocrite, and the man who pretends to govern, sunk into the humble and submissive memorialist?

What those essential rights and permanent interests are, on which the future strength and security of England must principally *depend,* are not so much as alluded to. They are words which impress nothing but the ear, and are calculated only for the sound.

But if they have any reference to America, then do they amount to the disgraceful confession, that England, who once assumed to be her protectress, has now become her *dependant.* The British King and ministry are constantly holding up the vast importance which America is of to England, in order to allure the nation to carry on the war: now, whatever ground there is for this idea, it ought to have operated as a reason for not beginning it; and, therefore, they support their present measures to their own disgrace, because the arguments which they now use, are a direct reflection on their former policy.

"The favorable appearance of affairs," continues the speech, "in the East Indies, and the safe arrival of the numerous commercial fleets of my kingdom, must have given you satisfaction."

That things are not *quite* so bad every where as in America may be some cause of consolation, but can be none for triumph. One broken leg is better than two, but still it is not a source of joy: and let the appearance of affairs in the East Indies be ever so favorable, they are nevertheless worse than at first, without a prospect of their ever being better. But the mournful story of Cornwallis was yet to be told, and it was necessary to give it the softest introduction possible.

"But in the course of this year," continues the speech, "my assiduous endeavors to guard the extensive dominions of my crown have not been attended with success equal to the justice and uprightness of my views." —What Justice and uprightness there was in beginning a war with America, the world will judge of, and the unequalled barbarity with

[3] The reference is to the German origin of George III.—*Editor.*

which it has been conducted, is not to be worn from the memory by the cant of snivelling hypocrisy.

"And it is with *great concern* that I inform you that the events of war have been very unfortunate to my arms in Virginia, having ended in the loss of my forces in that province."—And *our* great concern is that they are not all served in the same manner.

"No endeavors have been wanted on my part," says the speech, "to extinguish that spirit of rebellion which our enemies have found means to foment and maintain in the colonies; and to restore to my *deluded subjects* in America that happy and prosperous condition which they formerly derived from a due obedience to the laws."

The expression of *deluded subjects* is become so hacknied and contemptible, and the more so when we see them making prisoners of whole armies at a time, that the pride of not being laughed at would induce a man of common sense to leave it off. But the most offensive falsehood in the paragraph is the attributing the prosperity of America to a wrong cause. It was the unremitted industry of the settlers and their descendants, the hard labor and toil of persevering fortitude, that were the true causes of the prosperity of America. The former tyranny of England served to people it, and the virtue of the adventurers to improve it. Ask the man, who, with his axe, has cleared a way in the wilderness, and now possesses an estate, what made him rich, and he will tell you the labor of his hands, the sweat of his brow, and the blessing of heaven. Let Britain but leave America to herself and she asks no more. She has risen into greatness without the knowledge and against the will of England, and has a right to the unmolested enjoyment of her own created wealth.

"I will order," says the speech, "the estimates of the ensuing year to be laid before you. I rely on your wisdom and public spirit for such supplies as the circumstances of our affairs shall be found to require. Among the many ill consequences which attend the continuation of the present war, I most sincerely regret the additional burdens which it must unavoidably bring upon my faithful subjects."

It is strange that a nation must run through such a labyrinth of trouble, and expend such a mass of wealth to gain the wisdom which an hour's reflection might have taught. The final superiority of America over every attempt that an island might make to conquer her, was as naturally marked in the constitution of things, as the future ability of a giant over a dwarf is delineated in his features while an infant. How far providence, to accomplish purposes which no human wisdom could foresee, permitted such extraordinary errors, is still a secret in the womb of time, and must remain so till futurity shall give it birth.

"In the prosecution of this great and important contest," says the speech, "in which we are engaged, I retain a firm confidence in the *protection of divine providence,* and a perfect conviction in the justice of my cause, and I have no doubt, but, that by the concurrence and support of my Parliament, by the valour of my fleets and armies, and by a vigorous, animated, and united exertion of the faculties and resources of my people, I shall be enabled to restore the blessings of a safe and honorable peace to all my dominions."

The King of England is one of the readiest believers in the world. In the beginning of the contest he passed an act to put America out of the protection of the crown of England, and though providence, for seven years together, has put him out of *her* protection, still the man has no doubt. Like Pharaoh on the edge of the Red Sea, he sees not the plunge he is making, and precipitately drives across the flood that is closing over his head.

I think it is a reasonable supposition, that this part of the speech was composed before the arrival of the news of the capture of Cornwallis: for it certainly has no relation to their condition at the time it was spoken. But, be this as it may, it is nothing to us. Our line is fixed. Our lot is cast; and America, the child of fate, is arriving at maturity. We have nothing to do but by a spirited and quick exertion, to stand prepared for war or peace. Too great to yield, and too noble to insult; superior to misfortune, and generous in success, let us untaintedly preserve the character which we have gained, and show to future ages an example of unequalled magnanimity. There is something in the cause and consequence of America that has drawn on her the attention of all mankind. The world has seen her brave. Her love of liberty; her ardour in supporting it; the justice of her claims, and the constancy of her fortitude have won her the esteem of Europe, and attached to her interest the first power in that country.

Her situation now is such, that to whatever point, past, present or to come, she casts her eyes, new matter rises to convince her that she is right. In her conduct towards her enemy, no reproachful sentiment lurks in secret. No sense of injustice is left upon the mind. Untainted with ambition, and a stranger to revenge, her progress has been marked by providence, and she, in every stage of the conflict, has blest her with success.

But let not America wrap herself up in delusive hope and suppose the business done. The least remissness in preparation, the least relaxation in execution, will only serve to prolong the war, and increase expenses. If our enemies can draw consolation from misfortune, and exert themselves upon despair, how much more ought we, who are to win a continent by the conquest, and have already an earnest of success?

Having, in the preceding part, made my remarks on the several matters which the speech contains, I shall now make my remarks on what it does not contain.

There is not a syllable in its respecting alliances. Either the injustice of Britain is too glaring, or her condition too desperate, or both, for any neighboring power to come to her support. In the beginning of the contest, when she had only America to contend with, she hired assistance from Hesse, and other smaller states of Germany, and for nearly three years did America, young, raw, undisciplined and unprovided, stand against the power of Britain, aided by twenty thousand foreign troops, and made a complete conquest of one entire army. The remembrance of those things ought to inspire us with confidence and greatness of mind, and carry us through every remaining difficulty with content and cheerfulness. What are the little sufferings of the present day, compared with the hardships that are past? There was a time, when we had neither house nor home in safety; when every hour was the hour of alarm and danger; when the mind, tortured with anxiety, knew no repose, and every thing, but hope and fortitude, was bidding us farewell.

It is of use to look back upon these things; to call to mind the times of trouble and the scenes of complicated anguish that are past and gone. Then every expense was cheap, compared with the dread of conquest and the misery of submission. We did not stand debating upon trifles, or contending about the necessary and unavoidable charges of defence. Every one bore his lot of suffering, and looked forward to happier days, and scenes of rest.

Perhaps one of the greatest dangers which any country can be exposed to, arises from a kind of trifling which sometimes steals upon the mind, when it supposes the danger past; and this unsafe situation marks at this time the peculiar crisis of America. What would she once have given to have known that her condition at this day should be what it now is? And yet we do not seem to place a proper value upon it, nor vigorously pursue the necessary measures to secure it. We know that we cannot be defended, nor yet defend ourselves, without trouble and expense. We have no right to expect it; neither ought we to look for it. We are a people, who, in our situation, differ from all the world. We form one common floor of public good, and, whatever is our charge, it is paid for our own interest and upon our own account.

Misfortune and experience have now taught us system and method; and the arrangements for carrying on the war are reduced to rule and order. The quotas of the several states are ascertained, and I intend in a future publication to show what they are, and the necessity as well as the advantages of vigorously providing for them.

In the mean time, I shall conclude this paper with an instance of *British clemency,* from Smollett's History of England, vol. xi., p. 239, printed in London. It will serve to show how dismal the situation of a conquered people is, and that the only security is an effectual defence.

We all know that the Stuart family and the house of Hanover opposed each other for the crown of England. The Stuart family stood first in the line of succession, but the other was the most successful.

In July, 1745, Charles, the son of the exiled king, landed in Scotland, collected a small force, at no time exceeding five or six thousand men, and made some attempts to re-establish his claim. The late Duke of Cumberland, uncle to the present King of England, was sent against him, and on the 16th of April following, Charles was totally defeated at Culloden, in Scotland. Success and power are the only situations in which clemency can be shown, and those who are cruel, because they are victorious, can with the same facility act any other degenerate character.

"Immediately after the decisive action at Culloden, the Duke of Cumberland took possession of Inverness; where six and thirty deserters, convicted by a court martial, were ordered to be executed: then he detached several parties to ravage the country. One of these apprehended The Lady Mackintosh, who was sent prisoner to Inverness, plundered her house, and drove away her cattle, though her husband was actually in the service of the government. The castle of Lord Lovat was destroyed. The French prisoners were sent to Carlisle and Penrith: Kilmarnock, Balmerino, Cromartie, and his son, The Lord Macleod, were conveyed by sea to London; and those of an inferior rank were confined in different prisons. The Marquis of Tullibardine, together with a brother of the Earl of Dunmore, and Murray, the pretender's secretary, were seized and transported to the Tower of London, to which the Earl of Traquaire had been committed on suspicion; and the eldest son of Lord Lovat was imprisoned in the castle of Edinburgh. In a word, all the jails in Great Britain, from the capital, northwards, were filled with those unfortunate captives; and great numbers of them were crowded together in the holds of ships, where they perished in the most deplorable manner, for want of air and exercise. Some rebel chiefs escaped in two French frigates that arrived on the coast of Lochaber about the end of April, and engaged three vessels belonging to his Britannic majesty, which they obliged to retire. Others embarked on board a ship on the coast of Buchan, and were conveyed to Norway, from whence they travelled to Sweden. In the month of May, the Duke of Cumberland advanced with the army into the Highlands, as far as Fort Augustus, where he encamped; and sent off detachments on all hands, to hunt down the fugitives, and lay waste the country with fire and sword. The castles of Glengary and Lochiel were plundered and burned; every house, hut, or habitation, met with the same fate, without distinction; and all the cattle and provision were carried off; the men were either shot upon the mountains, like wild beasts, or put to death in cold blood, without form of trial; the women, after having seen their husbands and fathers murdered, were subjected to brutal violation, and then turned out naked, with their children, to starve on the barren heaths. One whole family was enclosed in a barn, and consumed to ashes. Those ministers of vengeance were so alert in the execution of their office, that in a few days there was neither house, cottage, man, nor beast, to be seen within the compass of fifty miles; all was ruin, silence, and desolation."

I have here presented the reader with one of the most shocking instances of cruelty ever practised, and I leave it, to rest on his mind, that he may be fully impressed with a sense of the destruction he has escaped, in case Britain had conquered America; and likewise, that he may see and feel the necessity, as well for his own personal safety, as for the honor, the interest, and happiness of the whole community, to omit or delay no one preparation necessary to secure the ground which we so happily stand upon.

To the People of America

On the expenses, arrangements and disbursements for carrying on the war, and finishing it with honor and advantage

When any necessity or occasion has pointed out the convenience of addressing the public, I have never made it a consideration whether the subject was popular or unpopular, but whether it was right or wrong;

for that which is right will become popular, and that which is wrong, though by mistake it may obtain the cry or fashion of the day, will soon lose the power of delusion, and sink into disesteem.

A remarkable instance of this happened in the case of Silas Deane; [4] and I mention this circumstance with the greater ease, because the poison of his hypocrisy spread over the whole country, and every man, almost without exception, thought me wrong in opposing him. The best friends I then had, except Mr. Laurens,[5] stood at a distance, and this tribute, which is due to his constancy, I pay to him with respect, and that the readier, because he is not here to hear it. If it reaches him in his imprisonment, it will afford him an agreeable reflection.

"As he rose like a rocket, he would fall like a stick," is a metaphor which I applied to Mr. Deane, in the first piece which I published respecting him, and he has exactly fulfilled the description. The credit he so unjustly obtained from the public, he lost in almost as short a time. The delusion perished as it fell, and he soon saw himself stripped of popular support. His more intimate acquaintances began to doubt, and to desert him long before he left America, and at his departure, he saw himself the object of general suspicion. When he arrived in France, he endeavored to effect by treason what he had failed to accomplish by fraud. His plans, schemes and projects, together with his expectation of being sent to Holland to negotiate a loan of money, had all miscarried. He then began traducing and accusing America of every crime, which could injure her reputation. "That she was a ruined country; that she only meant to make a tool of France, to get what money she could out of her, and then to leave her and accommodate with Britain." Of all which and much more, Colonel Laurens and myself, when in France, informed Dr. Franklin, who had not before heard of it.[6] And to com-

---

[4] Silas Deane, American commissioner in France, was in the pay of the British and worked actively for reunion with Great Britain. For an analysis of his activities for the British, see Carl Van Doren, *Secret History of the American Revolution,* pp. 62–63, 149, 170–171, 417–418.—*Editor.*

[5] Henry Laurens, President of Congress.—*Editor.*

[6] Paine sailed for France early in 1781, to ask the French Government for financial assistance for the American Republic. Colonel John Laurens had been appointed by Congress to negotiate a loan with France, but Laurens declared that he would only go if Paine went with him. Abandoning his project to write a history of the American Revolution for which he had been gathering material, Paine went with Laurens, arriving in France in March, 1781. They returned to America in August with two and a half livres and a boatload of stores and clothing. These funds and supplies enabled Washington to prosecute the campaign which resulted in the defeat of Cornwallis at Yorktown. Paine paid his own expenses during the mission to France.—*Editor.*

plete the character of traitor, he has, by letters to his country since, some of which, in his own handwriting, are now in the possession of Congress, used every expression and argument in his power, to injure the reputation of France, and to advise America to renounce her alliance, and surrender up her independence.[7] Thus in France he abuses America, and in his letters to America he abuses France; and is endeavoring to create disunion between two countries, by the same arts of double-dealing by which he caused dissensions among the commissioners in Paris, and distractions in America. But his life has been fraud, and his character has been that of a plodding, plotting, cringing mercenary, capable of any disguise that suited his purpose. His final detection has very happily cleared up those mistakes, and removed that uneasiness, which his unprincipled conduct occasioned. Every one now sees him in the same light; for towards friends or enemies he acted with the same deception and injustice, and his name, like that of *Arnold,* ought now to be forgotten among us.[8] As this is the first time that I have mentioned him since my return from France, it is my intention that it shall be the last. From this digression, which for several reasons I thought necessary to give, I now proceed to the purport of my address.

I consider the war of America against Britain as the country's war, the public's war, or the war of the people in their own behalf, for the security of their natural rights, and the protection of their own property. It is not the war of Congress, the war of the assemblies, or the war of government in any line whatever. The country first, by mutual compact, resolved to defend their rights and maintain their independence, *at the hazard of their lives and fortunes;* they elected their representatives, by whom they appointed their members of Congress, and said, *act you for us, and we will support you.* This is the true ground and principle of the war on the part of America, and, consequently, there remains nothing to do, but for every one to fulfil his obligation.

It was next to impossible that a new country, engaged in a new undertaking, could set off systematically right at first. She saw not the ex-

---

[7] Mr. William Marshall, of this city [Philadelphia], formerly a pilot, who had been taken at sea and carried to England, and got from thence to France, brought over letters from Mr. Deane to America, one of which was directed to "Robert Morris, Esq." Mr. Morris sent it unopened to Congress, and advised Mr. Marshall to deliver the others there, which he did. The letters were of the same purport with those which have been already published under the signature of S. Deane, to which they had frequent reference.—*Author.*

[8] Deane denied that there had been any intimacy between him and Arnold. The extent of his treachery was not revealed until the publication in 1867 of George the Third's correspondence. See also Van Doren, *op. cit.,* pp. 252–253, 417–418.—*Editor.*

tent of the struggle that she was involved in, neither could she avoid the beginning. She supposed every step that she took, and every resolution which she formed, would bring her enemy to reason and close the contest. Those failing, she was forced into new measures; and these, like the former, being fitted to her expectations, and failing in their turn, left her continually unprovided, and without system. The enemy, likewise, was induced to prosecute the war, from the temporary expedients we adopted for carrying it on. We were continually expecting to see their credit exhausted, and they were looking to see our currency fail; and thus, between their watching us, and we them, the hopes of both have been deceived, and the childishness of the expectation has served to increase the expense.

Yet who, through this wilderness of error, has been to blame? Where is the man who can say the fault, in part, has not been his? They were the natural, unavoidable errors of the day. They were the errors of a whole country, which nothing but experience could detect and time remove. Neither could the circumstances of America admit of system, till either the paper currency was fixed or laid aside. No calculation of a finance could be made on a medium failing without reason, and fluctuating without rule.

But there is one error which might have been prevented and was not; and as it is not my custom to flatter, but to serve mankind, I will speak it freely. It certainly was the duty of every assembly on the continent to have known, at all times, what was the condition of its treasury, and to have ascertained at every period of depreciation, how much the real worth of the taxes fell short of their nominal value. This knowledge, which might have been easily gained, in the time of it, would have enabled them to have kept their constituents well informed, and this is one of the greatest duties of representation. They ought to have studied and calculated the expenses of the war, the quota of each state, and the consequent proportion that would fall on each man's property for his defence; and this must have easily shown to them, that a tax of one hundred pounds could not be paid by a bushel of apples or an hundred of flour, which was often the case two or three years ago. But instead of this, which would have been plain and upright dealing, the little line of temporary popularity, the feather of an hour's duration, was too much pursued; and in this involved condition of things, every state, for the want of a little thinking, or a little information, supposed that it supported the whole expenses of the war, when in fact it fell, by the time the tax was levied and collected, above three-fourths short of its own quota.

Impressed with a sense of the danger to which the country was exposed by this lax method of doing business, and the prevailing errors of the day, I published, last October was a twelvemonth, the *Crisis Extraordinary,* on the revenues of America, and the yearly expense of carrying on the war. My estimation of the latter, together with the civil list of Congress, and the civil list of the several states, was two million pounds sterling, which is very nearly nine millions of dollars.

Since that time, Congress have gone into a calculation, and have estimated the expenses of the War Department and the civil list of Congress (exclusive of the civil list of the several governments) at eight millions of dollars; and as the remaining million will be fully sufficient for the civil list of the several states, the two calculations are exceedingly near each other.

The sum of eight millions of dollars have called upon the states to furnish, and their quotas are as follows, which I shall preface with the resolution itself.

"By the United States in Congress assembled.

"October 30, 1781.

"*Resolved,* That the respective states be called upon to furnish the treasury of the United States with their quotas of eight millions of dollars, for the War Department and civil list for the ensuing year, to be paid quarterly, in equal proportions, the first payment to be made on the first day of April next.

"*Resolved,* That a committee, consisting of a member from each state, be appointed to apportion to the several states the quota of the above sum.

"November 2d. The committee appointed to ascertain the proportions of the several states of the monies to be raised for the expenses of the ensuing year, report the following resolutions:

"That the sum of eight millions of dollars, as required to be raised by the resolutions of the 30th of October last, be paid by the states in the following proportion:

New Hampshire	$ 373,598
Massachusetts	1,307,596
Rhode Island	216,684
Connecticut	747,196
New York	373,598
New Jersey	485,679

Pennsylvania	1,120,794
Delaware	112,085
Maryland	933,996
Virginia	1,307,594
North Carolina	622,677
South Carolina	373,598
Georgia	24,905

$8,000,000

"Resolved, That it be recommended to the several states, to lay taxes for raising their quotas of money for the United States, separate from those laid for their own particular use."

On these resolutions I shall offer several remarks.

1st, On the sum itself, and the ability of the country.

2d, On the several quotas, and the nature of a union. And,

3d, On the manner of collection and expenditure.

1st, On the sum itself, and the ability of the country. As I know my own calculation is as low as possible, and as the sum called for by congress, according to their calculation, agrees very nearly therewith, I am sensible it cannot possibly be lower. Neither can it be done for that, unless there is ready money to go to market with; and even in that case, it is only by the utmost management and economy that it can be made to do.

By the accounts which were laid before the British Parliament last spring, it appeared that the charge of only subsisting, that is, feeding their army in America, cost annually four million pounds sterling, which is very nearly eighteen millions of dollars. Now if, for eight millions, we can feed, clothe, arm, provide for, and pay an army sufficient for our defence, the very comparison shows that the money must be well laid out.

It may be of some use, either in debate or conversation, to attend to the progress of the expenses of an army, because it will enable us to see on what part any deficiency will fall.

The first thing is, to feed them and prepare for the sick.

Second, to clothe them.

Third, to arm and furnish them.

Fourth, to provide means for removing them from place to place. And,

Fifth, to pay them.

The first and second are absolutely necessary to them as men. The third and fourth are equally as necessary to them as an army. And the fifth is their just due. Now if the sum which shall be raised should fall short, either by the several acts of the states for raising it, or by the manner of collecting it, the deficiency will fall on the fifth head, the soldiers' pay, which would be defrauding them, and eternally disgracing ourselves. It would be a blot on the councils, the country, and the revolution of America, and a man would hereafter be ashamed to own that he had any hand in it.

But if the deficiency should be still shorter, it would next fall on the fourth head, *the means of removing the army from place to place;* and, in this case, the army must either stand still where it can be of no use, or seize on horses, carts, wagons, or any means of transportation which it can lay hold of; and in this instance the country suffers. In short, every attempt to do a thing for less than it can be done for, is sure to become at last both a loss and a dishonor.

But the country cannot bear it, say some. This has been the most expensive doctrine that ever was held out, and cost America millions of money for nothing. Can the country bear to be overrun, ravaged, and ruined by an enemy? This will immediately follow where defence is wanting, and defence will ever be wanting where sufficient revenues are not provided. But this is only one part of the folly. The second is, that when the danger comes, invited in part by our not preparing against it, we have been obliged, in a number of instances, to expend double the sums to do that which at first might have been done for half the money. But this is not all. A third mischief has been, that grain of all sorts, flour, beef, fodder, horses, carts, wagons, or whatever was absolutely or immediately wanted, have been taken without pay. Now, I ask, why was all this done, but from that extremely weak and expensive doctrine, *that the country could not bear it?* That is, that she could not bear, in the first instance, that which would have saved her twice as much at last; or, in proverbial language, that she could not bear to pay a penny to save a pound; the consequence of which has been, that she has paid a pound for a penny. Why are there so many unpaid certificates in almost every man's hands, but from the parsimony of not providing sufficient revenues? Besides, the doctrine contradicts itself; because, if the whole country cannot bear it, how is it possible that a part should? And yet this has been the case: for those things have been had; and they must be had; but the misfortune is, that they have been obtained in a very unequal manner, and upon expensive credit, whereas, with ready money, they might have been purchased for half the price, and nobody distressed.

But there is another thought which ought to strike us, which is, how is the army to bear the want of food, clothing and other necessaries? The man who is at home, can turn himself a thousand ways, and find as many means of ease, convenience or relief: but a soldier's life admits of none of those: their wants cannot be supplied from themselves: for an army, though it is the defence of a state, is at the same time the child of a country, or must be provided for in every thing.

And lastly, the doctrine is false. There are not three millions of people in any part of the universe, who live so well, or have such a fund of ability, as in America. The income of a common laborer, who is industrious, is equal to that of the generality of tradesmen in England. In the mercantile line, I have not heard of one who could be said to be a bankrupt since the war began, and in England they have been without number. In America almost every farmer lives on his own lands, and in England not one in a hundred does. In short, it seems as if the poverty of that country had made them furious, and they were determined to risk all to recover all.

Yet, notwithstanding those advantages on the part of America, true it is, that had it not been for the operation of taxes for our necessary defence, we had sunk into a state of sloth and poverty: for there was more wealth lost by neglecting to till the earth in the years 1776, '77, and '78, than the quota of taxes amounts to. That which is lost by neglect of this kind, is lost for ever: whereas that which is paid, and continues in the country, returns to us again; and at the same time that it provides us with defence, it operates not only as a spur, but as a premium to our industry.

I shall now proceed to the second head, viz., *on the several quotas, and the nature of a union.*

There was a time when America had no other bond of union, than that of common interest and affection. The whole country flew to the relief of Boston, and, making her cause their own, participated in her cares and administered to her wants.[9] The fate of war, since that day,

---

[9] The reference is to the reaction of the colonies to the Coercive Acts of 1774, the first of which closed that town's harbor to all shipping. Every colony responded to Boston's call for help by sending food, clothing, and money. The deputy governor of Pennsylvania pointed out correctly: "They [the people] look upon the chastisement . . . of Boston to be purposely rigorous, and held up by way of intimidation to all *America*. . . ." (Peter Force, ed., *American Archives, Fourth Series* [Washington, 1837], Vol. I, p. 514.)

has carried the calamity in a ten-fold proportion to the southward; but in the mean time the union has been strengthened by a legal compact of the states, jointly and severally ratified, and that which before was choice, or the duty of affection, is now likewise the duty of legal obligation.

The union of America is the foundation-stone of her independence; the rock on which it is built; and is something so sacred in her constitution, that we ought to watch every word we speak, and every thought we think, that we injure it not, even by mistake. When a multitude, extended, or rather scattered, over a continent in the manner we were, mutually agree to form one common centre whereon the whole shall move to accomplish a particular purpose, all parts must act together and alike, or act not at all, and a stoppage in any one is a stoppage of the whole, at least for a time.

Thus the several states have sent representatives to assemble together in Congress, and they have empowered that body, which thus becomes their centre, and are no other than themselves in representation, to conduct and manage the war, while their constituents at home attend to the domestic cares of the country, their internal legislation, their farms, professions or employments, for it is only by reducing complicated things to method and orderly connection that they can be understood with advantage, or pursued with success. Congress, by virtue of this delegation, estimates the expense, and apportions it out to the several parts of the empire according to their several abilities; and here the debate must end, because each state has already had its voice, and the matter has undergone its whole portion of argument, and can no more be altered by any particular state, than a law of any state, after it has passed, can be altered by any individual. For with respect to those things which immediately concern the union, and for which the union was purposely established, and is intended to secure, each state is to the United States what each individual is to the state he lives in. And it is on this grand point, this movement upon one centre, that our existence as a nation, our happiness as a people, and our safety as individuals, depend.

It may happen that some state or other may be somewhat over or under rated, but this cannot be much. The experience which has been had upon the matter, has nearly ascertained their several abilities. But even in this case, it can only admit of an appeal to the United States, but cannot authorise any state to make the alteration itself, any more than our internal government can admit an individual to do so in the case of an act of assembly; for if one state can do it, then may another do the same, and the instant this is done the whole is undone.

Neither is it supposable that any single state can be a judge of all the comparative reasons which may influence the collective body in arranging the quotas of the continent. The circumstances of the several states are frequently varying, occasioned by the accidents of war and commerce, and it will often fall upon some to help others, rather beyond what their exact proportion at another time might be; but even this assistance is as naturally and politically included in the idea of a union as that of any particular assigned proportion; because we know not whose turn it may be next to want assistance, for which reason that state is the wisest which sets the best example.

Though in matters of bounden duty and reciprocal affection, it is rather a degeneracy from the honesty and ardor of the heart to admit any thing selfish to partake in the government of our conduct, yet in cases where our duty, our affections, and our interest all coincide, it may be of some use to observe their union. The United States will become heir to an extensive quantity of vacant land, and their several titles to shares and quotas thereof, will naturally be adjusted according to their relative quotas, during the war, exclusive of that inability which may unfortunately arise to any state by the enemy's holding possession of a part; but as this is a cold matter of interest, I pass it by, and proceed to my third head, viz., *on the manner of collection and expenditure.*

It has been our error, as well as our misfortune, to blend the affairs of each state, especially in money matters, with those of the United States; whereas it is our case, convenience and interest, to keep them separate. The expenses of the United States for carrying on the war, and the expenses of each state for its own domestic government, are distinct things, and to involve them is a source of perplexity and a cloak for fraud. I love method, because I see and am convinced of its beauty and advantage. It is that which makes all business easy and understood, and without which, everything becomes embarrassed and difficult.

There are certain powers which the people of each state have delegated to their legislative and executive bodies, and there are other powers which the people of every state have delegated to Congress, among which is that of conducting the war, and, consequently, of managing the expenses attending it; for how else can that be managed, which concerns each state, but by a delegation from each? When a state has furnished its quota, it has an undoubted right to know how it has been applied, and it is as much the duty of Congress to inform the state of the one, as it is the duty of the state to provide the other.

In the resolution of Congress already excited, it is recommended to the several states *to lay taxes for raising their quotas of money for the United States, separate from those laid for their own particular use.*

This is a most necessary point to be observed, and the distinction should follow all the way through. They should be levied, paid and collected, separately, and kept separate in every instance. Neither have the civil officers of any state, nor the government of that state, the least right to touch that money which the people pay for the support of their army and the war, any more than Congress has to touch that which each state raises for its own use.

This distinction will naturally be followed by another. It will occasion every state to examine nicely into the expenses of its civil list, and to regulate, reduce, and bring it into better order than it has hitherto been; because the money for that purpose must be raised apart, and accounted for to the public separately. But while the monies of both were blended, the necessary nicety was not observed, and the poor soldier, who ought to have been the first, was the last who was thought of.

Another convenience will be, that the people, by paying the taxes separately, will know what they are for; and will likewise know that those which are for the defence of the country will cease with the war, or soon after. For although, as I have before observed, the war is their own, and for the support of their own rights and the protection of their own property, yet they have the same right to know, that they have to pay, and it is the want of not knowing that is often the cause of dissatisfaction.

This regulation of keeping the taxes separate has given rise to a regulation in the office of finance, by which it is directed:

"That the receivers shall, at the end of every month, make out an exact account of the monies received by them respectively, during such month, specifying therein the names of the persons from whom the same shall have been received, the dates and the sums; which account they shall respectively cause to be published in one of the newspapers of the state; to the end that every citizen may know how much of the monies collected from him, in taxes, is transmitted to the treasury of the United States for the support of the war; and also, that it may be known what monies have been at the order of the superintendent of finance. It being proper and necessary, that, in a free country, the people should be as fully informed of the administration of their affairs as the nature of things will admit."

It is an agreeable thing to see a spirit of order and economy taking place, after such a series of errors and difficulties. A government or an administration, who means and acts honestly, has nothing to fear, and consequently has nothing to conceal; and it would be of use if a monthly or quarterly account was to be published, as well of the expenditures as of the receipts. Eight millions of dollars must be husbanded with an exceeding deal of care to make it do, and, therefore, as the management must be reputable, the publication would be serviceable.

I have heard of petitions which have been presented to the assembly of this state (and probably the same may have happened in other states) praying to have the taxes lowered. Now the only way to keep taxes low is, for the United States to have ready money to go to market with: and though the taxes to be raised for the present year will fall heavy, and there will naturally be some difficulty in paying them, yet the difficulty, in proportion as money spreads about the country, will every day grow less, and in the end we shall save some millions of dollars by it. We see what a bitter, revengeful enemy we have to deal with, and any expense is cheap compared to their merciless paw. We have seen the unfortunate Carolineans hunted like partridges on the mountains, and it is only by providing means for our defence, that we shall be kept from the same condition. When we think or talk about taxes, we ought to recollect that we lie down in peace and sleep in safety; that we can follow our farms or stores or other occupations, in prosperous tranquillity; and that these inestimable blessings are procured to us by the taxes that we pay. In this view, our taxes are properly our insurance money; they are what we pay to be made safe, and, in strict policy, are the best money we can lay out.

It was my intention to offer some remarks on the impost law of five per cent. recommended by Congress, and to be established as a fund for the payment of the loan-office certificates, and other debts of the United States; but I have already extended my piece beyond my intention. And as this fund will make our system of finance complete, and is strictly just, and consequently requires nothing but honesty to do it, there needs but little to be said upon it.

COMMON SENSE.

PHILADELPHIA, March 5, 1782.

THE AMERICAN CRISIS

XI

England sought frantically to break the alliance between America and France by making tempting offers to each nation in turn. Having discussed this matter with Washington over "a crust of bread and cheese" in his own lodgings, Paine produced *Crisis XI* in May, 1782. "Let the world and Britain know that we are neither to be bought nor sold," declared Paine. "Beaten," he adds, "but not humble; condemned but not penitent; they act like men trembling at fate and catching at a straw." No words could express the feelings of every decent man at this—the latest—example of British corruption. The answer of Americans was clear—"we have nothing to do but to go on with vigor and determination."—*Editor*.

On the Present State of News

SINCE the arrival of two, if not three packets in quick succession, at New York, from England, a variety of unconnected *news* has circulated through the country, and afforded as great a variety of speculation.

That something is the matter in the cabinet and councils of our enemies, on the other side of the water, is certain—that they have run their length of madness, and are under the necessity of changing their measures may easily be seen into; but to what this change of measures may amount, or how far it may correspond with our interest, happiness and duty, is yet uncertain; and from what we have hitherto experienced, we have too much reason to suspect them in every thing.

I do not address this publication so much to the people of America as to the British ministry, whoever they may be, for if it is their intention to promote any kind of negotiation, it is proper they should know beforehand, that the United States have as much honor as bravery; and that they are no more to be seduced from their alliance than their allegiance; that their line of politics is formed and not dependent, like that of their enemy, on chance and accident.

On our part, in order to know, at any time, what the British government will do, we have only to find out what they ought *not* to do, and this last will be their conduct. Forever changing and forever wrong; too distant from America to improve in circumstances, and too unwise to foresee them; scheming without principle, and executing without probability, their whole line of management has hitherto been blunder and baseness. Every campaign has added to their loss, and every year to their disgrace; till unable to go on, and ashamed to go back, their politics have come to a halt, and all their fine prospects to a halter.

Could our affections forgive, or humanity forget the wounds of an injured country—we might, under the influence of a momentary oblivion, stand still and laugh. But they are engraven where no amusement can conceal them, and of a kind for which there is no recompense. Can ye restore to us the beloved dead? Can ye say to the grave, give up the murdered? Can ye obliterate from our memories those who are no more? Think not then to tamper with our feelings by an insidious contrivance, nor suffocate our humanity by seducing us to dishonor.

In March 1780, I publshed part of the Crisis, No. VIII., in the newspapers, but did not conclude it in the following papers, and the remainder has lain by me till the present day.

There appeared about that time some disposition in the British cabinet to cease the further prosecution of the war, and as I had formed my opinion that whenever such a design should take place, it would be accompanied by a dishonorable proposition to America, respecting France, I had suppressed the remainder of that number, not to expose the baseness of any such proposition. But the arrival of the next news from England, declared her determination to go on with the war, and consequently as the political object I had then in view was not become a subject, it was unnecessary in me to bring it forward, which is the reason it was never published.

The matter which I allude to in the unpublished part, I shall now make a quotation of, and apply it as the more enlarged state of things, at this day, shall make convenient or necessary.

It was as follows:

"By the speeches which have appeared from the British Parliament, it is easy to perceive to what impolitic and imprudent excesses their passions and prejudices have, in every instance, carried them during the present war. Provoked at the upright and honorable treaty between America and France, they imagined that nothing more was necessary to be done to prevent its final ratification, than to promise, through the agency of their commissioners (Carlisle, Eden, and Johnstone) a repeal of their once offensive acts of Parliament. The vanity of the conceit, was as unpardonable as the experiment was impolitic. And so convinced am I of their wrong ideas of America, that I shall not wonder, if, in their last stage of political frenzy, they propose to her to break her alliance with France, and enter into one with them. Such a proposition, should it ever be made, and it has been already more than once hinted at in Parliament, would discover such a disposition to perfidiousness, and such disregard of honor and morals, as would add the finishing vice to national corruption.—I do not mention this to put America on the watch, but to put England on her guard, that she do not, in the looseness of her heart, envelop in disgrace every fragment of reputation."—Thus far the quotation.

By the complection of some part of the news which has transpired through the New York papers, it seems probable that this insidious era in the British politics is beginning to make its appearance. I wish it may not; for that which is a disgrace to human nature, throws something of a shade over all the human character, and each individual feels his share of the wound that is given to the whole.

The policy of Britain has ever been to divide America in some way or other. In the beginning of the dispute, she practised every art to prevent or destroy the union of the states, well knowing that could she once get them to stand singly, she could conquer them unconditionally. Failing in this project in America, she renewed it in Europe; and, after the alliance had taken place, she made secret offers to France to induce her to give up America; and what is still more extraordinary, she at the same time made propositions to Dr. Franklin, then in Paris, the very court to which she was secretly applying, to draw off America from France. But this is not all.

On the 14th of September, 1778, the British court, through their secretary, Lord Weymouth, made application to the Marquis d'Almadovar, the Spanish ambassador at London, to "ask the *mediation,*" for these

were the words, of the court of Spain, for the purpose of negotiating
a peace with France, leaving America (as I shall hereafter show) out of
the question. Spain readily offered her mediation, and likewise the city
of Madrid as the place of conference, but withal, proposed, that the
United States of America should be invited to the treaty, and considered
as independent during the time the business was negotiating. But this
was not the view of England. She wanted to draw France from the war,
that she might uninterruptedly pour out all her force and fury upon
America; and being disappointed in this plan, as well through the open
and generous conduct of Spain, as the determination of France, she refused the mediation which she had solicited.

I shall now give some extracts from the justifying memorial of the
Spanish court, in which she has set the conduct and character of Britain,
with respect to America, in a clear and striking point of light.

The memorial, speaking of the refusal of the British court to meet in
conference with commissioners from the United States, who were to be
considered as independent during the time of the conference, says,

"It is a thing very extraordinary and even ridiculous, that the court of
London, who treats the colonies as independent, not only in acting, but of
right, during the war, should have a repugnance to treat them as such only
in acting during a truce, or suspension of hostilities. The convention of Saratoga; the reputing General Burgoyne as a lawful prisoner, in order to suspend his trial; the exchange and liberation of other prisoners made from
the colonies; the having named commissioners to go and supplicate the Americans, at their own doors, request peace of them, and treat with them and
the Congress: and, finally, by a thousand other acts of this sort, authorized
by the court of London, which have been, and are true signs of the acknowledgment of their independence.

"In aggravation of all the foregoing, at the same time the British cabinet
answered the King of Spain in the terms already mentioned, they were in-
sinuating themselves at the court of France by means of secret emissaries,
and making very great offers to her, to abandon the colonies and make peace
with England. But there is yet more; for at this same time the English ministry were treating, by means of another certain emissary, with Dr. Franklin, minister plenipotentiary from the colonies, residing at Paris, to whom
they made various proposals to disunite them from France, and accommodate matters with England.

"From what has been observed, it evidently follows, that the whole of the
British politics was, to disunite the two courts of Paris and Madrid, by means
of the suggestions and offers which she separately made to them; and also

to separate the colonies from their treaties and engagements entered into with France, and induce them to arm against the house of Bourbon, or *more probably to oppress them when they found, from breaking their engagements, that they stood alone and without protection.*

"This, therefore, is the net they laid for the American states; that is to say, to tempt them with flattering and very magnificent promises to come to an accommodation with them, exclusive of any intervention of Spain or France, that the British ministry might always remain the arbiters of the fate of the colonies.

"But the Catholic king (the King of Spain) faithful on the one part of the engagements which bind him to the Most Christian king (the King of France) his nephew; just and upright on the other, to his own subjects, whom he ought to protect and guard against so many insults; and finally, full of humanity and compassion for the Americans and other individuals who suffer in the present war; he is determined to pursue and prosecute it, and to make all the efforts in his power, until he can obtain a solid and permanent peace, with full and satisfactory securities that it shall be observed."

Thus far the memorial; a translation of which into English, may be seen in full, under the head of State Papers, in the Annual Register, for 1779, p. 367.

The extracts I have here given, serve to show the various endeavors and contrivances of the enemy, to draw France from her connection with America, and to prevail on her to make a separate peace with England, leaving America totally out of the question, and at the mercy of a merciless, unprincipled enemy. The opinion, likewise, which Spain has formed of the British cabinet's character for meanness and perfidiousness, is so exactly the opinion of America respecting it, that the memorial, in this instance, contains our own statements and language; for people, however remote, who think alike, will unavoidably speak alike.

Thus we see the insidious use which Britain endeavored to make of the propositions of peace under the mediation of Spain. I shall now proceed to the second proposition under the mediation of the Emperor of Germany and the Empress of Russia; the general outline of which was, that a congress of the several powers at war should meet at Vienna, in 1781, to settle preliminaries of peace.

I could wish myself at liberty to make use of all the information which I am possessed of on this subject, but as there is a delicacy in the matter, I do not conceive it prudent, at least at present, to make references and quotations in the same manner as I have done with respect to the mediation of Spain, who published the whole proceedings herself;

and therefore, what comes from me, on this part of the business, must rest on my own credit with the public, assuring them, that when the whole proceedings, relative to the proposed Congress of Vienna shall appear, they will find my account not only true, but studiously moderate.

We know at the time this mediation was on the carpet, the expectation of the British king and ministry ran high with respect to the conquest of America. The English packet which was taken with the mail on board, and carried into l'Orient, in France, contained letters from Lord G. Germaine to Sir Henry Clinton, which expressed in the fullest terms the ministerial idea of a total conquest. Copies of those letters were sent to congress and published in the newspapers of last year. Colonel [John] Laurens brought over the originals, some of which, signed in the handwriting of the then secretary, Germaine, are now in my possession.

Filled with these high ideas, nothing could be more insolent towards America than the language of the British court on the proposed mediation. A peace with France and Spain she anxiously solicited; but America, as before, was to be left to her mercy, neither would she hear any proposition for admitting an agent from the United States into the congress of Vienna.

On the other hand, France, with an open, noble and manly determination, and a fidelity of a good ally, would hear no proposition for a separate peace, nor even meet in congress at Vienna, without an agent from America: and likewise that the independent character of the United States, represented by the agent, should be fully and unequivocally defined and settled before any conference should be entered on. The reasoning of the court of France on the several propositions of the two imperial courts, which relate to us, is rather in the style of an American than an ally, and she advocated the cause of America as if she had been America herself.—Thus the second mediation, like the first, proved ineffectual.

But since that time, a reverse of fortune has overtaken the British arms, and all their high expectations are dashed to the ground. The noble exertions to the southward under General [Nathanael] Greene;[1] the successful operations of the allied arms in the Chesapeake; the loss of most of their islands in the West Indies, and Minorca in the Mediter-

---

[1] The reference is to the victory scored by General Greene at Camden, South Carolina, May 10, 1781, and to his success in bottling up the British in Charleston until the end of the war.—*Editor*.

ranean; the persevering spirit of Spain against Gibraltar; the expected capture of Jamaica; the failure of making a separate peace with Holland, and the expense of an hundred millions sterling, by which all these fine losses were obtained, have read them a loud lesson of disgraceful misfortune, and necessity has called on them to change their ground.

In this situation of confusion and despair, their present councils have no fixed character. It is now the hurricane months of British politics. Every day seems to have a storm of its own, and they are scudding under the bare poles of hope. Beaten, but not humble; condemned, but not penitent; they act like men trembling at fate and catching at a straw. From this convulsion, in the entrails of their politics, it is more than probable, that the mountain groaning in labor, will bring forth a mouse, as to its size, and a monster in its make. They will try on America the same insidious arts they tried on France and Spain.

We sometimes experience sensations to which language is not equal. The conception is too bulky to be born alive, and in the torture of thinking, we stand dumb. Our feelings, imprisoned by their magnitude, find no way out—and, in the struggle of expression, every finger tries to be a tongue. The machinery of the body seems too little for the mind, and we look about for helps to show our thoughts by. Such must be the sensation of America, whenever Britain, teeming with corruption, shall propose to her to sacrifice her faith.

But, exclusive of the wickedness, there is a personal offence contained in every such attempt. It is calling us villains: for no man asks the other to act the villain unless he believes him inclined to be one. No man attempts to seduce the truly honest woman. It is the supposed looseness of her mind that starts the thoughts of seduction, and he who offers it calls her a prostitute. Our pride is always hurt by the same propositions which offend our principles; for when we are shocked at the crime, we are wounded by the suspicion of our compliance.

Could I convey a thought that might serve to regulate the public mind, I would not make the interest of the alliance the basis of defending it. All the world are moved by interest, and it affords them nothing to boast of. But I would go a step higher, and defend it on the ground of honor and principle. That our public affairs have flourished under the alliance—that it was wisely made, and has been nobly executed—that by its assistance we are enabled to preserve our country from conquest, and expel those who sought our destruction—that it is our true interest to maintain it unimpaired, and that while we do so no enemy can conquer us, are matters which experience has taught us, and the common good of ourselves, abstracted from principles of faith and honor, would lead us to maintain the connection.

But over and above the mere letter of the alliance, we have been nobly and generously treated, and have had the same respect and attention paid to us, as if we had been an old established country. To oblige and be obliged is fair work among mankind, and we want an opportunity of showing to the world that we are a people sensible of kindness and worthy of confidence. Character is to us, in our present circumstances, of more importance than interest. We are a young nation, just stepping upon the stage of public life, and the eye of the world is upon us to see how we act. We have an enemy who is watching to destroy our reputation, and who will go any length to gain some evidence against us, that may serve to render our conduct suspected, and our character odious; because, could she accomplish this, wicked as it is, the world would withdraw from us, as from a people not to be trusted, and our task would then become difficult.

There is nothing which sets the character of a nation in a higher or lower light with others, than the faithfully fulfilling, or perfidiously breaking, of treaties. They are things not to be tampered with: and should Britain, which seems very probable, propose to seduce America into such an act of baseness, it would merit from her some mark of unusual detestation. It is one of those extraordinary instances in which we ought not to be contented with the bare negative of Congress, because it is an affront on the multitude as well as on the government. It goes on the supposition that the public are not honest men, and that they may be managed by contrivance, though they cannot be conquered by arms. But, let the world and Britain know, that we are neither to be bought nor sold; that our mind is great and fixed; our prospect clear; and that we will support our character as firmly as our independence.

But I will go still further; General Conway, who made the motion, in the British Parliament, for discontinuing *offensive* war in America, is a gentleman of an amiable character. We have no personal quarrel with him. But he feels not as we feel; he is not in our situation, and that alone, without any other explanation, is enough.

The British Parliament suppose they have many friends in America, and that, when all chance of conquest is over, they will be able to draw her from her alliance with France. Now, if I have any conception of the human heart, they will fail in this more than in any thing that they have yet tried.

This part of the business is not a question of policy only, but of honor and honesty; and the proposition will have in it something so visibly low and base, that their partisans, if they have any, will be ashamed of it. Men are often hurt by a mean action who are not startled at a wicked one, and this will be such a confession of inability, such a declaration of servile thinking, that the scandal of it will ruin all their hopes.

In short, we have nothing to do but to go on with vigor and determination. The enemy is yet in our country. They hold New York, Charleston, and Savannah, and the very being in those places is an offence, and a part of offensive war, and until they can be driven from them, or captured in them, it would be folly in us to listen to an idle tale. I take it for granted that the British ministry are sinking under the impossibility of carrying on the war. Let them then come to a fair and open peace with France, Spain, Holland and America, in the manner they ought to do; but until then, we can have nothing to say to them.

COMMON SENSE.

PHILADELPHIA, May 22, 1782.

A SUPERNUMERARY CRISIS

This article was Paine's personal appeal to prevent the hanging of a young British officer by the Americans in retaliation for a crime of which he was not guilty.

After the defeat of Cornwallis, Sir Guy Carleton succeeded Sir Henry Clinton at New York.—*Editor*.

TO SIR GUY CARLETON

IT IS the nature of compassion to associate with misfortune; and I address this to you in behalf even of an enemy, a captain in the British service, now on his way to the headquarters of the American army, and unfortunately doomed to death for a crime not his own. A sentence so extraordinary, an execution so repugnant to every human sensation, ought never to be told without the circumstances which produced it: and as the destined victim is yet in existence, and in your hands rests his life or death, I shall briefly state the case, and the melancholy consequence.

Captain Huddy, of the Jersey militia, was attacked in a small fort on Tom's River, by a party of refugees in the British pay and service, was made prisoner, together with his company, carried to New York and lodged in the provost of that city: about three weeks after which, he was taken out of the provost down to the water-side, put into a boat, and brought again upon the Jersey shore, and there, contrary to the practice of all nations but savages, was hung up on a tree, and left hanging till found by our people who took him down and buried him.

The inhabitants of that part of the country where the murder was committed, sent a deputation to General Washington with a full and certified statement of the fact. Struck, as every human breast must be, with such brutish outrage, and determined both to punish and prevent it for the future, the General represented the case to General Clinton, who then commanded, and demanded that the refugee officer who ordered and attended the execution, and whose name is Lippincut, should be delivered up as a murderer; and in case of refusal, that the person of some British officer should suffer in his stead. The demand, though not refused, has not been complied with; and the melancholy lot (not by selection, but by casting lots) has fallen upon Captain Asgill, of the Guards, who, as I have already mentioned, is on his way from Lancaster to camp, a martyr to the general wickedness of the cause he engaged in, and the ingratitude of those whom he served.

The first reflection which arises on this black business is, what sort of men must Englishmen be, and what sort of order and discipline do they preserve in their army, when in the immediate place of their head-quarters, and under the eye and nose of their commander-in-chief, a prisoner can be taken at pleasure from his confinement, and his death made a matter of sport.

The history of the most savage Indians does not produce instances exactly of this kind. They, at least, have a formality in their punishments. With them it is the horridness of revenge, but with your army it is a still greater crime, the horridness of diversion.

The British generals who have succeeded each other, from the time of General Gage to yourself, have all affected to speak in language that they have no right to. In their proclamations, their addresses, their letters to General Washington, and their supplications to Congress (for they deserve no other name) they talk of British honor, British generosity, and British clemency, as if those things were matters of fact; whereas, we whose eyes are open, who speak the same language with yourselves, many of whom were born on the same spot with you, and who can no more be mistaken in your words than in your actions, can declare to all the world, that so far as our knowledge goes, there is not a more detestable character, nor a meaner or more barbarous enemy, than the present British one. With us, you have forfeited all pretensions to reputation, and it is only by holding you like a wild beast, afraid of your keepers, that you can be made manageable. But to return to the point in question.

Though I can think no man innocent who has lent his hand to destroy the country which he did not plant, and to ruin those that he could not enslave, yet, abstracted from all ideas of right and wrong on the original question, Captain Asgill, in the present case, is not the guilty man. The villain and the victim are here separated characters. You hold the one and we the other. You disown, or affect to disown and reprobate the conduct of Lippincut, yet you give him a sanctuary; and by so doing you as effectually become the executioner of Asgill, as if you had put the rope on his neck, and dismissed him from the world. Whatever your feelings on this interesting occasion may be are best known to yourself. Within the grave of your own mind lies buried the fate of Asgill. He becomes the corpse of your will, or the survivor of your justice. Deliver up the one, and you save the other; withhold the one, and the other dies by your choice.

On our part the case is exceeding plain; *an officer has been taken from his confinement and murdered, and the murderer is within your lines.* Your army has been guilty of a thousand instances of equal cruelty, but they have been rendered equivocal, and sheltered from personal detection. Here the crime is fixed; and is one of those extraordinary cases which can neither be denied nor palliated, and to which the custom of war does not apply; for it never could be supposed that such a brutal outrage would ever be committed. It is an original in the history of civilized barbarians, and is truly British.

On your part you are accountable to us for the personal safety of the prisoners within your walls. Here can be no mistake; they can neither be spies nor suspected as such; your security is not endangered, nor your operations subjected to miscarriage, by men immured within a dungeon. They differ in every circumstance from men in the field, and leave no pretence for severity of punishment. But if to the dismal condition of captivity with you must be added the constant apprehensions of death; if to be imprisoned is so nearly to be entombed; and if, after all, the murderers are to be protected, and thereby the crime encouraged, wherein do you differ from [American] Indians either in conduct or character?

We can have no idea of your honor, or your justice, in any future transaction, of what nature it may be, while you shelter within your lines an outrageous murderer, and sacrifice in his stead an officer of your own. If you have no regard to us, at least spare the blood which it is your duty to save. Whether the punishment will be greater on him, who, in this case, innocently dies, or on him whom sad necessity forces to retaliate, is, in the nicety of sensation, an undecided question? It rests with you to prevent the sufferings of both. You have nothing to do but to give up the murderer, and the matter ends.

But to protect him, be he who he may, is to patronize his crime, and to trifle it off by frivolous and unmeaning inquiries, is to promote it.

There is no declaration you can make, nor promise you can give that will obtain credit. It is the man and not the apology that is demanded.

You see yourself pressed on all sides to spare the life of your own officer, for die he will if you withhold justice. The murder of Captain Huddy is an offence not to be borne with, and there is no security which we can have, that such actions or similar ones shall not be repeated, but by making the punishment fall upon yourselves. To destroy the last security of captivity, and to take the unarmed, the unresisting prisoner to private and sportive execution, is carrying barbarity too high for silence. The evil *must* be put an end to; and the choice of persons rests with you. But if your attachment to the guilty is stronger than to the innocent, you invent a crime that must destroy your character, and if the cause of your king needs to be so supported, for ever cease, sir, to torture our remembrance with the wretched phrases of British honor, British generosity and British clemency.

From this melancholy circumstance, learn, sir, a lesson of morality. The refugees are men whom your predecessors have instructed in wickedness, the better to fit them to their master's purpose. To make them useful, they have made them vile, and the consequence of their tutored villainy is now descending on the heads of their encouragers. They have been trained like hounds to the scent of blood, and cherished in every species of dissolute barbarity. Their ideas of right and wrong are worn away in the constant habitude of repeated infamy, till, like men practised in execution, they feel not the value of another's life.

The task before you, though painful, is not difficult; give up the murderer, and save your officer, as the first outset of a necessary reformation.

COMMON SENSE.

PHILADELPHIA, May 31, 1782.

[1] In addition to his *Supernumerary Crisis* Paine wrote to Washington on September 7, 1782, urging that he spare the life of the British captain. "For my own part," he observed, "I am fully persuaded that a suspension of his fate, still holding it *in terrorem,* will operate on a greater quantity of their passions and vices, and restrain them more, than his execution would do. However, the change of measures which seems now to be taking place, gives somewhat of a new cast to former designs; and if the case, without the execution, can be so managed as to answer all the purposes of the last, it will look much better hereafter, when the sensations that now provoke, and the circumstances which would justify his exit shall be forgotten." On September 30th, Washington wrote to a member of Congress intimating that that body should release Asgill, and in a letter to Paine he wrote: "The case of Captain Asgill has indeed been spun out to a great length—but, with you, I hope that its termination will not be unfavourable to this country."—*Editor.*

THE AMERICAN CRISIS

XII

In September 1782, Americans learned that the new Shelburne ministry was opposed to granting independence, believing that the two countries could still be united. Paine wrote his new *Crisis* to disillusion the Earl of Shelburne who had become Prime Minister after Rockingham had died.

Paine came to know Shelburne well when he was in England after the war. In a letter to Thomas Jefferson, March 12, 1789, Paine writes: "I believe I am not so much in the good graces of the Marquis of Lansdowne as I used to be—I do not answer his purpose. He was always talking of a sort of reconnection of England and America, and my coldness and reserve on this subject checked communication."—*Editor.*

To the Earl of Shelburne

MY LORD,—A speech, which has been printed in several of the British and New York newspapers, as coming from your lordship, in answer to one from the Duke of Richmond, of the 10th of July last, contains expressions and opinions so new and singular, and so enveloped in mysterious reasoning, that I address this publication to you, for the purpose of giving them a free and candid examination. The speech I allude to is in these words:

"His lordship said, it had been mentioned in another place, that he had been guilty of inconsistency. To clear himself of this, he asserted that he still held the same principles in respect to American independence which he at first imbibed. He had been, and yet was of opinion, whenever the Parliament of Great Britain acknowledges that point, the sun of England's glory is set forever. Such were the sentiments he possessed on a former day, and such the sentiments he continued to hold at this hour. It was the opinion of Lord Chatham, as well as many other able statesmen. Other noble lords, however, think differently, and as the majority of the cabinet support them, he acquiesced in the measure, dissenting from the idea; and the point is settled for bringing the matter into the full discussion of Parliament, where it will be candidly, fairly, and impartially debated. The independence of America would end in the ruin of England; and that a peace patched up with France, would give that proud enemy the means of yet trampling on this country. The sun of England's glory he wished not to see set forever; he looked for a spark at least to be left, which might in time light us up to a new day. But if independence was to be granted, if Parliament deemed that measure prudent, he foresaw, in his own mind, that England was undone. He wished to God that he had been deputed to Congress, that he might plead the cause of that country as well as of this, and that he might exercise whatever powers he possessed as an orator, to save both from ruin, in a conviction to Congress, that, if their independence was signed, their liberties were gone forever.

"Peace, his lordship added, was a desirable object, but it must be an honorable peace, and not an humiliating one, dictated by France, or insisted on by America. It was very true, that this kingdom was not in a flourishing state, it was impoverished by war. But if we were not rich, it was evident that France was poor. If we were straitened in our finances, the enemy were exhausted in their resources. This was a great empire; it abounded with brave men, who were able and willing to fight in a common cause; the language of humiliation should not, therefore, be the language of Great Britain. His lordship said, that he was not afraid nor ashamed of those expressions going to America. There were numbers, great numbers there, who were of the same way of thinking, in respect to that country being dependent on this, and who, with his lordship, perceived ruin and independence linked together."

Thus far the speech; on which I remark—That his lordship is a total stranger to the mind and sentiments of America; that he has wrapped himself up in fond delusion, that something less than independence, may, under his administration, be accepted; and he wishes himself sent to Congress, to prove the most extraordinary of all doctrines, which is, that *independence,* the sublimest of all human conditions, is loss of liberty.

In answer to which we may say, that in order to know what the contrary word *dependence* means, we have only to look back to those years of severe humiliation, when the mildest of all petitions could obtain no other notice than the haughtiest of all insults; and when the base terms of unconditional submission were demanded, or undistinguishable destruction threatened. It is nothing to us that the ministry have been

changed, for they may be changed again. The guilt of a government is
the crime of a whole country; and the nation that can, though but for
a moment, think and act as England has done, can never afterwards
be believed or trusted. There are cases in which it is as impossible to
restore character to life, as it is to recover the dead. It is a phœnix that
can expire but once, and from whose ashes there is no resurrection. Some
offences are of such a slight composition, that they reach no further
than the temper, and are created or cured by a thought. But the sin of
England has struck the heart of America, and nature has not left in
our power to say we can forgive.

Your lordship wishes for an opportunity to plead before Congress
the cause of England and America, and to save, as you say, *both from
ruin.*

That the country, which, for more than seven years has sought our
destruction, should now cringe to solicit our protection, is adding the
wretchedness of disgrace to the misery of disappointment; and if England has the least spark of supposed honor left, that spark must be
darkened by asking, and extinguished by receiving, the smallest favor
from America; for the criminal who owes his life to the grace and mercy
of the injured, is more executed by living, than he who dies.

But a thousand pleadings, even from your lordship, can have no effect.
Honor, interest, and every sensation of the heart, would plead against
you. We are a people who think not as you think; and what is equally
true, you cannot feel as we feel. The situations of the two countries are
exceedingly different. Ours has been the seat of war; yours has seen
nothing of it. The most wanton destruction has been committed in our
sight; the most insolent barbarity has been acted on our feelings. We can
look round and see the remains of burnt and destroyed houses, once
the fair fruit of hard industry, and now the striking monuments of British brutality. We walk over the dead whom we loved, in every part of
America, and remember by whom they fell. There is scarcely a village
but brings to life some melancholy thought, and reminds us of what we
have suffered, and of those we have lost by the inhumanity of Britain. A
thousand images arise to us, which, from situation, you cannot see, and
are accompanied by as many ideas which you cannot know; and therefore your supposed system of reasoning would apply to nothing, and
all your expectations die of themselves.

The question whether England shall accede to the independence of
America, and which your lordship says is to undergo a parliamentary

discussion, is so very simple, and composed of so few cases, that it scarcely needs a debate.

It is the only way out of an expensive and ruinous war, which has no object, and without which acknowledgment there can be no peace.

But your lordship says, *the sun of Great Britain will set whenever she acknowledges the independence of America.*—Whereas the metaphor would have been strictly just, to have left the sun wholly out of the figure, and have ascribed her not acknowledging it to the influence of the moon.

But the expression, if true, is the greatest confession of disgrace that could be made, and furnishes America with the highest notions of sovereign independent importance. Mr. Wedderburne, about the year 1776, made use of an idea of much the same kind,—*Relinquish America!* says he—*What is it but to desire a giant to shrink spontaneously into a dwarf.*

Alas! are those people who call themselves Englishmen, of so little internal consequence, that when America is gone, or shuts her eyes upon them, their sun is set, they can shine no more, but grope about in obscurity, and contract into insignificant animals? Was America, then, the giant of the empire, and England only her dwarf in waiting! Is the case so strangely altered, but those who once thought we could not live without them, are now brought to declare that they cannot exist without us? Will they tell to the world, and that from their first minister of state, that America is their all in all; that it is by her importance only that they can live, and breathe, and have a being? Will they, who long since threatened to bring us to their feet, bow themselves to ours, and own that without us they are not a nation? Are they become so unqualified to debate on independence, that they have lost all idea of it themselves, and are calling to the rocks and mountains of America to cover their insignificance? Or, if America is lost, is it manly to sob over it like a child for its rattle, and invite the laughter of the world by declarations of disgrace? Surely, a more consistent line of conduct would be to bear it without complaint; and to show that England, without America, can preserve her independence, and a suitable rank with other European powers. You were not contented while you had her, and to weep for her now is childish.

But Lord Shelburne thinks something may yet be done. What that something is, or how it is to be accomplished, is a matter in obscurity. By arms there is no hope. The experience of nearly eight years, with the expense of an hundred million pounds sterling, and the loss of two armies, must positively decide that point. Besides, the British have lost their interest in America with the disaffected. Every part of it has been tried. There is no new scene left for delusion: and the thousands who have been ruined by adhering to them, and have now to quit the settlements which they had acquired, and be conveyed like transports to cultivate the deserts of Augustine and Nova Scotia, has put an end to all further expectations of aid.

If you cast your eyes on the people of England, what have they to console themselves with for the millions expended? Or, what encouragement is there left to continue throwing good money after bad? America can carry on the war for ten years longer, and all the charges of government included, for less than you can defray the charges of war and government for one year. And I, who know both countries, know well, that the people of America can afford to pay their share of the expense much better than the people of England can. Besides, it is their own estates and property, their own rights, liberties and government, that they are defending; and were they not to do it, they would deserve to lose all, and none would pity them. The fault would be their own, and their punishment just.

The British army in America care not how long the war lasts. They enjoy an easy and indolent life. They fatten on the folly of one country and the spoils of another; and, between their plunder and their prey, may go home rich. But the case is very different with the laboring farmer, the working tradesman, and the necessitous poor in England, the sweat of whose brow goes day after day to feed, in prodigality and sloth, the army that is robbing both them and us. Removed from the eye of that country that supports them, and distant from the government that employs them, they cut and carve for themselves, and there is none to call them to account.

But England will be ruined, says Lord Shelburne, if America is independent.

Then I say, is England already ruined, for America is already independent: and if Lord Shelburne will not allow this, he immediately denies the fact which he infers. Besides, to make England the mere creature of America, is paying too great a compliment to us, and too little to himself.

But the declaration is a rhapsody of inconsistency. For to say, as Lord Shelburne has numberless times said, that the war against America is ruinous, and yet to continue the prosecution of that ruinous war for the purpose of avoiding ruin, is a language which cannot be understood. Neither is it possible to see how the independence of America is to accomplish the ruin of England after the war is over, and yet not affect it before. America cannot be more independent of her, nor a greater enemy to her, hereafter than she now is; nor can England derive less advantages from her than at present: why then is ruin to follow in the best state of the case, and not in the worst? And if not in the worst, why is it to follow at all?

That a nation is to be ruined by peace and commerce, and fourteen or fifteen millions a-year less expenses than before, is a new doctrine in politics. We have heard much clamor of national savings and economy; but surely the true economy would be, to save the whole charge of a silly, foolish, and headstrong war; because, compared with this, all other retrenchments are baubles and trifles.

But is it possible that Lord Shelburne can be serious in supposing that the least advantage can be obtained by arms, or that any advantage can be equal to the expense or the danger of attempting it? Will not the capture of one army after another satisfy him, must all become prisoners? Must England ever be the sport of hope, and the victim of delusion? Sometimes our currency was to fail; another time our army was to disband; then whole provinces were to revolt. Such a general said this and that; another wrote so and so; Lord Chatham was of this opinion; and lord somebody else of another. To-day 20,000 Russians and 20 Russian ships of the line were to come; to-morrow the empress was abused without mercy or decency. Then the Emperor of Germany was to be bribed with a million of money, and the King of Prussia was to do wonderful things. At one time it was, Lo here! and then it was, Lo there! Sometimes this power, and sometimes that power, was to engage in the war, just as if the whole world was mad and foolish like Britain. And thus, from year to year, has every straw been catched at, and every Will-with-a-wisp led them a new dance.

This year a still newer folly is to take place. Lord Shelburne wishes to be sent to Congress, and he thinks that something may be done.

Are not the repeated declarations of Congress, and which all America supports, that they will not even hear any proposals whatever, until the unconditional and unequivocal independence of America is recognised; are not, I say, these declarations answer enough?

But for England to receive any thing from America now, after so many insults, injuries and outrages, acted towards us, would show such a spirit of meanness in her, that we could not but despise her for accepting it. And so far from Lord Shelburne's coming here to solicit it, it would be the greatest disgrace we could do them to offer it. England would appear a wretch indeed, at this time of day, to ask or owe any thing to the bounty of America. Has not the name of Englishman blots enough upon it, without inventing more? Even Lucifer would scorn to reign in heaven by permission, and yet an Englishman can creep for only an entrance into America. Or, has a land of liberty so many charms, that to be a doorkeeper in it is better than to be an English minister of state?

But what can this expected something be? Or, if obtained, what can it amount to, but new disgraces, contentions and quarrels? The people of America have for years accustomed themselves to think and speak so freely and contemptuously of English authority, and the inveteracy is so deeply rooted, that a person invested with any authority from that country, and attempting to exercise it here, would have the life of a toad under a harrow. They would look on him as an interloper, to whom their compassion permitted a residence. He would be no more than the Mungo of a farce; and if he disliked that, he must set off. It would be a station of degradation, debased by our pity, and despised by our pride, and would place England in a more contemptible situation than any she has yet been in during the war. We have too high an opinion of ourselves, even to think of yielding again the least obedience to outlandish authority; and for a thousand reasons, England would be the last country in the world to yield it to. She has been treacherous, and we know it. Her character is gone, and we have seen the funeral.

Surely she loves to fish in troubled waters, and drink the cup of contention, or she would not now think of mingling her affairs with those of America. It would be like a foolish dotard taking to his arms the bride that despises him, or who has placed on his head the ensigns of her disgust. It is kissing the hand that boxes his ears, and proposing to renew the exchange. The thought is as servile as the war is wicked, and shows the last scene of the drama to be as inconsistent as the first.

As America is gone, the only act of manhood is to *let her go*. Your lordship had no hand in the separation, and you will gain no honor by temporising politics. Besides, there is something so exceedingly whimsical, unsteady, and even insincere in the present conduct of England, that she exhibits herself in the most dishonorable colors.

On the second of August last, General Carleton and Admiral Digby wrote to General Washington in these words:

"The resolution of the House of Commons, of the 27th of February last, has been placed in Your Excellency's hands, and intimations given at the same time that further pacific measures were likely to follow. Since which, until the present time, we have had no direct communications with England; but a mail is now arrived, which brings us very important information. We are acquainted, sir, *by authority,* that negotiations for a general peace have already commenced at Paris, and that Mr. Grenville is invested with full powers to treat with all the parties at war, and is now at Paris in execution of his commission. And we are further, sir, made acquainted, *that His Majesty, in order to remove any obstacles to that peace which he so ardently wishes to restore, has commanded his ministers to direct Mr. Grenville, that the independence of the Thirteen United Provinces, should be proposed by him in the first instance, instead of making it a condition of a general treaty."*

Now, taking your present measures into view, and comparing them with the declaration in this letter, pray what is the word of your king, or his ministers, or the Parliament, good for? Must we not look upon you as a confederated body of faithless, treacherous men, whose assurances are fraud, and their language deceit? What opinion can we possibly form of you, but that you are a lost, abandoned, profligate nation, who sport even with your own character, and are to be held by nothing but the bayonet or the halter?

To say, after this, *that the sun of Great Britain will be set whenever she acknowledges the independence of America,* when the not doing it is the unqualified lie of government, can be no other than the language of ridicule, the jargon of inconsistency. There were thousands in America who predicted the delusion, and looked upon it as a trick of treachery, to take us from our guard, and draw off our attention from the only system of finance, by which we can be called, or deserve to be called, a sovereign, independent people. The fraud, on your part, might be worth attempting, but the sacrifice to obtain it is too high.

There are others who credited the assurance, because they thought it impossible that men who had their characters to establish, would begin with a lie. The prosecution of the war by the former ministry was savage and horrid; since which it has been mean, trickish, and delusive. The one went greedily into the passion of revenge, the other into the subtleties of low contrivance; till, between the crimes of both, there is scarcely left a man in America, be he Whig or Tory, who does not despise or detest the conduct of Britain.

The management of Lord Shelburne, whatever may be his views, is a caution to us, and must be to the world, never to regard British assurances. A perfidy so notorious cannot be hid. It stands even in the public papers of New York, with the names of Carleton and Digby affixed to it. It is a proclamation that the king of England is not to be believed; that the spirit of lying is the governing principle of the ministry. It is holding up the character of the House of Commons to public infamy, and warning all men not to credit them. Such are the consequences which Lord Shelburne's management has brought upon his country.

After the authorized declarations contained in Carleton and Digby's letter, you ought, from every motive of honor, policy and prudence, to have fulfilled them, whatever might have been the event. It was the least atonement that you could possibly make to America, and the greatest kindness you could do to yourselves; for you will save millions by a general peace, and you will lose as many by continuing the war.

COMMON SENSE.

PHILADELPHIA, Oct. 29, 1782.

P. S. The manuscript copy of this letter is sent your lordship, by the way of our head-quarters, to New York, inclosing a late pamphlet of mine, addressed to the Abbé Raynal,[1] which will serve to give your lordship some idea of the principles and sentiments of America.

C. S.

---

[1] A Frenchman whose work *On the Revolution of the English Colonies in North America* was carefully studied by Paine. The pamphlet referred to is, of course, his *Letter to Abbé Raynal.* It is printed in the second volume of this edition.—*Editor.*

THE AMERICAN CRISIS

XIII

In April, 1783, the war came to an end and American independence was recognized by the British. "The times that tried men's souls are over," Paine declares in the opening sentence of his last *Crisis*. Again as in his other articles, Paine warned his countrymen that everything in the future depended on the absolute sovereignty of the United States. This *Crisis* contains some of Paine's finest utterances in behalf of a centralized government, and a clearly formulated attack upon the theory of states' rights and sectional antagonisms.—*Editor*.

THOUGHTS ON THE PEACE, AND THE PROBABLE ADVANTAGES THEREOF

"THE times that tried men souls," [1] are over—and the greatest and completest revolution the world ever knew, gloriously and happily accomplished.

But to pass from the extremes of danger to safety—from the tumult of war to the tranquillity of peace, though sweet in contemplation, requires a gradual composure of the senses to receive it. Even calmness has the power of stunning, when it opens too instantly upon us. The long and raging hurricane that should cease in a moment, would leave us in a state rather of wonder than enjoyment; and some moments of recollection must pass, before we could be capable of tasting the felicity of repose. There are but few instances, in which the mind is fitted for sudden transitions: it takes in its pleasures by reflection and comparison and those must have time to act, before the relish for new scenes is complete.

---

[1] "These are the times that try men's souls," The Crisis No. I. published December, 1776.—*Author*.

In the present case—the mighty magnitude of the object—the various uncertainties of fate it has undergone—the numerous and complicated dangers we have suffered or escaped—the eminence we now stand on, and the vast prospect before us, must all conspire to impress us with contemplation.

To see it in our power to make a world happy—to teach mankind the art of being so—to exhibit, on the theatre of the universe a character hitherto unknown—and to have, as it were, a new creation intrusted to our hands, are honors that command reflection, and can neither be too highly estimated, nor too gratefully received.

In this pause then of recollection—while the storm is ceasing, and the long agitated mind vibrating to a rest, let us look back on the scenes we have passed, and learn from experience what is yet to be done.

Never, I say, had a country so many openings to happiness as this. Her setting out in life, like the rising of a fair morning, was unclouded and promising. Her cause was good. Her principles just and liberal. Her temper serene and firm. Her conduct regulated by the nicest steps, and everything about her wore the mark of honor. It is not every country (perhaps there is not another in the world) that can boast so fair an origin. Even the first settlement of America corresponds with the character of the revolution. Rome, once the proud mistress of the universe, was originally a band of ruffians. Plunder and rapine made her rich, and her oppression of millions made her great. But America need never be ashamed to tell her birth, nor relate the stages by which she rose to empire.

The remembrance, then, of what is past, if it operates rightly, must inspire her with the most laudable of all ambition, that of adding to the fair fame she began with. The world has seen her great in adversity; struggling, without a thought of yielding, beneath accumulated difficulties, bravely, nay proudly, encountering distress, and rising in resolution as the storm increased. All this is justly due to her, for her fortitude has merited the character. Let, then, the world see that she can bear prosperity: and that her honest virtue in time of peace, is equal to the bravest virtue in time of war.

She is now descending to the scenes of quiet and domestic life. Not beneath the cypress shade of disappointment, but to enjoy in her own land, and under her own vine, the sweet of her labors, and the reward of her toil.—In this situation, may she never forget that a fair national reputation is of as much importance as independence. That it possesses a charm that wins upon the world, and makes even enemies civil. That it gives a dignity which is often superior to power, and commands reverence where pomp and splendor fail.

It would be a circumstance ever to be lamented and never to be forgotten, were a single blot, from any cause whatever, suffered to fall on a revolution, which to the end of time must be an honor to the age that accomplished it: and which has contributed more to enlighten the world, and diffuse a spirit of freedom and liberality among mankind, than any human event (if this may be called one) that ever preceded it.

It is not among the least of the calamities of a long continued war, that it unhinges the mind from those nice sensations which at other times appear so amiable. The continual spectacle of woe blunts the finer feelings, and the necessity of bearing with the sight, renders it familiar. In like manner, are many of the moral obligations of society weakened, till the custom of acting by necessity becomes an apology, where it is truly a crime. Yet let but a nation conceive rightly of its character, and it will be chastely just in protecting it. None ever began with a fairer than America and none can be under a greater obligation to preserve it.

The debt which America has contracted, compared with the cause she has gained, and the advantages to flow from it, ought scarcely to be mentioned. She has it in her choice to do, and to live as happily as she pleases. The world is in her hands. She has no foreign power to monopolize her commerce, perplex her legislation, or control her prosperity. The struggle is over, which must one day have happened, and, perhaps, never could have happened at a better time.[2] And instead of a domineer-

[2] That the revolution began at the exact period of time best fitted to the purpose, is sufficiently proved by the event.—But the great hinge on which the whole machine turned, is the *Union of the States:* and this union was naturally produced by the inability of any one state to support itself against any foreign enemy without the assistance of the rest.

Had the states severally been less able than they were when the war began, their united strength would not have been equal to the undertaking, and they must in all human probability have failed.—And, on the other hand, had they severally been more able, they might not have seen, or, what is more, might not have felt, the necessity of uniting: and, either by attempting to stand alone or in small confederacies, would have been separately conquered.

Now, as we cannot see a time (and many years must pass away before it can arrive) when the strength of any one state, or several united, can be equal to the whole of the present United States, and as we have seen the extreme difficulty of collectively prosecuting the war to a successful issue, and preserving our national importance in the world, therefore, from the experience we have had, and the knowledge we have gained, we must, unless we make a waste of wisdom, be strongly impressed with the advantage, as well as the necessity of strengthening that happy union which had been our salvation, and without which we should have been a ruined people.

ing master, she has gained an *ally* whose exemplary greatness, and universal liberality, have extorted a confession even from her enemies.

With the blessings of peace, independence, and an universal commerce, the states, individually and collectively, will have leisure and opportunity to regulate and establish their domestic concerns, and to put it beyond the power of calumny to throw the least reflection on their honor. Character is much easier kept than recovered, and that man, if any such there be, who, from sinister views, or littleness of soul, lends unseen his hand to injure it, contrives a wound it will never be in his power to heal.

As we have established an inheritance for posterity, let that inheritance descend, with every mark of an honorable conveyance. The little it will cost, compared with the worth of the states, the greatness of the object, and the value of the national character, will be a profitable exchange.

But that which must more forcibly strike a thoughtful, penetrating mind, and which includes and renders easy all inferior concerns, is the UNION OF THE STATES. On this our great national character depends. It is this which must give us importance abroad and security at home. It is through this only that we are, or can be, nationally known in the world; it is the flag of the United States which renders our ships and commerce safe on the seas, or in a foreign port. Our Mediterranean passes must be obtained under the same style. All our treaties, whether of alliance, peace, or commerce, are formed under the sovereignty of the United States, and Europe knows us by no other name or title.

The division of the empire into states is for our own convenience, but abroad this distinction ceases. The affairs of each state are local. They can go no further than to itself. And were the whole worth of even the richest of them expended in revenue, it would not be sufficient to sup-

---

While I was writing this note, I cast my eye on the pamphlet, Common Sense, from which I shall make an extract, as it exactly applies to the case. It is as follows:

"I have never met with a man, either in England or America, who has not confessed it as his opinion that a separation between the countries would take place one time or other; and there is no instance in which we have shown less judgment, than in endeavoring to describe what we call the ripeness or fitness of the continent for independence.

"As all men allow the measure, and differ only in their opinion of the time, let us, in order to remove mistakes, take a general survey of things, and endeavor, if possible, to find out the *very time*. But we need not to go far, the inquiry ceases at once, for, *the time has found us*. The general concurrence, the glorious union of all things prove the fact.

"It is not in numbers, but in a union, that our great strength lies. The continent is just arrived at that pitch of strength, in which no single colony is able to support itself, and the whole, when united, can accomplish the matter; and either more or less than this, might be fatal in its effects."—*Author*.

port sovereignty against a foreign attack. In short, we have no other national sovereignty than as United States. It would even be fatal for us if we had—too expensive to be maintained, and impossible to be supported. Individuals, or individual states, may call themselves what they please; but the world, and especially the world of enemies, is not to be held in awe by the whistling of a name. Sovereignty must have power to protect all the parts that compose and constitute it: and as UNITED STATES we are equal to the importance of the title, but otherwise we are not. Our union, well and wisely regulated and cemented, is the cheapest way of being great—the easiest way of being powerful, and the happiest invention in government which the circumstances of America can admit of.—Because it collects from each state, that which, by being inadequate, can be of no use to it, and forms an aggregate that serves for all.

The states of Holland are an unfortunate instance of the effects of individual sovereignty. Their disjointed condition exposes them to numerous intrigues, losses, calamities, and enemies; and the almost impossibility of bringing their measures to a decision, and that decision into execution, is to them, and would be to us, a source of endless misfortune.

It is with confederated states as with individuals in society; something must be yielded up to make the whole secure. In this view of things we gain by what we give, and draw an annual interest greater than the capital.—I ever feel myself hurt when I hear the union, that great palladium of our liberty and safety, the least irreverently spoken of. It is the most sacred thing in the constitution of America, and that which every man should be most proud and tender of. Our citizenship in the United States is our national character. Our citizenship in any particular state is only our local distinction. By the latter we are known at home, by the former to the world. Our great title is AMERICANS—our inferior one varies with the place.

So far as my endeavors could go, they have all been directed to conciliate the affections, unite the interests, and draw and keep the mind of the country together; and the better to assist in this foundation work of the revolution, I have avoided all places of profit or office, either in the state I live in, or in the United States; [3] kept myself at a distance from all parties and party connections, and even disregarded all private and

---

[3] Paine, of course, is referring only to the previous two years. Prior to that time he had been Secretary of the Congressional Committee of Foreign Affairs, and Clerk of the Pennsylvania Legislature.—*Editor*.

inferior concerns: and when we take into view the great work which we have gone through, and feel, as we ought to feel, the just importance of it, we shall then see, that the little wranglings and indecent contentions of personal parley, are as dishonorable to our characters, as they are injurious to our repose.

It was the cause of America that made me an author. The force with which it struck my mind, and the dangerous condition the country appeared to me in, by courting an impossible and an unnatural reconciliation with those who were determined to reduce her, instead of striking out into the only line that could cement and save her, A DECLARATION OF INDEPENDENCE, made it impossible for me, feeling as I did, to be silent: and if, in the course of more than seven years, I have rendered her any service, I have likewise added something to the reputation of literature, by freely and disinterestedly employing it in the great cause of mankind, and showing that there may be genius without prostitution.

Independence always appeared to me practicable and probable, provided the sentiment of the country could be formed and held to the object: and there is no instance in the world, where a people so extended, and wedded to former habits of thinking, and under such a variety of circumstances, were so instantly and effectually pervaded, by a turn in politics, as in the case of independence; and who supported their opinion, undiminished, through such a succession of good and ill fortune, till they crowned it with success.

But as the scenes of war are closed, and every man preparing for home and happier times, I therefore take my leave of the subject. I have most sincerely followed it from beginning to end, and through all its turns and windings: and whatever country I may hereafter be in, I shall always feel an honest pride at the part I have taken and acted, and a gratitude to nature and providence for putting it in my power to be of some use to mankind.

COMMON SENSE.

PHILADELPHIA, April 19, 1783.[4]

[4] This date marked the eighth anniversary of the Battle of Lexington and Concord, where the shot heard around the world was fired.—*Editor.*

A SUPERNUMERARY CRISIS

To the People of America

IN "Rivington's New York Gazette," [1] of December 6th, is a publication, under the appearance of a letter from London, dated September 30th; and is on a subject which demands the attention of the United States.

The public will remember that a treaty of commerce between the United States and England was set on foot last spring, and that until the said treaty could be completed, a bill was brought into the British Parliament by the then chancellor of the exchequer, Mr. Pitt, to admit and legalize (as the case then required) the commerce of the United States into the British ports and dominions. But neither the one nor the other has been completed. The commercial treaty is either broken off, or remains as it began; and the bill in Parliament has been thrown aside. And in lieu thereof, a selfish system of English politics has started up, calculated to fetter the commerce of America, by engrossing to England the carrying trade of the American produce to the West India islands.

Among the advocates for this last measure is Lord Sheffield, a member of the British Parliament, who has published a pamphlet entitled "Observations on the Commerce of the American States." The pamphlet has two objects; the one is to allure the Americans to purchase British manufactures; [2] and the other to spirit up the British Parliament to

---

[1] A leading Tory newspaper.—*Editor*.

[2] English manufacturers did more than sponsor the publication of pamphlets to lure Americans to purchase British manufactures. They dumped goods on the American market even at a loss to destroy the industries that had arisen in this country during the war.—*Editor*.

prohibit the citizens of the United States from trading to the West India islands.

Viewed in this light, the pamphlet, though in some parts dexterously written, is an absurdity. It offends, in the very act of endeavoring to ingratiate; and his lordship, as a politician, ought not to have suffered the two objects to have appeared together. The latter alluded to, contains extracts from the pamphlet, with high encomiums on Lord Sheffield, for laboriously endeavoring (as the letter styles it) "to show the mighty advantages of retaining the carrying trade."

Since the publication of this pamphlet in England, the commerce of the United States to the West Indies, in American vessels, has been prohibited; and all intercourse, except in British bottoms, the property of and navigated by British subjects, cut off.

That a country has a right to be as foolish as it pleases, has been proved by the practice of England for many years past: in her island situation, sequestered from the world, she forgets that her whispers are heard by other nations; and in her plans of politics and commerce she seems not to know, that other votes are necessary besides her own. America would be equally as foolish as Britain, were she to suffer so great a degradation on her flag, and such a stroke on the freedom of her commerce, to pass without a balance.

We admit the right of any nation to prohibit the commerce of another into its own dominions, where there are no treaties to the contrary; but as this right belongs to one side as well as the other, there is always a way left to bring avarice and insolence to reason.

But the ground of security which Lord Sheffield has chosen to erect his policy upon, is of a nature which ought, and I think must, awaken in every American a just and strong sense of national dignity. Lord Sheffield appears to be sensible, that in advising the British nation and Parliament to engross to themselves so great a part of the carrying trade of America, he is attempting a measure which cannot succeed, if the politics of the United States be properly directed to counteract the assumption.

But, says he, in his pamphlet, "It will be a long time before the American states can be brought to act as a nation, neither are they to be feared as such by us."

What is this more or less than to tell us, that while we have no national system of commerce, the British will govern our trade by their own laws and proclamations as they please. The quotation discloses a

truth too serious to be overlooked, and too mischievous not to be remedied.

Among other circumstances which led them to this discovery none
could operate so effectually as the injudicious, uncandid and indecent
opposition made by sundry persons in a certain state,[3] to the recommendations of Congress last winter, for an import duty of five per cent.
It could not but explain to the British a weakness in the national power
of America, and encourage them to attempt restrictions on her trade,
which otherwise they would not have dared to hazard. Neither is there
any state in the union, whose policy was more misdirected to its interest
than the state I allude to, because her principal support is the carrying
trade, which Britain, induced by the want of a well-centred power in the
United States to protect and secure, is now attempting to take away. It
fortunately happened (and to no state in the union more than the state
in question) that the terms of peace were agreed on before the opposition appeared, otherwise, there cannot be a doubt, that if the same idea
of the diminished authority of America had occurred to them at that
time as has occurred to them since, but they would have made the same
grasp at the fisheries, as they have done at the carrying trade.

It is surprising that an authority which can be supported with so
much ease, and so little expense, and capable of such extensive advantages to the country, should be cavilled at by those whose duty it is to
watch over it, and whose existence as a people depends upon it. But this,
perhaps, will ever be the case, till some misfortune awakens us into reason, and the instance now before us is but a gentle beginning of what
America must expect, unless she guards her union with nicer care and
stricter honor. United, she is formidable, and that with the least possible
charge a nation can be so; separated, she is a medley of individual noth-
ings, subject to the sport of foreign nations.

It is very probable that the ingenuity of commerce may have found
out a method to evade and supersede the intentions of the British, in
interdicting the trade with the West India islands. The language of both
being the same, and their customs well understood, the vessels of one
country may, by deception, pass for those of another. But this would be
a practice too debasing for a sovereign people to stoop to, and too profligate not to be discountenanced. An illicit trade, under any shape it can
be placed, cannot be carried on without a violation of truth. America is

[3] The reference is to Rhode Island. Paine had already addressed six letters to this State
on the subject. These letters are reprinted in Volume II of the present edition.—*Editor.*

now sovereign and independent, and ought to conduct her affairs in a regular style of character. She has the same right to say that no British vessel shall enter ports, or that no British manufactures shall be imported, but in American bottoms, the property of, and navigated by American subjects, as Britain has to say the same thing respecting the West Indies. Or she may lay a duty of ten, fifteen, or twenty shillings per ton (exclusive of other duties) on every British vessel coming from any port of the West Indies, where she is not admitted to trade, the said tonnage to continue as long on her side as the prohibition continues on the other.

But it is only by acting in union, that the usurpations of foreign nations on the freedom of trade can be counteracted, and security extended to the commerce of America. And when we view a flag, which to the eye is beautiful, and to contemplate its rise and origin inspires a sensation of sublime delight, our national honor must unite with our interest to prevent injury to the one, or insult to the other.[4]

COMMON SENSE.

NEW YORK, December 9, 1783.

[4] It is quite fitting and in keeping with Paine's fundamental thoughts at this time that he should conclude the *Crisis* series by urging a stronger Union.—*Editor.*

RIGHTS OF MAN

EDITOR'S NOTE

What *Common Sense* meant for the people of America in their struggle for independence and democracy, the *Rights of Man* meant for all people everywhere struggling to overthrow oppression. As during the American Revolution, so during the French Revolution Thomas Paine brought home sharply to the people the most advanced thought of the age. Indeed, in some sections of this work Paine advocated social measures which were far in advance of his time and singularly prophetic of the future development of enlightened government. Paine boldly announced that it was the duty of the State to care for the indigent and the young, and declared that those who received such assistance were entitled to it, "not as a matter of grace and favour but as a right." These old-age pensions were to be paid for in part by those taxes to which every one contributed and in part by further exactions "from those whose circumstances did not require them to draw such support," and this program he defended as "not of the nature of a charity but of a right." Expenditures for public education, old age pensions, state aid to the youth, unemployment insurance and soldiers' bonus, he argued, were far better employed than in the support of useless royalty. "Is it then better," he asked, "that the lives of 144,000 aged persons be rendered comfortable or that one million a year of public money be expended on any one individual, and him often of the most worthless or insignificant character?" Equally interesting was his demand for the removal of all legislation restricting wages of workmen. "Several laws are in existence," he wrote, "for regulating and limiting workmen's wages. Why not leave them as free to make their own bargains as the lawmakers are to let their farms and houses? Personal labour is all the property they have. Why is that little and the little freedom they enjoy to be infringed?"

The *Rights of Man* was written as a defense of the French Revolution and its principles. Paine was visiting Europe when the great upheaval in France broke out. On November 1, 1790, Edmund Burke's pamphlet, *Reflections on the Revolution in France, and on the Proceedings of Certain Societies in London Relative to That Event* came off the press. Without hesitation Paine flung himself into the fight and at once set himself to answer Burke's reactionary attack on the French and English popular movements. But the *Rights of Man* was more than a vigorous answer to Burke's prejudiced arguments. It was also a clearcut statement of the philosophy of all democratic movements.

THE RIGHTS OF MAN

PART FIRST

Part I of *Rights of Man,* dedicated to George Washington, was published in London in February, 1791. The publisher became so frightened after a few copies were distributed that he refused to continue its publication, and it was transferred to J. S. Jordan, a Fleet Street printer. The pamphlet was immediately translated into French. The American edition featured a letter by Thomas Jefferson to the printer as a preface in which the author of the Declaration of Independence wrote: "I am extremely pleased to find it will be reprinted here, and that something is at length to be publicly said against the political heresies which have sprung up among us. I have no doubt our citizens will rally a second time to the standard of Common Sense." Several years later Andrew Jackson declared that the *"Rights of Man* will be more enduring than all the piles of marble and granite man can erect."

The pamphlet immediately reached a wide circulation, but once again Paine refused to profit from his writings in behalf of the democratic cause and turned the proceeds from the sale of the work over to the Constitutional Societies in the British Isles.

In Part I Paine ridicules Burke's contention that the English people of 1688 had entered into a solemn agreement binding them and their descendants forever, declaring that no one could barter away the rights of those not yet born. Government, Paine argues, must be based on the consent of the governed, and the masses must be allowed to direct their own affairs. He carefully examines the issues at stake in the French Revolution, describes the forces that made the Revolution inevitable and explains its aims. He analyzes in detail the famous "Declaration of the Rights of Man and of Citizens" adopted by the National Assembly of France, the authorship of which is usually attributed to Paine. The pamphlet ends on a note of great promise for mankind, the author envisioning, in "an age of revolutions, in which everything may be looked for," a confederation of nations to abolish war and "an European Congress, to patronize the progress of free government and promote the civilization of nations."—*Editor.*

TO

GEORGE WASHINGTON,

PRESIDENT OF THE UNITED STATES OF AMERICA.

SIR, I present you a small treatise in defense of those principles of freedom which your exemplary virtue hath so eminently contributed to establish. That the Rights of Man may become as universal as your benevolence can wish, and that you may enjoy the happiness of seeing the New World regenerate the Old, is the prayer of

SIR,

Your much obliged, and

Obedient humble servant,

THOMAS PAINE.

PREFACE TO THE ENGLISH EDITION

FROM the part Mr. Burke took in the American Revolution,[1] it was natural that I should consider him a friend to mankind; and as our acquaintance commenced on that ground, it would have been more agreeable to me to have had cause to continue in that opinion, than to change it.

At the time Mr. Burke made his violent speech last winter in the English Parliament against the French Revolution and the National Assembly, I was in Paris, and had written to him but a short time before, to inform him how prosperously matters were going on.[2] Soon after this, I saw his advertisement of the pamphlet he intended to publish.

---

[1] Burke frequently defended the American colonists during the critical years leading up to the War for Independence. His speech "On Reconciliation with America" in 1775 had earned him the reputation of America's greatest friend in England.

[2] All efforts to discover this letter have failed, and it may be assumed that it has disappeared. In Croly's life of Edmund Burke there is the following interesting statement: "Among his [Paine's] earliest missives was a letter [from Paris] to Burke, whom he

As the attack was to be made in a language but little studied, and less understood, in France, and as everything suffers by translation, I promised some of the friends of the Revolution in that country, that whenever Mr. Burke's pamphlet came forth, I would answer it.

This appeared to me the more necessary to be done, when I saw the flagrant misrepresentations which Mr. Burke's pamphlet contains; and that while it is an outrageous abuse on the French Revolution, and the principles of Liberty, it is an imposition on the rest of the world.

I am the more astonished and disappointed at this conduct of Mr. Burke, as (from the circumstance I am going to mention), I had formed other expectations.

I had seen enough of the miseries of war to wish it might never more have existence in the world, and that some other mode might be found out to settle the differences that should occasionally arise in the neighborhood of nations. This certainly might be done if courts were disposed to set honestly about it, or if countries were enlightened enough not to be made the dupes of courts.

The people of America had been bred up in the same prejudices against France, which at that time characterized the people of England; but experience and an acquaintance with the French nation have most effectually shown to the Americans the falsehood of those prejudices; and I do not believe that a more cordial and confidential intercourse exists between any two countries than between America and France.

When I came to France, in the spring of 1787, the Archbishop of Toulouse was then Minister, and at that time highly esteemed. I became much acquainted with the private secretary of that Minister, a man of an enlarged benevolent heart; and found that his sentiments and my own perfectly agreed with respect to the madness of war, and the wretched impolicy of two nations, like England and France, continually

---

eagerly urged to introduce Revolution into England, by its established name of 'Reform!' Burke threw back the temptation, or the insult, at once. 'Do you *really* imagine, Mr. Paine,' was his reply, 'that the constitution of this kingdom requires such innovations, or *could exist with them,* or that any *reflecting man would seriously engage in them?* You are aware that I have, all my life, opposed such schemes of reform, because *I know them not to be Reform.'* Paine, however, continued his ill-received correspondence; and whether from the delight of molesting Burke, or the expectation of making him a convert to a side which had the grand charm for the conviction of his own profligate heart, plunder; he sent him narratives of the rapidly recurring triumphs of democracy. In one of those he stated that the Reformers had already determined on the total overthrow of the [French] monarchy, etc." According to Croly this letter was written by Paine "exactly three days before the storming of the Bastille."—*Editor.*

worrying each other, to no other end than that of a mutual increase of burdens and taxes. That I might be assured I had not misunderstood him, nor he me, I put the substance of our opinions into writing, and sent it to him; subjoining a request, that if I should see among the people of England any disposition to cultivate a better understanding between the two nations than had hitherto prevailed, how far I might be authorized to say that the same disposition prevailed on the part of France?

He answered me by letter in the most unreserved manner, and that not for himself only, but for the Minister, with whose knowledge the letter was declared to be written.

I put this letter into the hands of Mr. Burke almost three years ago, and left it with him, where it still remains; hoping, and at the same time naturally expecting, from the opinion I had conceived of him, that he would find some opportunity of making a good use of it, for the purpose of removing those errors and prejudices, which two neighboring nations, from the want of knowing each other, had entertained, to the injury of both.

When the French Revolution broke out, it certainly afforded to Mr. Burke an opportunity of doing some good, had he been disposed to it; instead of which, no sooner did he see the old prejudices wearing away, than he immediately began sowing the seeds of a new inveteracy, as if he were afraid that England and France would cease to be enemies.

That there are men in all countries who get their living by war, and by keeping up the quarrels of nations, is as shocking as it is true; but when those who are concerned in the government of a country, make it their study to sow discord, and cultivate prejudices between nations, it becomes the more unpardonable.

With respect to a paragraph in this work, alluding to Mr. Burke's having a pension, the report has been some time in circulation, at least two months; and as a person is often the last to hear what concerns him the most to know, I have mentioned it, that Mr. Burke may have an opportunity of contradicting the rumor, if he thinks proper.

THOMAS PAINE.

PREFACE TO THE FRENCH EDITION

WE MAY regard the amazement occasioned throughout Europe by the French Revolution from two standpoints: its influence on foreign nations, and its influence on foreign governments.

Every country in Europe considers the cause of the French people as identical with the cause of its own people, or rather, as embracing the interests of the entire world. But those who rule those countries do not entertain quite the same opinion. Now, this is a difference to which we are bound to give the deepest attention. The people are not to be confounded with their government; and this is especially the case when the relation of the English Government to its people is considered.

The French Revolution has no more bitter enemy than the English Government. The evidence of its ill-feeling is plain to every eye; witness the gratitude expressed by the Elector of Hanover, sometimes styled King of England, a feeble and crazy personage, to Mr. Burke because the latter has, in his work, grossly libeled it, and also the slanderous' invectives of Mr. Pitt, the Prime Minister, in his parliamentary harangues.

The behavior of the English Government in its dealings with France is a palpable contradiction of all its pretensions of amity, however seemingly candid, and proves clearly that its official expressions of regard are illusory, that its court is a treacherous court, a demented court, which is a prominent factor in every European plot and quarrel, because it is in search of a war that will serve as an excuse for its insane prodigality.

But the people of England are actuated by entirely different motives: they applaud the French Revolution, and are anxious for the triumph of freedom in every land; when they have a fuller comprehension of the plots and stratagems of their Government, as well as of the principles of the French Revolution, this sentiment will become general and intensified. It would be well for French citizens to understand that the British journals, even when not actually subsidized by the English Government, are always controlled by its influence. Naturally, these journals continually assail the French Revolution and give an entirely false idea of its aims, solely with the view of misleading the people of England. Truth, however, is always ultimately victorious, and so the mendacity of these newspapers no longer produces the effect intended.

When it is known everywhere that the English Government prosecutes as a libel a public statement which is admittedly true, that this dictum, "The greater the truth, the greater the libel," is a legal maxim, constantly applied by the judges, it ought to be easy to satisfy the world that truth has always been suppressed in England. This insult to public morals has received the name of *law,* and there are vicious judges who actually sentence truth to punishment.

The spectacle at present afforded by the English Government is sufficiently strange: it perceives that the ill feeling which once existed between the French and English peoples, and which brought poverty and misfortune to both, is gradually fading away, so now it is looking in other directions for an enemy, because it will have no excuse for its enormous revenue and taxation, except it can prove that, somewhere or other, it has enemies.

As France, then, has declined to be an adversary of England, the Government of that country has no resource but in the supposed hostility of Russia. Apparently, it is communing with itself in some such fashion as this: "Should no nation show me sufficient kindness as to engage in hostilities against me, then fleets and armies will not be needed, and I shall be compelled to consent to a reduction of taxation. The war with America gave me an excuse for doubling my taxes; the affair with Holland contributed to the same purpose; that absurd Nootka business enabled me to collect three million pounds sterling. Times have changed, and unless I have a war with Russia, the taxation harvest for wars cannot be reaped. I played the chief rôle in egging on the Turks against the Russians; I think my present attitude will have the result of reaping another taxation harvest."

But for the fact that the devastation and misery which a war inflicts on a country restrain every tendency to gaiety, and must inspire everyone with sorrow rather than with merriment, the insane conduct of the English Government would only be a subject for mockery. But no one can regard with unconcern the sufferings that must necessarily spring from such a wicked policy. Moreover, it would be as absurd to argue rationally with the sorts of governments that have existed for centuries as it would be to argue with dumb animals. Whatever reforms are accomplished can only be accomplished by the nations, independent of their governments. It is at the present time pretty certain that the peoples of France, England and America, who are at once enlightened and enlightening, will be able in the future to serve as models of good government to the universe and will also have sufficient influence to compel the practical enforcement of it everywhere.

Among the incivilities by which nations or individuals provoke and irritate each other, Mr. Burke's pamphlet on the French Revolution is an extraordinary instance. Neither the people of France, nor the National Assembly, were troubling themselves about the affairs of England, or the English Parliament; and that Mr. Burke should commence an unprovoked attack upon them, both in Parliament and in public, is a conduct that cannot be pardoned on the score of manners, nor justified on that of policy. There is scarcely an epithet of abuse to be found in the English language, with which Mr. Burke has not loaded the French nation and the National Assembly. Every thing which rancor, prejudice, ignorance, or knowledge could suggest, are poured forth in the copious fury of near four hundred pages. In the strain and on the plan Mr. Burke was writing, he might have written on to as many thousands. When the tongue or the pen is let loose in a frenzy of passion, it is the man and not the subject that becomes exhausted.

Hitherto Mr. Burke has been mistaken and disappointed in the opinions he had formed of the affairs of France; but such is the ingenuity of his hope, or the malignancy of his despair, that it furnishes him with new pretenses to go on. There was a time when it was impossible to make Mr. Burke believe there would be any revolution in France. His opinion then was, that the French had neither spirit to undertake it, nor fortitude to support it; and now that there is one, he seeks an escape by condemning it.

Not sufficiently content with abusing the National Assembly, a great part of his work is taken up with abusing Dr. Price (one of the best-hearted men that lives), and the two societies in England known by the name of the Revolution Society, and the Society for Constitutional Information.

Dr. Price had preached a sermon on the 4th of November, 1789, being the anniversary of what is called in England the Revolution, which took place in 1688. Mr. Burke, speaking of this sermon, says, "The political divine proceeds dogmatically to assert that, by the principles of the Revolution, the people of England have acquired three fundamental rights:

"1. To choose our own governors.

"2. To cashier them for misconduct.

"3. To frame a government for ourselves."

Dr. Price does not say that the right to do these things exists in this or in that person, or in this or in that description of persons, but that it exists in the *whole;* that it is a right resident in the nation. Mr. Burke, on the contrary, denies that such a right exists in the nation, either in whole or in part, or that it exists any where; and, what is still more strange and marvelous, he says, "that the people of England utterly disclaim such a right, and that they will resist the practical assertion of it with their lives and fortunes."

That men should take up arms, and spend their lives and fortunes, *not* to maintain their rights, but to maintain they have *not* rights, is an entirely new species of discovery, and suited to the paradoxical genius of Mr. Burke.

The method which Mr. Burke takes to prove that the people of England had no such rights, and that such rights do not now exist in the nation, either in whole or in part, or any where at all, is of the same marvelous and monstrous kind with what he has already said; for his arguments are, that the persons, or the generation of persons, in whom they did exist, are dead, and with them the right is dead also.

To prove this, he quotes a declaration made by Parliament about a hundred years ago, to William and Mary, in these words: "The Lords Spiritual and Temporal, and Commons, do, in the name of the people aforesaid," (meaning the people of England then living) "most humbly and faithfully *submit* themselves, their *heirs* and *posterities,* for EVER." He also quotes a clause of another act of Parliament made in the same reign, the terms of which, he says, "bind us," (meaning the people of that day) "our *heirs* and our *posterity,* to *them,* their *heirs* and *posterity,* to the end of time."

Mr. Burke conceives his point sufficiently established by producing these clauses, which he enforces by saying that they exclude the right of the nation for *ever.* And not yet content with making such declarations, repeated over and over again, he further says, "that if the people of England possessed such a right before the Revolution," (which he acknowledges to have been the case, not only in England but throughout Europe, at an early period,) "yet that the *English nation* did, at the time of the Revolution, most solemnly renounce and abdicate it, for themselves, and for *all their posterity, for ever."*

As Mr. Burke occasionally applies the poison drawn from his horrid principles, not only to the English nation, but to the French Revolution and the National Assembly, and charges that august, illuminated and illuminating body of men with the epithet of *usurpers,* I shall, *sans cérémonie,* place another system of principles in opposition to his.

The English Parliament of 1688 did a certain thing, which, for themselves and their constituents, they had a right to do, and which it appeared right should be done: But, in addition to this right, which they possessed by delegation, *they set up another right by assumption,* that of binding and controlling posterity to the end of time.

The case, therefore, divides itself into two parts; the right which they possessed by delegation, and the right which they set up by assumption. The first is admitted; but with respect to the second, I reply:—

There never did, there never will, and there never can exist a parliament, or any description of men, or any generation of men, in any country, possessed of the right or the power of binding and controlling posterity to the *"end of time,"* or of commanding forever how the world shall be governed, or who shall govern it; and therefore, all such clauses, acts or declarations, by which the makers of them attempt to do what they have neither the right nor the power to do, nor the power to execute, are in themselves null and void.

Every age and generation must be as free to act for itself, *in all cases,* as the ages and generation which preceded it. The vanity and presumption of governing beyond the grave, is the most ridiculous and insolent of all tyrannies.

Man has no property in man; neither has any generation a property in the generations which are to follow. The Parliament or the people of 1688, or of any other period, had no more right to dispose of the people of the present day, or to bind or to control them *in any shape whatever,* than the Parliament or the people of the present day have to dispose of, bind, or control those who are to live a hundred or a thousand years hence.

Every generation is, and must be, competent to all the purposes which its occasions require. It is the living, and not the dead, that are to be accommodated. When man ceases to be, his power and his wants cease with him; and having no longer any participation in the concerns of this world, he has no longer any authority in directing who shall be its governors, or how its government shall be organized, or how administered.[3]

I am not contending for nor against any form of government, nor for nor against any party here or elsewhere. That which a whole nation chooses to do, it has a right to do. Mr. Burke says, No. Where then *does*

[3] It is interesting to compare these words with those of Thomas Jefferson who wrote in a letter to Samuel Kercheval, July 12, 1816: "Each generation is as independent of the

the right exist? I am contending for the rights of the *living,* and against their being willed away, and controlled and contracted for, by the manuscript assumed authority of the dead; and Mr. Burke is contending for the authority of the dead over the rights and freedom of the living.

There was a time when kings disposed of their crowns by will upon their death-beds, and consigned the people, like beasts of the field, to whatever successor they appointed. This is now so exploded as scarcely to be remembered, and so monstrous as hardly to be believed. But the parliamentary clauses upon which Mr. Burke builds his political church, are of the same nature.

The laws of every country must be analogous to some common principle. In England, no parent or master, nor all the authority of Parliament, omnipotent as it has called itself, can bind or control the personal freedom even of an individual beyond the age of twenty-one years. On what ground of right, then, could the Parliament of 1688, or any other parliament, bind all posterity for ever?

Those who have quitted the world, and those who are not yet arrived in it, are as remote from each other, as the utmost stretch of moral imagination can conceive. What possible obligation, then, can exist between them; what rule or principle can be laid down, that two nonentities, the one out of existence, and the other not in, and who never can meet in this world, that the one should control the other to the end of time?

In England, it is said that money cannot be taken out of the pockets of the people without their consent. But who authorized, or who could authorize the Parliament of 1688 to control and take away the freedom of posterity, and limit and confine their right of acting in certain cases for ever, who were not in existence to give or to withhold their consent?

A greater absurdity cannot present itself to the understanding of man, than what Mr. Burke offers to his readers. He tells them, and he tells the world to come, that a certain body of men, who existed a hundred years ago, made a law; and that there does not now exist in the nation, nor ever will, nor ever can, a power to alter it. Under how many subtilties, or absurdities, has the divine right to govern been imposed on the credulity of mankind!

---

preceding, as that was of all which had gone before. It has then, like them, a right to choose for itself the form of government it believes most promotive of its own happiness. . . . The dead have no rights. They are nothing, and nothing cannot own something. . . ." (Philip S. Foner, editor, *Thomas Jefferson: Selections from His Writings* [New York, 1943], p. 60.)—*Editor.*

Mr. Burke has discovered a new one, and he has shortened his journey to Rome, by appealing to the power of this infallible Parliament of former days; and he produces what it has done, as of divine authority; for that power most certainly be more than human, which no human power to the end of time can alter.

But Mr. Burke has done some service, not to his cause, but to his country, by bringing those clauses into public view. They serve to demonstrate how necessary it is at all times to watch against the attempted encroachment of power, and to prevent its running to excess.

It is somewhat extraordinary, that the offense for which James II was expelled, that of setting up power by *assumption*, should be reacted, under another shape and form, by the Parliament that expelled him. It shows that the rights of man were but imperfectly understood at the Revolution; for certain it is, that the right which that Parliament set up by *assumption* (for by the delegation it had it not, and could not have it, because none could give it) over the persons and freedom of posterity for ever, was the same tyrannical, unfounded kind which James attempted to set up over the Parliament and the nation, and for which he was expelled.

The only difference is (for in principle they differ not), that the one was an usurper over the living, and the other over the unborn; and as the one has no better authority to stand upon than the other, both of them must be equally null and void, and of no effect.

From what, or from whence, does Mr. Burke prove the right of any human power to bind posterity for ever? He has produced his clauses; but he must produce also his proofs that such a right existed, and show how it existed. If it ever existed, it must now exist; for whatever appertains to the nature of man, cannot be annihilated by man.

It is the nature of man to die, and he will continue to die as long as he continues to be born. But Mr. Burke has set up a sort of political Adam, in whom all posterity are bound for ever; he must therefore prove that his Adam possessed such a power, or such a right.

The weaker any cord is, the less it will bear to be stretched and the worse is the policy to stretch it, unless it is intended to break it. Had a person contemplated the overthrow of Mr. Burke's positions, he would have proceeded as Mr. Burke has done. He would have magnified the authorities, on purpose to have called the *right* of them into question; and the instant the question of right was started, the authorities must have been given up.

It requires but a very small glance of thought to perceive, that although laws made in one generation often continue in force through succeeding generations, yet they continue to derive their force from the consent of the living. A law not repealed continues in force, not because it *cannot* be repealed, but because it is *not* repealed; and the non-repealing passes for consent.

But Mr. Burke's clauses have not even this qualification in their favor. They become null, by attempting to become immortal. The nature of them precludes consent. They destroy the right which they *might* have, by grounding it on a right which they *cannot* have. Immortal power is not a human right, and therefore cannot be a right of Parliament.

The Parliament of 1688 might as well have passed an act to have authorized themselves to live for ever as to make their authority to live for ever. All therefore that can be said of them is, that they are a formality of words, of as much import as if those who used them had addressed a congratulation to themselves, and in the oriental style of antiquity, had said, O Parliament, live for ever!

The circumstances of the world are continually changing, and the opinions of men change also; and as government is for the living, and not for the dead, it is the living only that has any right in it. That which may be thought right and found convenient in one age, may be thought wrong and found inconvenient in another. In such cases, who is to decide, the living, or the dead?

As almost one hundred pages of Mr. Burke's book are employed upon these clauses, it will consequently follow, that if the clauses themselves, so far as they set up on *assumed, usurped* dominion over posterity for ever, are unauthoritative, and in their nature null and void; that all his voluminous inferences, and declamation drawn therefrom, or founded thereon, are null and void also: and on this ground I rest the matter.

We now come more particularly to the affairs of France. Mr. Burke's book has the appearance of being written as instruction to the French nation; but if I may permit myself the use of an extravagant metaphor, suited to the extravagance of the case, it is darkness attempting to illuminate light.

While I am writing this, there are accidentally before me some proposals for a declaration of rights by the Marquis de Lafayette (I ask his pardon for using his former address, and do it only for distinction's sake) to the National Assembly, on the 11th of July, 1789, three days before the taking of the Bastille, and I cannot but be struck by observing how op-

posite the sources are from which that gentleman and Mr. Burke draw
their principles.

Instead of referring to musty records and moldy parchments to prove
that the rights of the living are lost, "renounced and abdicated for ever,"
by those who are now no more, as Mr. Burke has done, M. de Lafayette
applies to the living world, and emphatically says:—"Call to mind the
sentiments which nature has engraved in the heart of every citizen, and
which take a new force when they are solemnly recognized by all: For
a nation to love liberty, it is sufficient that she knows it; and to be free,
it is sufficient that she wills it."

How dry, barren, and obscure is the source from which Mr. Burke
labors! and how ineffectual, though gay with flowers, are all his declamation and his argument, compared with these clear, concise, and soul-ani-
mating sentiments! Few and short as they are, they lead on to a vast field
of generous and manly thinking, and do not finish, like Mr. Burke's
periods, with music in the ear, and nothing in the heart.

As I have introduced M. de Lafayette, I will take the liberty of adding
an anecdote respecting his farewell address to the Congress of America
in 1783, and which occurred fresh to my mind, when I saw Mr. Burke's
thundering attack on the French Revolution.

M. de Lafayette went to America at an early period of the war, and
continued a volunteer in her service to the end. His conduct through the
whole of that enterprise is one of the most extraordinary that is to be
found in the history of a young man, scarcely twenty years of age.

Situated in a country that was like the lap of sensual pleasure, and
with the means of enjoying it, how few are there to be found who would
exchange such a scene for the woods and wilderness of America, and
pass the flowery years of youth in unprofitable danger and hardship;
but such is the fact.

When the war ended, and he was on the point of taking his final departure, he presented himself to Congress, and contemplating, in his
affectionate farewell, the Revolution he had seen, expressed himself in
these words: *May this great monument, raised to Liberty, serve as a
lesson to the oppressor, and an example to the oppressed!*

When this address came to the hands of Dr. Franklin, who was then
in France, he applied to Count Vergennes, to have it inserted in the
French *Gazette,* but never could obtain his consent. The fact was, that
Count Vergennes was an aristocratical despot at home, and dreaded the
example of the American Revolution in France, as certain other per-

sons now dread the example of the French Revolution in England; and Mr. Burke's tribute of fear, (for in this light his book must be considered) runs parallel with Count Vergennes' refusal. But, to return more particularly to his work—

"We have seen," says Mr. Burke, "the French rebel against a mild and lawful monarch, with more fury, outrage, and insult, than any people has been known to rise against the most illegal usurper, or the most sanguinary tyrant." This is one among a thousand other instances, in which Mr. Burke shows that he is ignorant of the springs and principles of the French Revolution.

It was not against Louis XVI, but against the despotic principles of the government, that the nation revolted. These principles had not their origin in him, but in the original establishment, many centuries back; and they were become too deeply rooted to be removed, and the Augean stable of parasites and plunderers too abominably filthy to be cleansed, by anything short of a complete and universal revolution.

When it becomes necessary to do a thing, the whole heart and soul should go into the measure, or not attempt it. That crisis was then arrived, and there remained no choice but to act with determined vigor, or not to act at all.

The King was known to be the friend of the nation, and this circumstance was favorable to the enterprise. Perhaps no man bred up in the style of an absolute king, ever possessed a heart so little disposed to the exercise of that species of power as the present King of France.

But the principles of the government itself still remained the same. The monarch and the monarchy were distinct and separate things; and it was against the established despotism of the latter, and not against the person or principles of the former, that the revolt commenced, and the Revolution has been carried.

Mr. Burke does not attend to the distinction between *men* and *principles;* and therefore, he does not see that a revolt may take place against the despotism of the latter, while there lies no charge of despotism against the former.

The natural moderation of Louis XVI contributed nothing to alter the hereditary despotism of the monarchy. All the tyrannies of the former reigns, acted under that hereditary despotism, were still liable to be revived in the hands of a successor. It was not the respite of a reign that would satisfy France, enlightened as she was then become.

A casual discontinuance of the *practise* of despotism, is not a discon
tinuance of its *principles;* the former depends on the virtue of the in
dividual who is in immediate possession of power; the latter, on the
virtue and fortitude of the nation. In the case of Charles I and James II
of England, the revolt was against the personal despotism of the men;
whereas in France, it was against the hereditary despotism of the estab·
lished government. But men who can consign over the rights of posterity
for ever, on the authority of a moldy parchment, like Mr. Burke, are not
qualified to judge of this Revolution. It takes in a field too vast for their
views to explore, and proceeds with a mightiness of reason they cannot
keep pace with.

But there are many points of view in which this Revolution may be
considered. When despotism has established itself for ages in a country,
as in France, it is not in the person of the king only that it resides. It has
the appearance of being so in show, and in nominal authority; but it is
not so in practise, and in fact. It has its standard everywhere.

Every office and department has its despotism, founded upon custom
and usage. Every place has its Bastille, and every Bastille its despot. The
original hereditary despotism, resident in the person of the king, divides
and subdivides itself into a thousand shapes and forms, till at last the
whole of it is acted by deputation.

This was the case in France; and against this species of despotism,
proceeding on through an endless labyrinth of office till the source of it
is scarcely perceptible, there is no mode of redress. It strengthens itself by
assuming the appearance of duty, and tyrannizes under the pretense of
obeying.

When a man reflects on the condition which France was in from the
nature of her government, he will see other causes for revolt than those
which immediately connect themselves with the person or character of
Louis XVI. There were, if I may so express it, a thousand despotisms
to be reformed in France, which had grown up under the hereditary
despotism of the monarchy, and became so rooted as to be in a great
measure independent of it. Between the monarchy, the parliament, and
the church, there was a *rivalship* of despotism; besides the feudal despotism operating locally, and the ministerial despotism operating everywhere.

But Mr. Burke, by considering the King as the only possible object of
a revolt, speaks as if France was a village, in which every thing that

passed must be known to its commanding officer, and no oppression could be acted but what he could conveniently control. Mr. Burke might have been in the Bastille his whole life, as well under Louis XVI and neither the one nor the other have known that such a man as Mr. Burke existed. The despotic principles of the government were the same in both reigns, though the dispositions of the men were as remote as tyranny and benevolence.

What Mr. Burke considers as a reproach to the French Revolution (that of bringing it forward under a reign more mild than the preceding ones), is one of its highest honors. The revolutions that have taken place in other European countries, have been excited by personal hatred. The rage was against the man, and he became the victim. But, in the instance of France, we see a revolution generated in the rational contemplation of the rights of man, and distinguishing from the beginning between persons and principles.

But Mr. Burke appears to have no idea of principles, when he is contemplating governments. "Ten years ago," says he, "I could have felicitated France on her having a government, without inquiring what the nature of that government was, or how it was administered."

Is this the language of a rational man? Is it the language of a heart feeling as it ought to feel for the rights and happiness of the human race? On this ground, Mr. Burke must compliment every government in the world, while the victims who suffer under them, whether sold into slavery, or tortured out of existence, are wholly forgotten.

It is power, and not principles, that Mr. Burke venerates; and under this abominable depravity, he is disqualified to judge between them. Thus much for his opinion as to the occasion of the French Revolution. I now proceed to other considerations.

I know a point in America called Point-no-Point; because as you proceed along the shore, gay and flowery as Mr. Burke's language, it continually recedes and presents itself at a distance before you; but when you have got as far as you can go, there is no point at all. Just thus it is with Mr. Burke's three hundred and fifty-six pages. It is therefore difficult to reply to him. But as the points he wishes to establish may be inferred from what he abuses, it is in his paradoxes that we must look for his arguments.

As to the tragic paintings by which Mr. Burke has outraged his own imagination, and seeks to work upon that of his readers, they are very well calculated for theatrical representation, where facts are manufactured for the sake of show, and accommodated to produce, through the weakness of sympathy, a weeping effect. But Mr. Burke should recollect that he is writing history, and not *plays;* and that his readers will expect truth, and not the spouting rant of high-toned declamation.

When we see a man dramatically lamenting in a publication intended to be believed, that, *"The age of chivalry is gone!* that *The glory of Europe is extinguished forever!* that *The unbought grace of life* (if any one knows what it is), *the cheap defense of nations, the nurse of manly sentiment and heroic enterprise, is gone!"* and all this because the Quixotic age of chivalric nonsense is gone, what opinion can we form of his judgment, or what regard can we pay to his facts?

In the rhapsody of his imagination, he has discovered a world of wind-mills, and his sorrows are, that there are no Quixotes to attack them. But if the age of aristocracy, like that of chivalry, should fall, and they had originally some connection, Mr. Burke, the trumpeter of the order, may continue his parody to the end, and finish with exclaiming, *"Othello's occupation's gone!"*

Notwithstanding Mr. Burke's horrid paintings, when the French Revolution is compared with that of other countries, the astonishment will be, that it is marked with so few sacrifices; but this astonishment will cease when we reflect that *principles* and not *persons,* were the meditated objects of destruction. The mind of the nation was acted upon by a higher stimulus than what the consideration of persons could inspire, and sought a higher conquest than could be produced by the downfall of an enemy.

Among the few who fell, there do not appear to be any that were intentionally singled out. They all of them had their fate in the circumstances of the moment, and were not pursued with that long, cold-blooded, unabated revenge which pursued the unfortunate Scotch, in the affair of 1745.

Through the whole of Mr. Burke's book I do not observe that the Bastille is mentioned more than once, and that with a kind of implication as if he were sorry it was pulled down, and wished it were built up again. "We have rebuilt Newgate," says he, "and tenanted the mansion; and we have prisons almost as strong as the Bastille for those who dare to libel the Queens of France." [4]

[4] Since writing the above, two other places occur in Mr. Burke's pamphlet in which the name of the Bastille is mentioned but in the same manner. In the one, he introduces it

As to what a madman, like the person called Lord George Gordon, might say, and to whom Newgate is rather a bedlam than a prison, it is unworthy a rational consideration.

It was a madman that libelled,—and that is sufficient apology; and it afforded an opportunity for confining him, which was the thing which was wished for; but certain it is that Mr. Burke, who does not call himself a madman, whatever other people may do, has libelled, in the most unprovoked manner, and in the grossest style of the most vulgar abuse, the whole representative authority of France; and yet Mr. Burke takes his seat in the British House of Commons!

From his violence and his grief, his silence on some points, and his excess on others, it is difficult not to believe that Mr. Burke is sorry, extremely sorry, that arbitrary power, the power of the Pope, and the Bastille, are pulled down.

Not one glance of compassion, not one commiserating reflection, that I can find throughout his book, has he bestowed on those who lingered out the most wretched of lives, a life without hope, in the most miserable of prisons.

It is painful to behold a man employing his talents to corrupt himself. Nature has been kinder to Mr. Burke than he is to her. He is not affected by the reality of distress touching his heart, but by the showy resemblage of it striking his imagination. He pities the plumage, but forgets the dying bird.

Accustomed to kiss the aristocratical hand that hath purloined him from himself, he degenerates into a composition of art, and the genuine soul of nature forsakes him. His hero or his heroine must be a tragedy-victim expiring in show, and not the real prisoner of mystery, sinking into death in the silence of a dungeon.

As Mr. Burke has passed over the whole transaction of the Bastille (and his silence is nothing in its favor), and has entertained his readers with reflections on supposed facts distorted into real falsehoods, I will give, since he has not, some account of the circumstances which preceded that transaction. They will serve to show, that less mischief could scarcely have accompanied such an event, when considered with the treacherous and hostile aggravations of the enemies of the Revolution.

in a sort of obscure question, and asks—"Will any ministers who now serve such a king with but a decent appearance of respect, cordially obey the orders of those whom but the other day, in his name, they had committed to the Bastille?" In the other, the taking it is mentioned as implying criminality in the French guards who assisted in demolishing it. "They have not," says he, "forgot the taking the king's castles at Paris." This is Mr. Burke, who pretends to write on constitutional freedom.—*Author.*

The mind can hardly picture to itself a more tremendous scene than which the city of Paris exhibited at the time of taking the Bastille, and for two days before and after, nor conceive the possibility of its quieting so soon. At a distance, this transaction has appeared only as an act of heroism, standing on itself; and the close political connection it had with the Revolution is lost in the brilliancy of the achievement.

But we are to consider it as the strength of the parties, brought man to man, and contending for the issue. The Bastille was to be either the prize or the prison of the assailants. The downfall of it included the idea of the downfall to despotism; and this compounded image was become as figuratively united as Bunyan's Doubting Castle and Giant Despair.

The National Assembly, before and at the time of taking the Bastille, were sitting at Versailles, twelve miles distant from Paris. About a week before the rising of the Parisians and their taking the Bastille, it was discovered that a plot was forming, at the head of which was the Count d'Artois, the King's youngest brother, for demolishing the National Assembly, seizing its members, and thereby crushing, by a *coup de main,* all hopes and prospects of forming a free government. For the sake of humanity, as well as of freedom, it is well this plan did not succeed. Examples are not wanting to show how dreadfully vindictive and cruel are all old governments, when they are successful against what they call a revolt.

This plan must have been some time in contemplation; because, in order to carry it into execution, it was necessary to collect a large military force around Paris, and to cut off the communication between that city and the National Assembly at Versailles. The troops destined for this service were chiefly the foreign troops in the pay of France, and who, for this particular purpose, were drawn from the distant provinces where they were then stationed. When they were collected, to the amount of between twenty-five and thirty thousand, it was judged time to put the plan into execution.

The ministry who were then in office, and who were friendly to the Revolution, were instantly dismissed, and a new Ministry formed of those who had concerted the project; among whom was Count de Broglio, and to his share was given the command of those troops. The character of this man, as described to me in a letter which I communicated to Mr. Burke before he began to write his book, and from an authority which Mr. Burke well knows was good, was that of "an high-flying aristocrat, cool, and capable of every mischief."

While these matters were agitating, the National Assembly stood in the most perilous and critical situation that a body of men can be supposed to act in. They were the devoted victims, and they knew it. They had the hearts and wishes of their country on their side, but military authority they had none. The guards of Broglio surrounded the hall where the Assembly sat, ready, at the word of command, to seize their persons, as had been done the year before to the Parliament of Paris.

Had the National Assembly deserted their trust, or had they exhibited signs of weakness or fear, their enemies had been encouraged, and the country depressed. When the situation they stood in, the cause they were engaged in, and the crisis then ready to burst which should determine their personal and political fate, and that of their country, and probably of Europe, are taken into one view, none but a heart callous with prejudice, or corrupted by dependence, can avoid interesting itself in their success.

The Archbishop of Vienne was at this time president of the National Assembly; a person too old to undergo the scene that a few days, or a few hours, might bring forth. A man of more activity, and bolder fortitude, was necessary; and the National Assembly chose (under the form of a vice-president, for the presidency still resided in the Archbishop) M. de Lafayette; and this is the only instance of a vice-president being chosen.

It was at the moment that this storm was pending (July 11) that a declaration of rights was brought forward by M. de Lafayette, and is the same which is alluded to in page 254. It was hastily drawn up, and makes only a part of a more extensive declaration of rights, agreed upon and adopted afterward by the National Assembly.

The particular reason for bringing it forward at this moment (M. de Lafayette has since informed me) was, that if the National Assembly should fall in the threatened destruction that then surrounded it, some traces of its principles might have the chance of surviving the wreck.

Every thing now was drawing to a crisis. The event was freedom or slavery. On one side, an army of nearly thirty thousand men; on the other, an unarmed body of citizens, for the citizens of Paris on whom the National Assembly must then immediately depend, were as unarmed and as undisciplined as the citizens of London are now. The French guards had given strong symptoms of their being attached to the national cause; but their numbers were small, not a tenth part of the force that Broglio commanded, and their officers were in the interest of Broglio.

Matters being now ripe for execution, the new Ministry made their appearance in office. The reader will carry in his mind, that the Bastille was taken the 14th of July; the point of time I am now speaking to, is the 12th. Immediately on the news of the change of the Ministry reaching Paris, in the afternoon, all the playhouses and places of entertainment, shops and houses, were shut up. The change of ministry was considered as the prelude of hostilities, and the opinion was rightly founded.

The foreign troops began to advance towards the city. The Prince de Lambesc, who commanded a body of German cavalry, approached by the Place of Louis XV which connects itself with some of the streets. In his march he insulted and struck an old man with his sword. The French are remarkable for their respect to old age, and the insolence, with which it appeared to be done, uniting with the general fermentation they were in, produced a powerful effect, and a cry of *To arms! to arms!* spread itself in a moment over the whole city.

Arms they had none, nor scarcely any who knew the use of them; but desperate resolution, when every hope is at stake, supplies for a while, the want of arms. Near where the Prince of Lambesc was drawn up, were large piles of stones collected for building the new bridge, and with these the people attacked the cavalry. A party of the French guards, upon hearing the firing, rushed from their quarters and joined the people; and night coming on, the cavalry retreated.

The streets of Paris, being narrow, are favorable for defense; and the loftiness of the houses, consisting of many stories, from which great annoyance might be given, secured them against nocturnal enterprises; and the night was spent in providing themselves with every sort of weapon they could make or procure: guns, swords, blacksmith's hammers, carpenter's axes, iron crows, pikes, halberds, pitchforks, spits, clubs, etc.

The incredible numbers with which they assembled the next morning, and the still more incredible resolution they exhibited, embarrassed and astonished their enemies. Little did the new Ministry expect such a salute. Accustomed to slavery themselves, they had no idea that liberty was capable of such inspiration, or that a body of unarmed citizens would dare to face the military force of thirty thousand men.

Every moment of this day was employed in collecting arms, concerting plans, and arranging themselves into the best order which such an instantaneous movement could afford. Broglio continued lying round the city, but made no further advances this day, and the succeeding night passed with as much tranquillity as such a scene could possibly produce.

But defense only was not the object of the citizens. They had a cause at stake, on which depended their freedom or their slavery. They every moment expected an attack, or to hear of one made on the National Assembly; and in such a situation, the most prompt measures are sometimes the best.

The object that now presented itself was the Bastille; and the *éclat* of carrying such a fortress in the face of such an army, could not fail to strike a terror into the new Ministry, who had scarcely yet had time to meet. By some intercepted correspondence this morning, it was discovered that the Mayor of Paris, M. de Flesselles, who appeared to be in their interest, was betraying them; and from this discovery, there remained no doubt, that Broglio would reinforce the Bastille the ensuing evening. It was therefore necessary to attack it that day; but before this could be done, it was first necessary to procure a better supply of arms than they were then possessed of.

There was, adjoining to the city, a large magazine of arms deposited at the Hospital of the Invalids, which the citizens summoned to surrender; and as the place was not defensible, nor attempted much defense, they soon succeeded.

Thus supplied, they marched to attack the Bastille; a vast, mixed multitude of all ages, and of all degrees, and armed with all sorts of weapons. Imagination would fail of describing to itself the appearance of such a procession, and of the anxiety for the events which a few hours or a few minutes might produce.

What plans the Ministry was forming, were as unknown to the people within the city, as what the citizens were doing was unknown to the Ministry; and what movements Broglio might make for the support or relief of the place, were to the citizens equally as unknown. All was mystery and hazard.

That the Bastille was attacked with an enthusiasm of heroism, such as only the highest animation of liberty could inspire, and carried in the space of a few hours, is an event which the world is fully possessed of. I am not undertaking a detail of the attack, but bringing into view the conspiracy against the nation which provoked it, and which fell with the Bastille.

The prison to which the new Ministry was dooming the National Assembly, in addition to its being the high altar and castle of despotism, became the proper object to begin with. This enterprise broke up the new Ministry, who began now to fly from the ruin they had prepared for others. The troops of Broglio dispersed, and himself fled also.

Mr. Burke has spoken a great deal about plots, but he has never once spoken of this plot against the National Assembly, and the liberties of the nation; and that he might not, he has passed over all the circumstances that might throw it in his way.

The exiles who have fled from France, whose cause he so much interests himself in, and from whom he has had his lesson, fled in consequence of a miscarriage of this plot. No plot was formed against them: they were plotting against others; and those who fell, met, not unjustly, the punishment they were preparing to execute.

But will Mr. Burke say, that if this plot, contrived with the subtility of an ambuscade, had succeeded, the successful party would have restrained their wrath so soon? Let the history of all old governments answer the question.

Whom has the National Assembly brought to the scaffold? None. They were themselves the devoted victims of this plot, and they have not retaliated; why then are they charged with revenge they have not acted? In the tremendous breaking forth of a whole people, in which all degrees, tempers and characters are confounded, and delivering themselves, by a miracle of exertion, from the destruction meditated against them, is it to be expected that nothing will happen?

When men are sore with the sense of oppressions, and menaced with the prospect of new ones, is the calmness of philosophy, or the palsy of insensibility to be looked for? Mr. Burke exclaims against outrage; yet the greatest is that which he has committed. His book is a volume of outrage, not apologized for by the impulse of a moment, but cherished through a space of ten months; yet Mr. Burke had no provocation, no life, no interest at stake.

More of the citizens fell in this struggle than of their opponents; but four or five persons were seized by the populace, and instantly put to death; the Governor of the Bastille, and the Mayor of Paris, who was detected in the act of betraying them; and afterwards Foulon, one of the new Ministry, and Berthier, his son-in-law, who had accepted the office of Intendant of Paris. Their heads were stuck upon spikes, and carried about the city; and it is upon this mode of punishment that Mr. Burke builds a great part of his tragic scenes. Let us therefore examine how men came by the idea of punishing in this manner.

They learn it from the governments they live under; and retaliate the punishments they have been accustomed to behold. The head stuck upon spikes, which remained for years upon Temple Bar, differed nothing in the horror of the scene from those carried about on spikes at Paris; yet this was done by the English Government.

It may perhaps be said, that it signifies nothing to a man what is done to him after he is dead; but it signifies much to the living. It either tortures their feelings, or it hardens their hearts; and in either case, it instructs them how to punish when power falls into their hands.

Lay then the axe to the root, and teach governments humanity. It is their sanguinary punishments which corrupt mankind. In England, the punishment in certain cases, is by *hanging, drawing* and *quartering;* the heart of the sufferer is cut out and held up to the view of the populace.

In France, under the former government, the punishments were not less barbarous. Who does not remember the execution of Damien, torn to pieces by horses? The effect of those cruel spectacles exhibited to the populace, is to destroy tenderness, or excite revenge, and by the base and false idea of governing men by terror, instead of reason, they become precedents.

It is over the lowest class of mankind that government by terror is intended to operate, and it is on them that it operates to the worst effect. They have sense enough to feel they are the objects aimed at; and they inflict in their turn the examples of terror they have been instructed to practise.

There is in all European countries, a large class of people of that description which in England is called the *"mob."* Of this class were those who committed the burnings and devastations in London in 1780,[5] and of this class were those who carried the heads upon the spikes in Paris.

Foulon and Berthier were taken up in the country and sent to Paris, to undergo their examination at the Hôtel de Ville; for the National Assembly, immediately on the new Ministry coming into office, passed a decree which they communicated to the King and the Cabinet, that they (the National Assembly) would hold the Ministry, of whom Foulon was one, responsible for the measures they were advising and pursuing; but the mob, incensed at the appearance of Foulon and Berthier,

[5] The reference is to the "Gordon riots" which reached a climax on June 7, 1780. The uprising arose from the opposition of the people to the oppressive measures of the Lord North ministry. During the uprising the homes of leading reactionaries were destroyed and prisons set afire. The demonstrations were finally suppressed by troops.—*Editor.*

tore them from their conductors before they were carried to the Hôtel de Ville, and executed them on the spot.

Why then does Mr. Burke charge outrages of this kind on a whole people? As well may he charge the riots and outrages of 1780 on all the people of London, or those in Ireland on all his countrymen.

But everything we see or hear offensive to our feelings and derogatory to the human character, should lead to other reflections than those of reproach. Even the beings who commit them have some claim to our consideration. How then is it that such vast classes of mankind as are distinguished by the appellation of the vulgar, or the ignorant, mob, are so numerous in all old countries?

The instant we ask ourselves this question, reflection finds an answer. They arise, as an unavoidable consequence, out of the ill construction of all old governments in Europe, England included with the rest. It is by distortedly exalting some men, that others are distortedly debased, till the whole is out of nature.

A vast mass of mankind are degradedly thrown into the background of the human picture, to bring forward, with greater glare, the puppet-show of state and aristocracy. In the commencement of a revolution, those men are rather the followers of the *camp* than of the *standard* of liberty, and have yet to be instructed how to reverence it.

I give Mr. Burke all his theatrical exaggerations for facts, and I then ask him, if they do not establish the certainty of what I here lay down? Admitting them to be true, they show the necessity of the French Revolution, as much as any one thing he could have asserted.

These outrages are not the effect of the principles of the Revolution, but of the degraded mind that existed before the Revolution, and which the Revolution is calculated to reform. Place them then to their proper cause, and take the reproach of them to your own side.

It is to the honor of the National Assembly, and the city of Paris, that during such a tremendous scene of arms and confusion, beyond the control of all authority, that they have been able, by the influence of example and exhortation, to restrain so much. Never were more pains taken to instruct and enlighten mankind, and to make them see that their interest consisted in their virtue, and not in their revenge, than what have been displayed in the Revolution of France. I now proceed to make some remarks on Mr. Burke's account of the expedition to Versailles, October the 5th and 6th.

I cannot consider Mr. Burke's book in scarcely any other light than a dramatic performance; and he must, I think, have considered it in the same light himself, by the poetical liberties he has taken of omitting some facts, distorting others, and making the machinery bend to produce a stage effect.

Of this kind is his account of the expedition to Versailles. He begins this account by omitting the only facts, which, as causes, are known to be true; everything beyond these is conjecture, even in Paris; and he then works up a tale accommodated to his own passions and prejudices.

It is to be observed throughout Mr. Burke's book, that he never speaks of plots *against* the Revolution; and it is from those plots that all the mischiefs have arisen. It suits his purpose to exhibit consequences without their causes. It is one of the arts of the drama to do so. If the crimes of men were exhibited with their sufferings, the stage effect would sometimes be lost, and the audience would be inclined to approve where it was intended they should commiserate.

After all the investigations that have been made into this intricate affair, (the expedition to Versailles,) it still remains enveloped in all that kind of mystery which ever accompanies events produced more from a concurrence of awkward circumstances, than from fixed design.

While the characters of men are forming, as is always the case in revolutions, there is a reciprocal suspicion, and a disposition to misinterpret each other; and even parties directly opposite in principle, will sometimes concur in pushing forward the same movement with very different views, and with the hope of its producing very different consequences.

A great deal of this may be discovered in this embarrassed affair, and yet the issue of the whole was what nobody had in view.

The only things certainly known are, that considerable uneasiness was at this time excited in Paris by the delay of the King in not sanctioning and forwarding the decrees of the National Assembly, particularly that of the *Declaration of the Rights of Man,* and the decrees of the *fourth of August,*[6] which contained the foundation principles on which the Constitution was to be erected.

The kindest, and perhaps the fairest, conjecture upon this matter is,

[6] The Declaration of the Rights of Man and of Citizens were adopted by the National Assembly of France on August 26, 1789.

On the evening of August 4, 1789, the liberal nobility in the National Assembly surrendered their hunting rights and their exemption from taxation, the cures yielded their tithes and their fees, the cities gave up the peculiar advantages which their ancient charters gave them, and the provinces surrendered their estates and their control of taxation.—*Editor.*

that some of the ministers intended to make remarks and observations upon certain parts of them, before they were finally sanctioned and sent to the provinces; but be this as it may, the enemies of the Revolution derived hopes from the delay, and the friends of the Revolution, uneasiness.

During this state of suspense, the *Garde du Corps,* which was composed, as such regiments generally are, of persons much connected with the Court, gave an entertainment at Versailles (Oct. 1,) to some foreign regiments then arrived; and when the entertainment was at its height, on a signal given, the *Garde du Corps* tore the national cockade from their hats, trampled it under foot, and replaced it with a counter-cockade prepared for the purpose.

An indignity of this kind amounted to defiance. It was like declaring war; and if men will give challenges, they must expect consequences. But all this Mr. Burke has carefully kept out of sight.

He begins his account by saying, "History will record, that on the sixth of October, 1789, the King and Queen of France, after a day of confusion, alarm, dismay and slaughter, lay down under the pledged security of public faith, to indulge nature in a few hours of respite, and troubled, melancholy repose."

This is neither the sober style of history, nor the intention of it. It leaves everything to be guessed at, and mistaken. One would at least think there had been a battle; and a battle there probably would have been, had it not been for the moderating prudence of those whom Mr. Burke involves in his censures. By his keeping the *Garde du Corps* out of sight, Mr. Burke has afforded himself the dramatic license of putting the King and Queen in their places, as if the object of the expedition was against them. But to return to my account—

This conduct of the *Garde du Corps,* as might well be expected, alarmed and enraged the Parisians. The colors of the cause, and the cause itself, were becoming too united to mistake the intention of the insult, and the Parisians were determined to call the *Garde du Corps* to an account.

There was certainly nothing of the cowardice of assassination in marching in the face of day to demand satisfaction (if such a phrase may be used) of a body of armed men who had voluntarily given defiance. But the circumstance which serves to throw this affair into embarrassment is, that the enemies of the Revolution appear to have encouraged it, as well as its friends.

The one hoped to prevent a civil war by checking it in time, and the other to make one. The hopes of those opposed to the Revolution rested in making the King of their party, and getting him from Versailles to Metz, where they expected to collect a force, and set up a standard.

We have therefore two different objects presenting themselves at the same time, and to be accomplished by the same means: the one, to chastise the *Garde du Corps,* which was the object of the Parisians; the other, to render the confusion of such a scene an inducement to the King to set off for Metz.

On October the fifth, a very numerous body of women, and men in the disguise of women, collected around the Hôtel de Ville or town-hall at Paris, and set off for Versailles. Their professed object was the *Garde du Corps;* but prudent men readily recollected that mischief is more easily begun than ended; and this impressed itself with the more force, from the suspicions already stated, and the irregularity of such a cavalcade.

As soon, therefore, as a sufficient force could be collected, M. de Lafayette, by orders from the civil authority of Paris, set off after them at head of twenty thousand of the Paris militia. The Revolution could derive no benefit from confusion, and its opposers might. By an amiable and spirited manner of address, he had hitherto been fortunate in calming disquietudes, and in this he was extraordinarily successful.

To frustrate, therefore, the hopes of those who might seek to improve this scene into a sort of justifiable necessity for the King's quitting Versailles and withdrawing to Metz, and to prevent at the same time, the consequences that might ensue between the *Garde du Corps* and this phalanx of men and women, he forwarded expresses to the King, that he was on his march to Versailles, at the orders of the civil authority of Paris, for the purpose of peace and protection, expressing at the same time, the necessity of restraining the *Garde du Corps* from firing on the people.[7]

He arrived at Versailles between ten and eleven at night. The *Garde du Corps* was drawn up, and the people had arrived some time before, but every thing had remained suspended. Wisdom and policy now consisted in changing a scene of danger into a happy event. M. de Lafayette became the mediator between the enraged parties; and the King, to remove the uneasiness which had arisen from the delay already stated, sent for the President of the National Assembly, and signed the *Declara-*

---

[7] I am warranted in asserting this, as I had it personally from M. de Lafayette, with whom I have lived in habits of friendship for fourteen years.—*Author.*

tion of the Rights of Man, and such other parts of the Constitution as were in readiness.

It was now about one in the morning. Every thing appeared to be composed, and a general congratulation took place. At the beat of drum a proclamation was made, that the citizens of Versailles would give the hospitality of their houses to their fellow-citizens of Paris. Those who could not be accommodated in this manner, remained in the streets, or took up their quarters in the churches; and at two o'clock the King and Queen retired.

In this state, matters passed till the break of day, when a fresh disturbance arose from the censurable conduct of some of both parties, for such characters there will be in all such scenes.

One of the *Garde du Corps* appeared at one of the windows of the palace, and the people, who had remained during the night in the streets, accosted him with reviling and provocative language. Instead of retiring, as in such a case prudence would have dictated, he presented his musket, fired and killed one of the Paris militia.

The peace being thus broken, the people rushed into the palace in quest of the offender. They attacked the quarters of the *Garde du Corps* within the palace, and pursued them through the avenues of it, and to the apartments of the King.

On this tumult, not the Queen only, as Mr. Burke has represented it, but every person in the palace, was awakened and alarmed; and M. de Lafayette had a second time to interpose between the parties, the event of which was, that the *Garde du Corps* put on the national cockade, and the matter ended, as by oblivion, after the loss of two or three lives.

During the latter part of the time in which this confusion was acting, the King and Queen were in public at the balcony, and neither of them concealed for safety's sake, as Mr. Burke insinuates.

Matters being thus appeased, and tranquillity restored, a general acclamation broke forth, of *Le Roi à Paris—Le Roi à Paris*—The King of Paris. It was the shout of peace, and immediately accepted on the part of the King. By this measure, all future projects of transporting the King to Metz, and setting up the standard of opposition to the Constitution, were prevented, and the suspicions extinguished.

The King and his family reached Paris in the evening, and were congratulated on their arrival by M. Bailley, the Mayor of Paris, in the name of the citizens. Mr. Burke, who throughout his book confounds things, persons, and principles, has in his remarks on M. Bailley's address, confounded time also. He censures M. Bailley for calling it, *"un bon jour,"* a good day.

Mr. Burke should have informed himself, that this scene took up the space of two days, the day on which it began with every appearance of danger and mischief, and the day on which it terminated without the mischiefs that threatened; and that it is to this peaceful termination that M. Bailley alludes, and to the arrival of the King at Paris.

Not less than three hundred thousand persons arranged themselves in the procession from Versailles to Paris, and not an act of molestation was committed during the whole march.

Mr. Burke, on the authority of M. Lally Tollendal, a deserter from the National Assembly, says, that on entering Paris, the people shouted, *"Tous les évêques à la lanterne."* All Bishops to be hanged at the lantern or lamp-posts.

It is surprising that nobody could bear this but Lally Tollendal, and that nobody should believe it but Mr. Burke. It has not the least connection with any part of the transaction, and is totally foreign to every circumstance of it.

The bishops have never been introduced before into any scene of Mr. Burke's drama: Why then are they, all at once, and altogether, *tout à coup et tous ensemble,* introduced now? Mr. Burke brings forward his bishops and his lantern, like figures in a magic lantern, and raises his scenes by contrast instead of connection.

But it serves to show, with the rest of his book, what little credit ought to be given, where even probability is set at defiance, for the purpose of defaming: and with this reflection, instead of a soliloquy in praise of chivalry, as Mr. Burke has done, I close the account of the expedition to Versailles.[8]

I have now to follow Mr. Burke through a pathless wilderness of rhapsodies, and a sort of descant upon governments, in which he asserts whatever he pleases, on the presumption of its being believed, without offering either evidence or reasons for so doing.

Before anything can be reasoned upon to a conclusion, certain facts, principles, or data, to reason from, must be established, admitted, or denied. Mr. Burke, with his usual outrage, abuses the *Declaration of the Rights of Man,* published by the National Assembly of France, as the

---

[8] An account of the expedition to Versailles may be seen in No. 13, of the "Révolution de Paris," containing the events from the 3d to the 10th of October, 1789.—*Author.*

basis on which the Constitution of France is built. This he calls "paltry and blurred sheets of paper about the rights of man."

Does Mr. Burke mean to deny that *man* has any rights? If he does, then he must mean that there are no such things as rights any where, and that he has none himself; for who is there in the world but man? But if Mr. Burke means to admit that man has rights, the question then will be, what are those rights, and how came man by them originally?

The error of those who reason by precedents drawn from antiquity, respecting the rights of man, is that they do not go far enough into antiquity. They do not go the whole way. They stop in some of the intermediate stages of an hundred or a thousand years, and produce what was then done as a rule for the present day. This is no authority at all.

If we travel still further into antiquity, we shall find a directly contrary opinion and practise prevailing; and, if antiquity is to be authority, a thousand such authorities may be produced, successively contradicting each other; but if we proceed on, we shall at last come out right; we shall come to the time when man came from the hand of his Maker. What was he then? Man. Man was his high and only title, and a higher cannot be given him. But of titles I shall speak hereafter.

We have now arrived at the origin of man, and at the origin of his rights. As to the manner in which the world has been governed from that day to this, it is no further any concern of ours than to make a proper use of the errors or the improvements which the history of it presents. Those who lived a hundred or a thousand years ago, were then moderns as we are now. They had *their* ancients, and those ancients had others, and we also shall be ancients in our turn.

If the mere name of antiquity is to govern in the affairs of life, the people who are to live an hundred or a thousand years hence, may as well take us for a precedent, as we make a precedent of those who lived an hundred or a thousand years ago.

The fact is, that portions of antiquity, by proving every thing, establish nothing. It is authority against authority all the way, till we come to the divine origin of the rights of man, at the Creation. Here our inquiries find a resting-place, and our reason finds a home.

If a dispute about the rights of man had arisen at a distance of an hundred years from the Creation, it is to this source of authority they must have referred, and it is to the same source of authority that we must now refer.

Though I mean not to touch upon any sectarian principle of religion, yet it may be worth observing, that the genealogy of Christ is traced to Adam. Why then not trace the rights of man to the creation of man? I will answer the question. Because there have been upstart governments, thrusting themselves between, and presumptuously working to *unmake* man.

If any generation of men ever possessed the right of dictating the mode by which the world should be governed for ever, it was the first generation that existed; and if that generation did it not, no succeeding generation can show any authority for doing it, nor can set any up.

The illuminating and divine principle of the equal rights of man (for it has its origin from the Maker of man), relates not only to the living individuals, but to generations of men succeeding each other. Every generation is equal in rights to the generations which preceded it, by the same rule that every individual is born equal in rights with his contemporary.

Every history of the Creation, and every traditionary account, whether from the lettered or unlettered world, however they may vary in their opinion or belief of certain particulars, all agree in establishing one point, *the unity of man;* by which I mean that men are all of *one degree.* and consequently that all men are born equal, and with equal natural rights, in the same manner as if posterity had been continued by *creation* instead of *generation,* the latter being only the mode by which the former is carried forward; and consequently, every child born into the world must be considered as deriving its existence from God. The world is as new to him as it was to the first man that existed, and his natural right in it is of the same kind.

The Mosaic account of the Creation, whether taken as divine authority or merely historical, is full to this point *the unity or equality of man.* The expressions admit of no controversy. "And God said, let us make man in our own image. In the image of God created he him; male and female created he them." The distinction of sexes is pointed out, but no other distinction is even implied. If this be not divine authority, it is at least historical authority, and shows that the equality of man, so far from being a modern doctrine, is the oldest upon record.

It is also to be observed, that all the religions known in the world are founded, so far as they relate to man, on the *unity of man,* as being all of one degree. Whether in heaven or in hell, or in whatever state man may be supposed to exist hereafter, the good and the bad are the only distinctions. Nay, even the laws of governments are obliged to slide into this principle, by making degrees to consist in crimes and not in persons.

It is one of the greatest of all truths, and of the highest advantage to cultivate. By considering man in this light, and by instructing him to consider himself in this light, it places him in a close connection with all his duties, whether to his Creator or to the creation, of which he is a part; and it is only when he forgets his origin, or, to use a more fashionable phrase, his *birth and family,* that he becomes dissolute.

It is not among the least of the evils of the present existing governments in all parts of Europe, that man, considered as man, is thrown back to a vast distance from his Maker, and the artificial chasm filled up by a succession of barriers, or a sort of turnpike gates, through which he has to pass.

I will quote Mr. Burke's catalogue of barriers that he has set up between man and his Maker. Putting himself in the character of a herald, he says—"We fear God—we look with *awe* to kings—with affection to parliaments—with duty to magistrates—with reverence to priests, and with respect to nobility." Mr. Burke has forgotten to put in *"chivalry."* He has also forgotten to put in Peter.

The duty of man is not a wilderness of turnpike gates, through which he is to pass by tickets from one to the other. It is plain and simple, and consists but of two points. His duty to God, which every man must feel; and with respect to his neighbor, to do as he would be done by. If those to whom power is delegated do well, they will be respected; if not, they will be despised; and with regard to those to whom no power is delegated, but who assume it, the rational world can know nothing of them.

Hitherto we have spoken only (and that but in part) of the natural rights of man. We have now to consider the civil rights of man, and to show how the one originates from the other. Man did not enter into society to become *worse* than he was before, nor to have fewer rights than he had before, but to have those rights better secured. His natural rights are the foundation of all his civil rights. But in order to pursue this distinction with more precision, it is necessary to make the different qualities of natural and civil rights.

A few words will explain this. Natural rights are those which appertain to man in right of his existence. Of this kind are all the intellectual rights, or rights of the mind, and also all those rights of acting as an individual for his own comfort and happiness, which are not injurious to the natural rights of others. Civil rights are those which appertain to man in right of his being a member of society.

Every civil right has for its foundation some natural right pre-existing in the individual, but to the enjoyment of which his individual power is not, in all cases, sufficiently competent. Of this kind are all those which relate to security and protection.

From this short review, it will be easy to distinguish between that class of natural rights which man retains after entering into society, and those which he throws into the common stock as a member of society.

The natural rights which he retains, are all those in which the *power* to execute is as perfect in the individual as the right itself. Among this class, as is before mentioned, are all the intellectual rights, or rights of the mind: consequently, religion is one of those rights.

The natural rights which are not retained, are all those in which, though the right is perfect in the individual, the power to execute them is defective. They answer not his purpose. A man, by natural right, has a right to judge in his own cause; and so far as the right of the mind is concerned, he never surrenders it: but what availeth it him to judge, if he has not power to redress? He therefore deposits his right in the common stock of society, and takes the arm of society, of which he is a part, in preference and in addition to his own. Society *grants* him nothing. Every man is proprietor in society, and draws on the capital as a matter of right.

From these premises, two or three certain conclusions will follow.

First, That every civil right grows out of a natural right; or, in other words, is a natural right exchanged.

Secondly, That civil power, properly considered as such, is made up of the aggregate of that class of the natural rights of man, which becomes defective in the individual in point of power, and answers not his purpose, but when collected to a focus, becomes competent to the purpose of every one.

Thirdly, That the power produced from the aggregate of natural rights, imperfect in power in the individual, cannot be applied to invade the natural rights which are retained in the individual, and in which the power to execute is as perfect as the right itself.

We have now, in a few words, traced man from a natural individual to a member of society, and shown, or endeavored to show, the quality of the natural rights retained, and those which are exchanged for civil rights. Let us now apply those principles to governments.

In casting our eyes over the world, it is extremely easy to distinguish the governments which have arisen out of society, or out of the social compact, from those which have not: but to place this in a clearer light than what a single glance may afford, it will be proper to take a review of the several sources from which the governments have arisen, and on which they have been founded.

They may be all comprehended under three heads. First, superstition. Secondly, power. Thirdly, the common interests of society, and the common rights of man.

The first was a government of priestcraft, the second of conquerors, and the third of reason.

When a set of artful men pretended, through the medium of oracles, to hold intercourse with the Deity, as familiarly as they now march up the back-stairs in European courts, the world was completely under the government of superstition. The oracles were consulted, and whatever they were made to say, became the law; and this sort of government lasted as long as this sort of superstition lasted.

After these a race of conquerors arose, whose government, like that of William the Conqueror, was founded in power, and the sword assumed the name of a sceptre. Governments thus established, last as long as the power to support them lasts; but that they might avail themselves of every engine in their favor, they united fraud to force, and set up an idol which they called *Divine Right,* and which, in imitation of the Pope, who affects to be spiritual and temporal, and in contradiction to the Founder of the Christian religion, twisted itself afterwards into an idol of another shape, called *Church and State.* The key of St. Peter, and the key of the Treasury, became quartered on one another, and the wondering, cheated multitude worshipped the invention.

When I contemplate the natural dignity of man; when I feel (for Nature has not been kind enough to me to blunt my feelings) for the honor and happiness of its character, I become irritated at the attempt to govern mankind by force and fraud, as if they were all knaves and fools, and can scarcely avoid disgust at those who are thus imposed upon.

We have now to review the governments which arise out of society, in contradistinction to those which arose out of superstition and conquest.

It has been thought a considerable advance toward establishing the principles of freedom, to say, that government is a compact between those who govern and those who are governed: but this cannot be true, because it is putting the effect before the cause; for as a man must have existed before governments existed, there necessarily was a time when governments did not exist, and consequently there could originally exist no governors to form such a compact with.

The fact therefore must be, that the *individuals themselves,* each in his own personal and sovereign right, *entered into a compact with each other* to produce a government: and this is the only mode in which governments have a right to arise, and the only principle on which they have a right to exist.

To possess ourselves of a clear idea of what government is, or ought to be, we must trace it to its origin. In doing this, we shall easily discover that governments must have arisen, either *out* of the people, or *over* the people. Mr. Burke has made no distinction.

He investigates nothing to its source, and therefore he confounds every thing; but he has signified his intention of undertaking at some future opportunity, a comparison between the constitutions of England and France.

As he thus renders it a subject of controversy by throwing the gauntlet, I take him upon his own ground. It is in high challenges that high truths have the right of appearing; and I accept it with the more readiness, because it affords me, at the same time, an opportunity of pursuing the subject with respect to governments arising out of society.

But it will be first necessary to define what is meant by a *constitution.* It is not sufficient that we adopt the word; we must fix also a standard signification to it.

A constitution is not a thing in name only, but in fact. It has not an ideal, but a real existence; and wherever it cannot be produced in a visible form, there is none. A constitution is a thing *antecedent* to a government, and a government is only the creature of a constitution. The constitution of a country is not the act of its government, but of the people constituting a government.

It is the body of elements, to which you can refer, and quote article by article; and which contains the principles on which the government shall be established, the manner in which it shall be organized, the powers it shall have, the mode of elections, the duration of parliaments, or by what other name such bodies may be called; the powers which the executive part of the government shall have; and, in fine, every thing that relates to the complete organization of a civil government, and the principles on which it shall act. and by which it shall be bound.

A constitution, therefore, is to a government, what the laws made afterwards by that government are to a court of judicature. The court of judicature does not make the laws, neither can it alter them; it only acts in conformity to the laws made: and the government is in like manner governed by the constitution.

Can then Mr. Burke produce the English Constitution? If he cannot, we may fairly conclude, that though it has been so much talked about, no such thing as a constitution exists, or ever did exist, and consequently that the people have yet a constitution to form. Mr. Burke will not, I presume, deny the position I have already advanced; namely, that governments arise, either *out* of the people, or *over* the people. The English Government is one of those which arose out of a conquest, and not out of society, and consequently it arose over the people; and though it has been much modified from the opportunity of circumstances since the time of William the Conqueror, the country has never yet regenerated itself, and is therefore without a constitution.

I readily perceive the reason why Mr. Burke declined going into the comparison between the English and French constitutions, because he could not but perceive, when he sat down to the task, that no such thing as a constitution existed on his side the question. His book is certainly bulky enough to have contained all he could say on this subject, and it would have been the best manner in which people could have judged of their separate merits.

Why then has he declined the only thing that was worth while to write upon? It was the strongest ground he could take, if the advantages were on his side; but the weakest, if they were not; and his declining to take it, is either a sign that he could not possess it, or could not maintain it. Mr. Burke said in a speech last winter in Parliament, That when the National Assembly first met in three Orders, (the Tiers États, the Clergy, and the Noblesse,) France had then a good constitution. This shows, among numerous other instances, that Mr. Burke does not understand what a constitution is. The persons so met, were not a *constitution,* but a *convention,* to make a constitution.

The present National Assembly of France is, strictly speaking, the personal social compact. The members of it are the delegates of the nation in its *original* character; future assemblies will be the delegates of the nation in its *organized* character.

The authority of the present Assembly is different to what the authority of future assemblies will be. The authority of the present one is to form a constitution; the authority of future assemblies will be to legislate according to the principles and forms prescribed in that constitution; and if experience should hereafter show that alterations, amendments, or additions are necessary, the constitution will point out the mode by which such things shall be done, and not leave it to the discretionary power of the future government.

A government on the principles on which constitutional governments, arising out of society are established, cannot have the right of altering itself. If it had, it would be arbitrary. It might make itself what it pleased; and wherever such a right is set up, it shows that there is no constitution.

The act by which the English Parliament empowered itself to sit for seven years, shows there is no constitution in England. It might, by the same self authority, have set any greater number of years or for life. The bill which the present Mr. Pitt brought into Parliament some years ago, to reform Parliament, was on the same erroneous principle.

The right of reform is in the nation in its original character, and the constitutional method would be by a general convention elected for the purpose. There is, moreover, a paradox in the idea of vitiated bodies reforming themselves.

From these preliminaries I proceed to draw some comparisons. I have already spoken of the Declaration of Rights; and as I mean to be as concise as possible, I shall proceed to other parts of the French Constitution.

The Constitution of France says, that every man who pays a tax of sixty sous per annum (2s. and 6d. English) is an elector. What article will Mr. Burke place against this? Can any thing be more limited, and at the same time more capricious, than what the qualifications are in England?

Limited—because not one man in a hundred (I speak much within compass) is admitted to vote: capricious—because the lowest character that can be supposed to exist, and who has not so much as the visible means of an honest livelihood, is an elector in some places while, in other places, the man who pays very large taxes, and with a known fair character, and the farmer who rents to the amount of three or four hundred pounds a year, and with a property on that farm to three or four times that amount, is not admitted to be an elector.

Every thing is out of nature, as Mr. Burke says on another occasion, in this strange chaos, and all sorts of follies are blended with all sorts of crimes. William the Conqueror, and his descendants, parcelled out the country in this manner, and bribed one part of it by what they called charters, to hold the other parts of it the better subjected to their will. This is the reason why so many of those charters abound in Cornwall.

The people were averse to the government established at the Conquest, and the towns were garrisoned and bribed to enslave the country. All the old charters are the badges of this conquest, and it is from this source that the capriciousness of election arises.

The French Constitution says, that the number of representatives for any place shall be in a ratio to the number of taxable inhabitants or electors. What article will Mr. Burke place against this? The county of Yorkshire, which contains near a million souls, sends two county members; and so does the county of Rutland, which contains not a hundredth part of that number.

The town of old Sarum which contains not three houses, sends two members; and the town of Manchester, which contains upward of sixty thousand souls, is not admitted to send any. Is there any principle in these things? [9] Is there any thing by which you can trace the marks of freedom or discover those of wisdom? No wonder, then, Mr. Burke has declined the comparison, and endeavored to lead his readers from the point by a wild, unsystematical display of paradoxical rhapsodies.

The French Constitution says, that the National Assembly shall be elected every two years. What article will Mr. Burke place against this? Why, that the nation has no right at all in the case: that the Government is perfectly arbitrary with respect to this point; and he can quote for his authority the precedent of a former parliament.

The French Constitution says, there shall be no game laws; that the farmer on whose land wild game shall be found (for it is by the produce of those lands they are fed) shall have a right to what he can take. That there shall be no monopolies of any kind, that all trades shall be free, and every man free to follow any occupation by which he can procure an honest livelihood, and in any place, town, or city, throughout the nation. What will Mr. Burke say to this?

In England game is made the property of those at whose expense it is not fed; and with respect to monopolies, the country is cut up into monopolies. Every chartered town is an aristocratic monopoly in itself, and the qualification of electors proceeds one of those chartered monopolies. Is this freedom? Is this what Mr. Burke means by a constitution?

In these chartered monopolies, a man coming from another part of the

---

[9] One of the leading demands of the English movement to extend democracy was the abolition of this rotten-borough system.—*Editor*.

282 COMPLETE WRITINGS OF THOMAS PAINE

country is hunted from them as if he were a foreign enemy. An English-man is not free in his own country: Every one of those places presents a barrier in his way, and tells him he is not a freeman—that he has no rights.

Within these monopolies are other monopolies. In a city, such for in-stance, as Bath, which contains between twenty and thirty thousand in-habitants, the right of electing representatives to Parliament is monopo-lized by about thirty-one persons. And within these monopolies are still others. A man, even of the same town, whose parents were not in circumstances to give him an occupation, is debarred, in many cases, from the natural right of acquiring one, be his genius or industry what it may.

Are these things examples to hold out to a country regenerating itself from slavery, like France? Certainly they are not; and certain am I, that when the people of England come to reflect upon them, they will, like France, annihilate those badges of ancient oppression, those traces of a conquered nation.

Had Mr. Burke possessed talents similar to the author of "On the Wealth of Nations," [10] he would have comprehended all the parts which enter into, and, by assemblage, form a constitution. He would have rea-soned from minutiæ to magnitude. It is not from his prejudices only, but from the disorderly cast of his genius, that he is unfitted for the sub-ject he writes upon.

Even his genius is without a constitution. It is a genius at random, and not a genius constituted. But he must say something. He has therefore mounted in the air like a balloon, to draw the eyes of the multitude from the ground they stand upon.

Much is to be learned from the French Constitution. Conquest and tyranny transplanted themselves with William the Conqueror from Nor-mandy into England, and the country is yet disfigured with the marks. May then the example of all France contribute to regenerate the freedom which a province of it destroyed!

The French Constitution says, That to preserve the national represen-tation from being corrupt, no member of the National Assembly shall be an officer of the government, a place-man, or a pensioner. What will Mr. Burke place against this? I will whisper his answer: *Loaves* and *Fishes*.

Ah! this government of loaves and fishes has more mischief in it than people have yet reflected on. The National Assembly has made the dis-

---

[10] The reference is to Adam Smith.—*Editor.*

covery, and it holds out the example to the world. Had governments agreed to quarrel on purpose to fleece their countries by taxes, they could not have succeeded better than they have done.

Many things in the English Government appear to me the reverse of what they ought to be, and of what they are said to be. The Parliament, imperfectly and capriciously elected as it is, is nevertheless *supposed* to hold the national purse in *trust* for the nation: but in the manner in which an English parliament is constructed, it is like a man being both mortgager and mortgagee; and in the case of misapplication of trust, it is the criminal sitting in judgment upon himself.

If those who vote the supplies are the same persons who receive the supplies when voted, and are to account for the expenditure of those supplies who voted them, it is *themselves accountable to themselves,* and the *Comedy of Errors* concludes with the Pantomime of *Hush.* Neither the ministerial party, nor the opposition, will touch upon this case. The national purse is the common hack which each mounts upon. It is like what the country people call, "Ride and tie—You ride a little way, and then I." [11] They order these things better in France.

The French Constitution says, that the right of war and peace is in the nation. Where else should it reside but in those who are to pay the expense?

In England, this right is said to reside in a *metaphor,* shown at the Tower for six-pence or a shilling a-piece: So are the lions; and it would be a step nearer to reason to say it resided in them, for any inanimate metaphor is no more than a hat or a cap. We can all see the absurdity of worshipping Aaron's molten calf, or Nebuchadnezzar's golden image; but why do men continue to practise on themselves the absurdities they despise in others?

It may with reason be said, that in the manner the English nation is represented, it signifies not where this right resides, whether in the Crown or in the Parliament. War is the common harvest of all those who participate in the division and expenditure of public money, in all countries.

It is the art of *conquering at home:* the object of it is an increase of revenue; and as revenue cannot be increased without taxes, a pretense

[11] It is a practise in some parts of the country, when two travellers have but one horse, which like the national purse will not carry double, that the one mounts and rides two or three miles a-head, and then ties the horse to a gate, and walks on. When the second traveller arrives, he takes the horse, rides on, and passes his companion a mile or two, and ties again; and so on—*Ride and tie.—Author.*

must be made for expenditures. In reviewing the history of the English Government, its wars and its taxes, a bystander, not blinded by prejudice, nor warped by interest, would declare, that taxes were not raised to carry on wars, but that wars were raised to carry on taxes.

Mr. Burke, as a member of the House of Commons, is a part of the English Government; and though he professes himself an enemy to war, he abuses the French Constitution, which seeks to explode it. He holds up the English Government as a model in all its parts, to France; but he should first know the remarks which the French make upon it.

They contend, in favor of their own, that the portion of liberty enjoyed in England, is just enough to enslave a country by, more productively than by despotism; and that as the real object of all despotism is revenue, a government so formed obtains more than it could do either by direct despotism, or in a full state of freedom, and is therefore, on the ground of interest, opposed to both.

They account also for the readiness which always appears in such governments for engaging in wars, by remarking on the different motives which produce them. In despotic governments, wars are the effect of pride; but in those governments in which they become the means of taxation, they acquire thereby a more permanent promptitude.

The French Constitution, therefore, to provide against both these evils, has taken away the power of declaring war from kings and ministers, and placed the right where the expense must fall.

When the question on the right of war and peace was agitating in the National Assembly, the people of England appeared to be much interested in the event, and highly to applaud the decision. As a principle, it applies as much to one country as to another. William the Conqueror, *as a conqueror,* held this power of war and peace in himself, and his descendants have ever since claimed it under him as a right.

Although Mr. Burke has asserted the right of the Parliament at the Revolution to bind and control the nation and posterity for *ever,* he denies, at the same time, that the Parliament or the nation had any right to alter what he calls the succession of the Crown, in any thing but in part, or by a sort of modification.

By his taking this ground, he throws the case back to the *Norman Conquest;* and by thus running a line of succession springing from William the Conqueror to the present day, he makes it necessary to inquire who and what William the Conqueror was, and where he came from; and into the origin, history, and nature of what are called prerogatives.

Every thing must have had a beginning, and the fog of time and antiquity should be penetrated to discover it. Let then Mr. Burke bring forward his William of Normandy, for it is to this origin that his argument goes. It also unfortunately happens, in running this line of succession, that another line, parallel thereto, presents itself, which is, that if the succession runs in the line of the Conquest, the nation runs in the line of being conquered, and it ought to rescue itself from this reproach.

But it will perhaps be said, that though the power of declaring war descends in the heritage of the Conquest, it is held in check by the right of the Parliament to withhold the supplies. It will always happen, when a thing is originally wrong, that amendments do not make it right; and it often happens, that they do as much mischief one way as good the other: and such is the case here; for if the one rashly declares war as a matter of right, and the other peremptorily withholds the supplies as a matter of right, the remedy becomes as bad, or worse than the disease.

The one forces the nation to a combat, and the other ties its hands: But the more probable issue is, that the contest will end in a collision between the parties, and be made a screen to both.

On this question of war, three things are to be considered. First, the right of declaring it: Secondly, the expense of supporting it: Thirdly, the mode of conducting it after it is declared. The French Constitution places the *right* where the *expense* must fall, and this union can be only in the nation. The mode of conducting it after it is declared, it consigns to the executive department. Were this the case in all countries, we should hear but little more of wars.

Before I proceed to consider other parts of the French Constitution, and by way of relieving the fatigue of argument, I will introduce an anecdote which I had from Dr. Franklin.

While the Doctor resided in France, as minister from America, during the war, he had numerous proposals made to him by projectors of every country and of every kind, who wished to go to the land that floweth with milk and honey, America; and among the rest, there was one who offered himself to be king. He introduced his proposal to the Doctor by letter, which is now in the hands of M. Beaumarchais, of Paris —stating, first, that as the Americans had dismissed or sent away [12] their king, they would want another. Secondly, that himself was a Norman. Thirdly, that he was of a more ancient family than the Dukes of Nor-

[12] The word he used was *renvoyé*, dismissed or sent away.—*Author*.

mandy, and of a more honorable descent, his line having never been bastardized. Fourthly, that there was already a precedent in England, of kings coming out of Normandy; and on these grounds he rested his offer, *enjoining* that the Doctor would forward it to America.

But as the Doctor did neither this, nor yet sent him an answer, the projector wrote a second letter; in which he did not, it is true, threaten to go over and conquer America, but only, with great dignity, proposed, that if his offer was not accepted, an acknowledgement of about £30,000 might be made to him for his generosity!

Now, as all arguments respecting succession must necessarily connect that succession with some beginning, Mr. Burke's arguments on this subject go to show that there is no English origin of kings, and that they are descendants of the Norman line in right of the Conquest.

It may, therefore, be of service to his doctrine to make this story known, and to inform him that in case of that natural distinction to which all mortality is subject, kings may again be had from Normandy, on more reasonable terms than William the Conqueror; and consequently, that the good people of England, at the Revolution of 1688, might have done much better, had such a generous Norman as *this* known *their* wants, and they *his*.

The chivalric character which Mr. Burke so much admires, is certainly much easier to make a bargain with than a hard-dealing Dutchman. But to return to the matters of the Constitution—

The French Constitution says, *there shall be no titles;* and of consequence, all that class of equivocal generation, which in some countries is called *"aristocracy,"* and in others *"nobility,"* is done away, and the *peer* is exalted into *man*.

Titles are but nicknames, and every nickname is a title. The thing is perfectly harmless in itself, but it marks a sort of foppery in the human character which degrades it. It renders man diminutive in things which are great, and the counterfeit of woman in things which are little. It talks about its fine blue *riband* like a girl, and shows its new *garter* like a child. A certain writer, of some antiquity, says, "When I was a child, I thought as a child: but when I became a man, I put away childish things."

It is, properly, from the elevated mind of France, that the folly of titles has been abolished. It has outgrown the babyclothes of *count* and *duke,* and breeched itself in manhood. France has not levelled, it has exalted. It has put down the dwarf to set up the man. The insignificance of a senseless word like *duke, count,* or *earl,* has ceased to please. Even those who possessed them, have disowned the gibberish, and, as they outgrew the rickets, have despised the rattle.

The genuine mind of man, thirsting for its native home, society, contemns the gewgaws that separate him from it. Titles are like circles drawn by the magician's wand, to contract the sphere of man's felicity. He lives immured within the Bastille of a word, and surveys at a distance the envied life of man.

Is it then any wonder that titles should fall in France? Is it not a greater wonder they should be kept up anywhere? What are they? What is their worth, and "what is their amount?" When we think or speak of a *judge* or a *general,* we associate with it the ideas of office and character; we think of gravity in the one, and bravery in the other; but when we use a word merely as a title, no ideas associate with it.

Through all the vocabulary of Adam, there is no such an animal as a duke or a count; neither can we connect any idea to the words. Whether they mean strength or weakness, wisdom or folly, a child or a man, or a rider or a horse, is all equivocal. What respect then can be paid to that which describes nothing, and which means nothing? Imagination has given figure and character to centaurs, satyrs, and down to all the fairy tribe; but titles baffle even the powers of fancy, and are a chimerical nondescript.

But this is not all. If a whole country is disposed to hold them in contempt, all their value is gone, and none will own them. It is common opinion only that makes them any thing or nothing, or worse than nothing. There is no occasion to take titles away, for they take themselves away when society concurs to ridicule them. This species of imaginary consequence has visibly declined in every part of Europe, and it hastens to its exit as the world of reason continues to rise.

There was a time when the lowest class of what are called nobility, was more thought of than the highest is now, and when a man in armor riding through Christendom in search of adventure was more stared at than a modern duke. The world has seen this folly fall, and it has fallen by being laughed at, and the farce of titles will follow its fate.

The patriots of France have discovered in good time, that rank and dignity in society must take a new ground. The old one has fallen through. It must now take the substantial ground of character, instead of the chimerical ground of titles; and they have brought their titles to the altar, and made of them a burnt-offering to Reason.

If no mischief had annexed itself to the folly of titles, they would not have been worth a serious and formal destruction, such as the National Assembly have decreed them: and this makes it necessary to inquire further into the nature and character of aristocracy.

That, then, which is called aristocracy in some countries, and nobility in others, arose out of the governments founded upon conquest. It was originally a military order, for the purpose of supporting military government (for such were all governments founded in conquest); and to keep up a succession of this order for the purpose for which it was established, all the younger branches of those families were disinherited, and the law of *primogenitureship* set up.

The nature and character of aristocracy shows itself to us in this law. It is a law against every law of nature, and nature herself calls for its destruction. Establish family justice, and aristocracy falls. By the aristocratical law of primogenitureship, in a family of six children, five are exposed. Aristocracy has never more than *one* child. The rest are begotten to be devoured. They are thrown to the cannibal for prey, and the natural parent prepares the unnatural repast.

As every thing which is out of nature in man, affects, more or less, the interest of society, so does this. All the children which the aristocracy disowns (which are all, except the eldest) are, in general, cast like orphans on a parish, to be provided for by the public, but at a greater charge. Unnecessary offices and places in governments and courts are created at the expense of the public, to maintain them.

With what kind of parental reflections can the father or mother contemplate their younger offspring? By nature they are children, and by marriage they are heirs; but by aristocracy they are bastards and orphans. They are the flesh and blood of their parents in one line, and nothing akin to them in the other. To restore, therefore, parents to their children, and children to their parents—relations to each other, and man to society—and to exterminate the monster, aristocracy, root and branch—the French Constitution has destroyed the law of *Primogenitureship*.[18] Here then lies the monster; and Mr. Burke, if he pleases, may write its epitaph.

Hitherto we have considered aristocracy chiefly in one point of view. We have now to consider it in another. But whether we view it before or behind, or sideways, or any way else, domestically or publicly, it is still a monster.

In France, aristocracy has one feature less, in its countenance, than

[18] According to the system of primogeniture the eldest son inherited all the land.—*Editor.*

what it has in some other countries. It did not compose a body of heredi-tary legislators. It was not *"a corporation of aristocracy,"* for such I have heard M. de Lafayette describe an English House of Peers. Let us then examine the grounds upon which the French Constitution has resolved against having such a House in France.

Because, in the first place, as is already mentioned, aristocracy is kept up by family tyranny and injustice.

Secondly, Because there is an unusual unfitness in an aristocracy to be legislators for a nation. Their ideas of *distributive justice* are corrupted at the very source. They begin life by trampling on all their younger brothers and sisters, and relations of every kind, and are taught and educated so to do. With what ideas of justice or honor can that man enter a house of legislation, who absorbs in his own person the inher-itance of a whole family of children, or doles out to them some pitiful portion with the insolence of a gift?

Thirdly, Because the idea of hereditary legislators is as inconsistent as that of hereditary judges, or hereditary juries; and as absurd as an heredi-tary mathematician, or an hereditary wise man; and as ridiculous as an hereditary poet-laureate.

Fourthly, Because a body of men holding themselves accountable to nobody, ought not to be trusted by any body.

Fifthly, Because it is continuing the uncivilized principles of the gov-ernments founded in conquest, and the base idea of man having property in man, and governing him by personal right.

Sixthly, Because aristocracy has a tendency to degenerate the human species. By the universal economy of nature it is known, and by the in-stance of the Jews it is proved, that the human species has a tendency to degenerate, in any small number of persons, when separated from the general stock of society, and intermarrying constantly with each other.

It defeats even its pretended end, and becomes in time the opposite of what is noble in man. Mr. Burke talks of nobility; let him show what it is. The greatest characters the world has known, have risen on the demo-cratic floor. Aristocracy has not been able to keep a proportionate pace with democracy.

The artificial NOBLE shrinks into a dwarf before the NOBLE of Nature; and in the few instances of those (for there are some in all countries) in whom nature, as by a miracle, has survived in aristocracy, THOSE MEN DESPISE IT. But it is time to proceed to a new subject.

The French Constitution has reformed the condition of the clergy. It has raised the income of the lower and middle classes, and taken from the higher. None is now less than twelve hundred livres (fifty pounds sterling), nor any higher than about two or three thousand pounds. What will Mr. Burke place against this? Hear what he says:

He says, "That the people of England can see without pain or grudging, an archbishop precede a duke; they can see a bishop of Durham, or a bishop of Winchester, in possession of £10,000 a year; and cannot see why it is in worse hands than estates to the like amount in the hands of this earl or that 'squire." And Mr. Burke offers this as an example to France.

As to the first part, whether the archbishop precedes the duke, or the duke the bishop, it is, I believe, to the people in general, somewhat like *Sternhold* and *Hopkins,* or *Hopkins* and *Sternhold;* [14] you may put which you please first; and as I confess that I do not understand the merits of this case, I will not contend it with Mr. Burke.

But with respect to the latter, I have something to say. Mr. Burke has not put the case right. The comparison is out of order by being put between the bishop and the earl or the 'squire. It ought to be put between the bishop and the curate, and then it will stand thus:—*The people of England can see without pain or grudging, a bishop of Durham, or a bishop of Winchester, in possession of ten thousand pounds a year, and a curate on thirty or forty pounds a year, or less.*

No, Sir, they certainly do not see those things without great pain or grudging. It is a case that applies itself to every man's sense of justice, and is one among many that calls aloud for a constitution.

In France, the cry of *"the church! the church!"* was repeated as often as in Mr. Burke's book, and as loudly as when the Dissenter's Bill was before the English Parliament; but the generality of the French clergy were not to be deceived by this cry any longer. They knew, that whatever the pretense might be, it was themselves who were one of the principal objects of it.

It was the cry of the high beneficed clergy, to prevent any regulation of income taking place between those of ten thousand pounds a year and the parish priest. They, therefore, joined their case to those of every other oppressed class of men, and by this union obtained redress.

The French Constitution has abolished tithes, that source of perpetual discontent between the tithe-holder and the parishioner. When land is held on tithe, it is in the condition of an estate held between two parties;

[14] Editors of a famous hymn-book.—*Editor.*

the one receiving one-tenth, and the other nine-tenths of the produce: and, consequently, on principles of equity, if the estate can be improved, and made to produce by that improvement double or treble what it did before, or in any other ratio, the expense of such improvement ought to be borne in like proportion between the parties who are to share the produce.

But this is not the case in tithes; the farmer bears the whole expense, and the tithe-holder takes a tenth of the improvement, in addition to the original tenth, and by this means gets the value of two-tenths instead of one. That is another case that calls for a constitution.

The French Constitution hath abolished or renounced *toleration,* and *intolerance* also, and hath established UNIVERSAL RIGHT OF CONSCIENCE.

Toleration is not the *opposite* of intoleration, but is the *counterfeit* of it. Both are despotisms. The one assumes to itself the right of withholding liberty of conscience, and the other of granting it. The one is the Pope, armed with fire and faggot, and the other is the Pope selling or granting indulgences. The former is church and state, and the latter is church and traffic.

But toleration may be viewed in a much stronger light. Man worships not himself, but his Maker: and the liberty of conscience which he claims, is not for the service of himself, but of his God. In this case, therefore, we must necessarily have the associated idea of two beings; the *mortal* who renders the worship, and the *immortal being* who is worshipped.

Toleration therefore, places itself not between man and man, nor between church and church, nor between one denomination of religion and another, but between God and man; between the being who worships, and the *being* who is worshipped; and by the same act of assumed authority by which it tolerates man to pay his worship, it presumptuously and blasphemously sets up itself to tolerate the Almighty to receive it.

Were a bill brought into Parliament, entitled, "An *act* to tolerate or grant liberty to the Almighty to receive the worship of a Jew or a Turk," or "to prohibit the Almighty from receiving it," all men would startle, and call it blasphemy. There would be an uproar. The presumption of toleration in religious matters would then, present itself unmasked; but the presumption is not the less because the name of "Man" only appears to those laws, for the associated idea of the *worshipper* and the *worshipped* cannot be separated.

Who, then, art thou, vain dust and ashes! by whatever name thou art called, whether a king, a bishop, a church or a state, a parliament or any thing else, that obtrudest thine insignificance between the soul of man and his Maker? Mind thine own concerns. If he believes not as thou believest, it is a proof that thou believest not as he believeth, and there is no earthly power can determine between you.

With respect to what are called denominations of religion, if every one is left to judge of his own religion, there is no such thing as a religion that is wrong; but if they are to judge of each other's religion, there is no such thing as a religion that is right; and therefore all the world is right, or all the world is wrong.

But with respect to religion itself, without regard to names, and as directing itself from the universal family of mankind to the divine object of all adoration, *it is man bringing to his Maker the fruits of his heart;* and though these fruits may differ from each other like the fruits of the earth, the grateful tribute of every one is accepted.

A bishop of Durham, or a bishop of Winchester, or the archbishop who heads the dukes, will not refuse a tithe-sheaf of wheat, because it is not a cock of hay; nor a cock of hay, because it is not a sheaf of wheat; nor a pig, because it is neither the one nor the other: but these same persons, under the figure of an established church, will not permit their Maker to receive the various tithes of man's devotion.

One of the continual choruses of Mr. Burke's book, is "church and state." He does not mean some one particular church, or some one particular state, but any church and state; and he uses the term as a general figure to hold forth the political doctrine of always uniting the church with the state in every country, and he censures the National Assembly for not having done this in France. Let us bestow a few thoughts on this subject.

All religions are in their nature mild and benign, and united with principles of morality. They could not have made proselytes at first, by professing anything that was vicious, cruel, persecuting or immoral. Like every thing else, they had their beginning; and they proceeded by persuasion, exhortation, and example. How then is it that they lose their native mildness, and become morose and intolerant?

It proceeds from the connection which Mr. Burke recommends. By engendering the church with the state, a sort of mule-animal, capable only of destroying, and not of breeding up, is produced, called, *The Church established by Law.* It is a stranger, even from its birth to any parent mother on which it is begotten, and whom in time it kicks out and destroys.

The Inquisition in Spain does not proceed from the religion originally professed, but from this mule-animal, engendered between the church and the state. The burnings in Smithfield proceeded from the same heterogeneous production; and it was the regeneration of this strange animal in England afterwards, that renewed rancor and irreligion among the inhabitants, and that drove the people called Quakers and Dissenters to America.

Persecution is not an original feature in *any* religion; but it is always the strongly marked feature of all law-religions, or religions established by law. Take away the law-establishment, and every religion reassumes its original benignity. In America, a Catholic priest is a good citizen, a good character, and a good neighbor; an Episcopal minister is of the same description: and this proceeds, independently of the men, from there being no law-establishment in America.

If also we view this matter in a temporal sense, we shall see the ill effects it has had on the prosperity of nations. The union of church and state has impoverished Spain. The revoking the edict of Nantes drove the silk manufacture from France into England; and church and state are now driving the cotton manufacture from England to America and France.

Let then Mr. Burke continue to preach his anti-political doctrine of Church and State. It will do some good. The National Assembly will not follow his advice, but will benefit by his folly. It was by observing the ill effects of it in England, that America has been warned against it; and it is by experiencing them in France, that the National Assembly have abolished it, and, like America, have established UNIVERSAL RIGHT OF CONSCIENCE, AND UNIVERSAL RIGHT OF CITIZENSHIP.[15]

[15] When in any country we see extraordinary circumstances taking place, they naturally lead any man who has a talent for observation and investigation, to inquire into the causes. The manufactures of Manchester, Birmingham and Sheffield, are the principal manufactures in England. From whence did this arise? A little observation will explain the case.

The principal, and the generality of the inhabitants of those places, are not of what is called in England, *the Church established by law;* and they, or their fathers (for it is within but a few years) withdrew from the persecution of the chartered towns, where test-laws more particularly operate, and established a sort of asylum for themselves in those places. It was the only asylum that then offered, for the rest of Europe was worse.

But the case is now changing. France and America bid all comers welcome, and initiate them into all the rights of citizenship. Policy and interest, therefore, will, but perhaps too late, dictate in England, what reason and justice could not. Those manufactures are with-

I will here cease the comparison with respect to the principles of the French Constitution, and conclude this part of the subject with a few observations on the organization of the formal parts of the French and English governments.

The executive power in each country is in the hands of a person styled the king; but the French Constitution distinguishes between the king and the sovereign: It considers the station of king as official, and places sovereignty in the nation.

The representatives of the nation, who compose the National Assembly, and who are the legislative power, originate in and from the people by election, as an inherent right in the people.

In England it is otherwise; and this arises from the original establishment of what is called its monarchy; for, as by the Conquest all the rights of the people or the nation were absorbed into the hands of the Conqueror, and who added the title of King to that of Conqueror, those same matters which in France are now held as rights in the people, or in the nation, are held in England as grants from what is called the Crown.

The Parliament in England, in both its branches, was erected by patents from the descendants of the Conqueror. The House of Commons did not originate as a matter of right in the people to delegate or elect, but as a grant or boon.

By the French Constitution, the nation is always named before the king. The third article of the Declaration of Rights says, *"The nation is essentially the source* (or fountain) *of all sovereignty."* Mr. Burke argues, that, in England, a king is the fountain—that he is the fountain

---

drawing, and are arising in other places. There is now [1791] erecting at Passy, three miles from Paris, a large cotton mill, and several are already erected in America. Soon after the rejecting the bill for repealing the test-law, one of the richest manufacturers in England said in my hearing, "England, Sir, is not a country for a Dissenter to live in— we must go to France."

These are truths, and it is doing justice to both parties to tell them. It is chiefly the Dissenters who have carried English manufactures to the height they are now at, and the same men have it in their power to carry them away; and though those manufactures would afterwards continue to be made in those places, the foreign market would be lost. There are frequently appearing in the London *Gazette,* extracts from certain acts to prevent machines, and, as far as it can extend to, persons, from going out of the country.

It appears from these, that the ill effects of the test-laws and church-establishment begin to be much suspected; but the remedy of force can never supply the remedy of reason. In the progress of less than a century, all the unrepresented part of England, of all denominations, which is at least a hundred times the most numerous, may begin to feel the necessity of a constitution, and then all those matters will come regularly before them.— *Author.*

of all honor. But as this idea is evidently descended from the Conquest, I shall make no other remark upon it, than that it is the nature of conquest to turn every thing upside down; and as Mr. Burke will not be refused the privilege of speaking twice, and as there are but two parts in the figure, the *fountain* and the *spout,* he will be right the second time.

The French Constitution puts the legislative before the executive; the Law before the King; *La Loi, Le Roi.* This also is in the natural order of things; because laws must have existence, before they can have execution.

A king in France does not in addressing himself to the National Assembly, say, "My assembly," similar to the phrase used in England of *my* "Parliament"; neither can he use it consistently with the Constitution, nor could it be admitted. There may be propriety in the use of it in England, because as is before mentioned, both Houses of Parliament originated from what is called the Crown by patent or boon—and not from the inherent rights of the people, as the National Assembly does in France, and whose name designates its origin.

The President of the National Assembly does not ask the King *to grant to the Assembly liberty of speech,* as is the case with the English House of Commons. The Constitutional dignity of the National Assembly cannot debase itself. Speech is, in the first place, one of the natural rights of man always retained; and with respect to the National Assembly, the use of it is their *duty,* and the nation is their *authority.*

They were elected by the greatest body of men exercising the right of election the European world ever saw. They sprung not from the filth of rotten boroughs, nor are they the vassal representatives of aristocratical ones. Feeling the proper dignity of their character, they support it. Their parliamentary language, whether for or against a question, is free, bold, and manly, and extends to all the parts and circumstances of the case.

If any matter or subject respecting the executive department, or the person who presides in it (the king) comes before them, it is debated on with the spirit of men, and the language of gentlemen; and their answer, or their address, is returned in the same style. They stand not aloof with the gaping vacuity of vulgar ignorance, nor bend with the cringe of sycophantic insignificance. The graceful pride of truth knows no extremes, and preserves, in every latitude of life, the right-angled character of man.

Let us now look to the other side of the question. In the addresses of the English Parliaments to their kings, we see neither the intrepid spirit of the old Parliaments of France, nor the serene dignity of the present National Assembly: neither do we see in them any thing of the style of English manners, which border somewhat on bluntness.

Since then they are neither of foreign extraction, nor naturally of English production, their origin must be sought for elsewhere, and that origin is the Norman Conquest. They are evidently of the vassalage class of manners, and emphatically mark the prostrate distance that exists in no other condition of men than between the conqueror and the conquered.

That this vassalage idea and style of speaking was not got rid of even at the Revolution of 1688, is evident from the declaration of Parliament to William and Mary, in these words: "We do most humbly and faithfully *submit* ourselves, our heirs and posterities for ever." Submission is wholly a vassalage term, repugnant to the dignity of freedom, and an echo of the language used at the Conquest.

As the estimation of all things is by comparison, the Revolution of 1688, however from circumstances it may have been exalted beyond its value, will find its level. It is already on the wane, eclipsed by the enlarging orb of reason, and the luminous revolutions of America and France. In less than another century, it will go, as well as Mr. Burke's labors, "to the family vault of all the Capulets." Mankind will then scarcely believe that a country calling itself free, would send to Holland for a man, and clothe him with power, on purpose to put themselves in fear of him, and give him almost a million sterling a year for leave to *submit* themselves and their posterity, like bond-men and bond-women, for ever.

But there is a truth that ought to be made known: I have had the opportunity of seeing it; which is, *that, notwithstanding appearances, there is not any description of men that despise monarchy so much as courtiers.* But they well know, that if it were seen by others, as it is by them, the juggle could not be kept up.

They are in the condition of men who get their living by a show, and to whom the folly of that show is so familiar that they ridicule it; but were the audience to be made as wise in this respect as themselves, there would be an end to the show and the profits with it.

The difference between a republican and a courtier with respect to monarchy, is, that the one opposes monarchy, believing it to be something, and the other laughs at it, knowing it to be nothing.

As I used sometimes to correspond with Mr. Burke, believing him then to be a man of sounder principles than his book shows him to be, I wrote to him last winter from Paris, and gave him an account how prosperously matters were going on. Among other subjects in that letter, I referred to the happy situation the National Assembly were placed in; that they had taken a ground on which their moral duty and their political interest were united.

They have not to hold out a language which they do not themselves believe, for the fraudulent purpose of making others believe it. Their station requires no artifice to support it, and can only be maintained by enlightening mankind. It is not their interest to cherish ignorance but to dispel it. They are not in the case of a ministerial or an opposition party in England, who, though they are opposed, are still united to keep up the common mystery.

The National Assembly must throw open a magazine of light. It must show man the proper character of man; and the nearer it can bring him to that standard, the stronger the National Assembly becomes.

In contemplating the French Constitution, we see in it a rational order of things. The principles harmonize with the forms, and both with their origin. It may perhaps be said as an excuse for bad forms, that they are nothing more than forms; but this is a mistake. Forms grow out of principles, and operate to continue the principles they grow from. It is impossible to practise a bad form on any thing but a bad principle. It cannot be ingrafted on a good one; and wherever the forms in any government are bad, it is a certain indication that the principles are bad also.

I will here finally close the subject. I began it by remarking that Mr. Burke had *voluntarily* declined going into a comparison of the English and French constitutions. He apologizes (in p. 241) for not doing it, by saying that he had not time. Mr. Burke's book was upwards of eight months in hand, and it extended to a volume of three hundred and sixty-six pages.

As his omission does injury to his cause, his apology makes it worse; and men on the English side of the water will begin to consider, whether there is not some radical defect in what is called the English Constitution, that made it necessary for Mr. Burke to suppress the comparison, to avoid bringing it into view.

As Mr. Burke has not written on constitutions, so neither has he written on the French Revolution. He gives no account of its commencement or its progress.

He only expresses his wonder. "It looks," says he, "to me as if I were in a great crisis, not of the affairs of France alone, but of all Europe, perhaps of more than Europe. All circumstances taken together, the French Revolution is the most astonishing that has hitherto happened in the world."

As wise men are astonished at foolish things, and other people at wise ones, I know not on which ground to account for Mr. Burke's astonishment; but certain it is that he does not understand the French Revolution. It has apparently burst forth like a creation from a chaos, but it is no more than the consequence of a mental revolution previously existing in France.

The mind of the nation had changed beforehand, and the new order of things had naturally followed the new order of thoughts. I will here, as concisely as I can, trace out the growth of the French Revolution, and mark the circumstances that have contributed to produce it.

The despotism of Louis XIV, united with the gaiety of his court, and the gaudy ostentation of his character, had so humbled, and at the same time so fascinated the mind of France, that the people appear to have lost all sense of their own dignity, in contemplating that of their Grand Monarch: and the whole reign of Louis XV, remarkable only for weakness and effeminacy, made no other alteration than that of spreading a sort of lethargy over the nation, from which it showed no disposition to rise.

The only signs which appeared of the spirit of liberty during those periods, are to be found in the writings of the French philosophers. Montesquieu,[16] President of the Parliament of Bordeaux, went as far as a writer under a despotic government could well proceed: and being obliged to divide himself between principle and prudence, his mind often appears under a veil, and we ought to give him credit for more than he has expressed.

Voltaire,[17] who was both the flatterer and satirist of despotism, took

[16] Charles de Secondat Montesquieu, famous French philosopher, author of the celebrated *Spirit of the Laws* published in 1782.—*Editor.*

[17] Jean-François-Marie Aronet Voltaire, famous French philosopher noted for his wit.—*Editor.*

another line. His forte lay in exposing and ridiculing the superstitions which priestcraft, united with statecraft, had interwoven with governments.

It was not from the purity of his principles, or his love of mankind (for satire and philanthropy are not naturally concordant), but from his strong capacity of seeing folly in its true shape, and his irresistible propensity to expose it, that he made those attacks. They were however as formidable as if the motives had been virtuous; and he merits the thanks rather than the esteem of mankind.

On the contrary, we find in the writings of Rousseau and the Abbé Raynal, a loveliness of sentiment in favor of liberty, that excites respect, and elevates the human faculties; but having raised his animation, they do not direct its operations, but leave the mind in love with an object, without describing the means of possessing it.

The writings of Quesnay,[18] Turgot,[19] and the friends of these authors, are of a serious kind; but they labored under the same disadvantage with Montesquieu; their writings abound with moral maxims of government, but are rather directed to economize and reform the administration of the government, than the government itself.

But all those writings and many others had their weight; and by the different manner in which they treated the subject of government—Montesquieu by his judgment and knowledge of laws, Voltaire by his wit, Rosseau [20] and Raynal [21] by their animation, and Quesnay and Turgot by their moral maxims and systems of economy, readers of every class met with something to their taste, and a spirit of political inquiry began to diffuse itself through the nation at the time the dispute between England and the then colonies of America broke out.

In the war which France afterwards engaged in, it is very well known that the nation appeared to be beforehand with the French Ministry. Each of them had its view: but those views were directed to different objects; the one sought liberty, and the other retaliation on England. The French officers and soldiers who after this went to America, were

[18] François Quesnay, leader of the physiocrats in France.—*Editor.*

[19] Baron de l'Aulne Turgot, follower of the physiocrats, minister of finance under Louis XVI, who introduced a number of economic reforms during his brief stay in office. He abolished the *corvèe*, re-established free commerce in grain within the kingdom, abolished many iniquitous taxes, and checked many useless expenditures.—*Editor.*

[20] Jean-Jacques Rousseau, author of *Contrat Social* (Social Contract) and other works on the nature of government and society.—*Editor.*

[21] M. Raynal, a former Roman Catholic clergyman, who became the editor of *Mercure de France* and a specialist in philosophy and history.—*Editor.*

eventually placed in the school of Freedom, and learned the practise as well as the principles of it by heart.

As it was impossible to separate the military events which took place in America from the principles of the American Revolution, the publication of those events in France necessarily connected themselves with the principles which produced them. Many of the facts were in themselves principles; such as the declaration of American independence, and the treaty of alliance between France and America, which recognized the natural right of man, and justified resistance to oppression.

The then Minister of France, Count Vergennes, was not the friend of America; and it is both justice and gratitude to say, that it was the Queen of France who gave the cause of America a fashion at the French Court. Count Vergennes was the personal and social friend of Dr. Franklin; and the Doctor had obtained, by his sensible gracefulness, a sort of influence over him; but with respect to principles, Count Vergennes was a despot.

The situation of Dr. Franklin as Minister from America to France, should be taken into the chain of circumstances. The diplomatic character is of itself the narrowest sphere of society that man can act in. It forbids intercourse by a reciprocity of suspicion; and a diplomatist is a sort of unconnected atom, continually repelling and repelled. But this was not the case with Dr. Franklin. He was not the diplomatist of a court, but of a MAN. His character as a philosopher had been long established, and his circle of society in France was universal.

Count Vergennes resisted for a considerable time the publication in France of the American Constitutions, translated into the French language; but even in this he was obliged to give way to public opinion, and a sort of propriety in admitting to appear what he had undertaken to defend. The American Constitutions were to liberty, what a grammar is to language: they define its parts of speech, and practically construct them into syntax.

The peculiar situation of the then Marquis de Lafayette is another link in the great chain. He served in America as an American officer under a commission of Congress, and by the universality of his acquaintance, was in close friendship with the civil government of America, as well as with the military line. He spoke the language of the country, entered into the discussions on the principles of government, and was always a welcome friend at any election.

When the war closed, a vast reinforcement to the cause of liberty spread itself over France, by the return of the French officers and soldiers. A knowledge of the practise was then joined to the theory; and all that was wanting to give it a real existence was opportunity. Man cannot, properly speaking, make circumstances for his purpose, but he always has it in his power to improve them when they occur; and this was the case in France.

M. Necker was displaced in May, 1781; and by the ill management of the finances afterward, and particularly during the extravagant administration of M. Calonne, the revenue of France, which was nearly twenty-four millions sterling *per* year, was become unequal to the expenditure, not because the revenue had decreased, but because the expenses had increased; and this was the circumstance which the nation laid hold of to bring forward a revolution.

The English Minister, Mr. Pitt, has frequently alluded to the state of the French finances in his budgets without understanding the subject. Had the French parliaments been as ready to register edicts for new taxes, as an English parliament is to grant them, there had been no derangement in the finances, nor yet any revolution; but this will better explain itself as I proceed.

It will be necessary here to show how taxes were formerly raised in France. The king, or rather the court or ministry acting under the use of that name, framed the edicts for taxes at their own discretion, and sent them to the parliaments to be registered; for until they were registered by the parliaments, they were not operative.

Disputes had long existed between the court and the parliaments with respect to the extent of the parliament's authority on this head. The court insisted that the authority of parliaments went no farther than to remonstrate or show reasons against the tax, reserving to itself the right of determining whether the reasons were well or ill-founded; and in consequence thereof, either to withdraw the edict as a matter of choice, or to order it to be enregistered as a matter of authority.

The parliaments on their part insisted, that they had not only a right to remonstrate, but to reject; and on this ground they were always supported by the nation.

But, to return to the order of my narrative, M. Calonne wanted money; and as he knew the sturdy disposition of the parliaments with respect to new taxes, he ingeniously sought either to approach them by a more gentle means than that of direct authority, or to get over their heads by a maneuver: and, for this purpose, he revived the project of assem-

302 COMPLETE WRITINGS OF THOMAS PAINE

bling a body of men from the several provinces, under the style of an
"Assembly of the Notables," or Men of Note, who met in 1787, and who
were either to recommend taxes to the parliaments, or to act as a parliament themselves. An Assembly under this name had been called in
1617.

As we are to view this as the first practical step towards the Revolution, it will be proper to enter into some particulars respecting it. The
Assembly of the Notables has in some places been mistaken for the
States-General, but was wholly a different body; the States-General
being always by election.

The persons who composed the Assembly of the Notables were all
nominated by the King, and consisted of one hundred and forty members. But as M. Calonne could not depend upon a majority of this Assembly in his favor, he very ingeniously arranged them in such a
manner as to make forty-four a majority of one hundred and forty: to
effect this, he disposed of them into seven separate committees, of
twenty members each.

Every general question was to be decided, not by a majority of persons
but by a majority of committees; and as eleven votes would make a
majority in a committee, and four committees a majority of seven, M.
Calonne had good reason to conclude, that as forty-four would determine any general question, he could not be out-voted. But all his plans
deceived him, and in the event became his overthrow.

The then Marquis de Lafayette was placed in the second committee,
of which Count D'Artois was President: and as money-matters was the
object, it naturally brought into view every circumstance connected with
it. M. de Lafayette made a verbal charge against Calonne, for selling
crown-lands to the amount of two millions of livres, in a manner that
appeared to be unknown to the King.

The Count D'Artois (as if to intimidate, for the Bastille was then in
being) asked the Marquis if he would render the charge in writing?
He replied that he would. The Count D'Artois did not demand it, but
brought a message from the King to that purport.

M. de Lafayette then delivered his charge in writing, to be given to the
King, undertaking to support it. No farther proceedings were had upon
this affair; but M. Calonne was soon after dismissed by the King, and set
off to England.

As M. de Lafayette, from the experience of what he had seen in
America, was better acquainted with the science of civil government

than the generality of the members who composed the Assembly of the Notables could then be, the brunt of the business fell considerably to his share.

The plan of those who had a constitution in view, was to contend with the Court on the ground of taxes, and some of them openly professed their object. Disputes frequently arose between Court D'Artois and M. de Lafayette, upon various subjects.

With respect to the arrears already incurred, the latter proposed to remedy them, by accommodating the expenses to the revenue, instead of the revenue to the expenses; and as objects of reform, he proposed to abolish the Bastille, and all the state-prisons throughout the nation, (the keeping of which was attended with great expense), and to suppress *Lettres de Cachet.*[22] But those matters were not then much attended to; and with respect to *Lettres de Cachet, a majority of the nobles appeared to be in favor of them.*

On the subject of supplying the treasury by new taxes the Assembly declined taking the matter on themselves, concurring in the opinion that they had not authority. In a debate on this subject, M. de Lafayette said that raising money by taxes could only be done by a National Assembly, freely elected by the people, and acting as their representatives. "Do you mean," said Count D'Artois, "the *States-General?*" M. de Lafayette replied, that he did. "Will you," said the Count D'Artois, "sign what you say, to be given to the King?" The other replied, that he not only would do this, but that he would go farther, and say that the effectual mode would be, for the King to agree to the establishment of a constitution.

As one of the plans had thus failed, that of getting the Assembly to act as a parliament, the other came into view, that of recommending. On his subject, the Assembly agreed to recommend two new taxes to be enregistered by the parliament, the one a stamp tax and the other a territorial tax, or sort of land tax. The two have been estimated at about five millions sterling per annum. We have now to turn our attention to the parliaments, on whom the business was again developing.

The Archbishop of Toulouse (since Archbishop of Sens, and now a Cardinal) was appointed to the administration of the finances, soon after the dismission of Calonne. He was also made Prime Minister, an office that did not always exist in France. When this office did not exist,

[22] Sealed letters which might order the police to arrest and imprison any subject of the king.—*Editor.*

the chief of each of the principal departments transacted business immediately with the king; but when a prime minister was appointed, they did business only with him. The Archbishop arrived to more state-authority than any minister since the Duke de Choiseul, and the nation was strongly disposed in his favor; but by a line of conduct scarcely to be accounted for, he perverted every opportunity, turned out a despot, and sunk into disgrace, and a Cardinal.

The Assembly of Notables having broken up, the new minister sent the edicts for the two new taxes recommended by the Assembly to the Parliaments, to be enregistered. They of course came first before the Parliament of Paris, who returned for answer; *That with such a revenue as the nation then supported, the name of taxes ought not to be mentioned, but for the purpose of reducing them;* and threw both the edicts out.[23]

On this refusal, the Parliament was ordered to Versailles, where in the usual form, the King held, what under the old government was called a Bed of Justice: and the two edicts were enregistered in presence of the Parliament, by an order of State, in the manner mentioned in page 301.

On this the Parliament immediately returned to Paris, renewed their session in form, and ordered the enregistering to be struck out, declaring that everything done at Versailles was illegal. All the members of Parliament were then served with *Lettres de Cachet,* and exiled to Trois; but as they continued as inflexible in exile as before, and as vengeance did not supply the place of taxes, they were after a short time recalled to Paris.

The edicts were again tendered to them, and the Count D'Artois undertook to act as representative of the King. For this purpose, he came from Versailles to Paris, in a train of procession; and the Parliament was assembled to receive him.

But show and parade had lost their influence in France; and whatever ideas of importance he might set off with, he had to return with those of mortification and disappointment. On alighting from his carriage to ascend the steps of the Parliament House, the crowd (which was numerously collected) threw out trite expressions, saying: "This is Monsieur D'Artois, who wants more of our money to spend."

The marked disapprobation which he saw, impressed him with ap-

[23] When the English Minister, Mr. Pitt, mentions the French finances again in the English Parliament, it would be well that he noticed this as an example.—*Author.*

prehensions; and the word *Aux arms! (To arms!)* was given out by the officer of the guard who attended him. It was so loudly vociferated, that it echoed through the avenues of the House, and produced a temporary confusion: I was then standing in one of the apartments through which he had to pass, and could not avoid reflecting how wretched was the condition of a disrespected man.

He endeavored to impress the Parliament by great words, and opened his authority by saying: "The King, our Lord and Master." The Parliament received him very coolly, and with their usual determination not to register the taxes; and in this manner the interview ended.

After this a new subject took place. In the various debates and contests that arose between the Court and the Parliaments on the subject of taxes, the Parliament of Paris at last declared, that although it had been customary for Parliaments to enregister edicts for taxes as a matter of convenience, the right belonged only to the States-General; and that, therefore, the Parliaments could no longer with propriety continue to debate on what it had not authority to act.

The King, after this, came to Paris, and held a meeting with the Parliament, in which he continued from ten in the morning till about six in the evening; and, in a manner that appeared to proceed from him, as if unconsulted upon with the Cabinet or the Ministry, gave his word to the Parliament, that the States-General should be convened.

But after this, another scene arose, on a ground different from all the former. The Minister and the Cabinet were averse to calling the States-General: they well knew, that if the States-General were assembled, that themselves must fall; and as the King had not mentioned *any time,* they hit on a project calculated to elude, without appearing to oppose.

For this purpose, the Court set about making a sort of constitution itself; it was principally the work of M. Lamoignon, Keeper of the Seals, who afterwards shot himself. This new arrangement consisted in establishing a body under the name of a *Cour plénière,* or full Court, in which were invested all the power that the government might have occasion to make use of.

The persons composing this Court were to be nominated by the King; the contended right of taxation was given up on the part of the King, and a new criminal code of laws, and law proceedings, was substituted in the room of the former. The thing, in many points, contained better principles than those upon which the government had hitherto been administered: but, with respect to the *Cour plénière,* it was no other than a medium through which despotism was to pass, without appearing to act directly from itself.

The Cabinet had high expectations from their new contrivance. The persons who were to compose the *Cour plénière* were already nominated, and as it was necessary to carry a fair appearance, many of the best characters in the nation were appointed among the number. It was to commence on the eighth of May, 1788: but an opposition arose to it, on two grounds—the one as to principle, the other as to form.

On the ground of principle it was contended, that government had not a right to alter itself; and that if the practise was once admitted, it would grow into a principle, and be made a precedent for any alterations the government might wish to establish; that the right of altering the government was a national right, and not a right of government. And on the ground of form, it was contended that the *Cour plénière* was nothing more than a larger cabinet.

The then Dukes de la Rouchefoucault, Luxembourg, de Noailles, and many others, refused to accept the nomination, and strenuously opposed the whole plan. When the edict for establishing this new court was sent to the Parliaments to be enregistered and put into execution, they resisted also. The Parliament of Paris not only refused but denied the authority; and the contest renewed itself between the Parliament and the Cabinet more strongly than ever.

While the Parliament was sitting in debate on this subject, the Ministry ordered a regiment of soldiers to surround the house and form a blockade. The members sent out for beds and provision, and lived as in a besieged citadel; and as this had no effect, the commanding officer was ordered to enter the Parliament House and seize them, which he did, and some of the principal members were shut up in different prisons.

About the same time a deputation of persons arrived from the province of Brittany, to remonstrate against the establishment of the *Cour plénière;* and those the Archbishop sent to the Bastille. But the spirit of the nation was not to be overcome; and it was so fully sensible of the strong ground it had taken, that of withholding taxes, that it contented itself with keeping up a sort of quiet resistance, which effectually overthrew all the plans at that time formed against it. The project of the *Cour plénière* was at last obliged to be given up, and the Prime Minister not long afterwards followed its fate; and M. Necker was recalled into office.

The attempt to establish the *Cour plénière* had an effect upon the nation which was not anticipated. It was a sort of new form of government, that insensibly served to put the old one out of sight, and to unhinge it from the superstitious authority of antiquity. It was government dethroning government; and the old one, by attempting to make a new one, made a chasm.

The failure of this scheme renewed the subject of convening the States-General: and this gave rise to a new series of politics. There was no settled form for convening the States-General; all that it positively meant, was a deputation from what was then called the Clergy, the Nobility and the Commons; but their numbers, or their proportions, had not been always the same. They had been convened only on extraordinary occasions, the last of which was in 1614; their numbers were then in equal proportions, and they voted by orders.

It could not well escape the sagacity of M. Necker, that the mode of 1614 would answer neither the purpose of the then Government, nor of the nation. As matters were at that time circumstanced, it would have been too contentious to agree upon anything. The debates would have been endless upon privileges and exemptions, in which neither the wants of the Government, nor the wishes of the nation for a constitution, would have been attended to. But as he did not choose to take the decision upon himself, he summoned again the Assembly of the Notables, and referred it to them. This body was in general interested in the decision, being chiefly of the aristocracy and the high paid clergy; and they decided, in favor of the mode of 1614.

This decision was against the sense of the nation, and also against the wishes of the Court; for the aristocracy opposed itself to both, and contended for privileges independent of either. The subject was then taken up by the Parliament, who recommended that the number of the Commons should be equal to the other two; and that they should all sit in one house, and vote in one body.

The number finally determined on was twelve hundred: six hundred to be chosen by the Commons (and this was less than their proportion ought to have been when their worth and consequence is considered on a national scale), three hundred by the clergy, and three hundred by the aristocracy; but with respect to the mode of assembling themselves, whether together or apart, or the manner in which they should vote, those matters were referred.[24]

[24] Mr. Burke (and I must take the liberty of telling him he is very unacquainted with French affairs,) speaking upon this subject, says, "The first thing that struck me in the

The election that followed, was not a contested election, but an animated one. The candidates were not men but principles. Societies were formed in Paris, and committees of correspondence and communication established throughout the nation, for the purpose of enlightening the people, and explaining to them the principles of civil government; and so orderly was the election conducted, that it did not give rise even to the rumor of tumult.

The States-General were to meet at Versailles in April, 1789, but did not assemble till May. They situated themselves in three separate chambers, or rather the clergy and the aristocracy withdrew each into a separate chamber. The majority of the aristocracy claimed what they called the privilege of voting as a separate body, and of giving their consent or their negative in that manner; and many of the bishops and the high-beneficed clergy claimed the same privilege on the part of their order.

The *Tiers État* (as they were then called) disowned any knowledge of artificial orders and artificial privileges; and they were not only resolute on this point, but somewhat disdainful. They began to consider aristocracy as a kind of fungus growing out of the corruption of society, that could not be admitted even as a branch of it; and from the disposition the aristocracy had shown by upholding *Lettres de Cachet,* and in sundry other instances, it was manifest that no constitution could be formed by admitting men in any other character than as national men.

After various altercations on this head, the *Tiers État or Commons* (as they were then called) declared themselves (on motion made for

---

calling the States-General, was a great departure from the ancient course"; and he soon after says, "From the moment I read the list, I saw distinctly, and very nearly as it has happened, all that was to follow." Mr. Burke certainly did not see all that was to follow. I endeavored to impress him, as well before as after the States-General met, .hat there would be a *revolution;* but was not able to make him see it, neither would he believe it. How then he could distinctly see all the parts, when the whole was out of sight, is beyond my comprehension. And with respect to the "departure" from the ancient "course," besides the natural weakness of the remark, it shows that he is unacquainted with circumstances. The departure was necessary, from the experience had upon it, that the ancient course was a bad one.

The States-General of 1614 were called at the commencement of the civil war in the minority of Louis III. But by the clash of arranging them by orders, they increased the confusion they were called to compose. The author of *L'Intrigue du Cabinet* (Intrigue of the Cabinet), who wrote before any revolution was thought of in France, speaking of the States-General of 1614, says, "They held the public in suspense five months; and by the questions agitated therein, and the heat with which they were put, it appears that the great (*les grands*) thought more to satisfy their *particular* passions, than to procure the good of the nations; and the whole time passed away in altercations, ceremonies and parade."—*Author*.

that purpose by the Abbé Sieyès) "THE REPRESENTATIVES OF THE NATION; *and that the two Orders could be considered but as deputies of corporations, and could only have a deliberative voice when they assembled in a national character with the national representatives."* This proceeding extinguished the style of *États Généraux,* or States-General, and erected it into the style it now bears, that of *L'Assemblée Nationale,* or National Assembly.

This motion was not made in a precipitate manner: It was the result of cool deliberation, and concerted between the national representatives and the patriotic members of the two chambers, who saw into the folly, mischief and injustice of artificial privileged distinctions.

It was become evident, that no constitution, worthy of being called by that name, could be established on any thing less than a national ground. The aristocracy had hitherto opposed the despotism of the court and affected the language of patriotism; but it opposed it as its rival (as the English barons opposed King John), and it now opposed the nation from the same motives.

On carrying this motion, the national representatives, as had been concerted, sent an invitation to the two chambers, to unite with them in a national character, and proceed to business. A majority of the clergy, chiefly of the parish priests, withdrew from the clerical chamber, and joined the nation; and forty-five from the other chamber joined in like manner.

There is a sort of secret history belonging to this last circumstance, which is necessary to its explanation: It was not judged prudent that all the patriotic members of the chamber styling itself the Nobles, should quit it at once; and in consequence of this arrangement, they drew off by degrees, always leaving some, as well to reason the case, as to watch the suspected.

In a little time, the numbers increased from forty-five to eighty, and soon after to a greater number; which, with a majority of the clergy, and the whole of the national representatives, put the malcontents in a very diminutive condition.

The King, who, very different from the general class called by that name, is a man of a good heart, showed himself disposed to recommend a union of the three chambers, on the ground the National Assembly had taken; but the malcontents exerted themselves to prevent it, and began now to have another project in view.

Their numbers consisted of a majority of the aristocratical chamber, and a minority of the clerical chamber, chiefly of bishops and high-beneficed clergy; and these men were determined to put everything to issue, as well by strength as by stratagem. They had no objection to a constitution; but it must be such an one as themselves should dictate, and suited to their own views and particular situations.

On the other hand, the nation disowned knowing any thing of them but as citizens, and was determined to shut out all such upstart pretensions. The more aristocracy appeared, the more it was despised; there was a visible imbecility and want of intellects in the majority, a sort of *je ne sais quoi,* that while it affected to be more than citizen, was less than man. It lost ground from contempt more than from hatred; and was rather jeered at as an ass, than dreaded as a lion. This is the general character of aristocracy, or what are called nobles or nobility, or rather no-ability, in all countries.

The plan of the malcontents consisted now of two things; either to deliberate and vote by chambers, (or orders), more especially on all questions respecting a constitution, (by which the aristocratical chamber would have a negative on any article of the constitution); or, in case they could not accomplish this object, to overthrow the National Assembly entirely.

To effect one or other of these objects, they began now to cultivate a friendship with the despotism they had hitherto attempted to rival, and the Count D'Artois became their chief. The King (who has since declared himself deceived into their measures) held, according to the old form, *a Bed of Justice,* in which he accorded to the deliberation and vote *par téte* (by head) upon several subjects; but reserved the deliberation and vote upon all questions respecting a constitution, to the three chambers separately.

The declaration of the King was made against the advice of M. Necker, who now began to perceive that he was growing out of Fashion at Court, and that another minister was in contemplation.

As the form of sitting in separate chambers was yet apparently kept up, though essentially destroyed, the national representatives, immediately after this declaration of the King, resorted to their own chambers to consult on a protest against it; and the minority of the chamber (calling itself the Nobles), who had joined the national cause, retired to a private house to consult in like manner. The malcontents had by this time concerted their measures with the Court, which Count D'Artois undertook to conduct; and as they saw from the discontent which the declaration excited, and the opposition making against it, that they could not obtain a control over the intended constitution by a separate vote, they prepared themselves for their final object—that of conspiring against the National Assembly and overthrowing it.

The next morning, the door of the chamber of the National Assembly was shut against them, and guarded by troops; and the members were refused admittance. On this they withdrew to a tennis-ground in the neighborhood of Versailles, as the most convenient place they could find, and, after renewing their session, took an oath never to separate from each other, under any circumstances whatever, death excepted, until they had established a constitution.

As the experiment of shutting up the House had no other effect than that of producing a closer connection in the members, it was opened again the next day, and the public business recommenced in the usual place.

We are now to have in view the forming of the new Ministry, which was to accomplish the overthrow of the National Assembly. But as force would be necessary, orders were issued to assemble thirty thousand troops, the command of which was given to Broglio, one of the new-intended Ministry, who was recalled from the country for this purpose. But as some management was necessary to keep this plan concealed till the moment it should be ready for execution, it is to this policy that a declaration made by the Count D'Artois must be attributed, and which is here proper to be introduced.

It could not but occur, that while the malcontents continued to resort to their chambers separate from the National Assembly, that more jealousy would be excited than if they were mixed with it, and that the plot might be suspected. But as they had taken their ground, and now wanted a pretense for quitting it, it was necessary that one should be devised.

This was effectually accomplished by a declaration made by Count D'Artois, *"that if they took not a part in the National Assembly, the life of the King would be endangered,"* on which they quitted their chambers, and mixed with the Assembly in one body.

At the time this declaration was made, it was generally treated as a piece of absurdity in the Count D'Artois, and calculated merely to relieve the outstanding members of the two chambers from the diminutive situation they were put in; and if nothing more had followed, this conclusion would have been good. But as things best explain themselves by their events, this apparent union was only a cover to the machinations that were secretly going on; and the declaration accommodated itself to answer that purpose.

In a little time the National Assembly found itself surrounded by troops, and thousands more daily arriving. On this a very strong declaration was made by the National Assembly to the King, remonstrating on the impropriety of the measure, and demanding the reason. The King, who was not in the secret of this business, as himself afterwards declared, gave substantially for answer, that he had no other object in view than to preserve public tranquillity, which appeared to be much disturbed.

But in a few days from this time, the plot unravelled itself. M. Necker and the Ministry were displaced, and a new one formed of the enemies of the Revolution; and Broglio, with between twenty-five to thirty thousand foreign troops, was arrived to support them. The mask was now thrown off, and matters were come to a crisis. The event was, that in the space of three days, the new Ministry, and all their abettors found it prudent to fly the nation; the Bastille was taken, and Broglio and his foreign troops dispersed; as is already related in a former part of this work.

There are some curious circumstances in the history of this short-lived Ministry, and this brief attempt at a counter-revolution. The palace of Versailles, where the Court was sitting, was not more than four hundred yards distant from the hall where the National Assembly was sitting. The two places were at this moment like the separate headquarters of two combatant armies; yet the Court was as perfectly ignorant of the information which had arrived from Paris to the National Assembly, as if it had resided at an hundred miles distance.

The then Marquis de Lafayette, who (as has been already mentioned) was chosen to preside in the National Assembly on this particular occasion, named, by order of the Assembly, three successive deputations to the King, on the day, and up to the evening on which the Bastille was taken, to inform and confer with him on the state of affairs; but the Ministry, who knew not so much as that it was attacked, precluded all communication, and were solacing themselves how dexterously they had succeeded: but in a few hours the accounts arrived so thick and fast, that they had to start from their desks and run: some set off in one disguise, and some in another, and none in their own character. Their anxiety now was to outride the news, lest they should be stopped, which, though it flew fast, flew not so fast as themselves.

It is worth remarking, that the National Assembly neither pursued those fugitive conspirators, nor took any notice of them, nor sought to retaliate in any shape whatever. Occupied with establishing a constitution, founded on the rights of man and the authority of the people, the only authority on which government has a right to exist in any country, the National Assembly felt none of those mean passions which mark the character of impertinent governments, founding themselves on their own authority, or on the absurdity of hereditary succession. It is the faculty of the human mind to become what it contemplates, and to act in unison with its object.

The conspiracy being thus dispersed, one of the first works of the National Assembly, instead of vindictive proclamations, as has been the case with other governments, published a Declaration of the Rights of Man, as the basis on which the new Constitution was to be built, and which is here subjoined.

DECLARATION

OF THE

RIGHTS OF MAN AND OF CITIZENS

BY THE NATIONAL ASSEMBLY OF FRANCE

THE Representatives of the people of FRANCE, *formed into a* NATIONAL ASSEMBLY, considering that ignorance, neglect, or contempt of human rights, are the sole causes of public misfortunes and corruptions of government, have resolved to set forth in a solemn declaration, these natural, imprescriptible, and unalienable rights: that this declaration, being constantly present to the minds of the members of the body social, they may be ever kept attentive to their rights and their duties: that the acts of the legislative and executive powers of government, being capable of being every moment compared with the end of political institutions, may be more respected: and also, that the future claims of the citizens, being directed by simple and incontestible principles, may always tend to the maintenance of the Constitution, and the general happiness.

"For these reasons the NATIONAL ASSEMBLY doth recognize and declare, in the presence of the Supreme Being, and with the hope of His blessing and favor, the following *sacred* rights of men and of citizens:

"I. *Men are born, and always continue, free, and equal in respect of their rights. Civil distinctions, therefore, can be founded only on public utility.*

"II. *The end of all political associations, is, the preservation of the natural and imprescriptible rights of man; and these rights are liberty, property, security, and resistance of oppression.*

"III. *The nation is essentially the source of all sovereignty; nor can any* INDIVIDUAL, *or* ANY BODY OF MEN, *be entitled to any authority which is not expressly derived from it.*

"IV. Political liberty consists in the power of doing whatever does not injure another. The exercise of the natural rights of every man has no other limits than those which are necessary to secure to every *other* man the free exercise of the same rights; and these limits are determinable only by the law.

"V. The law ought to prohibit only actions hurtful to society. What is not prohibited by the law, should not be hindered; nor should any one be compelled to that which the law does not require.

"VI. The law is an expression of the will of the community. All citizens have a right to concur, either personally, or by their representatives, in its formation. It should be the same to all, whether it protects or punishes; and *all being equal in its sight, are equally eligible to all honors, places, and employments, according to their different abilities, without any other distinction than that created by their virtues and talents.*

"VII. No man should be accused, arrested, or held in confinement, except in cases determined by the law, and according to the forms which it has prescribed. All who promote, solicit, execute, or cause to be executed, arbitrary orders, ought to be punished; and every citizen called upon or apprehended by virtue of the law, ought immediately to obey, and renders himself culpable by resistance.

"VIII. The law ought to impose no other penalties but such as are absolutely and evidently necessary: and no one ought to be punished, but in virtue of a law promulgated before the offense, and legally applied.

"IX. Every man being presumed innocent till he has been convicted, whenever his detention becomes indispensable, all rigor to him, more than is necessary to secure his person, ought to be provided against by the law.

"X. No man ought to be molested on account of his opinions, not even on account of his *religious* opinions, provided his avowal of them does not disturb the public order established by the law.

"XI. The unrestrained communication of thoughts and opinions being one of the most precious rights of man, every citizen may speak, write, and publish freely, provided he is responsible for the abuse of this liberty in cases determined by the law.

"XII. A public force being necessary to give security to the rights of men and of citizens, that force is instituted for the benefit of the community, and not for the particular benefit of the persons with whom it is intrusted.

"XIII. A common contribution being necessary for the support of the public force, and for defraying the other expenses of government, it ought to be divided equally among the members of the community, according to their abilities.

"XIV. Every citizen has a right, either by himself or his representative, to a free voice in determining the necessity of public contributions, the appropriation of them, and their amount, mode of assessment, and duration.

"XV. Every community has a right to demand of all its agents, an account of their conduct.

"XVI. Every community in which a separation of powers and a security of rights is not provided for, wants a constitution.

"XVII. The rights to property being inviolable and sacred, no one ought to be deprived of it, except in cases of evident public necessity, legally ascertained, and on condition of a previous just indemnity."

OBSERVATIONS

ON THE

DECLARATION OF RIGHTS

THE three first articles comprehend in general terms the whole of a Declaration of Rights: All the succeeding articles either originate from them, or follow as elucidations. The fourth, fifth, and sixth define more particularly what is only generally expressed in the first, second, and third.

The seventh, eighth, ninth, tenth, and eleventh articles, are declaratory of *principles* upon which laws shall be constructed, conformable to *rights* already declared. But it is questioned by some very good people in France, as well as in other countries, whether the tenth article sufficiently guarantees the right it is intended to accord with: besides which, it takes off from the divine dignity of religion, and weakens its operative force upon the mind, to make it a subject of human laws. It then presents itself to man, like light intercepted by a cloudy medium, in which the source of it is obscured from his sight, and he sees nothing to reverence in the dusky ray.[25]

The remaining articles, beginning with the twelfth, are substantially contained in the principles of the preceding articles; but, in the particular situation in which France then was, having to undo what was wrong, as well as to set up what was right, it was proper to be more particular than what in another condition of things would be necessary.

While the Declaration of Rights was before the National Assembly, some of its members remarked, that if a Declaration of Rights was published, it should be accompanied by a Declaration of Duties. The observation discovered a mind that reflected, and it only erred by not reflecting far enough. A Declaration of Rights is, by reciprocity, a Declaration of Duties also. Whatever is my right as a man, is also the right of another; and it becomes my duty to guarantee, as well as to possess.

The three first articles are the basis of liberty, as well individual as national; nor can any country be called free, whose government does not take its beginning from the principles they contain, and continue to preserve them pure; and the whole of the Declaration of Rights is of more value to the world, and will do more good, than all the laws and statutes that have yet been promulgated.

[25] There is a single idea, which, if it strikes rightly upon the mind, either in a legal or a religious sense, will prevent any man, or any body of men, or any government, from going wrong on the subject of religion; which is, that before any human institutions of government were known in the world, there existed, if I may so express it, a compact between God and man, from the beginning of time; and that as the relation and condition which man in his *individual person* stands in toward his Maker cannot be changed, or any ways altered by any human laws or human authority, that religious devotion, which is a part of this compact, cannot so much as be made a subject of human laws; and that all laws must conform themselves to this prior existing compact, and not assume to make the compact conform to the laws, which, besides being human, are subsequent thereto. The first act of man, when he looked around and saw himself a creature which he did not make, and a world furnished for his reception, must have been devotion; and devotion must ever continue sacred to every individual man, *as it appears right to him;* and governments do mischief by interfering.—*Author.*

In the declaratory exordium which prefaces the Declaration of Rights, we see the solemn and majestic spectacle of a nation opening its commission, under the auspices of its Creator, to establish a Government; a scene so new, and so transcendently unequalled by any thing in the European world, that the name of a revolution is diminutive of its character, and it rises into a regeneration of man.

What are the present governments of Europe, but a scene of iniquity and oppression? What is that of England? Do not its own inhabitants say, It is a market where every man has his price, and where corruption is common traffic, at the expense of a deluded people? No wonder, then, that the French Revolution is traduced.

Had it confined itself merely to the destruction of flagrant despotism, perhaps Mr. Burke and some others had been silent. Their cry now is, "It is gone too far": that is, it has gone too far for them. It stares corruption in the face, and the venal tribe are all alarmed. Their fear discovers itself in their outrage, and they are but publishing the groans of a wounded vice.

But from such opposition, the French Revolution, instead of suffering, receives an homage. The more it is struck, the more sparks it will emit; and the fear is, it will not be struck enough. It has nothing to dread from attacks: Truth has given it an establishment; and Time will record it with a name as lasting as his own.

Having now traced the progress of the French Revolution through most of its principal stages, from its commencement, to the taking of the Bastille, and its establishment by the Declaration of Rights, I will close the subject with the energetic apostrophe of M. de Lafayette—*May this great monument, raised to Liberty, serve as a lesson to the oppressor, and an example to the oppressed!* [26]

MISCELLANEOUS CHAPTER

TO PREVENT interrupting the argument of the preceding part of this work, or the narrative that follows it, I reserved some observations to be thrown together into a Miscellaneous Chapter; by which

[26] See page 255 of this work.—N. B. Since the taking of the Bastille, the occurrences have been published; but the matters recorded in this narrative are prior to that period; and some of them, as may be easily seen, can be but very little known.—*Author.*

variety might not be censured for confusion. Mr. Burke's book is *all* Miscellany. His intention was to make an attack on the French Revolution; but instead of proceeding with an orderly arrangement, he has stormed it with a mob of ideas tumbling over and destroying one another.

But this confusion and contradiction in Mr. Burke's book is easily accounted for. When a man in a long cause attempts to steer his course by any thing else than some polar truth or principle, he is sure to be lost. It is beyond the compass of his capacity to keep all the parts of an argument together, and make them unite in one issue by any other means than having this guide always in view. Neither memory nor invention will supply the want of it. The former fails him, and the latter betrays him.

Notwithstanding the nonsense, for it deserves no better name, that Mr. Burke has asserted about hereditary rights, and hereditary succession, and that a nation has not a right to form a government for itself; it happened to fall in his way to give some account of what Government is. *"Government,"* says he, *"is a contrivance of human wisdom."*

Admitting that Government is a contrivance of human *wisdom,* it must necessarily follow, that hereditary succession, and hereditary rights (as they are called), can make no part of it, because it is impossible to make wisdom hereditary; and on the other hand, *that* cannot be a wise contrivance, which in its operation may commit the government of a nation to the wisdom of an idiot. The ground which Mr. Burke now takes, is fatal to every part of his cause.

The argument changes from hereditary rights to hereditary wisdom; and the question is, Who is the wisest man? He must now show that every one in the line of hereditary succession was a Solomon, or his title is not good to be a king. What a stroke has Mr. Burke now made! To use a sailor's phrase, he has *swabbed the deck,* and scarcely left a name legible in the list of kings; and he has mowed down and thinned the House of Peers, with a scythe as formidable as Death and Time. But Mr. Burke appears to have been aware of this retort, and he has taken care to guard against it, by making government to be not only a *contrivance* of human wisdom, but a *monopoly* of wisdom. He puts the nation as fools on one side, and places his government of wisdom, all wise men of Gotham, on the other side; and he then proclaims, and says, that *"men have a* RIGHT *that their* WANTS *should be provided for by this wisdom."*

Having thus made proclamation, he next proceeds to explain to them what their *wants* are, and also what their *rights* are.

In this he has succeeded dexterously, for he makes their wants to be a *want* of wisdom; but as this is but cold comfort, he then informs them, that they have a *right* (not to any of the wisdom) but to be governed by it; and in order to impress them with a solemn reverence for this monopoly-government of wisdom, and of its vast capacity for all purposes, possible or impossible, right or wrong, he proceeds with astrological, mysterious importance, to tell them its powers in these words—

"The Rights of Man in government are their advantages; and these are often in balances between differences of good; and in compromises sometimes between *good* and *evil,* and sometimes between *evil* and *evil.* Political reason is a *computing principle;* adding, subtracting, multiplying, and dividing, morally and not metaphysically, or mathematically, true moral demonstrations."

As the wondering audience whom Mr. Burke supposes himself talking to, may not understand all this learned jargon, I will undertake to be its interpreter. The meaning then, good people, of all this, is, *that government is governed by no principle whatever; that it can make evil good, or good evil, just as it pleases. In short, that government is arbitrary power.*

But there are some things which Mr. Burke has forgotten. First, he has not shown where the wisdom originally came from; and, secondly, he has not shown by what authority it first began to act. In the manner he introduces the matter, it is either government stealing wisdom, or wisdom stealing government. It is without an origin, and its powers without authority. In short, it is usurpation.

Whether it be from a sense of shame, or from a consciousness of some radical defect in a government necessary to be kept out of sight, or from both, or from some other cause, I undertake not to determine; but so it is, that a monarchical reasoner never traces government to its source, or from its source. It is one of the *shibboleths* by which he may be known.

A thousand years hence, those who shall live in America, or in France, will look back with contemplative pride on the origin of their governments, and say, *this was the work of our glorious ancestors!* But what can a monarchical talker say? What has he to exult in? Alas! he has nothing. A certain something forbids him to look back to a beginning, lest some robber, or some Robin Hood, should rise from the long obscurity of time, and say, *I am the origin!*

Hard as Mr. Burke labored under the Regency Bill and Hereditary Succession two years ago, and much as he dived for precedents, he still had not boldness enough to bring up William of Normandy and say, *there is the head of the list! there is the fountain of honor!* the son of a prostitute, and the plunderer of the English nation.

The opinions of men, with respect to government, are changing fast in all countries. The revolutions of America and France have thrown a beam of light over the world, which reaches into man. The enormous expense of governments has provoked people to think by making them feel; and when once the veil begins to rend, it admits not of repair.

Ignorance is of a peculiar nature; once dispelled, it is impossible to reestablish it. It is not originally a thing of itself, but is only the absence of knowledge; and though man may be *kept* ignorant, he cannot be *made* ignorant.

The mind, in discovering truth, acts in the same manner as it acts through the eye in discovering objects; when once any object has been seen, it is impossible to put the mind back to the same condition it was in before it saw it. Those who talk of a counter-revolution in France show how little they understand of man.

There does not exist in the compass of language, an arrangement of words to express so much as the means of effecting a counter-revolution. The means must be an obliteration of knowledge; and it has never yet been discovered how to make a man *unknow* his knowledge, or *unthink* his thoughts.

Mr. Burke is laboring in vain to stop the progress of knowledge; and it comes with the worse grace from him, as there is a certain transaction known in the City, which renders him suspected of being a pensioner in a fictitious name. This may account for some strange doctrine he has advanced in his book, which, though he points it at the Revolution Society, is effectually directed against the whole nation.

"The King of England," says he, "holds *his* crown (for it does not belong to the nation, according to Mr. Burke) in *contempt* of the choice of the Revolution Society, who have not a single vote for a king among them either *individually or collectively;* and His Majesty's heirs, each in their time and order, will come to the crown *with the same contempt* of their choice, with which His Majesty has succeeded to that which he now wears."

As to who is king of England or elsewhere or whether there is any at all, or whether the people choose a Cherokee chief, or a Hessian hussar for a king, is not a matter that I trouble myself about,—be that to themselves; but with respect to the doctrine, so far as it relates to the rights of men and nations, it is as abominable as any thing ever uttered in the most enslaved country under heaven.

Whether it sounds worse to my ear, by not being accustomed to hear such despotism, than it does to the ear of another person, I am not so well a judge of; but of its abominable principle, I am at no loss to judge.

It is not the Revolution Society that Mr. Burke means; it is the nation, as well in its *original,* as in its *representative* character; and he has taken care to make himself understood, by saying, that they have not a vote either *collectively* or *individually.*

The Revolution Society is composed of citizens of all denominations, and of members of both Houses of Parliament; and consequently, if there is not a right to vote in any of the characters, there can be no right to any, either in the nation or in its Parliament.

This ought to be a caution to every country, how it imports foreign families to be kings. It is somewhat curious to observe, that although the people of England have been in the habit of talking about kings, it is always a foreign house of kings; hating foreigners, yet governed by them. It is now the House of Brunswick, one of the petty tribes of Germany.

It has hitherto been the practise of the English Parliaments, to regulate what was called the succession, (taking it for granted, that the nation then continued to accord to the form of annexing a monarchical branch to its government; for without this, the Parliament could not have had the authority to have sent either to Holland or to Hanover,[27] or to impose a king upon a nation against its will). And this must be the utmost limit to which Parliament can go upon the case; but the right of the nation goes to the *whole* case, because it has the right of changing its *whole* form of government.

The right of a parliament is only a right in trust, a right by delegation, and that but of a very small part of the nation; and one of its Houses has not even this. But the right of the nation is an original right, as universal as taxation. The nation is the paymaster of every thing, and every thing must conform to its general will.

I remember taking notice of a speech in what is called the English House of Peers, by the then Earl of Shelburne, and I think it was at the

[27] The reference is to the fact that William III came from Holland and George I from Hanover.—*Editor.*

time he was Minister, which is applicable to this case. I do not directly charge my memory with every particular; but the words and the purport, as nearly as I remember, were these: *That the form of a government was a matter wholly at the will of the nation at all times: that if it chose a monarchial form, it had a right to have it so; and if it afterwards chose to be a republic, it had a right to be a republic, and to say to a king, "We have no longer any occasion for you."*

When Mr. Burke says that "His Majesty's heirs and successors, each in their time and order, will come to the crown with the *same contempt* of their choice with which His Majesty has succeeded to that he wears," it is saying too much even to the humblest individual in the country; part of whose daily labor goes toward making up the million sterling a year, which the country gives the person it styles a king. Government with insolence is despotism; but when contempt is added, it becomes worse; and to pay for contempt is the excess of slavery.

This species of government comes from Germany; and reminds me of what one of the Brunswick soldiers told me, who was taken prisoner by the Americans in the late war. "Ah!" said he, "America is a fine, free country; it is worth the people's fighting for; I know the difference by knowing my own: in my country, if the Prince says, Eat straw, we eat straw." God help that country, thought I, be it England or elsewhere, whose liberties are to be protected by German principles of government, and Princes of Brunswick.

As Mr. Burke sometimes speaks of England, sometimes of France, and sometimes of the world, and of government in general, it is difficult to answer his book without apparently meeting him on the same ground. Although principles of government are general subjects, it is next to impossible in many cases to separate them from the idea of place and circumstance; and the more so when circumstances are put for arguments, which is frequently the case with Mr. Burke.

In the former part of his book, addressing himself to the people of France, he says, "No experience has taught us, (meaning the English), that in any other course or method than that of an *hereditary crown,* can our liberties be regularly perpetuated and preserved sacred as our *hereditary right.*" I ask Mr. Burke who is to take them away. M. de Lafayette, in speaking to France says, *"For a nation to be free, it is sufficient that she wills it."*

But Mr. Burke represents England as wanting capacity to take care of itself, and that its liberties must be taken care of by a king, holding it in "contempt." If England is sunk to this, it is preparing itself to eat straw, as in Hanover or in Brunswick. But besides the folly of the declaration, it happens that the facts are all against Mr. Burke. It was by the government *being hereditary,* that the liberties of the people were endangered. Charles I and James II are instances of this truth; yet neither of them went so far as to hold the nation in contempt.

As it is sometimes of advantage to the people of one country, to hear what those of other countries have to say respecting it, it is possible that the people of France may learn something from Mr. Burke's book, and and that the people of England may also learn something from the answers it will occasion. When nations fall out about freedom, a wide field of debate is opened. The argument commences with the rights of war, without its evils; and as knowledge is the object contended for, the party that sustains the defeat obtains the prize. Mr. Burke talks about what he calls an hereditary crown, as if it were some production of nature; or as if, like Time, it had a power to operate, not only independently, but in spite of man; or as if it were a thing or a subject universally consented to. Alas! it has none of those properties, but is the reverse of them all. It is a thing of imagination, the propriety of which is more than doubted, and the legality of which in a few years will be denied.

But, to arrange this matter in a clearer view than what general expressions can convey, it will be necessary to state the distinct heads under which (what is called) an hereditary crown, or, more properly speaking, an hereditary succession to the government of a nation, can be considered; which are,

First, The right of a particular family to establish itself.

Secondly, The right of a nation to establish a particular family.

With respect to the *first* of these heads, that of a family establishing itself with hereditary powers on its own authority, and independent of the consent of a nation, all men will concur in calling it despotism; and it would be trespassing on their understanding to attempt to prove it.

But the *second* head, that of a nation establishing a particular family with *hereditary powers,* does not present itself as despotism on the first reflection; but if men will permit a second reflection to take place, and carry that reflection forward but one remove out of their own persons to that of their offspring, they will then see that hereditary succession becomes in its consequences the same despotism to others, which they reprobated for themselves. It operates to preclude the consent of the succeeding generations; and the preclusion of consent is despotism.

When the person who at any time shall be in possession of a government, or those who stand in succession to him, shall say to a nation, I hold this power in "contempt" of you, it signifies not on what authority he pretends to say it. It is no relief, but an aggravation to a person in slavery, to reflect that he was sold by his parent; and as that which heightens the criminality of an act cannot be produced to prove the legality of it, hereditary succession cannot be established as a legal thing.

In order to arrive to a more perfect decision on this head, it will be proper to consider the generation which undertakes to establish a family with *hereditary powers,* apart and separate from the generations which are to follow; and also to consider the character in which the *first* generation acts with respect to succeeding generations.

The generation which first selects a person, and puts him at the head of its government, either with the title of king, or any other distinction, acts its *own choice,* be it wise or foolish, as a free agent for itself. The person so set up is not hereditary, but selected and appointed; and the generation who sets him up, does not live under an hereditary government, but under a government of its own choice and establishment. Were the generation who sets him up, and the person so set up, to live for ever, it never could become hereditary succession; and of consequence, hereditary succession can only follow on the death of the first parties.

As therefore hereditary succession is out of the question with respect to the *first* generation, we have now to consider the character in which *that* generation acts with respect to the commencing generation, and to all succeeding ones.

It assumes a character, to which it has neither right nor title. It changes itself from a *legislator* to a *testator,* and affects to make its will, which is to have operation after the demise of the makers, to bequeath the government; and it not only attempts to bequeath, but to establish on the succeeding generation, a new and different form of government under which itself lived.

Itself, as is already observed, lived not under an hereditary government, but under a government of its own choice and establishment; and it now attempts, by virtue of a will and testament, (which it has not authority to make), to take from the commencing generation, and all future ones, the rights and free agency by which itself acted.

But, exclusive of the right which any generation has to act collectively as a testator, the objects to which it applies itself in this case, are not within the compass of any law, or of any will or testament.

The rights of men in society are neither devisable, nor transferable, nor annihilable, but are descendible only; and it is not in the power of any generation to intercept finally and cut off the descent. If the present generation, or any other, are disposed to be slaves, it does not lessen the right of the succeeding generation to be free: wrongs cannot have a legal descent. When Mr. Burke attempts to maintain, that the *English nation did at the Revolution of 1688, most solemnly renounce and abdicate their rights for themselves, and for all their posterity for ever;* he speaks a language that merits not reply, and which can only excite contempt for his prostitute principles, or pity for his ignorance.

In whatever light hereditary succession, as growing out of the will and testament of some former generation, presents itself, it is an absurdity. A cannot make a will to take from B the property of B, and give it to C; yet this is the manner in which (what is called) hereditary succession by law operates.

A certain former generation made a will, to take away the rights of the commencing generation, and all future ones, and to convey those rights to a third person, who afterwards comes forward, and tells them, in Mr. Burke's language, that they have *no rights,* that their rights are already bequeathed to him, and that he will govern in *contempt* of them. From such principles, and such ignorance, Good Lord deliver the world!

But, after all, what is this metaphor, called a crown, or rather what is monarchy? Is it a thing, or is it a name, or is it a fraud? Is it a "contrivance of human wisdom," or human craft, to obtain money from a nation under specious pretenses? Is it a thing necessary to a nation? If it is, in what does that necessity consist, what service does it perform, what is its business, and what are its merits?

Doth the virtue consist in the metaphor, or in the man? Doth the goldsmith that makes the crown, make the virtue also? Doth it operate like Fortunatus' wishing cap or Harlequin's wooden sword? Doth it make a man a conjuror? In fine, what is it? It appears to be a something going much out of fashion, falling into ridicule, and rejected in some countries both as unnecessary and expensive. In America it is considered as an absurdity, and in France it has so far declined, that the goodness of the man, and the respect for his personal character are the only things that preserve the appearance of its existence.

If government be what Mr. Burke describes it, "a contrivance of human wisdom," I might ask him if wisdom was at such a low ebb in England, that it was become necessary to import it from Holland and from

Hanover? But I will do the country the justice to say, that was not the case; and even if it was, it mistook the cargo. The wisdom of every country, when properly exerted, is sufficient for all its purposes; and there could exist no more real occasion in England to have sent for a Dutch stadtholder, or a German elector, than there was in America to have done a similar thing.

If a country does not understand its own affairs, how is a foreigner to understand them, who knows neither its laws, its manners, nor its language? If there existed a man so transcendently wise above all others, that his wisdom was necessary to instruct a nation, some reason might be offered for monarchy; but when we cast our eyes about a country, and observe how every part understands its own affairs; and when we look around the world, and see that of all men in it, the race of kings are the most insignificant in capacity, our reason cannot fail to ask us—What are those men kept for?

If there is any thing in monarchy which we people of America do not understand, I wish Mr. Burke would be so kind as to inform us. I see in America, a government extending over a country ten times as large as England, and conducted with regularity for a fortieth part of the expense which government costs in England. If I ask a man in America, if he wants a king, he retorts, and asks me if I take him for an idiot. How is it that this difference happens? Are we more or less wise than others? I see in America, the generality of the people living in a style of plenty unknown in monarchial countries; and I see that the principle of its government, which is that of the *equal Rights of Man,* is making a rapid progress in the world.

If monarchy is a useless thing, why is it kept up any where? and if a necessary thing, how can it be dispensed with? That *civil government* is necessary, all civilized nations will agree; but civil government is republican government. All that part of the government of England which begins with the office of constable, and proceeds through the departments of magistrate, quarter-session, and general assize, including the trial by jury, is republican government. Nothing of monarchy appears in any part of it, except the name which William the Conqueror imposed upon the English, that of obliging them to call him "their Sovereign Lord the King."

It is easy to conceive, that a band of interested men, such as placemen, pensioners, lords of the bed-chamber, lords of the kitchen, lords of the necessary-house, and the Lord knows what besides, can find as many reasons for monarchy as their salaries, paid at the expense of the country, amount to; but if I ask the farmer, the manufacturer, the merchant, the tradesman, and down through all the occupations of life to the common laborer, what service monarchy is to him? He can give me no answer. If I ask him what monarchy is, he believes it is something like a sinecure.

Notwithstanding the taxes of England amount to almost seventeen millions a year, said to be for the expenses of government, it is still evident that the sense of the nation is left to govern itself, and does govern itself by magistrates and juries, almost at its own charge, on republican principles, exclusive of the expense of taxes. The salaries of the judges are almost the only charge that is paid out of the revenue. Considering that all the internal government is executed by the people, the taxes of England ought to be the lightest of any nation in Europe; instead of which, they are the contrary. As this cannot be accounted for on the score of civil government, the subject necessarily extends itself to the monarchial part.

When the people of England sent for George I (and it would puzzle a wiser man than Mr. Burke to discover for what he could be wanted or what service he could render), they ought at least to have conditioned for the abandonment of Hanover. Besides the endless German intrigues that must follow from a German elector being king of England, there is a natural impossibility of uniting in the same person the principles of freedom and the principles of despotism, or, as it is usually called in England, arbitrary power. A German elector is, in his electorate, a despot: how then could it be expected that he should be attached to principles of liberty in one country, while his interest in another was to be supported by despotism? The union cannot exist; and it might easily have been foreseen, that German electors would make German kings, or, in Mr. Burke's words, would assume government with "contempt."

The English have been in the habit of considering a king of England only in the character in which he appears to them; whereas the same person, while the connection lasts, has a home-seat in another country, the interest of which is different to their own, and the principles of the governments are in opposition to each other. To such a person England will appear as a town-residence, and the electorate as the estate. The English may wish, as I believe they do, success to the principles of liberty in France, or in Germany; but a German elector trembles for the fate of despotism in his electorate; and the Duchy of Mecklenburg, where the present Queen's family governs, is under the same wretched state of arbitrary power, and the people in slavish vassalage.

There never was a time when it became the English to watch continental intrigues more circumspectly than at the present moment, and to distinguish the politics of the electorate from the politics of the nation. The Revolution of France has entirely changed the ground with respect to England and France, as nations: but the German despots with Prussia at their head, are combining against liberty; and the fondness of Mr. Pitt for office, and the interest which all his family connections have obtained, do not give sufficient security against this intrigue.

As every thing which passes in the world becomes matter for history, I will now quit this subject, and take a concise review of the state of parties and politics in England, as Mr. Burke has done in France.

Whether the present reign commenced with contempt, I leave to Mr. Burke: certain however it is, that it had strongly that appearance. The animosity of the English nation, it is very well remembered, ran high; and, had the true principles of liberty been as well understood then as they now promise to be, it is probable the nation would not have patiently submitted to so much. George I and II were sensible of a rival in the remains of the Stuarts; and as they could not but consider themselves as standing on their good behavior, they had prudence to keep their German principles of government to themselves; but as the Stuart family wore away, the prudence became less necessary.

The contest between rights, and what were called prerogatives, continued to heat the nation till some time after the conclusion of the American War, when all at once it fell calm; execration exchanged itself for applause, and court popularity sprung up like a mushroom in a night.

To account for this sudden transition, it is proper to observe, that there are two distinct species of popularity; the one excited by merit, the other by resentment. As the nation had formed itself into two parties, and each was extolling the merits of its parliamentary champions for and against prerogative, nothing could operate to give a more general shock than an immediate coalition of the champions themselves.[28]

The partisans of each being thus suddenly left in the lurch, and mutually heated with disgust at the measure, felt no other relief than

[28] Paine is referring to the fact that Burke and Charles James Fox had joined with Lord North even though they had once proposed to impeach him.—*Editor*.

uniting in a common execration against both. A higher stimulus of resentment being thus excited, than what the contest of prerogatives had occasioned, the nation quitted all former objects of rights and wrongs, and sought only that of gratification.

The indignation at the coalition, so effectually superseded the indignation against the Court, as to extinguish it; and without any change of principles on the part of the Court, the same people who had reprobated its despotism, united with it, to revenge themselves on the Coalition Parliament. The case was not, which they liked best,—but, which they hated most; and the least hatred passed for love. The dissolution of the Coalition Parliament, as it afforded the means of gratifying the resentment of the nation, could not fail to be popular; and from hence arose the popularity of the Court.

Transitions of this kind exhibit a nation under the government of temper, instead of a fixed and steady principle, and having once committed itself, however rashly, it feels itself urged along, to justify by continuance its first proceeding. Measures which at other times it would censure, it now approves, and acts persuasion upon itself to suffocate its judgment.

On the return of a new Parliament, the new Minister, Mr. Pitt found himself in a secure majority: and the nation gave him credit, not out of regard to himself, but because it had resolved to do it out of resentment to another. He introduced himself to public notice by a proposed reform of Parliament, which in its operation would have amounted to a public justification of corruption. The nation was to be at the expense of buying up the rotten boroughs, whereas it ought to punish the persons who deal in the traffic.

Passing over the two bubbles, of the Dutch business, and the million a year to sink the national debt, the matter which most presents itself, is the affair of the Regency. Never, in the course of my observation, was delusion more successfully acted, nor a nation more completely deceived. But, to make this appear, it will be necessary to go over the circumstances.

Mr. Fox had stated in the House of Commons, that the Prince of Wales, as heir in succession, had a right in himself to assume the government. This was opposed by Mr. Pitt; and, so far as the opposition was confined to the doctrine, it was just. But the principles which Mr. Pitt maintained on the contrary side, were as bad, or worse in their extent, than those of Mr. Fox; because they went to establish an aristocracy over the nation, and over the small representation it has in the House of Commons.[29]

Whether the English form of government be good or bad, is not in this case the question; but, taking it as it stands, without regard to its merits or demerits, Mr. Pitt was farther from the point than Mr. Fox.

It is supposed to consist of three parts; while, therefore, the nation is disposed to continue this form, the parts have a *national standing,* independent of each other, and are not the creatures of each other. Had Mr. Fox passed through Parliament, and said that the person alluded to claimed on the ground of the nation, Mr. Pitt must then have contended (what he called) the right of the Parliament, against the right of the nation.

By the appearance which the contest made, Mr. Fox took the hereditary ground, and Mr. Pitt the parliamentary ground; but the fact is, they both took hereditary ground, and Mr. Pitt took the worst of the two.

What is called the Parliament is made up of two Houses; one of which is more hereditary, and more beyond the control of the nation, than what the Crown (as it is called) is supposed to be. It is an hereditary aristocracy, assuming and asserting indefeasible, irrevocable rights and authority, wholly independent of the nation. Where then was the merited popularity of exalting this hereditary power over another hereditary power less independent of the nation than what itself assumed to be, and of absorbing the rights of the nation into a House over which it has neither election nor control?

The general impulse of the nation was right; but it acted without reflection. It approved the opposition made to the right set up by Mr. Fox, without perceiving that Mr. Pitt was supporting another indefeasible right, more remote from the nation, in opposition to it.

With respect to the House of Commons, it is elected but by a small part of the nation; but were the election as universal as taxation, which it ought to be, it would still be only the organ of the nation, and cannot possess inherent rights. When the National Assembly of France resolves a matter, the resolve is made in right of the nation; but Mr. Pitt, on all national questions, so far as they refer to the House of Commons,

---

[29] In 1788 George II became insane, and Fox and Burke argued that the Prince of Wales automatically succeeded to the throne. Pitt, on the other hand, contended that the Prince had no more right to rule than any private individual unless chosen by the two Houses of Parliament — *Editor.*

absorbs the rights of the nation into the organ, and makes the organ into a nation, and the nation itself into a cipher.

In a few words, the question on the Regency was a question on a million a year, which is appropriated to the executive department; and Mr. Pitt could not possess himself of any management of this sum, without setting up the supremacy of Parliament; and when this was accomplished, it was indifferent who should be Regent, as he must be Regent at his own cost. Among the curiosities which this contentious debate afforded, was that of making the Great Seal into a King; the affixing of which to an act, was to be royal authority. If, therefore, royal authority is a great seal, it consequently is in itself nothing; and a good constitution would be of infinitely more value to the nation, than what the three Nominal Powers, as they now stand, are worth.

The continual use of the word *Constitution* in the English Parliament, shows there is none; and that the whole is merely a form of government without a constitution, and constituting itself with what power it pleases. If there were a constitution, it certainly could be referred to; and the debate on any constitutional point, would terminate by producing the constitution. One member says, "this is constitution"; and another says, "that is constitution." To-day it is one thing; and to-morrow, it is something else—while the maintaining of the debate proves there is none. Constitution is now the cant word of Parliament, tuning itself to the ear of the nation. Formerly it was the *universal supremacy of Parliament*—the *omnipotence of Parliament*. But since the progress of liberty in France, those phrases have a despotic harshness in their note; and the English Parliament has caught the fashion from the National Assembly, but without the substance, of speaking of a *Constitution*.

As the present generation of people in England did not make the Government, they are not accountable for its defects; but that sooner or later it must come into their hands to undergo a national reformation, is as certain as that the same thing has happened in France.

If France, with a revenue of nearly twenty-four million sterling, with an extent of rich and fertile country above four times larger than England, with a population of twenty-four millions of inhabitants to support taxation, with upwards of ninety millions sterling of gold and silver circulating in the nation, and with a debt less than the present debt of England—still found it necessary, from whatever cause, to come to a settlement of its affairs, it solves the problem of funding for both countries.

It is out of the question to say how long what is called the English Constitution has lasted, and to argue from thence how long it is to last; the question is, how long can the funding system last? It is a thing but of modern invention, and has not yet continued beyond the life of a man; yet in that short space it has so far accumulated, that, together with the current expenses, it requires an amount of taxes at least equal to the whole landed rental of the nation in acres, to defray the annual expenditure. That a government could not always have gone on by the same system which has been followed for the last seventy years, must be evident to every man; and for the same reason it cannot always go on.

The funding system is not money; neither is it, properly speaking, credit. It in effect creates upon paper the sum which it appears to borrow, and lays on a tax to keep the imaginary capital alive by the payment of interest, and sends the annuity to market, to be sold for paper already in circulation. If any credit is given, it is to the disposition of the people to pay the tax, and not to the government which lays it on. When this disposition expires, what is supposed to be the credit of government expires with it. The instance of France under the former Government, shows that it is impossible to compel the payment of taxes by force, when a whole nation is determined to take its stand upon that ground.

Mr. Burke, in his review of the finances of France, states the quantity of gold and silver in France, at about eighty-eight millions sterling. In doing this, he has, I presume, divided by the difference of exchange, instead of the standard of twenty-four livres to a pound sterling; for M. Necker's statement, from which Mr. Burke's is taken, is *two thousand two hundred millions of livres,* which is upwards of ninety-one millions and a half sterling.

M. Necker in France, and Mr. George Chalmers of the Office of Trade and Plantation in England, of which Lord Hawkesbury is president, published nearly about the same time (1786) an account of the quantity of money in each nation, from the returns of the mint of each nation. Mr. Chalmers, from the returns of the English Mint at the Tower of London, states the quantity of money in England, including Scotland and Ireland, to be twenty millions sterling.

M. Necker says [30] that the amount of money in France, recoined from the old coin which was called in, was two thousand and five hundred millions of livres, (upwards of one hundred and four millions sterling); and, after deducting for waste, and what may be in the West Indies,

[30] Paine is referring to Necker's *Administration of the Finances of France.—Editor.*

and other possible circumstances, states the circulation quantity at home, to be ninety-one millions and a half sterling; but, taking it as Mr. Burke has put it, it is sixty-eight millions more than the national quantity in England.

That the quantity of money in France cannot be under this sum, may at once be seen from the state of the French revenue, without referring to the records of the French Mint for proofs. The revenue of France prior to the Revolution, was nearly twenty-four millions sterling; and as paper had then no existence in France, the whole revenue was collected upon gold and silver; and it would have been impossible to have collected such a quantity of revenue upon a less national quantity than M. Necker has stated.

Before the establishment of paper in England, the revenue was about a fourth part of the national amount of gold and silver, as may be known by referring to the revenue prior to King William, and the quantity of money stated to be in the nation at that time, which was nearly as much as it is now.

It can be of no real service to a nation, to impose upon itself, or to permit itself to be imposed upon; but the prejudices of some, and the imposition of others, have always represented France as a nation possessing but little money, whereas the quantity is not only more than four times what the quantity is in England, but is considerably greater on a proportion of numbers.

To account for this deficiency on the part of England, some reference should be had to the English system of funding. It operates to multiply paper and to substitute it in the room of money, in various shapes; and the more paper is multiplied, the more opportunities are afforded to export the specie; and it admits of a possibility (by extending it to small notes) of increasing paper till there is no money left.

I know this is not a pleasant subject to English readers; but the matters I am going to mention, are so important in themselves, as to require the attention of men interested in money-transactions of a public nature. There is a circumstance stated by M. Necker, in his treatise on the administration of the finances, which has never been attended to in England, but which forms the only basis whereon to estimate the quantity of money (gold and silver) which ought to be in every nation in Europe, to preserve a relative proportion with other nations.

Lisbon and Cadiz are the ports into which (money) gold and silver from South America are imported, and which afterwards divides and spreads itself over Europe by means of commerce, and increases the quantity of money in all parts of Europe. If, therefore, the amount of the annual importation into Europe can be known, and the relative proportion of the foreign commerce of the several nations by which it is distributed can be ascertained, they give a rule, sufficiently true, to ascertain the quantity of money which ought to be found in any nation, at any given time.

M. Necker shows from the registers of Lisbon and Cadiz, that the importation of gold and silver into Europe, is five millions sterling annually. He has not taken it on a single year, but on an average of fifteen succeeding years, from 1763 to 1777, both inclusive; in which time, the amount was one thousand eight hundred million livres, in which is seventy-five millions sterling.

From the commencement of the Hanover Succession in 1714, to the time Mr. Chalmers published, is seventy-two years; and the quantity imported into Europe, in that time, would be three hundred and sixty millions sterling.

If the foreign commerce of Great Britain be stated at a sixth part of what the whole foreign commerce of Europe amounts to, (which is probably an inferior estimation to what the gentlemen at the Exchange would allow), the proportion which Britain should draw by commerce of this sum, to keep herself on a proportion with the rest of Europe, would be also a sixth part, which is sixty millions sterling; and if the same allowance for waste and accident be made for England which M. Necker makes for France, the quantity remaining after these deductions would be fifty-two millions. This sum ought to have been in the nation (at the time Mr. Chalmers published) in addition to the sum which was in the nation at the commencement of the Hanover Succession, and to have made in the whole at least sixty-six millions sterling; instead of which, there were but twenty millions, which is forty-six millions below its proportionate quantity.

As the quantity of gold and silver imported into Lisbon and Cadiz is more exactly ascertained than that of any commodity imported into England, and as the quantity of money coined at the Tower of London is still more positively known, the leading facts do not admit of controversy. Either, therefore, the commerce of England is unproductive of profit, or the gold and silver which it brings in, leak continually away by unseen means, at the average rate of about three-quarters of a million a year, which, in the course of seventy-two years, accounts for the deficiency; and its absence is supplied by paper.[31]

The Revolution of France is attended with many novel circumstances, not only in the political sphere, but in the circle of money transactions. Among others, it shows that a government may be in a state of insolvency, and a nation rich. So far as the fact is confined to the late

[31] Whether the English commerce does not bring in money, or whether the Government sends it out after it is brought in, is a matter which the parties concerned can best explain; but that the deficiency exists, is not in the power of either to disprove. While Dr. Price, Mr. Eden (now Auckland), Mr. Chalmers, and others, were debating whether the quantity of money was greater or less than at the Revolution, the circumstance was not adverted to, that since the Revolution, there cannot have been less than four hundred millions sterling imported into Europe; and therefore, the quantity in England ought at least to have been four times greater than it was at the Revolution, to be on a proportion with Europe.

What England is now doing by paper, is what she should have been able to do by solid money, if gold and silver had come into the nation in the proportion it ought, or had not been sent out; and she is endeavoring to restore by paper, the balance she has lost by money. It is certain, that the gold and silver which arrive annually in the register-ships to Spain and Portugal, do not remain in those countries. Taking the value half in gold and half in silver, it is about four hundred tons annually; and from the number of ships and galloons employed in the trade of bringing those metals from South America to Portugal and Spain, the quantity sufficiently proves itself, without referring to the registers.

In the situation England now is, it is impossible she can increase in money. High taxes not only lessen the property of the individuals, but they lessen also the money-capital of a nation, by inducing smuggling, which can only be carried on by gold and silver. By the politics which the British Government have carried on with the inland powers of Germany and the Continent, it has made an enemy of all the maritime powers, and is therefore obliged to keep up a large navy; but though the navy is built in England, the naval stores must be purchased from abroad, and that from countries where the greatest part must be paid for in gold and silver.

Some fallacious rumors have been set afloat in England to induce a belief of money, and, among others, that of the French refugees bringing great quantities. The idea is ridiculous. The general part of the money in France is silver; and it would take upward of twenty of the largest broad-wheel wagons, with ten horses each, to remove one million sterling of silver. Is it then to be supposed, that a few people fleeing on horse-back, or in post-chaises, in a secret manner, and having the French custom house to pass, and the sea to cross, could bring even a sufficiency for their own expenses?

When millions of money are spoken of, it should be recollected, that such sums can only accumulate in a country by slow degrees, and a long procession of time. The most frugal system that England could now adopt, would not recover, in a century, the balance she has lost in money since the commencement of the Hanover Succession. She is seventy millions behind France, and she must be in some considerable proportion behind every country in Europe, because the returns of the English Mint do not show an increase of money, while the registers of Lisbon and Cadiz show an European increase of between three and four hundred millions sterling.—*Author.*

Government of France, it was insolvent; because the nation would no longer support its extravagance, and therefore it could no longer support itself; but with respect to the nation, all the means existed. A government may be said to be insolvent, every time it applies to a nation to discharge its arrears. The insolvency of the late Government of France, and the present Government of England, differed in no other respect than as the disposition of the people differ. The people of France refused their aid to the old Government; and the people of England submit to taxation without inquiry. What is called the Crown in England, has been insolvent several times; the last of which, publicly known, was in May, 1777, when it applied to the nation to discharge upwards of £600,000, private debts, which otherwise it could not pay.

It was the error of Mr. Pitt, Mr. Burke, and all those who were unacquainted with the affairs of France, to confound the French nation with the French Government. The French nation, in effect, endeavored to render the late Government insolvent, for the purpose of taking government into its own hands; and it reserved its means for the support of the new Government. In a country of such vast extent and population as France, the natural means cannot be wanting; and the political means appear the instant the nation is disposed to permit them.

When Mr. Burke, in a speech last winter in the British Parliament, *cast his eyes over the map of Europe, and saw the chasm that once was France,* he talked like a dreamer of dreams. The same natural France existed as before, and all the natural means existed with it. The only chasm was that which the extinction of despotism had left, and which was to be filled up with a constitution more formidable in resources than the power which had expired.

Although the French nation rendered the late Government insolvent, it did not permit the insolvency to act toward the creditors; and the creditors considering the nation as the real paymaster, and the Government only as the agent, rested themselves on the nation, in preference to the Government.

This appears greatly to disturb Mr. Burke, as the precedent is fatal to the policy by which governments have supposed themselves secure. They have contracted debts, with a view of attaching what is called the monied interest of a nation to their support; but the example in France shows, that the permanent security of the creditor is in the nation, and not in the government; and that in all possible revolutions that may happen in governments, the means are always with the nation, and the nation always in existence. Mr. Burke argues, that the creditors ought to have abided the fate of the Government which they trusted; but the National Assembly considered them as the creditors of the nation, and not of the Government—of the master, and not of the steward.

Notwithstanding the late Government could not discharge the current expenses, the present Government has paid off a great part of the capital. This has been accomplished by two means; the one by lessening the expenses of government, and the other by the sale of the monastic and ecclesiastical landed estates. The devotees and penitent debauchees, extortioner and misers of former days, to ensure themselves of a better world than that which they were about to leave, had bequeathed immense property in trust to the priesthood, for *pious uses;* and the priesthood kept it for themselves. The National Assembly has ordered it to be sold for the good of the whole nation, and the priesthood to be decently provided for.

In consequence of the Revolution, the annual interest of the debt of France will be reduced at least six millions sterling, by paying off upwards of one hundred millions of the capital; which, with lessening the former expenses of government at least three millions, will place France in a situation worthy the imitation of Europe.

Upon a whole review of the subject, how vast is the contrast? While Mr. Burke has been talking of a general bankruptcy in France, the National Assembly has been paying off the capital of its debt; and while taxes have increased nearly a million a year in England, they have lowered several millions a year in France. Not a word has either Mr. Burke or Mr. Pitt said about French affairs, or the state of the French finances, in the present session of Parliament. The subject begins to be too well understood, and imposition serves no longer.

There is a general enigma running through the whole of Mr. Burke's book. He writes in a rage against the National Assembly; but what is he enraged about? If his assertions were as true as they are groundless, and that France, by her Revolution, had annihilated her power, and become what he calls a *chasm,* it might excite the grief of a Frenchman (considering himself as a national man), and provoke his rage against the National Assembly; but why should it excite the rage of Mr. Burke?

Alas! it is not the nation of France that Mr. Burke means, but the *Court;* and every court in Europe, dreading the same fate, is in mourning. He writes neither in the character of a Frenchman nor an Englishman, but in the fawning character of that creature known in all countries, and a friend to none, a *Courtier*. Whether it be the Court of Versailles, or the Court of St. James or Carlton-House, or the Court in expectation, signifies not; for the caterpillar principles of all courts and courtiers are alike. They form a common policy throughout Europe, detached and separate from the interest of nations: and while they appear to quarrel, they agree to plunder. Nothing can be more terrible to a court or a courtier, than the Revolution of France. That which is a blessing to nations, is bitterness to them; and as their existence depends on the duplicity of a country, they tremble at the approach of principles, and dread the precedent that threatens their overthrow.

CONCLUSION

REASON and Ignorance, the opposites of each other, influence the great bulk of mankind. If either of these can be rendered sufficiently extensive in a country, the machinery of government goes easily on. Reason obeys itself; and Ignorance submits to whatever is dictated to it.

The two modes of government which prevail in the world, are, *First,* government by election and representation: *Secondly,* government by hereditary succession. The former is generally known by the name of republic; the latter by that of monarchy and aristocracy.

Those two distinct and opposite forms, erect themselves on the two distinct and opposite bases of Reason and Ignorance. As the exercise of government requires talents and abilities, and as talents and abilities cannot have hereditary descent, it is evident that hereditary succession requires a belief from man, to which his reason cannot subscribe, and which can only be established upon his ignorance; and the more ignorant any country is, the better it is fitted for this species of government.

On the contrary, government in a well constituted republic, requires no belief from man beyond what his reason can give. He sees the *rationale* of the whole system, its origin and its operation; and as it is best supported when best understood, the human faculties act with boldness, and acquire, under this form of government, a gigantic manliness.

As, therefore, each of those forms acts on a different base, the one moving freely by the aid of reason, the other by ignorance; we have next to consider, what it is that gives motion to that species of government which is called mixed government, or, as it is sometimes ludicrously styled, a government of *this, that,* and *t'other.*

The moving power of this species of government, is of necessity, corruption. However imperfect election and representation may be in mixed governments, they still give exercise to a greater portion of reason than is convenient to the hereditary part; and therefore it becomes necessary to buy the reason up. A mixed government is an imperfect everything, cementing and soldering the discordant parts together by corruption, to act as a whole. Mr. Burke appears highly disgusted, that France, since she had resolved on a revolution, did not adopt what he calls, *"A British Constitution,"* and the regretful manner in which he expresses himself on this occasion, implies a suspicion, that the British Constitution needed something to keep its defects in countenance.

In mixed governments there is no responsibility: the parts cover each other till responsibility is lost; and the corruption which moves the machine, contrives at the same time its own escape. When it is laid down as a maxim, that *a king can do no wrong,* it places him in a state of similar security with that of idiots and persons insane, and responsibility is out of the question with respect to himself. It then descends upon the minister, who shelters himself under a majority in Parliament, which, by places, pensions, and corruption, he can always command; and that majority justifies itself by the same authority with which it protects the minister. In this rotary motion, responsibility is thrown off from the parts, and from the whole.

When there is a part in a government which can do no wrong, it implies that it does nothing; and is only the machine of another power, by whose advice and direction it acts. What is supposed to be the king in mixed governments is the cabinet; and as the cabinet is always a part of the parliament, and the members justifying in one character what they advise and act in another, a mixed government becomes a continual enigma; entailing upon a country, by the quantity of corruption necessary to solder the parts, the expense of supporting all the forms of government at once, and finally resolving itself into a government by committee; in which the advisers, the actors, the approvers, the justifiers, the persons responsible, and the persons not responsible, are the same persons.

By this pantomimical contrivance, and change of scene and character, the parts help each other out in matters which neither of them singly would assume to act. When money is to be obtained, the mass of variety apparently dissolves, and a profusion of parliamentary praises passes between the parts. Each admires with astonishment, the wisdom, the liberality, the disinterestedness of the other; and all of them breathe a pitying sigh at the burdens of the nation.

But in a well constituted republic, nothing of this soldering, praising, and pitying, can take place; the representation being equal throughout the country, and complete in itself, however it may be arranged into legislative and executive, they have all one and the same natural source. The parts are not foreigners to each other, like democracy, aristocracy, and monarchy. As there are no discordant distinctions, there is nothing to corrupt by compromise, nor confound by contrivance.

Public measures appeal of themselves to the understanding of the nation, and, resting on their own merits, disown any flattering application to vanity. The continual whine of lamenting the burden of taxes, however successfully it may be practised in mixed governments, is inconsistent with the sense and spirit of a republic. If taxes are necessary, they are of course advantageous; but if they require an apology, the apology itself implies an impeachment. Why then is man thus imposed upon, or why does he impose upon himself?

When men are spoken of as kings and subjects, or when government is mentioned under the distinct or combined heads of monarchy, aristocracy, and democracy, what is it that *reasoning* man is to understand by the terms? If there really existed in the world two or more distinct and separate *elements* of human power, we should then see the several origins to which those terms would descriptively apply; but as there is but one species of man, there can be but one element of human power, and that element is man himself. Monarchy, aristocracy, and democracy, are but creatures of imagination; and a thousand such may be contrived, as well as three.

From the Revolutions of America and France, and the symptoms that have appeared in other countries, it is evident that the opinion of the world is changed with respect to systems of government, and that revolutions are not within the compass of political calculations. The progress of time and circumstances, which men assign to the accomplishment of great changes, is too mechanical to measure the force of the mind, and the rapidity of reflection, by which revolutions are generated. All the old governments have received a shock from those that already appear, and which were once more improbable, and are a greater subject of wonder, than a general revolution in Europe would be now.

When we survey the wretched condition of man under the monarchical and hereditary systems of government, dragged from his home by one power, or driven by another, and impoverished by taxes more than by enemies, it becomes evident that those systems are bad, and that a general revolution in the principle and construction of governments is necessary.

What is government more than the management of the affairs of a nation? It is not, and from its nature cannot be, the property of any particular man or family, but of the whole community, at whose expense it is supported; and though by force or contrivance it has been usurped into an inheritance, the usurpation cannot alter the right of things. Sovereignty, as a matter of right, appertains to the nation only, and not to any individual; and a nation has at all times an inherent indefeasible right to abolish any form of government it finds inconvenient, and establish such as accords with its interest, disposition, and happiness. The romantic and barbarous distinction of [making] men into kings and subjects, though it may suit the condition of courtiers, cannot that of citizens; and is exploded by the principle upon which governments are now founded. Every citizen is a member of the sovereignty, and, as such, can acknowledge no personal subjection; and his obedience can be only to the laws.

When men think of what government is, they must necessarily suppose it to possess a knowledge of all the objects and matters upon which its authority is to be exercised. In this view of government the republican system, as established by America and France, operates to embrace the whole of a nation; and the knowledge necessary to the interest of all the parts, is to be found in the center which the parts by representation form. But the old governments are on a construction that excludes knowledge as well as happiness; government by monks, who know nothing of the world beyond the walls of a convent, is as consistent as government by kings.

What were formerly called revolutions, were little more than a change of persons, or an alteration of local circumstances. They rose and fell like things of course, and had nothing in their existence or their fate that could influence beyond the spot that produced them. But what we now see in the world, from the revolutions of America and France, is a renovation of the natural order of things, a system of principles as universal as truth and the existence of man, and combining moral with political happiness and national prosperity.

"I. *Men are born and always continue free and equal in respect to their rights. Civil distinctions, therefore, can be founded only on public utility.*

"II. *The end of all political associations is the preservation of the natural and imprescriptible rights of man; and these rights are liberty, property, security, and resistance of oppression.*

"III. *The Nation is essentially the source of all Sovereignty; nor can any individual or any body of men, be entitled to any authority which is not expressly derived from it."*

In these principles, there is nothing to throw a nation into confusion by inflaming ambition. They are calculated to call forth wisdom and abilities, and to exercise them for the public good, and not for the emolument or aggrandizement of particular descriptions of men or families. Monarchial sovereignty, the enemy of mankind, and the source of misery, is abolished; and sovereignty itself is restored to its natural and original place, the nation. Were this the case throughout Europe, the cause of wars would be taken away.

It is attributed to Henry IV of France, a man of an enlarged and benevolent heart, that he proposed, about the year 1610, a plan of abolishing war in Europe. The plan consisted in constituting an European Congress, or as the French authors style it, a Pacific Republic; by appointing delegates from the several nations, who were to act as a court of arbitration in any disputes that might arise between nation and nation. Had such a plan been adopted at the time it was proposed, the taxes of England and France, as two of the parties, would have been at least ten millions sterling annually to each nation less than they were at the commencement of the French Revolution.

To conceive a cause why such a plan has not been adopted (and that instead of a congress for the purpose of *preventing* war, it has been called only to *terminate* a war, after fruitless expense of several years), it will be necessary to consider the interest of governments as a distinct interest to that of nations.

Whatever is the cause of taxes to a nation, becomes also the means of revenue to a government. Every war terminates with an addition of taxes, and consequently with an addition of revenue; and in any event of war, in the manner they are now commenced and concluded, the power and interest of governments are increased.

War, therefore, from its productiveness, as it easily furnishes the pretence of necessity for taxes and appointments to places and offices, becomes a principal part of the system of old governments; and to establish any mode to abolish war, however advantageous it might be to nations, would be to take from such government the most lucrative of its branches. The frivolous matters upon which war is made, show the disposition and avidity of governments to uphold the system of war, and betray the motives upon which they act.

Why are not republics plunged into war, but because the nature of their government does not admit of an interest distinct from that of the nation? Even Holland, though an ill-constructed republic, and with a commerce extending over the world, existed nearly a century without war: and the instant the form of government was changed in France, the republican principles of peace and domestic prosperity and economy arose with the new Government; and the same consequences would follow the same causes in other nations.

As war is the system of government on the old construction, the animosity which nations reciprocally entertain, is nothing more than what the policy of their governments excites, to keep up the spirit of the system. Each government accuses the other of perfidy, intrigue, and ambition, as a means of heating the imagination of their respective nations, and increasing them to hostilities. Man is not the enemy of man, but through the medium of a false system of government. Instead, therefore, of exclaiming against the ambition of kings, the exclamation should be directed against the principle of such governments; and instead of seeking to reform the individual, the wisdom of a nation should apply itself to reform the system.

Whether the forms and maxims of governments which are still in practise, were adapted to the condition of the world at the period they were established, is not in this case the question. The older they are, the less correspondence can they have with the present state of things. Time, and change of circumstances and opinions, have the same progressive effect in rendering modes of government obsolete, as they have upon customs and manners. Agriculture, commerce, manufactures, and the tranquil arts, by which the prosperity of nations is best promoted, require a different system of government, and a different species of knowledge to direct its operations, than what might have been required in the former condition of the world.

As it is not difficult to perceive, from the enlightened state of mankind, that hereditary governments are verging to their decline, and that revolutions on the broad basis of national sovereignty, and government by representation, are making their way in Europe, it would be an act of wisdom to anticipate their approach, and produce revolutions by reason and accommodation, rather than commit them to the issue of convulsions.

From what we now see, nothing of reform on the political world ought to be held improbable. It is an age of revolutions, in which every thing may be looked for. The intrigue of courts, by which the system of war is kept up, may provoke a confederation of nations to abolish it: and an European Congress, to patronize the progress of free government, and promote the civilization of nations with each other, is an event nearer in probability, than once were the revolutions and alliance of France and America.

RIGHTS OF MAN

PART SECOND

Part II of *Rights of Man,* inscribed to Lafayette, was published in London in February, 1792. It met with an instant response and its circulation even exceeded that of Part I, close to a million and a half copies being published in England during the author's lifetime.

The work was acclaimed by the people on both sides of the English Channel and in America. But its vivid presentation of the doctrines and practices of democratic government, its vigorous attack upon British monarchial usurpations and aristocratic institutions, and its open call for world revolution for the achievement of democracy terrified the ruling class in England. The defenders of reaction struck back quickly. Having failed to prevent the publication of Part II by bribing the publisher, Premier Pitt launched a vicious campaign of slander against Paine. A biography, paid for by the Crown, vilified the democratic leader. The book was signed by "Francis Oldys, A.M., of the University of Pennsylvania," but it was soon discovered that the author was in reality George Chalmers, a London government clerk who had been well paid to paint a slanderous picture of Paine. While Court-inspired mobs burned Paine in effigy, a royal proclamation against seditious writings stopped the sale of the book. The last step in the persecution of the spokesman for the common people was his indictment for sedition.

But at the very time that British royalty was persecuting him, the French nation hailed Paine as a noble defender of the struggle for freedom and claimed him as their own citizen. Three Departments chose him as their deputy to the National Assembly. "Come, friend of the people," they wrote him, "to swell the number of patriots in an assembly which will decide the destiny of a great people, perhaps of the human race. The happy period you have predicted for the nation has arrived. Come! do not deceive their hopes." In his letter of thanks, addressed to his "Fellow-Citizens of France," Paine replied: "The scene that now opens itself in France extends far beyond the boundaries of her own dominions. Every nation is becoming her colleague, and every court is becoming her enemy. It is now the cause of all nations against the cause of all courts."

Paine was soon to join his friends in France. Warned by the poet William Blake that he was about to be arrested, he departed secretly for France having been persuaded by his friends and a Frenchman sent by the municipality of Calais that it was dangerous for him to remain any longer in England. He left behind him a pamphlet in reply to the charges of seditious libel. In his *Letter to the Addressers,* he declared: "If to expose the fraud and imposition of monarchy and every species of hereditary government—to lessen the oppression of taxes—to propose plans for the education of helpless infancy, and the comfortable support of the aged and distressed—to endeavor to conciliate nations to each other—to extirpate the horrid practice of war—to promote universal peace, civilization, and commerce—and to break the chains of political superstition, and raise degraded man to his proper rank;—if these things be libellous, let me live the life of a libeller, and let the name of *libeller* be engraven on my tomb!"

In December 1792, three months after Paine had departed for France, a packed jury in a London court found him guilty of seditious libel for having written the revolutionary work. The publishers and booksellers were also found guilty and sentenced to three years in prison. Thomas Clio Rickman, one of the men sentenced to prison, escaped to France.

Unlike Part I, the second part of *Rights of Man* is primarily an exposition of Paine's principles of government.—*Editor.*

FRENCH TRANSLATOR'S PREFACE

THE work of which we offer a translation to the public has created the greatest sensation in England. Paine, that man of freedom, who seems born to preach "Common Sense" to the whole world with the same success as in America, explains in it to the people of England the theory of the practice of the Rights of Man.

Owing to the prejudices that still govern *that nation,* the author has been obliged to condescend to answer Mr. Burke. He has done so more especially in an extended preface which is nothing but a piece of very tedious controversy, in which he shows himself very sensitive to criticisms that do not really affect him. To translate it seemed an insult to the *free French people,* and similar reasons have led the editors to suppress also a dedicatory epistle addressed by Paine to Lafayette.[1]

The French can no longer endure dedicatory epistles. A man should write privately to those he esteems: when he publishes a book his thoughts should be offered to the public alone. Paine, that uncorrupted friend of freedom, believed too in the sincerity of Lafayette. So easy is it to deceive men of single-minded purpose! Bred at a distance from courts, that austere American does not seem any more on his guard against the artful ways and speech of courtiers than some Frenchmen who resemble him.

TO

M. DE LAFAYETTE

AFTER an acquaintance of nearly fifteen years, in difficult situations in America, and various consultations in Europe, I feel a pleasure in presenting to you this small treatise, in gratitude for your services to my beloved America, and as a testimony of my esteem for the virtues, public and private, which I know you to possess.

The only point upon which I could ever discover that we differed was not as to principles of government, but as to time. For my own part, I think it equally as injurious to good principles to permit them to linger, as to push them on too fast. That which you suppose accomplishable in fourteen or fifteen years, I may believe practicable in a much shorter period. Mankind, as it appears to me, are always ripe enough to understand their true interest, provided it be presented clearly to their understanding, and that in a manner not to create suspicion by any thing like self-design, nor offend by assuming too much. Where we would wish to reform we must not reproach.

When the American Revolution was established, I felt a disposition to sit serenely down and enjoy the calm. It did not appear to me that any

---

[1] The French translator who wrote this preface was F. Lanthenas. By the time the second part of *Rights of Man* was written, Lafayette had lost his early popularity among the French masses. His popularity declined after he used officers against the soldiers and the people, and approved the massacre at Navey by his appointee General Boulée.—*Editor.*

object could afterwards arise great enough to make me quit tranquillity, and feel as I had felt before. But when principle, and not place, is the energetic cause of action, a man, I find, is everywhere the same.

I am now once more in the public world; and as I have not a right to contemplate on so many years of remaining life as you have, I am resolved to labor as fast as I can; and as I am anxious for your aid and your company, I wish you to hasten your principles and overtake me.

If you make a campaign the ensuing spring,[2] which it is most probable there will be no occasion for, I will come and join you. Should the campaign commence, I hope it will terminate in the extinction of German despotism, and in establishing the freedom of all Germany. When France shall be surrounded with revolutions, she will be in peace and safety, and her taxes, as well as those of Germany, will consequently become less.

Your sincere,
Affectionate Friend,
THOMAS PAINE.

LONDON, Feb. 9, 1792.

PREFACE

WHEN I began the chapter entitled the "Conclusion" in the former part of the "Rights of Man," published last year, it was my intention to have extended it to a greater length; but in casting the whole matter in my mind which I wished to add, I found that I must either make the work too bulky, or contract my plan too much. I therefore brought it to a close as soon as the subject would admit, and reserved what I had further to say to another opportunity.

Several other reasons contributed to produce this determination. I wished to know the manner in which a work, written in a style of thinking and expression different to what had been customary in England,

---

[2] France at this time was on the verge of war with Prussia and Austria. In the "ensuing spring campaign," to which Paine is referring, Lafayette was in command of the Army of Ardennes, and scored several victories.—*Editor.*

would be received before I ventured farther. A great field was opening to the view of mankind by means of the French Revolution. Mr. Burke's outrageous opposition thereto brought the controversy into England. He attacked principles which he knew (from information) I would contest with him, because they are principles which I believe to be good, and which I have contributed to establish, and conceive myself bound to defend. Had he not urged the controversy, I had most probably been a silent man.

Another reason for deferring the remainder of the work, was that Mr. Burke promised in his first publication to renew the subject at another opportunity, and to make a comparison of what he called the English and French constitutions. I therefore held myself in reserve for him. He has published two works since, without doing this; which he certainly would not have omitted, had the comparison been in his favor.

In his last work, his "Appeal from the New to the Old Whigs," he has quoted about ten pages from the "Rights of Man," and having given himself the trouble of doing this, says he "shall not attempt in the smallest degree to refute them," meaning the principles therein contained. I am enough acquainted with Mr. Burke, to know, that he would if he could. But instead of contesting them, he immediately after consoles himself with saying, that he "has done his part." He has not done his part. He has not performed his promise of a comparison of constitutions. He started the controversy, he gave the challenge, and has fled from it; and he is now a *case in point* with his own opinion, that, *"the age of chivalry is gone!"* The title, as well as the substance of his last work, his "Appeal," is his condemnation. Principles must stand on their own merits, and if they are good they certainly will. To put them under the shelter of other men's authority, as Mr. Burke has done, serves to bring them into suspicion. Mr. Burke is not very fond of dividing his honors, but in this case he is artfully dividing the disgrace.

But who are those to whom Mr. Burke has made his appeal? A set of childish thinkers and half-way politicians born in the last century; men who went no farther with any principle than as it suited their purpose as a party; the nation was always left out of the question; and this has been the character of every party from that day to this. The nation sees nothing in such works, or such politics, worthy its attention. A little matter will move a party, but it must be something great that moves a nation.

Though I see nothing in Mr. Burke's "Appeal" worth taking much notice of, there is, however, one expression upon which I shall offer a few remarks. After quoting largely from the "Rights of Man," and declining to contest the principles contained in that work, he says, "This will most probably be done (*if such writings shall be thought to deserve any other refutation than that of criminal justice*) by others, who may think with Mr. Burke and with the same zeal." [3]

In the first place, it has not yet been done by anybody. Not less, I believe, than eight or ten pamphlets, intended as answer to the former part of the "Rights of Man," have been published by different persons, and not one of them, to my knowledge, has extended to a second edition, nor are even the titles of them so much as generally remembered. As I am averse to unnecessarily multiplying publications, I have answered none of them. And as I believe that a man may write himself out of reputation when nobody else can do it, I am careful to avoid that rock.

But as I would decline unnecessary publications on the one hand, so would I avoid every thing that might appear like sullen pride on the other. If Mr. Burke, or any person on his side the question, will produce an answer to the "Rights of Man," that shall extend to a half, or even to a fourth part of the number of copies to which the "Rights of Man" extended, I will reply to his work. But until this be done, I shall so far take the sense of the public for my guide (and the world knows I am not a flatterer) that what they do not think worth while to read, is not worth mine to answer. I suppose the number of copies to which the first part of the "Rights of Man" extended, taking England, Scotland, and Ireland, is not less than between forty and fifty thousand.

I now come to remark on the remaining part of the quotation I have made from Mr. Burke.

"If," says he, "such writings shall be thought to deserve any other refutation than that of *criminal* justice."

Pardoning the pun, it must be *criminal* justice indeed that should condemn a work as a substitute for not being able to refute it. The greatest condemnation that could be passed upon it would be a refutation. But in proceeding by the method Mr. Burke alludes to, the condemnation would, in the final event, pass upon the criminality of the process and not upon the work, and in this case, I had rather be the author, than be either the judge, or the jury, that should condemn it.

But to come at once to the point. I have differed from some professional

[3] In his *Appeal from the New to the Old Whigs,* Burke referred to himself in the third person.—*Editor.*

gentlemen on the subject of prosecutions, and I since find they are fall-ing into my opinion, which I will here state as fully, but as concisely as I can.

I will first put a case with respect to any law, and then compare it with a government, or with what in England is, or has been, called a con-stitution.

It would be an act of despotism, or what in England is called arbitrary power, to make a law to prohibit investigating the principles, good or bad, on which such a law, or any other is founded.

If a law be bad, it is one thing to oppose the practise of it, but it is quite a different thing to expose its errors, to reason on its defects. and to show cause why it should be repealed, or why another ought to be substituted in its place. I have always held it an opinion (making it also my practise) that it is better to obey a bad law, making use at the same time of every argument to show its errors and procure its repeal, than forcibly to violate it; because the precedent of breaking a bad law might weaken the force, and lead to a discretionary violation of those which are good.

The case is the same with respect to principles and forms of govern-ment, or to what are called constitutions, and the parts of which they are composed.

It is for the good of nations, and not for the emolument or aggrandize-ment of particular individuals, that government ought to be established, and that mankind are at the expense of supporting it. The defects of every government and constitution, both as to principle and form must, on a parity of reasoning, be as open to discussion as the defects of a law, and it is a duty which every man owes to society to point them out. When those defects, and the means of remedying them are generally seen by a nation, that nation will reform its government or its constitution in the one case, as the government repealed or reformed the law in the other.

The operation of government is restricted to the making and the ad-ministering of laws; but it is to a nation that the right of forming or re-forming, generating or regenerating constitutions and governments be-long; and consequently those subjects, as subjects of investigation. are always before a country *as a matter of right,* and cannot, without invad-ing the general rights of that country, be made subjects for prosecution. On this ground I will meet Mr. Burke whenever he pleases. It is better that the whole argument should come out, than to seek to stifle it. It was himself that opened the controversy, and he ought not to desert it.

I do not believe that monarchy and aristocracy will continue seven years longer in any of the enlightened countries in Europe.[4] If better reasons can be shown for them than against them, they will stand; if the contrary, they will not. Mankind are not now to be told they shall not think, or they shall not read; and publications that go no farther than to investigate principles of government, to invite men to reason and to reflect, and to show the errors and excellencies of different systems, have a right to appear. If they do not excite attention, they are not worth the trouble of a prosecution; and if they do, the prosecution will amount to nothing, since it cannot amount to a prohibition of reading. This would be a sentence of the public, instead of the author, and would also be the most effectual mode of making or hastening revolutions.

On all cases that apply universally to a nation, with respect to systems of government, a jury of *twelve* men is not competent to decide. Where there are no witnesses to be examined, no facts to be proved, and where the whole matter is before the whole public and the merits or demerits of it resting on their opinion; and where there is nothing to be known in a court, but what every body knows out of it, every twelve men are equally as good a jury as the other, and would most probably reverse each other's verdict; or from the variety of their opinions not be able to form one.

It is one case, whether a nation approve a work, or a plan; but it is quite another case, whether it will commit to any such jury the power of determining whether that nation have a right to, or shall reform its government, or not. I mention these cases, that Mr. Burke may see I have not written on government without reflecting on what is law, as well as on what are rights. The only effectual jury in such cases would be, a convention of the whole nation fairly elected; for in all such cases the whole nation is the vicinage. If Mr. Burke will propose such a jury, I will waive all privileges of being the citizen of any other country, and, defending its principles, abide the issue, provided he will do the same; for my opinion is, that his work and his principles would be condemned instead of mine.

As to the prejudices which men have from education and habit, in favor of any particular form or system of government, those prejudices have yet to stand the test of reason and reflection. In fact, such prejudices

---

[4] This sentence reveals that Paine was a romantic rather than a realistic revolutionary. Unlike Jefferson, he failed to consider the tremendous strength of reaction in many European countries.—*Editor.*

are nothing. No man is prejudiced in favor of a thing, knowing it to be wrong. He is attached to it on the belief of its being right; and when he sees it is not so, the prejudice will be gone. We have but a defective idea what prejudice is. It might be said that until men think for themselves the whole is prejudice, and *not opinion;* for that only is opinion which is the result of reason and reflection. I offer this remark, that Mr. Burke may not confide too much in what has been the customary prejudices of the country.

I do not believe that the people of England have ever been fairly and candidly dealt by. They have been imposed upon by parties, and by men assuming the character of leaders. It is time that the nation should rise above those trifles. It is time to dismiss that inattention which has so long been the encouraging cause of stretching taxation to excess. It is time to dismiss all those songs and toasts which are calculated to enslave, and operate to suffocate reflection.

On all such subjects men have only to think, and they will neither act wrong nor be misled. To say that any people are not fit for freedom, is to make poverty their choice, and to say they had rather be loaded with taxes than not. If such a case could be proved, it would equally prove, that those who govern are not fit to govern them, for they are a part of the same national mass.

But admitting governments to be changed all over Europe, it certainly may be done without convulsion and revenge. It is not worth making changes or revolutions, unless it be for some great national benefit; and when this shall appear to a nation, the danger will be, as in America and France, to those who oppose; and with this reflection I close my Preface.

THOMAS PAINE.

LONDON, Feb. 9, 1792.

INTRODUCTION

WHAT Archimedes said of the mechanical powers, may be applied to reason and liberty: *"Had we,"* said he, *"a place to stand upon, we might raise the world."*

The Revolution of America presented in politics what was only theory in mechanics. So deeply rooted were all the governments of the old world, and so effectually had the tyranny and the antiquity of habit established itself over the mind, that no beginning could be made in Asia, Africa, or Europe, to reform the political condition of man. Freedom had been hunted round the globe; reason was considered as rebellion; and the slavery of fear had made men afraid to think.

But such is the irresistible nature of truth, that all it asks, and all it wants, is the liberty of appearing. The sun needs no inscription to distinguish him from darkness; and no sooner did the American governments display themselves to the world, than despotism felt a shock, and man began to contemplate redress.

The independence of America, considered merely as a separation from England, would have been a matter but of little importance, had it not been accompanied by a revolution in the principles and practise of governments. She made a stand, not for herself only, but for the world, and looked beyond the advantages herself could receive. Even the Hessian, though hired to fight against her, may live to bless his defeat; and England, condemning the viciousness of its government, rejoice in its miscarriage.

As America was the only spot in the political world, where the principles of universal reformation could begin, so also was it the best in the natural world. An assemblage of circumstances conspired, not only to give birth, but to add gigantic maturity to its principles.

The scene which that country presents to the eye of a spectator, has something in it which generates and encourages great ideas. Nature appears to him in magnitude. The mighty objects he beholds, act upon his mind by enlarging it, and he partakes of the greatness he contemplates. Its first settlers were emigrants from different European nations, and of diversified professions of religion, retiring from the governmental persecutions of the old world, and meeting in the new, not as enemies, but as brothers. The wants which necessarily accompany the cultivation of a wilderness, produced among them a state of society, which countries. long harassed by the quarrels and intrigues of governments, had neglected to cherish. In such a situation man becomes what he ought. He sees his species, not with the inhuman idea of a natural enemy, but as kindred; and the example shows to the artificial world, that man must go back to nature for information.[5]

---

[5] While Paine tends to romanticize early American History, it is interesting to note that he understood the significance of the frontier in moulding American democracy.—*Editor.*

From the rapid progress which America makes in every species of improvement, it is rational to conclude, that if the governments of Asia, Africa, and Europe, had begun on a principle similar to that of America, or had not been very early corrupted therefrom, that those countries must, by this time, have been in a far superior condition to what they are. Age after age has passed away, for no other purpose than to behold their wretchedness. Could we suppose a spectator who knew nothing of the world, and who was put into it merely to make his observations, he would take a great part of the old world to be new, just struggling with the difficulties and hardships of an infant settlement. He could not suppose that the hordes of miserable poor, with which old countries abound, could be any other than those who had not yet had time to provide for themselves. Little would he think they were the consequence of what in such countries is called government.

If, from the more wretched parts of the old world, we look at those which are in an advanced stage of improvement, we still find the greedy hand of government thrusting itself into every corner and crevice of industry, and grasping the spoil of the multitude. Invention is continually exercised, to furnish new pretenses for revenue and taxation. It watches prosperity as its prey, and permits none to escape without tribute.

As revolutions have begun (and the probability is always greater against a thing beginning, than of proceeding after it has begun), it is natural to expect that other revolutions will follow. The amazing and still increasing expenses with which old governments are conducted, the numerous wars they engage in or provoke, the embarrassment they throw in the way of universal civilization and commerce, and the oppression and usurpation they practise at home, have wearied out the patience, and exhausted the property of the world. In such a situation, and with the examples already existing, revolutions are to be looked for. They are become subjects of universal conversation, and may be considered as the *order of the day*.

If systems of government can be introduced, less expensive, and more productive of general happiness, than those which have existed, all attempts to oppose their progress will in the end be fruitless. Reason, like time, will make its own way, and prejudice will fall in a combat with interest. If universal peace, civilization, and commerce, are ever to be the happy lot of man, it cannot be accomplished but by a revolution in the system of governments. All the monarchial governments are military. War is their trade, plunder and revenue their objects. While such governments continue, peace has not the absolute security of a day.

What is the history of all monarchical governments, but a disgustful picture of human wretchedness, and the accidental respite of a few years' repose? Wearied with war, and tired with human butchery, they sat down to rest, and called it peace. This certainly is not the condition that heaven intended for man; and if *this be monarchy,* well might monarchy be reckoned among the sins of the Jews.

The revolutions which formerly took place in the world, had nothing in them that interested the bulk of mankind. They extended only to a change of persons and measures, but not of principles, and rose or fell among the common transactions of the moment. What we now behold, may not improperly be called a *"counter-revolution."*

Conquest and tyranny, at some early period, dispossessed man of his rights, and he is now recovering them. And as the tide of all human affairs has its ebb and flow in directions contrary to each other, so also is it in this. Government founded on a *moral theory, on a system of universal peace, on the indefeasible, hereditary rights of man,* is now revolving from West to East, by a stronger impulse than the government of the sword revolved from East to West. It interests not particular individuals, but nations, in its progress, and promises a new era to the human race.

The danger to which the success of revolutions is most exposed, is that of attempting them before the principles on which they proceed, and the advantages to result from them, are sufficiently seen and understood. Almost everything appertaining to the circumstances of a nation, has been absorbed and confounded under the general and mysterious word *government.* Though it avoids taking to its account the errors it commits, and the mischiefs it occasions, it fails not to arrogate to itself whatever has the appearance of prosperity. It robs industry of its honors, by pedantically making itself the cause of its effects; and purloins from the general character of man, the merits that appertain to him as a social being.

It may therefore be of use, in this day of revolutions, to discriminate between those things which are the effect of government, and those which are not. This will best be done by taking a review of society and civilization, and the consequences resulting therefrom, as things distinct from what are called governments. By beginning with this investigation, we shall be able to assign effects to their proper cause, and analyze the mass of common errors.

CHAPTER I

GREAT part of that order which reigns among mankind is not the effect of government. It had its origin in the principles of society and the natural constitution of man. It existed prior to government, and would exist if the formality of government was abolished. The mutual dependence and reciprocal interest which man has upon man, and all parts of a civilized community upon each other, create that great chain of connection which holds it together. The landholder, the farmer, the manufacturer, the merchant, the tradesman, and every occupation, prospers by the aid which each receives from the other, and from the whole. Common interest regulates their concerns, and forms their laws; and the laws which common usage ordains, have a greater influence than the laws of government. In fine, society performs for itself almost every thing which is ascribed to government.

To understand the nature and quantity of government proper for man, it is necessary to attend to his character. As Nature created him for social life, she fitted him for the station she intended. In all cases she made his natural wants greater than his individual powers. No one man is capable, without the aid of society, of supplying his own wants; and those wants acting upon every individual, impel the whole of them into society, as naturally as gravitation acts to a center.

But she has gone further. She has not only forced man into society, by a diversity of wants, which the reciprocal aid of each other can supply, but she has implanted in him a system of social affections, which, though not necessary to his existence, are essential to his happiness. There is no period in life when this love for society ceases to act. It begins and ends with our being.

If we examine, with attention, into the composition and constitution of man, the diversity of his wants, and the diversity of talents in different men for reciprocally accommodating the wants of each other, his propensity to society, and consequently to preserve the advantages resulting from it, we shall easily discover that a great part of what is called government is mere imposition.

Government is no farther necessary than to supply the few cases to which society and civilization are not conveniently competent; and instances are not wanting to show, that every thing which government can usefully add thereto, has been performed by the common consent of society, without government.

For upward of two years from the commencement of the American War, and to a longer period in several of the American states, there were no established forms of government. The old governments had been abolished, and the country was too much occupied in defense, to employ its attention in establishing new governments; yet during this interval, order and harmony were preserved as inviolate as in any country in Europe.

There is a natural aptness in man, and more so in society, because it embraces a greater variety of abilities and resources, to accommodate itself to whatever situation it is in. The instant formal government is abolished, society begins to act. A general association takes place, and common interest produces common security.

So far is it from being true, as has been pretended, that the abolition of any formal government is the dissolution of society, that it acts by a contrary impulse, and brings the latter the closer together. All that part of its organization which it had committed to its government, devolves again upon itself, and acts through its medium.

When men, as well from natural instinct, as from reciprocal benefits, have habituated themselves to social and civilized life, there is always enough of its principles in practise to carry them through any changes they may find necessary or convenient to make in their government. In short, man is so naturally a creature of society, that it is almost impossible to put him out of it.

Formal government makes but a small part of civilized life; and when even the best that human wisdom can devise is established, it is a thing more in name and idea, than in fact. It is to the great and fundamental principles of society and civilization—to the common usage universally consented to, and mutually and reciprocally maintained—to the unceasing circulation of interest, which, passing through its million channels, invigorates the whole mass of civilized man—it is to these things, infinitely more than to any thing which even the best instituted government can perform, that the safety and prosperity of the individual and of the whole depends.

The more perfect civilization is, the less occasion has it for government, because the more does it regulate its own affairs, and govern itself; but so contrary is the practise of old governments to the reason of the case, that the expenses of them increase in the proportion they ought to diminish. It is but few general laws that civilized life requires, and those of such common usefulness, that whether they are enforced by the forms of government or not, the effect will be nearly the same. If we consider what the principles are that first condense men into society, and what the motives that regulate their mutual intercourse afterwards, we shall find, by the time we arrive at what is called government, that nearly the whole of the business is performed by the natural operation of the parts upon each other.

Man, with respect to all those matters, is more a creature of consistency than he is aware, or that governments would wish him to believe. All the great laws of society are laws of nature. Those of trade and commerce, whether with respect to the intercourse of individuals, or of nations, are laws of mutual and reciprocal interest. They are followed and obeyed because it is the interest of the parties so to do, and not on account of any formal laws their governments may impose or interpose.

But how often is the natural propensity to society disturbed or destroyed by the operations of government. When the latter, instead of being ingrafted on the principles of the former, assumes to exist for itself, and acts by partialities of favor and oppression, it becomes the cause of the mischiefs it ought to prevent.

If we look back to the riots and tumults, which at various times have happened in England, we shall find, that they did not proceed from the want of a government, but that government was itself the generating cause; instead of consolidating society, it divided it; it deprived it of its natural cohesion, and engendered discontents and disorders, which otherwise would not have existed.

In those associations which men promiscuously form for the purpose of trade, or of any concern, in which government is totally out of the question, and in which they act merely on the principles of society, we see how naturally the various parties unite; and this shows, by comparison, that governments, so far from being always the cause or means of order, are often the destruction of it. The riots of 1780 had no other source than the remains of those prejudices, which the government itself had encouraged. But with respect to England there are also other causes.

Excess and inequality of taxation, however disguised in the means, never fail to appear in their effects. As a great mass of the community are thrown thereby into poverty and discontent, they are constantly on the brink of commotion; and deprived, as they unfortunately are, of the means of information, are easily heated to outrage. Whatever the apparent cause of any riots may be, the real one is always want of happiness. It shows that something is wrong in the system of government, that injures the felicity by which society is to be preserved.

But as fact is superior to reasoning, the instance of America presents itself to confirm these observations. If there is a country in the world, where concord, according to common calculation, would be least expected, it is America. Made up, as it is, of people from different nations,[6] accustomed to different forms and habits of government, speaking different languages, and more different in their modes of worship, it would appear that the union of such a people was impracticable; but by the simple operation of constructing government on the principles of society and the rights of man, every difficulty retires, and all the parts are brought into cordial unison. There the poor are not oppressed, the rich are not privileged. Industry is not mortified by the splendid extravagance of a court rioting at its expense. Their taxes are few, because their government is just; and as there is nothing to render them wretched, there is nothing to engender riots and tumults.

A metaphysical man, like Mr. Burke, would have tortured his invention to discover how such a people could be governed. He would have supposed that some must be managed by fraud, others by force, and all by some contrivance; that genius must be hired to impose upon ignorance, and show and parade to fascinate the vulgar. Lost in the abundance of his researches, he would have resolved and re-resolved, and finally overlooked the plain and easy road that lay directly before him.

One of the great advantages of the American Revolution has been, that it led to a discovery of the principles, and laid open the imposition, of governments. All the revolutions till then had been worked within the atmosphere of a court, and never on the great floor of a nation. The parties were always of the class of courtiers; and whatever was their rage

[6] That part of America which is generally called New England, including New Hampshire, Massachusetts, Rhode Island, and Connecticut, is peopled chiefly by English descendants. In the State of New York, about half are Dutch, the rest English, Scotch and Irish. In New Jersey, a mixture of English and Dutch, with some Scotch and Irish. In Pennsylvania, about one-third are English, another Germans, and the remainder Scotch and Irish, with some Swedes. The states to the Southward have a greater proportion of English than the Middle States, but in all of them there is a mixture; and besides those enumerated, there are a considerable number of French, and some few of all the European nations, lying on the coast. The most numerous religious denomination is the Presbyterian; but no one sect is established above another, and all men are equally citizens.—*Author.*

for reformation, they carefully preserved that fraud of the profession.

In all cases they took care to represent government as a thing made up of mysteries, which only themselves understood, and they hid from the understanding of the nation, the only thing that was beneficial to know, namely, *That government is nothing more than a national association acting on the principles of society.*

Having thus endeavored to show that the social and civilized state of man is capable of performing within itself, almost every thing necessary to its protection and government, it will be proper, on the other hand, to take a review of the present old governments, and examine whether their principles and practise are correspondent thereto.

CHAPTER II

On the Origin of the Present Old Governments

IT IS impossible that such governments as have hitherto existed in the world, could have commenced by any other means than a total violation of every principle, sacred and moral. The obscurity in which the origin of all the present old governments is buried, implies the iniquity and disgrace with which they began. The origin of the present governments of America and France will ever be remembered, because it is honorable to record it; but with respect to the rest, even flattery has consigned them to the tomb of time, without an inscription.

It could have been no difficult thing in the early and solitary ages of the world, while the chief employment of men was that of attending flocks and herds, for a banditti of ruffians to overrun a country, and lay it under contributions. Their power being thus established, the chief of the band contrived to lose the name of robber in that of monarch; and hence the origin of monarchy and kings.

The origin of the government of England, so far as relates to what is called its line of monarchy, being one of the lastest, is perhaps the best recorded. The hatred which the Norman invasion and tyranny begat, must have been deeply rooted in the nation, to have outlived the contrivance to obliterate it. Though not a courtier will talk of the curfew-bell, not a village in England has forgotten it.

Those bands of robbers having parcelled out the world and divided it into dominions, began, as is naturally the case, to quarrel with each other. What at first was obtained by violence, was considered by others as lawful to be taken, and a second plunderer succeeded the first. They alternately invaded the dominions which each had assigned to himself, and the brutality with which they treated each other explains the original character of monarchy. It was ruffian torturing ruffian.

The conqueror considered the conquered, not as his prisoner, but as his property. He led him in triumph, rattling in chains, and doomed him, at pleasure, to slavery or death. As time obliterated the history of their beginning, their successors assumed new appearances, to cut off the entail of their disgrace, but their principles and objects remained the same. What at first was plunder, assumed the softer name of revenue; and the power originally usurped, they affected to inherit.

From such beginning of governments, what could be expected, but a continual system of war and extortion? It has established itself into a trade. The vice is not peculiar to one more than to another, but is the common principle of all. There does not exist within such government sufficient stamina whereon to ingraft reformation; and the shortest, easiest, and most effectual remedy, is to begin anew.

What scenes of horror, what perfection of iniquity, present themselves in contemplating the character, and reviewing the history of such governments! If we would delineate human nature with a baseness of heart, and hypocrisy of countenance, that reflection would shudder at and humanity disown, it is kings, courts, and cabinets, that must sit for the portrait. Man, naturally as he is, with all his faults about him, is not up to the character.

Can we possibly suppose that if governments had originated in a right principle, and had not an interest in pursuing a wrong one, that the world could have been in the wretched and quarrelsome condition we have seen it? What inducement has the farmer, while following the plough, to lay aside his peaceful pursuit, and go to war with the farmer of another country? Or what inducement has the manufacturer? What is dominion to them, or to any class of men in a nation? Does it add an acre to any man's estate, or raise its value? Are not conquest and defeat each of the same price, and taxes the never failing consequence? Though this reasoning may be good to a nation, it is not so to a government. War is the faro-table of governments, and nations the dupes of the games.

If there is any thing to wonder at in this miserable scene of governments, more than might be expected, it is the progress which the peaceful arts of agriculture, manufacture and commerce have made, beneath such a long accumulating load of discouragement and oppression. It serves to show, that instinct in animals does not act with stronger impulse, than the principles of society and civilization operate in man. Under all discouragements, he pursues his object, and yields to nothing but impossibilities.

CHAPTER III

On the Old and New Systems of Government

NOTHING can appear more contradictory than the principles on which the old governments began, and the condition to which society, civilization and commerce, are capable of carrying mankind. Government on the old system is an assumption of power, for the aggrandizement of itself; on the new, a delegation of power, for the common benefit of society. The former supports itself by keeping up a system of war; the latter promotes a system of peace, as the true means of enriching a nation. The one encourages national prejudices; the other promotes universal society, as the means of universal commerce. The one measures its prosperity, by the quantity of revenue it extorts; the other proves its excellence, by the small quantity of taxes it requires.

Mr. Burke has talked of old and new Whigs. If he can amuse himself with childish names and distinctions, I shall not interrupt his pleasure. It is not to him, but to Abbé Sieyès, that I address this chapter. I am already engaged to the latter gentleman, to discuss the subject of monarchical government; [7] and as it naturally occurs in comparing the old and

[7] Paine is referring to the fact that in July, 1791, he criticized the Abbé Sieyès' insistence on the continuation of the monarchy in France. "I am not the personal enemy of Kings," Paine wrote on that occasion. ". . . but I am the avowed, open, and intrepid enemy of what is called monarchy; and I am such by principles which nothing can either alter or corrupt—by my attachment to humanity; by the anxiety which I feel within myself for the dignity and honor of the human race; by the disgust which I experience when I observe men directed by children and governed by brutes; by the horror which all the evils that monarchy has spread over the earth excite within my breast; ⎱ by those sentiments which make me shudder at the calamities, the exactions, the wars, and the massacres with which monarchy has crushed mankind; in short, it is against all the hell of monarchy that I have declared war." Sieyès replied that he had "no leisure to enter into controversy with republican *polycrats.*"—*Editor.*

new systems, I make this the opportunity of presenting to him my observations. I shall occasionally take Mr. Burke in my way.

Though it might be proved that the system of government now called
the NEW, is the most ancient in principle of all that have existed, being
founded on the original inherent Rights of Man: yet, as tyranny and the
sword have suspended the exercise of those rights for many centuries
past, it serves better the purpose of distinction to call it a *new*, than to
claim the right of calling it the old.

The first general distinction between those two systems is, that the one
now called the old is *hereditary*, either in whole or in part; and the new
is entirely *representative*. It rejects all hereditary government:

First, as being an imposition on mankind.

Secondly, as being inadequate to the purposes for which government is
necessary.

With respect to the first of these heads. It cannot be proved by what
right hereditary government could begin: neither does there exist within
the compass of mortal power a right to establish it. Man has no authority
over posterity in matters of personal right; and therefore, no man, or
body of men, had, or can have, a right to set up hereditary government.
Were even ourselves to come again into existence, instead of being succeeded by posterity, we have not now the right of taking from ourselves
the rights which would then be ours. On what ground, then, do we pretend to take them from others?

All hereditary government is in its nature tyranny. An heritable crown,
or an heritable throne, or by what other fanciful name such things may
be called, have no other significant explanation than that mankind are
heritable property. To inherit a government, is to inherit the people, as
if they were flocks and herds.

With respect to the second head, that of being inadequate to the purposes for which government is necessary, we have only to consider what
government essentially is, and compare it with the circumstances to
which hereditary succession is subject. Government ought to be a thing
always in maturity. It ought to be so constructed as to be superior to all
the accidents to which individual man is subject; and therefore, hereditary succession, by being *subject to them all*, is the most irregular and
imperfect of all the systems of government.

We have heard the Rights of Man called a *levelling* system; but the
only system to which the word *levelling* is truly applicable, is the hereditary monarchical system. It is a system of *mental levelling*. It indis-

criminately admits every species of character to the same authority. Vice and virtue, ignorance and wisdom, in short, every quality, good or bad, is put on the same level. Kings succeed each other, not as rationals, but as animals. It signifies not what their mental or moral characters are.

Can we then be surprised at the abject state of the human mind in monarchical countries, when the government itself is formed on such an abject levelling system? It has no fixed character. To-day it is one thing; to-morrow it is something else. It changes with the temper of every succeeding individual, and is subject to all the varieties of each. It is government through the medium of passions and accidents.

It appears under all the various characters of childhood, decrepitude, dotage, a thing at nurse, in leading-strings, or on crutches. It reverses the wholesome order of nature. It occasionally puts children over men, and the conceits of non-age over wisdom and experience. In short, we cannot conceive a more ridiculous figure of government than hereditary succession, in all its cases, presents.

Could it be made a decree in nature, or an edict registered in heaven, and man could know it, that virtue and wisdom should invariably appertain to hereditary succession, the objections to it would be removed; but when we see that nature acts as if she disowned and sported with the hereditary system; that the mental characters of successors, in all countries, are below the average of human understanding; that one is a tyrant, another an idiot, a third insane, and some all three together, it is impossible to attach confidence to it, when reason in man has power to act.

It is not to the Abbé Sieyès that I need apply this reasoning; he has already saved me that trouble, by giving his own opinion upon the case. "If it be asked," says he, "what is my opinion with respect to hereditary right, I answer, without hesitation, that, in good theory, an hereditary transmission of any power or office, can never accord with the laws of a true representation. Hereditaryship is, in this sense, as much an attaint upon principle, as an outrage upon society. But let us," continues he, "refer to the history of all elective monarchies and principalities: is there one in which the elective mode is not worse than the hereditary succession?"

As to debating on which is the worse of the two, is admitting both to be bad; and herein we are agreed. The preference which the Abbé has given is a condemnation of the thing he prefers. Such a mode of reasoning on such a subject is inadmissible, because it finally amounts to an accusation upon Providence, as if she had left to man no other choice with respect to government than between two evils, the best of which he admits to be *"an attaint upon principle, and an outrage upon society."*

Passing over, for the present, all the evils and mischiefs which monarchy has occasioned in the world, nothing can more effectually prove its uselessness in a state of *civil government,* than making it hereditary. Would we make any office hereditary that required wisdom and abilities to fill it? And where wisdom and abilities are not necessary, such an office, whatever it may be, is superfluous or insignificant.

Hereditary succession is a burlesque upon monarchy. It puts it in the most ridiculous light, by presenting it as an office, which any child or idiot may fill. It requires some talents to be a common mechanic; but to be a king, requires only the animal figure of a man—a sort of breathing automaton. This sort of superstition may last a few years more, but it cannot long resist the awakened reason and interest of man.

As to Mr. Burke, he is a stickler for monarchy, not altogether as a pensioner, if he is one, which I believe, but as a political man. He has taken up a contemptible opinion of mankind, who in their turn, are taking up the same of him. He considers them as a herd of beings that must be governed by fraud, effigy, and show; and an idol would be as good a figure of monarchy with him, as a man. I will, however, do him the justice to say, that, with respect to America, he has been very complimentary. He always contended, at least in my hearing, that the people of America are more enlightened than those of England, or of any other country in Europe; and that therefore the imposition of show was not necessary in their government.

Though the comparison between hereditary and elective monarchy, which the Abbé has made, is unnecessary to the case, because the representative system rejects both; yet, were I to make the comparison, I should decide contrary to what he has done.

The civil wars which have originated from contested hereditary claims are numerous, and have been more dreadful, and of longer continuance, than those which have been occasioned by election. All the civil wars in France arose from the hereditary system; they were either produced by hereditary claims, or by the imperfection of the hereditary form, which admits of regencies, or monarchies at nurse.

With respect to England, its history is full of the same misfortunes. The contests for succession between the houses of York and Lancaster, lasted a whole century; and others of a similar nature, have renewed themselves since that period. Those of 1715 and 1745, were of the same kind. The Succession-war for the crown of Spain, embroiled almost half of Europe. The disturbances in Holland are generated from the hereditaryship of the stadtholder. A government calling itself free, with an hereditary office, is like a thorn in the flesh, that produces a fermentation which endeavors to discharge it.

But I might go further, and place also foreign wars, of whatever kind, to the same cause. It is by adding the evil of hereditary succession to that of monarchy, that a permanent family interest is created, whose constant objects are dominion and revenue. Poland, though an elective monarchy, has had fewer wars than those which are hereditary; and it is the only government that has made a voluntary essay, though but a small one, to reform the condition of the country.

Having thus glanced at a few of the defects of the old, or hereditary system of government, let us compare it with the new, or representative system.

The representative system takes society and civilization for its basis; nature, reason, and experience for its guide.

Experience, in all ages, and in all countries, has demonstrated, that it is impossible to control Nature in her distribution of mental powers. She gives them as she pleases. Whatever is the rule by which she, apparently to us, scatters them among mankind, that rule remains a secret to man. It would be as ridiculous to attempt to fix the hereditaryship of human beauty, as of wisdom.

Whatever wisdom constituently is, it is like a seedless plant; it may be reared when it appears, but it cannot be voluntarily produced. There is always a sufficiency somewhere in the general mass of society for all purposes; but with respect to the parts of society, it is continually changing its place. It rises in one to-day, in another to-morrow, and has most probably visited in rotation every family of the earth, and again withdrawn.

As this is the order of nature, the order of government must necessarily follow it, or government will, as we see it does, degenerate into ignorance. The hereditary system, therefore, is as repugnant to human wisdom, as to human rights, and is as absurd, as it is unjust.

As the republic of letters brings forward the best literary productions, by giving to genius a fair and universal chance; so the representative system of government is calculated to produce the wisest laws, by collecting wisdom where it can be found. I smile to myself when I contemplate the ridiculous insignificance into which literature and all the sciences would sink, were they made hereditary; and I carry the same idea into governments. An hereditary governor is as inconsistent as an hereditary author. I know not whether Homer or Euclid had sons; but I will venture an opinion, that if they had, and had left their works unfinished, those sons could not have completed them.

Do we need a stronger evidence of the absurdity of hereditary government, than is seen in the descendants of those men, in any line of life, who once were famous? Is there scarcely an instance in which there is not a total reverse of character? It appears as if the tide of mental faculties flowed as far as it could in certain channels, and then forsook its course, and arose in others. How irrational then is the hereditary system which establishes channels of power, in company with which wisdom refuses to flow! By continuing this absurdity, man is perpetually in contradiction with himself; he accepts, for a king, or a chief magistrate, or a legislator, a person whom he would not elect for a constable.

It appears to general observation, that revolutions create genius and talents; but those events do no more than bring them forward. There is existing in man, a mass of sense lying in a dormant state, and which, unless something excites it to action, will descend with him, in that condition, to the grave. As it is to the advantage of society that the whole of its faculties should be employed, the construction of government ought to be such as to bring forward, by a quiet and regular operation, all that extent of capacity which never fails to appear in revolutions.

This cannot take place in the insipid state of hereditary government, not only because it prevents, but because it operates to benumb. When the mind of a nation is bowed down by any political superstition in its government, such as hereditary succession is, it loses a considerable portion of its powers on all other subjects and objects.

Hereditary succession requires the same obedience to ignorance, as to wisdom; and when once the mind can bring itself to pay this indiscriminate reverence, it descends below the stature of mental manhood. It is fit to be great only in little things. It acts a treachery upon itself, and suffocates the sensations that urge to detection.

Though the ancient governments present to us a miserable picture of the condition of man, there is one which above all others exempts itself from the general description. I mean the democracy of the Athenians. We see more to admire, and less to condemn, in that great, extraordinary people, than in any thing which history affords.

Mr. Burke is so little acquainted with constituent principles of government, that he confounds democracy and representation together. Representation was a thing unknown in the ancient democracies. In those the mass of the people met and enacted laws (grammatically speaking) in the first person.

Simple democracy was no other than the common hall of the ancients. It signifies the *form,* as well as the public principle of the government. As these democracies increased in population, and the territory extended, the simple democratical form became unwieldy and impracticable; and as the system of representation was not known, the consequence was, they either degenerated convulsively into monarchies, or became absorbed into such as then existed.

Had the system of representation been then understood, as it now is, there is no reason to believe that those forms of government, now called monarchical and aristocratical, would ever have taken place. It was the want of some method to consolidate the parts of society, after it became too populous, and too extensive for the simple democratical form, and also the lax and solitary condition of shepherds and herdsmen in other parts of the world, that afforded opportunities to those unnatural modes of government to begin.

As it is necessary to clear away the rubbish of errors, into which the subject of government has been thrown, I shall proceed to remark on some others.

It has always been the political craft of courtiers and court-governments, to abuse something which they called republicanism; but what republicanism was, or is, they never attempt to explain. Let us examine a little into this case.

The only forms of government are, the democratical, the aristocratical, the monarchical, and what is now called the representative.

What is called a *republic,* is not any *particular form* of government. It is wholly characteristical of the purport, matter, or object for which government ought to be instituted, and on which it is to be employed, *res-publica,* the public affairs, or the public good; or, literally translated, the *public thing.*

It is a word of a good original, referring to what ought to be the character and business of government; and in this sense it is naturally opposed to the word *monarchy,* which has a base original signification. It means arbitrary power in an individual person; in the exercise of which, *himself,* and not the *res-publica,* is the object.

Every government that does not act on the principle of a *republic,* or in other words, that does not make the *res-publica* its whole and sole object, is not a good government. Republican government is no other than government established and conducted for the interest of the public, as well individually as collectively. It is not necessarily connected with any particular form, but it most naturally associates with the representative form, as being best calculated to secure the end for which a nation is at the expense of supporting it.

Various forms of government have affected to style themselves a republic. Poland calls itself a republic, which is an hereditary aristocracy, with what is called an elective monarchy. Holland calls itself a republic which is chiefly aristocratical, with an hereditary stadtholdership.

But the government of America, which is wholly on the system of representation, is the only real republic in character and practise, that now exists. Its government has no other object than the public business of the nation, and therefore it is properly a republic; and the Americans have taken care that *this,* and no other, shall always be the object of the government, by their rejecting everything hereditary, and establishing government on the system of representation only.

Those who have said that a republic is not a *form* of government calculated for countries of great extent, mistook, in the first place, the *business* of a government for a *form* of government; for the *res-publica* equally appertains to every extent of territory and population. And, in the second place, if they meant any thing with respect to *form,* it was the simple democratical form, such as was the mode of government in the ancient democracies, in which there was no representation. The case therefore, is not, that a republic cannot be extensive, but that it cannot be extensive on the simple democratical form; and the question naturally presents itself, *What is the best form of government for conducting the* RES-PUBLICA, *or the* PUBLIC BUSINESS *of a nation, after it becomes too extensive and populous for the simple democratical form?*

It cannot be monarchy, because monarchy is subject to an objection of the same amount to which the simple democratical form was subject.

It is possible that an individual may lay down a system of principles, on which government shall be constitutionally established to any extent of territory. This is no more than an operation of the mind, acting by its own powers. But the practise upon those principles, as applying to the various and numerous circumstances of a nation, its agriculture, manufacture, trade, commerce, etc., requires a knowledge of a different kind, and which can be had only from the various parts of society.

It is an assemblage of practical knowledge, which no one individual can possess; and therefore the monarchical form is as much limited, in useful practise, from the incompetency of knowledge, as was the democratical form, from the multiplying of population. The one degenerates, by extension, into confusion; the other, into ignorance and incapacity, of which all the great monarchies are an evidence. The monarchical form, therefore, could not be a substitute for the democratical, because it has equal inconveniences.

Much less could it when made hereditary. This is the most effectual of all forms to preclude knowledge. Neither could the high democratical mind have voluntarily yielded itself to be governed by children and idiots, and all the motley insignificance of character, which attends such a mere animal system, the disgrace and the reproach of reason and of man.

As to the aristocratical form, it has the same vices and defects with the monarchical, except that the chance of abilities is better from the proportion of numbers, but there is still no security for the right use and application of them.[8]

Referring, then, to the original simple democracy, it affords the true data from which government on a large scale can begin. It is incapable of extension, not from its principle, but from the inconvenience of its form; and monarchy and aristocracy, from their incapacity. Retaining, then, democracy as the ground, and rejecting the corrupt systems of monarchy and aristocracy, the representative system naturally presents itself; remedying at once the defects of the simple democracy as to form, and the incapacity of the other two with respect to knowledge.

Simple democracy was society governing itself without the aid of secondary means. By ingrafting representation upon democracy, we arrive at a system of government capable of embracing and confederating all the various interests and every extent of territory and population; and that also with advantages as much superior to hereditary government, as the republic of letters is to hereditary literature.

It is on this system that the American government is founded. It is representation ingrafted upon democracy. It has fixed the form by a scale parallel in all cases to the extent of the principle. What Athens was

[8] For a character of aristocracy, the reader is referred to "Rights of Man," Part I., page 286.—*Author.*

in miniature, America will be in magnitude. The one was the wonder of the ancient world; the other is becoming the admiration and model of the present. It is the easiest of all the forms of government to be understood, and the most eligible in practise; and excludes at once the ignorance and insecurity of the hereditary mode, and the inconvenience of the simple democracy.

It is impossible to conceive a system of government capable of acting over such an extent of territory, and such a circle of interests, as is immediately produced by the operation of representation. France, great and popular as it is, is but a spot in the capaciousness of the system. It adapts itself to all possible cases. It is preferable to simple democracy even in small territories. Athens, by representation, would have outrivalled her own democracy.

That which is called government, or rather that which we ought to conceive government to be, is no more than some common center, in which all the parts of society unite. This cannot be accomplished by any method so conducive to the various interests of the community, as by the representative system.

It concentrates the knowledge necessary to the interests of the parts, and of the whole. It places government in a state of constant maturity. It is, as has been already observed, never young, never old. It is subject neither to nonage, nor dotage. It is never in the cradle, nor on crutches. It admits not of a separation between knowledge and power, and is superior, as government always ought to be, to all the accidents of individual man, and is therefore superior to what is called monarchy.

A nation is not a body, the figure of which is to be represented by the human body; but is like a body contained within a circle, having a common center, in which every radius meets; and that center is formed by representation. To connect representation with what is called monarchy is eccentric government. Representation is of itself the delegated monarchy of a nation, and cannot debase itself by dividing it with another.

Mr. Burke has two or three times, in his parliamentary speeches, and in his publications, made use of a jingle of words that convey no ideas. Speaking of government, he says, "it is better to have monarchy for its basis, and republicanism for its corrective, than republicanism for its basis, and monarchy for its corrective." If he means that it is better to correct folly with wisdom, than wisdom with folly, I will not otherwise contend with him, than that it would be much better to reject the folly entirely.

But what is this thing that Mr. Burke calls monarchy? Will he explain it? All men can understand what representation is; and that it must necessarily include a variety of knowledge and talents. But what security is there for the same qualities on the part of monarchy? Or, when this monarchy is a child, where then is the wisdom? What does it know about government? Who then is the monarch, or where is the monarchy? If it is to be performed by regency, it proves to be a farce.

A regency is a mock species of republic, and the whole of monarchy deserves no better description. It is a thing as various as imagination can paint. It has none of the stable character that government ought to possess. Every succession is a revolution, and every regency a counter-revolution. The whole of it is a scene of perpetual court cabal and intrigue, of which Mr. Burke is himself an instance.

To render monarchy consistent with government, the next in succession should not be born a child, but a man at once, and that man a Solomon. It is ridiculous that nations are to wait, and government be interrupted, till boys grow to be men.

Whether I have too little sense to see, or too much to be imposed upon; whether I have too much or too little pride, or of anything else, I leave out of the question; but certain it is, that what is called monarchy, always appears to me a silly, contemptible thing. I compare it to something kept behind a curtain, about which there is a great deal of bustle and fuss, and a wonderful air of seeming solemnity; but when, by any accident, the curtain happens to open, and the company see what it is, they burst into laughter.

In the representative system of government, nothing of this can happen. Like the nation itself, it possesses a perpetual stamina, as well of body as of mind, and presents itself on the open theater of the world in a fair and manly manner. Whatever are its excellencies or its defects, they are visible to all. It exists not by fraud and mystery; it deals not in cant and sophistry; but inspires a language, that, passing from heart to heart, is felt and understood.

We must shut our eyes against reason, we must basely degrade our understanding, not to see the folly of what is called monarchy. Nature is orderly in all her works; but this is a mode of government that counteracts nature. It turns the progress of the human faculties upside down. It subjects age to be governed by children, and wisdom by folly. On the contrary, the representative system is always parallel with the order and immutable laws of nature, and meets the reason of man in every part. For example:

In the American Federal Government, more power is delegated to the President of the United States, than to any other individual member of Congress.[9] He cannot, therefore, be elected to this office under the age of thirty-five years. By this time the judgment of man becomes matured, and he has lived long enough to be acquainted with men and things, and the country with him.

But on the monarchial plan, (exclusive of the numerous chances there are against every man born into the world, of drawing a prize in the lottery of human faculties), the next in succession, whatever he may be, is put at the head of a nation, and of a government, at the age of eighteen years.

Does this appear like an act of wisdom? Is it consistent with the proper dignity and the manly character of a nation? Where is the propriety of calling such a lad the father of the people? In all other cases, a person is a minor until the age of twenty-one years. Before this period, he is not trusted with the management of an acre of land, or with the heritable property of a flock of sheep, or an herd of swine; but, wonderful to tell! he may, at the age of eighteen years, be trusted with a nation.

That monarchy is all a bubble, a mere court artifice to procure money, is evident (at least to me) in every character in which it can be viewed. It would be impossible, on the rational system of representative government, to make out a bill of expenses to such an enormous amount as this deception admits. Government is not of itself a very chargeable institution. The whole expense of the Federal Government of America, founded, as I have already said, on the system of representation, and extending over a country nearly ten times as large as England, is but six hundred thousand dollars, or one hundred and thirty thousand pounds sterling.

I presume, that no man in his sober senses will compare the character of any of the kings of Europe with that of General Washington. Yet, in France, and also in England, the expense of the civil list only, for the support of one man, is eight times greater than the whole expense of the

[9] Paine is following the custom in England of referring to the President of the United States as "the President of Congress."—*Editor*.

Federal Government in America. To assign a reason for this, appears almost impossible. The generality of people in America, especially the poor, are more able to pay taxes, than the generality of people either in France or England. But the case is, that the representative system diffuses such a body of knowledge throughout a nation, on the subject of government, as to explode ignorance and preclude imposition. The craft of courts cannot be acted on that ground. There is no place for mystery; nowhere for it to begin. Those who are not in the representation, know as much of the nature of business as those who are. An affectation of mysterious importance would there be scouted. Nations can have no secrets; and the secrets of courts, like those of individuals, are always their defects.

In the representative system, the reason for everything must publicly appear. Every man is a proprietor in government and considers it a necessary part of his business to understand. It concerns his interest, because it affects his property. He examines the cost, and compares it with the advantages; and above all, he does not adopt the slavish custom of following what in other governments are called LEADERS.

It can only be by blinding the understanding of man, and making him believe that government is some wonderful mysterious thing, that excessive revenues are obtained. Monarchy is well calculated to ensure this end. It is the popery of government; a thing kept up to amuse the ignorant, and quiet them into paying taxes.

The government of a free country, properly speaking, is not in the persons, but in the laws. The enacting of those requires no great expense; and when they are administered, the whole of civil government is performed—the rest is all court contrivance.

CHAPTER IV

ON CONSTITUTIONS

THAT men mean distinct and separate things when they speak of constitutions and of government, is evident; or why are those terms distinctly and separately used? A constitution is not the act of a government, but of a people constituting a government; and government without a constitution, is power without a right.

All power exercised over a nation, must have some beginning. It must be either delegated, or assumed. There are no other sources. All delegated power is trust, and all assumed power is usurpation. Time does not alter the nature and quality of either.

In viewing this subject, the case and circumstances of America present themselves as in the beginning of the world; and our inquiry into the origin of government is shortened, by referring to the facts that have arisen in our own day. We have no occasion to roam for information into the obscure field of antiquity, nor hazard ourselves upon conjecture. We are brought at once to the point of seeing government begin, as if we had lived in the beginning of time. The real volume, not of history, but of facts, is directly before us, unmutilated by contrivance, or the errors of tradition.

I will here concisely state the commencement of the American constitutions; by which the difference between constitutions and government will sufficiently appear.

It may not be improper to remind the reader, that the United States of America consist of thirteen separate states, each of which established a government for itself, after the Declaration of Independence, done the fourth of July, 1776. Each state acted independently of the rest, in forming its government; but the same general principle pervades the whole. When the several state governments were formed, they proceeded to form the Federal Government, that acts over the whole in all matters which concern the interest of the whole, or which relate to the intercourse of the several states with each other, or with foreign nations. I will begin with giving an instance from one of the state governments, (that of Pennsylvania) and then proceed to the Federal Government.

The State of Pennsylvania, though nearly of the same extent of territory as England, was then divided into only twelve counties. Each of those counties had elected a committee at the commencement of the dispute with the English Government; and as the city of Philadelphia, which also had its committee, was the most central for intelligence, it became the center of communication to the several county committees. When it became necessary to proceed to the formation of a government, the Committee of Philadelphia proposed a conference of all the county committees, to be held in that city, and which met the latter end of July, 1776.[10]

[10] For a scholarly analysis of the formation of the Pennsylvania Constitution discussed by Paine, see John Paul Selsam, *The Pennsylvania Constitution of 1776*, Philadelphia, 1936.

Though these committees had been elected by the people, they were not elected expressly for the purpose, nor invested with the authority of forming a constitution; and as they could not, consistently with the American idea of rights, assume such a power, they could only confer upon the matter, and put it into a train of operation. The conferees, therefore, did no more than state the case, and recommend to the several counties to elect six representatives for each county, to meet in convention at Philadelphia, with powers to form a constitution, and propose it for public consideration.

This convention, of which Benjamin Franklin was president, having met and deliberated, and agreed upon a constitution, they next ordered it to be published, not as a thing established, but for the consideration of the whole people, their approbation or rejection, and then adjourned to a stated time.

When the time of adjournment was expired, the convention reassembled, and as the general opinion of the people in approbation of it was then known, the constitution was signed, sealed, and proclaimed on the *authority of the people;* and the original instrument deposited as a public record.

The convention then appointed a day for the general election of the representatives who were to compose the Government, and the time it should commence; and having done this, they dissolved, and returned to their several homes and occupations.

In this constitution were laid down, first, a declaration of rights. Then followed the form which the Government should have, and the powers it should possess—the authority of the courts of judicature, and of juries—the manner in which elections should be conducted, and the proportion of representatives to the number of electors—the time which each succeeding assembly should continue, which was one year—the mode of levying, and of accounting for the expenditure, of public money—of appointing public officers, etc.

No article of this Constitution could be altered or infringed at the discretion of the Government that was to ensue. It was to that Government a law. But as it would have been unwise to preclude the benefit of experience, and in order also to prevent the accumulation of errors, if any should be found, and to preserve a unison of government with the circumstances of the State at all times, the Constitution provided, that, at the expiration of every seven years, a convention should be elected, for the express purpose of revising the Constitution, and making alterations, additions, or abolitions therein, if any such should be found necessary.

Here we see a regular process—a government issuing out of a constitution, formed by the people in their original character; and that constitution serving, not only as an authority, but as a law of control to the government. It was the political bible of the State. Scarcely a family was without it. Every member of the Government had a copy; and nothing was more common when any debate arose on the principle of a bill, or on the extent of any species of authority, than for the members to take the printed Constitution out of their pocket, and read the chapter with which such matter in debate was connected.

Having thus given an instance from one of the states, I will show the proceedings by which the Federal Constitution of the United States arose and was formed.

Congress, at its two first meetings, in September 1774, and May 1775, was nothing more than a deputation from the legislatures of the several provinces, afterwards states; and had no other authority than what arose from common consent, and the necessity of its acting as a public body. In every thing which related to the internal affairs of America, Congress went no farther than to issue recommendations to the several provincial assemblies, who at discretion adopted them or not.

Nothing on the part of Congress was compulsive; yet, in this situation, it was more faithfully and affectionately obeyed, than was any government in Europe. This instance, like that of the National Assembly of France, sufficiently shows that the strength of government does not consist in any thing *within* itself, but in the attachment of a nation, and the interest which the people feel in supporting it. When this is lost, government is but a child in power; and though, like the old government of France, it may harass individuals for a while, it but facilitates its own fall.

After the Declaration of Independence, it became consistent with the principle on which representative government is founded, that the authority of Congress should be defined and established. Whether that authority should be more or less than Congress then discretionally exercised, was not the question. It was merely the rectitude of the measure.

For this purpose, the act, called the Act of Confederation (which was a sort of imperfect federal constitution), was proposed, and, after long deliberation, was concluded in the year 1781. It was not the act of Congress, because it is repugnant to the principles of representative government that a body should give power to itself. Congress first informed the several states of the powers which it conceived were necessary to be invested in the union, to enable it to perform the duties and services required from it; and the states severally agreed with each other, and concentrated in Congress those powers.

It may not be improper to observe, that in both those instances (the one of Pennsylvania, and the other of the United States), there is no such thing as the idea of a compact between the people on one side, and the government on the other. The compact was that of the people with each other, to produce and constitute a government.

To suppose that any government can be a party in a compact with the whole people, is to suppose it to have existence before it can have a right to exist. The only instance in which a compact can take place between the people and those who exercise the government, is, that the people shall pay them, while they choose to employ them.

Government is not a trade which any man or body of men has a right to set up and exercise for his own emolument, but is altogether a trust, in right of those by whom that trust is delegated, and by whom it is always resumable. It has of itself no rights; they are altogether duties.

Having thus given two instances of the original formation of a constitution, I will show the manner in which both have been changed since their first establishment.

The powers vested in the governments of the several States, by the State constitutions, were found, upon experience, to be too great; and those vested in the Federal Government, by the Act of Confederation, too little. The defect was not in the principle, but in the distribution of power.

Numerous publications, in pamphlets and in the newspapers, appeared on the propriety and necessity of new modelling the Federal Government. After some time of public discussion, carried on through the channel of the press, and in conversations, the State of Virginia, experiencing some inconvenience with respect to commerce, proposed holding a continental conference; in consequence of which, a deputation from five or six of the State assemblies met at Annapolis in Maryland in 1786.

This meeting, not conceiving itself sufficiently authorized to go into the business of a reform, did no more than state their general opinions of the propriety of the measure, and recommended that a convention of all the States should be held the year following.

This convention met at Philadelphia in May, 1787, of which General

Washington was elected President. He was not at that time connected with any of the State governments, or with Congress. He delivered up his commission when the war ended,[11] and since then had lived a private citizen. The convention went deeply into all the subjects; and having, after a variety of debate and investigation, agreed among themselves upon the several parts of a Federal Constitution, the next question was, the manner of giving it authority and practise.

For this purpose, they did not, like a cabal of courtiers, send for a Dutch stadtholder, or a German elector; [12] but they referred the whole matter to the sense and interest of the country.

They first directed that the proposed Constitution should be published. Secondly, that each State should elect a convention, expressly for the purpose of taking it into consideration, and of ratifying or rejecting it; and that as soon as the approbation and ratification of any nine States should be given, that those States should proceed to the election of their proportion of members to the new Federal Government; and that the operation of it should then begin, and the former Federal Government cease.

The several States proceeded accordingly to elect their conventions. Some of those conventions ratified the Constitution by very large majorities, and two or three unanimously. In others there were much debate and division of opinion. In the Massachusetts Convention, which met at Boston, the majority was not above nineteen or twenty, in about three hundred members; but such is the nature of representative government, that it quietly decides all matters by majority.

After the debate in the Massachusetts Convention was closed, and the vote taken, the objecting members rose, and declared, *"That though they had argued and voted against it, because certain parts appeared to them in a different light to what they appeared to other members: yet, as the vote had decided in favor of the Constitution as proposed, they should give it the same practical support as if they had voted for it."*

As soon as nine States had concurred (and the rest followed in the order their conventions were elected), the old fabric of the Federal Government was taken down, and the new one elected, of which General Washington is President. In this place I cannot help remarking,

[11] Washington resigned his commission as commander of the army to the Continental Congress at Annapolis, Maryland, on December 23, 1783.—*Editor.*

[12] The reference is to William III, who came from Holland to assume the throne in England; and to George I, who came from Hanover to become the King of England.— *Editor.*

that the character and services of this gentleman are sufficient to put all those men called kings to shame.

While they are receiving from the sweat and labors of mankind, a prodigality of pay, to which neither their abilities nor their services can entitle them, he is rendering every service in his power, and refusing every pecuniary reward. He accepted no pay as Commander-in-Chief; he accepts none as President of the United States.[13]

After the new Federal Constitution was established, the State of Pennsylvania, conceiving that some parts of its own Constitution required to be altered, elected a convention for that purpose. The proposed alterations were published, and the people concurring therein, they were established.

In forming those constitutions, or in altering them, little or no inconvenience took place. The ordinary course of things was not interrupted, and the advantages have been much. It is always the interest of a far greater number of people in a nation to have things right, than to let them remain wrong; and when public matters are open to debate, and the public judgment free, it will not decide wrong, unless it decides too hastily.

In the two instances of changing the constitutions, the governments then in being were not actors either way.[14] Government has no right to make itself a party in any debates respecting the principles or mode of forming or of changing, constitutions.

It is not for the benefit of those who exercise the powers of government, that constitutions, and the governments issuing from them, are established. In all those matters the right of judging and acting are in those who pay, and not in those who receive.

A constitution is the property of a nation, and not of those who exercise the government. All the constitutions of America are declared to be established on the authority of the people. In France, the word nation is used instead of the people; but in both cases, a constitution is a thing antecedent to the government, and always distinct therefrom.

[13] Washington accepted nothing but his expenses for his revolutionary services, and announced in his first inaugural address that he wished not to receive a salary while President of the United States. He was finally convinced, however, to accept $25,000 per year.—*Editor.*

[14] Paine is not entirely accurate in his discussion of the Federal Constitution. Congress under the Articles of Confederation invited the States to send delegates to the Constitutional Convention, appointed the day of meeting, and submitted the document to the several States for ratification.—*Editor.*

In England, it is not difficult to perceive that every thing has a constitution, except the nation. Every society and association that is established, first agreed upon a number of original articles, digested into form, which are its constitution. It then appointed its officers, whose powers and authorities are described in that constitution, and the government of that society then commenced. Those officers, by whatever name they are called, have no authority to add to, alter, or abridge the original articles. It is only to the constituting power that this right belongs.

From the want of understanding the difference between a constitution and a government, Dr. Johnson, and all writers of his description, have always bewildered themselves. They could not but perceive, that there must necessarily be a *controlling* power existing somewhere, and they placed this power in the discretion of the persons exercising the government, instead of placing it in a constitution formed by the nation.

When it is in a constitution, it has the nation for its support, and the natural and controlling powers are together. The laws which are enacted by governments, control men only as individuals, but the nation, through its constitution, controls the whole government, and has a natural ability so to do. The final controlling power, therefore, and the original constituting power, are one and the same power.

Dr. Johnson could not have advanced such a position in any country where there was a constitution; and he is himself an evidence, that no such thing as a constitution exists in England. But it may be put as a question, not improper to be investigated, that if a constitution does not exist, how came the idea of its existence so generally established?

In order to decide this question, it is necessary to consider a constitution in both cases:—First, as creating a government and giving it powers. Secondly, as regulating and restraining the powers so given.

If we begin with William of Normandy, we find that the government of England was originally a tyranny, founded on an invasion and conquest of the country. This being admitted, it will then appear, that the exertion of the nation, at different periods, to abate that tyranny, and render it less intolerable, has been credited for a constitution.

Magna Charta, as it was called, (it is now like an almanac of the same date), was no more than compelling the Government to renounce a part of its assumptions. It did not create and give powers to Government in the manner a constitution does; but was, as far as it went, of the nature of a re-conquest, and not of a constitution; for could the nation have totally expelled the usurpation, as France has done its despotism, it would then have had a constitution in form.[15]

The history of the Edwards and the Henrys, and up to the commencement of the Stuarts, exhibits as many instances of tyranny as could be acted within the limits to which the nation has restricted it. The Stuarts endeavored to pass those limits, and their fate is well known. In all those instances we see nothing of a constitution, but only of restrictions on assumed power. After this, another William, descended from the same stock, and claiming from the same origin, gained possession; and of the two evils, James and William, the nation preferred what it thought the least; since, from the circumstances, it must take one.

The act, called the Bill of Rights, comes here into view. What is it but a bargain, which the parts of government made with each other to divide powers, profits and privileges? You shall have so much, and I will have the rest; and with respect to the nation, it said, for *your share*, YOU *shall have the right of petitioning.*

This being the case, the Bill of Rights is more properly a bill of wrongs, and of insult. As to what is called the Convention-parliament, it was a thing that made itself, and then made the authority by which it acted. A few persons got together, and called themselves by that name. Several of them had never been elected, and none of them for that purpose.

From the time of William, a species of government arose, issuing out of this coalition Bill of Rights; and more so, since the corruption introduced at the Hanover succession, by the agency of Walpole: that can be described by no other name than a despotic legislation. Though the parts may embarrass each other, the whole has no bounds; and the only right it acknowledges out of itself, is the right of petitioning. Where then is the constitution that either gives or restrains power?

[15] The following four paragraphs were omitted by Paine in the Symonds edition of 1792 with the following statement by the author: "Here follow, on page 52 of the original edition, four paragraphs. As those paragraphs are put into information, and will publicly appear with the pleadings thereon, when the prosecution shall be brought to an issue, they are not verbally recited here, except the first of them, which is added in the annexed note, for the purpose of shewing the spirit of the prosecuting party, and the sort of matter which has been selected from the work for prosecution." After the note Paine adds: "Query. Does the prosecuting party mean to deny that instances of tyranny were acted by the Edwards and Henries? Does he mean to deny that the Stuarts endeavoured to pass the limits which the nation had prescribed? Does he mean to prove it libellous in any person to say that they did?"—*Editor.*

It is not because a part of the government is elective, that makes it less a despotism, if the persons so elected, possess afterwards, as a parliament, unlimited powers. Election, in this case, becomes separated from representation, and the candidates are candidates for despotism.

I cannot believe that any nation, reasoning on its own rights, would have thought of calling those things *a constitution,* if the cry of constitution had not been set up by the Government. It has got into circulation like the words *bore* and *quoz,* by being chalked up in the speeches of Parliament, as those words were on the window-shutters and door-posts; but whatever the Constitution may be in other respects, it has undoubtedly been *the most productive machine for taxation that was ever invented.*

The taxes in France under the new Constitution are not quite thirteen shillings per head,[16] and the taxes in England, under what is called its present Constitution, are forty-eight shillings and sixpence per head, men, women, and children, amounting to nearly seventeen millions sterling, besides the expense of collection, which is upwards of a million more.

In a country like England, where the whole of the civil government is executed by the people of every town and country, by means of parish officers, magistrates, quarterly sessions, juries, and assize, without any trouble to what is called government, or any other expense to the revenue than the salary of the judges, it is astonishing how such a mass of taxes can be employed.

Not even the internal defense of the country is paid out of the revenue. On all occasions, whether real or contrived, recourse is continually had to new loans and new taxes. No wonder, then, that a machine of government so advantageous to the advocates of a court, should be so triumphantly extolled!

No wonder, that St. James's or St. Stephen's should echo with the continual cry of constitution! No wonder, that the French Revolution should be reprobated, and the *res-publica* treated with reproach! The

[16] The whole amount of the assessed taxes of France, for the present year [1792], is three hundred millions of francs, which is twelve millions and a half sterling; and the incidental taxes are estimated at three millions, making in the whole fifteen millions and a half; which among twenty-four millions of people, is not quite thirteen shillings per head.

France has lessened her taxes since the Revolution, nearly nine millions sterling annually. Before the Revolution, the city of Paris paid a duty of upwards of thirty per cent on all articles brought into the city. This tax was collected at the city gates. It was taken off on the first of last May, and the gates taken down.—*Author.*

red book of England, like the red book of France, will explain the reason.[17]

I will now, by way of relaxation, turn a thought or two to Mr. Burke. I ask his pardon for neglecting him so long.

"America," says he, (in his speech on the Canada Constitution Bill) "never dreamed of such absurd doctrine as the *Rights of Man.*"

Mr. Burke is such a bold presumer, and advances his assertions and his premises with such a deficiency of judgment, that, without troubling ourselves about principles of philosophy or politics, the mere logical conclusions they produce, are ridiculous. For instance:

If governments, as Mr. Burke asserts, are not founded on the *rights of man,* and are founded on *any rights* at all, they consequently must be founded on the rights of *something* that is *not man.* What then is that something?

Generally speaking, we know of no other creatures that inhabit the earth than man and beast; and in all cases, where only two things offer themselves, and one must be admitted, a negation proved on any one, amounts to an affirmative on the other; and therefore, Mr. Burke, by proving against the rights of *man,* proves in behalf of the *beast;* and consequently proves that government is a beast; and as difficult things sometimes explain each other, we now see the origin of keeping wild beasts in the Tower; for they certainly can be of no other use than to show the origin of the government. They are in the place of a constitution.

O! John Bull, what honors thou hast lost by not being a wild beast. Thou mightest, on Mr. Burke's system, have been in the Tower for life.

If Mr. Burke's arguments have not weight enough to keep one serious, the fault is less mine than his; and as I am willing to make an apology to the reader for the liberty I have taken, I hope Mr. Burke will also make his for giving the cause.

Having thus paid Mr. Burke the compliment of remembering him, I return to the subject.

From the want of a Constitution in England to restrain and regulate the wild impulse of power, many of the laws are irrational and tyrannical, and the administration of them vague and problematical.

The attention of the Government of England (for I rather choose to

---

[17] What was called the *livre rouge,* or the red book, in France, was not exactly similar to the court calendar in England; but it sufficiently showed how a great part of the taxes were lavished.—*Author.*

call it by this name, than the English Government) appears, since its political connection with Germany, to have been so completely engrossed and absorbed by foreign affairs, and the means of raising taxes, that it seems to exist for no other purposes. Domestic concerns are neglected; and with respect to regular law, there is scarcely such a thing.

Almost every case must now be determined by some precedent, be that precedent good or bad, or whether it properly applies or not; and the practise has become so general, as to suggest a suspicion, that it proceeds from a deeper policy than at first sight appears.

Since the Revolution of America, and more so since that of France, this preaching up the doctrine of precedents, drawn from times and circumstances antecedent to those events, has been the studied practise of the English Government. The generality of those precedents are founded on principles and opinions, the reverse of what they ought to be; and the greater distance of time they are drawn from, the more they are to be suspected.

But by associating those precedents with a superstitious reverence for ancient things, as monks show relics and call them holy, the generality of mankind are deceived into the design. Governments now act as if they were afraid to awaken a single reflection in man. They are softly leading him to the sepulchre of precedents, to deaden his faculties and call his attention from the scene of revolutions.

They feel that he is arriving at knowledge faster than they wish, and their policy of precedents is the barometer of their fears. This political popery, like the ecclesiastical popery of old, has had its day, and is hastening to its exit. The ragged relic and the antiquated precedent, the monk and the monarch, will molder together.

Government by precedent, without any regard to the principle of the precedent, is one of the vilest systems that can be set up. In numerous instances, the precedent ought to operate as a warning, and not as an example, and requires to be shunned instead of imitated; but instead of this, precedents are taken in the lump, and put at once for constitution and for law.

Either the doctrine of precedents is policy to keep a man in a state of ignorance, or it is a practical confession that wisdom degenerates in governments as governments increase in age, and can only hobble along by the stilts and crutches of precedents.

How is it that the same persons who would proudly be thought wiser than their predecessors, appear at the same time only as the ghosts of departed wisdom? How strangely is antiquity treated! To answer some purposes, it is spoken of as the times of darkness and ignorance, and to answer others, it is put for the light of the world.

If the doctrine of precedents is to be followed, the expenses of government need not continue the same. Why pay men extravagantly, who have but little to do? If every thing that can happen is already in precedent, legislation is at an end, and precedent, like a dictionary, determines every case. Either, therefore, government has arrived at its dotage, and requires to be renovated, or all the occasions for exercising its wisdom have occurred.

We now see all over Europe, and particularly in England, the curious phenomenon of a nation looking one way, and the Government the other—the one forward and the other backward. If governments are to go on by precedent, while nations go on by improvement, they must at last come to a final separation; and the sooner, and the more civilly they determine this point, the better it will be for them.[18]

Having thus spoken of constitutions generally, as things distinct from actual governments, let us proceed to consider the parts of which a constitution is composed.

Opinions differ more on this subject, than with respect to the whole. That a nation ought to have a constitution, as a rule for the conduct of its government, is a simple question to which all men, not directly courtiers, will agree. It is only on the component parts that questions and opinions multiply.

But this difficulty, like every other, will diminish when put into a train of being rightly understood. The first thing is, that a nation has a right to establish a constitution.

Whether it exercises this right in the most judicious manner at first, it is quite another case. It exercises it agreeably to the judgment it possesses; and by continuing to do so, all errors will at last be exploded.

When this right is established in a nation, there is no fear that it will

---

[18] In England the improvements in agriculture, useful arts, manufactures, and commerce have been made in opposition to the genius of its government, which is that of following precedents. It is from the enterprise and industry of the individuals, and their numerous associations, in which, tritely speaking, government is neither pillow nor bolster, that these improvements have proceeded.

No man thought about the Government, or who was *in,* or who was *out,* when he was planning or executing those things, and all he had to hope, with respect to government, was, that it would let him alone. Three or four very silly ministerial newspapers are continually offending against the spirit of national improvement, by ascribing it to a minister. They may with as much truth ascribe this book to a minister.—*Author.*

be employed to its own injury. A nation can have no interest in being wrong.

Though all the constitutions of America are on one general principle, yet no two of them are exactly alike in their component parts, or in the distribution of the powers which they give to the actual governments. Some are more and others less complex.

In forming a constitution, it is first necessary to consider what are the ends for which government is necessary: secondly, what are the best means, and the least expensive, for accomplishing those ends.

Government is nothing more than a national association; and the object of this association is the good of all, as well individually as collectively. Every man wishes to pursue his occupation, and enjoy the fruits of his labors, and the produce of his property, in peace and safety, and with the least possible expense. When these things are accomplished, all the objects for which government ought to be established are answered.

It has been customary to consider government under three distinct general heads: The legislative, the executive, and the judicial.

But if we permit our judgment to act unincumbered by the habit of multiplied terms, we can perceive no more than two divisions of power, of which civil government is composed, namely, that of legislating, or enacting laws, and that of executing or administering them. Every thing, therefore, appertaining to civil government, classes itself under one or other of these two divisions.

So far as regards the execution of the laws, that which is called the judicial power, is strictly and properly the executive power of every country. It is that power to which every individual has an appeal, and which causes the laws to be executed; neither have we any other clear idea with respect to the official execution of the laws. In England, and also in America and France, this power begins with the magistrate, and proceeds up through all the courts of judicature.

I leave to courtiers to explain what is meant by calling monarchy the executive power. It is merely a name in which acts of government are done; and any other, or none at all, would answer the same purpose.

Laws have neither more nor less authority on this account. It must be from the justness of their principles, and the interest which a nation feels therein, that they derive support; if they require any other than this, it is a sign that something in the system of government is imperfect. Laws difficult to be executed cannot be generally good.

With respect to the organization of the *legislative power,* different modes have been adopted in different countries. In America it is generally composed of two houses. In France it consists of but one, but in both countries, it is wholly by representation.

The case is, that mankind (from the long tyranny of assumed power) have had so few opportunities of making the necessary trials on modes and principles of government, in order to discover the best, *that government is but now beginning to be known,* and experience is yet wanting to determine many particulars.

The objections against two houses are, first, that there is an inconsistency in any part of a whole legislature coming to a final determination by vote on any matter, whilst *that matter,* with respect to *that whole,* is yet only in a train of deliberation, and consequently open to new illustrations.

Secondly, That by taking the vote on each, as a separate body, it always admits of the possibility, and is often the case in practise, that the minority governs the majority, and that, in some instances, to a great degree of inconsistency.

Thirdly, That two houses arbitrarily checking or controlling each other, is inconsistent; because it cannot be proved, on the principles of just representation, that either should be wiser or better than the other. They may check in the wrong as well as in the right; and therefore, to give the power where we cannot give the wisdom to use it, nor be assured of its being rightly used, renders the hazard at least equal to the precaution.[19]

[19] With respect to the two Houses, of which the English Parliament is composed, they appear to be effectually influenced into one, and, as a legislature, to have no temper of its own. The minister, whoever he at any time may be, touches it as with an opium wand, and it sleeps obedience.

But if we look at the distinct abilities of the two Houses, the difference will appear so great, as to show the inconsistency of placing power where there can be no certainty of the judgment to use it. Wretched as the state of representation is in England, it is manhood compared with what is called the House of Lords; and so little is this nick-named House regarded, that the people scarcely inquire at any time what it is doing. It appears also to be most under influence, and the furthest removed from the general interest of the nation. In the debate on engaging in the Russian and Turkish war, the majority in the House of Peers in favor of it was upwards of ninety, when in the other House, which was more than double its numbers, the majority was sixty-three.

The proceedings on Mr. Fox's bill, respecting the rights of juries, merits also to be noticed. The persons called the peers, were not the objects of that bill. They are already in possession of more privileges than that bill gave to others. They are their own jury, and if any one of that House were prosecuted for a libel, he would not suffer, even upon conviction, for the first offense. Such inequality in laws ought not to exist in any country.

The objection against a single house is, that it is always in a condition of committing itself too soon. But it should at the same time be remembered that when there is a constitution which defines the power, and establishes the principles within which a legislature shall act, there is already a more effectual check provided, and more powerfully operating, than any other check can be. For example:

Were a bill brought into any of the American legislatures, similar to that which was passed into an act of the English Parliament, at the commencement of the reign of George I, tò extend the duration of the assemblies to a longer period than they now sit, the check is in the constitution, which in effect says, *thus far shalt thou go and no further.*

But in order to remove the objection against a single House (that of acting with too quick an impulse), and at the same time to avoid the inconsistencies, in some cases absurdities, arising from the two Houses, the following method has been proposed as an improvement on both:

First: To have but one representation.

Secondly: To divide that representation, by lot, into two or three parts.

Thirdly: That every proposed bill shall first be debated in those parts, by succession, that they may become hearers of each other, but without taking any vote. After which the whole representation to assemble, for a general debate and determination, by vote.

To this proposed improvement has been added another, for the purpose of keeping the representation in a state of constant renovation; which is, that one-third of the representation of each county, shall go out at the expiration of one year, and the number be replaced by new elections. Another third at the expiration of the second year, replaced in like manner, and every third year to be a general election.[20]

But in whatever manner the separate parts of a constitution may be arranged, there is one general principle that distinguishes freedom from slavery, which is, that all *hereditary government over a people is to them a species of slavery, and representative government is freedom.*

Considering government in the only light in which it should be considered, that of a NATIONAL ASSOCIATION, it ought to be so constructed as

---

The French Constitution says, that *the law is the same to every individual, whether to protect or to punish. All are equal in its sight.—Author.*

[20] As to the state of representation in England, it is too absurd to be reasoned upon. Almost all the represented parts are decreasing in population, and the unrepresented parts are increasing. A general convention of the nation is necessary to take the whole state of its government into consideration.—*Author.*

not to be disordered by any accident happening among the parts; and therefore, no extraordinary power, capable of producing such an effect, should be lodged in the hands of any individual.

The death, sickness, absence, or defection of any one individual in a government, ought to be a matter of no more consequence, with respect to the nation, than if the same circumstance had taken place in a member of the English Parliament, or the French National Assembly.

Scarcely anything presents a more degrading character of national greatness, than its being thrown into confusion by any thing happening to, or acted by an individual; and the ridiculousness of the scene is often increased by the natural insignificance of the person by whom it is occasioned.

Were a government so constructed, that it could not go on unless a goose or a gander were present in the senate, the difficulties would be just as great and as real on the flight or sickness of the goose or the gander, as if they were called a king. We laugh at individuals for the silly difficulties they make to themselves, without perceiving that the greatest of all ridiculous things are acted in governments.[21]

All the constitutions of America are on a plan that excludes the childish embarrassments which occur in monarchial countries. No suspension of government can there take place for a moment, from any circumstance whatever. The system of representation provides for every thing, and is the only system in which nations and governments can always appear in their proper character.

As extraordinary power ought not to be lodged in the hands of any individual, so ought there to be no appropriations of public money to any person beyond what his services in a state may be worth.

It signifies not whether a man be called a president, a king, an emperor,

---

[21] It is related, that in the canton of Berne, in Switzerland, it had been customary from time immemorial, to keep a bear at the public expense, and the people had been taught to believe, that if they had not a bear, they should all be undone. It happened some years ago, that the bear, then in being, was taken sick, and died too suddenly to have his place immediately supplied with another.

During the interregnum the people discovered, that the corn grew and the vintage flourished, and the sun and moon continued to rise and set, and every thing went on the same as before, and, taking courage from these circumstances, they resolved not to keep any more bears; "for," said they, "a bear is a very voracious, expensive animal, and we were obliged to pull out his claws, lest he should hurt the citizens."

The story of the bear of Berne was related in some of the French newspapers, at the time of the flight of Louis XVI, and the application of it to monarchy could not be mistaken in France; but it seems that the aristocracy of Berne applied it to themselves, and have since prohibited the reading of French newspapers.—*Author.*

a senator, or by any other name which propriety or folly may devise, or arrogance assume! it is only a certain service he can perform in the state; and the service of any such individual in the routine of office, whether such office be called monarchial, presidential, senatorial, or by any other name or title, can never exceed the value of ten thousand pounds a year.

All the great services that are done in the world are performed by volunteer characters, who accept no pay for them; but the routine of office is always regulated to such a general standard of abilities as to be within the compass of numbers in every country to perform, and therefore cannot merit very extraordinary recompense. *"Government,"* says Swift, *"is a plain thing, and fitted to the capacity of many heads."* [22]

It is inhuman to talk of a million sterling a year, paid out of the public taxes of any country, for the support of any individual, while thousands, who are forced to contribute thereto, are pining with want, and struggling with misery. Government does not consist in a contrast between prisons and palaces, between poverty and pomp; it is not instituted to rob the needy of his mite, and increase the wretchedness of the wretched. But of this part of the subject I shall speak hereafter, and confine myself at present to political observations.

When extraordinary power and extraordinary pay are allotted to any individual in a government, he becomes the center, round which every kind of corruption generates and forms. Give to any man a million a year, and add thereto the power of creating and disposing of places, at the expense of a country, and the liberties of that country are no longer secure. What is called the splendor of a throne, is no other than the corruption of the state. It is made up of a band of parasites, living in luxurious indolence, out of the public taxes.

When once such a vicious system is established, it becomes the guard and protection of all inferior abuses. The man who is in the receipt of a million a year is the last person to promote a spirit of reform, lest, in the event, it should reach to himself. It is always his interest to defend inferior abuses, as so many outworks to protect the citadel, and in this species of political fortification, all the parts have such a common dependence, that it is never to be expected they will attack each other. [23]

[22] The reference is to Jonathan Swift, the English satirist.—*Editor.*

[23] It is scarcely possible to touch on any subject, that will not suggest an allusion to some corruption in governments. The simile of *"fortifications,"* unfortunately involves with it a circumstance, which is directly in point with the matter alluded to.

Among the numerous instances of abuse which have been acted or protected by gov-

Monarchy would not have continued so many ages in the world, had it not been for the abuses it protects. It is the master fraud which shelters all others. By admitting a participation of the spoil, it makes itself friends; and when it ceases to do this, it will cease to be the idol of courtiers.

As the principle on which constitutions are now formed, rejects all hereditary pretensions to government, it also rejects all that catalogue of assumptions known by the name of prerogatives.

If there is any government where prerogatives might with apparent safety be intrusted to any individual, it is in the Federal Government of America. The President of the United States of America is elected only for four years. He is not only responsible in the general sense of the word, but a particular mode is laid down in the Constitution for trying him. He cannot be elected under thirty-five years of age; and he must be a native of the country.

In a comparison of these cases with the government of England, the difference when applied to the latter amounts almost to an absurdity. In England, the person who exercises this prerogative is often a foreigner; always half a foreigner, and always married to a foreigner. He is never in full natural or political connection with the country, is not responsible for anything, and becomes of age at eighteen years; yet such a person is permitted to form foreign alliances, without even the knowledge of the nation; and to make war and peace without its consent.

But this is not all. Though such a person cannot dispose of the government, in the manner of a testator, he dictates the marriage connections, which, in effect, accomplishes a great part of the same end. He cannot directly bequeath half the government to Prussia, but he can form a marriage partnership that will produce the same effect.

---

ernments, ancient or modern, there is not a greater than that of quartering a man and his heirs upon the public, to be maintained at its expense.

Humanity dictates a provision for the poor; but by what right, moral, or political, does any government assume to say, that the person called the Duke of Richmond, shall be maintained by the public? Yet, if common report is true, not a beggar in London can purchase his wretched pittance of coal, without paying towards the civil list of the Duke of Richmond.

Were the whole produce of this imposition but a shilling a year, the iniquitous principle would be still the same; but when it amounts, as it is said to do, to not less than twenty thousand pounds per annum, the enormity is too serious to be permitted to remain. This is one of the effects of monarchy and aristocracy.

In stating this case, I am led by no personal dislike. Though I think it mean in any man to live upon the public, the vice originates in the government; and so general is it become, that whether the parties are in the ministry or in the opposition, it makes no difference; they are sure of the guaranty of each other.—*Author*.

Under such circumstances, it is happy for England that she is not situated on the Continent, or she might, like Holland, fall under the dictatorship of Prussia. Holland, by marriage, is as effectually governed by Prussia, as if the old tyranny of bequeathing the government had been the means.

The presidency in America (or, as it is sometimes called, the executive,) is the only office from which a foreigner is excluded; and in England, it is the only one to which he is admitted. A foreigner cannot be a Member of Parliament, but he may be what is called a king. If there is any reason for excluding foreigners, it ought to be from those offices where most mischief can be acted, and where, by uniting every bias of interest and attachment, the trust is best secured.

But as nations proceed in the great business of forming constitutions, they will examine with more precision into the nature and business of that department which is called the executive. What the legislative and judicial departments are, every one can see; but with respect to what, in Europe, is called the executive, as distinct from those two, it is either a political superfluity, or a chaos of unknown things. Some kind of official department, to which reports shall be made from different parts of the nation, or from abroad, to be laid before the national representatives, is all that is necessary; but there is no consistency in calling this the executive; neither can it be considered in any other light than as inferior to the legislature. The sovereign authority in any country is the power of making laws, and every thing else is an official department.

Next to the arrangement of the principles and the organization of the several parts of a constitution, is the provision to be made for the support of the persons to whom the nation shall confide the administration of the constitutional powers.

A nation can have no right to the time and services of any person at his own expense, whom it may choose to employ or intrust in any department whatever; neither can any reason be given for making provision for the support of any one part of the government and not for the other.

But, admitting that the honor of being intrusted with any part of a government, is to be considered a sufficient reward, it ought to be so to every person alike. If the members of the legislature of any country are to serve at their own expense, that which is called the executive, whether monarchial, or by any other name, ought to serve in like manner. It is inconsistent to pay the one, and accept the service of the other gratis.

In America, every department in the government is decently provided for; but no one is extravagantly paid. Every Member of Congress, and of the State Assemblies, is allowed a sufficiency for his expenses. Whereas, in England, a most prodigal provision is made for the support of one part of the government and none for the other; the consequence of which is, that the one is furnished with the means of corruption, and the other is put into the condition of being corrupted. Less than a fourth part of such expense, applied as it is in America, would remedy a great part of the corruption.

Another reform in the American Constitution is the exploding all oaths of personality. The oath of allegiance is to the nation only. The putting any individual as a figure for a nation is improper. The happiness of a nation is the first object, and therefore the intention of an oath of allegiance ought not to be obscured by being figuratively taken, to, or in the name of, any person. The oath, called the civic oath, in France, *viz*. the *"nation, the law, and the king,"* is improper. If taken at all, it ought to be as in America, to the nation only.

The law may or may not be good; but, in this place, it can have no other meaning, than as being conducive to the happiness of the nation, and therefore is included in it. The remainder of the oath is improper, on the ground that all person oaths ought to be abolished. They are the remains of tyranny on one part, and slavery on the other; and the name of the Creator ought not to be introduced to witness the degradation of his creation; or if taken, as is already mentioned, as figurative of the nation, it is in this place redundant.

But whatever apology may be made for oaths at the first establishment of a government, they ought not to be permitted afterwards. If a government requires the support of oaths, it is a sign that it is not worth supporting, and ought not to be supported. Make government what it ought to be, and it will support itself.

To conclude this part of the subject:—One of the greatest improvements that has been made for the perpetual security and progress of constitutional liberty, is the provision which the new constitutions make for occasionally revising, altering and amending them.

The principle upon which Mr. Burke formed his political creed, that *"of binding and controlling posterity to the end of time, and renouncing and abdicating the rights of all posterity for ever,"* is now become too detestable to be made a subject for debate; and, therefore, I pass it over with no other notice than exposing it.

Government is but now beginning to be known. Hitherto it has been the mere exercise of power, which forbade all effectual inquiry into rights, and grounded itself wholly on possession. While the enemy of liberty was its judge, the progress of its principles must have been small indeed.

The constitutions of America, and also that of France, have either fixed a period for their revision, or laid down the mode by which improvements shall be made.

It is perhaps impossible to establish any thing that combines principles with opinions and practise, which the progress of circumstances, through a length of years, will not in some measure derange, or render inconsistent; and therefore, to prevent inconveniences accumulating, till they discourage reformations or provoke revolutions, it is best to regulate them as they occur.

The rights of man are the rights of all generations of men, and cannot be monopolized by any. That which is worth following, will be followed for the sake of its worth; and it is in this that its security lies, and not in any conditions with which it may be incumbered. When a man leaves property to his heirs, he does not connect it with an obligation that they shall accept it. Why then should we do otherwise with respect to constitutions?

The best constitution that could now be devised, consistent with the condition of the present moment, may be far short of that excellence which a few years may afford.[24] There is a morning of reason rising upon man, on the subject of government, that has not appeared before. As the barbarism of the present old governments expires, the moral condition of the nations, with respect to each other, will be changed.

Man will not be brought up with the savage idea of considering his species as enemies, because the accident of birth gave the individuals existence in countries distinguished by different names; and as constitutions have always some relation to external as well as domestic cir-

---

[24] It is interesting again to compare Paine's views with those of Jefferson, for the resemblance is striking. In his letter to Samuel Kercheval, cited above, Jefferson also wrote: "Some men look at constitutions with sanctimonious reverence, and deem them like the ark of the covenant, too sacred to be touched. They ascribe to the men of the preceding age a wisdom more than human, and suppose what they did to be beyond amendment. . . . Laws and institutions must go hand in hand with the progress of the human mind. As that becomes more developed, more enlightened, as new discoveries are made, new truths disclosed, and manners and opinions change with the circumstances, institutions must advance also, and keep pace with the times."—*Editor*.

cumstances, the means of benefiting by every change, foreign or domestic, should be a part of every constitution.

We already see an alteration in the national disposition of England and France toward each other, which, when we look back only a few years, is itself a revolution. Who could have foreseen, or who would have believed, that a French National Assembly would ever have been a popular toast in England, or that a friendly alliance of the two nations should become the wish of either? [25]

It shows, that man, were he not corrupted by governments, is naturally the friend of man, and that human nature is not of itself vicious. That spirit of jealousy and ferocity, which the governments of the two countries inspired, and which they rendered subservient to the purpose of taxation, is now yielding to the dictates of reason, interest and humanity.

The trade of courts is beginning to be understood, and the affectation of mystery, with all the artificial sorcery by which they imposed upon mankind, is on the decline. It has received its death wound; and though it may linger, it will expire.

Government ought to be as much open to improvement as anything which appertains to man, instead of which it has been monopolized from age to age, by the most ignorant and vicious of the human race. Need we any other proof of their wretched management, than the excess of debt and taxes with which every nation groans, and the quarrels into which they have precipitated the world?

Just emerging from such a barbarous condition, it is too soon to determine to what extent of improvement government may yet be carried. For what we can foresee, all Europe may form but one great republic, and man be free of the whole.

[25] Paine is not referring here to the attitude of the British Government which was one of extreme hostility to the French Revolution, but to the enthusiasm of the British people for the uprising of the French people and the acclaim with which they received the news from France.—*Editor.*

CHAPTER V

IN CONTEMPLATING a subject that embraces with equatorial magnitude the whole region of humanity, it is impossible to confine the pursuit in one single direction. It takes ground on every character and condition that appertains to man, and blends the individual, the nation, and the world.

From a small spark kindled in America, a flame has arisen not to be extinguished. Without consuming, like the *Ultima Ratio Regum,* it winds its progress from nation to nation, and conquers by a silent operation. Man finds himself changed, he scarcely perceives how. He acquires a knowledge of his rights by attending justly to his interest, and discovers in the event that the strength and powers of despotism consist wholly in the fear of resisting it, and that in order, *"to be free, it is sufficient that he wills it."*

Having in all the preceding parts of this work endeavored to establish a system of principles as a basis on which governments ought to be erected, I shall proceed in this to the ways and means of rendering them into practise. But in order to introduce this part of the subject with more propriety and stronger effect, some preliminary observations, deducible from or connected with those principles, are necesssary.

Whatever the form or constitution of government may be, it ought to have no other object than the *general* happinesss. When, instead of this, it operates to create and increase wretchedness in any of the parts of society, it is on a wrong system, and reformation is necessary.

Customary language has classed the condition of man under the two descriptions of civilized and uncivilized life. To the one it has ascribed felicity and affluence; to the other hardship and want. But, however our imagination may be impressed by painting and comparison, it is nevertheless true, that a great portion of mankind in what are called civilized countries, are in a state of poverty and wretchedness, far below the condition of an Indian. I speak not of one country, but of all. It is so in England, it is so all over Europe. Let us inquire into the cause.

It lies not in any natural defect in the principles of civilization, but in preventing those principles having an universal operation; the consequence of which is a perpetual system of war and expense, that drains the country, and defeats the general felicity of which civilization is capable.

All the European governments (France now excepted) are constructed not on the principle of universal civilization, but on the reverse of it. So far as those governments relate to each other, they are in the same condition as we conceive of savage, uncivilized life; they put themselves beyond the law as well of God as of man, and are, with respect to principle and reciprocal conduct, like so many individuals in a state of nature.

The inhabitants of every country, under the civilization of laws, easily associate together, but governments being yet in an uncivilized state, and almost continually at war, they pervert the abundance which civilized life produces to carry on the uncivilized part to a greater extent.

By thus ingrafting the barbarism of government upon the internal civilization of a country, it draws from the latter, and more especially from the poor, a great portion of those earnings which should be applied to their own subsistence and comfort. Apart from all reflections of morality and philosophy it is a melancholy fact, that more than one-fourth of the labor of mankind is annually consumed by this barbarous system. What has served to continue this evil, is the pecuniary advantage which all the governments of Europe have found in keeping up this state of uncivilization. It affords to them pretenses for power and revenue, for which there would be neither occasion nor apology, if the circle of civilization were rendered complete.

Civil government alone, or the government of laws, is not productive of pretenses for many taxes; it operates at home, directly under the eye of the country, and precludes the possibility of much imposition. But when the scene is laid in the uncivilized contention of governments, the field of pretenses is enlarged, and the country, being no longer a judge, is open to every imposition, which governments please to act.

Not a thirtieth, scarcely a fortieth, part of the taxes which are raised in England are either occasioned by, or applied, to the purposes of civil government. It is not difficult to see that the whole which the actual government does in this respect is to enact laws, and that the country administers and executes them, at its own expense, by means of magistrates, juries, sessions, and assize, over and above the taxes which it pays.

In this view of the case, we have two distinct characters of government; the one, the civil government, or the government of laws, which operates at home; the other, the court or cabinet government, which operates abroad, on the rude plan of uncivilized life; the one attended with little charge, the other with boundless extravagance; and so distinct are the two, that if the latter were to sink, as it were, by a sudden opening of the earth, and totally disappear, the former would not be deranged. It would still proceed, because it is the common interest of the nation that it should, and all the means are in practise.

Revolutions, then, have for their object a change in the moral condition of governments, and with this change the burden of public taxes will lessen, and civilization will be left to the enjoyment of that abundance of which it is now deprived.

In contemplating the whole of this subject, I extend my views into the department of commerce. In all my publications, where the matter would admit, I have been an advocate for commerce, because I am a friend to its effects. It is a pacific system, operating to unite mankind by rendering nations, as well as individuals, useful to each other. As to the mere theoretical reformation, I have never preached it up. The most effectual process is that of improving the condition of man by means of his interest; and it is on this ground that I take my stand.

If commerce were permitted to act to the universal extent it is capable of, it would extirpate the system of war, and produce a revolution in the uncivilized state of governments. The invention of commerce has arisen since those governments began, and is the greatest approach toward universal civilization, that has yet been made by any means not immediately flowing from moral principles.

Whatever has a tendency to promote the civil intercourse of nations by an exchange of benefits is a subject as worthy of philosophy as of politics. Commerce is no other than the traffic of two individuals, multiplied on a scale of numbers; and by the same rule that nature intended the intercourse of two, she intended that of all. For this purpose she has distributed the materials of manufacturers and commerce in various and distant parts of a nation and of the world; and as they cannot be procured by war so cheaply or so commodiously as by commerce, she has rendered the latter the means of extirpating the former.

As the two are nearly the opposites of each other, consequently the uncivilized state of European governments is injurious to commerce. Every kind of destruction or embarrassment serves to lessen the quantity, and it matters but little in what part of the commercial world the reduction begins. Like blood, it cannot be taken from any of the parts without being taken from the whole mass in circulation, and all partake of the loss. When the ability in any nation to buy is destroyed, it equally involves the seller. Could the government of England destroy the commerce of all other nations, she would most effectually ruin her own.

It is possible that a nation may be the carrier for the world, but she cannot be the merchant. She cannot be the seller and the buyer of her own merchandise. The ability to buy must reside out of herself; and, therefore, the prosperity of any commercial nation is regulated by the prosperity of the rest. If they are poor, she cannot be rich; and her condition, be it what it may, is an index of the height of the commercial tide in other nations.

That the principles of commerce, and its universal operation may be understood without understanding the practise, is a position that reason will not deny; and it is on this ground only that I argue the subject. It is one thing in the counting house, in the world it is another.

With respect to its operation, it must necessarily be contemplated as a reciprocal thing, that only one-half its power resides within the nation, and that the whole is as effectually destroyed by destroying the half that resides without, as if the destruction had been committed on that which is within, for neither can act without the other.

When in the last, as well as in the former wars, the commerce of England sunk, it was because the general quantity was lessened everywhere; and it now rises because commerce is in a rising state in every nation. If England, at this day, imports or exports more than at any former period, the nations with which she trades must necessarily do the same; her imports are their exports, and *vice versa*.

There can be no such thing as a nation flourishing alone in commerce; she can only participate; and the destruction of it in any part must necessarily affect all. When, therefore, governments are at war, the attack is made upon the common stock of commerce, and the consequence is the same as if each had attacked his own.

The present increase of commerce is not to be attributed to ministers, or to any political contrivances, but to its own natural operations in consequence of peace. The regular markets have been destroyed, the channels of trade broken up, the high road of the seas infested with robbers of every nation, and the attention of the world called to other objects. Those interruptions have ceased, and peace has restored the deranged condition of things to their proper order.[26]

[26] In America the increase of commerce is greater in proportion than in England. It is, at this time, at least one-half more than at any period prior to the Revolution. The greatest

It is worth remarking that every nation reckons the balance of trade in its own favor; and therefore something must be irregular in the common ideas upon this subject.

The fact, however, is true, according to what is called a balance; and it is from this cause that commerce is universally supported. Every nation feels the advantage, or it would abandon the practise: but the deception lies in the mode of making up the accounts, and attributing what are called profits to a wrong cause.

Mr. Pitt has sometimes amused himself, by showing what he called a balance of trade from the custom-house books. This mode of calculation, not only affords no rule that is true, but one that is false.

In the first place, every cargo that departs from the custom-house, appears on the books as an export; and according to the custom-house balance, the losses at sea, and by foreign failures, are all reckoned on the side of profit, because they appear as exports.

Secondly, Because the importation by the smuggling trade does not appear on the custom-house books to arrange against the exports.

No balance, therefore, as applying to superior advantages, can be drawn from these documents; and if we examine the natural operation of commerce, the idea is fallacious; and if true, would soon be injurious. The great support of commerce consists in the balance being a level of benefits among all nations.

Two merchants of different nations trading together, will both become rich, and each makes the balance in his own favor; consequently, they do not get rich out of each other; and it is the same with respect to the nations in which they reside. The case must be, that each nation must get rich out of its own means, and increases that riches by something it procures from another in exchange.

If a merchant in England sends an article of English manufacture abroad, which costs him a shilling at home, and imports something which sells for two, he makes a balance of one shilling in his own favor; but this is not gained out of the foreign nation, or the foreign merchant, for he also does the same by the article he receives, and neither has a balance of advantage upon the other.

---

number of vessels cleared out of the port of Philadelphia, before the commencement of the war was between eight and nine hundred. In the year 1788, the number was upwards of twelve hundred. As the State of Pennsylvania is estimated as an eighth part of the United States in population, the whole number of vessels must now be nearly ten thousand.—*Author.*

The original value of the two articles in their proper countries was but two shillings; but by changing their places, they acquire a new idea of value, equal to double what they had at first, and that increased value is equally divided.

There is not otherwise a balance on foreign than on domestic commerce. The merchants of London and Newcastle trade on the same principles as if they resided in different nations, and make their balances in the same manner: yet London does not get rich out of Newcastle, any more than Newcastle out of London: but coals, the merchandise of Newcastle, have an additional value at London, and London merchandise has the same at Newcastle.

Though the principle of all commerce is the same, the domestic, in a national view, is the part most beneficial; because the whole of the advantages, on both sides, rests within the nation; whereas, in foreign commerce, it is only a participation of one-half.

The most unprofitable of all commerce is that connected with foreign dominion. To a few individuals it may be beneficial, merely because it is commerce; but to the nation it is a loss. The expense of maintaining dominion more than absorbs the profits of any trade. It does not increase the general quantity in the world, but operates to lessen it; and as a greater mass would be afloat by relinquishing dominion, the participation without the expense would be more valuable than a greater quantity with it.

But it is impossible to engross commerce by dominion; and therefore it is still more fallacious. It cannot exist in confined channels, and necessarily breaks out by regular or irregular means that defeat the attempt, and to succeed would be still worse. France, since the Revolution, has been more than indifferent as to foreign possessions; and other nations will become the same, when they investigate the subject with respect to commerce.

To the expense of dominion is to be added that of navies, and when the amount of the two is subtracted from the profits of commerce, it will appear that what is called the balance of trade, even admitting it to exist, is not enjoyed by the nation, but absorbed by the government.

The idea of having navies for the protection of commerce is delusive. It is putting the means of destruction for the means of protection. Commerce needs no other protection than the reciprocal interest which every nation feels in supporting it—it is common stock—it exists by a balance of advantages to all; and the only interruption it meets, is from the present uncivilized state of governments, and which is its common interest to reform.[27]

Quitting this subject, I now proceed to other matters. As it is necessary to include England in the prospect of a general reformation, it is proper to inquire into the defects of its government. It is only by each nation reforming its own, that the whole can be improved, and the full benefit of reformation enjoyed. Only partial advantages can flow from partial reforms. France and England are the only two countries in Europe where a reformation in government could have successfully begun. The one secure by the ocean, and the other by the immensity of its internal strength, could defy the malignancy of foreign despotism. But it is with revolutions as with commerce, the advantages increase by their becoming general, and double to either what each would receive alone.

As a new system is now opening to the view of the world, the European courts are plotting to counteract it. Alliances, contrary to all former systems, are agitating, and a common interest of courts is forming against the common interest of man.

This combination draws a line that runs throughout Europe, and presents a case so entirely new as to exclude all calculations from former circumstances. While despotism warred with despotism, man had no interest in the contest; but in a cause that unites the soldier with the citizen, and nation with nation, the despotism of courts, though it feels the danger, and meditates revenge, is afraid to strike.

No question has arisen within the records of history that pressed with the importance of the present. It is not whether this or that party shall be in or out, or Whig or Tory, or high or low shall prevail; but whether man shall inherit his rights, and universal civilization take place? Whether the fruits of his labor shall be enjoyed by himself, or consumed by the profligacy of governments? Whether robbery shall be banished from courts, and wretchedness from countries?

When, in countries that are called civilized, we see age going to the work-house, and youth to the gallows, something must be wrong in the system of government. It would seem, by the exterior appearance of such

---

[27] When I saw Mr. Pitt's mode of estimating the balance of trade, in one of his parliamentary speeches, he appeared to me to know nothing of the nature and interest of commerce; and no man has more wantonly tortured it than himself. During a period of peace, it has been shackled with the calamities of war. Three times has it been thrown into stagnation, and the vessels unmanned by impressing, within less than four years of peace.— *Author.*

countries, that all was happiness; but there lies hidden from the eye of common observation, a mass of wretchedness that has scarcely any other chance than to expire in poverty or infamy. Its entrance into life is marked with the presage of its fate; and until this is remedied, it is in vain to punish.

Civil government does not consist in executions; but in making that provision for the instruction of youth, and the support of age, as to exclude, as much as possible, profligacy from the one, and despair from the other. Instead of this, the resources of a country are lavished upon kings, upon courts, upon hirelings, impostors, and prostitutes; and even the poor themselves, with all their wants upon them, are compelled to support the fraud that oppresses them.

Why is it that scarcely any are executed but the poor? The fact is a proof, among other things, of a wretchedness in their condition. Bred up without morals, and cast upon the world without a prospect, they are the exposed sacrifice of vice and legal barbarity. The millions that are superfluously wasted upon governments are more than sufficient to reform those evils, and to benefit the condition of every man in the nation, not included within the purlieus of a court. This I hope to make appear in the progress of this work.

It is the nature of compassion to associate with misfortune. In taking up this subject, I seek no recompense—I fear no consequences. Fortified with that proud integrity that disdains to triumph or to yield, I will advocate the Rights of Man.

At an early period, little more than sixteen years of age, raw and adventurous, and heated with the false heroism of a master [28] who had served in a man-of-war, I began the carver of my own fortune, and entered on board the *Terrible* privateer, Captain Death. From this adventure I was happily prevented by the affectionate and moral remonstrance of a good father, who, from his own habits of life, being of the Quaker profession, must have begun to look upon me as lost. But the impression, much as it effected at the time, began to wear away, and I entered afterwards in the *King of Prussia* privateer, Captain Mendez, and went in her to sea.

Yet, from such a beginning, and with all the inconveniences of early life against me, I am proud to say that with a perseverance undismayed by difficulties, a disinterestedness that compelled respect, I have not only contributed to raise a new empire in the world, founded on a new system

[28] Rev. William Knowle, master of the grammar school at Thetford, in Norfolk.—*Author.*

of government, but I have arrived at an eminence in political literature, the most difficult of all lines to succeed and excel in, which aristocracy, with all its aids, has not been able to reach or to rival.

Knowing my own heart, and feeling myself, as I now do, superior to all the skirmish of party, the inveteracy of interested or mistaken opponents, I answer not to falsehood or abuse, but proceed to the defects of the English Government.[29]

[29] Politics and self-interest have been so uniformly connected, that the world, from being so often deceived, has a right to be suspicious of public characters: but with regard to myself, I am perfectly easy on this head. I did not, at my first setting out in public life, nearly seventeen years ago, turn my thoughts to subjects of government from motives of interest; and my conduct from that moment to this, proves the fact. I saw an opportunity, in which I thought I could do some good, and I followed exactly what my heart dictated. I neither read books, nor studied other people's opinions. I thought for myself. The case was this:

During the suspension of the old governments in America, both prior to and at the breaking out of hostilities, I was struck with the order and decorum with which everything was conducted; and impressed with the idea, that a little more than what society naturally performed, was all the government that was necessary, and that monarchy and aristocracy were frauds and impositions upon mankind.

On these principles I published the pamphlet "Common Sense." The success it met with was beyond anything since the invention of printing. I gave the copy-right to every State in the Union, and the demand ran to not less than one hundred thousand copies. I continued the subject in the same manner, under the title of the "Crisis," till the complete establishment of the Revolution.

After the Declaration of Independence, Congress, unanimously and unknown to me, appointed me secretary in the Foreign Department. This was agreeable to me because it gave me an opportunity of seeing into the abilities of foreign courts, and their manner of doing business. But a misunderstanding arising between Congress and me, respecting one of their commissioners, then in Europe, Mr. Silas Deane, I resigned the office, and declined, at the same time, the pecuniary offers made me by the Ministers of France and Spain, M. Gerard and Don Juan Mirralles.

I had by this time so completely gained the ear and confidence of America, and my independence was become so visible, as to give me a range of political writings, beyond, perhaps, what any man ever possessed in any country; and what is more extraordinary, I held it undiminished to the end of the war, and enjoy it in the same manner to the present moment. As my object was not myself, I set out with the determination, and happily with the disposition, of not being moved by praise or censure, friendship or calumny, nor of being drawn from my purpose by any personal altercation; and the man who cannot do this, is not fit for a public character.

When the war ended, I went from Philadelphia to Bordentown, on the East bank of the Delaware, where I have a small place. Congress was at this time at Princeton, fifteen miles distant; and General Washington had taken his head-quarters at Rocky Hill, within the neighborhood of Congress, for the purpose of resigning his commission (the object for which he accepted it being accomplished) and of retiring to private life. While he was on this business, he wrote me the letter which I here subjoin.

Rocky Hill, Sept. 10, 1783.

I have learned since I have been at this place, that you are at Bordentown. Whether

I begin with charters and corporations.[30]

It is a perversion of terms to say that a charter gives rights. It operates by a contrary effect, that of taking rights away. Rights are inherently in all the inhabitants; but charters, by annulling those rights in the majority, leave the right, by exclusion, in the hands of a few. If charters

---

for the sake of retirement or economy, I know not. Be it for either, for both, or whatever it may, if you will come to this place, and partake with me, I shall be exceedingly happy to see you.

Your presence may remind Congress of your past services to this country; and if it is in my power to impress them, command my best exertions with freedom, as they will be rendered cheerfully by one, who entertains a lively sense of the importance of your works, and who, with much pleasure, subscribes himself,

Your sincere friend,   G. WASHINGTON.

During the war, in the latter end of the year 1780, I formed to myself the design of coming over to England, and communicated it to General Greene, who was then in Philadelphia, on his route to the Southward, General Washington being then at too great a distance to communicate with immediately. I was strongly impressed with the idea, that, if I could get over to England, without being known, and only remain in safety till I could get out a publication, I could open the eyes of the country with respect to the madness and stupidity of its government. I saw that the parties in Parliament had pitted themselves as far as they could go, and could make no new impressions on each other. General Greene entered fully into my views, but the affair of Arnold and André happening just after, he changed his mind, and, under strong apprehensions for my safety, wrote very pressingly to me from Annapolis, in Maryland, to give up the design, which, with some reluctance, I did.

Soon after this I accompanied Colonel Laurens, (son of Mr. Laurens, who was then in the Tower), to France, on business from Congress. We landed at L'Orient, and while I remained there, he being gone forward, a circumstance occurred that renewed my former design. An English packet from Falmouth to New York, with government despatches on board, was brought into L'Orient.

That a packet should be taken, is no very extraordinary thing, but that the despatches should be taken with it, will scarcely be credited, as they are always slung at the cabin window, in a bag loaded with cannon ball and ready to be sunk in a moment. The fact, however, is as I have stated it, for the despatches came into my hands, and I read them.

The capture, as I was informed, succeeded by the following stratagem:—The captain of the privateer *Madame,* who spoke English, on coming up with the packet, passed himself for the captain of an English frigate, and invited the captain of the packet on board, which, when done, he sent some of his own hands and secured the mail. But be the circumstance of the capture what it may, I speak with certainty as to the government despatches. They were sent up to Paris to Count Vergennes, and when Colonel Laurens and myself returned to America, we took the originals to Congress.

By these despatches I saw into the stupidity of the English Cabinet far more than I otherwise could have done, and I renewed my former design. But Colonel Laurens was so unwilling to return alone, more especially, as among other matters, he had a charge of upwards of two hundred thousand pounds sterling in money, that I gave in to his wishes, and finally gave up my plan. But I am now certain, that if I could have executed it, it would not have been altogether unsuccessful.—*Author.*

[30] Paine had already discussed this subject at some length. At a meeting of the Society

were constructed so as to express in direct terms, *"that every inhabitant, who is not a member of a corporation, shall not exercise the right of voting,"* such charters would in the face be charters, not of rights, but of exclusion. The effect is the same under the form they now stand; and the only persons on whom they operate, are the persons whom they exclude.

Those whose rights are guaranteed, by not being taken away, exercise no other rights than as members of the community they are entitled to without a charter; and, therefore, all charters have no other than an indirect negative operation. They do not give rights to A, but they make a difference in favor of A, by taking away the rights of B, and consequently are instruments of injustice.

But charters and corporations have a more extensive evil effect than what relates merely to elections. They are sources of endless contention in the places where they exist; and they lessen the common rights of national society. A native of England, under the operation of these charters and corporations, cannot be said to be an Englishman in the full sense of the word. He is not free of the nation, in the same manner that a Frenchman is free of France, and an American of America.

His rights are circumscribed to the town, and, in some cases, to the parish of his birth; and all other parts, though in his native land, are to him as a foreign country. To acquire a residence in these, he must undergo a local naturalization by purchase, or he is forbidden or expelled the place. This species of feudality is kept up to aggrandize the corporations at the ruin of the towns; and the effect is visible.

The generality of corporation towns are in a state of solitary decay, and prevented from further ruin only by some circumstance in their situation, such as a navigable river, or a plentiful surrounding country. As population is one of the chief sources of wealth, (for without it, land itself has no value), every thing which operates to prevent it, must lessen the value of property; and as corporations have not only this tendency, but directly this effect, they cannot but be injurious.

If any policy were to be followed, instead of that of general freedom, to every person to settle where he chose, (as in France or in America), it would be more consistent to give encouragement to new comers,

---

for Political Inquiries which met at Benjamin Franklin's house in Philadelphia in 1787, he had read a paper entitled "On the inexpediency of incorporating towns." Unfortunately, this essay has never been found.—*Editor.*

than to preclude their admission by exacting premiums from them.[31]

The persons most immediately interested in the abolition of corporations, are the inhabitants of the towns where corporations are established. The instances of Manchester, Birmingham and Sheffield, show, by contrast, the injury which those Gothic institutions are to property and commerce. A few examples may be found, such as that of London, whose natural and commercial advantages, owing to its situation on the Thames, is capable of bearing up against the political evils of a corporation; but in almost all other cases the fatality is too visible to be doubted or denied.

Though the whole nation is not so directly affected by the depression of property in corporation towns as the inhabitants themselves, it partakes of the consequences. By lessening the value of property, the quantity of national commerce is curtailed. Every man is a customer in proportion to his ability; and as all parts of a nation trade with each other, whatever affects any of the parts must necessarily communicate to the whole.

As one of the Houses of the English Parliament is, in a great measure, made up by elections from these corporations; and as it is unnatural that a pure stream should flow from a foul fountain, its vices are but a continuation of the vices of its origin. A man of moral honor and good political principles, cannot submit to the mean drudgery and disgraceful arts, by which such elections are carried. To be a successful candidate, he must be destitute of the qualities that constitute a just legislator: and being thus disciplined to corruption by the mode of entering into Parliament, it is not to be expected that the representative should be better than the man.

Mr. Burke, in speaking of the English representation, has advanced as bold a challenge as ever was given in the days of chivalry. "Our representation," says he, "has been found *perfectly adequate to all the pur-*

[31] It is difficult to account for the origin of charter and corporation towns, unless we suppose them to have arisen out of, or having been connected with some species of garrison services. The times in which they began justify this idea. The generality of those towns have been garrisons, and the corporations were charged with the care of the gates of the town, when no military garrison was present. Their refusing or granting admission to strangers, which has produced the custom of giving, selling, and buying freedom, has more of the nature of garrison authority than civil government. Soldiers are free of all corporations throughout the nation, by the same propriety that every soldier is free of every garrison, and no other persons are. He can follow any employment, with the permission of his officers, in any corporation town throughout the nation.—*Author.*

poses for which a representation of the people can be desired or devised. I defy," continues he, "the enemies of our Constitution to show the contrary." This declaration from a man who has been in constant opposition to all the measures of Parliament the whole of his political life, a year or two excepted, is most extraordinary, and, comparing him with himself, admits of no other alternative, than that he acted against his judgment as a member, or has declared contrary to it as an author.

But it is not in the representation only that the defects lie, and therefore I proceed in the next place to aristocracy.

What is called the House of Peers is constituted on a ground very similar to that against which there is a law in other cases. It amounts to a combination of persons in one common interest. No reason can be given, why a house of legislation should be composed entirely of men whose occupation consists in letting landed property, than why it should be composed of those who hire, or of brewers, or bakers, or any other separate class of men.

Mr. Burke calls this House *"the great ground and pillar of security to the landed interest."* Let us examine this idea.

What pillar of security does the landed interest require, more than any other interest in the state, or what right has it to a distinct and separate representation from the general interest of a nation? The only use to be made of this power, (and which it has always made), is to ward off taxes from itself, and throw the burden upon such articles of consumption by which itself would be least affected. That this has been the consequence (and will always be the consequence of constructing governments on combinations), is evident, with respect to England, from the history of its taxes.

Notwithstanding taxes have increased and multiplied upon every article of common consumption, the land tax, which more particularly affects this "pillar," has diminished. In 1788, the amount of the land-tax was £1,950,000 which is half a million less than it produced almost a hundred years ago,[32] notwithstanding the rentals are in many instances doubled since that period.

Before the coming of the Hanoverians, the taxes were divided in nearly equal proportions between the land and articles of consumption, the land bearing rather the largest share; but since that era, nearly thirteen millions annually of new taxes have been thrown upon consump-

[32] See Sir John Sinclair's "History of the Revenue." The land-tax in 1646 was £2,473,499.—*Author.*

tion. The consequence of which has been a constant increase in the number and wretchedness of the poor, and in the amount of the poor-rates.

Yet here again the burden does not fall in equal proportions on the aristocracy with the rest of the community. Their residences, whether in town or country, are not mixed with the habitations of the poor. They live apart from distress, and the expense of relieving it. It is in the manufacturing towns and laboring villages that those burdens press the heaviest; in many of which it is one class of poor supporting another.

Several of the most heavy and productive taxes are so contrived as to give an exemption of this pillar, thus standing in its own defense. The tax upon beer brewed for sale does not affect the aristocracy, who brew their own beer free of this duty. It falls only on those who have not conveniency or ability to brew, and who must purchase it in small quantities.

But what will mankind think of the justice of taxation, when they know, that this tax alone, from which the aristocracy are from circumstances exempt, is nearly equal to the whole of the land-tax, being in the year 1788, (and it is not less now), £1,666,152, and with its proportion of the taxes on malt and hops, it exceeds it. That a single article thus partially consumed, and that chiefly by the working part, should be subject to a tax equal to that on the whole rental of a nation, is, perhaps, a fact not to be paralleled in the history of revenues.

This is one of the consequences resulting from a house of legislation composed on the ground of a combination of common interest; for whatever their separate politics as to parties may be, in this they are united. Whether a combination acts to raise the price of an article for sale, or the rate of wages; or whether it acts to throw taxes from itself upon another class of the community, the principle and the effect are the same; and if the one be illegal, it will be difficult to show that the other ought to exist.

It is no use to say that the taxes are first proposed in the House of Commons; for as the other House has always a negative, it can always defend itself; and it would be ridiculous to suppose that its acquiescence in the measures to be proposed were not understood beforehand. Besides which, it has obtained so much influence by borough traffic, and so many of its relations and connections are distributed on both sides of the Commons, as to give it, besides an absolute negative in the House, a preponderancy in the other, in all matters of common concern.

It is difficult to discover what is meant by the *landed interest,* if it does not mean a combination of aristocratical land-holders, opposing their own pecuniary interest to that of the farmer, and every branch of trade, commerce, and manufacture. In all other respects, it is the only interest that needs no partial protection. It enjoys the general protection of the world.

Every individual, high or low, is interested in the fruits of the earth; men, women, and children, of all ages and degrees, will turn out to assist the farmer, rather than a harvest should not be got in; and they will not act thus by any other property. It is the only one for which the common prayer of mankind is put up, and the only one that can never fail from the want of means. It is the interest, not of the policy, but of the existence of man, and when it ceases, he must cease to be.

No other interest in a nation stands on the same united support. Commerce, manufactures, arts, sciences and everything else, compared with this, are supported but in parts. Their prosperity or their decay has not the same universal influence. When the valleys laugh and sing, it is not the farmer only, but all creation that rejoices. It is a prosperity that excludes all envy; and this cannot be said of anything else.

Why then does Mr. Burke talk of this House of Peers, as the pillar of the landed interest? Were that pillar to sink into the earth, the same landed property would continue, and the same plowing, sowing and reaping would go on. The aristocracy are not the farmers who work the land, and raise the produce, but are the mere consumers of the rent; and when compared with the active world, are the drones, a seraglio of males, who neither collect the honey nor form the hive, but exist only for lazy enjoyment.

Mr. Burke, in his first essay, called aristocracy *"the Corinthian capital of polished society."* Toward completing the figure, he has now added the *pillar,* but still the base is wanting; and whenever a nation chooses to act a Samson, not blind, but bold, down goes the temple of Dagon, the Lords and the Philistines.

If a house of legislation is to be composed of men of one class, for the purpose of protecting a distinct interest, all the other interests, should have the same. The inequality as well as the burden of taxation, arises from admitting it in one case and not in all. Had there been a house of farmers, there had been no game laws; or a house of merchants and manufacturers, the taxes had neither been so unequal nor so excessive. It is from the power of taxation being in the hands of those who can throw so great a part of it from their own shoulders, that it has raged without a check.

Men of small or moderate estates are more injured by the taxes being thrown on articles of consumption, than they are eased by warding it from landed property, for the following reasons:

First, They consume more of the productive taxable articles, in proportion to their property, than those of large estates.

Secondly, Their residence is chiefly in towns, and their property in houses; and the increase of the poor-rates, occasioned by taxes on consumption, is in much greater proportion than the land-tax has been favored. In Birmingham, the poor-rates are not less than seven shillings in the pound. From this, as is already observed, the aristocracy are in a great measure exempt.

These are but a part of the mischiefs flowing from the wretched scheme of an house of peers.

As a combination, it can always throw a considerable portion of taxes from itself; and as an hereditary house, accountable to nobody, it resembles a rotten borough, whose consent is to be courted by interest. There are but few of its members who are not in some mode or other participators, or disposers of the public money. One turns a candle-holder, or a lord in waiting; another a lord of the bed-chamber, a groom of the stole, or any insignificant nominal office, to which a salary is annexed, paid out of the public taxes, and which avoids the direct appearance of corruption. Such situations are derogatory to the character of man; and where they can be submitted to, honor cannot reside.

To all these are to be added the numerous dependents, the long list of the younger branches and distant relations, who are to be provided for at the public expense: in short, were an estimation to be made of the charge of the aristocracy to a nation, it will be found nearly equal to that of supporting the poor. The Duke of Richmond alone (and there are cases similar to his) takes away as much for himself as would maintain two thousand poor and aged persons. Is it, then, any wonder that under such a system of government, taxes and rates have multiplied to their present extent?

In stating these matters, I speak an open and disinterested language, dictated by no passion but that of humanity. To me, who have not only refused offers, because I thought them improper, but have declined rewards I might with reputation have accepted, it is no wonder that meanness and imposition appear disgusting. Independence is my happiness, and I view things as they are, without regard to place or person; my country is the world, and my religion is to do good.[33]

Mr. Burke, in speaking of the aristocratical law of primogeniture, says, "It is the standard law of our landed inheritance; and which, without question has a tendency, and I think," continues he, "a happy tendency to preserve a character of weight and consequence."

Mr. Burke may call this law what he pleases, but humanity and impartial reflection will pronounce it a law of brutal injustice. Were we not accustomed to the daily practise, and did we only hear of it, as the law of some distant part of the world, we should conclude that the legislators of such countries had not yet arrived at a state of civilization.

As to its preserving a character of *weight and consequence,* the case appears to me directly the reverse. It is an attaint upon character; a sort of privateering upon family property. It may have weight among dependent tenants, but it gives none on a scale of national, and much less of universal character. Speaking for myself, my parents were not able to give me a shilling, beyond what they gave me in education; and to do this they distressed themselves; yet I possess more 'of what is called consequence, in the world than any one in Mr. Burke's catalogue of aristocrats. Having thus glanced at some of the defects of the two Houses of Parliament, I proceed to what is called the Crown, upon which I shall be very concise.[34]

It signifies a nominal office of a million sterling a year, the business of which consists in receiving the money. Whether the person be wise or foolish, sane or insane, a native or a foreigner, matters not. Every ministry acts upon the same idea that Mr. Burke writes, namely, that the people must be hoodwinked, and held in superstitious ignorance by some bugbear or other; and what is called the Crown answers this purpose,

[33] This is one of Paine's most famous utterances and was to be quoted on the mastheads of progressive journals for many years.—*Editor.*

[34] The following two paragraphs were also omitted by Paine in the Symonds edition of 1792, the author observing: "Those two short paragraphs are taken into the information as prosecutable matter; but on what ground such a prosecution can be supported I am at a loss to discover. Every part of which a government is composed must be alike open to examination and investigation; and where this is not the case the country is not in a state of freedom; for it is only by the free and rational exercise of this right, that errors, impositions, and absurdities can be detected and rendered either in the parts severally, or in the whole.—If there be an part in a government on which the exercise of this right ought to be more fully insisted upon by a nation than on another part, it is on that part for which a nation pays the most money, and which, in England, is the crown." —*Editor.*

and therefore it answers all the purposes to be expected from it. This is more than can be said of the other two branches.

The hazard to which this office is exposed in all countries is not from anything that can happen to the man, but from what may happen to the nation,—the danger of its coming to its senses.

It has been customary to call the Crown the executive power, and the custom has continued, though the reason has ceased.

It was called the *excutive,* because the person whom it signifies used, formerly, to sit in the character of a judge, in administering or executing the laws. The tribunals were then a part of the court. The power, therefore, which is now called the judicial, is what was called the executive; and, consequently, one or the other of the terms is redundant, and one of the offices useless. When we speak of the Crown, now, it means nothing; it signifies neither a judge nor a general; besides which, it is the laws that govern, and not the man. The old terms are kept up, and give an appearance of consequence to empty forms; and the only effect they have is that of increasing expenses.

Before I proceed to the means of rendering governments more conducive to the general happiness of mankind than they are at present, it will not be improper to take a review of the progress of taxation in England.

It is a general idea, that when taxes are once laid on, they are never taken off. However true this may have been of late, it was not always so. Either, therefore, the people of former times were more watchful over government than those of the present, or government was administered with less extravagance.

It is now seven hundred years since the Norman Conquest, and the establishment of what is called the Crown. Taking this portion of time in seven separate periods of one hundred years each, the amount of annual taxes, at each period, will be as follows:

Annual amount of taxes levied by William the Conqueror, beginning in the year 1066	£400,000
Annual amount of taxes at one hundred years from the Conquest, (1166)	200,000
Annual amount of taxes at two hundred years from the Conquest, (1266)	150,000
Annual amount of taxes at three hundred years from the Conquest, (1366)	130,000

Annual amount of taxes at four hundred years from the Conquest, (1466) 100,000

These statements, and those which follow, are taken from Sir John Sinclair's "History of the Revenue"; by which it appears that taxes continued decreasing for four hundred years, at the expiration of which time they were reduced three-fourths, *viz.* from four hundred thousand pounds to one hundred thousand. The people of England, of the present day, have a traditionary and historical idea of the bravery of their ancestors; but whatever their virtues or vices might have been, they certainly were a people who would not be imposed upon, and who kept government in awe as to taxation, if not as to principle. Though they were not able to expel the monarchical usurpation, they restricted it to a republican economy of taxes.

Let us now review the remaining three hundred years.

Annual amount of taxes at five hundred years from the Conquest, (1566) £500,000
Annual amount of taxes at six hundred years from the Conquest, (1666) 1,800,000
Annual amount of taxes at the present time, (1791) 17,000,000

The difference between the first four hundred years and the last three, is so astonishing, as to warrant the opinion, that the national character of the English has changed. It would have been impossible to have dragooned the former English into the excess of taxation that now exists; and when it is considered that the pay of the army, the navy, and of all the revenue-officers, is the same now as it was above a hundred years ago, when the taxes were not above a tenth part of what they are at present, it appears impossible to account for the enormous increase and expenditure, on any other ground than extravagance, corruption, and intrigue.[35]

[35] Several of the court newspapers have of late made frequent mention of Wat Tyler. That his memory should be traduced by court sycophants, and all those who live on the spoil of a public, is not to be wondered at. He was, however, the means of checking the rage and injustice of taxation in his time, and the nation owed much to his valor. The history is concisely this:—In the time of Richard II a poll-tax was levied, of one shilling per head, upon every person in the nation, of whatever estate or condition, on poor as well as rich, above the age of fifteen years.

If any favor was shown in the law, it was to the rich rather than to the poor; as no person could be charged more than twenty shillings for himself, family and servants, though ever so numerous; while all other families, under the number of twenty, were

With the Revolution of 1688, and more so since the Hanover Succession, came the destructive system of continental intrigues, and the rage of foreign wars and foreign dominion; systems of such secure mystery, that the expenses admit of no accounts; a single line stands for millions. To what excess taxation might have extended, had not the French Revolution contributed to break up the system, and put an end to pretenses, it is impossible to say.

Viewed as that revolution ought to be, as the fortunate means of lessening the load of taxes of both countries, it is of as much importance to England as to France; and, if properly improved to all the advantages of which it is capable, and to which it leads, deserves as much celebration in one country as the other.

In pursuing this subject, I shall begin with the matter that first presents itself, that of lessening the burden of taxes; and shall then add such matters and propositions, respecting the three countries of England, France, and America, as the present prospect of things appears to justify; I mean an alliance of the three, for the purposes that will be mentioned in their proper place.

What has happened may happen again. By the statement before

---

charged per head. Poll-taxes had always been odious; but this, being also oppressive and unjust, it excited, as it naturally must, universal detestation among the poor and middle classes.

The person known by the name of Wat Tyler, whose proper name was Walter, and a tyler by trade, lived at Deptford. The gatherer of the poll-tax, on coming to his house, demanded tax for one of his daughters, whom Tyler declared was under the age of fifteen. The tax-gatherer insisted on satisfying himself, and began an indecent examination of the girl, which enraging the father, he struck him with a hammer, that brought him to the ground, and was the cause of his death.

This circumstance served to bring the discontents to an issue. The inhabitants of the neighborhood espoused the cause of Tyler, who in a few days was joined, according to some histories, by upwards of fifty thousand men, and chosen their chief. With this force he marched to London, to demand an abolition of the tax, and a redress of their grievances. The court, finding itself in a forlorn condition, and unable to make resistance, agreed, with Richard at its head, to hold a conference with Tyler in Smithfield, making many fair professions, courtier-like, of its disposition to redress the oppressions.

While Richard and Tyler were in conversation on these matters, each being on horseback, Walworth, then Mayor of London, and one of the creatures of the court, watched an opportunity, and like a cowardly assassin, stabbed Tyler with a dagger; and two or three others falling upon him, he was instantly sacrificed.

Tyler appears to have been an intrepid, disinterested man, with respect to himself. All his proposals made to Richard, were on a more just and public ground, than those which had been made to John by the barons; and notwithstanding the sycophancy of historians, and men like Mr. Burke, who seek to gloss over a base action of the court by traducing Tyler, his fame will outlive their falsehood. If the barons merited a monument to be erected in Runneymede, Tyler merits one in Smithfield.—*Author.*

shown, of the progress of taxation, it is seen, that taxes have been lessened to a fourth part of what they had formerly been. Though the present circumstances do not admit of the same reduction, yet they admit of such a beginning, as may accomplish that end in a less time, than in the former case.

The amount of taxes for the year, ending at Michaelmas, 1788, was as follows:

Land tax	£1,950,000
Customs	3,789,274
Excise (including old and new malt)	6,751,727
Stamps	1,278,214
Miscellaneous taxes and incidents	1,803,755
	£15,572,970

Since the year 1788, upwards of one million, new taxes, have been laid on, besides the produce of the lotteries; and as the taxes have in general been more productive since than before, the amount may be taken, in round numbers, at £17,000,000.

N. B. The expense of collection and the drawbacks, which together amount to nearly two millions, are paid out of the gross amount; and the above is the net sum paid into the exchequer.

This sum of seventeen millions is applied to two different purposes; the one to pay the interest of the national debt, the other to pay the current expenses of each year. About nine millions are appropriated to the former; and the remainder, being nearly eight millions, to the latter. As to the million, said to be applied to the reduction of the debt, it is so much like paying with one hand and taking out with the other, as not to merit much notice.

It happened, fortunately for France, that she possessed national domains for paying off her debt, and thereby lessening her taxes; but as this is not the case in England, her reduction of taxes can only take place by reducing the current expenses, which may now be done to the amount of four or five millions annually, as will hereafter appear. When this is accomplished, it will more than counterbalance the enormous charge of the American War; and the saving will be from the same source from whence the evil rose.

As to the national debt, however heavy the interest may be in taxes, yet, as it serves to keep alive a capital, useful to commerce, it balances by its effects a considerable part of its own weight; and as the quantity of gold and silver in England is, by some means or other, short of its proper proportion [36] (being not more than twenty millions, whereas it should be sixty), it would, besides the injustice, be bad policy to extinguish a capital that serves to supply that defect. But, with respect to the current expense, whatever is saved therefrom is gain. The excess may serve to keep corruption alive, but it has no reaction on credit and commerce, like the interest of the debt.

It is now very probable, that the English Government (I do not mean the nation) is unfriendly to the French Revolution. Whatever serves to expose the intrigue and lessen the influence of courts, by lessening taxation, will be unwelcome to those who feed upon the spoil. Whilst the clamor of French intrigue, arbitrary power, popery, and wooden shoes, could be kept up, the nations were easily allured and alarmed into taxes. Those days are now past; deception, it is to be hoped, has reaped its last harvest, and better times are in prospect for both countries, and for the world.

Taking it for granted that an alliance may be formed between England, France and America, for the purposes hereafter to be mentioned, the national expenses of France and England may consequently be lessened. The same fleets and armies will no longer be necessary to either, and the reduction can be made ship for ship on each side. But to accomplish these objects, the governments must necessarily be fitted to a common correspondent principle. Confidence can never take place while a hostile disposition remains in either, or where mystery and secrecy on one side is opposed to candor and openness on the other.

These matters admitted, the national expenses might be put back, *for the sake of a precedent,* to what they were at some period when France and England were not enemies. This, consequently must be prior to the Hanover Succession, and also to the Revolution of 1688.[37] The first

[36] Foreign intrigues, foreign wars, and foreign dominions, will in a great measure account for the deficiency.—*Author.*

[37] I happened to be in England at the celebration of the centenary of the Revolution of 1688. The characters of William and Mary have always appeared to me detestable; the one seeking to destroy his uncle, and the other her father, to get possession of power themselves: yet, as the nation was disposed to think something of that event, I felt hurt at seeing it ascribe the whole reputation of it to a man who had undertaken it as a job, and who, besides what he otherwise got, charged £600,000 for the expense of the little fleet that brought him from Holland.

George I acted the same close-fisted part as William had done, and bought the Duchy of Bremen with the money he got from England, two hundred and fifty thousand instance that presents itself, antecedent to those dates, is in the very wasteful and profligate times of Charles II, at which time England and France acted as allies. If I have chosen a period of great extravagance, it will serve to show modern extravagance in a still worse light; especially, as the pay of the navy, the army, and the revenue-officers has not increased since that time.

The peace establishment was then as follows: (See Sir John Sinclair's "History of the Revenue").

Navy	£300,000
Army	212,000
Ordnance	40,000
Civil List	462,115
	£1,014,115

The Parliament, however, settled the whole annual peace establishment of £1,200,000.[38] If we go back to the time of Elizabeth, the amount of all the taxes was but half a million, yet the nation sees nothing, during that period, but reproaches it with want of consequence.

All circumstances, then, taken together, arising from the French Revolution, from the approaching harmony and reciprocal interest of the two nations, the abolition of court intrigue on both sides, and the progress of knowledge in the science of government, the annual expenditure might be put back to one million and a half, *viz.*

Navy	£500,000
Army	500,000
Expenses of government	500,000
	£1,500,000

Even this sum is six times greater than the expenses of government are in America, yet the civil internal government of England (I mean

---

pounds over and above his pay as king; and having thus purchased it at the expense of England, added it to his Hanoverian dominions for his own private benefit. In fact, every nation that does not govern itself, is governed as a job. England has been the prey of jobs ever since the Revolution.—*Author*.

[38] Charles, like his predecessors and successors, finding that war was the harvest of governments, engaged in a war with the Dutch, the expense of which increased the annual expenditure to £1,800,000 as stated under the date of 1666; but the peace establishment was but £1,200,000.—*Author*.

that administered by means of quarter-sessions, juries, and assize, and which, in fact, is nearly the whole, and is performed by the nation), is less expense upon the revenue, than the same species and portion of government is in America.

It is time that nations should be rational, and not be governed like animals for the pleasure of their riders. To read the history of kings, a man would be almost inclined to suppose that government consisted in stag-hunting, and that every nation paid a million a year to the huntsman. Man ought to have pride or shame enough to blush at being thus imposed upon, and when he feels his proper character, he will.

Upon all subjects of this nature, there is often passing in the mind a train of ideas he has not yet accustomed himself to encourage and communicate. Restrained by something that puts on the character of prudence, he acts the hypocrite upon himself as well as to others. It is, however, curious to observe how soon this spell can be dissolved. A single expression, boldly conceived and uttered, will sometimes put a whole company into their proper feelings, and whole nations are acted upon in the same manner.

As to the offices of which any civil government may be composed, it matters but little by what names they are described. In the routine of business, as before observed, whether a man be styled a president, a king, an emperor, a senator, or any thing else, it is impossible that any service he can perform, can merit from a nation more than ten thousand pounds a year; and as no man should be paid beyond his services, so every man of a proper heart will not accept more.

Public money ought to be touched with the most scrupulous consciousness of honor. It is not the produce of riches only, but of the hard earnings of labor and poverty. It is drawn even from the bitterness of want and misery. Not a beggar passes, or perishes in the streets, whose mite is not in that mass.

Were it possible that the Congress of America, could be so lost to their duty, and to the interest of their constituents, as to offer General Washington, as President of America, a million a year, he would not, and he could not accept it. His sense of honor is of another kind. It has cost England almost seventy millions sterling, to maintain a family imported from abroad, of very inferior capacity to thousands in the nation; and scarcely a year has passed that has not produced some new mercenary application. Even the physicians' bills have been sent to the public to be paid.

No wonder that jails are crowded, and taxes and poor-rates increased. Under such systems, nothing is to be looked for but what has already happened; and as to reformation, whenever it comes, it must be from the nation, and not from the government.

To show that the sum of five hundred thousand pounds is more than sufficient to defray all the expenses of government, exclusive of navies and armies, the following estimate is added for any country, of the same extent as England.

In the first place, three hundred representatives, fairly elected, are sufficient for all the purposes to which legislation can apply, and preferable to a larger number. They may be divided into two or three houses, or meet in one, as in France, or in any manner a constitution shall direct.

As representation is always considered in free countries as the most honorable of all stations, the allowance made to it is merely to defray the expenses which the representatives incur by that service, and not to it as an office.

If an allowance at the rate of five hundred pounds per annum be made to every representative, deducting for non-attendance, the expense, if the whole number attended for six months each year would be .... £ 75,000

The official departments cannot reasonably exceed the following number, with the salaries annexed:

Three offices, at ten thousand pounds each	30,000
Ten ditto, at five thousand pounds each	50,000
Twenty ditto, at two thousand pounds each	40,000
Forty ditto, at one thousand pounds each	40,000
Two hundred ditto, at five hundred pounds each	100,000
Three hundred ditto, at two hundred pounds each	60,000
Five hundred ditto, at one hundred pounds each	50,000
Seven hundred ditto, at seventy-five pounds each	52,500
	£497,500

If a nation chooses, it can deduct four per cent from all offices, and make one of twenty thousand per annum.

All revenue-officers are paid out of the monies they collect, and therefore, are not included in this estimation.

The foregoing is not offered as an exact detail of offices, but to show the number and rate of salaries which five hundred thousand pounds will support; and it will, on experience, be found impracticable to find business sufficient to justify even this expense. As to the manner in which office business is now performed, the chiefs in several offices, such as the postoffice, and certain offices in the exchequer, etc., do little more than sign their names three or four times a year; and the whole duty is performed by under-clerks.

Taking, therefore, one million and a half as a sufficient peace establishment for all the honest purposes of government, which is three thousand pounds more than the peace establishment in the profligate and prodigal times of Charles II (notwithstanding, as has been already observed, the pay and salaries of the army, navy, and revenue-officers, continue the same as at that period), there will remain a surplus of upwards of six millions out of the present current expenses. The question then will be, how to dispose of this surplus.

Whoever has observed the manner in which trade and taxes twist themselves together, must be sensible of the impossibility of separating them suddenly.

First, Because the articles now on hand are already charged with the duty, and the reduction cannot take place on the present stock.

Secondly, Because, on all those articles on which the duty is charged in the gross, such as per barrel, hogshead, hundred weight, or ton, the abolition of the duty does not admit of being divided down so as fully to relieve the consumer, who purchases by the pint, or the pound. The last duty paid on strong beer and ale, was three shillings per barrel, which, if taken off, would lessen the purchase only half a farthing per pint, and consequently, would not reach to practical relief.

This being the condition of a greater part of the taxes, it will be necessary to look for such others as are free from this embarrassment, and where the relief will be direct and visible, and capable of immediate operation.

In the first place, then, the poor-rates are a direct tax which every housekeeper feels, and who knows also, to a farthing, the sum which he pays. The national amount of the whole of the poor-rates is not positively known, but can be procured. Sir John Sinclair in his "History of the Revenue," has stated it at £2,100,587, a considerable part of which is expended in litigations, in which the poor, instead of being relieved, are tormented. The expense, however, is the same to the parish, from whatever cause it arises.

In Birmingham, the amount of the poor-rates is fourteen thousand pounds a year. This, though a large sum, is moderate compared with the population. Birmingham is said to contain seventy thousand souls, and on a proportion of seventy thousand to fourteen thousand pounds poor-rates, the national amount of poor-rates, taking the population of England at seven millions, would be but one million four hundred thousand pounds. It is, therefore, most probable, that the population of Birmingham is over-rated. Fourteen thousand pounds is the proportion upon fifty thousand souls, taking two millions of poor-rates as the national amount.

Be it, however, what it may, it is no other than the consequence of the excessive burden of taxes, for, at the time when the taxes were very low, the poor were able to maintain themselves; and there were no poor-rates.[39] In the present state of things, a laboring man, with a wife and two or three children, does not pay less than between seven and eight pounds a year in taxes. He is not sensible of this, because it is disguised to him in the articles which he buys, and he thinks only of their dearness; but as the taxes take from him, at least, a fourth part of his yearly earnings, he is consequently disabled from providing for a family, especially if himself, or any of them, are afflicted with sickness.

The first step, therefore, of practical relief, would be to abolish the poor-rates entirely, and, in lieu thereof, to make a remission of taxes to the poor to double the amount of the present poor-rates, viz., four millions annually out of the surplus taxes. By this measure, the poor would be benefited two millions, and the housekeepers two millions. This alone would be equal to a reduction of one hundred and twenty millions of the national debt, and consequently equal to the whole expense of the American War.

It will then remain to be considered, which is the most effectual mode of distributing the remission of four millions.

It is easily seen, that the poor are generally composed of large families of children, and old people unable to labor. If these two classes are provided for, the remedy will so far reach to the full extent of the case, that what remains will be incidental, and, in a great measure, fall within the compass of benefit clubs, which, though of humble invention, merit to be ranked among the best of modern institutions.

Admitting England to contain seven millions of souls; if one-fifth thereof are of that class of poor which need support, the number will be

[39] Poor-rates began about the time of Henry VIII when taxes began to increase, and they have increased as the taxes increased ever since.—*Author*.

one million four hundred thousand. Of this number, one hundred and forty thousand will be aged poor, as will be hereafter shown, and for which a distinct provision will be proposed.

There will then remain one million two hundred and sixty thousand, which, at five souls to each family, amount to two hundred and fifty-two thousand families, rendered poor from the expense of children and the weight of taxes.

The number of children under fourteen years of age, in each of those families, will be found to be about five to every two families; some having two, others three; some one, and others four; some none, and others five; but it rarely happens that more than five are under fourteen years of age, and after this age they are capable of service, or of being apprenticed.

Allowing five children (under fourteen years) to every two families,

The number of children will be 630,000
The number of parents (were they all living) would be 504,000

It is certain that if the children are provided for, the parents are relieved of consequence, because it is from the expense of bringing up children that their poverty arises.

Having thus ascertained the greatest number that can be supposed to need support on account of young families, I proceed to the mode of relief, or distribution, which is,

To pay as a remission of taxes to every poor family, out of the surplus taxes and in room of poor-rates, four pounds a year for every child under fourteen years of age; enjoining the parents of such children to send them to school, to learn reading, writing, and common arithmetic; the ministers of every parish, of every denomination, to certify jointly to an office, for this purpose, that the duty is performed. The amount of this expense will be:

For six hundred and thirty thousand children at four
pounds each per annum £2,520,000

By adopting this method, not only the poverty of the parents will be relieved, but ignorance will be banished from the rising generation, and the number of poor will hereafter become less, because their abilities, by the aid of education, will be greater. Many a youth, with good natural genius, who is apprenticed to a mechanical trade, such as a carpenter, joiner, millwright, blacksmith, etc., is prevented getting forward the whole of his life, from the want of a little common education when a boy.

I now proceed to the case of the aged.

I divide age into two classes. First, the approach of old age, beginning at fifty. Secondly, old age commencing at sixty.

At fifty, though the mental faculties of man are in full vigor, and his judgment better than at any preceding date, the bodily powers are on the decline. He cannot bear the same quantity of fatigue as at an earlier period. He begins to earn less, and is less capable of enduring the wind and weather; and in those retired employments where much sight is required, he fails apace, and feels himself like an old horse, beginning to be turned adrift.

At sixty, his labor ought to be over, at least from direct necessity. It is painful to see old age working itself to death, in what are called civilized countries, for its daily bread.

To form some judgment of the number of those above fifty years of age, I have several times counted the persons I met in the streets of London, men, women, and children, and have generally found that the average is one in about sixteen or seventeen. If it be said that aged persons do not come much into the streets, so neither do infants; and a great proportion of grown children are in schools, and in the work-shops as apprentices. Taking then sixteen for a divisor, the whole number of persons, in England, of fifty years and upwards, of both sexes, rich and poor, will be four hundred and twenty thousand.

The persons to be provided for out of this gross number will be husbandmen, common laborers, journeymen of every trade and their wives, sailors, and disbanded soldiers, worn-out servants of both sexes, and poor widows.

There will be also a considerable number of middling tradesmen, who, having lived decently in the former part of life, begin, as age approaches, to lose their business, and at last fall into decay.

Besides these, there will be constantly thrown off from the revolutions of that wheel, which no man can stop, nor regulate, a number from every class of life connected with commerce and adventure.

To provide for all those accidents, and whatever else may befall, I take the number of persons, who at one time or other of their lives, after fifty years of age, may feel it necessary or comfortable to be better supported, than they can support themselves, and that not as a matter of grace and favor, but of right, at one-third of the whole number, which is one hundred and forty thousand, as stated in a previous page, and for whom a distinct provision was to be made. If there be more, society, notwithstanding the show and pomposity of government, is in a deplorable condition in England.

Of this one hundred and forty thousand, I take one-half, seventy thousand, to be of the age of fifty and under sixty, and the other half to be sixty years and upwards. Having thus ascertained the probable proportion of the number of aged persons, I proceed to the mode of rendering their condition comfortable, which is,

To pay to every such person of the age of fifty years, and until he shall arrive at the age of sixty, the sum of six pounds per annum out of the surplus taxes; and ten pounds per annum during life, after the age of sixty. The expense of which will be:

Seventy thousand persons at six pounds per annum	£420,000
Seventy thousand persons at ten pounds per annum	700,000
	£1,120,000

This support, as already remarked, is not of the nature of charity, but of a right. Every person in England, male or female, pays on an average of taxes, two pounds eight shillings and sixpence per annum from the day of his (or her) birth; and if the expense of collection be added, he pays two pounds, eleven shillings and sixpence; consequently, at the end of fifty years, he has paid one hundred and twenty-eight pounds fifteen shillings; and at sixty, one hundred and fifty-four pounds ten shillings.

Converting, therefore, his (or her) individual tax into a tontine, the money he shall receive after fifty years, is but little more than the legal interest of the net money he has paid; the rest is made up from those whose circumstances do not require them to draw such support, and the capital in both cases defrays the expenses of government.

It is on this ground that I have extended the probable claims to one-third of the number of aged persons in the nation. Is it then better that the lives of one hundred and forty thousand aged persons be rendered comfortable, or that a million a year of public money be expended on any one individual, and he often of the most worthless and insignificant character? Let reason and justice, let honor and humanity, let even hypocrisy, sycophancy, and Mr. Burke, let George, let Louis, Leopold, Frederic, Catherine, Cornwallis, or Tippoo Saib, answer the question.[40]

The sum thus remitted to the poor will be:

To two hundred and fifty-two thousand poor families, containing six hundred and thirty thousand children.......	£2,520,000
To one hundred and fifty thousand aged persons	1,120,000
	£3,640,000

There will then remain three hundred and sixty thousand pounds out of the four millions, part of which may be applied as follows:

After all the above cases are provided for, there will still be a number of families who, though not properly of the class of poor, yet find it difficult to give education to their children, and such children, under such a case, would be in a worse condition than if their parents were actually poor. A nation under a well regulated government should permit none to remain uninstructed. It is monarchical and aristocratical governments, only, that require ignorance for their support.

Suppose then four hundred thousand children to be in this condition, which is a greater number than ought to be supposed, after the provisions already made, the method will be:

To allow for each of those children ten shillings a year for the expense of schooling, for six years each, which will give them six months schooling each year, and half a crown a year for paper and spelling books.

---

[40] Reckoning the taxes by families, five to a family, each family pays on an average £12 17 6 per annum: To this sum are to be added the poor-rates. Though all pay taxes in the articles they consume, all do not pay poor-rates. About two millions are exempted, some as not being housekeepers, others as not being able, and the poor themselves who receive the relief. The average, therefore, of poor-rates on the remaining number, is forty shillings for every family of five persons, which makes the whole average amount of taxes and rates £14 17 6. For six persons, £17 17. For seven persons, £20 16 6.

The average of taxes in America, under the new or representative system of government, including the interest of the debt contracted in the war, and taking the population at four millions of souls, which it now amounts to, and is daily increasing, is five shillings per head, men, women and children. The difference, therefore, between the two governments, is as under:

	England.	America.
For a family of five persons	£14 17 6	£1 5 0
For a family of six persons	17 17 0	1 10 0
For a family of seven persons	20 16 6	1 15 0

—*Author.*

The expense of this will be annually [41] £250,000.

There will then remain one hundred and ten thousand pounds.

Notwithstanding the great modes of relief which the best instituted and best principled government may devise, there will still be a number of smaller cases, which it is good policy as well as beneficence in a nation to consider.

Were twenty shillings to be given to every woman immediately on the birth of a child, who should make the demand, and none will make it whose circumstances do not require it, it might relieve a great deal of instant distress.

There are about two hundred thousand births yearly in England; and if claimed by one-fourth,

The amount would be £50,000

And twenty shillings to every new married couple who should claim in like manner. This would not exceed the sum of £20,000

Also twenty thousand pounds to be appropriated to defray the funeral expenses of persons, who, traveling for work, may die at a distance from their friends. By relieving parishes from this charge, the sick stranger will be better treated.

I shall finish this part of my subject with a plan adapted to the particular condition of a metropolis, such as London.

Cases are continually occurring in a metropolis different from those which occur in the country, and for which a different, or rather an additional mode of relief is necessary. In the country, even in large towns, people have a knowledge of each other and distress never rises to that extreme height it sometimes does in a metropolis. There is no such thing in the country as persons, in the literal sense of the word, starved to death, or dying with cold from the want of a lodging. Yet such cases, and others equally as miserable, happen in London.

[41] Public schools do not answer the general purpose of the poor. They are chiefly in corporation-towns, from which the country towns and villages are excluded; or, if admitted, the distance occasions a great loss of time. Education, to be useful to the poor, should be on the spot; and the best method, I believe, to accomplish this, is to enable the parents to pay the expense themselves. There are always persons of both sexes to be found in every village, especially when growing into years, capable of such an undertaking. Twenty children, at ten shillings each (and that not more than six months in each year), would be as much as some livings amount to in the remote parts of England; and there are often distressed clergymen's widows to whom such an income would be acceptable. Whatever is given on this account to children answers two purposes: to them it is education, to those who educate them it is a livelihood.—*Author.*

Many a youth comes up to London full of expectations, and little or no money, and unless he gets employment he is already half undone; and boys bred up in London without any means of a livelihood, and, as it often happens, of dissolute parents, are in a still worse condition, and servants long out of place are not much better off. In short, a world of little cases is continually arising, which busy or affluent life knows not of, to open the first door to distress. Hunger is not among the postponable wants, and a day, even a few hours, in such a condition, is often the crisis of a life of ruin.

These circumstances, which are the general cause of the little thefts and pilferings that lead to greater, may be prevented. There yet remain twenty thousand pounds out of the four millions of surplus taxes, which, with another fund hereafter to be mentioned, amounting to about twenty thousand pounds more, cannot be better applied than to this purpose. The plan then will be:

First, To erect two or more buildings, or take some already erected, capable of containing at least six thousand persons, and to have in each of these places as many kinds of employment as can be contrived, so that every person who shall come, may find something which he or she can do.

Secondly, To receive all who shall come, without inquiring who or what they are. The only condition to be, that for so much or so many hours work, each person shall receive so many meals of wholesome food, and a warm lodging, at least as good as a barrack. That a certain portion of what each person's work shall be worth shall be reserved, and given to him, or her, on their going away; and that each person shall stay as long, or as short time, or come as often as he chooses, on these conditions.

If each person staid three months, it would assist by rotation twenty-four thousand persons annually, though the real number, at all times, would be but six thousand. By establishing an asylum of this kind, such persons, to whom temporary distresses occur, would have an opportunity to recruit themselves, and be enabled to look out for better employment.

Allowing that their labor paid but one-half the expense of supporting them, after reserving a portion of their earnings for themselves, the sum of forty thousand pounds additional would defray all other charges for even a greater number than six thousand.

The fund properly convertible to this purpose, in addition to the twenty thousand pounds, remaining of the former fund, will be the produce of the tax upon coals, and so iniquitously and wantonly applied to the support of the Duke of Richmond. It is horrid that any man, more especially at the price coals now are, should live on the distresses of a community; and any government permitting such an abuse deserves to be dissolved. This fund is said to be about twenty thousand pounds per annum.

I shall now conclude this plan with enumerating the several particulars, and then proceed to other matters.

The enumeration is as follows:

First, Abolition of two millions poor-rates.

Secondly, Provision for two hundred and fifty-two thousand poor families.

Thirdly, Education for one million and thirty thousand children.

Fourthly, Comfortable provision for one hundred and forty thousand aged persons.

Fifthly, Donation of twenty shillings each for fifty thousand births.

Sixthly, Donation of twenty shillings each for twenty thousand marriages.

Seventhly, Allowance of twenty thousand pounds for the funeral expenses of persons traveling for work, and dying at a distance from their friends.

Eighthly, Employment, at all times, for the casual poor in the cities of London and Westminster.

By the operation of this plan, the poor laws, those instruments of civil torture, will be superseded, and the wasteful expense of litigation prevented. The hearts of the humane will not be shocked by ragged and hungry children, and persons of seventy and eighty years of age begging for bread. The dying poor will not be dragged from place to place to breathe their last, as a reprisal of parish upon parish.

Widows will have maintenance for their children, and will not be carted away, on the death of their husbands, like culprits and criminals; and children will no longer be considered as increasing the distress of their parents. The haunts of the wretched will be known, because it will be to their advantage; and the number of petty crimes, the offspring of distress and poverty, will be lessened. The poor, as well as the rich, will then be interested in the support of government, and the cause and apprehension of riots and tumults will cease.

Ye who sit in ease, and solace yourselves in plenty, and such there are in Turkey and Russia, as well as in England, and who say to yourselves, "Are we not well off," have ye thought of these things? When ye do, ye will cease to speak and feel for yourselves alone.

The plan is easy of practise. It does not embarrass trade by a sudden interruption in the order of taxes, but effects the relief by changing the application of them; and the money necessary for the purpose can be drawn from the excise collections, which are made eight times a year in every market town in England.

Having now arranged and concluded this subject, I proceed to the next.

Taking the present current expenses at seven millions and a half, which is the least amount they are now at, there will remain (after the sum of one million and a half be taken for the new current expenses, and four millions for the before mentioned service) the sum of two millions, part of which to be applied as follows:

Though fleets and armies, by an alliance with France, will, in a great measure, become useless, yet the persons who have devoted themselves to those services, and have thereby unfitted themselves for other lines of life, are not to be sufferers by the means that make others happy. They are a different description of men to those who form or hang about a court.

A part of the army will remain at least for some years, and also of the navy, for which a provision is already made, in the former part of this plan, of one million, which is almost half a million more than the peace establishment of the army and navy in the prodigal times of Charles II.

Suppose, then, fifteen thousand soldiers to be disbanded, and to allow to each of those men three shillings a week during life, clear of all deductions, to be paid in the same manner as the Chelsea college pensioners are paid, and for them to return to their trades and their friends; and also to add fifteen thousand sixpences per week to the pay of the soldiers who shall remain; the annual expense will be:

To the pay of fifteen thousand disbanded soldiers, at three
shillings per week £117,000
Additional pay to the remaining soldiers 19,500
Suppose the pay to the officers of the disbanded corps be of
the same amount as the sum allowed to the men 117,000
                                                          _____
                                                          £253,500

To prevent bulky estimations, admit the same sum to the
disbanded navy as to the army, and the same increase of
pay 253,500

Total, £507,000

Every year some part of this sum of half a million (I omit the odd
seven thousand pounds, for the purpose of keeping the account unem-
barrassed) will fall in, and the whole of it in time, as it is on the ground
of life annuities, except the increased pay of thirty-nine thousand pounds.
As it falls in, a part of the taxes may be taken off; for instance, when
thirty thousand pounds fall in, the duty on hops may be wholly taken
off; and as other parts fall in, the duties on candles and soap may be
lessened, till at last they will totally cease. There now remains at least
one million and a half of surplus taxes.

The tax on houses and windows is one of those direct taxes, which,
like the poor-rates, is not confounded with trade; and when taken off,
the relief will be instantly felt. This tax falls heavy on the middle class
of people.

The amount of this tax by the returns of 1788, was:

Houses and windows by the act of 1766 .... £385,459 11 7
Houses and windows by the act of 1779 .... 130,739 14 5½

Total, £516,199 6 0½

If this tax be struck off, there will then remain about one million of
surplus taxes, and as it is always proper to keep a sum in reserve, for
incidental matters, it may be best not to extend reductions further, in
the first instance, but to consider what may be accomplished by other
modes of reform.

Among the taxes most heavily felt is the commutation tax. I shall,
therefore, offer a plan for its abolition, by substituting another in its place
which will effect three objects at once:

First, That of removing the burden to where it can best be borne.

Secondly, Restoring justice among families by distribution of property.

Thirdly, Extirpating the overgrown influence arising from the unnatural law of primogeniture, and which is one of the principal sources
of corruption at elections.

The amount of the commutation tax by the returns of 1788, was £771,657.

When taxes are proposed, the country is amused by the plausible language of taxing luxuries. One thing is called a luxury at one time, and something else at another; but the real luxury does not consist in the article, but in the means of procuring it, and this is always kept out of sight.

I know not why any plant or herb of the field should be a greater luxury in one country than in another, but an overgrown estate in either is a luxury at all times, and, as such, is the proper object of taxation. It is, therefore, right to take those kind, tax-making gentlemen upon their own word, and argue on the principle themselves have laid down, that of *taxing luxuries*. If they or their champion, Mr. Burke, who, I fear, is growing out of date like the man in armor, can prove that an estate of twenty, thirty, or forty thousand pounds a year is not a luxury, I will give up the argument.

Admitting that any annual sum, say for instance, one thousand pounds, is necessary or sufficient for the support of a family, consequently the second thousand is of the nature of a luxury, the third still more so, and by proceeding on, we shall at last arrive at a sum that may not improperly be called a prohibitable luxury. It would be impolitic to set bounds to property acquired by industry, and therefore it is right to place the prohibition beyond the probable acquisition to which industry can extend; but there ought to be a limit to property, or the accumulation of it by bequest. It should pass in some other line. The richest in every nation have poor relations, and those very often near in consanguinity.

The following table of progressive taxation is constructed on the above principles, and as a substitute for the commutation tax. It will reach the point of prohibition by a regular operation, and thereby supersede the aristocratical law of primogeniture.

TABLE I

A tax on all estates of the clear yearly value of fifty pounds, after deducting the land tax, and up.

To £500 .... 0s 3d per pound.
From 500 to 1000 .... 0 6 "   "

On the second thousand .... 0s 9d per pound.
On the third   "   .... 1 0 " "
On the fourth   "   .... 1 6 " "
On the fifth   "   .... 2 0 " "
On the sixth   "   .... 3 0 " "
On the seventh   "   .... 4 0 " "
On the eighth   "   .... 5 0 " "
On the ninth   "   .... 6 0 " "
On the tenth   "   .... 7 0 " "
On the eleventh   "   .... 8 0 " "
On the twelfth   "   .... 9 0 " "
On the thirteenth   "   .... 10 0 " "
On the fourteenth   "   .... 11 0 " "
On the fifteenth   "   .... 12 0 " "
On the sixteenth   "   .... 13 0 " "
On the seventeenth   "   .... 14 0 " "
On the eighteenth   "   .... 15 0 " "
On the nineteenth   "   .... 16 0 " "
On the twentieth   "   .... 17 0 " "
On the twenty-first   "   .... 18 0 " "
On the twenty-second "   .... 19 0 " "
On the twenty-third   "   .... 20 0 " "

The foregoing table shows the progression per pound on every progressive thousand. The following table shows the amount of the tax on every thousand separately, and in the last column, the total amount of all the separate sums collected.

TABLE II

An estate of £50 per an. at 3d per pound pays £0 12 6

100	"	"	3	"	"	"	1 5 0
200	"	"	3	"	"	"	2 10 0
300	"	"	3	"	"	"	3 15 0
400	"	"	3	"	"	"	5 0 0
500	"	"	3	"	"	"	7 5 0

After £500—the tax of sixpence per pound takes place on the second £500,—consequently an estate of £1000 per annum pays £21 15 and so on.

For the 1st	£500	at	0s	3d	per pound	£7	5	}	£21	15
2d	500	at	0	6	" "	14	10	}		
2d	1000	at	0	9	" "	37	10		59	5
3d	1000	at	1	0	" "	50	0		109	5
4th	1000	at	1	6	" "	75	0		184	5
5th	1000	at	2	0	" "	100	0		284	5
6th	1000	at	3	0	" "	150	0		434	5
7th	1000	at	4	0	" "	200	0		634	5
8th	1000	at	5	0	" "	250	0		880	5
9th	1000	at	6	0	" "	300	0		1180	5
10th	1000	at	7	0	" "	350	0		1530	5
11th	1000	at	8	0	" "	400	0		1930	5
12th	1000	at	9	0	" "	450	0		2380	5
13th	1000	at	10	0	" "	500	0		2880	5
14th	1000	at	11	0	" "	550	0		3430	5
15th	1000	at	12	0	" "	600	0		4030	5
16th	1000	at	13	0	" "	650	0		4680	5
17th	1000	at	14	0	" "	700	0		5380	5
18th	1000	at	15	0	" "	750	0		6130	5
19th	1000	at	16	0	" "	800	0		6930	5
20th	1000	at	17	0	" "	850	0		7780	5
21st	1000	at	18	0	" "	900	0		8680	5
22d	1000	at	19	0	" "	950	0		9630	5
23d	1000	at	20	0	" "	1000	0		10630	5

At the twenty-third thousand the tax becomes twenty shillings in the pound, and, consequently, every thousand beyond that sum, can produce no profit but by dividing the estate. Yet, formidable as this tax appears, it will not, I believe, produce so much as the commutation tax; should it produce more, it ought to be lowered to that amount upon estates under two or three thousand a year.

On small and middling estates it is lighter (as it is intended to be) than the commutation tax. It is not till after seven or eight thousand a year that it begins to be heavy. The object is not so much the produce of the tax as the justice of the measure. The aristocracy has screened itself too much, and this serves to restore a part of the lost equilibrium.

As an instance of screening itself, it is only necessary to look back to the first establishment of the excise laws, at what is called the Revolution, or the coming of Charles II. The aristocratical interest then in power, commuted the feudal services itself was under, by laying a tax on beer brewed for *sale;* that is, they compounded with Charles for an exemption from those services for themselves and their heirs, by a tax to be paid by other people. The aristocracy do not purchase beer brewed for sale, but brew their own beer free of the duty, and if any commutation at that time was necessary, it ought to have been at the expense of those for whom the exemptions from those services were intended; [42] instead of which, it was thrown on an entire different class of men.

But the chief object of this progressive tax (besides the justice of rendering taxes more equal than they are) is, as already stated, to extirpate the overgrown influence arising from the unnatural law of primogeniture, and which is one of the principal sources of corruption at elections.

It would be attended with no good consequences to inquire how such vast estates as thirty, forty, or fifty thousand a year could commence, and that at a time when commerce and manufactures were not in a state to admit of such acquisitions. Let it be sufficient to remedy the evil by putting them in a condition of descending again to the community by the quiet means of apportioning them among all the heirs and heiresses of those families. This will be the more necessary, because hitherto the aristocracy have quartered their younger children and connections upon the public, in useless posts, places and offices, which, when abolished, will leave them destitute, unless the law of primogeniture be also abolished or superseded.

A progressive tax will, in a great measure, effect this object, and that as a matter of interest to the parties most immediately concerned, as will be seen by the following table; which shows the net produce upon every estate, after substracting the tax.

By this it will appear, that after an estate exceeds thirteen or fourteen thousand a year, the remainder produces but little profit to the holder, and consequently, will either pass to the younger children or to other kindred.

---

[42] The tax on beer brewed for sale, from which the aristocracy are exempt, is almost one million more than the present commutation tax, being by the returns of 1788, £1,666,152, and consequently they ought to take on themselves the amount of the commutation tax, as they are already exempted from one which is almost a million greater.— *Author.*

TABLE III

Showing the net produce of every estate from one thousand to twenty-three thousand pounds a year.

No. of thousands per annum.	Total tax subtracted.	Net produce.
£1000	£21	£979
2000	59	1941
3000	109	2891
4000	184	3816
5000	284	4716
6000	434	5566
7000	634	6366
8000	880	7120
9000	1180	7820
10,000	1530	8480
11,000	1930	9070
12,000	2380	9620
13,000	2880	10,120
14,000	3430	10,670
15,000	4030	10,970
16,000	4680	11,320
17,000	5380	11,620
18,000	6130	11,870
19,000	6930	12,170
20,000	7780	12,220
21,000	8680	12,320
22,000	9630	12,370
23,000	10,630	12,370

N.B. The odd shillings are dropped in this table.

According to this table, an estate cannot produce more than £12,370 clear of the land tax and the progressive tax, and therefore the dividing such estates will follow as a matter of family interest. An estate of £23,000 a year, divided into five estates of four thousand each and one of three, will be charged only £1,129, which is but five per cent, but if held by any one possessor, will be charged £10,630.

Although an inquiry into the origin of those estates be unnecessary, the continuation of them in their present state is another subject. It is a matter of national concern. As hereditary estates, the law has created the evil, and it ought also to provide the remedy. Primogeniture ought to be abolished, not only because it is unnatural and unjust, but because the country suffers by its operation.

By cutting off (as before observed) the younger children from their proper portion of inheritance, the public is loaded with the expense of maintaining them; and the freedom of elections violated by the overbearing influence which this unjust monopoly of family property produces. Nor is this all. It occasions a waste of national property. A considerable part of the land of the country is rendered unproductive, by the great extent of parks and chases which this law serves to keep up, and this at a time when the annual production of grain is not equal to the national consumption.[43]

In short the evils of the aristocratical system are so great and numerous, and so inconsistent with every thing that is just, wise, natural, and beneficent, that when they are considered, there ought not to be a doubt that many, who are now classed under that description, will wish to see such a system abolished.

What pleasure can they derive from contemplating the exposed condition and almost certain beggary of their younger offspring? Every aristocratical family has an appendage of family beggars hanging round it, which, in a few ages, or a few generations, are shook off, and console themselves with telling their tale in almshouses, work-houses and prisons. This is the natural consequence of aristocracy. The peer and the beggar are often of the same family. One extreme produces the other; to make one rich many must be made poor; neither can the system be supported by other means.

There are two classes of people to whom the laws of England are particularly hostile, and those the most helpless: younger children and the poor. Of the former I have just spoken; of the latter I shall mention one instance out of the many that might be produced, and with which I shall close this subject.

Several laws are in existence for regulating and limiting workmen's wages. Why not leave them as free to make their own bargains, as the law-makers are to let their farms and houses? Personal labor is all the property they have. Why is that little, and the little freedom they enjoy,

[43] See the Reports on the Corn Trade.—*Author.*

to be infringed? But the injustice will appear stronger, if we consider the operation and effect of such laws. When wages are fixed by what is called a law, the legal wages remain stationary, while every thing else is in progression; and as those who make that law, still continue to lay on new taxes by other laws, they increase the expense of living by one law, and take away the means by another.

But if these gentlemen law-makers and tax-makers thought it right to limit the poor pittance which personal labor can produce, and on which a whole family is to be supported, they certainly must feel themselves happily indulged in a limitation on their own part, of not less than twelve thousand a year, and that of property they never acquired (nor probably any of their ancestors), and of which they have made so ill a use.

Having now finished this subject, I shall bring the several particulars into one view, and then proceed to other matters.

The first eight articles are brought forward from p. 431.

1. Abolition of two millions poor-rates.

2. Provision for two hundred and fifty-two thousand poor families, at the rate of four pounds per head for each child under fourteen years of age; which, with the addition of two hundred and fifty thousand pounds, provides also education for one million and thirty thousand children.

3. Annuity of six pounds per annum each for all poor persons, decayed tradesmen, and others, supposed seventy thousand, of the age of fifty years and until sixty.

4. Annuity of ten pounds each for life for all poor persons, decayed tradesmen and others, supposed seventy thousand, of the age of sixty years.

5. Donation of twenty shillings each for fifty thousand births.

6. Donation of twenty shillings each for twenty thousand marriages.

7. Allowance of twenty thousand pounds for the funeral expenses of persons traveling for work, and dying at a distance from their friends.

8. Employment at all times for the casual poor in the cities of London and Westminster.

Second enumeration.

9. Abolition of the tax on houses and windows.

10. Allowance of three shillings per week for life to fifteen thousand disbanded soldiers, and a proportionate allowance to the officers of the disbanded corps.

11. Increase of pay to the remaining soldiers of £19,500 annually.

12. The same allowance to the disbanded navy, and the same increase of pay, as to the army.

13. Abolition of the commutation tax.

14. Plan of a progressive tax, operating to extirpate the unjust and unnatural law of primogeniture, and the vicious influence of the aristocratical system.[44]

There yet remains, as already stated, one million of surplus taxes. Some part of this will be required for circumstances that do not immediately present themselves, and such part as shall not be wanted, will admit of a further reduction of taxes equal to that amount.

Among the claims that justice requires to be made, the condition of the inferior revenue-officers will merit attention. It is a reproach to any government to waste such an immensity of revenue in sinecures and nominal and unnecessary places and offices, and not allow even a decent livelihood to those on whom the labor falls. The salary of the inferior officers of the revenue has stood at the petty pittance of less than fifty pounds a year, for upwards of one hundred years. It ought to be seventy. About one hundred and twenty thousand pounds applied to this purpose, will put all those salaries in a decent condition.

This was proposed to be done almost twenty years ago, but the Treasury Board then in being, startled at it, as it might lead to similar expectations from the army and navy; and the event was, that the King, or somebody for him, applied to Parliament to have his own salary

[44] When inquiries are made into the condition of the poor, various degrees of distress will most probably be found, to render a different arrangement preferable to that which is already proposed. Widows with families will be in greater want than where there are husbands living. There is also a difference in the expense of living in different countries; and more so in fuel.

Suppose fifty thousand extraordinary cases at the rate of ten pounds per family per annum	£500,000
100,000 families, at £8 per family per annum	800,000
100,000 families, at 7 " "	700,000
104,000 families, at 5 " "	520,000
And instead of ten shillings per head for the education of other children, to allow fifty shillings per family for that purpose to 50,000 families	250,000
	2,770,000
140,000 aged persons as before.	1,120,000
	£3,890,000

The arrangement amounts to the same sum as stated in p. 428, including the £250,000 for education; but it provides (including the aged people) for four hundred and four thousand families, which is almost one-third of all families in England.—*Author.*

raised a hundred thousand pounds a year, which being done, every thing else was laid aside.[45]

With respect to another class of men, the inferior clergy, I forbear to enlarge on their condition; but all partialities and prejudices for, or against, different modes and forms of religion aside, common justice will determine, whether there ought to be an income of twenty or thirty pounds a year to one man, and of ten thousand to another. I speak on this subject with the more freedom, because I am known not to be a Presbyterian; and therefore the cant cry of court sycophants, about church and meeting, kept up to amuse and bewilder the nation, cannot be raised against me.

Ye simple men on both sides the question, do you not see through this courtly craft? If ye can be kept disputing and wrangling about church and meeting, ye just answer the purpose of every courtier, who lives the while on the spoil of the taxes, and laughs at your credulity. Every religion is good that teaches man to be good; and I know of none that instructs him to be bad.

All the before-mentioned calculations suppose only sixteen millions and a half of taxes paid into the exchequer, after the expense of collection and drawbacks at the custom-house and excise-office are deducted; whereas the sum paid into the exchequer, is very nearly, if not quite, seventeen millions. The taxes raised in Scotland and Ireland are expended in those countries, and therefore their savings will come out of their own taxes; but if any part be paid into the English exchequer, it might be remitted. This will not make one hundred thousand pounds a year difference.

There now remains only the national debt to be considered. In the year 1789, the interest, exclusive of the tontine, was £9,150,138. How much the capital has been reduced since that time the Minister best knows. But after paying the interest, abolishing the tax on houses and windows, the commutation tax and the poor-rates, and making all the provisions for the poor, for the education of children, the support of the aged, the disbanded part of the army and navy, and increasing the pay of the remainder, there will be a surplus of one million.

[45] Paine himself had been involved in the matter under discussion, for in 1772, when he was Exciseman at Lewes, he had written *The Case of the officers of Excise; with remarks on the qualifications of officers; and of the numerous evils arising to the Revenue from the insufficiency of the present salary. Humbly addressed to the Hon. and Right Hon. Members of both Houses of Parliament.* The pamphlet was printed but was not released to the public until 1793. It is published separately in Volume II of the present edition.—*Editor.*

The present scheme of paying off the national debt appears to me, speaking as an indifferent person, to be an ill concerted, if not a fallacious job. The burden of the national debt consists not in its being so many millions, or so many hundred millions, but in the quantity of taxes collected every year to pay the interest. If this quantity continues the same, the burden of the national debt is the same to all intents and purposes, be the capital more or less.

The only knowledge the public can have of the reduction of the debt, must be through the reduction of taxes for paying the interest. The debt, therefore, is not reduced one farthing to the public by all the millions that have been paid; and it would require more money now to purchase up the capital, than when the scheme began.

Digressing for a moment at this point, to which I shall return again, I look back to the appointment of Mr. Pitt as Minister.

I was then in America. The war was over; and though resentment had ceased, memory was still alive.

When the news of the coalition arrived, though it was a matter of no concern to me as a citizen of America, I felt it as a man. It had something in it which shocked, by publicly sporting with decency, if not with principle. It was impudence in Lord North; it was a want of firmness in Mr. Fox.

Mr. Pitt was, at that time, what may be called a maiden character in politics. So far from being hackneyed, he appeared not to be initiated into the first mysteries of court intrigue. Every thing was in his favor. Resentment against the coalition served as friendship to him, and his ignorance of vice was credited for virtue. With the return of peace, commerce and prosperity would rise of itself; yet even this increase was thrown to his account.

When he came to the helm, the storm was over, and he had nothing to interrupt his course. It required even ingenuity to be wrong, and he succeeded. A little time showed him the same sort of man as his predecessors had been. Instead of profiting by those errors which had accumulated a burden of taxes unparalleled in the world, he sought, I might almost say, he advertised for enemies, and provoked means to increase taxation. Aiming at something, he knew not what, he ransacked Europe and India for adventures, and abandoning the fair pretensions he began with, became the knight-errant of modern times.

It is unpleasant to see a character throw itself away. It is more so to see one's self deceived. Mr. Pitt had merited nothing, but he promised much.

He gave symptoms of a mind superior to the meanness and corruption of courts. His apparent candor encouraged expectations; and the public confidence, stunned, wearied, and confounded by a chaos of parties, revived and attached itself to him. But mistaking, as he has done, the disgust of the nation against the coalition, for merit in himself, he has rushed into measures, which a man less supported would not have presumed to act.

All this seems to show that change of ministers amounts to nothing. One goes out, another comes in, and still the same measures, vices, and extravagance are pursued. It signifies not who is minister. The defect lies in the system. The foundation and superstructure of the government is bad. Prop it as you please, it continually sinks into court government, and ever will.

I return, as I promised, to the subject of the national debt, that offspring of the Dutch-Anglo Revolution, and its handmaid, the Hanover Succession.

But it is now too late to inquire how it began. Those to whom it is due have advanced the money; and whether it was well or ill spent, or pocketed, is not their crime. It is, however, easy to see, that as the nation proceeds in contemplating the nature and principles of government, and to understand taxes, and makes comparisons between those of America, France, and England, it will be next to impossible to keep it in the same torpid state it has hitherto been. Some reform must, from the necessity of the case, soon begin. It is not whether these principles press with little or much force in the present moment. They are out. They are abroad in the world, and no force can stop them. Like a secret told, they are beyond recall; and he must be blind indeed that does not see that a change is already beginning.

Nine millions of dead taxes is a serious thing; and this not only for bad, but in a great measure for foreign government. By putting the power of making war into the hands of foreigners who came for what they could get, little else was to be expected than what has happened.

Reasons are already advanced in this work, showing that whatever the reforms in the taxes may be, they ought to be made in the current expenses of government, and not in the part applied to the interest of the national debt. By remitting the taxes of the poor, *they* will be totally relieved and all discontent will be taken away; and by striking off such of the taxes as are already mentioned, the nation will more than recover the whole expense of the mad American War.

There will then remain only the national debt as a subject of discontent, and in order to remove, or rather prevent this, it would be good policy in the stockholders themselves to consider it as property, subject like all other property, to bear some portion of the taxes. It would give to it both popularity and security, and, as a great part of its present inconvenience is balanced by the capital which it keeps alive, a measure of this kind would so far add to that balance as to silence objections.

This may be done by such gradual means as to accomplish all that is necessary with the greatest ease and convenience.

Instead of taxing the capital, the best method would be to tax the interest by some progressive ratio, and to lessen the public taxes in the same proportion as the interest diminished.

Suppose the interest was taxed one half-penny in the pound the first year, a penny more the second, and to proceed by a certain ratio to be determined upon, always less than any other tax upon property. Such a tax would be subtracted from the interest at the time of payment, without any expense of collection.

One halfpenny in the pound would lessen the interest and consequently the taxes, twenty thousand pounds. The tax on wagons amounts to this sum, and this tax might be taken off the first year. The second year the tax on female servants, or some other of the like amount, might also be taken off, and by proceeding in this manner, always applying the tax raised from the property of the debt towards its extinction, and not carrying it to the current services, it would liberate itself.

The stockholders, notwithstanding this tax, would pay less taxes than they do now. What they would save by the extinction of the poor-rates and the tax on houses and windows, and the commutation tax, would be considerably greater than what this tax, slow, but certain in its operation, amounts to.

It appears to me to be prudence to look out for measures that may apply under any circumstances that may approach. There is, at this moment, a crisis in the affairs of Europe that requires it. Preparation now is wisdom. If taxation be once let loose, it will be difficult to reinstate it; neither would the relief be so effectual, as if it proceeded by some certain and gradual reduction.

The fraud, hypocrisy, and imposition of governments are now beginning to be too well understood to promise them any longer career. The farce of monarchy and aristocracy, in all countries, is following that of chivalry, and Mr. Burke is dressing for the funeral. Let it then pass quietly to the tomb of all other follies, and the mourners be comforted.

The time is not very distant, when England will laugh at itself for sending to Holland, Hanover, Zell, or Brunswick for men, at the expense of a million a year, who understood neither her laws, her language, nor her interest, and whose capacities would scarcely have fitted them for the office of a parish constable. If government could be trusted to such hands, it must be some easy and simple thing indeed, and materials fit for all the purposes may be found in every town and village in England.

When it shall be said in any country in the world, "My poor are happy; neither ignorance nor distress is to be found among them; my jails are empty of prisoners, my streets of beggars; the aged are not in want, the taxes are not oppressive; the rational world is my friend, because I am a friend of its happiness":—when these things can be said, then may that country boast of its constitution and its government. Within the space of a few years we have seen two revolutions, those of America and France. In the former, the contest was long and the conflict severe; in the latter, the nation acted with such a consolidated impulse, that having no foreign enemy to contend with, the revolution was complete in power the moment it appeared.

From both those instances it is evident, that the greatest forces that can be brought into the field of revolutions, are reason and common interest. Where these can have the opportunity of acting, opposition dies with fear, or crumbles away by conviction. It is a great standing which they have now universally obtained; and we may hereafter hope to see revolutions, or changes in governments, produced with the same quiet operation by which any measure, determinable by reason and discussion, is accomplished.

When a nation changes its opinion and habits of thinking, it is no longer to be governed as before; but it would not only be wrong, but bad policy, to attempt by force what ought to be accomplished by reason. Rebellion consists in forcibly opposing the general will of a nation, whether by a party or by a government. There ought, therefore, to be in every nation a method of occasionally ascertaining the state of public opinion with respect to government.

On this point the old Government of France was superior to the present Government of England, because, on extraordinary occasions, recourse could be had to what was then called the States-General. But in England there are no such occasional bodies; and as to those who are now called representatives, a great part of them are mere machines of the court, placemen and dependents.

I presume, that though all the people of England pay taxes, not a hundredth part of them are electors, and the members of one of the Houses of Parliament represent nobody but themselves. There is, therefore, no power but the voluntary will of the people that has a right to act in any matter respecting a general reform; and by the same right that two persons can confer on such a subject, a thousand may. The object, in all such preliminary proceedings, is to find out what the general sense of a nation is, and to be governed by it.

If it prefer a bad or defective government to a reform, or choose to pay ten times more taxes than there is any occasion for, it has a right to do so; and so long as the majority do not impose conditions on the minority, different from what they impose upon themselves, though there may be much error, there is no injustice. Neither will the error continue long. Reason and discussion will soon bring things right, however wrong they may begin.

By such a process no tumult is to be apprehended. The poor in all countries are naturally both peaceable and grateful in all reforms in which their interest and happiness are included. It is only by neglecting and rejecting them that they become tumultuous.

The objects that now press on the public attention are the French Revolution, and the prospect of a general revolution in governments. Of all nations in Europe, there is none so much interested in the French Revolution as England. Enemies for ages, and that at a vast expense, and without any national object, the opportunity now presents itself of amicably closing the scene, and joining their efforts to reform the rest of Europe.

By doing this, they will not only prevent the further effusion of blood, and increase of taxes, but be in a condition of getting rid of a considerable part of their present burdens, as has been already stated. Long experience, however, has shown that reforms of this kind are not those which old governments wish to promote, and therefore, it is to nations, and not to such governments, that these matters present themselves.

In the preceding part of this work I have spoken of an alliance between England, France and America, for purposes that were to be afterwards mentioned. Though I have no direct authority on the part of America, I have good reason to conclude, that she is disposed to enter into a consideration of such a measure, provided that the governments with which she might ally, acted as national governments and not as courts enveloped in intrigue and mystery.

That France as a nation and a national government would prefer an alliance with England, is a matter of certainty. Nations, like individuals, who have long been enemies, without knowing each other, or knowing why, become better friends when they discover the errors and impositions under which they had acted.

Admitting, therefore, the probability of such a connection, I will state some matters by which such an alliance, together with that of Holland, might render service, not only to the parties immediately concerned, but to all parts of Europe.

It is, I think, quite certain, that if the fleets of England, France and Holland were confederated, they could propose, with effect, a limitation to, and a general dismantling of, all the navies in Europe, to a certain proportion to be agreed upon.

First, That no new ship of war should be built by any power in Europe, themselves included.

Secondly, That all the navies now in existence shall be put back, suppose to one-tenth of their present force. This will save to France and England at least two millions annually to each, and their relative force be in the same proportion as it is now. If men will permit themselves to think, as rational beings ought to think, nothing can appear more ridiculous and absurd, exclusive of all moral reflections, than to be at the expense of building navies, filling them with men, and then hauling them into the ocean, to try which can sink each other fastest.

Peace, which costs nothing, is attended with infinitely more advantage than any victory with all its expense. But this, though it best answers the purpose of nations, does not that of court governments, whose habitual policy is pretense for taxation, places and offices.

It is, I think, also certain, that the above confederated powers, together with that of the United States of America, can propose, with effect, to Spain, the independence of South America, and the opening those countries, of immense extent and wealth, to the general commerce of the world, as North America now is.

With how much more glory and advantage to itself does a nation act, when it exerts its powers to rescue the world from bondage, and to create to itself friends, than when it employs those powers to increase ruin, desolation and misery. The horrid scene that is now acting by the

English Government in the East Indies, is fit only to be told of Goths and Vandals, who, destitute of principle, robbed and tortured the world which they were incapable of enjoying.

The opening of South America would produce an immense field for commerce, and a ready money market for manufactures, which the Eastern world does not. The East is already a country of manufactures, the importation of which is not only an injury to the manufactures of England, but a drain upon its specie. The balance against England by this trade is regularly upward of half a million annually sent out in the East India ships, in silver; and this is the reason, together with German intrigue, and German subsidies, that there is so little silver in England.

But any war is harvest to such governments, however ruinous it may be to a nation. It serves to keep up deceitful expectations, which prevent people from looking into the defects and abuses of government. It is the *lo here!* and the *lo there!* that amuses and cheats the multitude.

Never did so great an opportunity offer itself to England, and to all Europe, as is produced by the two revolutions of America and France. By the former, freedom has a national champion in the Western world; and by the latter, in Europe. When another nation shall join France, despotism and bad government will scarcely dare to appear. To use a trite expression, the iron is becoming hot all over Europe. The insulted German and the enslaved Spaniard, the Russ and the Pole are beginning to think. The present age will hereafter merit to be called the Age of Reason,[46] and the present generation will appear to the future as the Adam of a new world.

When all the governments of Europe shall be established on the representative system, nations will become acquainted, and the animosities and prejudices fomented by the intrigues and artifice of courts will cease. The oppressed soldier will become a free man; and the tortured sailor, no longer dragged through the streets like a felon, will pursue his mercantile voyage in safety. It would be better that nations should continue the pay of their soldiers during their lives, and give them their discharge and restore them to freedom and their friends, and cease recruiting, than retain such multitudes at the same expense, in a condition useless to society and to themselves.

As soldiers have hitherto been treated in most countries, they might

[46] A year later Paine used this phrase as the title of his great work on religion which was published in 1794.—*Editor.*

be said to be without a friend. Shunned by the citizen on an apprehension of their being enemies to liberty, and too often insulted by those who commanded them, their condition was a double oppression. But where genuine principles of liberty pervade a people, everything is restored to order; and the soldier civilly treated, returns the civility.

In contemplating revolutions, it is easy to perceive that they may arise from two distinct causes; the one, to avoid or get rid of some calamity, the other, to obtain some great and positive good; and the two may be distinguished by the names of active and passive revolutions. In those which proceed from the former cause, the temper becomes incensed and soured; and the redress, obtained by danger, is too often sullied by revenge.

But in those which proceed from the latter, the heart, rather animated than agitated, enters serenely upon the subject. Reason and discussion, persuasion and conviction, become the weapons in the contest, and it is only when those are attempted to be suppressed that recourse is had to violence.

When men unite in agreeing that a *thing is good,* could it be obtained, such as relief from a burden of taxes and the extinction of corruption, the object is more than half accomplished. What they approve as the end, they will promote in the means.

Will any man say in the present excess of taxation, falling so heavily on the poor, that a remission of five pounds annually of taxes to one hundred and four thousand poor families is not a *good thing?* Will he say that a remission of seven pounds annually to one hundred thousand other poor families; of eight pounds annually to another hundred thousand poor families, and of ten pounds annually to fifty thousand poor and widowed families, are not *good things?*

And, to proceed a step further in this climax, will he say, that to provide against the misfortunes to which all human life is subject, by securing six pounds annually for all poor, distressed, and reduced persons of the age of fifty and until sixty, and of ten pounds annually after sixty, is not a *good thing?*

Will he say that an abolition of two millions of poor-rates to the housekeepers, and of the whole of the house and window-light tax and of the commutation tax, is not a *good thing?* Or will he say, that to abolish corruption is a *bad thing?*

If, therefore, the good to be obtained be worthy of a passive, rational and costless revolution, it would be bad policy to prefer waiting for a calamity that should force a violent one. I have no idea, considering the reforms which are now passing and spreading throughout Europe, that England will permit herself to be the last; and where the occasion and the opportunity quietly offer, it is better than to wait for a turbulent necessity. It may be considered as an honor to the animal faculties of man to obtain redress by courage and danger, but it is far greater honor to the rational faculties to accomplish the same object by reason, accommodation, and general consent.[47]

As reforms, or revolutions, call them which you please, extend themselves among nations, those nations will form connections and conventions, and when a few are thus confederated, the progress will be rapid, till despotism and corrupt government be totally expelled, at least out of two quarters of the world, Europe and America. The Algerine piracy may then be commanded to cease, for it is only by the malicious policy of old governments against each other that it exists.

Throughout this work, various and numerous as the subjects are, which I have taken up and investigated, there is only a single paragraph upon religion, *viz. "that every religion is good that teaches man to be good."*

I have carefully avoided to enlarge upon the subject, because I am inclined to believe that what is called the present Ministry wish to see contentions about religion kept up, to prevent the nation turning its attention to subjects of government. It is as if they were to say, *"look that way, or any way but this."*

But as religion is very improperly made a political machine, and the

---

[47] I know it is the opinion of many of the most enlightened characters in France (there always will be those who see further into events than others), not only among the general mass of citizens, but of many of the principal members of the former National Assembly, that the monarchical plan will not continue many years in that country. They have found out, that, as wisdom cannot be made hereditary, power ought not; and that for a man to merit a million sterling a year from a nation, he ought to have a mind capable of comprehending from an atom to a universe, which, if he had, he would be above receiving the pay.

But they wished not to appear to lead the nation faster than its own reason and interest dictated. In all the conversations where I have been present upon this subject, the idea always was, that when such a time, from the general opinion of the nation, shall arrive, that the honorable and liberal method would be, to make a handsome present in fee simple to the person, whoever he may be, that shall then be in the monarchical office, and for him to retire to the enjoyment of private life, possessing his share of general rights and privileges, and to be no more accountable to the public for his time and his conduct than any other citizen.—*Author.*

On September 21, 1792, monarchy was formally abolished in France.—*Editor.*

reality of it is thereby destroyed, I will conclude this work with stating in what light religion appears to me.

If we suppose a large family of children, who, on any particular day, or particular occasion, make it a custom to present to their parents some token of their affection and gratitude, each of them would make a different offering, and most probably in a different manner.

Some would pay their congratulations in themes of verse and prose, by some little devices, as their genius dictated, or according to what they thought would please; and, perhaps, the least of all, not able to do any of those things, would ramble into the garden, or the field, and gather what it thought the prettiest flower it could find, though, perhaps, it might be but a simple weed. The parents would be more gratified by such a variety than if the whole of them had acted on a concerted plan, and each had made exactly the same offering.

This would have the cold appearance of contrivance, or the harsh one of control. But of all unwelcome things, nothing would more afflict the parent than to know that the whole of them had afterwards gotten together by the ears, boys and girls, fighting, reviling, and abusing each other about which was the best or the worst present.

Why may we not suppose that the great Father of all is pleased with variety of devotion; and that the greatest offense we can act is that by which we seek to torment and render each other miserable? For my own part I am fully satisfied that what I am now doing, with an endeavor to conciliate mankind, to render their condition happy, to unite nations that have hitherto been enemies, and to extirpate the horrid practise of war and break the chains of slavery and oppression, is acceptable in His sight, and being the best service I can perform I act it cheerfully.

I do not believe that any two men, on what are called doctrinal points, think alike who think at all. It is only those who have not thought that appear to agree. It is in this case as with what is called the British Constitution; it has been taken for granted to be good, and encomiums have supplied the place of proof. But when the nation comes to examine into its principles and the abuses it admits, it will be found to have more defects than I have pointed out in this work and the former.

As to what are called national religions, we may, with as much propriety, talk of national gods. It is either political craft or the remains of the pagan system, when every nation had its separate and particular deity.

Among all the writers of the English Church clergy, who have treated on the general subject of religion, the present Bishop of Llandaff has not been excelled, and it is with much pleasure that I take this opportunity of expressing this token of respect.[48]

I have now gone through the whole of the subject, at least, as far as it appears to me at present.

It has been my intention for the five years I have been in Europe to offer an address to the people of England on the subject of government, if the opportunity presented itself before I returned to America. Mr. Burke has thrown it in my way, and I thank him. On a certain occasion, three years ago, I pressed him to propose a national convention, to be fairly elected, for the purpose of taking the state of the nation into consideration; but I found that however strongly the parliamentary current was then setting against the party he acted with, their policy was to keep everything within that field of corruption, and trust to accidents. Long experience had shown that parliaments would follow any change of ministers, and on this they rested their hopes and their expectations.

Formerly, when divisions arose respecting governments, recourse was had to the sword, and a civil war ensued. That savage custom is exploded by the new system, and reference is had to national conventions. Discussion and the general will arbitrates the question, and to this private opinion yields with a good grace, and order is preserved uninterrupted.

Some gentlemen have affected to call the principles upon which this work and the former part of the "Rights of Man" are founded "a new fangled doctrine." The question is not whether these principles are new or old, but whether they are right or wrong. Suppose the former, I will show their effect by a figure easily understood.

It is now toward the middle of February. Were I to take a turn into the country, the trees would present a leafless, wintery appearance. As people are apt to pluck twigs as they go along, I perhaps might do the same, and by chance might observe that a *single bud* on that twig has begun to swell. I should reason very unnaturally, or rather not reason at all, to suppose *this* was the *only bud* in England which had this appearance.

Instead of deciding thus, I should instantly conclude that the same appearance was beginning, or about to begin, everywhere; and though

[48] Paine is referring to Richard Watson (1737–1816). Four years later the Bishop wrote a bitter attack on Paine's *Age of Reason*, entitled, *An Apology for the Bible in a series of letters, addressed to Thomas Paine, author of a book entitled, The age of reason. . . .* London, 1796.—*Editor.*

the vegetable sleep will continue longer on some trees and plants than on others, and though some of them may not *blossom* for two or three years, all will be in leaf in the summer, except those which are *rotten*. What pace the political summer may keep with the natural, no human foresight can determine. It is, however, not difficult to perceive that the spring is begun.

Thus wishing, as I sincerely do, freedom and happiness to all nations, I close the SECOND PART.

APPENDIX

As the publication of this work has been delayed beyond the time intended, I think it not improper, all circumstances considered, to state the causes that have occasioned that delay.

The reader will probably observe that some parts in the plan contained in this work for reducing the taxes, and certain parts in Mr. Pitt's speech at the opening of the present session, Tuesday, January 31, are so much alike, as to induce a belief that either the author had taken the hint from Mr. Pitt, or Mr. Pitt from the author. I will first point out the parts that are similar, and then state such circumstances as I am acquainted with, leaving the reader to make his own conclusion.

Considering it as almost an unprecedented case that taxes should be proposed to be taken off, it is equally extraordinary that such a measure should occur to two persons at the same time; and still more so (considering the vast variety and multiplicity of taxes) that they should hit on the same specific taxes. Mr. Pitt has mentioned, in his speech, the tax on *carts and wagons;* that on *female servants;* the lowering the tax on *candles,* and the taking off the tax of three shillings on *houses* having under seven windows.

Every one of those specific taxes are a part of the plan contained in this work, and proposed also to be taken off. Mr. Pitt's plan, it is true, goes no further than to a reduction of three hundred and twenty thousand pounds; and the reduction proposed in this work, to nearly six millions. I have made my calculations on only sixteen millions and an half of revenue, still asserting that it was very nearly, if not quite, seventeen millions. Mr. Pitt states it at £16,690,000. I know enough of the matter to say, that he has not *over*stated it. Having thus given the particulars, which correspond in this work and his speech, I will state a chain of circumstances that may lead to some explanation.

The first hint for lessening the taxes, and that as a consequence flowing from the French Revolution, is to be found in the Address and Declaration of the gentlemen who met at the Thatched-House tavern, August 20, 1791. Among many other particulars stated in that address, is the following, put as an interrogation to the government opposers of the French Revolution. *"Are they sorry that the pretense for new oppressive taxes, and the occasion for continuing many old taxes will be at an end?"*

It is well known, that the persons who chiefly frequent the Thatched-House tavern, are men of court connections, and so much did they take this address and declaration respecting the French Revolution and the reduction of taxes, in disgust, that the landlord was under the necessity of informing the gentlemen, who composed the meeting of the 20th of August, and who proposed holding another meeting, that he could not receive them.[49]

What was only hinted at in the *"Address and Declaration"*[50] respecting taxes and principles of government, will be found reduced to a regular system in this work. But as Mr. Pitt's speech contains some of the same things respecting taxes, I now come to give the circumstances before alluded to.

The case is this: This work was intended to be published just before the meeting of Parliament, and for that purpose a considerable part of the copy was put into the printer's hands in September, and all the remaining copy, as far as page 160 [first English edition], which contains the part to which Mr. Pitt's speech is similar, was given to him full six weeks before the meeting of Parliament, and he was informed of

[49] The gentleman who signed the *Address and Declaration* as chairman of the meeting, Mr. Horne Tooke, being generally supposed to be the person who drew it up, and having spoken much in commendation of it, has been jocularly accused of praising his own work. To free him from this embarrassment, and to save him the repeated trouble of mentioning the author, as he had not failed to do, I make no hesitation in saying, that as the opportunity of benefiting by the French Revolution easily occurred to me, I drew up the publication in question, and showed it to him and some other gentlemen; who, fully approving it, held a meeting for the purpose of making it public, and subscribed to the amount of fifty guineas to defray the expense of advertising.

I believe there are at this time in England a greater number of men acting on disinterested principles and determined to look into the nature and practises of government themselves, and not blindly trust, as has hitherto been the case, either to government generally, or to parliaments, or to parliamentary opposition, than at any former period. Had this been done a century ago, corruption and taxation had not arrived at the height they are now at.—*Author.*

[50] Paine is referring to the *Address and Declaration. At a select Meeting of the Friends of Universal Peace and Liberty, held at the Thatched House Tavern, St. James's Street, August 20, 1791, the following address was agreed on and ordered to be published.* It is published separately in Volume II of the present edition.—*Editor.*

the time at which it was to appear. He had composed nearly the whole about a fortnight before the time of Parliament's meeting, and had printed as far as page 112, and had given me a proof of the next sheet, up to page 128.

It was then in sufficient forwardness to be out at the time proposed, as two other sheets were ready for striking off. I had before told him, that if he thought he should be straitened for time, I could get part of the work done at another press, which he desired me not to do. In this manner the work stood on the Tuesday fortnight preceding the meeting of Parliament, when all at once, without any previous intimation, though I had been with him the evening before, he sent me by one of his workmen, all the remaining copy, from page 112, declining to go on with the work *on any consideration.*

To account for this extraordinary conduct I was totally at a loss, as he stopped at the part where the arguments on systems and principles of government closed, and where the plan for the reduction of taxes, the education of children, and the support of the poor and the aged begins; and still more especially, as he had, at the time of his beginning to print, and before he had seen the whole copy, offered a thousand pounds for the copy-right, together with the future copy-right of the former part of the "Rights of Man."

I told the person who brought me this offer that I should not accept it, and wished it not to be renewed, giving him as my reason, that though I believed the printer to be an honest man, I would never put it in the power of any printer or publisher to suppress or alter a work of mine, by making him master of the copy, or give to him the right of selling it to any minister, or to any other person, or to treat as a mere matter of traffic, that which I intended should operate as a principle.

His refusal to complete the work (which he could not purchase) obliged me to seek for another printer, and this of consequence would throw the publication back until after the meeting of Parliament, otherwise it would have appeared that Mr. Pitt had only taken up a part of the plan which I had more fully stated.

Whether that gentleman, or any other, had seen the work or any part of it, is more than I have authority to say. But the manner in which the work was returned, and the particular time at which this was done, and that after the offers he had made, are suspicious circumstances. I know what the opinion of booksellers and publishers is upon such a case, but as to my own opinion, I choose to make no declaration. There are many ways by which proof sheets may be procured by other persons before a work publicly appears; to which I shall add a certain circumstance, which is,

A Ministerial bookseller in Piccadilly who has been employed, as common report says, by a clerk of one of the boards closely connected with the Ministry (the Board of Trade and Plantations, of which Hawksbury is president,) to publish what he calls my life,[51] (I wish his own life and that those of the Cabinet were as good,) used to have his books printed at the same printing office that I employed; but when the former part of the "Rights of Man" came out, he took his work away in a dudgeon; and about a week or ten days before the printer returned my copy, he came to make him an offer of his work again, which was accepted.

This would consequently give him admission into the printing office where the sheets of this work were then lying; and as booksellers and printers are free with each other, he would have the opportunity of seeing what was going on. Be the case, however, as it may, Mr. Pitt's plan, little and diminutive as it is, would have made a very awkward appearance, had this work appeared at the time the printer had engaged to finish it.

I have now stated the particulars which occasioned the delay, from the proposal to purchase, to the refusal to print. If all the gentlemen are innocent, it is very unfortunate for them that such a variety of suspicious circumstances should, without any design, arrange themselves together.

Having now finished this part, I will conclude with stating another circumstance.

About a fortnight or three weeks before the meeting of Parliament, a small addition, amounting to about twelve shillings and sixpence a year, was made to the pay of the soldiers, or rather their pay was docked so much less. Some gentleman who knew in part that this work would contain a plan of reforms respecting the oppressed condition of soldiers, wished me to add a note to the work, signifying that the part upon that subject had been in the printer's hands some weeks before that addition of pay was proposed.

I declined doing this, lest it should be interpreted into an air of vanity, or an endeavor to excite suspicion (for which perhaps there might be no grounds) that some of the Government gentlemen had, by some

---

[51] Paine is referring to the scurrilous biography by George Chalmers who was subsidized by the crown to attack the author of the *Rights of Man.—Editor.*

means or other, made out what this work would contain; and had not the printing been interrupted so as to occasion a delay beyond the time fixed for publication, nothing contained in this appendix would have appeared.

THOMAS PAINE.

THE AGE OF REASON

EDITOR'S NOTE

The first edition of *The Age of Reason* was printed by Barras in Paris in :794. Written when the author was in his fifty-seventh year, this famous theological treatise represented the results of years of study and reflection on the place of religion in society. Paine always made it his practice to keep abreast of the latest developments in the field of science, so that when he prepared to begin writing *The Age of Reason* he was in the position to apply all the discoveries in the field of scientific knowledge to incidents related in the Old and New Testaments. In essence, therefore, the work is an application of reason to the Bible, in the light of the Newtonian principles of science, and is devoted chiefly to a careful analysis of the revelations, prophecies, miracles and stories related in that book. Actually, Paine was doing for the English world what had already been done in France by men like Voltaire and Diderot. Moreover, he was doing what Jefferson had advised his nephew Peter Carr to do as early as August 10, 1787. "Fix reason firmly in her seat," wrote Jefferson in his letter of advice, "and call to her tribunal every fact, every opinion. Question with boldness even the existence of a God; because if there be one, He must more approve of the homage of reason, than that of blindfold fear. You will naturally examine first, the religion of your own country. Read the Bible, then, as you would read Livy or Tacitus. . . . Your own reason is the only oracle given you by heaven, and you are answerable, not for the rightness, but the uprightness of the decision." (Philip S. Foner, editor, *Thomas Jefferson: Selections from His Writings*, p. 76.)

Paine was not an atheist. Indeed, in the "Profession of Faith" with which he opens his book he states emphatically: "I believe in one God, and no more; and I hope for happiness beyond this life." Together with many other progressive leaders of the age of enlightenment, Paine was a deist, who believed in "a God of moral truth, and not a God of mystery or obscurity." Well grounded in the science of his day, he conceived of God as the "first cause, the cause of all things." The universe itself, he observed, seemed a singular proof of the beneficence of God: "The Almighty Lecturer, by displaying the principles of science in the structure of the universe, has invited man to study and to imitation. It is as if He had said to the inhabitants of this globe we call ours: I have made an earth for man to dwell upon, and I have rendered the starry heavens visible, to teach him science and the arts. He can now provide for his own comfort, and learn from my munificence to all to be kind to each other."

Organized religion, Paine wrote, was "set up to terrify and enslave mankind, and monopolize power and profit." The only true theology was "natural philosophy, embracing the whole circle of science." The only true religion was that of deism. "The only religion that has not been invented," he wrote, "and that has in it every evidence of divine originality, is pure and simple deism. It must have been the first and will probably be the last that man believes. . . ."

Paine's interest in religious issues was an essential part of his political thinking. Since the clergy in many countries were on the side of oppression and served the vested interests as a valuable bulwark against democratic reforms, it was essential for the future of progress that these defenders of aristocracy and hereditary privilege be exposed and their influence destroyed. During the French Revolution, Paine became even more convinced of the reactionary role played by the clergy in political affairs as he observed the close alliance that existed between the higher clergy of France and the forces of aristocracy and monarchy. In order to break this alliance and to preserve republican and liberal principles, he determined to destroy the priesthood by exposing the false character of the source of its authority—the Scriptural revelation. Still another motive influenced Paine in writing *The Age of Reason*. He was genuinely alarmed by the growth of atheism, and was convinced that the growing disbelief in God and a future life was due primarily to the disgust men felt for the reactionary and rigid conduct of the clergy. Fearing that the growth of atheism threatened the existence of the only true religion, deism, and determined to save republicanism from despotism, Paine published *The Age of Reason*.

Whereas the first part of *The Age of Reason* deals with revelation in general (possibly because the author did not have a Bible at hand while writing this section), the second discusses the Judaic-Christian account in detail. Examining the books of the Old Testament (with which he was now equipped) in the light of reason, he found them all wanting. He argues that Moses, Joshua, Samuel, David and Solomon did not compose the books bearing their names, and asserts that the Pentateuch was written "by some very ignorant and stupid pretenders to authorship, several hundred years after the death of Moses. . . ."

Paine deals just as sharply with the New Testament, a copy of which was also at his side when he wrote the section. He holds that the Gospels were not written by the apostles and that they appeared centuries after the death of

Christ. Of the existence of Jesus, Paine has no doubt, nor of his crucifixion. He admits the greatness of Jesus as a man but denies that he was a God. "The morality that he preached and practised," he writes, "was of the most benevolent kind, and though similar systems of morality had been preached by Confucius and by some of the Greek philosophers many years before, by the Quakers since, and by many good men in all ages, it has not been exceeded by any." But the immaculate conception was a pure piece of fiction, and the resurrection exceedingly doubtful. Thus Paine repudiates the divine origin of Christianity on the ground that it was too "absurd for belief, too impossible to convince and too inconsistent to practice. . . ."

Since the Christian religion was "an engine of power" functioning in behalf of despotism as well as "a species of Atheism," Paine suggests the introduction of deism which he defines as follows: "Were a man impressed as fully and as strongly as he ought to be with the belief of a God, his moral life would be regulated by the forces of this belief, he would stand in awe of God and of himself, and would not do the thing that could not be concealed from either. To give this belief the full opportunity of force it is necessary that it acts alone. This is deism."

So profoundly were the royalists and reactionaries shocked by Paine's vigorous attack upon one of the principal bulwarks of feudal despotism, that the author was treated with such deep and relentless hatred as to earn for him a discredit which the lapse of more than a century has scarcely succeeded in modifying. A century after his death, Theodore Roosevelt could still speak of Paine as "a filthy little atheist." Volumes were written in reply to *The Age of Reason;* the publisher of the book was found guilty of blasphemy; the work was suppressed and the author again hanged in effigy. Not only was the publisher imprisoned, but anyone who distributed, read or discussed *The Age of Reason* was persecuted by the British ministry, and some were even arrested simply for displaying the portrait of the author.

The chief reason for the campaign of slander and vilification launched against Paine was that he had succeeded in carrying the message of deism to the people. Up to this point the deistic movement had been influential solely among people of education and social prominence. Now it was being spread among the masses. Written in a style easily understood by the average man, distributed free of charge in America and Europe by deistic organizations, the work gained an extensive circulation in cities, villages and towns. Overnight deism became a mass movement, and since it allied itself naturally with republicanism in the political arena it became a vital force in the struggle against reaction.

For detailed and scholarly treatments of the deistic movements and the influence of *The Age of Reason,* see Herbert M. Morais, *Deism in Eighteenth Century America,* New York, 1934, and G. A. Koch, *Republican Religion,* New York, 1933.—*Editor.*

THE AGE OF REASON

BEING AN INVESTIGATION OF TRUE
AND FABULOUS THEOLOGY

PART FIRST

TO MY FELLOW-CITIZENS OF THE UNITED
STATES OF AMERICA

I PUT the following work under your protection. It contains my opinion upon religion. You will do me the justice to remember, that I have always strenuously supported the right of every man to his own opinion, however different that opinion might be to mine. He who denies to another this right, makes a slave of himself to his present opinion, because he precludes himself the right of changing it.

The most formidable weapon against errors of every kind is reason. I have never used any other, and I trust I never shall.

Your affectionate friend and fellow-citizen,

THOMAS PAINE.

Paris, 8th Pluvôise.
Second year of the French Republic, one and indivisible.
January 27th, O. S. 1794.

THE AUTHOR'S PROFESSION OF FAITH

IT HAS been my intention, for several years past, to publish my thoughts upon religion. I am well aware of the difficulties that attend the subject, and from that consideration, had reserved it to a more advanced period of life. I intended it to be the last offering I should make to my fellow-citizens of all nations, and that at a time when the purity of the motive that induced me to it could not admit of a question, even by those who might disapprove the work. The circumstance that has now taken place in France of the total abolition of the whole national order of priesthood, and of everything appertaining to compulsive systems of religion, and compulsive articles of faith, has not only precipitated my intention, but rendered a work of this kind exceedingly necessary, lest in the general wreck of superstition, of false systems of government and false theology, we lose sight of morality, of humanity and of the theology that is true.

As several of my colleagues, and others of my fellow-citizens of France, have given me the example of making their voluntary and individual profession of faith, I also will make mine; and I do this with all that sincerity and frankness with which the mind of man communicates with itself.

I believe in one God, and no more; and I hope for happiness beyond this life.

I believe in the equality of man; and I believe that religious duties consist in doing justice, loving mercy, and endeavoring to make our fellow-creatures happy.

But, lest it should be supposed that I believe many other things in addition to these, I shall, in the progress of this work, declare the things I do not believe, and my reasons for not believing them.

I do not believe in the creed professed by the Jewish Church, by the Roman Church, by the Greek Church, by the Turkish Church, by the Protestant Church, nor by any church that I know of. My own mind is my own church.

All national institutions of churches, whether Jewish, Christian or Turkish, appear to me no other than human inventions, set up to terrify and enslave mankind, and monopolize power and profit.

I do not mean by this declaration to condemn those who believe otherwise; they have the same right to their belief as I have to mine. But it is necessary to the happiness of man that he be mentally faithful to himself. Infidelity does not consist in believing, or in disbelieving; it consists in professing to believe what he does not believe.

It is impossible to calculate the moral mischief, if I may so express it, that mental lying has produced in society. When a man has so far corrupted and prostituted the chastity of his mind as to subscribe his professional belief to things he does not believe he has prepared himself for the commission of every other crime.

He takes up the trade of a priest for the sake of.gain, and in order to qualify himself for that trade he begins with a perjury. Can we conceive any thing more destructive to morality than this?

Soon after I had published the pamphlet "Common Sense," in America, I saw the exceeding probability that a revolution in the system of government would be followed by a revolution in the system of religion. The adulterous connection of church and state, wherever it has taken place, whether Jewish, Christian or Turkish, has so effectually prohibited by pains and penalties every discussion upon established creeds, and upon first principles of religion, that until the system of government should be changed, those subjects could not be brought fairly and openly before the world; but that whenever this should be done, a revolution in the system of religion would follow. Human inventions and priestcraft would be detected; and man would return to the pure, unmixed and unadulterated belief of one God, and no more.

Concerning Missions and Revelations

Every national church or religion has established itself by pretending some special mission from God, communicated to certain individuals. The Jews have their Moses; the Christians their Jesus Christ, their apostles and saints; and the Turks their Mahomet, as if the way to God was not open to every man alike.

Each of those churches show certain books, which they call *revelation,* or the Word of God. The Jews say that their Word of God was given by God to Moses, face to face; the Christians say that their Word of God came by divine inspiration; and the Turks say that their Word of God (the Koran) was brought by an angel from heaven. Each of those churches accuses the other of unbelief; and for my own part, I disbelieve them all.

As it is necessary to affix right ideas to words, I will, before I proceed further into the subject, offer some observations on the word *revelation.* Revelation, when applied to religion, means something communicated *immediately* from God to man.

No one will deny or dispute the power of the Almighty to make such a communication, if He pleases. But admitting, for the sake of a case, that something has been revealed to a certain person, and not revealed to any other person, it is revelation to that person only. When he tells it to a second person, a second to a third, a third to a fourth, and so on, it ceases to be a revelation to all those persons. It is revelation to the first person only, and *hearsay* to every other, and consequently they are not obliged to believe it.

It is a contradiction in terms and ideas, to call anything a revelation that comes to us at second-hand, either verbally or in writing. Revelation is necessarily limited to the first communication—after this it is only an account of something which that person says was a revelation made to him; and though he may find himself obliged to believe it, it cannot be incumbent on me to believe it in the same manner; for it was not a revelation made to *me,* and I have only his word for it that it was made to him. When Moses told the children of Israel that he received the two tables of the commandments from the hands of God, they were not obliged to believe him, because they had no other authority for it than his telling them so; and I have no other authority for it than some historian telling me so. The commandments carry no internal evidence of divinity with them; they contain some good moral precepts, such as any man qualified to be a lawgiver, or a legislator, could produce himself, without having recourse to supernatural intervention.[1]

When I am told that the Koran was written in heaven and brought to Mahomet by an angel, the account comes too near the same kind of hearsay evidence and second-hand authority as the former. I did not see the angel myself and, therefore, I have a right not to believe it.

When also I am told that a woman called the Virgin Mary, said, or gave out, that she was with child without any cohabitation with a man, and that her betrothed husband, Joseph, said that an angel told him so, I have a right to believe them or not; such a circumstance required a much stronger evidence than their bare word for it; but we have not even this—for neither Joseph nor Mary wrote any such matter themselves; it is only reported by others that *they said so*—it is hearsay upon hearsay, and I do not choose to rest my belief upon such evidence.

It is, however, not difficult to account for the credit that was given to the story of Jesus Christ being the Son of God. He was born at a time when the heathen mythology had still some fashion and repute in the world, and that mythology had prepared the people for the belief of such

---

[1] It is, however, necessary to except the declaration which says that God *visits the sins of the fathers upon the children;* it is contrary to every principle of moral justice.—*Author.*

a story. Almost all the extraordinary men that lived under the heathen mythology were reputed to be the sons of some of their gods. It was not a new thing, at that time, to believe a man to have been celestially begotten; the intercourse of gods with women was then a matter of familiar opinion.

Their Jupiter, according to their accounts, had cohabited with hundreds: the story, therefore, had nothing in it either new, wonderful or obscene; it was conformable to the opinions that then prevailed among the people called Gentiles, or Mythologists, and it was those people only that believed it.

The Jews, who had kept strictly to the belief of one God, and no more, and who had always rejected the heathen mythology, never credited the story.

It is curious to observe how the theory of what is called the Christian Church sprung out of the tail of the heathen mythology. A direct incorporation took place in the first instance, by making the reputed founder to be celestially begotten. The trinity of gods that then followed was no other than a reduction of the former plurality, which was about twenty or thirty thousand; the statue of Mary succeeded the statue of Diana of Ephesus; the deification of heroes changed into the canonization of saints; the Mythologists had gods for everything; the Christian Mythologists had saints for everything; the Church became as crowded with the one as the Pantheon had been with the other, and Rome was the place of both. The Christian theory is little else than the idolatry of the ancient Mythologists, accommodated to the purposes of power and revenue; and it yet remains to reason and philosophy to abolish the amphibious fraud.

An Appreciation of the Character of Jesus Christ, and His History

Nothing that is here said can apply, even with the most distant disrespect, to the real character of Jesus Christ. He was a virtuous and an amiable man. The morality that he preached and practised was of the most benevolent kind; and though similar systems of morality had been preached by Confucius, and by some of the Greek philosophers, many years before; by the Quakers since; and by many good men in all ages, it has not been exceeded by any.

Jesus Christ wrote no account of himself, of his birth, parentage, or anything else; not a line of what is called the New Testament is of his own writing. The history of him is altogether the work of other people; and as to the account given of his resurrection and ascension, it was the necessary counterpart to the story of his birth. His historians, having brought him into the world in a supernatural manner, were obliged to take him out again in the same manner, or the first part of the story must have fallen to the ground.

The wretched contrivance with which this latter part is told exceeds every thing that went before it. The first part, that of the miraculous conception, was not a thing that admitted of publicity; and therefore the tellers of this part of the story had this advantage, that though they might not be credited, they could not be detected. They could not be expected to prove it, because it was not one of those things that admitted of proof, and it was impossible that the person of whom it was told could prove it himself.

But the resurrection of a dead person from the grave, and his ascension through the air, is a thing very different as to the evidence it admits of, to the invisible conception of a child in the womb. The resurrection and ascension, supposing them to have taken place, admitted of public and ocular demonstration, like that of the ascension of a balloon, or the sun at noon-day, to all Jerusalem at least.

A thing which everybody is required to believe requires that the proof and evidence of it should be equal to all, and universal; and as the public visibility of this last related act was the only evidence that could give sanction to the former part, the whole of it falls to the ground, because that evidence never was given. Instead of this, a small number of persons, not more than eight or nine, are introduced as proxies for the whole world to say they saw it, and all the rest of the world are called upon to believe it. But it appears that Thomas did not believe the resurrection, and, as they say, would not believe without having ocular and manual demonstration himself. *So neither will I,* and the reason is equally as good for me, and for every other person, as for Thomas.

It is in vain to attempt to palliate or disguise this matter. The story, so far as relates to the supernatural part, has every mark of fraud and imposition stamped upon the face of it. Who were the authors of it is as impossible for us now to know, as it is for us to be assured that the books in which the account is related were written by the persons whose names they bear; the best surviving evidence we now have respecting this affair is the Jews. They are regularly descended from the people who lived in the times this resurrection and ascension is said to have happened, and they say, *it is not true*. It has long appeared to me a strange inconsistency to cite the Jews as a proof of the truth of the story. It is just the same as if a man were to say, I will prove the truth of what I have told you by producing the people who say it is false.

That such a person as Jesus Christ existed, and that he was crucified, which was the mode of execution at that day, are historical relations strictly within the limits of probability. He preached most excellent morality and the equality of man; but he preached also against the corruptions and avarice of the Jewish priests, and this brought upon him the hatred and vengeance of the whole order of priesthood.

The accusation which those priests brought against him was that of sedition and conspiracy against the Roman government, to which the Jews were then subject and tributary; and it is not improbable that the Roman government might have some secret apprehensions of the effects of his doctrine, as well as the Jewish priests; neither is it improbable that Jesus Christ had in contemplation the delivery of the Jewish nation from the bondage of the Romans. Between the two, however, this virtuous reformer and revolutionist lost his life.

FABULOUS BASES OF CHRISTIANITY

It is upon this plain narrative of facts, together with another case I am going to mention, that the Christian Mythologists, calling themselves the Christian Church, have erected their fable, which, for absurdity and extravagance, is not exceeded by anything that is to be found in the mythology of the ancients.

The ancient Mythologists tell that the race of Giants made war against Jupiter, and that one of them threw a hundred rocks against him at one throw; that Jupiter defeated him with thunder, and confined him afterward under Mount Etna, and that every time the giant turns himself Mount Etna belches fire. It is here easy to see that the circumstance of the mountain, that of its being a volcano, suggested the idea of the fable; and that the fable is made to fit and wind itself up with that circumstance.

The Christian Mythologists tell that their Satan made war against the Almighty, who defeated him, and confined him afterward, not under a mountain, but in a pit. It is here easy to see that the first fable suggested the idea of the second; for the fable of Jupiter and the Giants was told many hundred years before that of Satan.

Thus far the ancient and the Christian Mythologists differ very little from each other. But the latter have contrived to carry the matter much farther.

They have contrived to connect the fabulous part of the story of Jesus Christ with the fable originating from Mount Etna; and in order to make all the parts of the story tie together they have taken to their aid the traditions of the Jews; for the Christian mythology is made up partly from the ancient mythology and partly from the Jewish traditions.

The Christian Mythologists, after having confined Satan in a pit, were obliged to let him out again to bring on the sequel of the fable. He is then introduced into the Garden of Eden, in the shape of a snake or a serpent, and in that shape he enters into familiar conversation with Eve, who is no way surprised to hear a snake talk; and the issue of this *tête-à-tête* is that he persuades her to eat an apple, and the eating of that apple damns all mankind.

After giving Satan this triumph over the whole creation, one would have supposed that the Church Mythologists would have been kind enough to send him back again to the pit; or, if they had not done this, that they would have put a mountain upon him (for they say that their faith can remove a mountain), or have put him *under* a mountain, as the former mythologists had done, to prevent his getting again among the women and doing more mischief. But instead of this they leave him at large, without even obliging him to give his parole—the secret of which is that they could not do without him; and after being at the trouble of making him, they bribed him to stay. They promised him ALL the Jews, ALL the Turks by anticipation, nine-tenths of the world beside, and Mahomet into the bargain. After this, who can doubt the bountifulness of the Christian Mythology?

Having thus made an insurrection and a battle in heaven, in which none of the combatants could be either killed or wounded—put Satan into the pit—let him out again—gave him a triumph over the whole creation—damned all mankind by the eating of an apple, these Christian Mythologists bring the two ends of their fable together. They represent this virtuous and amiable man, Jesus Christ, to be at once both God and Man, and also the Son of God, celestially begotten, on purpose to be sacrificed, because they say that Eve in her longing had eaten an apple.

EXAMINATION OF THE PRECEDING BASES

Putting aside everything that might excite laughter by its absurdity, or detestation by its profaneness, and confining ourselves merely to an examination of the parts, it is impossible to conceive a story more derogatory to the Almighty, more inconsistent with His wisdom, more contradictory to His power, than this story is.

In order to make for it a foundation to rise upon, the inventors were under the necessity of giving to the being whom they call Satan, a power equally as great, if not greater than they attribute to the Almighty. They have not only given him the power of liberating himself from the pit, after what they call his fall, but they have made that power increase afterward to infinity. Before this fall they represent him only as an angel of limited existence, as they represent the rest. After his fall, he becomes, by their account, omnipresent. He exists everywhere, and at the same time. He occupies the whole immensity of space.

Not content with this deification of Satan, they represent him as defeating, by stratagem, in the shape of an animal of the creation, all the power and wisdom of the Almighty. They represent him as having compelled the Almighty to the *direct necessity* either of surrendering the whole of the creation to the government and sovereignty of this Satan, or of capitulating for its redemption by coming down upon earth, and exhibiting Himself upon a cross in the shape of a man.

Had the inventors of this story told it the contrary way, that is, had they represented the Almighty as compelling Satan to exhibit *himself* on a cross, in the shape of a snake, as a punishment for his new transgression, the story would have been less absurd—less contradictory. But instead of this, they make the transgressor triumph, and the Almighty fall.

That many good men have believed this strange fable, and lived very good lives under that belief (for credulity is not a crime), is what I have no doubt of. In the first place, they were educated to believe it, and they would have believed anything else in the same manner.

There are also many who have been so enthusiastically enraptured by what they conceived to be the infinite love of God to man, in making a sacrifice of Himself, that the vehemence of the idea has forbidden and deterred them from examining into the absurdity and profaneness of the story. The more unnatural anything is, the more it is capable of becoming the object of dismal admiration.

OF THE TRUE THEOLOGY

But if objects for gratitude and admiration are our desire, do they not present themselves every hour to our eyes? Do we not see a fair creation prepared to receive us the instant we are born—a world furnished to our hands, that cost us nothing? Is it we that light up the sun, that pour down the rain, and fill the earth with abundance? Whether we sleep or wake, the vast machinery of the universe still goes on.

Are these things, and the blessings they indicate in future, nothing to us? Can our gross feelings be excited by no other subjects than tragedy and suicide? Or is the gloomy pride of man become so intolerable, that nothing can flatter it but a sacrifice of the Creator?

I know that this bold investigation will alarm many, but it would be paying too great a compliment to their credulity to forbear it upon that account; the times and the subject demand it to be done. The suspicion that the theory of what is called the Christian Church is fabulous is becoming very extensive in all countries; and it will be a consolation to men staggering under that suspicion, and doubting what to believe and what to disbelieve, to see the object freely investigated. I therefore pass on to an examination of the books called the Old and New Testaments.

EXAMINATION OF THE OLD TESTAMENT

These books, beginning with Genesis and ending with Revelation (which, by the bye, is a book of riddles that requires a revelation to explain it), are, we are told, the Word of God. It is, therefore, proper for us to know who told us so, that we may know what credit to give to the report. The answer to this question is that nobody can tell, except that we tell one another so. The case, however, historically appears to be as follows:

When the Church Mythologists established their system, they collected all the writings they could find and managed them as they pleased. It is a matter altogether of uncertainty to us whether such of the writings as now appear under the name of the Old and New Testaments are in the same state in which those collectors say they found them, or whether they added, altered, abridged or dressed them up.

Be this as it may, they decided by *vote* which of the books out of the collection they had made should be the WORD OF GOD, and which should not. They rejected several; they voted others to be doubtful, such as the books called the Apocrypha; and those books which had a majority of votes were voted to be the Word of God. Had they voted otherwise, all the people, since calling themselves Christians, had believed otherwise— for the belief of the one comes from the vote of the other. Who the people were that did all this, we know nothing of; they called themselves by the general name of the Church, and this is all we know of the matter.

As we have no other external evidence or authority for believing these books to be the Word of God than what I have mentioned, which is no evidence or authority at all, I come in the next place to examine the internal evidence contained in the books themselves.

In the former part of this essay, I have spoken of revelation; I now proceed further with that subject for the purpose of applying it to the books in question.

Revelation is a communication of something which the person to whom that thing is revealed did not know before. For if I have done a thing, or seen it done, it needs no revelation to tell me I have done it, or seen it, nor to enable me to tell it, or to write it.

Revelation, therefore, cannot be applied to anything done upon earth, of which man himself is the actor or the witness; and consequently all the historical and anecdotal parts of the Bible, which is almost the whole of it, is not within the meaning and compass of the word revelation, and, therefore, is not the Word of God.

When Samson ran off with the gate-posts of Gaza, if he ever did so (and whether he did or not is nothing to us), or when he visited his Delilah, or caught his foxes, or did anything else, what has revelation to do with these things? If they were facts, he could tell them himself, or his secretary, if he kept one, could write them, if they were worth either telling or writing; and if they were fictions, revelation could not make them true; and whether true or not, we are neither the better nor the wiser for knowing them. When we contemplate the immensity of that Being who directs and governs the incomprehensible WHOLE, of which the utmost ken of human sight can discover but a part, we ought to feel shame at calling such paltry stories the Word of God.

As to the account of the Creation, with which the book of Genesis opens, it has all the appearance of being a tradition which the Israelites had among them before they came into Egypt; and after their departure from that country they put it at the head of their history, without telling (as it is most probable) that they did not know how they came by it. The manner in which the account opens shows it to be traditionary. It begins abruptly; it is nobody that speaks; it is nobody that hears; it is addressed to nobody; it has neither first, second, nor third person; it has every criterion of being a tradition; it has no voucher. Moses does not take it upon himself by introducing it with the formality that he used on other occasions, such as that of saying, *"The Lord spake unto Moses, saying."*

Why it has been called the Mosaic account of the Creation, I am at a loss to conceive. Moses, I believe, was too good a judge of such subjects to put his name to that account. He had been educated among the Egyptians, who were a people as well skilled in science, and particularly in astronomy, as any people of their day; and the silence and caution that Moses observes in not authenticating the account is a good negative evidence that he neither told it nor believed it.

The case is that every nation of people has been world-makers, and the Israelites had as much right to set up the trade of world-making as any of the rest; and as Moses was not an Israelite, he might not choose to contradict the tradition. The account, however, is harmless; and this is more than can be said for many other parts of the Bible.[2]

Whenever we read the obscene stories, the voluptuous debaucheries, the cruel and torturous executions, the unrelenting vindictiveness, with which more than half the Bible is filled, it would be more consistent that we called it the word of a demon than the Word of God. It is a history of wickedness that has served to corrupt and brutalize mankind; and, for my part, I sincerely detest it as I detest everything that is cruel.

We scarcely meet with anything, a few phrases excepted, but what deserves either our abhorrence or our contempt, till we come to the miscellaneous parts of the Bible. In the anonymous publications, the Psalms, and the book of Job, more particularly in the latter, we find a great deal of elevated sentiment reverentially expressed of the power and benignity of the Almighty; but they stand on no higher rank than many other compositions on similar subjects, as well before that time as since.

The Proverbs which are said to be Solomon's, though most probably a collection (because they discover a knowledge of life which his situation excluded·him from knowing), are an instructive table of ethics. They are inferior in keenness to the proverbs of the Spaniards, and

[2] When Paine refers to the "Bible" he means the Old Testament only.—*Editor.*

not more wise and economical than those of the American Franklin.[8]

All the remaining parts of the Bible, generally known by the name of the Prophets, are the works of the Jewish poets and itinerant preachers, who mixed poetry,[4] anecdote, and devotion together—and those works still retain the air and style of poetry, though in translation.

There is not, throughout the whole book called the Bible, any word that describes to us what we call a poet, nor any word which describes what we call poetry. The case is that the word *prophet,* to which latter times have affixed a new idea, was the Bible word for poet, and the word *prophesying* meant the art of making poetry. It also meant the art of playing poetry to a tune upon any instrument of music.

We read of prophesying with pipes, tabrets and horns—of prophesying with harps, with psalteries, with cymbals and with every other instrument of music then in fashion. Were we now to speak of prophesying with a fiddle, or with a pipe and tabor, the expression would have no meaning or would appear ridiculous, and to some people contemptuous, because we have changed the meaning of the word.

We are told of Saul being among the *prophets,* and also that he prophesied; but we are not told what *they prophesied* nor what *he*

[8] Paine is referring to the proverbs in Benjamin Franklin's *Poor Richard's Almanack.*—*Editor.*

[4] As there are many readers who do not see that a composition is poetry unless it be in rhyme, it is for their information that I add this note.

Poetry consists principally in two things—imagery and composition. The composition of poetry differs from that of prose in the manner of mixing long and short syllables together. Take a long syllable out of a line of poetry, and put a short one in the room of it, or put a long syllable where a short one should be, and that line will lose its poetical harmony. It will have an effect upon the line like that of misplacing a note in a song. The imagery in those books, called the Prophets, appertains altogether to poetry. It is fictitious, and often extravagant, and not admissible in any other kind of writing than poetry. To show that these writings are composed in poetical numbers, I will take ten syllables, as they stand in the book, and make a line of the same number of syllables, (heroic measure) that shall rhyme with the last word. It will then be seen that the composition of these books is poetical measure. The instance I shall produce is from Isaiah:

> *"Hear, O ye heavens, and give ear, O earth!"*
> 'Tis God himself that calls attention forth.

Another instance I shall quote is from the mournful Jeremiah, to which I shall add two other lines, for the purpose of carrying out the figure, and showing the intention of the poet:

> *"O! that mine head were waters and mine eyes"*
> Were fountains flowing like the liquid skies;
> Then would I give the mighty flood release,
> And weep a deluge for the human race.—*Author.*

prophesied. The case is, there was nothing to tell; for these prophets were a company of musicians and poets, and Saul joined in the concert, and this was called *prophesying.*

The account given of this affair in the book called Samuel is that Saul met a *company* of prophets; a whole company of them! coming down with a psaltery, a tabret, a pipe and a harp, and that they prophesied, and that he prophesied with them. But it appears afterward that Saul prophesied badly; that is, he performed his part badly; for it is said, that an *"evil spirit from God"* [5] came upon Saul, and he prophesied.

Now, were there no other passage in the book called the Bible than this to demonstrate to us that we have lost the original meaning of the word *prophesy,* and substituted another meaning in its place, this alone would be sufficient; for it is impossible to use and apply the word *prophesy,* in the place it is here used and applied, if we give to it the sense which latter times have affixed to it. The manner in which it is here used strips it of all religious meaning, and shows that a man might then be a prophet, or he might *prophesy,* as he may now be a poet or a musician, without any regard to the morality or immorality of his character. The word was originally a term of science, promiscuously applied to poetry and to music, and not restricted to any subject upon which poetry and music might be exercised.

Deborah and Barak are called prophets, not because they predicted anything, but because they composed the poem or song that bears their name in celebration of an act already done. David is ranked among the prophets, for he was a musician, and was also reputed to be (though perhaps very erroneously) the author of the Psalms. But Abraham, Isaac and Jacob are not called prophets; it does not appear from any accounts we have that they could either sing, play music or make poetry.

We are told of the greater and the lesser prophets. They might as well tell us of the greater and the lesser God; for there cannot be degrees in prophesying consistently with its modern sense. But there are degrees in poetry, and therefore the phrase is reconcilable to the case, when we understand by it the greater and the lesser poets.

It is altogether unnecessary, after this, to offer any observations upon what those men, styled prophets, have written. The axe goes at once to

---

[5] As those men who call themselves divines and commentators are very fond of puzzling one another, I leave them to contest the meaning of the first part of the phrase, that of *an evil spirit from God.* I keep to my text—I keep to the meaning of the word prophesy.— *Author.*

the root, by showing that the original meaning of the word has been mistaken; and consequently all the inferences that have been drawn from those books, the devotional respect that has been paid to them, and the labored commentaries that have been written upon them, under that mistaken meaning, are not worth disputing about. In many things, however, the writings of the Jewish poets deserve a better fate than that of being bound up, as they now are with the trash that accompanies them, under the abused name of the Word of God.

If we permit ourselves to conceive right ideas of things, we must necessarily affix the idea, not only of unchangeableness, but of the utter impossibility of any change taking place, by any means or accident whatever, in that which we would honor with the name of the Word of God; and therefore the Word of God cannot exist in any written or human language.

The continually progressive change to which the meaning of words is subject, the want of a universal language which renders translation necessary, the errors to which translations are again subject, the mistakes of copyists and printers, together with the possibility of willful alteration, are of themselves evidences that the human language, whether in speech or in print, cannot be the vehicle of the Word of God. The Word of God exists in something else.

Did the book called the Bible excel in purity of ideas and expression all the books that are now extant in the world, I would not take it for my rule of faith, as being the Word of God, because the possibility would nevertheless exist of my being imposed upon. But when I see throughout the greater part of this book scarcely anything but a history of the grossest vices and a collection of the most paltry and contemptible tales, I cannot dishonor my Creator by calling it by His name.

OF THE NEW TESTAMENT

Thus much for the Bible; I now go on to the book called the New Testament. The *New* Testament! that is, the *new* will, as if there could be two wills of the Creator.

Had it been the object or the intention of Jesus Christ to establish a new religion, he would undoubtedly have written the system himself, or *procured it to be written* in his life-time. But there is no publication extant authenticated with his name. All the books called the New Testament were written after his death. He was a Jew by birth and by profession; and he was the Son of God in like manner that every other person is—for the Creator is the Father of All.

The first four books, called Matthew, Mark, Luke and John, do not give a history of the life of Jesus Christ, but only detached anecdotes of him. It appears from these books that the whole time of his being a preacher was not more than eighteen months; and it was only during this short time that those men became acquainted with him. They make mention of him at the age of twelve years, sitting, they say, among the Jewish doctors, asking and answering them questions. As this was several years before their acquaintance with him began, it is most probable they had this anecdote from his parents.

From this time there is no account of him for about sixteen years. Where he lived, or how he employed himself during this interval, is not known. Most probably he was working at his father's trade, which was that of a carpenter. It does not appear that he had any school education, and the probability is that he could not write, for his parents were extremely poor, as appears from their not being able to pay for a bed when he was born.

It is somewhat curious that the three persons whose names are the most universally recorded, were of very obscure parentage. Moses was a foundling; Jesus Christ was born in a stable; and Mahomet was a mule driver. The first and last of these men were founders of different systems of religion; but Jesus Christ founded no new system. He called men to the practice of moral virtues and the belief of one God. The great trait in his character is philanthropy.

The manner in which he was apprehended shows that he was not much known at that time; and it shows also, that the meetings he then held with his followers were in secret; and that he had given over or suspended preaching publicly. Judas could not otherwise betray him than by giving information where he was, and pointing him out to the officers that went to arrest him; and the reason for employing and paying Judas to do this could arise only from the cause already mentioned, that of his not being much known and living concealed.

The idea of his concealment not only agrees very ill with his reputed divinity, but associates with it something of pusillanimity; and his being betrayed or, in other words, his being apprehended on the information of one of his followers shows that he did not intend to be apprehended, and consequently that he did not intend to be crucified.

The Christian Mythologists tell us that Christ died for the sins of the world, and that he came on *purpose to die*. Would it not then have been the same if he had died of a fever or of the small-pox, of old age, or of anything else?

The declaratory sentence which, they say, was passed upon Adam, in case he ate of the apple, was not, that *thou shalt surely be crucified,* but, *thou shalt surely die*—the sentence of death, and not the manner of dying. Crucifixion, therefore, or any other particular manner of dying, made no part of the sentence that Adam was to suffer, and consequently, even upon their own tactics, it could make no part of the sentence that Christ was to suffer in the room of Adam. A fever would have done as well as a cross, if there was any occasion for either.

The sentence of death, which they tell us was thus passed upon Adam, must either have meant dying naturally, that is, ceasing to live, or have meant what these Mythologists call damnation; and, consequently, the act of dying on the part of Jesus Christ, must, according to their system, apply as a prevention to one or other of these two *things* happening to Adam and to us.

That it does not prevent our dying is evident, because we all die; and if their accounts of longevity be true, men die faster since the crucifixion than before; and with respect to the second explanation (including with it the *natural death* of Jesus Christ as a substitute for the *eternal death or damnation* of all mankind), it is impertinently representing the Creator as coming off, or revoking the sentence, by a pun or a quibble upon the word *death*.

That manufacturer of quibbles, St. Paul, if he wrote the books that bear his name, has helped this quibble on by making another quibble upon the word *Adam*. He makes there to be two Adams; the one who sins in fact and suffers by proxy; the other who sins by proxy and suffers in fact. A religion thus interlarded with quibble, subterfuge and pun has a tendency to instruct its professors in the practise of these arts. They acquire the habit without being aware of the cause.

If Jesus Christ was the being which those Mythologists tell us he was, and that he came into this world to *suffer,* which is a word they sometimes use instead of *to die,* the only real suffering he could have endured would have been *to live*. His existence here was a state of exilement or transportation from heaven, and the way back to his original country was to die. In fine, everything in this strange system is the reverse of what it pretends to be. It is the reverse of truth, and I become so tired of examining into its inconsistencies and absurdities that I hasten to the conclusion of it in order to proceed to something better.

How much or what parts of the books called the New Testament were written by the persons whose names they bear is what we can know nothing of; neither are we certain in what language they were originally written. The matters they now contain may be classed under two heads—anecdote and epistolary correspondence.

The four books already mentioned, Matthew, Mark, Luke and John, are altogether anecdotal. They relate events after they have taken place. They tell what Jesus Christ did and said, and what others did and said to him; and in several instances they relate the same event differently. Revelation is necessarily out of the question with respect to those books; not only because of the disagreement of the writers, but because revelation cannot be applied to the relating of facts by the person who saw them done, nor to the relating or recording of any discourse or conversation by those who heard it. The book called the Acts of the Apostles (an anonymous work) belongs also to the anecdotal part.

All the other parts of the New Testament, except the book of enigmas called the Revelations, are a collection of letters under the name of epistles; and the forgery of letters has been such a common practise in the world that the probability is at least equal, whether they are genuine or forged.

One thing, however, is much less equivocal, which is, that out of the matters contained in those books, together with the assistance of some old stories, the Church has set up a system of religion very contradictory to the character of the person whose name it bears. It has set up a religion of pomp and of revenue, in pretended imitation of a person whose life was humility and poverty.

The invention of a purgatory, and of the releasing of souls therefrom by prayers bought of the church with money; the selling of pardons, dispensations and indulgences, are revenue laws, without bearing that name or carrying that appearance.

But the case nevertheless is that those things derive their origin from the paroxysm of the crucifixion and the theory deduced therefrom, which was that one person could stand in the place of another, and could perform meritorious services for him.

The probability, therefore, is that the whole theory or doctrine of what is called the redemption (which is said to have been accomplished by the act of one person in the room of another) was originally fabricated on purpose to bring forward and build all those secondary and pecuniary redemptions upon; and that the passages in the books upon which the idea or theory of redemption is built have been manufactured and fabricated for that purpose.

Why are we to give this Church credit when she tells us that those books are genuine in every part, any more than we give her credit for everything else she has told us, or for the miracles she says she has performed? That she *could* fabricate writings is certain, because she could write; and the composition of the writings in question is of that kind that anybody might do it; and that she *did* fabricate them is not more inconsistent with probability than that she should tell us, as she has done, that she could and did work miracles.

Since, then, no external evidence can, at this long distance of time, be produced to prove whether the Church fabricated the doctrine called redemption or not (for such evidence whether for or against, would be subject to the same suspicion of being fabricated), the case can only be referred to the internal evidence which the thing carries of itself; and this affords a very strong presumption of its being a fabrication. For the internal evidence is that the theory or doctrine of redemption has for its basis an idea of pecuniary justice and not that of moral justice.

If I owe a person money and cannot pay him, and he threatens to put me in prison, another person can take the debt upon himself and pay it for me; but if I have committed a crime, every circumstance of the case is changed; moral justice cannot take the innocent for the guilty, even if the innocent would offer itself. To suppose justice to do this is to destroy the principle of its existence, which is the thing itself; it is then no longer justice, it is indiscriminate revenge. This single reflection will show that the doctrine of redemption is founded on a mere pecuniary idea corresponding to that of a debt which another person might pay; and as this pecuniary idea corresponds again with the system of second redemption, obtained through the means of money given to the church for pardons, the probability is that the same persons fabricated both the one and the other of those theories; and that in truth there is no such thing as redemption—that it is fabulous, and that man stands in the same relative condition with his Maker as he ever did stand since man existed, and that it is his greatest consolation to think so.

Let him believe this, and he will live more consistently and morally than by any other system; it is by his being taught to contemplate himself as an outlaw, as an outcast, as a beggar, as a mumper, as one thrown, as it were, on a dunghill at an immense distance from his Creator, and who must make his approaches by creeping and cringing to intermediate beings, that he conceives either a contemptuous disregard for everything under the name of religion, or becomes indifferent, or turns what he calls devout.

In the latter case, he consumes his life in grief, or the affectation of it; his prayers are reproaches; his humility is ingratitude; he calls himself a worm, and the fertile earth a dunghill; and all the blessings of life by the thankless name of vanities; he despises the choicest gift of God to man, the GIFT OF REASON; and having endeavored to force upon himself the belief of a system against which reason revolts, he ungratefully calls it *human reason,* as if man could give reason to himself.

Yet, with all this strange appearance of humility and this contempt for human reason, he ventures into the boldest presumptions; he finds fault with everything; his selfishness is never satisfied; his ingratitude is never at an end.

He takes on himself to direct the Almighty what to do, even in the government of the universe; he prays dictatorially; when it is sunshine, he prays for rain, and when it is rain, he prays for sunshine; he follows the same idea in everything that he prays for; for what is the amount of all his prayers but an attempt to make the Almighty change His mind, and act otherwise than He does? It is as if he were to say: Thou knowest not so well as I.

Defining the True Revelation

But some, perhaps, will say: Are we to have no Word of God—no revelation? I answer, Yes; there is a Word of God; there is a revelation.

THE WORD OF GOD IS THE CREATION WE BEHOLD and it is in *this word,* which no human invention can counterfeit or alter, that God speaketh universally to man.

Human language is local and changeable, and is therefore incapable of being used as the means of unchangeable and universal information. The idea that God sent Jesus Christ to publish, as they say, the glad tidings to all nations, from one end of the earth unto the other, is consistent only with the ignorance of those who knew nothing of the extent of the world, and who believed, as those world-saviors believed, and continued to believe for several centuries (and that in contradiction to the discoveries of philosophers and the experience of navigators), that the earth was flat like a trencher, and that man might walk to the end of it.

But how was Jesus Christ to make anything known to all nations? He could speak but one language, which was Hebrew, and there are in the world several hundred languages. Scarcely any two nations speak the same language, or understand each other; and as to translations, every man who knows anything of languages knows that it is impossible to translate from one language into another, not only without losing a great part of the original, but frequently mistaking the sense; and besides all this, the art of printing was wholly unknown at the time Christ lived.

It is always necessary that the means that are to accomplish any end be equal to the accomplishment of that end, or the end cannot be accomplished. It is in this that the difference between finite and infinite power and wisdom discovers itself. Man frequently fails in accomplishing his ends, from a natural inability of the power to the purpose, and frequently from the want of wisdom to apply power properly. But it is impossible for infinite power and wisdom to fail as man faileth. The means it uses are always equal to the end; but human language, more especially as there is not an universal language, is incapable of being used as an universal means of unchangeable and uniform information, and therefore it is not the means that God uses in manifesting himself universally to man.

It is only in the CREATION that all our ideas and conceptions of a *Word of God* can unite. The Creation speaks a universal language, independently of human speech or human language, multiplied and various as they be. It is an ever-existing original, which every man can read. It cannot be forged; it cannot be counterfeited; it cannot be lost; it cannot be altered; it cannot be suppressed. It does not depend upon the will of man whether it shall be published or not; it publishes itself from one end of the earth to the other. It preaches to all nations and to all worlds; and this *Word of God* reveals to man all that is necessary for man to know of God.

Do we want to contemplate His power? We see it in the immensity of the creation. Do we want to contemplate His wisdom? We see it in the unchangeable order by which the incomprehensible whole is governed. Do we want to contemplate His munificence? We see it in the abundance with which He fills the earth. Do we want to contemplate His mercy? We see it in His not withholding that abundance even from the unthankful. In fine, do we want to know what God is? Search not the book called the Scripture, which any human hand might make, but the Scripture called the creation.

Concerning God, and the Lights Cast on His Existence and Attributes by the Bible

The only idea man can affix to the name of God is that of a *first cause*, the cause of all things. And incomprehensible and difficult as it is for a man to conceive what a first cause is, he arrives at the belief of it from the tenfold greater difficulty of disbelieving it.

It is difficult beyond description to conceive that space can have no end; but it is more difficult to conceive an end. It is difficult beyond the power of man to conceive an eternal duration of what we call time; but it is more impossible to conceive a time when there shall be no time.

In like manner of reasoning, everything we behold carries in itself the internal evidence that it did not make itself. Every man is an evidence to himself that he did not make himself; neither could his father make himself, nor his grandfather, nor any of his race; neither could any tree, plant or animal make itself; and it is the conviction arising from this evidence that carries us on, as it were, by necessity to the belief of a first cause eternally existing, of a nature totally different to any material existence we know of, and by the power of which all things exist; and this first cause man calls God.

It is only by the exercise of reason that man can discover God. Take away that reason, and he would be incapable of understanding anything; and, in this case, it would be just as consistent to read even the book called the Bible to a horse as to a man. How, then, is it that people pretend to reject reason?

Almost the only parts of the book called the Bible that convey to us any idea of God are some chapters in Job and the 19th Psalm; I recollect no other. Those parts are true *deistical* compositions, for they treat of the *Deity* through His works. They take the book of creation as the Word of God, they refer to no other book, and all the inferences they make are drawn from that volume.

I insert in this place the 19th Psalm, as paraphrased into English verse by Addison. I recollect not the prose, and where I write this I have not the opportunity of seeing it.

"The spacious firmament on high,
With all the blue ethereal sky,
And spangled heavens, a shining frame
Their great original proclaim.
The unwearied sun, from day to day,
Does his Creator's power display;
And publishes to every land
The work of an Almighty hand.

"Soon as the evening shades prevail,
The moon takes up the wondrous tale,
And nightly to the list'ning earth
Repeats the story of her birth;
While all the stars that round her burn,
And all the planets in their turn,
Confirm the tidings as they roll,
And spread the truth from pole to pole.

"What, though in solemn silence all
Move round this dark, terrestrial ball?
What though no real voice, nor sound,
Amidst their radiant orbs be found?
In reason's ear they all rejoice
And utter forth a glorious voice,
Forever singing, as they shine,
THE HAND THAT MADE US IS DIVINE."

What more does man want to know than that the hand or power that made these things is divine, is omnipotent? Let him believe this with the force it is impossible to repel, if he permits his reason to act, and his rule of moral life will follow of course.

The allusions in Job have, all of them, the same tendency with this Psalm; that of deducing or proving a truth that would be otherwise unknown, from truths already known.

I recollect not enough of the passages in Job to insert them correctly; but there is one occurs to me that is applicable to the subject I am speaking upon. "Canst thou by searching find out God? Canst thou find out the Almighty to perfection?"

I know not how the printers have pointed this passage, for I keep no Bible; but it contains two distinct questions that admit of distinct answers.

First,—Canst thou by searching find out God? Yes; because, in the first place, I know I did not make myself, and yet I have existence; and by *searching* into the nature of other things, I find that no other thing could make itself; and yet millions of other things exist; therefore it is, that I know, by positive conclusion resulting from this search, that there is a power superior to all those things, and that power is God.

Secondly,—Canst thou find out the Almighty to *perfection?* No; not only because the power and wisdom He has manifested in the structure of the creation that I behold is to me incomprehensible, but because even this manifestation, great as it is, is probably but a small display of that immensity of power and wisdom by which millions of other worlds, to me invisible by their distance, were created and continue to exist.

It is evident that both these questions were put to the reason of the person to whom they are supposed to have been addressed; and it is only by admitting the first question to be answered affirmatively that the second could follow. It would have been unnecessary, and even absurd, to have put a second question, more difficult than the first, if the first question had been answered negatively.

The two questions have different objects; the first refers to the existence of God; the second to His attributes; reason can discover the one, but it falls infinitely short in discovering the whole of the other.

I recollect not a single passage in all the writings ascribed to the men called apostles that conveys any idea of what God is. Those writings are chiefly controversial; and the subjects they dwell upon, that of a man dying in agony on a cross, is better suited to the gloomy genius of a monk in a cell, by whom it is not impossible they were written, than to any man breathing the open air of the creation.

The only passage that occurs to me that has any reference to the works of God, by which only His power and wisdom can be known, is related to have been spoken by Jesus Christ as a remedy against distrustful care. "Behold the lilies of the field, they toil not, neither do they spin." This, however, is far inferior to the allusions in Job and in the 19th Psalm; but it is similar in idea, and the modesty of the imagery is correspondent to the modesty of the man.

TRUE THEOLOGY AND THAT OF SUPERSTITION

As to the Christian system of faith, it appears to me a species of Atheism—a sort of religious denial of God. It professes to believe in a man rather than in God. It is a compound made up chiefly of Manism with but little Deism, and is as near to Atheism as twilight is to darkness. It introduces between man and his Maker an opaque body, which it calls a Redeemer, as the moon introduces her opaque self between the earth and the sun, and it produces by this means a religious, or an irreligious, eclipse of light. It has put the whole orbit of reason into shade.

The effect of this obscurity has been that of turning everything upside down, and representing it in reverse, and among the revolutions it has thus magically produced it has made a revolution in theology.

That which is now called natural philosophy, embracing the whole circle of science, of which astronomy occupies the chief place, is the study of the works of God, and of the power and wisdom of God in His works, and is the true theology.

As to the theology that is now studied in its place, it is the study of human opinions and of human fancies *concerning* God. It is not the study of God Himself in the works that He has made, but in the works or writings that man has made; and it is not among the least of the mischiefs that the Christian system has done to the world, that it has abandoned the original and beautiful system of theology, like a beautiful innocent, to distress and reproach, to make room for the hag of superstition.

The Book of Job and the 19th Psalm, which even the Church admits to be more ancient than the chronological order in which they stand in the book called the Bible, are theological orations conformable to the original system of theology.

The internal evidence of those orations proves to a demonstration that the study and contemplation of the works of creation, and of the power and wisdom of God, revealed and manifested in those works, made a great part in the religious devotion of the times in which they were written; and it was this devotional study and contemplation that led to the discovery of the principles upon which what are now called sciences are established; and it is to the discovery of these principles that almost all the arts that contribute to the convenience of human life owe their existence.

Every principal art has some science for its parent, though the person who mechanically performs the work does not always, and but very seldom, perceive the connection.

It is a fraud of the Christian system to call the sciences *human invention;* it is only the application of them that is human. Every science has for its basis a system of principles as fixed and unalterable as those by which the universe is regulated and governed. Man cannot make principles, he can only discover them.

For example: Every person who looks at an almanac sees an account when an eclipse will take place, and he sees also that it never fails to take place according to the account there given. This shows that man is acquainted with the laws by which the heavenly bodies move. But it would be something worse than ignorance, were any church on earth to say that those laws are a human invention.

It would also be ignorance, or something worse, to say that the scientific principles by the aid of which man is enabled to calculate and foreknow when an eclipse will take place are a human invention. Man cannot invent anything that is eternal and immutable; and the scientific principles he employs for this purpose must be, and are of necessity, as eternal and immutable as the laws by which the heavenly bodies move, or they could not be used as they are to ascertain the time when, and the manner how, an eclipse will take place.

The scientific principles that man employs to obtain the foreknowledge of an eclipse, or of anything else relating to the motion of the heavenly bodies, are contained chiefly in that part of science which is called trigonometry, or the properties of a triangle, which, when applied to the study of the heavenly bodies, is called astronomy; when applied to direct the course of a ship on the ocean it is called navigation; when applied to the construction of figures drawn by rule and compass it is called geometry; when applied to the construction of plans or edifices it is called architecture; when applied to the measurement of any portion of the surface of the earth it is called land surveying. In fine, it is the soul of science; it is an eternal truth; it contains the *mathematical demonstration* of which man speaks, and the extent of its uses is unknown.

It may be said that man can make or draw a triangle, and therefore a triangle is a human invention.

But the triangle, when drawn, is no other than the image of the principle; it is a delineation to the eye, and from thence to the mind, of a principle that would otherwise be imperceptible. The triangle does not make the principle, any more than a candle taken into a room that was dark makes the chairs and tables that before were invisible. All the properties of a triangle exist independently of the figure, and existed before any triangle was drawn or thought of by man. Man had no more to do in the formation of these properties or principles than he had to do in making the laws by which the heavenly bodies move; and therefore the one must have the same divine origin as the other.

In the same manner, as it may be said, that man can make a triangle, so also, may it be said, he can make the mechanical instrument called a lever; but the principle by which the lever acts is a thing distinct from the instrument, and would exist if the instrument did not; it attaches itself to the instrument after it is made; the instrument, therefore, cannot act otherwise than it does act; neither can all the efforts of human invention make it act otherwise—that which, in all such cases, man calls the *effect* is no other than the principle itself rendered perceptible to the senses.

Since, then, man cannot make principles, from whence did he gain a knowledge of them, so as to be able to apply them, not only to things on earth, but to ascertain the motion of bodies so immensely distant from him as all the heavenly bodies are? From whence, I ask, *could* he gain that knowledge, but from the study of the true theology?

It is the structure of the universe that has taught this knowledge to man. That structure is an ever-existing exhibition of every principle upon which every part of mathematical science is founded. The offspring of this science is mechanics; for mechanics is no other than the principles of science applied practically.

The man who proportions the several parts of a mill uses the same scientific principles as if he had the power of constructing a universe; but as he cannot give to matter that invisible agency by which all the component parts of the immense machine of the universe have influence upon each other and act in motional unison together, without any apparent contact, and to which man has given the name of attraction, gravitation and repulsion, he supplies the place of that agency by the humble imitation of teeth and cogs.

All the parts of a man's microcosm must visibly touch; but could he gain a knowledge of that agency so as to be able to apply it in practise we might then say that another *canonical book* of the Word of God had been discovered.

If man could alter the properties of the lever, so also could he alter the properties of the triangle, for a lever (taking that sort of lever which is called a steelyard, for the sake of explanation) forms, when in motion, a triangle. The line it descends from (one point of that line being in the fulcrum), the line it descends to, and the chord of the arc which the end of the lever describes in the air, are the three sides of a triangle.

The other arm of the lever describes also a triangle; and the corresponding sides of those two triangles, calculated scientifically, or measured geometrically, and also the sines, tangents and secants generated from the angles, and geometrically measured, have the same proportions to each other as the different weights have that will balance each other on the lever, leaving the weight of the lever out of the case.

It may also be said that man can make a wheel and axis; that he can put wheels of different magnitudes together, and produce a mill. Still the case comes back to the same point, which is that he did not make the principle that gives the wheels those powers. That principle is as unalterable as in the former cases, or rather it is the same principle under a different appearance to the eye.

The power that two wheels of different magnitudes have upon each other is in the same proportion as if the semi-diameter of the two wheels were joined together and made into that kind of lever I have described, suspended at the part where the semi-diameters join; for the two wheels, scientifically considered, are no other than the two circles generated by the motion of the compound lever.

It is from the study of the true theology that all our knowledge of science is derived, and it is from that knowledge that all the arts have originated.

The Almighty Lecturer, by displaying the principles of science in the structure of the universe, has invited man to study and to imitation. It is as if He had said to the inhabitants of this globe that we call ours, "I have made an earth for man to dwell upon, and I have rendered the starry heavens visible, to teach him science and the arts. He can now provide for his own comfort, AND LEARN FROM MY MUNIFICENCE TO ALL, TO BE KIND TO EACH OTHER."

Of what use is it, unless it be to teach man something, that his eye is endowed with the power of beholding to an incomprehensible distance an immensity of worlds revolving in the ocean of space? Of what use is it that this immensity of worlds is visible to man? What has man to do with the Pleiades, with Orion, with Sirius, with the star he calls the North Star, with the moving orbs he has named Saturn, Jupiter, Mars, Venus, and Mercury, if no uses are to follow from their being visible? A less power of vision would have been sufficient for man, if the immensity he now possesses were given only to waste itself, as it were, on an immense desert of space glittering with shows.

It is only by contemplating what he calls the starry heavens, as the book and school of science, that he discovers any use in their being visible to him, or any advantage resulting from his immensity of vision. But when he contemplates the subject of this light, he sees an additional motive for saying, that *nothing was made in vain;* for in vain would be this power of vision if it taught man nothing.

CHRISTIANITY AND EDUCATION, IN THE LIGHT OF HISTORY

As the Christian system of faith has made a revolution in theology, so also has it made a revolution in the state of learning. That which is now called learning was not learning originally. Learning does not consist, as the schools now make it consist, in the knowledge of languages, but in the knowledge of things to which language gives names.

The Greeks were a learned people, but learning with them did not consist in speaking Greek any more than in a Roman's speaking Latin, or a Frenchman's speaking French, or an Englishman's speaking English. From what we know of the Greeks, it does not appear that they knew or studied any language but their own, and this was one cause of their becoming so learned; it afforded them more time to apply themselves to better studies. The schools of the Greeks were schools of science and philosophy, and not of languages; and it is in the knowledge of the things that science and philosophy teach, that learning consists.

Almost all the scientific learning that now exists came to us from the Greeks, or the people who spoke the Greek language. It, therefore, became necessary to the people of other nations who spoke a different language that some among them should learn the Greek language in order that the learning of the Greeks might be made known in those nations, by translating the Greek books of science and philosophy into the mother tongue of each nation.

The study, therefore, of the Greek language (and in the same manner for the Latin) was no other than the drudgery business of a linguist; and the language thus obtained was no other than the means, as it were the tools, employed to obtain the learning the Greeks had. It made no part of the learning itself, and was so distinct from it as to make it exceedingly probable that the persons who had studied Greek sufficiently to translate those works, such, for instance, as Euclid's "Elements," did not understand any of the learning the works contained.

As there is now nothing new to be learned from the dead languages, all the useful books being already translated, the language are become useless, and the time expended in teaching and learning them is wasted. So far as the study of languages may contribute to the progress and communication of knowledge (for it has nothing to do with the *creation* of knowledge), it is only in the living languages that new knowledge is to be found; and certain it is that, in general, a youth will learn more of a living language in one year than of a dead language in seven, and it is but seldom that the teacher knows much of it himself.

The difficulty of learning the dead languages does not arise from any superior abstruseness in the languages themselves, but in their *being dead,* and the pronunciation entirely lost. It would be the same with any other language when it becomes dead. The best Greek linguist that now exists does not understand Greek so well as a Grecian plowman did or a Grecian milkmaid; and the same for the Latin, compared with a plowman or milkmaid of the Romans; and with respect to pronunciation and idiom, not so well as the cows that she milked. It would therefore be advantageous to the state of learning to abolish the study of dead languages and to make learning consist, as it originally did, in scientific knowledge.

The apology that is sometimes made for continuing to teach the dead languages is that they are taught at a time when a child is not capable of exerting any other mental faculty than that of memory; but that is altogether erroneous. The human mind has a natural disposition to scientific knowledge and to the things connected with it.

The first and favorite amusement of a child, even before it begins to play, is that of imitating the works of man. It builds houses with cards or sticks: it navigates the little ocean of a bowl of water with a paper boat, or dams the stream of a gutter and contrives something which it calls a mill; and it interests itself in the fate of its works with a care that resembles affection. It afterwards goes to school, where its genius is killed by the barren study of a dead language, and the philosopher is lost in the linguist.

But the apology that is now made for continuing to teach the dead languages could not be the cause, at first, of cutting down learning to the narrow and humble sphere of linguistry; the cause, therefore, must be sought for elsewhere. In all researches of this kind the best evidence that can be produced is the internal evidence the thing carries with itself, and the evidence of circumstances that unite with it; both of which, in this case, are not difficult to be discovered.

Putting then aside, as a matter of distinct consideration, the outrage

offered to the moral justice of God by supposing Him to make the innocent suffer for the guilty, and also the loose morality and low contrivance of supposing Him to change Himself into the shape of a man, in
order to make an excuse to Himself for not executing His supposed
sentence upon Adam—putting, I say, those things aside as matter of
distinct consideration, it is certain that what is called the Christian system of faith, including in it the whimsical account of the Creation—the
strange story of Eve—the snake and the apple—the ambiguous idea of
a man-god—the corporeal idea of the death of a god—the mythological
idea of a family of gods, and the Christian system of arithmetic, that
three are one, and one is three, are all irreconcilable, not only to the
divine gift of reason that God has given to man, but to the knowledge
that man gains of the power and wisdom of God, by the aid of the sciences and by studying the structure of the universe that God has made.

The setters-up, therefore, and the advocates of the Christian system
of faith could not but foresee that the continually progressive knowledge
that man would gain, by the aid of science, of the power and wisdom
of God, manifested in the structure of the universe and in all the works
of creation, would militate against, and call into question, the truth of
their system of faith; and therefore it became necessary to their purpose
to cut learning down to a size less dangerous to their project, and this
they effected by restricting the idea of learning to the dead study of dead
languages.

They not only rejected the study of science out of the Christian
schools, but they persecuted it, and it is only within about the last two
centuries that the study has been revived. So late as 1610, Galileo, a
Florentine, discovered and introduced the use of telescopes, and by
applying them to observe the motions and appearances of the heavenly
bodies afforded additional means for ascertaining the true structure of
the universe.

Instead of being esteemed for those discoveries, he was sentenced to
renounce them, or the opinions resulting from them, as a damnable
heresy. And, prior to that time, Virgilius was condemned to be burned
for asserting the antipodes, or in other words that the earth was a globe,
and habitable in every part where there was land; yet the truth of this
is now too well known even to be told.

If the belief of errors not morally bad did no mischief, it would make
no part of the moral duty of man to oppose and remove them. There
was no moral ill in believing the earth was flat like a trencher, any more

than there was moral virtue in believing it was round like a globe; neither was there any moral ill in believing that the Creator made no other world than this, any more than there was moral virtue in believing that He made millions and that the infinity of space is filled with worlds.

But when a system of religion is made to grow out of a supposed system of creation that is not true, and to unite itself therewith in a manner almost inseparable therefrom, the case assumes an entirely different ground. It is then that errors not morally bad become fraught with the same mischiefs as if they were. It is then that the truth, though otherwise indifferent itself, becomes an essential by becoming the criterion that either confirms by corresponding evidence, or denies by contradictory evidence the reality of the religion itself.

In this view of the case, it is the moral duty of man to obtain every possible evidence that the structure of the heavens or any other part of creation affords, with respect to systems of religion. But this, the supporters or partisans of the Christian system, as if dreading the result, incessantly opposed, and not only rejected the sciences, but persecuted the professors.

Had Newton or Descartes lived three or four hundred years ago and pursued their studies as they did, it is most probable they would not have lived to finish them; and had Franklin drawn lightning from the clouds at the same time, it would have been at the hazard of expiring for it in the flames.

Later times have laid all the blame upon the Goths and the Vandals; but, however unwilling the partisans of the Christian system may be to believe or to acknowledge it, it is nevertheless true that the age of ignorance commenced with the Christian system. There was more knowledge in the world before that period than for many centuries afterwards; and as to religious knowledge, the Christian system, as already said, was only another species of mythology, and the mythology to which it succeeded was a corruption of an ancient system of theism.[6]

[6] It is impossible for us now to know at what time the heathen mythology began; but it is certain, from the internal evidence that it carries, that it did not begin in the same state or condition in which it ended. All the gods of that mythology, except Saturn, were of modern invention. The supposed reign of Saturn was prior to that which is called the heathen mythology, and was so far a species of theism, that it admitted the belief of only one God. Saturn is supposed to have abdicated the government in favor of his three sons and one daughter, Jupiter, Pluto, Neptune and Juno; after this, thousands of other gods and demi-gods were imaginarily created, and the calendar of gods increased as fast as the calendar of saints and the calendars of courts have increased since.

All the corruptions that have taken place in theology and in religion have been produced

It is owing to this long interregnum of science, *and to no other cause,* that we have now to look back through a vast chasm of many hundred years to the respectable characters we call the ancients. Had the progression of knowledge gone on proportionably with that stock that before existed, that chasm would have been filled up with characters rising superior in knowledge to each other; and those ancients we now so much admire would have appeared respectably in the background of the scene. But the Christian system laid all waste; and if we take our stand about the beginning of the sixteenth century, we look back through that long chasm to the times of the ancients, as over a vast sandy desert, in which not a shrub appears to intercept the vision to the fertile hills beyond.

It is an inconsistency scarcely possible to be credited that anything should exist, under the name of a religion, that held it to be *irreligious* to study and contemplate the structure of the universe that God has made. But the fact is too well established to be denied. The event that served more than any other to break the first link in this long chain of despotic ignorance is that known by the name of the Reformation by Luther.

From that time, though it does not appear to have made any part of the intention of Luther, or of those who are called reformers, the sciences began to revive, and liberality, their natural associate, began to appear. This was the only public good the Reformation did; for with respect to religious good it might as well not have taken place. The mythology still continued the same, and a multiplicity of National Popes grew out of the downfall of the Pope of Christendom.

Comparing Christianism With Pantheism

Having thus shown from the internal evidence of things the cause that produced a change in the state of learning, and the motive for sub-

---

by admitting of what man calls *revealed religion.* The Mythologists pretended to more revealed religion than the Christians do. They had their oracles and their priests, who were supposed to receive and deliver the word of God verbally, on almost all occasions.

Since then, all corruptions, down from Moloch to modern predestinarianism, and the human sacrifices of the heathens to the Christian sacrifice of the Creator, have been produced by admitting of what is called *revealed religion.* The most effectual means to prevent all such evils and impositions is not to admit of any other revelation than that which is manifested in the book of creation, and to contemplate the creation as the only true and real Word of God that ever did or ever will exist; and that everything else, called the Word of God, is fable and imposition.—*Author.*

stituting the study of the dead languages in the place of the sciences, I proceed, in addition to the several observations already made in the former part of this work, to compare, or rather to confront, the evidence that the structure of the universe affords with the Christian system of religion; but, as I cannot begin this part better than by referring to the ideas that occurred to me at an early part of life, and which I doubt not have occurred in some degree to almost every person at one time or other, I shall state what those ideas were and add thereto such other matter as shall arise out of the subject, giving to the whole, by way of preface, a short introduction.

My father being of the Quaker profession, it was my good fortune to have an exceedingly good moral education, and a tolerable stock of useful learning. Though I went to the grammar school,[7] I did not learn Latin, not only because I had no inclination to learn languages, but because of the objection the Quakers have against the books in which the language is taught. But this did not prevent me from being acquainted with the subjects of all the Latin books used in the school.

The natural bent of my mind was to science. I had some turn, and I believe some talent, for poetry; but this I rather repressed than encouraged, as leading too much into the field of imagination. As soon as I was able I purchased a pair of globes, and attended the philosophical lectures of Martin and Ferguson, and became afterward acquainted with Dr. Bevis, of the society called the Royal Society, then living in the Temple, and an excellent astronomer.

I had no disposition for what is called politics. It presented to my mind no other idea than as contained in the word Jockeyship. When, therefore, I turned my thoughts toward matter of government I had to form a system for myself that accorded with the moral and philosophic principles in which I have been educated. I saw, or at least I thought I saw, a vast scene opening itself to the world in the affairs of America, and it appeared to me that unless the Americans changed the plan they were pursuing with respect to the government of England, and declared themselves independent, they would not only involve themselves in a multiplicity of new difficulties, but shut out the prospect that was then offering itself to mankind through their means. It was from these motives that I published the work known by the name of "Common Sense," which was the first work I ever did publish; and so far as I can judge of

[7] The same school, Thetford in Norfolk that the present Counsellor Mingay went to and under the same master.—*Author.*

myself, I believe I should never have been known in the world as an author on any subject whatever had it not been for the affairs of America. I wrote "Common Sense" the latter end of the year 1775, and published it the first of January, 1776. Independence was declared the fourth of July following.

Any person who has made observations on the state and progress of the human mind by observing his own cannot but have observed that there are two distinct classes of what are called thoughts—those that we produce in ourselves by reflection and the act of thinking, and those that bolt into the mind of their own accord. I have always made it a rule to treat these voluntary visitors with civility, taking care to examine, as well as I was able, if they were worth entertaining, and it is from them I have acquired almost all the knowledge that I have. As to the learning that any person gains from school education, it serves only, like a small capital, to put him in a way of beginning learning for himself afterward.

Every person of learning is finally his own teacher, the reason of which is that principles, being a distinct quality to circumstances, cannot be impressed upon the memory; their place of mental residence is the understanding and they are never so lasting as when they begin by conception. Thus much for the introductory part.

From the time I was capable of conceiving an idea and acting upon it by reflection, I either doubted the truth of the Christian system or thought it to be a strange affair; I scarcely knew which it was, but I well remember, when about seven or eight years of age, hearing a sermon read by a relation of mine, who was a great devotee of the Church, upon the subject of what is called *redemption by the death of the Son of God*.

After the sermon was ended, I went into the garden, and as I was going down the garden steps (for I perfectly recollect the spot) I revolted at the recollection of what I had heard, and thought to myself that it was making God Almighty act like a passionate man who killed His son when He could not revenge Himself in any other way, and, as I was sure a man would be hanged who did such a thing, I could not see for what purpose they preached such sermons.

This was not one of that kind of thoughts that had anything in it of childish levity; it was to me a serious reflection, arising from the idea I had that God was too good to do such an action, and also too almighty to be under any necessity of doing it. I believe in the same manner at this moment; and I moreover believe that any system of religion that has anything in it that shocks the mind of a child cannot be a true system.

It seems as if parents of the Christian profession were ashamed to tell their children anything about the principles of their religion. They sometimes instruct them in morals and talk to them of the goodness of what they call Providence, for the Christian mythology has five deities—there is God the Father, God the Son, God the Holy Ghost, the God Providence and the Goddess Nature. But the Christian story of God the Father putting His son to death, or employing people to do it (for that is the plain language of the story) cannot be told by a parent to a child; and to tell him that it was done to make mankind happier and better is making the story still worse—as if mankind could be improved by the example of murder; and to tell him that all this is a mystery is only making an excuse for the incredibility of it.

How different is this to the pure and simple profession of Deism! The true Deist has but one Deity, and his religion consists in contemplating the power, wisdom and benignity of the Deity in His works, and in endeavoring to imitate Him in everything moral, scientifical and mechanical.

The religion that approaches the nearest of all others to true Deism, in the moral and benign part thereof, is that professed by the Quakers; but they have contracted themselves too much by leaving the works of God out of their system. Though I reverence their philanthropy, I cannot help smiling at the conceit that if the taste of a Quaker could have been consulted at the Creation what a silent and drab-colored Creation it would have been! Not a flower would have blossomed its gayeties, nor a bird been permitted to sing.

Quitting these reflections, I proceed to other matters. After I had made myself master of the use of the globes and of the orrery,[8] and conceived an idea of the infinity of space, and the eternal divisibility of matter, and obtained at least a general knowledge of what is called natural philosophy, I began to compare, or, as I have before said, to confront the eternal evidence those things afford with the Christian system of faith.

Though it is not a direct article of the Christian system, that this world

---

[8] As this book may fall into the hands of persons who do not know what an orrery is, it is for their information I add this note, as the name gives no idea of the uses of the thing. The orrery has its name from the person who invented it. It is a machinery of clock-work, representing the universe in miniature, and in which the revolution of the earth round itself and round the sun, the revolution of the moon round the earth, the revolution of the planets round the sun, their relative distances from the sun, as the center of the whole system, their relative distances from each other and their different magnitudes, are represented as they really exist in what we call the heavens.—*Author*.

that we inhabit is the whole of the habitable creation, yet it is so worked up therewith, from what is called the Mosaic account of the Creation, the story of Eve and the apple, and the counterpart of that story, the death of the Son of God, that to believe otherwise, that is, to believe that God created a plurality of worlds, at least as numerous as what we call stars, renders the Christian system of faith at once little and ridiculous, and scatters it in the mind like feathers in the air. The two beliefs cannot be held together in the same mind, and he who thinks that he believes both has thought but little of either.

Though the belief of a plurality of worlds was familiar to the ancients, it is only within the last three centuries that the extent and dimensions of this globe that we inhabit have been ascertained. Several vessels following the tract of the ocean have sailed entirely around the world, as a man may march in a circle and come round by the contrary side of the circle to the spot he set out from.

The circular dimensions of our world, in the widest part, as a man would measure the widest round of an apple or ball, is only twenty-five thousand and twenty English miles, reckoning sixty-nine miles and a half to an equatorial degree, and may be sailed round in the space of about three years.[9]

A world of this extent may, at first thought, appear to us to be great; but if we compare it with the immensity of space in which it is suspended, like a bubble or balloon in the air, it is infinitely less in proportion than the smallest grain of sand is to the size of the world, or the finest particle of dew to the whole ocean, and is therefore but small; and, as will be hereafter shown, is only one of a system of worlds of which the universal creation is composed.

It is not difficult to gain some faint idea of the immensity of space in which this and all other worlds are suspended if we follow a progression of ideas. When we think of the size or dimensions of a room our ideas limit themselves to the walls, and there they stop; but when our eye or our imagination darts into space, that is, when it looks upward into what we call the open air, we cannot conceive any walls or boundaries it can have, and if for the sake of resting our ideas we suppose a boundary, the question immediately renews itself, and asks what is beyond that boundary? —and in the same manner, what is beyond the next boundary? And so

[9] Allowing a ship to sail, on an average, three miles in an hour, she would sail entirely round the world in less than one year, if she could sail in a direct circle; but she is obliged to follow the course of the ocean.—*Author.*

on till the fatigued imagination returns and says, *There is no end.* Certainly, then, the Creator was not pent for room when He made this world no larger than it is, and we have to seek the reason in something else.

If we take a survey of our own world, or rather of this of which the Creator has given us the use as our portion of the immense system of creation, we find every part of it—the earth, the waters, and the air that surrounds it—filled, and, as it were, crowded with life, down from the largest animals that we know of to the smallest insects the naked eye can behold, and from thence to others still smaller, and totally invisible without the assistance of the microscope. Every tree, every plant, every leaf serves not only as a habitation but as a world to some numerous race, till animal existence becomes so exceedingly refined that the effluvia of a blade of grass would be food for thousands.

Since, then, no part of our earth is left unoccupied, why is it to be supposed that the immensity of space is a naked void, lying in eternal waste? There is room for millions of worlds as large or larger than ours, and each of them millions of miles apart from each other. Having now arrived at this point, if we carry our ideas only one thought further, we shall see, perhaps, the true reason, at least a very good reason for our happiness, why the Creator, instead of making one immense world extending over an immense quantity of space, has preferred dividing that quantity of matter into several distinct and separate worlds, which we call planets, of which our earth is one. But before I explain my ideas upon this subject, it is necessary (not for the sake of those who already know, but for those who do not) to show what the system of the universe is.

The Plan and Order of the Universe

That part of the universe that is called the solar system (meaning the system of worlds to which our earth belongs, and of which Sol, or in English language, the Sun, is the center) consists, besides the Sun, of six distinct orbs, or planets, or worlds, besides the secondary bodies, called the satellites or moons, of which our earth has one that attends her in her annual revolution around the Sun, in like manner as the other satellites or moons attend the planets or worlds to which they severally belong, as may be seen by the assistance of the telescope.

The Sun is the center, round which those six worlds or planets revolve at different distances therefrom, and in circles concentric to each other. Each world keeps constantly in nearly the same track round the Sun, and continues, at the same time, turning round itself in nearly an upright position, as a top turns round itself when it is spinning on the ground, and leans a little sideways.

It is this leaning of the earth (23½ degrees) that occasions summer and winter, and the different length of days and nights. If the earth turned round itself in a position perpendicular to the plane or level of the circle it moves in around the Sun, as a top turns round when it stands erect on the ground, the days and nights would be always of the same length, twelve hours day and twelve hours night, and the seasons would be uniformly the same throughout the year.

Every time that a planet (our earth for example) turns round itself, it makes what we call day and night; and every time it goes entirely round the Sun it makes what we call a year; consequently our world turns three hundred and sixty-five times round itself in going once round the Sun.[10]

The names that the ancients gave to those six worlds, and which are still called by the same names, are Mercury, Venus, this world that we call ours, Mars, Jupiter and Saturn. They appear larger to the eye than the stars, being many million miles nearer to our earth than any of the stars are. The planet Venus is that which is called the evening star, and sometimes the morning star, as she happens to set after or rise before the Sun, which in either case is never more than three hours.

The Sun, as before said, being the center, the planet or world nearest the Sun is Mercury; his distance from the Sun is thirty-four million miles, and he moves round in a circle always at that distance from the Sun, as a top may be supposed to spin round in the track in which a horse goes in a mill.

The second world is Venus; she is fifty-seven million miles distant from the Sun, and consequently moves round in a circle much greater than that of Mercury. The third world is this that we inhabit, and which is eighty-eight million miles distant from the Sun, and consequently moves round in a circle greater than that of Venus.

The fourth world is Mars; he is distant from the Sun one hundred and thirty-four million miles, and consequently moves round in a circle greater than that of our earth. The fifth is Jupiter; he is distant from the

[10] Those who supposed that the sun went round the earth every 24 hours made the same mistake in idea that a cook would do in fact, that should make the fire go round the meat, instead of the meat turning round itself toward the fire.—*Author*.

Sun five hundred and fifty-seven million miles, and consequently moves round in a circle greater than that of Mars.

The sixth world is Saturn; he is distant from the Sun seven hundred and sixty-three million miles, and consequently moves round in a circle that surrounds the circles, or orbits, of all the other worlds or planets.

The space, therefore, in the air, or in the immensity of space, that our solar system takes up for the several worlds to perform their revolutions in round the Sun, is of the extent in a straight line of the whole diameter of the orbit, or circle, in which Saturn moves round the Sun, which being double his distance from the Sun, is fifteen hundred and twenty-six million miles and its circular extent is nearly five thousand million, and its globular contents are almost three thousand five hundred million times three thousand five hundred million square miles.[11]

But this, immense as it is, is only one system of worlds. Beyond this, at a vast distance into space, far beyond all power of calculation, are the stars called the fixed stars. They are called fixed because they have no revolutionary motion, as the six worlds or planets have that I have been describing. Those fixed stars continue always at the same distance from each other, and always in the same place, as the Sun does in the center of our system. The probability, therefore, is that each of those fixed stars is also a Sun, round which another system of worlds or planets, though too remote for us to discover, performs its revolutions, as our system of worlds does round our central Sun.

By this easy progression of ideas, the immensity of space will appear to us to be filled with systems of worlds, and that no part of space lies at waste, any more than any part of the globe of earth and water is left unoccupied.

Having thus endeavored to convey, in a familiar and easy manner, some idea of the structure of the universe, I return to explain what I

[11] If it should be asked, how can man know these things? I have one plain answer to give, which is, that man knows how to calculate an eclipse, and also how to calculate to a minute of time when the planet Venus in making her revolutions around the sun will come in a straight line between our earth and the sun, and will appear to us about the size of a large pea passing across the face of the sun. This happens but twice in about a hundred years, at the distance of about eight years from each other, and has happened twice in our time, both of which were foreknown by calculation. It can also be known when they will happen again for a thousand years to come, or to any other portion of time. As, therefore, man could not be able to do these things if he did not understand the solar system, and the manner in which the revolutions of the several planets or worlds are performed, the fact of calculating an eclipse, or a transit of Venus, is a proof in point that the knowledge exists; and as to a few thousand, or even a few million miles, more or less, it makes scarcely any sensible difference in such immense distances.—*Author.*

before alluded to, namely, the great benefits arising to man in consequence of the Creator having made a *plurality* of worlds, such as our
system is, consisting of a central Sun and six worlds, besides satellites, in
preference to that of creating one world only of a vast extent.

ADVANTAGES OF LIFE IN A PLURALITY OF WORLDS

It is an idea I have never lost sight of that all our knowledge of science
is derived from the revolutions (exhibited to our eye and from thence to
our understanding) which those several planets or worlds of which our
system is composed make in their circuit round the Sun.

Had, then, the quantity of matter which these six worlds contain been
blended into one solitary globe, the consequence to us would have been
that either no revolutionary motion would have existed, or not a sufficiency of it to give to us the idea and the knowledge of science we now
have; and it is from the sciences that all the mechanical arts that contribute so much to our earthly felicity and comfort are derived.

As, therefore, the Creator made nothing in vain, so also must it be believed that He organized the structure of the universe in the most advantageous manner for the benefit of man; and as we see, and from experience feel, the benefits we derive from the structure of the universe formed
as it is, which benefits we should not have had the opportunity of enjoying, if the structure, so far as relates to our system, had been a solitary
globe—we can discover at least one reason why a *plurality* of worlds has
been made, and that reason calls forth the devotional gratitude of man
as well as his admiration.

But it is not to us, the inhabitants of this globe, only, that the benefits
arising from a plurality of worlds are limited. The inhabitants of each of
the worlds of which our system is composed enjoy the same opportunities
of knowledge as we do. They behold the revolutionary motions of our
earth, as we behold theirs. All the planets revolve in sight of each other
and, therefore, the same universal school of science presents itself to all.
Neither does the knowledge stop here. The system of worlds next to us
exhibits, in its revolutions, the same principles and school of science to
the inhabitants of their system as our system does to us, and in like manner throughout the immensity of space.

Our ideas, not only of the almightiness of the Creator, but of His
wisdom and His beneficence, become enlarged in proportion as we contemplate the extent and the structure of the universe. The solitary idea

of a solitary world rolling or at rest in the immense ocean of space gives place to the cheerful idea of a society of worlds so happily contrived as to administer, even by their motion, instruction to man. We see our own earth filled with abundance, but we forget to consider how much of that abundance is owing to the scientific knowledge the vast machinery of the universe has unfolded.

But, in the midst of those reflections, what are we to think of the Christian system of faith that forms itself upon the idea of only one world, and that of no greater extent, as is before shown, than twenty-five thousand miles? An extent which a man walking at the rate of three miles an hour, for twelve hours in the day, could he keep on in a circular direction, would walk entirely round in less than two years. Alas! what is this to the mighty ocean of space, and the almighty power of the Creator?

From whence, then, could arise the solitary and strange conceit that the Almighty, who had millions of worlds equally dependent on His protection, should quit the care of all the rest, and come to die in our world, because, they say, one man and one woman had eaten an apple?

And, on the other hand, are we to suppose that every world in the boundless creation had an Eve, an apple, a serpent and a redeemer? In this case, the person who is irreverently called the Son of God, and sometimes God Himself, would have nothing else to do than to travel from world to world, in an endless succession of deaths, with scarcely a momentary interval of life.

Concerning the Multiplicity of Religions

It has been by rejecting the evidence that the world or works of God in the creation afford to our senses, and the action of our reason upon that evidence, that so many wild and whimsical systems of faith and of religion have been fabricated and set up.

There may be many systems of religion that, so far from being morally bad, are in many respects morally good; but there can be but ONE that is true; and that one necessarily must, as it ever will, be in all things consistent with the ever-existing word of God that we behold in His works. But such is the strange construction of the Christian system of faith that every evidence the heavens afford to man either directly contradicts it or renders it absurd.

It is possible to believe, and I always feel pleasure in encouraging myself to believe it, that there have been men in the world who persuade themselves that what is called a *pious fraud* might, at least under particular circumstances, be productive of some good. But the fraud being once established, could not afterward be explained, for it is with a pious fraud as with a bad action, it begets a calamitous necessity of going on.

The persons who first preached the Christian system of faith, and in some measure combined with it the morality preached by Jesus Christ, might persuade themselves that it was better than the heathen mythology that then prevailed. From the first preachers the fraud went on to the second and to the third, till the idea of its being a pious fraud became lost in the belief of its being true; and that belief became again encouraged by the interests of those who made a livelihood by preaching it.

But though such a belief might by such means be rendered almost general among the laity, it is next to impossible to account for the continued persecution carried on by the Church for several hundred years against the sciences and against the professors of science, if the Church had not some record or some tradition that it was originally no other than a pious fraud, or did not foresee that it could not be maintained against the evidence that the structure of the universe afforded.

Having thus shown the irreconcilable inconsistencies between the real word of God existing in the universe and that which is called *the Word of God,* as shown to us in a printed book that any man might make, I proceed to speak of the three principal means that have been employed in all ages, and perhaps in all countries, to impose upon mankind.

Those three means are mystery, miracle and prophecy. The two first are incompatible with true religion, and the third ought always to be suspected.

With respect to mystery, everything we behold is, in one sense, a mystery to us. Our own existence is a mystery; the whole vegetable world is a mystery. We cannot account how it is that an acorn, when put into the ground, is made to develop itself and become an oak. We know not how it is that the seed we sow unfolds and multiplies itself, and returns to us such an abundant interest for so small a capital.

The fact, however, as distinct from the operating cause, is not a mystery, because we see it, and we know also the means we are to use, which is no other than putting the seed into the ground. We know, therefore, as much as is necessary for us to know; and that part of the operation that we do not know, and which, if we did, we could not perform, the Creator takes upon Himself and performs it for us. We are, therefore, better off than if we had been let into the secret, and left to do it for ourselves.

But though every created thing is, in this sense a mystery, the word mystery cannot be applied to *moral truth,* any more than obscurity can be applied to light. The God in whom we believe is a God of moral truth, and not a God of mystery or obscurity. Mystery is the antagonist of truth. It is a fog of human invention, that obscures truth, and represents it in distortion. Truth never envelops *itself* in mystery, and the mystery in which it is at any time enveloped is the work of its antagonist, and never of itself.

The Best Way to Serve God

Religion, therefore, being the belief of a God and the practise of moral truth, cannot have connection with mystery. The belief of a God, so far from having anything of mystery in it, is of all beliefs the most easy, because it arises to us, as is before observed, out of necessity. And the practise of moral truth, or, in other words, a practical imitation of the moral goodness of God, is no other than our acting toward each other as He acts benignly toward all.

We cannot *serve* God in the manner we serve those who cannot do without such service; and, therefore, the only idea we can have of serving God is that of contributing to the happiness of the living creation that God has made. This cannot be done by retiring ourselves from the society of the world and spending a recluse life in selfish devotion.

The very nature and design of religion, if I may so express it, prove even to demonstration that it must be free from everything of mystery, and unencumbered with everything that is mysterious. Religion, considered as a duty, is incumbent upon every living soul alike, and, therefore, must be on a level with the understanding and comprehension of all.

Man does not learn religion as he learns the secrets and mysteries of a trade. He learns the theory of religion by reflection. It arises out of the action of his own mind upon the things which he sees, or upon what he may happen to hear or to read, and the practise joins itself thereto.

When men, whether from policy or pious fraud, set up systems of religion incompatible with the word or works of God in the creation, and not only above, but repugnant to human comprehension, they were under the necessity of inventing or adopting a word that should serve as a bar to all questions, inquiries and speculations. The word *mystery* answered this purpose, and thus it has happened that religion, which is in itself without mystery, has been corrupted into a fog of mysteries.

As *mystery* answered all general purposes, *miracle* followed as an occasional auxiliary. The former served to bewilder the mind, the latter to puzzle the senses. The one was the lingo, the other the legerdemain.

But before going further into this subject, it will be proper to inquire what is to be understood by a miracle.

In the same sense that everything may be said to be a mystery, so also may it be said that everything is a miracle, and that no one thing is a greater miracle than another. The elephant, though larger, is not a greater miracle than a mite, nor a mountain a greater miracle than an atom. To an almighty power, it is no more difficult to make the one than the other, and no more difficult to make millions of worlds than to make one.

Everything, therefore, is a miracle in one sense, while in the other sense there is no such thing as a miracle. It is a miracle when compared to our power and to our comprehension, it is not a miracle compared to the power that performs it; but as nothing in this description conveys the idea that is affixed to the word miracle, it is necessary to carry the inquiry further.

Mankind have conceived to themselves certain laws by which what they call nature is supposed to act; and that a miracle is something contrary to the operation and effect of those laws; but unless we know the whole extent of those laws, and of what are commonly called the powers of nature, we are not able to judge whether anything that may appear to us wonderful or miraculous be within, or be beyond, or be contrary to, her natural power of acting.

The ascension of man several miles high in the air would have everything in it that constitutes the idea of a miracle if it were not known that a species of air can be generated several times lighter than the common atmospheric air and yet possess elasticity enough to prevent the balloon in which that light air is inclosed from being compressed into as many times less bulk by the common air that surrounds it.

In like manner, extracting flashes or sparks of fire from the human body, as visibly as from a steel struck with a flint, and causing iron or steel to move without any visible agent, would also give the idea of a miracle if we were not acquainted with electricity and magnetism. So also would many other experiments in natural philosophy, to those who are not acquainted with the subject.

The restoring of persons to life who are to appearance dead, as is practised upon drowned persons, would also be a miracle if it were not known that animation is capable of being suspended without being extinct.

Besides these, there are performances by sleight-of-hand, and by persons acting in concert that have a miraculous appearance, which when known are thought nothing of. And besides these, there are mechanical and optical deceptions. There is now an exhibition in Paris of ghosts or spectres, which, though it is not imposed upon the spectators as a fact, has an astonishing appearance. As, therefore, we know not the extent to which either nature or art can go, there is no positive criterion to determine what a miracle is, and mankind, in giving credit to appearances, under the idea of there being miracles, are subject to be continually imposed upon.

Since, then, appearances are so capable of deceiving, and things not real have a strong resemblance to things that are, nothing can be more inconsistent than to suppose that the Almighty would make use of means such as are called miracles that would subject the person who performed them to the suspicion of being an impostor, and the person who related them to be suspected of lying, and the doctrine intended to be supported thereby to be suspected as a fabulous invention.

Of all the modes of evidence that ever were invented to obtain belief to any system or opinion to which the name of religion has been given, that of miracle, however successful the imposition may have been, is the most inconsistent. For, in the first place, whenever recourse is had to show, for the purpose of procuring that belief (for a miracle, under any idea of the word, is a show), it implies a lameness or weakness in the doctrine that is preached.

And, in the second place, it is degrading the Almighty into the character of a showman, playing tricks to amuse and make the people stare and wonder. It is also the most equivocal sort of evidence that can be set up; for the belief is not to depend upon the thing called a miracle, but upon the credit of the reporter who says that he saw it; and, therefore, the thing, were it true, would have no better chance of being believed than if it were a lie.

Suppose I were to say that when I sat down to write this book a hand presented itself in the air, took up the pen and wrote every word that is herein written; would anybody believe me? Certainly they would not. Would they believe me a whit more if the thing had been a fact? Certainly they would not.

Since, then, a real miracle, were it to happen, would be subject to the same fate as the falsehood, the inconsistency becomes the greater of supposing the Almighty would make use of means that would not answer the purpose for which they were intended, even if they were real.

If we are to suppose a miracle to be something so entirely out of the course of what is called nature that she must go out of that course to accomplish it, and we see an account given of such miracle by the person who said he saw it, it raises a question in the mind very easily decided, which is, is it more probable that nature should go out of her course or that a man should tell a lie? We have never seen, in our time, nature go out of her course; but we have good reason to believe that millions of lies have been told in the same time; it is, therefore, at least millions to one that the reporter of a miracle tells a lie.

The story of the whale swallowing Jonah, though a whale is large enough to do it, borders greatly on the marvelous; but it would have approached nearer to the idea of a miracle if Jonah had swallowed the whale. In this, which may serve for all cases of miracles, the matter would decide itself, as before stated, namely, is it more probable that a man should have swallowed a whale or told a lie?

But suppose that Jonah had really swallowed the whale, and gone with it in his belly to Nineveh and, to convince the people that it was true, had cast it up in their sight, of the full length and size of a whale, would they not have believed him to have been the devil instead of a prophet? Or, if the whale had carried Jonah to Nineveh, and cast him up in the same public manner, would they not have believed the whale to have been the devil, and Jonah one of his imps?

The most extraordinary of all the things called miracles, related in the New Testament, is that of the devil flying away with Jesus Christ, and carrying him to the top of a high mountain, and to the top of the highest pinnacle of the temple, and showing him and promising to him *all the kingdoms of the World.* How happened it that he did not discover America, or is it only with *kingdoms* that his sooty highness has any interest?

I have too much respect for the moral character of Christ to believe that he told this whale of a miracle himself; neither is it easy to account for what purpose it could have been fabricated, unless it were to impose upon the connoisseurs of miracles as is sometimes practised upon the connoisseurs of Queen Anne's farthings and collectors of relics and antiquities; or to render the belief of miracles ridiculous by outdoing miracles, as Don Quixote outdid chivalry; or to embarrass the belief of miracles by making it doubtful by what power, whether of God or of the devil, anything called a miracle was performed. It requires, however, a great deal of faith in the devil to believe this miracle

In every point of view in which those things called miracles can be placed and considered, the reality of them is improbable and their existence unnecessary. They would not, as before observed, answer any useful purpose even if they were true; for it is more difficult to obtain belief to a miracle than to a principle evidently moral without any miracle.

Moral principle speaks universally for itself. Miracle could be but a thing of the moment, and seen but by a few; after this it requires a transfer of faith from God to man to believe a miracle upon man's report. Instead, therefore, of admitting the recitals of miracles as evidence of any system of religion being true, they ought to be considered as symptoms of its being fabulous. It is necessary to the full and upright character of truth that it rejects the crutch, and it is consistent with the character of fable to seek the aid that truth rejects. Thus much for mystery and miracle.

As mystery and miracle took charge of the past and the present, prophecy took charge of the future and rounded the tenses of faith. It was not sufficient to know what had been done, but what would be done. The supposed prophet was the supposed historian of times to come; and if he happened, in shooting with a long bow of a thousand years, to strike within a thousand miles of a mark, the ingenuity of posterity could make it point-blank; and if he happened to be directly wrong, it was only to suppose, as in the case of Jonah and Nineveh, that God had repented Himself and changed His mind. What a fool do fabulous systems make of man!

PROPHETS AND THEIR PROPHECIES

It has been shown, in a former part of this work, that the original meaning of the words *prophet* and *prophesying* has been changed, and that a prophet, in the sense of the word as now used, is a creature of modern invention; and it is owing to this change in the meaning of the words, that the flights and metaphors of the Jewish poets, and phrases and expressions now rendered obscure by our not being acquainted with the local circumstances to which they applied at the time they were used, have been erected into prophecies and made to bend to explanations at the will and whimsical conceits of sectaries, expounders and commentators.

Everything unintelligible was prophetical, and everything insignificant was typical. A blunder would have served for a prophecy, and a dish-clout for a type.

If by a prophet we are to suppose a man to whom the Almighty com-municated some event that would take place in future, either there were such men or there were not. If there were, it is consistent to believe that the event so communicated would be told in terms that could be understood, and not related in such a loose and obscure manner as to be out of the comprehension of those that heard it, and so equivocal as to fit almost any circumstance that might happen afterward. It is conceiving very irreverently of the Almighty to suppose that He would deal in this jesting manner with mankind, yet all the things called prophecies in the book called the Bible come under this description.

But it is with prophecy as it is with miracle; it could not answer the purpose even if it were real. Those to whom a prophecy should be told, could not tell whether the man prophesied or lied, or whether it had been revealed to him, or whether he conceited it; and if the thing that he prophesied, or intended to prophesy, should happen, or something like it, among the multitude of things that are daily happening, nobody could again know whether he foreknew it, or guessed at it, or whether it was accidental.

A prophet, therefore, is a character useless and unnecessary; and the safe side of the case is to guard against being imposed upon by not giving credit to such relations.

Upon the whole, mystery, miracle and prophecy are appendages that belong to fabulous and not to true religion. They are the means by which so many *Lo, heres!* and *Lo, theres!* have been spread about the world, and religion been made into a trade. The success of one impostor gave encouragement to another, and the quieting salvo of doing *some good* by keeping up a *pious fraud* protected them from remorse.

RECAPITULATION

Having now extended the subject to a greater length than I first in-tended, I shall bring it to a close by abstracting a summary from the whole.

First—That the idea or belief of a Word of God existing in print, or in writing, or in speech, is inconsistent in itself for reasons already assigned. These reasons, among many others, are the want of a uni-versal language; the mutability of language; the errors to which translations are subject; the possibility of totally suppressing such a word; the probability of altering it, or of fabricating the whole, and imposing it upon the world.

Secondly—That the creation we behold is the real and ever-existing Word of God, in which we cannot be deceived. It proclaims His power, it demonstrates His wisdom, it manifests His goodness and beneficence.

Thirdly—That the moral duty of man consists in imitating the moral goodness and beneficence of God, manifested in the creation toward all His creatures. That seeing, as we daily do, the goodness of God to all men, it is an example calling upon all men to practise the same toward each other; and, consequently, that everything of persecution and revenge between man and man, and everything of cruelty to animals, is a violation of moral duty.

I trouble not myself about the manner of future existence. I content myself with believing, even to positive conviction, that the Power that gave me existence is able to continue it, in any form and manner He pleases, either with or without this body; and it appears more probable to me that I shall continue to exist hereafter, than that I should have had existence, as I now have, before that existence began.

It is certain that, in one point, all the nations of the earth and all religions agree—all believe in a God; the things in which they disagree are the redundancies annexed to that belief; and, therefore, if ever a universal religion should prevail, it will not be by believing anything new, but in getting rid of redundancies and believing as man believed at first. Adam, if ever there were such a man, was created a Deist; but in the meantime, let every man follow, as he has a right to do, the religion and the worship he prefers.

END OF THE FIRST PART

AUTOBIOGRAPHICAL INTERLUDE

Thus far I had written on the 28th of December, 1793. In the evening I went to the Hotel Philadelphia (formerly White's Hotel), Passage des Petits Pères, where I lodged when I came to Paris in consequence of being elected a member of the Convention, but had left the lodging about nine months, and taken lodgings in the Rue Fauxbourg St. Denis, for the sake of being more retired than I could be in the middle of the town.

Meeting with a company of Americans at the Hotel Philadelphia, I agreed to spend the evening with them; and as my lodging was distant about a mile and a half, I bespoke a bed at the hotel. The company broke up about twelve o'clock and I went directly to bed. About four in the morning I was awakened by a rapping at my chamber door; when I opened it, I saw a guard and the master of the hotel with them. The guard told me they came to put me under arrestation and to demand the key of my papers. I desired them to walk in, and I would dress myself and go with them immediately.

It happened that Archilles Audibert, of Calais, was then in the hotel; and I desired to be conducted into his room. When we came there I told the guard that I had only lodged at the hotel for that night; that I was printing a work, and that part of that work was at the Maison Bretagne, Rue Jacob; and desired they would take me there first, which they did.

The printing office at which the work was printing was near the Maison Bretagne, where Colonel Blackden and Joel Barlow, of the United States of America, lodged; and I had desired Joel Barlow to compare the proof sheets with the copy as they came from the press. The remainder of the manuscript from page 32 to 76 was at my lodging. But besides the necessity of my collecting all the parts of the work together that the publication might not be interrupted by my imprisonment or by any event that might happen to me, it was highly proper that I should have a fellow-citizen of America with me during the examination of my papers, as I had letters of correspondence in my possession of the President of Congress, General Washington; the Minister of Foreign Affairs to Congress, Mr. Jefferson; and the late Benjamin Franklin; and it might be necessary for me to make a pròces-verbal to send to Congress.

It happened that Joel Barlow had received only one proof sheet of the work, which he had compared with the copy and sent it back to the printing office.

We then went in company with Joel Barlow to my lodging; and the guard, or commissaires, took with them the interpreter to Committee of Surety-General. It was satisfactory to me that they went through the examination of my papers with the strictness they did; and it is but justice that I say they did it not only with civility, but with tokens of respect to my character.

I showed them the remainder of the manuscript of the foregoing work. The interpreter examined it and returned it to me saying, *"It is an interesting work; it will do much good."* I also showed him another manuscript, which I had intended for the Committee of Public Safety. It is entitled, "Observations on the Commerce between the United States of America and France."

After the examination of my papers was finished, the guard conducted me to the prison of the Luxembourg where they left me as they would a man whose undeserved fate they regretted. I offered to write under the procès-verbal they had made that they had executed their orders with civility, but they had declined it.

THE AGE OF REASON

PART SECOND

PREFACE

I HAVE mentioned in the former part of "The Age of Reason" that it had long been my intention to publish my thoughts upon religion; but that I had originally reserved it to a later period in life, intending it to be the last work I should undertake. The circumstances, however, which existed in France in the latter end of the year 1793 determined me to delay it no longer. The just and humane principles of the Revolution, which philosophy had first diffused, had been departed from. The idea, always dangerous to society, as it is derogatory to the Almighty, that priests could forgive sins, though it seemed to exist no longer, had blunted the feelings of humanity and prepared men for the commission of all crimes.

The intolerant spirit of Church persecutions had transferred itself into politics; the tribunal styled revolutionary supplied the place of an inquisition; and the guillotine of the stake. I saw many of my most intimate friends destroyed, others daily carried to prison, and I had reason to believe, and had also intimations given me that the same danger was approaching myself.

Under these disadvantages, I began the former part of "The Age of Reason"; I had, besides, neither Bible nor Testament [1] to refer to, though I was writing against both; nor could I procure any; notwithstanding which, I have produced a work that no Bible believer, though

---

[1] Paine continually refers to the Old Testament as the "Bible," and to the New Testament as the Testament.—*Editor.*

writing at his ease, and with a library of Church books about him, can refute.

Toward the latter end of December of that year a motion was made and carried to exclude foreigners from the Convention. There were but two in it, Anacharsis Cloots [2] and myself; and I saw I was particularly pointed at by Bourbon de l'Oise, in his speech on that motion.

Conceiving, after this, that I had but a few days of liberty, I sat down and brought the work to a close as speedily as possible; and I had not finished it more than six hours, in the state it has since appeared, before a guard came there, about three in the morning, with an order signed by the two Committees of Public Safety and Surety-General for putting me in arrestation as a foreigner, and conveyed me to the prison of the Luxembourg.

I contrived, on my way there, to call on Joel Barlow,[3] and I put the manuscript of the work into his hands, as more safe than in my possession in prison; and, not knowing what might be the fate in France either of the writer or the work, I addressed it to the protection of the citizens of the United States.

It is with justice that I say that the guard who executed this order, and the interpreter of the Committee of General Surety who accompanied them to examine my papers, treated me not only with civility, but with respect. The keeper of the Luxembourg, Bennoit, a man of a good heart, showed to me every friendship in his power, as did also all his family, while he continued in that station. He was removed from it, put into arrestation, and carried before the tribunal upon a malignant accusation, but acquitted.

After I had been in the Luxembourg about three weeks, the Americans then in Paris went in a body to the Convention to reclaim me as their countryman and friend; but were answered by the President, Vadier, who was also President of the Committee of Surety-General, and had signed the order for my arrestation, that I was born in England. I heard no more, after this, from any person out of the walls of the prison till the fall of Robespierre, on the ninth of Thermidor—July 27, 1794.

About two months before this event I was seized with a fever that in

[2] Anacharsis Clootz was a leader of the Girondins in France and the author of a pamphlet entitled *Ni Marat ni Roland.*—*Editor.*
[3] Joel Barlow was the author of the great poem, *The Columbiad* and a close friend of Paine.—*Editor.*

its progress had every symptom of becoming mortal, and from the effects of which I am not recovered. It was then that I remembered with renewed satisfaction, and congratulated myself most sincerely, on having written the former part of "The Age of Reason." I had then but little expectation of surviving, and those about me had less. I know, therefore, by experience, the conscientious trial of my own principles.

I was then with three chamber comrades, Joseph Vanhuele, of Bruges; Charles Bastini and Michael Rubyns, of Louvain. The unceasing and anxious attention of these three friends to me, by night and by day, I remember with gratitude and mention with pleasure. It happened that a physician (Dr. Graham) and a surgeon (Mr. Bond), part of the suite of General O'Hara,[4] were then in the Luxembourg. I ask not myself whether it be convenient to them, as men under the English Government, that I express to them my thanks, but I should reproach myself if I did not; and also to the physician of the Luxembourg, Dr. Markoski.

I have some reason to believe, because I cannot discover any other, that this illness preserved me in existence. Among the papers of Robespierre that were examined and reported upon to the Convention by a Committee of Deputies is a note in the handwriting of Robespierre, in the following words:

"Demander que Thomas Paine soit décrété d'accusation, pour l'intérêts de l'Amerique autant que de la France."

To demand that a decree of accusation be passed against Thomas Paine, for the interest of America, as well as of France.

From what cause it was that the intention was not put in execution I know not, and cannot inform myself, and therefore I ascribe it to impossibility, on account of that illness.

The Convention, to repair as much as lay in their power the injustice I had sustained, invited me publicly and unanimously to return into the Convention, and which I accepted, to show I could bear an injury without permitting it to injure my principles or my disposition. It is not because right principles have been violated that they are to be abandoned.

I have seen, since I have been at liberty, several publications written,

---

[4] O'Hara was a British officer who officiated for Cornwallis at the Yorktown surrender. He was in prison with Paine and the latter loaned him about $1,500 when he (O'Hara) was released from the jail ahead of Paine.—*Editor.*

some in America and some in England, as answers to the former part of "The Age of Reason." If the authors of these can amuse themselves by so doing, I shall not interrupt them. They may write against the work, and against me, as much as they please; they do me more service than they intend, and I can have no objection that they write on. They will find, however, by this second part, without its being written as an answer to them, that they must return to their work, and spin their cobweb over again. The first is brushed away by accident.

They will now find that I have furnished myself with a Bible and a Testament; and I can say also that I have found them to be much worse books than I had conceived. If I have erred in anything in the former part of "The Age of Reason," it has been by speaking better of some parts of those books than they have deserved.

I observe that all my opponents resort, more or less, to what they call Scripture evidence and Bible authority to help them out. They are so little masters of the subject as to confound a dispute about authenticity with a dispute about doctrines; I will, however, put them right, that if they should be disposed to write any more, they may know how to begin.

THOMAS PAINE.

October, 1795.

CHAPTER I

As to the Old Testament

IT HAS often been said, that anything may be proved from the Bible, but before anything can be admitted as proved by the Bible, the Bible itself must be proved to be true; for if the Bible be not true, or the truth of it be doubtful, it ceases to have authority, and cannot be admitted as proof of anything.

It has been the practise of all Christian commentators on the Bible, and of all Christian priests and preachers, to impose the Bible on the world as a mass of truth and as the Word of God; they have disputed and wrangled, and anathematized each other about the supposeable meaning of particular parts and passages therein; one has said and insisted that such a passage meant such a thing; another that it meant directly the contrary; and a third, that it meant neither one nor the other, but something different from both; and this they have called *understanding* the Bible.

It has happened that all the answers which I have seen to the former part of "The Age of Reason" have been written by priests; and these pious men, like their predecessors, contend and wrangle, and *understand* the Bible; each understands it differently, but each understands it best; and they have agreed in nothing but in telling their readers that Thomas Paine understands it not.

Now, instead of wasting their time and heating themselves in fractious disputations about doctrinal points drawn from the Bible, these men ought to know, and if they do not, it is civility to inform them, that the first thing to be understood is whether there is sufficient authority for believing the Bible to be the Word of God or whether there is not.

There are matters in that book, said to be done by the *express command* of God, that are as shocking to humanity and to every idea we have of moral justice as anything done by Robespierre, by Carrier, by Joseph le Bon, in France, by the English Government in the East Indies, or by any other assassin in modern times. When we read in the books ascribed to Moses, Joshua, etc., that they (the Israelites) came by stealth upon whole nations of people, who, as history itself shows, had given them no offense; *that they put all those nations to the sword; that they spared neither age nor infancy; that they utterly destroyed men, women and children; that they left not a soul to breathe*—expressions that are repeated over and over again in those books, and that, too, with exulting ferocity—are we sure these things are facts? Are we sure that the Creator of man commissioned these things to be done? And are we sure that the books that tell us so were written by His authority?

It is not the antiquity of a tale that is any evidence of its truth; on the contrary, it is a symptom of its being fabulous; for the more ancient any history pretends to be the more it has the resemblance of a fable. The origin of every nation is buried in fabulous tradition, and that of the Jews is as much to be suspected as any other.

To charge the commission of acts upon the Almighty, which, in their own nature and by every rule of moral justice, are crimes, as all assassination is, and more especially the assassination of infants, is matter of serious concern. The Bible tells us, that those assassinations were done by the *express command of God*.

To believe, therefore, the Bible to be true, we must *unbelieve* all our belief in the moral justice of God; for wherein could crying or smiling infants offend? And to read the Bible without horror, we must undo everything that is tender, sympathizing and benevolent in the heart of man. Speaking for myself, if I had no other evidence that the Bible is fabulous than the sacrifice I must make to believe it to be true, that alone would be sufficient to determine my choice.

But in addition to all the moral evidence against the Bible, I will in the progress of this work produce such other evidence as even a priest cannot deny, and show, from that evidence, that the Bible is not entitled to credit as being the Word of God.

But, before I proceed to this examination, I will show wherein the Bible differs from all other ancient writings with respect to the nature of the evidence necessary to establish its authenticity; and this is the more proper to be done, because the advocates of the Bible, in their answers to the former part of "The Age of Reason," undertake to say, and they put some stress thereon, that the authenticity of the Bible is as well established as that of any other ancient book; as if our belief of the one could become any rule for our belief of the other.

I know, however, but of one ancient book that authoritatively challenges universal consent and belief, and that is Euclid's "Elements of Geometry" [5] and the reason is, because it is a book of self-evident demonstration, entirely independent of its author, and of everything relating to time, place and circumstance. The matters contained in that book would have the same authority they now have, had they been written by any other person, or had the work been anonymous, or had the author never been known; for the identical certainty of who was the author makes no part of our belief of the matters contained in the book.

But it is quite otherwise with respect to the books ascribed to Moses, to Joshua, to Samuel, etc.; those are books of *testimony,* and they testify of things naturally incredible; and, therefore, the whole of our belief as to the authenticity of those books rests, in the first place, upon the *certainty* that they were written by Moses, Joshua and Samuel; secondly, upon the credit we give to their testimony.

We may believe the first, that is, we may believe the certainty of the authorship, and yet not the testimony; in the same manner that we may believe that a certain person gave evidence upon a case and yet not believe the evidence that he gave.

But if it should be found that the books ascribed to Moses, Joshua

---

[5] Euclid, according to Chronological history, lived three years before Christ, and about one hundred years before Archimedes; he was of the city of Alexandria in Egypt.—*Author.*

and Samuel were not written by Moses, Joshua and Samuel, every part of the authority and authenticity of those books is gone at once; for there can be no such thing as forged or invented testimony; neither can there be anonymous testimony, more especially as to things naturally incredible, such as that of talking to God face to face, or that of the sun and moon standing still at the command of a man.

The greatest part of the other ancient books are works of genius, of which kind are those ascribed to Homer, to Plato, to Aristotle, to Demosthenes, to Cicero, etc. Here, again, the author is not an essential in the credit we give to any of those works, for, as works of genius, they would have the same merit they have now, were they anonymous.

Nobody believes the Trojan story, as related by Homer, to be true—for it is the poet only that is admired, and the merit of the poet will remain, though the story be fabulous. But if we disbelieve the matters related by the Bible authors (Moses, for instance), as we disbelieve the things related by Homer, there remains nothing of Moses in our estimation, but an impostor.

As to the ancient historians, from Herodotus to Tacitus, we credit them as far as they relate things probable and credible, and no further; for if we do, we must believe the two miracles which Tacitus relates were performed by Vespasian, that of curing a lame man and a blind man in just the same manner as the same things are told of Jesus Christ by his historians. We must also believe the miracle cited by Josephus, that of the sea of Pamphilia opening to let Alexander and his army pass, as is related of the Red Sea in Exodus.

These miracles are quite as well authenticated as the Bible miracles, and yet we do not believe them; consequently the degree of evidence necessary to establish our belief of things naturally incredible, whether in the Bible or elsewhere, is far greater than that which obtains our belief to natural and probable things; and therefore the advocates for the Bible have no claim to our belief of the Bible, because that we believe the things stated in other ancient writings; since that we believe the things stated in these writings no further than they are probable and credible, or because they are self-evident, like Euclid; or admire them because they are elegant, like Homer; or approve of them because they are sedate, like Plato; or judicious, like Aristotle.

Having premised those things, I proceed to examine the authenticity of the Bible, and I begin with what are called the five books of Moses, Genesis, Exodus, Leviticus, Numbers and Deuteronomy. My intention is to show that those books are spurious, and that Moses is not the author of them; and still further, that they were not written in the time of Moses, nor till several hundred years afterward; that they are no other than an attempted history of the life of Moses, and of the times in which he is said to have lived, and also of the times prior thereto, written by some very ignorant and stupid pretenders to authorship several hundred years after the death of Moses, as men now write histories of things that happened, or are supposed to have happened, several hundred or several thousand years ago.

The evidence that I shall produce in this case is from the books themselves, and I shall confine myself to this evidence only. Were I to refer for proof to any of the ancient authors whom the advocates of the Bible call profane authors, they would controvert that authority, as I controvert theirs; I will therefore come on their own ground, and oppose them with their own weapon, the Bible.

In the first place, there is no affirmative evidence that Moses is the author of those books; and that he is the author, is altogether an unfounded opinion, got abroad nobody knows how. The style and manner in which those books are written give no room to believe, or even to suppose, they were written by Moses, for it is altogether the style and manner of another person speaking of Moses.

In Exodus, Leviticus and Numbers (for everything in Genesis is prior to the time of Moses, and not the least allusion is made to him therein), the whole, I say, of these books is in the third person; it is always, *the Lord said unto Moses,* or *Moses said unto the Lord,* or *Moses said unto the people* or *the people said unto Moses;* and this is the style and manner that historians use in speaking of the persons whose lives and actions they are writing. It may be said that a man may speak of himself in the third person, and therefore it may be supposed that Moses did; but supposition proves nothing; and if the advocates for the belief that Moses wrote those books himself have nothing better to advance than supposition, they may as well be silent.

But granting the grammatical right that Moses might speak of himself in the third person, because any man might speak of himself in that manner, it cannot be admitted as a fact in those books that it is Moses who speaks, without rendering Moses truly ridiculous and absurd. For example, Numbers, chap. xii. ver. 3. *Now the man Moses was very meek, above all the men which were upon the face of the earth.*

If Moses said this of himself, instead of being the meekest of men, he was one of the most vain and arrogant of coxcombs; and the advocates for those books may now take which side they please, for both sides are against them; if Moses was not the author, the books are without authority; and if he was the author, the author is without credit, because to boast of *meekness* is the reverse of meekness, and is *a lie in sentiment*.

In Deuteronomy, the style and manner of writing marks more evidently than in the former books that Moses is not the writer. The manner here used is dramatical; the writer opens the subject by a short introductory discourse, and then introduces Moses as in the act of speaking, and when he has made Moses finish his harangue, he (the writer) resumes his own part, and speaks till he brings Moses forward again, and at last closes the scene with an account of the death, funeral and character of Moses.

This interchange of speakers occurs four times in this book; from the first verse of the first chapter to the end of the fifth verse it is the writer who speaks; he then introduces Moses as in the act of making his harangue, and this continues to the end of the 40th verse of the fourth chapter; here the writer drops Moses and speaks historically of what was done in consequence of what Moses, when living, is supposed to have said, and which the writer had dramatically rehearsed.

The writer opens the subject again in the first verse of the fifth chapter, though it is only by saying that Moses called the people of Israel together; he then introduces Moses as before, and continues him, as in the act of speaking, to the end of the 26th chapter. He does the same thing at the beginning of the 27th chapter; and continues Moses, as in the act of speaking, to the end of the 28th chapter. At the 29th chapter the writer speaks again through the whole of the first verse and the first line of the second verse, where he introduces Moses for the last time and continues him, as in the act of speaking, to the end of the 33d chapter.

The writer, having now finished the rehearsal on the part of Moses, comes forward and speaks through the whole of the last chapter; he begins by telling the reader that Moses went to the top of Pisgah; that he saw from thence the land which (the writer says) had been promised to Abraham, Isaac and Jacob; that he, Moses, died there in the land of Moab, but that no man knows of his sepulchre unto this day; that is, unto the time in which the writer lived who wrote the book of Deuteronomy. The writer then tells us, that Moses was 110 years of age when he died—that his eye was not dim, nor his natural force abated;

and he concludes by saying that there arose not a prophet *since* in Israel like unto Moses, whom, says this anonymous writer, the Lord knew face to face.

Having thus shown, as far as grammatical evidence applies, that Moses was not the writer of those books, I will, after making a few observations on the inconsistencies of the writer of the book of Deuteronomy, proceed to show from the historical and chronological evidence contained in those books, that Moses was not, because *he could not be,* the writer of them, and consequently that there is no authority for believing that the inhuman and horrid butcheries of men, women and children, told of in those books, were done, as those books say they were, at the command of God. It is a duty incumbent on every true Deist, that he vindicate the moral justice of God against the calumnies of the Bible.

The writer of the book of Deuteronomy, whoever he was (for it is an anonymous work), is obscure, and also in contradiction with himself, in the account he has given of Moses.

After telling that Moses went to the top of Pisgah (and it does not appear from any account that he ever came down again), he tells us that Moses died *there* in the land of Moab, and that *he* buried him in a valley in the land of Moab; but as there is no antecedent to the pronoun *he,* there is no knowing who *he* was that did bury him. If the writer meant that *He* (God) buried him, how should *he* (the writer) know it? or why should we (the readers) believe him? since we know not who the writer was that tells us so, for certainly Moses could not himself tell where he was buried.

The writer also tells us, that no man knows where the sepulchre of Moses is *unto this day,* meaning the time in which this writer lived; how then should he know that Moses was buried in a valley in the land of Moab? for as the writer lived long after the time of Moses, as is evident from his using the expression of *unto this day,* meaning a great length of time after the death of Moses, he certainly was not at his funeral; and on the other hand, it is impossible that Moses himself could say that *no man knows where the sepulchre is unto this day.* To make Moses the speaker would be an improvement on the play of a child that hides himself and cries *nobody can find me;* nobody can find Moses!

This writer has nowhere told us how he came by the speeches which he has put into the mouth of Moses to speak, and therefore we have a right to conclude that he either composed them himself or wrote them from oral tradition. One or the other of these is the more probable, since he has given in the fifth chapter a table of commandments in which that called the fourth commandment is different from the fourth commandment in the twentieth chapter of Exodus.

In that of Exodus the reason given for keeping the seventh day is, "because (says the commandment) God made the heavens and the earth in six days, and rested on the seventh"; but in that of Deuteronomy, the reason given is that it was the day on which the children of Israel came out of Egypt and *therefore*, says this commandment, *the Lord thy God commanded thee to keep the sabbath day*. This makes no mention of the Creation, nor *that* of the coming out of Egypt.

There are also many things given as laws of Moses in this book that are not to be found in any of the other books; among which is that inhuman and brutal law, chapter xxi., verses 18, 19, 20 and 21, which authorizes parents, the father and the mother, to bring their own children to have them stoned to death for what it is pleased to call stubbornness.

But priests have always been fond of preaching up Deuteronomy, for Deuteronomy preaches up tithes; and it is from this book, chap. xxv., ver. 4, that they have taken the phrase, and applied it to tithing, that *"thou shalt not muzzle the ox when he treadeth out the corn"*; and that this might not escape observation, they have noted it in the table of contents at the head of the chapter, though it is only a single verse of less than two lines. Oh, priests! priests! ye are willing to be compared to an ox, for the sake of tithes.

Though it is impossible for us to know *identically* who the writer of Deuteronomy was, it is not difficult to discover him *professionally*, that he was some Jewish priest, who lived, as I shall show in the course of this work, at least three hundred and fifty years after the time of Moses.

I come now to speak of the historical and chronological evidence. The chronology that I shall use is the Bible chronology, for I mean not to go out of the Bible for evidence of anything, but to make the Bible itself prove, historically and chronologically, that Moses is not the author of the books ascribed to him. It is, therefore, proper that I inform the reader (such at least as may not have the opportunity of knowing it), that in the larger Bibles, and also in some smaller ones, there is a series of chronology printed in the margin of every page, for the purpose of showing how long the historical matters stated in each page happened, or are supposed to have happened, before Christ, and, consequently, the distance of time between one historical circumstance and another.

I begin with the book of Genesis. In the 14th chapter of Genesis, the writer gives an account of Lot being taken prisoner in a battle between the four kings against five, and carried off; and that when the account of Lot being taken came to Abraham, he armed all his household and marched to rescue Lot from the captors, and that he pursued them unto Dan (ver. 14).

To show in what manner this expression of *pursuing them unto Dan* applies to the case in question, I will refer to two circumstances, the one in America, the other in France.

The city now called New York, in America, was originally New Amsterdam; and the town in France, lately called Havre Marat, was before called Havre de Grace. New Amsterdam was changed to New York in the year 1664; Havre de Grace to Havre Marat in the year 1793. Should, therefore, any writing be found, though without date, in which the name of New York should be mentioned, it would be certain evidence that such a writing could not have been written before, but must have been written after New Amsterdam was changed to New York, and consequently, not till after the year 1664, or at least during the course of that year. And, in like manner, any dateless writing with the name Havre Marat would be certain evidence that such a writing must have been written after Havre de Grace became Havre Marat, and consequently not till after the year 1793, or at least during the course of that year.

I now come to the application of those cases, and to show that there was no such place as *Dan*, till many years after the death of Moses, and consequently that Moses could not be the writer of the book of Genesis, where this account of pursuing them unto *Dan* is given. The place that is called Dan in the Bible was originally a town of the Gentiles called Laish; and when the tribe of Dan seized upon this town they changed its name to Dan, in commemoration of Dan, who was the father of that tribe and the great-grandson of Abraham.

To establish this in proof, it is necessary to refer from Genesis, to the 18th chapter of the book called the book of Judges. It is there said (ver. 27) *that they* (the Danites) *came unto Laish to a people that were quiet and secure, and they smote them with the edge of the sword* (the Bible is filled with murder) *and burned the city with fire; and they built a city* (ver. 28), and dwelt therein, *and they called the name of the city*

Dan, after the name of Dan, their father, howbeit the name of the city was Laish at the first.

This account of the Danites taking possession of Laish and changing it to Dan is placed in the book of Judges immediately after the death of Samson. The death of Samson is said to have happened 1120 years before Christ, and that of Moses 1451 before Christ; and, therefore, according to the historical arrangement, the place was not called Dan till 331 years after the death of Moses.

There is a striking confusion between the historical and the chronological arrangement in the book of Judges. The five last chapters, as they stand in the book, 17, 18, 19, 20, 21, are put chronologically before all the preceding chapters; they are made to be 28 years before the 16th chapter, 266 before the 15th, 245 before the 13th, 195 before the 9th, 90 before the 4th, and 15 years before the 1st chapter. This shows the uncertain and fabulous state of the Bible.

According to the chronological arrangement, the taking of Laish and giving it the name of Dan is made to be 20 years after the death of Joshua, who was the successor of Moses; and by the historical order as it stands in the book, it is made to be 306 years after the death of Joshua, and 331 after that of Moses; but they both exclude Moses from being the writer of Genesis, because, according to either of the statements, no such a place as Dan existed in the time of Moses; and therefore the writer of Genesis must have been some person who lived after the town of Laish had the name of Dan; and who that person was nobody knows, and consequently the book of Genesis is anonymous and without authority.

I proceed now to state another point of historial and chronological evidence, and to show therefrom, as in the preceding case, that Moses is not the author of the book of Genesis.

In the 36th chapter of Genesis there is given a genealogy of the sons and descendants of Esau, who are called Edomites, and also a list, by name, of the kings of Edom, in enumerating of which, it is said (ver. 31), *And these are the kings that reigned in Edom, before there reigned any king over the children of Israel.*

Now, were any dateless writings to be found in which, speaking of any past events, the writer should say, These things happened before there was any Congress in America, or before there was any Convention in France, it would be evidence that such writing could not have been written before, and could only be written after there was a Congress in

America, or a Convention in France, as the case might be; and, consequently, that it could not be written by any person who died before there was a Congress in the one country or a Convention in the other.

Nothing is more frequent, as well in history as in conversation, than to refer to a fact in the room of a date; it is most natural so to do, first, because a fact fixes itself in the memory better than a date; secondly, because the fact includes the date and serves to excite two ideas at once; and this manner of speaking by circumstances implies as positively that the fact alluded to is *past* as if it were so expressed.

When a person speaking upon any matter, says, it was before I was married, or before my son was born, or before I went to America, or before I went to France, it is absolutely understood, and intended to be understood, that he had been married, that he has had a son, that he has been in America or been in France. Language does not admit of using this mode of expression in any other sense; and whenever such an expression is found anywhere it can only be understood in the sense in which it only could have been used.

The passage, therefore, that I have quoted—"that these are the kings that reigned in Edom, before there reigned *any* king over the children of Israel"—could only have been written after the first king began to reign over them; and, consequently, that the book of Genesis, so far from having been written by Moses, could not have been written till the time of Saul at least.

This is the positive sense of the passage; but the expression, *any* king, implies more kings than one, at least it implies two, and this will carry it to the time of David; and if taken in a general sense, it carries itself through all times of the Jewish monarchy.

Had we met with this verse in any part of the Bible that *professed* to have been written after kings began to reign in Israel, it would have been impossible not to have seen the application of it. It happens then that this is the case; the two books of Chronicles which give a history of all the kings of Israel are *professedly,* as well as in fact, written after the Jewish monarchy began; and this verse that I have quoted, and all the remaining verses of the 36th chapter of Genesis, are word for word in the first chapter of Chronicles, beginning at the 43d verse.

It was with consistency that the writer of the Chronicles could say, as he has said, 1st Chron., chap. i., ver. 43, *These are the kings that reigned in the land of Edom, before any king reigned over the children of Israel,* because he was going to give, and has given, a list of the kings that had reigned in Israel; but as it is impossible that the same expression could have been used before that period, it is as certain as anything that can be proved from historical language that this part of Genesis is taken from Chronicles, and that Genesis is not so old as Chronicles, and probably not so old as the book of Homer, or as Æsop's "Fables," admitting Homer to have been, as the tables of chronology state, contemporary with David or Solomon, and Æsop to have lived about the end of the Jewish monarchy.

Take away from Genesis the belief that Moses was the author, on which only the strange belief that it is the Word of God has stood, and there remains nothing of Genesis but an anonymous book of stories, fables and traditionary or invented absurdities, or of downright lies. The story of Eve and the serpent, and of Noah and his ark, drops to a level with the Arabian tales, without the merit of being entertaining; and the account of men living to eight and nine hundred years becomes as fabulous as the immortality of the giants of the Mythology.

Besides, the character of Moses, as stated in the Bible, is the most horrid that can be imagined. If those accounts be true, he was the wretch that first began and carried on wars on the score or on the pretense of religion; and under that mask, or that infatuation, committed the most unexampled atrocities that are to be found in the history of any nation, of which I will state only one instance.

When the Jewish army returned from one of their plundering and murdering excursions, the account goes on as follows: Numbers, chap. xxxi., ver. 13:

"And Moses, and Eleazar the priest, and all the princes of the congregation, went forth to meet them without the camp; and Moses was wroth with the officers of the host, with the captains over thousands, and captains over hundreds, which came from the battle; and Moses said unto them, *Have ye saved all the women alive?* behold, these caused the children of Israel, through the council of Balaam, to commit trespass against the Lord in the matter of Peor, and there was a plague among the congregation of the Lord. Now, therefore, *kill every male among the little ones, and kill every woman that hath known a man by lying with him; but all the women-children, that have not known a man by lying with him, keep alive for yourselves.*"

Among the detestable villains that in any period of the world have disgraced the name of man, it is impossible to find a greater than Moses, if this account be true. Here is an order to butcher the boys, to massacre the mothers and debauch the daughters.

Let any mother put herself in the situation of those mothers; one child murdered, another destined to violation, and herself in the hands of an executioner; let any daughter put herself in the situation of those daughters, destined as a prey to the murderers of a mother and a brother, and what will be their feelings? It is in vain that we attempt to impose upon nature, for nature will have her course, and the religion that tortures all her social ties is a false religion.

After this detestable order, follows an account of the plunder taken, and the manner of dividing it; and here it is that the profaneness of priestly hypocrisy increases the catalogue of crimes. Ver. 37, *"And the Lord's tribute* of the sheep was six hundred and three score and fifteen; and the beeves were thirty and six thousand, of which the *Lord's tribute* was three score and twelve; and the asses were thirty thousand, of which the *Lord's tribute* was three score and one; and the persons were sixteen thousand, of which the *Lord's tribute* was thirty and two."

In short, the matters contained in this chapter, as well as in many other parts of the Bible, are too horrid for humanity to read or for decency to hear, for it appears, from the 35th verse of this chapter, that the number of women-children consigned to debauchery by the order of Moses was thirty-two thousand.

People in general do not know what wickedness there is in this pretended Word of God. Brought up in habits of superstition, they take it for granted that the Bible is true, and that it is good; they permit themselves not to doubt of it, and they carry the ideas they form of the benevolence of the Almighty to the book which they have been taught to believe was written by His authority. Good heavens! it is quite another thing; it is a book of lies, wickedness and blasphemy; for what can be greater blasphemy than to ascribe the wickedness of man to the orders of the Almighty?

But to return to my subject, that of showing that Moses is not the author of the books ascribed to him, and that the Bible is spurious. The two instances I have already given would be sufficient without any additional evidence to invalidate the authenticity of any book that pretended to be four or five hundred years more ancient than the matters it speaks of, or refers to, as facts; for in the case of *pursuing them unto Dan,* and of *the kings that reigned over the children of Israel,* not even the flimsy pretense of prophecy can be pleaded. The expressions are in the preterite tense, and it would be downright idiotism to say that a man could prophesy in the preterite tense.

But there are many other passages scattered throughout those books that unite in the same point of evidence. It is said in Exodus (another of the books ascribed to Moses), chap. xvi. ver. 34, "And the children of Israel did eat manna forty years *until they came to a land inhabited;* they did eat manna *until they came unto the borders of the land of Canaan."*

Whether the children of Israel ate manna or not, or what manna was, or whether it was anything more than a kind of fungus or small mushroom, or other vegetable substance common to that part of the country, makes no part my argument; all that I mean to show is that it is not Moses that could write this account, because the account extends itself beyond the life and time of Moses. Moses, according to the Bible (but it is such a book of lies and contradictions there is no knowing which part to believe, or whether any), died in the wilderness and never came upon the borders of the land of Canaan; and consequently it could not be he that said what the children of Israel did, or what they ate when they came there.

This account of eating manna, which they tell us was written by Moses, extends itself to the time of Joshua, the successor of Moses; as appears by the account given in the book of Joshua, after the children of Israel had passed the river Jordan, and came unto the borders of the land of Canaan. Joshua, chap. v., ver. 12. *"And the manna ceased on the morrow, after they had eaten of the old corn of the land; neither had the children of Israel manna any more, but they did eat of the fruit of the land of Canaan that year."*

But a more remarkable instance than this occurs in Deuteronomy, which, while it shows that Moses could not be the writer of that book, shows also the fabulous notions that prevailed at that time about giants. In the third chapter of Deuteronomy, among the conquests said to be made by Moses, is an account of the taking of Og, king of Bashan, v. 12. "For only Og, king of Bashan, remained of the race of giants; behold, his bedstead was a bedstead of iron; is it not in Rabbath of the children of Ammon? Nine cubits was the length thereof, and four cubits the breadth of it, after the cubit of a man."

A cubit is 1 foot 9 888-1000ths inches; the length, therefore, of the bed was 16 feet 4 inches, and the breadth 7 feet 4 inches; thus much for this giant's bed. Now for the historical part, which, though the evidence is not so direct and positive as in the former cases, it is nevertheless very presumable and corroborating evidence, and is better than the *best* evidence on the contrary side.

The writer, by way of proving the existence of this giant, refers to his bed as an *ancient relic,* and says, Is it not in Rabbath (or Rabbah) of the children of Ammon? meaning that it is; for such is frequently the Bible method of affirming a thing. But it could not be Moses that said this, because Moses could know nothing about Rabbah nor of what was in it.

Rabbah was not a city belonging to this giant king, nor was it one of the cities that Moses took. The knowledge, therefore, that this bed was at Rabbah, and of the particulars of its dimensions, must be referred to the time when Rabbah was taken, and this was not till four hundred years after the death of Moses; for which see 2 Sam. chap. xii., ver. 26. "And Joab (David's general) fought against *Rabbah of the children of Ammon,* and took the royal city."

As I am not undertaking to point out all the contradictions in time, place, and circumstance that abound in the books ascribed to Moses, and which prove to demonstration that those books could not have been written by Moses, nor in the time of Moses, I proceed to the book of Joshua, and to show that Joshua is not the author of that book, and that it is anonymous and without authority. The evidence I shall produce is contained in the book itself; I will not go out of the Bible for proof against the supposed authenticity of the Bible. False testimony is always good against itself.

Joshua, according to the first chapter of Joshua, was the immediate successor of Moses; he was, moreover, a military man, which Moses was not, and he continued as chief of the people of Israel 25 years, that is, from the time that Moses died, which, according to the Bible chronology, was 1451 years before Christ, until 1426 years before Christ, when, according to the same chronology, Joshua died.

If, therefore, we find in this book, said to have been written by Joshua, reference to *facts done* after the death of Joshua, it is evidence that Joshua could not be the author; and also that the book could not have been written till after the time of the latest fact which it records. As to the character of the book, it is horrid; it is a military history of rapine and murder, as savage and brutal as those recorded of his predecessor in villainy and hypocrisy, Moses; and the blasphemy consists, as in the former books, in ascribing those deeds to the orders of the Almighty.

In the first place, the book of Joshua, as is the case in the preceding books, is written in the third person; it is the historian of Joshua that speaks, for it would have been absurd and vainglorious that Joshua should say of himself, as is said of him in the last verse of the sixth chapter, that *"his fame was noised throughout all the country."* I now come more immediately to the proof.

In the 24th chapter, ver. 31, it is said, "And Israel served the Lord all the days of Joshua, and *all the days of the elders that overlived Joshua."* Now, in the name of common sense, can it be Joshua that relates what people had done after he was dead? This account must not only have been written by some historian that lived after Joshua, but that lived also after the elders that had outlived Joshua.

There are several passages of a general meaning with respect to time scattered throughout the book of Joshua, that carries the time in which the book was written to a distance from the time of Joshua, but without marking by exclusion any particular time, as in the passage above quoted. In that passage, the time that intervened between the death of Joshua and the death of the elders is excluded descriptively and absolutely, and the evidence substantiates that the book could not have been written till after the death of the last.

But though the passages to which I allude, and which I am going to quote, do not designate any particular time by exclusion, they imply a time far more distant from the days of Joshua than is contained between the death of Joshua and the death of the elders. Such is the passage, chap. x., ver. 14, where, after giving an account that the sun stood still upon Gibeon, and the moon in the valley of Ajalon, at the command of Joshua (a tale only fit to amuse children), the passage says, "And there was no day like that, before it, or after it, that the Lord hearkened unto the voice of a man."

This tale of the sun standing still upon mount Gibeon, and the moon in the valley of Ajalon, is one of those fables that detects itself. Such a circumstance could not have happened without being known all over the world. One half would have wondered why the sun did not rise, and the other why it did not set; and the tradition of it would be universal, whereas there is not a nation in the world that knows anything about it.

But why must the moon stand still? What occasion could there be for moonlight in the daytime, and that, too, while the sun shone? As a poetical figure, the whole is well enough; it is akin to that in the song of Deborah and Barak, *The stars in their courses fought against Sisera;* but it is inferior to the figurative declaration of Mahomet to the persons who came to expostulate with him on his goings on: *"Wert thou,"* said he, *"to come to me with the sun in thy right hand and the moon in thy left, it should not alter my career."*

For Joshua to have exceeded Mahomet, he should have put the sun and moon one in each pocket, and carried them as Guy Fawkes carried his dark lantern, and taken them out to shine as he might happen to want them.

The sublime and the ridiculous are often so nearly related that it is difficult to class them separately. One step above the sublime makes the ridiculous, and one step above the ridiculous makes the sublime again; the account, however, abstracted from the poetical fancy, shows the ignorance of Joshua, for he should have commanded the earth to have stood still.

The time implied by the expression *after* it, that is, after that day, being put in comparison with all the time that passed *before* it, must, in order to give any expressive signification to the passage, mean a *great length of time;* for example, it would have been ridiculous to have said so the next day, or the next week, or the next month, or the next year; to give, therefore, meaning to the passage, comparative with the wonder it relates and the prior time it alludes too, it must mean centuries of years; less, however, than one would be trifling, and less than two would be barely admissible.

A distant but general time is also expressed in the 8th chapter, where, after giving an account of the taking of the city of Ai, it is said, ver. 28, "And Joshua burned Ai, and made it a heap forever, a desolation *unto this day";* and again, ver. 29, where, speaking of the king of Ai, whom Joshua had hanged, and buried at the entering of the gate, it is said, "And he raised thereon a great heap of stones, which remaineth unto this day," that is, unto the day or time in which the writer of the book of Joshua lived. And again, in the 10th chapter, where, after speaking of the five kings whom Joshua had hanged on five trees, and then thrown in a cave, it is said, "And he laid great stones on the cave's mouth, which remain unto this very day."

In enumerating the several exploits of Joshua, and of the tribes, and of the places which they conquered or attempted, it is said, chap. xv., ver. 63: "As for the Jebusites, the inhabitants of Jerusalem, the children of Judah could not drive them out; but the Jebusites dwell with the children of Judah *at Jerusalem unto this day."* The question upon this passage is, at what time did the Jebusites and the children of Judah dwell together at Jerusalem? As this matter occurs again in the first chapter of Judges, I shall reserve my observations until I come to that part.

Having thus shown from the book of Joshua itself, without any auxiliary evidence whatever, that Joshua is not the author of that book, and that it is anonymous, and consequently without authority, I proceed as before mentioned, to the book of Judges.

The book of Judges is anonymous on the face of it; and therefore, even the pretense is wanting to call it the Word of God; it has not so much as a nominal voucher; it is altogether fatherless.

This book begins with the same expression as the book of Joshua. That of Joshua begins, chap. i., ver. 1, *"Now after the death of Moses,"* etc., and this of the Judges begins, *"Now after the death of Joshua,"* etc. This and the similarity of style between the two books indicate that they are the work of the same author, but who he was is altogether unknown; the only point that the book proves is that the author lived long after the time of Joshua; for though it begins as if it followed immediately after his death, the second chapter is an epitome or abstract of the whole book, which, according to the Bible chronology, extends its history through a space of 306 years; that is, from the death of Joshua, 1426 years before Christ, to the death of Samson, 1120 years before Christ, and only 25 years before Saul went *to seek his father's asses, and was made king.* But there is good reason to believe, that it was not written till the time of David, at least, and that the book of Joshua was not written before the same time.

In the first chapter of Judges, the writer, after announcing the death of Joshua, proceeds to tell what happened between the children of Judah and the native inhabitants of the land of Canaan. In this statement, the writer, having abruptly mentioned Jerusalem in the 7th verse, says immediately after, in the 8th verse, by way of explanation, "Now the children of Judah *had* fought against Jerusalem and *taken* it"; consequently this book could not have been written before Jerusalem had been taken. The reader will recollect the quotation I have just before made from the 15th chapter of Joshua, ver. 63, where it is said that *the Jebusites dwell with the children of Judah at Jerusalem at this day,* meaning the time when the book of Joshua was written.

The evidence I have already produced to prove that the books I have hitherto treated of were not written by the person to whom they are ascribed, nor till many years after their death, if such persons ever lived, is already so abundant that I can afford to admit this passage with less weight than I am entitled to draw from it. For the case is, that so far as the Bible can be credited as a history, the city of Jerusalem was not taken till the time of David; and consequently that the books of Joshua and of Judges were not written till after the commencement of the reign of David, which was 370 years after the death of Joshua.

The name of the city that was afterward called Jerusalem was originally Jebus, or Jebusi, and was the capital of the Jebusites. The account of David's taking this city is given in II. Samuel, chap. v., ver. 4, etc.; also in I. Chron., chap. xiv., ver. 4, etc. There is no mention in any part of the Bible that it was ever taken before, nor any account that favors such an opinion.

It is not said, either in Samuel or in Chronicles, that they *utterly destroyed men, women and children; that they left not a soul to breathe,* as is said of their other conquests; and the silence here observed implies that it was taken by capitulation, and that the Jebusites, the native inhabitants, continued to live in the place after it was taken. The account, therefore, given in Joshua, that *the Jebusites dwell with the children of Judah* at Jerusalem *at this day* corresponds to no other time than after the taking of the city by David.

Having now shown that every book in the Bible, from Genesis to Judges, is without authenticity, I come to the book of Ruth, an idle, bungling story, foolishly told, nobody knows by whom, about a strolling country-girl, creeping slyly to bed with her cousin Boaz. Pretty stuff indeed, to be called the Word of God! It is, however, one of the best books in the Bible, for it is free from murder and rapine.

I come next to the two books of Samuel, and to show that those books were not written by Samuel, nor till a great length of time after the death of Samuel; and that they are, like all former books, anonymous and without authority.

To be convinced that these books have been written much later than the time of Samuel, and consequently not by him, it is only necessary to read the account which the writer gives of Saul going to seek his father's asses, and of his interview with Samuel, of whom Saul went to inquire about those lost asses, as foolish people nowadays go to a conjuror to inquire after lost things.

The writer, in relating this story of Saul, Samuel and the asses, does not tell it as a thing that has just then happened, but as an ancient *story in the time this writer lived;* for he tells it in the language or terms used at the time that *Samuel* lived, which obliges the writer to explain the story in the terms or language used in the time the *writer* lived.

Samuel, in the account given of him, in the first of those books, chap. ix., is called *the seer;* and it is by this term that Saul inquires after him, ver. 11, "And as they (Saul and his servant) went up the hill to the city, they found young maidens going out to draw water; and they said unto them, *Is the seer here?*" Saul then went according to the direction of these maidens, and met Samuel without knowing him, and said unto him, ver. 18, "Tell me, I pray thee, where the *seer's house is?* and Samuel answered Saul, and said, *I am the seer.*"

As the writer of the book of Samuel relates these questions and answers, in the language or manner of speaking used in the time they are said to have been spoken, and as that manner of speaking was out of use when this author wrote, he found it necessary, in order to make the story understood, to explain the terms in which these questions and answers are spoken; and he does this in the 9th verse, when he says "*Before-time,* in Israel, when a man went to inquire of God, thus he spake, Come, and let us go to the seer; for he that is now called a prophet, was *before-time* called a seer."

This proves, as I have before said, that this story of Saul, Samuel and the asses, was an ancient story at the time the book of Samuel was written, and consequently that Samuel did not write it, and that that book is without authenticity.

But if we go further into those books the evidence is still more positive that Samuel is not the writer of them; for they relate things that did not happen till several years after the death of Samuel. Samuel died before Saul; for the 1st Samuel, chap. xxviii., tells that Saul and the witch of Endor conjured Samuel up after he was dead; yet the history of the matters contained in those books is extended through the remaining part of Saul's life, and to the latter end of the life of David, who succeeded Saul.

The account of the death and burial of Samuel (a thing which he could not write himself) is related in the 25th chapter of the first book of Samuel, and the chronology affixed to this chapter makes this to be 1060 years before Christ; yet the history of this *first* book is brought down to 1056 years before Christ; that is, to the death of Saul, which was not till four years after the death of Samuel.

The second book of Samuel begins with an account of things that did not happen till four years after Samuel was dead; for it begins with the reign of David, who succeeded Saul, and it goes on to the end of David's reign, which was forty-three years after the death of Samuel; and, therefore, the books are in themselves positive evidence that they were not written by Samuel.

I have now gone through all the books in the first part of the Bible to which the names of persons are affixed, as being the authors of those books, and which the Church, styling itself the Christian Church, has imposed upon the world as the writings of Moses, Joshua and Samuel, and I have detected and proved the falsehood of this imposition.

And now, ye priests of every description, who have preached and written against the former part of "The Age of Reason," what have ye to say? Will ye, with all this mass of evidence against you, and staring you in the face, still have the assurance to march into your pulpits and continue to impose these books on your congregations as the works of *inspired penmen,* and the Word of God, when it is as evident as demonstration can make truth appear that the persons who ye say are the authors are *not* the authors, and that ye know not who the authors are?

What shadow of pretense have ye now to produce for continuing the blasphemous fraud? What have ye still to offer against the pure and moral religion of Deism, in support of your system of falsehood, idolatry and pretended revelation? Had the cruel and murderous orders with which the Bible is filled, and the numberless torturing executions of men, women and children, in consequence of those orders, been ascribed to some friend whose memory you revered, you would have glowed with satisfaction at detecting the falsehood of the charge, and gloried in defending his injured fame.

Is it because ye are sunk in the cruelty of superstition, or feel no interest in the honor of your Creator, that ye listen to the horrid tales of the Bible, or hear them with callous indifference? The evidence I have produced, and shall produce in the course of this work, to prove that the Bible is without authority, will, while it wounds the stubbornness of a priest, relieve and tranquillize the minds of millions; it will free them from all those hard thoughts of the Almighty which priestcraft and the Bible had infused into their minds, and which stood in everlasting opposition to all their ideas of His moral justice and benevolence.

I come now to the two books of Kings, and the two books of Chronicles. Those books are altogether historical, and are chiefly confined to the lives and actions of the Jewish kings, who in general were a parcel of rascals; but these are matters with which we have no more concern than we have with the Roman emperors or Homer's account of the Trojan War.

Besides which, as those works are anonymous, and as we know nothing of the writer, or of his character, it is impossible for us to know what degree of credit to give to the matters related therein. Like all other ancient histories, they appear to be a jumble of fable and of fact, and of probable and of improbable things; but which distance of time and place, and change of circumstances in the world, have rendered obsolete and uninteresting.

The chief use I shall make of those books will be that of comparing them with each other, and with other parts of the Bible, to show the confusion, contradiction and cruelty in this pretended Word of God.

The first book of Kings begins with the reign of Solomon, which, according to the Bible chronology, was 1015 years before Christ; and the second book ends 588 years before Christ, being a little after the reign of Zedekiah, whom Nebuchadnezzar, after taking Jerusalem and conquering the Jews, carried captive to Babylon. The two books include a space of 427 years.

The two books of Chronicles are a history of the same times, and in general of the same persons, by another author; for it would be absurd to suppose that the same author wrote the history twice over. The first book of Chronicles (after giving the genealogy from Adam to Saul, which takes up the first nine chapters), begins with the reign of David; and the last book ends as in the last book of Kings, soon after the reign of Zedekiah, about 588 years before Christ. The two last verses of the last chapter bring the history more forward 52 years, that is, to 536. But these verses do not belong to the book, as I shall show when I come to speak of the book of Ezra.

The two books of Kings, besides the history of Saul, David and Solomon, who reigned over *all* Israel, contain an abstract of the lives of 17 kings and one queen, who are styled kings of Judah, and of 19, who are styled kings of Israel; for the Jewish nation, immediately on the death of Solomon, split into two parties, who chose separate kings, and who carried on most rancorous wars against each other.

These two books are little more than a history of assassinations, treachery and wars. The cruelties that the Jews had accustomed themselves to practise on the Canaanites, whose country they had savagely invaded under a pretended gift from God, they afterward practised as furiously on each other. Scarcely half their kings died a natural death, and in some instances whole families were destroyed to secure possession to the successor, who, after a few years, and sometimes only a few months or less, shared the same fate. In the tenth chapter of the second book of Kings, an account is given of two baskets full of children's heads, seventy in number, being exposed at the entrance of the city; they were the children of Ahab, and were murdered by the order of Jehu, whom Elisha, the pretended man of God, had anointed to be king over Israel, on purpose to commit this bloody deed, and assassinate his predecessor.

And in the account of the reign of Menahem, one of the kings of Israel who had murdered Shallum, who had reigned but one month, it is said, II. Kings, chap. xv., ver. 16, that Menahem smote the city of Tiphsah, because they opened not the city to him, *and all the women therein that were with child he ripped up.*

Could we permit ourselves to suppose that the Almighty would distinguish any nation of people by the name of *His chosen people,* we must suppose that people to have been an example to all the rest of the world of the purest piety and humanity, and not such a nation of ruffians and cut-throats as the ancient Jews were; a people who, corrupted by and copying after such monsters and imposters as Moses and Aaron, Joshua, Samuel and David, had distinguished themselves above all others on the face of the known earth for barbarity and wickedness.

If we will not stubbornly shut our eyes and steel our hearts, it is impossible not to see, in spite of all that long-established superstition imposes upon the mind, that the flattering appellation of *His chosen people* is no other than a *lie* which the priests and leaders of the Jews had invented to cover the baseness of their own characters, and which Christian priests, sometimes as corrupt and often as cruel, have professed to believe.

The two books of Chronicles are a repetition of the same crimes, but the history is broken in several places by the author leaving out the reign of some of their kings; and in this, as well as in that of Kings, there is such a frequent transition from kings of Judah to kings of Israel, and from kings of Israel to kings of Judah, that the narrative is obscure in the reading.

In the same book the history sometimes contradicts itself; for example, in the second book of Kings, chap. i., ver. 17, we are told, but in rather ambiguous terms, that after the death of Ahaziah, king of Israel, Jehoram, or Joram (who was of the house of Ahab), reigned in his stead, in the *second year* of Jehoram, or Joram, son of Jehoshaphat, king of Judah; and in chap. viii., ver. 16, of the same book, it is said, and in the *fifth year* of Joram, the son of Ahab, king of Israel, Jehoshaphat being then king of Judah, began to reign; that is, one chapter says Joram of Judah began to reign in the *second year* of Joram of Israel; and the other chapter says that Joram of Israel began to reign in the *fifth year* of Joram of Judah.

Several of the most extraordinary matters related in one history, as having happened during the reign of such and such of their kings, are not to be found in the other, in relating the reign of the same king; for example, the two first rival kings, after the death of Solomon, were Rehoboam and Jeroboam; and in I. Kings, chaps. xii. and xiii., an account is given of Jeroboam making an offering of burnt incense, and that a man, who was there called a man of God, cried out against the altar, chap. xiii., ver. 2: "O altar, altar! thus saith the Lord; Behold, a child shall be born unto the house of David, Josiah by name; and upon thee shall he offer the priests of the high places that burn incense upon thee, and men's bones shall be burnt upon thee." Verse 3: "And it came to pass, when King Jeroboam heard the saying of the man of God, which had cried against the altar in Bethel, that he put forth his hand from the altar, saying, *Lay hold on him.* And his hand which he put out against him *dried up, so that he could not pull it in again to him.*"

One would think that such an extraordinary case as this (which is spoken of as a judgment), happening to the chief of one of the parties, and that at the first moment of the separation of the Israelites into two nations, would, if it had been true, have been recorded in both histories. But though men in latter times have believed *all that the prophets have said unto them,* it does not appear that these prophets or historians believed each other; they knew each other too well.

A long account also is given in Kings about Elijah. It runs through several chapters, and concludes with telling, II. Kings, chap. ii., ver. 11,

"And it came to pass, as they (Elijah and Elisha) still went on, and talked, that, behold, there appeared *a chariot of fire and horses of fire, and parted them both asunder, and Elijah *went up by a whirlwind into heaven.*" Hum! this the author of Chronicles, miraculous as the story is, makes no mention of, though he mentions Elijah by name; neither does he say anything of the story related in the second chapter of the same book of Kings, of a parcel of children calling Elisha *bald head, bald head;* and that this *man of God,* verse 24, "Turned back, and looked on them, *and cursed them in the name of the Lord;* and there came forth two she-bears out of the wood, and tore forty-and-two children of them."

He also passed over in silence the story told, II. Kings, chap. xiii., that when they were burying a man in the sepulchre where Elisha had been buried, it happened that the dead man, as they were letting him down (ver. 21), touched the bones of Elisha, and he (the dead man) *"revived and stood upon his feet."*

The story does not tell us whether they buried the man, notwithstanding he revived and stood upon his feet, or drew him up again. Upon all these stories the writer of Chronicles is as silent as any writer of the present day who did not choose to be accused of *lying,* or at least of romancing, would be about stories of the same kind.

But, however these two historians may differ from each other with respect to the tales related by either, they are silent alike with respect to those men styled prophets, whose writings fill up the latter part of the Bible.

Isaiah, who lived in the time of Hezekiah, is mentioned in Kings, and again in Chronicles, when these historians are speaking of that reign; but, except in one or two instances at most, and those very slightly, none of the rest are so much as spoken of, or even their existence hinted at; although, according to the Bible chronology, they lived within the time those histories were written; some of them long before.

If those prophets, as they are called, were men of such importance in their day as the compilers of the Bible and priests and commentators have since represented them to be, how can it be accounted for that not one of these histories should say anything about them?

The history in the books of Kings and of Chronicles is brought forward, as I have already said, to the year 588 before Christ; it will therefore be proper to examine which of these prophets lived before that period.

Here follows a table of all the prophets, with the times in which they lived before Christ, according to the chronology affixed to the first chapter of each of the books of the prophets; and also of the number of years they lived before the books of Kings and Chronicles were written.

TABLE OF THE PROPHETS

Names.	Years before Christ.	Years before Kings and Chronicles.	Observations.
Isaiah	760	172	mentioned.
Jeremiah	629	41	{ mentioned only in the last chap. of Chron.
Ezekiel	595	7	not mentioned.
Daniel	607	19	not mentioned.
Hosea	785	97	not mentioned.
Joel	800	212	not mentioned.
Amos	789	199	not mentioned.
Obadiah	789	199	not mentioned.
Jonah	862	274	see the note.[6]
Micah	750	162	not mentioned.
Nahum	713	125	not mentioned.
Habakkuk	620	38	not mentioned.
Zephaniah	630	42	not mentioned.
Haggai Zachariah Malachi { after the year 588			

This table is either not very honorable for the Bible historians, or not very honorable for the Bible prophets; and I leave to priests and commentators, who are very learned in little things, to settle the point of *etiquette* between the two, and to assign a reason why the authors of Kings and Chronicles have treated those prophets whom, in the former part of "The Age of Reason," I have considered as poets, with as much

[6] In II. Kings, chap. xiv., ver. 25, the name of Jonah is mentioned on account of the restoration of a tract of land by Jeroboam; but nothing further is said of him, nor is any allusion made to the book of Jonah, nor to his expedition to Nineveh, nor to his encounter with the whale.—*Author.*

degrading silence as any historian of the present day would treat Peter Pindar.

I have one observation more to make on the book of Chronicles, after which I shall pass on to review the remaining books of the Bible.

In my observations on the book of Genesis, I have quoted a passage from the 36th chapter, verse 31, which evidently refers to a time *after* that kings began to reign over the children of Israel; and I have shown that as this verse is verbatim the same as in Chronicles, chap. i, ver. 43, where it stands consistently with the order of history, which in Genesis it does not, that the verse in Genesis, and a great part of the 36th chapter, have been taken from Chronicles; and that the book of Genesis, though it is placed first in the Bible, and ascribed to Moses, has been manufactured by some unknown person after the book of Chronicles was written, which was not until at least eight hundred and sixty years after the time of Moses.

The evidence I proceed by to substantiate this is regular and has in it but two stages. First, as I have already stated that the passage in Genesis refers itself for *time* to Chronicles; secondly, that the book of Chronicles, to which this passage refers itself, was not *begun* to be written until at least eight hundred and sixty years after the time of Moses. To prove this, we have only to look into the thirteenth verse of the third chapter of the first book of Chronicles, where the writer, in giving the genealogy of the descendants of David, mentions Zedekiah; and it was in the time of Zedekiah that Nebuchadnezzar conquered Jerusalem, 588 years before Christ, and consequently more than 860 years after Moses.

Those who have superstitiously boasted of the antiquity of the Bible, and particularly of the books ascribed to Moses, have done it without examination, and without any other authority than that of one credulous man telling it to another; for, so far as historical and chronological evidence applies, the very first book in the Bible is not so ancient as the book of Homer by more than three hundred years, and is about the same age with Æsop's "Fables."

I am not contending for the morality of Homer; on the contrary, I think it a book of false glory, tending to inspire immoral and mischievous notions of honor; and with respect to Æsop, though the moral is in general just, the fable is often cruel; and the cruelty of the fable does more injury to the heart, especially in a child, than the moral does good to the judgment.

Having now dismissed Kings and Chronicles, I come to the next in course, the book of Ezra.

As one proof, among others I shall produce, to show the disorder in which this pretended word of God, the Bible, has been put together, and the uncertainty of who the authors were, we have only to look at the three first verses in Ezra, and the last two in Chronicles; for by what kind of cutting and shuffling has it been that the three first verses in Ezra should be the two last verses in Chronicles, or that the two last in Chronicles should be the three first in Ezra? Either the authors did not know their own works, or the compilers did not know the authors.

Two last verses of Chronicles.	*Three first verses of Ezra.*
Ver. 22. Now in the first year of Cyrus, king of Persia, that the word of the Lord, spoken by the mouth of Jeremiah, might be accomplished, the Lord stirred up the spirit of Cyrus, king of Persia, that he made a proclamation throughout all his kingdom, and put it also in writing, saying,	Ver. 1. Now in the first year of Cyrus, king of Persia, that the word of the Lord, by the mouth of Jeremiah, might be fulfilled, the Lord stirred up the spirit of Cyrus, king of Persia, that he made a proclamation throughout all his kingdom, and put it also in writing, saying,
23. Thus saith Cyrus, king of Persia, All the kingdoms of the earth hath the Lord God of heaven given me: and he hath charged me to build him an house in Jerusalem, which is in Judah. Who is there among you of all his people? the Lord his God be with him, and let him go up.	2. Thus saith Cyrus, king of Persia, the Lord God of heaven hath given me all the kingdoms of the earth; and he hath charged me to build him an house at Jerusalem, which is in Judah.
	3. Who is there among you of all his people? his God be with him, and let him go up *to Jerusalem, which is in Judah, and build the house of the Lord God of Israel, (he is the God,) which is in Jerusalem.*

The last verse in Chronicles is broken abruptly, and ends in the middle of the phrase, with the word *up,* without signifying to what place. This abrupt break, and the appearance of the same verses, in different books, show, as I have already said, the disorder and ignorance in which the Bible has been put together, and that the compilers of it had no authority for what they were doing, nor we any authority for believing what they have done.[7]

The only thing that has any appearance of certainty in the book of Ezra, is the time in which it was written, which was immediately after the return of the Jews from the Babylonian captivity, about 536 years before Christ. Ezra (who, according to the Jewish commentators, is the same person as is called Esdras in the Apocrypha) was one of the persons who returned, and who, it is probable, wrote the account of that affair.

Nehemiah, whose book follows next to Ezra, was another of the returned persons; and who, it is also probable, wrote the account of the same affair in the book that bears his name. But these accounts are nothing to us, nor to any other persons, unless it be to the Jews, as a part of the history of their nation; and there is just as much of the word of God in these books as there is in any of the histories of France, or

---

[7] I observed, as I passed along, several broken and senseless passages in the Bible, without thinking them of consequence enough to be introduced in the body of the work; such as that, I. Samuel, chap. xiii. ver. 1, where it is said, "Saul reigned one year; and when he had reigned two years over Israel, Saul chose him three thousand men," etc. The first part of the verse, that Saul reigned one year, has no sense, since it does not tell us what Saul did, nor say anything of what happened at the end of that one year; and it is, besides, mere absurdity to say he reigned one year, when the very next phrase says he had reigned two; for if he had reigned two, it was impossible not to have reigned one.

Another instance occurs in Joshua, chap. v, where the writer tells us a story of an angel (for such the table of contents at the head of the chapter calls him) appearing unto Joshua; and the story ends abruptly, and without any conclusion. The story is as follows: Verse 13, "And it came to pass, when Joshua was by Jericho, that he lifted up his eyes and looked, and behold there stood a man over against him with his sword drawn in his hand; and Joshua went unto him and said unto him, Art thou for us or for our adversaries?" Verse 14, "And he said, Nay; but as captain of the hosts of the Lord am I now come. And Joshua fell on his face to the earth, and did worship, and said unto him, What saith my Lord unto his servant?" Verse 15, "And the captain of the Lord's host said unto Joshua, Loose thy shoe from off thy foot; for the place whereon thou standeth is holy. And Joshua did so." And what then? nothing, for here the story ends, and the chapter too.

Either the story is broken off in the middle, or it is a story told by some Jewish humorist, in ridicule of Joshua's pretended mission from God; and the compilers of the Bible, not perceiving the design of the story, have told it as a serious matter. As a story of humor and ridicule it has a great deal of point, for it pompously introduces an angel in the figure of a man, with a drawn sword in his hand, before whom Joshua falls on his face to the earth and worships (which is contrary to their second commandment); and then this most important embassy from heaven ends in telling Joshua to pull off his shoe. It might as well have told him to pull up his breeches.

It is certain, however, that the Jews did not credit everything their leaders told them, as appears from the cavalier manner in which they speak of Moses, when he was gone into the mount. "As for this Moses," say they, "we wot not what is become of him." Exod. chap. xxxii, ver. 1.—*Author.*

Rapin's "History of England," or the history of any other country.

But even in matters of historical record, neither of those writers are to be depended upon. In the second chapter of Ezra, the writer gives a list of the tribes and families, and of the precise number of souls of each, that returned from Babylon to Jerusalem: and this enrollment of the persons so returned appears to have been one of the principal objects for writing the book; but in this there is an error that destroys the intention of the undertaking.

The writer begins his enrollment in the following manner, chap. ii., ver. 3: "The children of Parosh, two thousand one hundred seventy and four." Ver. 4, "The children of Shephatiah, three hundred seventy and two." And in this manner he proceeds through all the families; and in the 64th verse, he makes a total, and says, "The whole congregation together was *forty and two thousand three hundred and threescore.*"

But whoever will take the trouble of casting up the several particulars will find that the total is but 29,818; so that the error is 12,542.[8] What certainty, then, can there be in the Bible for anything?

Nehemiah, in like manner, gives a list of the returned families, and of the number of each family. He begins, as in Ezra, by saying, chap. vii., ver. 8, "The children of Parosh, two thousand three hundred seventy and two;" and so on through all the families. The list differs in several of the particulars from that of Ezra. In the 66th verse, Nehemiah makes a total, and says, as Ezra had said, "The whole congregation together was forty and two thousand three hundred and threescore." But the particulars of this list make a total of but 31,089, so that the error here is

---

[8] *Particulars of the Families from the second Chapter of Ezra.*

Chap. ii.		Bro't for. 12,243		Bro't for. 15,953		Bro't for. 24,144	
Verse 3	2172	Verse 14	2056	Verse 25	743	Verse 36	973
4	372	15	454	26	621	37	1052
5	775	16	98	27	122	38	1247
6	2812	17	323	28	223	39	1017
7	1254	18	112	29	52	40	74
8	945	19	223	30	156	41	128
9	760	20	95	31	1254	42	139
10	642	21	123	32	320	53	392
11	623	22	56	33	725	60	652
12	1222	23	128	34	345		
13	666	24	42	35	3630		
	12,243		15,953		24,144	Total,	29,818

—*Author*

THE AGE OF REASON

11,271. These writers may do well enough for Bible-makers, but not for anything where truth and exactness is necessary.

The next book in course is the book of Esther. If Madame Esther thought it any honor to offer herself as a kept mistress to Ahasuerus, or as a rival to Queen Vashti who had refused to come to a drunken king in the midst of a drunken company, to be made a show of (for the account says they had been drinking seven days and were merry), let Esther and Mordecai look to that; it is no business of ours; at least it is none of mine; besides which the story has a great deal the appearance of being fabulous, and is also anonymous. I pass on to the book of Job.

The book of Job differs in character from all the books we have hitherto passed over. Treachery and murder make no part of this book; it is the meditations of a mind strongly impressed with the vicissitudes of human life, and by turns sinking under, and struggling against the pressure.

It is a highly wrought composition, between willing submission and involuntary discontent, and shows man, as he sometimes is, more disposed to be resigned than he is capable of being. Patience has but a small share in the character of the person of whom the book treats; on the contrary, his grief is often impetuous, but he still endeavors to keep a guard upon it, and seems determined in the midst of accumulating ills, to impose upon himself the hard duty of contentment.

I have spoken in a respectful manner of the book of Job in the former part of the "Age of Reason," but without knowing at that time what I have learned since, which is, that from all the evidence that can be collected the book of Job does not belong to the Bible.

I have seen the opinion of two Hebrew commentators, Abenezra and Spinoza, upon this subject. They both say that the book of Job carries no internal evidence of being a Hebrew book; that the genius of the composition and the drama of the piece are not Hebrew; that it has been translated from another language into Hebrew, and that the author of the book was a Gentile; that the character represented under the name of Satan (which is the first and only time this name is mentioned in the Bible) does not correspond to any Hebrew idea, and that the two convocations which the Deity is supposed to have made of those whom the poem calls Sons of God, and the familiarity which this supposed Satan is stated to have with the Deity, are in the same case.

It may also be observed, that the book shows itself to be the production of a mind cultivated in science, which the Jews, so far from being famous for, were very ignorant of. The allusions to objects of natural philosophy are frequent and strong, and are of a different cast to anything in the books known to be Hebrew.

The astronomical names, Pleiades, Orion and Arcturus, are Greek and not Hebrew names, and it does not appear from anything that is to be found in the Bible that the Jews knew anything of astronomy, or that they studied it; they had no translation of those names into their own language, but adopted the names as they found them in the poem.

That the Jews did translate the literary productions of the Gentile nations into the Hebrew language, and mix them with their own, is not a matter of doubt; the thirty-first chapter of Proverbs is an evidence of this; it is there said, v. 1: *"The words of King Lemuel, the prophecy that his mother taught him."* This verse stands as a preface to the Proverbs that follow, and which are not the proverbs of Solomon, but of Lemuel; and this Lemuel was not one of the kings of Israel, nor of Judah, but of some other country, and consequently a Gentile.

The Jews, however, have adopted his proverbs, and as they cannot give any account who the author of the book of Job was, nor how they came by the book, and as it differs in character from the Hebrew writings, and stands totally unconnected with every other book and chapter in the Bible, before it and after it, it has all the circumstantial evidence of being originally a book of the Gentiles.[9]

The Bible-makers and those regulators of time, the chronologists, appear to have been at a loss where to place and how to dispose of the book of Job; for it contains no one historical circumstance, nor allusion to any, that might serve to determine its place in the Bible.

But it would not have answered the purpose of these men to have informed the world of their ignorance, and, therefore, they have affixed

[9] The prayer known by the name of *Agur's prayer,* in the 30th chapter of Proverbs, immediately preceding the proverbs of Lemuel, and which is the only sensible, well-conceived and well-expressed prayer in the Bible, has much the appearance of being a prayer taken from the Gentiles. The name of Agur occurs on no other occasion than this; and he is introduced, together with the prayer ascribed to him, in the same manner, and nearly in the same words, that Lemuel and his proverbs are introduced in the chapter that follows. The first verse of the 30th chapter says, "The words of Agur, the son of Jakeh, even the prophecy." Here the word prophecy is used in the same application it has in the following chapter of Lemuel, unconnected with any thing of prediction. The prayer of Agur is in the 8th and 9th verses, "Remove far from me vanity and lies; give me neither riches nor poverty; feed me with food convenient for me; lest I be full and deny thee, and say, Who is the Lord? or lest I be poor and steal, and take the name of my God in vain." This has not any of the marks of being a Jewish prayer, for the Jews never prayed but when they were in trouble, and never for anything but victory, vengeance or riches.—*Author.*

it to the era of 1520 years before Christ, which is during the time the Israelites were in Egypt, and for which they have just as much authority and no more than I should have for saying it was a thousand years before that period. The probability, however, is that it is older than any book in the Bible; and it is the only one that can be read without indignation or disgust.

We know nothing of what the ancient Gentile world (as it is called) was before the time of the Jews, whose practise has been to calumniate and blacken the character of all other nations; and it is from the Jewish accounts that we have learned to call them heathens.

But, as far as we know to the contrary, they were a just and moral people, and not addicted, like the Jews, to cruelty and revenge, but of whose profession of faith we are unacquainted. It appears to have been their custom to personify both virtue and vice by statues and images, as is done nowadays both by statuary and by paintings; but it does not follow from this that they worshipped them, any more than we do.

I pass on to the book of Psalms, of which it is not necessary to make much observation. Some of them are moral, and others are very revengeful; and the greater part relates to certain local circumstances of the Jewish nation at the time they were written, with which we have nothing to do.

It is, however, an error or an imposition to call them the Psalms of David. They are a collection, as song-books are nowadays, from different song-writers, who lived at different times. The 137th Psalm could not have been written till more than 400 years after the time of David, because it was written in commemoration of an event, the captivity of the Jews in Babylon, which did not happen till that distance of time. *"By the rivers of Babylon we sat down; yea, we wept, when we remembered Zion. We hanged our harps upon the willows, in the midst thereof; for there they that carried us away captive required of us a song, saying, Sing us one of the songs of Zion."* As a man would say to an American, or to a Frenchman, or to an Englishman, "Sing us one of your American songs, or of your French songs, or of your English songs."

This remark, with respect to the time this Psalm was written, is of no other use than to show (among others already mentioned) the general imposition the world has been under in respect to the authors of the Bible.

No regard has been paid to time, place and circumstance, and the names of persons have been affixed to the several books, which it was as impossible they should write as that a man should walk in procession at his own funeral.

The Book of Proverbs. These, like the Psalms, are a collection, and that from authors belonging to other nations than those of the Jewish nation, as I have shown in the observations upon the book of Job; besides which some of the proverbs ascribed to Solomon did not appear till two hundred and fifty years after the death of Solomon; for it is said in the 1st verse of the 25th chapter, *"These are also proverbs of Solomon, which the men of Hezekiah, king of Judah, copied out."*

It was two hundred and fifty years from the time of Solomon to the time of Hezekiah. When a man is famous and his name is abroad, he is made the putative father of things he never said or did, and this, most probably, has been the case with Solomon. It appears to have been the fashion of that day to make proverbs, as it is now to make jest-books and father them upon those who never saw them.

The book of Ecclesiastes, or the Preacher, is also ascribed to Solomon, and that with much reason, if not with truth. It is written as the solitary reflections of a worn-out debauchee, such as Solomon was, who, looking back on scenes he can no longer enjoy, cries out, *"All is vanity!"*

A great deal of the metaphor and of the sentiment is obscure, most probably by translation; but enough is left to show they were strongly pointed in the original.[10] From what is transmitted to us of the character of Solomon, he was witty, ostentatious, dissolute and at last melancholy. He lived fast, and died, tired of the world, at the age of fifty-eight years.

Seven hundred wives and three hundred concubines are worse than none, and, however it may carry with it the appearance of heightened enjoyment, it defeats all the felicity of affection by leaving it no point to fix upon. Divided love is never happy. This was the case with Solomon, and if he could not, with all his pretensions to wisdom, discover it beforehand, he merited, unpitied, the mortification he afterward endured.

In this point of view, his preaching is unnecessary, because, to know the consequences, it is only necessary to know the case. Seven hundred wives, and three hundred concubines would have stood in place of the whole book. It was needless, after this, to say that all was vanity and

---

[10] *Those that look out of the window shall be darkened,* is an obscure figure in translation for loss of sight.—*Author.*

vexation of spirit; for it is impossible to derive happiness from the company of those whom we deprive of happiness.

To be happy in old age, it is necessary that we accustom ourselves to objects that can accompany the mind all the way through life, and that we take the rest as good in their day. The mere man of pleasure is miserable in old age, and the mere drudge in business is but little better; whereas, natural philosophy, mathematical and mechanical science are a continual source of tranquil pleasure, and in spite of the gloomy dogmas of priests and of superstition, the study of those things is the study of the true theology; it teaches man to know and to admire the Creator, for the principles of science are in the creation, and are unchangeable and of divine origin.

Those who knew Benjamin Franklin will recollect that his mind was ever young, his temper ever serene; science, that never grows gray, was always his mistress. He was never without an object, for when we cease to have an object, we become like an invalid in a hospital waiting for death.

Solomon's Songs are amorous and foolish enough, but which wrinkled fanaticism has called divine. The compilers of the Bible have placed these songs after the book of Ecclesiastes, and the chronologists have affixed to them the era of 1014 years before Christ, at which time Solomon, according to the same chronology, was nineteen years of age, and was then forming his seraglio of wives and concubines.

The Bible-makers and the chronologists should have managed this matter a little better, and either have said nothing about the time, or chosen a time less inconsistent with the supposed divinity of those songs; for Solomon was then in the honeymoon of one thousand debaucheries.

It should also have occurred to them that, as he wrote, if he did write, the book of Ecclesiastes long after these songs, and in which he exclaims, that all is vanity and vexation of spirit, that he included those songs in that description. This is the more probable, because he says, or somebody for him, Ecclesiastes, chap. ii. ver. 8, "*I gat me men singers and women singers* (most probably to sing those songs), *as musical instruments and that of all sorts;* and behold (ver. 11), all was vanity and vexation of spirit." The compilers, however, have done their work but by halves, for as they have given us the songs, they should have given us the tunes, that we might sing them.

The books called the books of the Prophets fill up all the remaining parts of the Bible; they are sixteen in number, beginning with Isaiah, and ending with Malachi, of which I have given a list in the observations upon Chronicles. Of these sixteen prophets, all of whom, except the three last, lived within the time the books of Kings and Chronicles were written, two only, Isaiah and Jeremiah, are mentioned in the history of those books. I shall begin with those two, reserving what I have to say on the general character of the men called prophets to another part of the work.

Whoever will take the trouble of reading the book ascribed to Isaiah will find it one of the most wild and disorderly compositions ever put together; it has neither beginning, middle nor end; and, except a short historical part and a few sketches of history in two or three of the first chapters, is one continued, incoherent, bombastical rant, full of extravagant metaphor, without application, and destitute of meaning; a school-boy would scarcely have been excusable for writing such stuff; it is (at least in the translation) that kind of composition and false taste that is properly called prose run mad.

The historical part begins at the 36th chapter, and is continued to the end of the 39th chapter. It relates to some matters that are said to have passed during the reign of Hezekiah, king of Judah; at which time Isaiah lived. This fragment of history begins and ends abruptly; it has not the least connection with the chapter that precedes it, nor with that which follows it, nor with any other in the book.

It is probable that Isaiah wrote this fragment himself, because he was an actor in the circumstances it treats of; but, except this part, there are scarcely two chapters that have any connection with each other; one is entitled, at the beginning of the first verse, "The burden of Babylon;" another, "The burden of Moab;" another, "The burden of Damascus;" another, "The burden of Egypt;" another, "The burden of the desert of the sea;" another, "The burden of the valley of vision" [11]—as you would say, "The story of the Knight of the Burning Mountain," "The story of Cinderella or The Glass Slipper"; the story of "The Sleeping Beauty in the Woods," etc., etc.

I have already shown, in the instance of the two last verses of Chronicles, and the three first in Ezra, that the compilers of the Bible mixed and confounded the writings of different authors with each other, which alone, were there no other cause, is sufficient to destroy the authenticity of any compilation, because it is more than presumptive evidence that

---

[11] See beginning of chapters xiii, xv, xvii, xix, xxi and xxii.—*Author.*

the compilers were ignorant who the authors were. A very glaring instance of this occurs in the book ascribed to Isaiah; the latter part of the 44th chapter and the beginning of the 45th, so far from having been written by Isaiah, could only have been written by some person who lived at least a hundred and fifty years after Isaiah was dead.

These chapters are a compliment to Cyrus, who permitted the Jews to return to Jerusalem from the Babylonian captivity, to rebuild Jerusalem and the temple, as is stated in Ezra. The last verse of the 44th chapter and the beginning of the 45th, are in the following words: *"That saith of Cyrus; He is my shepherd, and shall perform all my pleasure; even saying to Jerusalem, Thou shalt be built, and to the temple, Thy foundation shall be laid. Thus saith the Lord to His anointed, to Cyrus, whose right hand I have holden, to subdue nations before him; and I will loose the loins of kings, to open before him the two-leaved gates, and the gates shall not be shut; I will go before thee,"* etc.

What audacity of church and priestly ignorance it is to impose this book upon the world as the writing of Isaiah, when Isaiah, according to their own chronology, died soon after the death of Hezekiah, which was 693 years before Christ, and the decree of Cyrus, in favor of the Jews returning to Jerusalem, was, according to the same chronology, 536 years before Christ, which is a distance of time between the two of 162 years.

I do not suppose that the compilers of the Bible made these books, but rather that they picked up some loose anonymous essays, and put them together under the names of such authors as best suited their purpose. They have encouraged the imposition, which is next to inventing it, for it was impossible but they must have observed it.

When we see the studied craft of the Scripture-makers, in making every part of this romantic book of school-boy's eloquence bend to the monstrous idea of a Son of God begotten by a ghost on the body of a virgin, there is no imposition we are not justified in suspecting them of. Every phrase and circumstance is marked with the barbarous hand of superstitious torture, and forced into meanings it was impossible they could have. The head of every chapter and the top of every page are blazoned with the names of Christ and the Church, that the unwary reader might suck in the error before he began to read.

"Behold a virgin shall conceive, and bear a son," Isaiah, chap. vii. ver. 14, has been interpreted to mean the person called Jesus Christ, and his mother Mary, and has been echoed through Christendom for more

than a thousand years; and such has been the rage of this opinion that scarcely a spot in it but has been stained with blood, and marked with desolation in consequence of it. Though it is not my intention to enter into controversy on subjects of this kind, but to confine myself to show that the Bible is spurious, and thus, by taking away the foundation, to overthrow at once the whole structure of superstition raised thereon, I will, however, stop a moment to expose the fallacious application of this passage.

Whether Isaiah was playing a trick with Ahaz, king of Judah, to whom this passage is spoken, is no business of mine; I mean only to show the misapplication of the passage, and that it has no more reference to Christ and his mother than it has to me and my mother.

The story is simply this: The king of Syria and the king of Israel (I have already mentioned that the Jews were split into two nations, one of which was called Judah, the capital of which was Jerusalem, and the other Israel), made war jointly against Ahaz, king of Judah, and marched their armies toward Jerusalem. Ahaz and his people became alarmed, and the account says, ver. 2, *"And his heart was moved, and the heart of his people, as the trees of the wood are moved with the wind."*

In this situation of things, Isaiah addresses himself to Ahaz, and assures him in the *name of the Lord* (the cant phrase of all the prophets) that these two kings should not succeed against him; and to satisfy Ahaz that this should be the case, tells him to ask a sign. This, the account says, Ahaz declined doing, giving as a reason that he would not tempt the Lord; upon which Isaiah, who is the speaker, says, ver. 14, "Therefore the Lord himself shall give you a sign, *Behold, a virgin shall conceive, and bear a son"*; and the 16th verse says, *"For before this child shall know to refuse the evil, and choose the good, the land that thou abhorrest* [or dreadest, meaning Syria and the kingdom of Israel], *shall be forsaken of both her kings."* Here then was the sign, and the time limited for the completion of the assurance or promise, namely, before this child should know to refuse the evil and choose the good.

Isaiah having committed himself thus far, it became necessary to him, in order to avoid the imputation of being a false prophet and the consequence thereof, to take measures to make this sign appear. It certainly was not a difficult thing, in any time of the world, to find a girl with child, or to make her so, and perhaps Isaiah knew of one beforehand; for I do not suppose that the prophets of that day were any more to be trusted than the priests of this. Be that, however, as it may, he says in the next chapter, ver. 2, "And I took unto me faithful witnesses to record, Uriah the priest, and Zechariah the son of Jeberechiah, and *I went unto the prophetess, and she conceived and bare a son.*"

Here, then, is the whole story, foolish as it is, of this child and this virgin; and it is upon the barefaced perversion of this story, that the book of Matthew, and the impudence and sordid interests of priests in later times, have founded a theory which they call the Gospel; and have applied this story to signify the person they call Jesus Christ, begotten, they say, by a ghost, whom they call holy, on the body of a woman, engaged in marriage, and afterward married, whom they call a virgin, 700 years after this foolish story was told; a theory which, speaking for myself, I hesitate not to disbelieve, and to say, is as fabulous and as false as God is true.[12]

But to show the imposition and falsehood of Isaiah, we have only to attend to the sequel of this story, which, though it is passed over in silence in the book of Isaiah, is related in the 28th chapter of the second Chronicles, and which is, that instead of these two kings failing in their attempt against Ahaz, king of Judah, as Isaiah had pretended to foretell in the name of the Lord, they succeeded; Ahaz was defeated and destroyed, a hundred and twenty thousand of his people were slaughtered, Jerusalem was plundered, and two hundred thousand women, and sons and daughters, carried into captivity. Thus much for this lying prophet and impostor, Isaiah, and the book of falsehoods that bears his name.

I pass on to the book of Jeremiah. This prophet, as he is called, lived in the time that Nebuchadnezzar besieged Jerusalem, in the reign of Zedekiah, the last king of Judah; and the suspicion was strong against him that he was a traitor in the interests of Nebuchadnezzar. Everything relating to Jeremiah shows him to have been a man of an equivocal character; in his metaphor of the potter and the clay, chap. xviii., he guards his prognostications in such a crafty manner as always to leave himself a door to escape by, in case the event should be contrary to what he had predicted.

In the 7th and 8th verses of that chapter he makes the Almighty to say, "At what instant I shall speak concerning a nation, and concerning

[12] In the 14th verse of the 7th chapter, it is said that the child should be called Immanuel; but this name was not given to either of the children otherwise than as a character which the word signifies. That of the prophetess was called Maher-shalal-hash-baz, and that of Mary was called Jesus.—*Author.*

a kingdom, to pluck up, and to pull down, and destroy it. If that nation, against whom I have pronounced, turn from their evil, I will repent of the evil that I thought to do unto them." Here was a proviso against one side of the case; now for the other side.

Verses 9 and 10, "And at what instant I shall speak concerning a nation, and concerning a kingdom, to build and to plant it, if it do evil in my sight, that it obey not my voice; then I shall repent of the good wherewith I said I would benefit them." Here is a proviso against the other side; and, according to this plan of prophesying, a prophet could never be wrong, however mistaken the Almighty might be. This sort of absurd subterfuge, and this manner of speaking of the Almighty, as one would speak of a man, is consistent with nothing but the stupidity of the Bible.

As to the authenticity of the book, it is only necessary to read it in order to decide positively that, though some passages recorded therein may have been spoken by Jeremiah, he is not the author of the book. The historical parts, if they can be called by that name, are in the most confused condition; the same events are several times repeated, and that in a manner different, and sometimes in contradiction to each other; and this disorder runs even to the last chapter, where the history upon which the greater part of the book has been employed begins anew, and ends abruptly.

The book has all the appearance of being a medley of unconnected anecdotes respecting persons and things of that time, collected together in the same rude manner as if the various and contradictory accounts that are to be found in a bundle of newspapers respecting persons and things of the present day were put together without date, order or explanation. I will give two or three examples of this kind.

It appears, from the account of the 37th chapter, that the army of Nebuchadnezzar, which is called the army of the Chaldeans, had besieged Jerusalem some time, and on their hearing that the army of Pharaoh, of Egypt, was marching against them they raised the siege and retreated for a time.

It may here be proper to mention, in order to understand this confused history, that Nebuchadnezzar had besieged and taken Jerusalem during the reign of Jehoiakim, the predecessor of Zedekiah; and that it was Nebuchadnezzar who had made Zedekiah king, or rather viceroy; and that this second siege, of which the book of Jeremiah treats, was in consequence of the revolt of Zedekiah against Nebuchadnezzar. This will in some measure account for the suspicion that affixes to Jeremiah of being a traitor in the interest of Nebuchadnezzar, whom Jeremiah calls, in the 43d chapter, ver. 10, the servant of God. The 11th verse of this chapter (the 37th), says, "And it came to pass, that, when the army of the Chaldeans was broken up from Jerusalem, for fear of Pharaoh's army, that Jeremiah went forth out of Jerusalem, to go (as this account states) into the land of Benjamin, to separate himself thence in the midst of the people, and when he was in the gate of Benjamin, a captain of the ward was there, whose name was Irijah, the son of Shelemiah, the son of Hananiah, and he took Jeremiah the prophet, saying, Thou fallest away to the Chaldeans. Then said Jeremiah, It is false; I fall not away to the Chaldeans." Jeremiah being thus stopped and accused, was, after being examined, committed to prison on suspicion of being a traitor, where he remained, as is stated in the last verse of this chapter.

But the next chapter gives an account of the imprisonment of Jeremiah which has no connection with this account, but ascribes his imprisonment to another circumstance, and for which we must go back to the 21st chapter. It is there stated, ver. 1, that Zedekiah sent Pashur, the son of Malchiah, and Zephaniah, the son of Maaseiah the priest, to Jeremiah to inquire of him concerning Nebuchadnezzar, whose army was then before Jerusalem; and Jeremiah said unto them, ver. 8 and 9, "Thus saith the Lord, Behold I set before you the way of life, and the way of death; he that abideth in this city shall die by the sword, and by the famine, and by the pestilence; but he that goeth out and falleth to the Chaldeans that besiege you, he shall live, and his life shall be unto him for a prey."

This interview and conference breaks off abruptly at the end of the 10th verse of the 21st chapter; and such is the disorder of this book that we have to pass over sixteen chapters, upon various subjects, in order to come at the continuation and event of this conference, and this brings us to the first verse of the 38th chapter, as I have just mentioned.

The 38th chapter opens with saying, "Then Shephatiah, the son of Mattan; Gedaliah, the son of Pashur; and Jucal, the son of Shelemiah; and Pashur, the son of Malchiah (here are more persons mentioned than in the 21st chapter), heard the words that Jeremiah had spoken unto all the people, saying, *Thus saith the Lord, He that remaineth in this city, shall die by the sword, by the famine, and by the pestilence; but he that goeth forth to the Chaldeans shall live, for he shall have his life for a prey, and shall live"* (which are the words of the conference); therefore (they say to Zedekiah), "We beseech thee, let us put this man to death, *for thus he weakeneth the hands of the men of war that remain in this city, and the hands of all the people in speaking such words unto them; for this man seeketh not the welfare of the people, but the hurt."* And at the 6th verse it is said, "Then took they Jeremiah, and cast him into the dungeon of Malchiah."

These two accounts are different and contradictory. The one ascribes his imprisonment to his attempt to escape out of the city; the other to his preaching and prophesying in the city; the one to his being seized by the guard at the gate; the other to his being accused before Zedekiah, by the conferees.[13]

In the next chapter (the 39th) we have another instance of the disordered state of this book; for notwithstanding the siege of the city by Nebuchadnezzar has been the subject of several of the preceding chapters, particularly the 37th and 38th, the 39th chapter begins as if not a word had been said upon the subject; and as if the reader was to be informed of every particular respecting it, for it begins with saying,

---

[13] I observed two chapters, 16th and 17th, in the first book of Samuel, that contradict each other with respect to David, and the manner he became acquainted with Saul; as the 37th and 38th chapters of the book of Jeremiah contradict each other with respect to the cause of Jeremiah's imprisonment.

In the 16th chapter of Samuel, it is said, that an evil spirit of God troubled Saul, and that his servants advised him (as a remedy) "to seek out a man who was a cunning player upon the harp." And Saul said [ver. 17], "Provide me now a man that can play well, and bring *him* to me. Then answered one of the servants, and said, Behold I have seen a son of Jesse the Bethlehemite, *that is* cunning in playing, and a mighty valiant man, and a man of war, and prudent in matters, and a comely person, and the LORD is with him. Wherefore Saul sent messengers unto Jesse, and said, "Send me David thy son." "And [ver. 21] David came to Saul, and stood before him, and he loved him greatly, and he became his armor-bearer. And when the evil spirit from God was upon Saul [ver. 23] David took an harp, and played with his hand: so Saul was refreshed, and was well."

But the next chapter [17] gives an account, all different to this, of the manner that Saul and David became acquainted. Here it is ascribed to David's encounter with Golia[t]h, when David was sent by his father to carry provision to his brethren in the camp. In the 55th verse of this chapter it is said, "And when Saul saw David go forth against the Philistine [Golia[t]h], he said unto Abner, the captain of the host, Abner, whose son is this youth? And Abner said, *As* thy soul liveth, O king, I cannot tell. And the king said, Enquire thou whose son the stripling *is*. And as David returned from the slaughter of the Philistine, Abner took him, and brought him before Saul with the head of the Philistine in his hand. And Saul said to him, Whose son *art* thou, *thou* young man? And David answered, *I am* the son of thy servant Jesse the Bethlehemite." These two accounts belie each other, because each of them supposes Saul and David not to have known each other before. This book, the Bible, is too ridiculous even for criticism.—*Author.*

ver. 1, "In the ninth year of Zedekiah, king of Judah, in the tenth month, came Nebuchadnezzar, king of Babylon, and all his army, against Jerusalem, and they besieged it," etc.

But the instance in the last chapter (the 52d) is still more glaring, for though the story has been told over and over again, this chapter still supposes the reader not to know anything of it, for it begins by saying, ver. 1, *"Zedekiah was one and twenty years old when he began to reign, and he reigned eleven years in Jerusalem, and his mother's name was Hamutal, the daughter of Jeremiah of Libnah. (Ver. 4.) And it came to pass in the ninth year of his reign, in the tenth month, in the tenth day of the month, that Nebuchadnezzar, king of Babylon, came, he and all his army, against Jerusalem, and pitched against it, and built forts against it,"* etc.

It is not possible that any one man, and more particularly Jeremiah, could have been the writer of this book. The errors are such as could not have been committed by any person sitting down to compose a work. Were I, or any other man, to write in such a disordered manner, nobody would read what was written; and everybody would suppose that the writer was in a state of insanity. The only way, therefore, to account for this disorder is that the book is a medley of detached, unauthenticated anecdotes put together by some stupid book-maker under the name of Jeremiah, because many of them refer to him and to the circumstances of the times he lived in.

Of the duplicity, and of the false prediction of Jeremiah, I shall mention two instances, and then proceed to review the remainder of the Bible.

It appears from the 38th chapter, that when Jeremiah was in prison, Zedekiah sent for him, and at this interview, which was private, Jeremiah pressed it strongly on Zedekiah to surrender himself to the enemy. *"If,"* says he (ver. 17), *"thou wilt assuredly go forth unto the king of Babylon's princes, then thy soul shall live,"* etc. Zedekiah was apprehensive that what passed at this conference should be known, and he said to Jeremiah (ver. 25), "If the princes [meaning those of Judah] hear that I have talked with thee, and they come unto thee, and say unto thee, Declare unto us now what thou hast said unto the king; hide it not from us, and we will not put thee to death; and also what the king said unto thee; then thou shalt say unto them, I presented my supplication before the king, that he would not cause me to return to Jonathan's house to die there. Then came all the princes unto Jeremiah, and asked him: and *he told them according to all the words the king had commanded.*"

Thus, this man of God, as he is called, could tell a lie or very strongly prevaricate, when he supposed it would answer his purpose; for certainly he did not go to Zedekiah to make his supplication, neither did he make it; he went because he was sent for, and he employed that opportunity to advise Zedekiah to surrender himself to Nebuchadnezzar.

In the 34th chapter is a prophecy of Jeremiah to Zedekiah, in these words (ver. 2), "Thus saith the Lord, Behold I will give this city into the hands of the king of Babylon, and he shall burn it with fire; and thou shalt not escape out of his hand, but shalt surely be taken, and delivered into his hand; and thine eyes shall behold the eyes of the king of Babylon, and he shall speak with thee mouth to mouth, and thou shalt go to Babylon. *Yet hear the word of the Lord, O Zedekiah, king of Judah, Thus saith the Lord, of thee, Thou shalt not die by the sword, but thou shalt die in peace; and with the burnings of thy fathers, the former kings which were before thee, so shall they burn odors for thee, and they will lament thee, saying, Ah, lord; for I have pronounced the word, saith the Lord.*"

Now, instead of Zedekiah beholding the eyes of the king of Babylon, and speaking with him mouth to mouth, and dying in peace, and with the burning of odors, as at the funeral of his fathers (as Jeremiah had declared the Lord himself had pronounced), the reverse, according to the 52nd chapter, was the case; it is there said (ver. 10), "And the king of Babylon slew the son of Zedekiah before his eyes; then he put out the eyes of Zedekiah, and the king of Babylon bound him in chains, and carried him to Babylon, and put him in prison till the day of his death." What, then, can we say of these prophets, but that they were impostors and liars?

As for Jeremiah, he experienced none of those evils. He was taken into favor by Nebuchadnezzar, who gave him in charge to the captain of the guard (chap. xxxix. ver. 12), "Take him (said he) and look well to him, and do him no harm; but do unto him even as he shall say unto thee." Jeremiah joined himself afterward to Nebuchadnezzar, and went about prophesying for him against the Egyptians, who had marched to the relief of Jerusalem while it was besieged. Thus much for another of the lying prophets, and the book that bears his name.

I have been the more particular in treating of the books ascribed to

Isaiah and Jeremiah, because those two are spoken of in the books of Kings and Chronicles, which the others are not. The remainder of the books ascribed to the men called prophets I shall not trouble myself much about, but take them collectively into the observations I shall offer on the character of the men styled prophets.

In the former part of "The Age of Reason," I have said that the word prophet was the Bible word for poet, and that the flights and metaphors of Jewish poets have been foolishly erected into what are now called prophecies. I am sufficiently justified in this opinion, not only because the books called the prophecies are written in poetical language, but because there is no word in the Bible, except it be the word prophet, that describes what we mean by a poet.

I have also said that the word signifies a performer upon musical instruments, of which I have given some instances, such as that of a company of prophets prophesying with psalteries, with tabrets, with pipes, with harps, etc., and that Saul prophesied with them, I. Sam., chap. x., ver. 5.

It appears from this passage, and from other parts in the book of Samuel, that the word prophet was confined to signify poetry and music; for the person who was supposed to have a visionary insight into concealed things, was not a prophet but a *seer* [14] (I. Sam., chap. ix., ver. 9); and it was not till after the word *seer* went out of use (which most probably was when Saul banished those he called wizards) that the profession of the seer, or the art of seeing, became incorporated into the word prophet.

According to the *modern* meaning of the words prophet and prophesying, it signifies foretelling events to a great distance of time, and it became necessary to the inventors of the Gospel to give it this latitude of meaning, in order to apply or to stretch what they call the prophecies of the Old Testament to the times of the New; but according to the Old Testament, the prophesying of the seer, and afterward of the prophet, so far as the meaning of the word seer, incorporated into that of prophet, had reference only to things of the time then passing, or very closely connected with it, such as the event of a battle they were going to engage in, or of a journey, or of any enterprise they were going

---

[14] I know not what is the Hebrew word that corresponds to the word seer in English; but I observe it is translated into French by *la voyant*, from the verb *voir*, to *see*; and which means the person who *sees*, or the seer.—*Author.*

The Hebrew word for *Seer*, in I Samuel ix., is *chozéh*, the gazer.—*Editor.*

to undertake, or of any circumstance then pending, or of any difficulty they were then in; all of which had immediate reference to themselves (as in the case already mentioned of Ahaz and Isaiah with respect to the expression, *"Behold a virgin shall conceive and bear a son"*), and not to any distant future time.

It was that kind of prophesying that corresponds to what we call fortune-telling, such as casting nativities, predicting riches, fortunate or unfortunate marriages, conjuring for lost goods, etc.; and it is the fraud of the Christian Church, not that of the Jews, and the ignorance and the superstition of modern, not that of ancient, times, that elevated those poetical, musical, conjuring, dreaming, strolling gentry into the rank they have since had.

But, besides this general character of all the prophets, they had also a particular character. They were in parties, and they prophesied for or against, according to the party they were with, as the poetical and political writers of the present day write in defense of the party they associate with against the other.

After the Jews were divided into two nations, that of Judah and that of Israel, each party had its prophets, who abused and accused each other of being false prophets, lying prophets, impostors, etc.

The prophets of the party of Judah prophesied against the prophets of the party of Israel; and those of the party of Israel against those of Judah. This party prophesying showed itself immediately on the separation under the first two rival kings, Rehoboam and Jeroboam.

The prophet that cursed or prophesied against the altar that Jeroboam had built in Bethel was of the party of Judah, where Rehoboam was king; and he was waylaid on his return home, by a prophet of the party of Israel, who said unto him (I. Kings, chap. x.), *"Art thou the man of God that came from Judah? and he said, I am."* Then the prophet of the party of Israel said to him, *"I am a prophet also, as thou art* [signifying of Judah], *and an angel spake unto me by the word of the Lord, saying, Bring him back with thee into thine house, that he may eat bread and drink water: but* (says the 18th verse) *he lied unto him."*

This event, however, according to the story, is that the prophet of Judah never got back to Judah, for he was found dead on the road, by the contrivance of the prophet of Israel, who, no doubt, was called a true prophet by his own party, and the prophet of Judah a lying prophet.

In the third chapter of the second of Kings, a story is related of prophesying or conjuring that shows, in several particulars, the character of a prophet. Jehoshaphat, king of Judah, and Jehoram, king of Israel, had for a while ceased their party animosity, and entered into an alliance; and these two, together with the king of Edom, engaged in a war against the king of Moab.

After uniting and marching their armies, the story says, they were in great distress for water; upon which Jehoshaphat said, *"Is there not here a prophet of the Lord, that we may inquire of the Lord by him? and one of the servants of the king of Israel said, Here is Elisha."* [Elisha was one of the party of Judah.] *"And Jehoshaphat, the king of Judah, said, The word of the Lord is with him."*

The story then says, that these three kings went down to Elisha; and when Elisha (who, as I have said, was a Judahmite prophet) saw the king of Israel, he said unto him, *"What have I to do with thee? get thee to the prophets of thy father, and to the prophets of thy mother. And the king of Israel said unto him, Nay, for the Lord hath called these three kings together, to deliver them into the hand of Moab."* [Meaning because of the distress they were in for water.] Upon which Elisha said, *"As the Lord of hosts liveth, before whom I stand, surely, were it not that I regard the presence of Jehoshaphat, the king of Judah, I would not look towards thee, nor see thee."* Here is all the venom and vulgarity of a party prophet. We have now to see the performance, or manner of prophesying.

Verse 15. *"Bring me* (said Elisha), *a minstrel: And it came to pass, when the minstrel played, that the hand of the Lord came upon him."* Here is the farce of the conjurer. Now for the prophecy: *"And Elisha said,* [singing most probably to the tune he was playing,] *Thus saith the Lord, make this valley full of ditches";* which was just telling them what every countryman could have told them, without either fiddle or farce, that the way to get water was to dig for it.

But as every conjurer is not famous alike for the same thing, so neither were those prophets; for though all of them, at least those I have spoken of, were famous for lying, some of them excelled in cursing. Elisha, whom I have just mentioned, was a chief in this branch of prophesying; it was he that cursed the forty-two children in the name of the Lord, whom the two she-bears came and devoured. We are to suppose that those children were of the party of Israel; but as those who will curse will lie, there is just as much credit to be given to this story of Elisha's two she-bears as there is to that of the Dragon of Wantley, of whom it is said:

"Poor children three devoured he,
    That could not with him grapple;
And at one sup he ate them up,
    As a man would eat an apple."

There was another description of men called prophets that amused themselves with dreams and visions; but whether by night or by day we know not. These, if they were not quite harmless, were but little mischievous. Of this class are:

Ezekiel and Daniel; and the first question upon those books, as upon all the others, is, are they genuine? that is, were they written by Ezekiel and Daniel?

Of this there is no proof, but so far as my own opinion goes, I am more inclined to believe they were than that they were not. My reasons for this opinion are as follows: First, Because those books do not contain internal evidence to prove they were not written by Ezekiel and Daniel, as the books ascribed to Moses, Joshua, Samuel, etc. prove they were not written by Moses, Joshua, Samuel, etc.

Secondly, Because they were not written till after the Babylonian captivity began, and there is good reason to believe that not any book in the Bible was written before that period; at least it is proveable from the books themselves, as I have already shown, that they were not written till after the commencement of the Jewish monarchy.

Thirdly, Because the manner in which the books ascribed to Ezekiel and Daniel are written agrees with the condition these men were in at the time of writing them.

Had the numerous commentators and priests, who have foolishly employed or wasted their time in pretending to expound and unriddle those books, been carried into captivity, as Ezekiel and Daniel were, it would have greatly improved their intellects in comprehending the reason for this mode of writing, and have saved them the trouble of racking their invention, as they have done, to no purpose; for they would have found that themselves would be obliged to write whatever they had to write respecting their own affairs or those of their friends or of their country, in a concealed manner, as those men have done.

These two books differ from all the rest, for it is only these that are filled with accounts of dreams and visions; and this difference arose from the situation the writers were in as prisoners of war, or prisoners of state, in a foreign country, which obliged them to convey even the most trifling information to each other, and all their political projects or opinions, in obscure and metaphorical terms. They pretended to have dreamed dreams and seen visions, because it was unsafe for them to speak facts or plain language.

We ought, however, to suppose that the persons to whom they wrote understood what they meant, and that it was not intended anybody else should. But these busy commentators and priests have been puzzling their wits to find out what it was not intended they should know, and with which they have nothing to do.

Ezekiel and Daniel were carried prisoners to Babylon under the first captivity, in the time of Jehoiakim, nine years before the second captivity in the time of Zedekiah.

The Jews were still numerous, and had considerable force at Jerusalem; and as it is natural to suppose that men in the situation of Ezekiel and Daniel would be meditating the recovery of their country and their own deliverance, it is reasonable to suppose that the accounts of dreams and visions with which those books are filled are no other than a disguised mode of correspondence, to facilitate those objects —it served them as a cipher or secret alphabet. If they are not this, they are tales, reveries and nonsense; or, at least, a fanciful way of wearing off the wearisomeness of captivity; but the presumption is they are the former.

Ezekiel begins his book by speaking of a vision of *cherubims* and of a *wheel within a wheel,* which he says he saw by the river Chebar, in the land of his captivity. Is it not reasonable to suppose, that by the cherubims he meant the temple at Jerusalem, where they had figures of cherubims? And by a wheel within a wheel (which, as a figure, has always been understood to signify political contrivance) the project or means of recovering Jerusalem?

In the latter part of this book he supposes himself transported to Jerusalem and into the temple; and he refers back to the vision on the river Chebar, and says (chap. xliii, ver. 3), that this last vision was like the vision on the river Chebar; which indicates that those pretended dreams and visions had for their object the recovery of Jerusalem, and nothing further.

As to the romantic interpretations and applications, wild as the dreams and visions they undertake to explain, which commentators and priests have made of those books, that of converting them into things which they call prophecies, and making them bend to times and circumstances as far remote even as the present day, it shows the fraud or the extreme folly to which credulity or priestcraft can go.

Scarcely anything can be more absurd than to suppose that men situated as Ezekiel and Daniel were, whose country was overrun and in the possession of the enemy, all their friends and relations in captivity abroad, or in slavery at home, or massacred, or in continual danger of it; scarcely anything, I say, can be more absurd than to suppose that such men should find nothing to do but that of employing their time and their thoughts about what was to happen to other nations a thousand or two thousand years after they were dead; at the same time, nothing is more natural than that they should meditate the recovery of Jerusalem and their own deliverance; and that this was the sole object of all the obscure and apparently frantic writings contained in those books.

In this sense, the mode of writing used in those two books, being forced by necessity, and not adopted by choice, is not irrational; but, if we are to view the books as prophecies, they are false. In the 29th chapter of Ezekiel, speaking of Egypt, it is said (ver. 11), *"No foot of man shall pass through it, nor foot of beast shall pass through it; neither shall it be inhabited for forty years."* This is what never came to pass, and consequently it is false, as all the books I have already reviewed are: I here close this part of the subject.

In the former part of "The Age of Reason" I have spoken of Jonah, and of the story of him and the whale. A fit story for ridicule, if it was written to be believed; or of laughter, if it was intended to try what credulity could swallow; for if it could swallow Jonah and the whale, it could swallow anything.

But, as is already shown in the observations on the book of Job and of Proverbs, it is not always certain which of the books in the Bible are originally Hebrew, or only translations from the books of the Gentiles into Hebrew; and as the book of Jonah, so far from treating of the affairs of the Jews, says nothing upon that subject, but treats altogether of the Gentiles, it is more probable that it is a book of the Gentiles than of the Jews, and that it has been written as a fable, to expose the nonsense and satirize the vicious and malignant character of a Bible prophet, or a predicting priest.

Jonah is represented, first, as a disobedient prophet, running away from his mission, and taking shelter aboard a vessel of the Gentiles, bound from Joppa to Tarshish; as if he ignorantly supposed, by such a paltry contrivance, he could hide himself where God could not find him. The vessel is overtaken by a storm at sea, and the mariners, all of whom are Gentiles, believing it to be a judgment, on account of some one on board who had committed a crime, agreed to cast lots to discover the offender, and the lot fell upon Jonah. But, before this, they had cast all their wares and merchandise overboard to lighten the vessel, while Jonah, like a stupid fellow, was fast asleep in the hold.

After the lot had designated Jonah to be the offender, they questioned him to know who and what he was? and he told them *he was a Hebrew;* and the story implies that he confessed himself to be guilty.

But these Gentiles, instead of sacrificing him at once, without pity or mercy, as a company of Bible prophets or priests would have done by a Gentile in the same case, and as it is related Samuel had done by Agag, and Moses by the women and children, they endeavored to save him, though at the risk of their own lives, for the account says, *"Nevertheless* [that is, though Jonah was a Jew and a foreigner, and the cause of all their misfortunes and the loss of their cargo], *the men rowed hard to bring it* [*the boat*] *to land, but they could not, for the sea wrought and was tempestuous against them."*

Still they were unwilling to put the fate of the lot into execution, and they cried (says the account) unto the Lord, saying (ver. 14), *"We beseech Thee, O Lord, we beseech Thee, let us not perish for this man's life, and lay not upon us innocent blood; for Thou, O Lord, hast done as it pleased Thee."* Meaning, thereby, that they did not presume to judge Jonah guilty, since that he might be innocent; but that they considered the lot that had fallen upon him as a decree of God, or as it *pleased God.*

The address of this prayer shows that the Gentiles worshipped one *Supreme Being,* and that they were not idolaters, as the Jews represented them to be. But the storm still continuing and the danger increasing, they put the fate of the lot into execution, and cast Jonah into the sea, where, according to the story, a great fish swallowed him up whole and alive.

We have now to consider Jonah securely housed from the storm in the fish's belly. Here we are told that he prayed; but the prayer is a made-up prayer, taken from various parts of the Psalms, without any connection or consistency, and adapted to the distress, but not at all to the condition Jonah was in. It is such a prayer as a Gentile, who might know something of the Psalms, could copy out for him.

This circumstance alone, were there no other, is sufficient to indicate that the whole is a made-up story. The prayer, however, is supposed to have answered the purpose, and the story goes on (taking up at the same time the cant language of a Bible prophet), saying: (chap. ii, ver. 10), *"And the Lord spake unto the fish,* and it vomited out Jonah upon the dry land."

Jonah then received a second mission to Nineveh, with which he sets out; and we have now to consider him as a preacher. The distress he is represented to have suffered, the remembrance of his own disobedience as the cause of it, and the miraculous escape he is supposed to have had, were sufficient, one would conceive, to have impressed him with sympathy and benevolence in the execution of his mission; but, instead of this, he enters the city with denunciation and malediction in his mouth, crying (chap. iii, ver. 4): *"Yet forty days, and Nineveh shall be over-thrown."*

We have now to consider this supposed missionary in the last act of his mission; and here it is that the malevolent spirit of a Bible-prophet, or of a predicting priest, appears in all that blackness of character that men ascribe to the being they call the devil.

Having published his predictions, he withdrew, says the story, to the East side of the city. But for what? Not to contemplate, in retirement, the mercy of his Creator to himself or to others, but to wait, with malignant impatience, the destruction of Nineveh.

It came to pass, however, as the story relates, that the Ninevites reformed, and that God, according to the Bible phrase, repented Him of the evil He had said He would do unto them, and did it not. This, saith the first verse of the last chapter, *"displeased Jonah exceedingly, and he was very angry."* His obdurate heart would rather that all Nineveh should be destroyed, and every soul, young and old, perish in its ruins, than that his prediction should not be fulfilled.

To expose the character of a prophet still more, a gourd is made to grow up in the night, that promised him an agreeable shelter from the heat of the sun, in the place to which he had retired, and the next morning it dies.

Here the rage of the prophet becomes excessive, and he is ready to destroy himself. *"It is better, said he, for me to die than to live."* This brings on a supposed expostulation between the Almighty and the prophet, in which the former says, *"Doest thou well to be angry for the gourd? And Jonah said, I do well to be angry even unto death; Then, said the Lord, Thou hast had pity on the gourd, for which thou hast*

*not labored, neither madest it grow; which came up in a night, and
perished in a night; and should not I spare Nineveh that great city,
in which are more than threescore thousand persons that cannot discern between their right hand and their left hand?"*

Here is both the winding up of the satire and the moral of the fable.
As a satire, it strikes against the character of all the Bible prophets,
and against all the indiscriminate judgments upon men, women and
children, with which this lying book, the Bible, is crowded; such as
Noah's flood, the destruction of the cities of Sodom and Gomorrah, the
extirpation of the Canaanites, even to the sucking infants and women
with child, because the same reflection, *that there are more than threescore thousand persons that cannot discern between their right hand and
their left hand,* meaning young children, apply to all the cases. It
satirizes also the supposed partiality of the Creator for one nation more
than for another.

As a moral, it preaches against the malevolent spirit of prediction;
for as certainly as a man predicts ill, he becomes inclined to wish it.
The pride of having his judgment right hardens his heart, till at last
he beholds with satisfaction, or sees with disappointment, the accomplishment or the failure of his predictions.

The book ends with the same kind of strong and well-directed point
against prophets, prophecies and indiscriminate judgment, as the chapter
that Benjamin Franklin made for the Bible, about Abraham and the
stranger, ends against the intolerant spirit of religious persecution. Thus
much for the book of Jonah.

Of the poetical parts of the Bible, that are called prophecies, I have
spoken in the former part of "The Age of Reason," and already in this,
where I have said that the word *prophet* is the Bible word for *poet,* and
that the flights and metaphors of those poets, many of which have
become obscure by the lapse of time and the change of circumstances,
have been ridiculously erected into things called prophecies, and applied
to purposes the writers never thought of.

When a priest quotes any of those passages, he unriddles it agreeably
to his own views, and imposes that explanation upon his congregation
as the meaning of the writer. The *whore of Babylon* has been the common whore of all the priests, and each has accused the other of keeping
the strumpet; so well do they agree in their explanations.

There now remain only a few books, which they call books of the
lesser prophets, and as I have already shown that the greater are im-

postors, it would be cowardice to disturb the repose of the little ones. Let them sleep, then, in the arms of their nurses, the priests, and both be forgotten together.

I have now gone through the Bible, as a man would go through a wood with an axe on his shoulder and fell trees. Here they lie; and the priests, if they can, may replant them. They may, perhaps, stick them in the ground, but they will never make them grow. I pass on to the books of the New Testament.

CHAPTER II

Turning to the New Testament

THE New Testament, they tell us, is founded upon the prophecies of the Old; if so, it must follow the fate of its foundation.

As it is nothing extraordinary that a woman should be with child before she was married, and that the son she might bring forth should be executed, even unjustly, I see no reason for not believing that such a woman as Mary, and such a man as Joseph, and Jesus existed; their mere existence is a matter of indifference about which there is no ground either to believe or to disbelieve, and which comes under the common head of, *It may be so; and what then?*

The probability, however, is that there were such persons, or at least such as resembled them in part of the circumstances, because almost all romantic stories have been suggested by some actual circumstance; as the adventures of Robinson Crusoe, not a word of which is true, were suggested by the case of Alexander Selkirk.

It is not the existence, or non-existence, of the persons that I trouble myself about; it is the fable of Jesus Christ, as told in the New Testament, and the wild and visionary doctrine raised thereon, against which I contend. The story, taking it as it is told, is blasphemously obscene.

It gives an account of a young woman engaged to be married, and while under this engagement she is, to speak plain language, debauched by a ghost, under the impious pretense (Luke, chap. i., ver. 35), that *"the Holy Ghost shall come upon thee, and the power of the Highest shall overshadow thee."* Notwithstanding which, Joseph afterward marries her, cohabits with her as his wife, and in his turn rivals the ghost. This is putting the story into intelligible language, and when told in this manner, there is not a priest but must be ashamed to own it.[15]

Obscenity in matters of faith, however wrapped up, is always a token of fable and imposture; for it is necessary to our serious belief of God that we do not connect it with stories that run, as this does, into ludicrous interpretations. This story is upon the face of it, the same kind of story as that of Jupiter and Leda, or Jupiter and Europa, or any of the amorous adventures of Jupiter; and shows, as is already stated in the former part of "The Age of Reason," that the Christian faith is built upon the heathen mythology.

As the historical parts of the New Testament, so far as concerns Jesus Christ, are confined to a very short space of time, less than two years, and all within the same country, and nearly to the same spot, the discordance of time, place and circumstance, which detects the fallacy of the books of the Old Testament, and proves them to be impositions, cannot be expected to be found here in the same abundance. The New Testament compared with the Old, is like a farce of one act, in which there is not room for very numerous violations of the unities. There are, however, some glaring contradictions, which, exclusive of the fallacy of the pretended prophecies, are sufficient to show the story of Jesus Christ to be false.

I lay it down as a position which cannot be controverted, first, that the *agreement* of all the parts of a story does not prove that story to be true, because the parts may agree and the whole may be false; secondly, that the *disagreement* of the parts of a story proves *the whole cannot be true*. The agreement does not prove true, but the disagreement proves falsehood positively.

The history of Jesus Christ is contained in the four books ascribed to Matthew, Mark, Luke and John. The first chapter of Matthew begins with giving a genealogy of Jesus Christ; and in the third chapter of Luke there is also given a genealogy of Jesus Christ. Did those two agree, it would not prove the genealogy to be true, because it might, nevertheless, be a fabrication; but as they contradict each other in every particular, it proves falsehood absolutely.

If Matthew speaks truth, Luke speaks falsehood, and if Luke speaks truth, Matthew speaks falsehood; and as there is no authority for be-

---

[15] Mary, the supposed virgin-mother of Jesus, had several other children, sons and daughters. See Matthew, chap. xiii, verses 55, 56.—*Author*.

lieving one more than the other, there is no authority for believing either; and if they cannot be believed even in the very first thing they say and set out to prove, they are not entitled to be believed in anything they say afterward.

Truth is a uniform thing; and as to inspiration and revelation, were we to admit it, it is impossible to suppose it can be contradictory. Either, then, the men called apostles are impostors, or the books ascribed to them have been written by other persons and fathered upon them, as is the case in the Old Testament.

The book of Matthew gives (chap. i., ver. 6) a genealogy by name from David up through Joseph, the husband of Mary, to Christ; and makes there to be *twenty-eight* generations. The book of Luke gives also a genealogy by name from Christ, through Joseph, the husband of Mary, down to David, and makes there to be *forty-three* generations; besides which, there are only the two names of David and Joseph that are alike in the two lists.

I here insert both genealogical lists, and for the sake of perspicuity and comparison, have placed them both in the same direction, that is from Joseph down to David.

Now, if these men, Matthew and Luke, set out with a falsehood between them (as these two accounts show they do) in the very commencement of their history of Jesus Christ, and of whom and what he was, what authority (as I have before asked) is there left for believing the strange things they tell us afterward? If they cannot be believed in their account of his natural genealogy, how are we to believe them when they tell us he was the Son of God begotten by a ghost, and that an angel announced this in secret to his mother? If they lied in one genealogy, why are we to believe them in the other?

If his natural genealogy be manufactured, which it certainly is, why are we not to suppose that his celestial genealogy is manufactured also, and that the whole is fabulous? Can any man of serious reflection hazard his future happiness upon the belief of a story naturally impossible, repugnant to every idea of decency, and related by persons already detected of falsehood? Is it not more safe that we stop ourselves at the plain, pure and unmixed belief of one God, which is Deism, than that we commit ourselves on an ocean of improbable, irrational, indecent and contradictory tales?

The first question, however, upon the books of the New Testament, as upon those of the Old, is: Are they genuine? Were they written by

Genealogy according to Matthew		Genealogy according to Luke	
Christ	23 Josaphat	Christ	23 Neri
2 Joseph	24 Asa	2 Joseph	24 Melchi
3 Jacob	25 Abia	3 Heli	25 Addi
4 Matthan	26 Roboam	4 Matthat	26 Cosam
5 Eleazar	27 Solomon	5 Levi	27 Elmodam
6 Eliud	28 David [16]	6 Melchi	28 Er
7 Achim		7 Janna	29 Jose
8 Sadoc		8 Joseph	30 Eliezer
9 Azor		9 Mattathias	31 Jorim
10 Eliakim		10 Amos	32 Matthat
11 Abiud		11 Naum	33 Levi
12 Zorobabel		12 Esli	34 Simeon
13 Salathiel		13 Nagge	35 Juda
14 Jechonias		14 Maath	36 Joseph
15 Josias		15 Mattathias	37 Jonan
16 Amon		16 Semei	38 Eliakim
17 Manasses		17 Joseph	39 Melea
18 Ezekias		18 Juda	40 Menan
19 Achaz		19 Joanna	41 Mattatha
20 Joatham		20 Rhesa	42 Nathan
21 Ozias		21 Zorobabel	43 David
22 Joram		22 Salathiel	

the persons to whom they are ascribed? for it is upon this ground only that the strange things related therein have been credited. Upon this point there is no *direct proof for or against,* and all that this state of a case proves is *doubtfulness,* and doubtfulness is the opposite of belief. The state, therefore, that the books are in, proves against themselves as far as this kind of proof can go.

[16] From the birth of David to the birth of Christ is upwards of 1080 years; and as the lifetime of Christ is not included, there are but 27 full generations. To find, therefore, the average age of each person mentioned in the list, at the time his first son was born, it is only necessary to divide 1080 years by 27, which gives 40 years for each person. As the lifetime of man was then but of the same extent it is now, it is an absurdity to suppose that 27 following generations should all be old bachelors, before they married; and the more so, when we are told, that Solomon, the next in succession to David, had a house full of wives and mistresses before he was twenty-one years of age. So far from this genealogy being a solemn truth, it is not even a reasonable lie. This list of Luke gives about twenty-six years for the average age, and this is too much.—*Author.*

But exclusive of this, the presumption is that the books called the Evangelists, and ascribed to Matthew, Mark, Luke and John, were not written by Matthew, Mark, Luke and John, and that they are impositions. The disordered state of the history in those four books, the silence of one book upon matters related in the other, and the disagreement that is to be found among them, implies that they are the production of some unconnected individuals, many years after the things they pretend to relate, each of whom made his own legend; and not the writings of men living intimately together, as the men called the apostles are supposed to have done—in fine, that they have been manufactured, as the books of the Old Testament have been, by other persons than those whose names they bear.

The story of the angel announcing what the Church calls the *immaculate conception* is not so much as mentioned in the books ascribed to Mark and John; and is differently related in Matthew and Luke. The former says the angel appeared to Joseph; the latter says it was to Mary; but either Joseph or Mary was the worst evidence that could have been thought of, for it was others that should have testified *for them,* and not they for themselves.

Were any girl that is now with child to say, and even to swear it, that she was gotten with child by a ghost, and that an angel told her so, would she be believed? Certainly she would not. Why, then, are we to believe the same thing of another girl, whom we never saw, told by nobody knows who, nor when, nor where? How strange and inconsistent it is, that the same circumstance that would weaken the belief even of a probable story should be given as a motive for believing this one, that has upon the face of it every token of absolute impossibility and imposture!

The story of Herod destroying all the children under two years old belongs altogether to the book of Matthew; not one of the rest mentions anything about it. Had such a circumstance been true, the universality of it must have made it known to all the writers, and the thing would have been too striking to have been omitted by any.

This writer tells us that Jesus escaped this slaughter because Joseph and Mary were warned by an angel to flee with him unto Egypt; but he forgot to make any provision for John, who was then under two years of age. John, however, who stayed behind, fared as well as Jesus, who fled; and, therefore, the story circumstantially belies itself.

Not any two of these writers agree in reciting, *exactly in the same words,* the written inscription, short as it is, which they tell us was put over Christ when he was crucified; and besides this, Mark says: He was crucified at the third hour (nine in the morning), and John says it was the sixth hour (twelve at noon).[17]

The inscription is thus stated in these books:

MATTHEW .... *This is Jesus, the King of the Jews.*
MARK .... *The King of the Jews.*
LUKE .... *This is the King of the Jews.*
JOHN .... *Jesus of Nazareth, King of the Jews.*

We may infer from these circumstances, trivial as they are, that those writers, whoever they were, and in whatever time they lived, were not present at the scene. The only one of the men called apostles who appears to have been near the spot was Peter, and when he was accused of being one of Jesus' followers, it is said (Matthew, chap. xxvi., ver. 74), *"Then he [Peter] began to curse and to swear, saying, I know not the man!"* yet we are now called upon to believe the same Peter, convicted, by their own account, of perjury. For what reason, or on what authority, shall we do this?

The accounts that are given of the circumstances that they tell us attended the crucifixion are differently related in these four books.

The book ascribed to Matthew says (chap. xxvii, v. 45), *"Now from the sixth hour there was darkness over all the land unto the ninth hour."* (Ver. 51, 52, 53), *"And, behold, the veil of the temple was rent in twain from the top to the bottom; and the earth did quake, and the rocks rent; and the graves were opened; and many bodies of the saints which slept arose, and came out of the graves after his resurrection, and went into the holy city and appeared unto many."* Such is the account which this dashing writer of the book of Matthew gives, but in which he is not supported by the writers of the other books.

The writer of the book ascribed to Mark, in detailing the circumstances of the crucifixion, makes no mention of any earthquake, nor of the rocks rending, nor of the graves opening, nor of the dead men walking out. The writer of the book of Luke is silent also upon the same

[17] According to John, the sentence was not passed till about the sixth hour (noon), and, consequently, the execution could not be till the afternoon; but Mark says expressly, that he was crucified at the third hour (nine in the morning), chap. xv, verse 25. John, chap. xix, verse 14.—*Author.*

points. And as to the writer of the book of John, though he details all the circumstances of the crucifixion down to the burial of Christ, he says nothing about either the darkness—the veil of the temple—the earthquake—the rocks—the graves—nor the dead men.

Now, if it had been true that those things had happened, and if the writers of these books had lived at the time they did happen, and had been the persons they are said to be, namely, the four men called apostles, Matthew, Mark, Luke and John, it was not possible for them, as true historians, even without the aid of inspiration, not to have recorded them.

The things, supposing them to have been facts, were of too much notoriety not to have been known, and of too much importance not to have been told. All these supposed apostles must have been witnesses of the earthquake, if there had been any; for it was not possible for them to have been absent from it; the opening of the graves and the resurrection of the dead men, and their walking about the city, is of still greater importance than the earthquake.

An earthquake is always possible and natural, and proves nothing; but this opening of the graves is supernatural, and directly in point to their doctrine, their cause and their apostleship. Had it been true, it would have filled up whole chapters of those books, and been the chosen theme and general chorus of all the writers; but instead of this, little and trivial things, and mere prattling conversations of, *he said this,* and *he said that,* are often tediously detailed, while this, most important of all, had it been true, is passed off in a slovenly manner by a single dash of the pen, and that by one writer only and not so much as hinted at by the rest.

It is an easy thing to tell a lie, but it is difficult to support the lie after it is told. The writer of the book of Matthew should have told us who the saints were that came to life again and went into the city, and what became of them afterward, and who it was that saw them—for he is not hardy enough to say he saw them himself; whether they came out naked, and all in natural buff, he-saints and she-saints; or whether they came full dressed, and where they got their dresses; whether they went to their former habitations, and reclaimed their wives, their husbands and their property, and how they were received; whether they entered ejectments for the recovery of their possessions, or brought actions of *crim. con.* against the rival interlopers; whether they remained on earth, and followed their former occupation of preaching or working; or whether they died again, or went back to their graves alive and buried themselves.

Strange, indeed, that an army of saints should return to life and nobody know who they were, nor who it was that saw them, and that not a word more should be said upon the subject, nor these saints have anything to tell us!

Had it been the prophets who (as we are told) had formerly prophesied of these things, *they* must have had a *great deal* to say. They could have told us everything and we should have had posthumous prophecies, with notes and commentaries upon the first, a little better at least than we have now. Had it been Moses and Aaron and Joshua and Samuel and David, not an unconverted Jew had remained in all Jerusalem. Had it been John the Baptist, and the saints of the time then present, everybody would have known them, and they would have out-preached and out-famed all the other apostles. But, instead of this, these saints were made to pop up, like Jonah's gourd in the night, for no purpose at all but to wither in the morning. Thus much for this part of the story.

The tale of the resurrection follows that of the crucifixion, and in this as well as in that, the writers, whoever they were, disagree so much as to make it evident that none of them were there.

The book of Matthew states that when Christ was put in the sepulchre, the Jews applied to Pilate for a watch or a guard to be placed over the sepulchre, to prevent the body being stolen by the disciples; and that, in consequence of this request, the sepulchre *was made sure, sealing the stone* that covered the mouth, and setting a watch.

But the other books say nothing about this application, nor about the sealing, nor the guard, nor the watch; and, according to their accounts, there were none. Matthew, however, follows up this part of the story of the guard or the watch with a second part that I shall notice in the conclusion, as it serves to detect the fallacy of those books.

The book of Matthew continues its account, and says (chap. xxviii., ver. 1) that at the end of the Sabbath, as it began to dawn toward the first day of the week, came Mary Magdalene and the other Mary, to see the sepulchre. Mark says it was sun-rising, and John says it was dark. Luke says it was Mary Magdalene and Joanna, and Mary, the mother of James, and other women, that came to the sepulchre; and John states that Mary Magdalene came alone. So well do they agree about

their first evidence! they all, however, appear to have known most about
Mary Magdalene; she was a woman of a large acquaintance, and it was
not an ill conjecture that she might be upon the stroll.

The book of Matthew goes on to say (ver. 2), "And behold there was
a great earthquake, for the angel of the Lord descended from heaven,
and came and rolled back the stone from the door, and sat upon it." But
the other books say nothing about any earthquake, nor about the angel
rolling back the stone and sitting upon it, and according to their account, there was no angel sitting there. Mark says the angel was within
the sepulchre, sitting on the right side. Luke says there were two, and
they were both standing up; and John says they were both sitting down,
one at the head and the other at the feet.

Matthew says that the angel that was sitting upon the stone on the
outside of the sepulchre told the two Marys that Christ was risen, and
that the women went away quickly. Mark says that the women, upon
seeing the stone rolled away and wondering at it, went into the sepulchre, and that it was the angel that was sitting within on the right side
that told them so. Luke says it was the two angels that were standing up;
and John says it was Jesus Christ himself that told it to Mary Magdalene,
and that she did not go into the sepulchre, but only stooped down and
looked in.

Now, if the writers of those four books had gone into a court of justice
to prove an *alibi* (for it is of the nature of an alibi that is here attempted
to be proved, namely, the absence of a dead body by supernatural
means), and had they given their evidence in the same contradictory
manner as it is here given, they would have been in danger of having
their ears cropped for perjury, and would have justly deserved it. Yet this
is the evidence, and these are the books that have been imposed upon
the world as being given by divine inspiration and as the unchangeable
Word of God.

The writer of the book of Matthew, after giving this account, relates
a story that is not to be found in any of the other books, and which is
the same I have just before alluded to.

"Now," says he [that is, after the conversation the women had with
the angel sitting upon the stone], "behold some of the watch [meaning
the watch that he had said had been placed over the sepulchre] came
into the city, showed unto the chief priests all the things that were done;
and when they were assembled with the elders and had taken counsel
they gave large money unto the soldiers, saying, Say ye, His disciples

came by night, and stole him away while we *slept;* and if this come
to the governor's ears, we will persuade him, and secure you. So they
took the money, and did as they were taught; and this saying [that his
disciples stole him away] is commonly reported among the Jews until
this day."

The expression, *until this day,* is an evidence that the book ascribed
to Matthew was not written by Matthew, and that it had been manufactured long after the time and things of which it pretends to treat;
for the expression implies a great length of intervening time. It would
be inconsistent in us to speak in this manner of anything happening in
our own time. To give, therefore, intelligible meaning to the expression,
we must suppose a lapse of some generations at least, for this manner
of speaking carries the mind back to ancient time.

The absurdity also of the story is worth noticing; for it shows the
writer of the book of Matthew to have been an exceedingly weak and
foolish man. He tells a story that contradicts itself in point of possibility;
for though the guard, if there were any, might be made to say that the
body was taken away while they were *asleep,* and to give that as a reason
for their not having prevented it, that same sleep must also have prevented their knowing how and by whom it was done, and yet they were
made to say that it was the disciples who did it.

Were a man to tender his evidence of something that he should say
was done, and of the manner of doing it, and of the persons who did it,
while he was asleep, and could know nothing of the matter, such evidence could not be received; it will do well enough for Testament evidence, but not for anything where truth is concerned.

I come now to that part of the evidence in those books that respects
the pretended appearance of Christ after this pretended resurrection.

The writer of the book of Matthew relates that the angel that was
sitting on the stone at the mouth of the sepulchre said to the two Marys
(chap. xxviii, ver. 7), *"Behold Christ has gone before you into Galilee,
there shall ye see him; lo, I have told you."* And the same writer at
the next two verses (8, 9), makes Christ himself to speak to the same
purpose to these women immediately after the angel had told it to
them, and that they ran quickly to tell it to the disciples; and at the
16th verse it is said, *"Then the eleven disciples went away into Galilee,
into a mountain where Jesus had appointed them; and when they saw
him, they worshiped him."*

But the writer of the book of John tells us a story very different to this; for he says (chap. xx., ver. 19), *"Then the same day at evening, being the first day of the week* [that is, the same day that Christ is said to have risen], *when the doors were shut, where the disciples were assembled, for fear of the Jews, came Jesus and stood in the midst of them."*

According to Matthew the eleven were marching to Galilee to meet Jesus in a mountain, by his own appointment, at the very time when, according to John, they were assembled in another place, and that not by appointment, but in secret, for fear of the Jews.

The writer of the book of Luke contradicts that of Matthew more pointedly than John does; for he says expressly that the meeting was in *Jerusalem* the evening of the same day that he [Christ] rose, and that the *eleven* were *there*. See Luke, chap. xxiv, ver. 13, 33.

Now, it is not possible, unless we admit these supposed disciples the right of willful lying, that the writer of those books could be any of the eleven persons called disciples; for if, according to Matthew, the eleven went into Galilee to meet Jesus in a mountain by his own appointment, on the same day that he is said to have risen, Luke and John must have been two of that eleven; yet the writer of Luke says expressly, and John implies as much, that the meeting was that same day in a house in Jerusalem; and, on the other hand, if, according to Luke and John, the *eleven* were assembled in a house in Jerusalem, Matthew must have been one of that eleven; yet Matthew says the meeting was in a mountain in Galilee, and consequently the evidence given in those books destroys each other.

The writer of the book of Mark says nothing about any meeting in Galilee; but he says (chap. xvi, ver. 12), that Christ, after his resurrection, appeared in another form to two of them as they walked into the country, and that these two told it to the residue, who would not believe them.

Luke also tells a story in which he keeps Christ employed the whole day of this pretended resurrection until the evening, and which totally invalidates the account of going to the mountain in Galilee. He says that two of them, without saying which two, went that same day to a village called Emmaus, three score furlongs (seven miles and a half) from Jerusalem, and that Christ, in disguise, went with them, and stayed with them unto the evening, and supped with them, and then vanished out of their sight, and re-appeared that same evening at the meeting of the eleven in Jerusalem.

This is the contradictory manner in which the evidence of this pretended re-appearance of Christ is stated; the only point in which the writers agree is the skulking privacy of that re-appearance; for whether it was in the recess of a mountain in Galilee, or a shut-up house in Jerusalem, it was still skulking. To what cause, then, are we to assign this skulking? On the one hand it is directly repugnant to the supposed or pretended end—that of convincing the world that Christ was risen; and, on the other hand, to have asserted the publicity of it would have exposed the writers of those books to public detection, and, therefore, they have been under the necessity of making it a private affair.

As to the account of Christ being seen by more than five hundred at once, it is Paul only who says it, and not the five hundred who say it for themselves. It is, therefore, the testimony of but one man, and that, too, of a man who did not, according to the same account, believe a word of the matter himself at the time it is said to have happened.

His evidence, supposing him to have been the writer of the 15th chapter of Corinthians, where this account is given, is like that of a man who comes into a court of justice to swear that what he had sworn before is false. A man may often see reason, and he has, too, always the right of changing his opinion; but this liberty does not extend to matters of fact.

I now come to the last scene, that of the ascension into heaven. Here all fear of the Jews, and of everything else, must necessarily have been out of the question: it was that which, if true, was to seal the whole, and upon which the reality of the future mission of the disciples was to rest for proof.

Words, whether declarations or promises, that passed in private, either in the recess of a mountain in Galilee, or in a shut-up house in Jerusalem, even supposing them to have been spoken, could not be evidence in public; it was therefore necessary that this last scene should preclude the possibility of denial and dispute, and that it should be, as I have stated in the former part of "The Age of Reason," as public and as visible as the sun at noonday; at least it ought to have been as public as the crucifixion is reported to have been. But to come to the point.

In the first place, the writer of the book of Matthew does not say a syllable about it; neither does the writer of the book of John. This being the case, is it possible to suppose that those writers, who affect to be even minute in other matters, would have been silent upon this, had it been true?

The writer of the book of Mark passes it off in a careless, slovenly manner, with a single dash of the pen, as if he was tired of romancing or ashamed of the story. So also does the writer of Luke. And even between these two there is not an apparent agreement as to the place where his final parting is said to have been.

The book of Mark says that Christ appeared to the eleven as they sat at meat, alluding to the meeting of the eleven at Jerusalem; he then states the conversation that he says passed at that meeting; and immediately after says (as a schoolboy would finish a dull story) *"So then, after the Lord had spoken unto them, he was received up into heaven and sat on the right hand of God."*

But the writer of Luke says, that the ascension was from Bethany; that *he* [Christ] *led them out as far as Bethany, and was parted from them, and was carried up into heaven.* So also was Mahomet; and as to Moses, the apostle Jude says (ver. 9) *"that Michael and the devil disputed about his body."* While we believe such fables as these, or either of them, we believe unworthily of the Almighty.

I have now gone through the examination of the four books ascribed to Matthew, Mark, Luke and John; and when it is considered that the whole space of time from the crucifixion to what is called the ascension is but a few days, apparently not more than three or four, and that all the circumstances are reported to have happened nearly about the same spot, Jerusalem, it is, I believe, impossible to find in any story upon record so many and such glaring absurdities, contradictions and falsehoods as are in those books. They are more numerous and striking than I had any expectation of finding when I began this examination, and far more so than I had any idea of when I wrote the former part of "The Age of Reason."

I had neither Bible nor Testament to refer to, nor could I procure any. My own situation, even as to existence, was becoming every day more precarious, and as I was willing to leave something behind me on the subject, I was obliged to be quick and concise.

The quotations I then made were from memory only, but they are correct; and the opinions I have advanced in that work are the effect of the most clear and long-established conviction that the Bible and the Testament are impositions upon the world, that the fall of man, the account of Jesus Christ being the Son of God, and of his dying to appease the wrath of God, and of salvation by that strange means are all fabulous inventions, dishonorable to the wisdom and power of the

Almighty; that the only true religion is Deism, by which I then meant, and mean now, the belief of one God, and an imitation of His moral character, or the practise of what are called moral virtues—and that it was upon this only (so far as religion is concerned) that I rested all my hopes of happiness hereafter. So I say now—and so help me God.

But to return to the subject. Though it is impossible, at this distance of time, to ascertain as a fact who were the writers of those four books (and this alone is sufficient to hold them in doubt, and where we doubt we do not believe), it is not difficult to ascertain negatively that they were not written by the persons to whom they are ascribed. The contradictions in those books demonstrate two things:

First, that the writers could not have been eye-witnesses and ear-witnesses of the matters they relate, or they would have related them without those contradictions; and consequently that the books have not been written by the persons called apostles, who are supposed to have been witnesses of this kind.

Secondly, that the writers, whoever they were, have not acted in concerted imposition; but each writer separately and individually for himself, and without the knowledge of the other.

The same evidence that applies to prove the one, applies equally to prove both those cases; that is, that the books were not written by the men called apostles, and also that they are not a concerted imposition. As to inspiration, it is altogether out of the question; we may as well attempt to unite truth and falsehood as inspiration and contradiction.

If four men are eye-witnesses and ear-witnesses to a scene, they will, without any concert between them, agree as to time and place when and where that scene happened. Their individual knowledge of the *thing,* each one knowing it for himself, renders concert totally unnecessary; the one will not say it was in a mountain in the country, and the other at a house in town: the one will not say it was at sunrise, and the other that it was dark. For in whatever place it was, at whatever time it was, they know it equally alike.

And, on the other hand, if four men concert a story, they will make their separate relations of that story agree and corroborate with each other to support the whole. *That* concert supplies the want of fact in the one case, as the knowledge of the fact supersedes, in the other case, the necessity of a concert.

The same contradictions, therefore, that prove that there has been no concert, prove also that the reporters had no knowledge of the fact (or rather of that which they relate as a fact), and detect also the falsehood of their reports. These books, therefore, have neither been written by the men called apostles, nor by impostors in concert. How then have they been written?

I am not one of those who are fond of believing there is much of that which is called willful lying, or lying originally, except in the case of men setting up to be prophets, as in the Old Testament; for prophesying is lying professionally. In almost all other cases, it is not difficult to discover the progress by which even simple supposition, with the aid of credulity, will, in time, grow into a lie, and at last be told as a fact; and whenever we can find a charitable reason for a thing of this kind, we ought not to indulge a severe one.

The story of Jesus Christ appearing after he was dead is the story of an apparition, such as timid imaginations can always create in vision, and credulity believe. Stories of this kind had been told of the assassination of Julius Caesar, not many years before; and they generally have their origin in violent deaths, or in the execution of innocent persons.

In cases of this kind, compassion lends its aid and benevolently stretches the story. It goes on a little and a little further till it becomes *a most certain truth*. Once start a ghost and credulity fills up the history of its life and assigns the cause of its appearance! One tells it one way, another another way, till there are as many stories about the ghost and about the proprietor of the ghost, as there are about Jesus Christ in these four books.

The story of the appearance of Jesus Christ is told with that strange mixture of the natural and impossible that distinguishes legendary tale from fact. He is represented as suddenly coming in and going out when the doors were shut, and of vanishing out of sight and appearing again, as one would conceive of an unsubstantial vision; then again he is hungry, sits down to meat and eats his supper. But as those who tell stories of this kind never provide for all the cases, so it is here; they have told us that when he arose he left his grave clothes behind him; but they have forgotten to provide other clothes for him to appear in afterward, or to tell us what he did with them when he ascended—whether he stripped them off, or went up clothes and all.

In the case of Elijah, they have been careful enough to make him throw down his mantle; how it happened not to be burned in the chariot of fire they also have not told us. But as imagination supplies all deficiencies of this kind, we may suppose, if we please, that it was made of salamander's wool.

Those who are not much acquainted with ecclesiastical history may suppose that the book called the New Testament has existed ever since the time of Jesus Christ, as they suppose that the books ascribed to Moses have existed ever since the time of Moses. But the fact is historically otherwise. There was no such book as the New Testament till more than three hundred years after the time that Christ is said to have lived.

At what time the books ascribed to Matthew, Mark, Luke and John began to appear is altogether a matter of uncertainty. There is not the least shadow of evidence of who the persons were that wrote them, nor at what time they were written; and they might as well have been called by the names of any of the other supposed apostles, as by the names they are now called. The originals are not in the possession of any Christian Church existing, any more than the two tables of stone written on, they pretend, by the finger of God, upon Mount Sinai, and given to Moses, are in the possession of the Jews. And even if they were, there is no possibility of proving the handwriting in either case.

At the time those books were written there was no printing, and consequently there could be no publication, otherwise than by written copies, which any man might make or alter at pleasure, and call them originals.[18] Can we suppose it is consistent with the wisdom of the Almighty, to commit Himself and His will to man upon such precarious means as these, or that it is consistent we should pin our faith upon such uncertainties? We cannot make, nor alter, nor even imitate so much as one blade of grass that He has made, and yet we can make or alter *words of God* as easily as words of man.

About three hundred and fifty years after the time that Christ is

[18] The former part of "The Age of Reason" has not been published two years, and there is already an expression in it that is not mine. The expression is, *The book of Luke was carried by a majority of one voice only*. It may be true, but it is not I that have said it. Some person, who might know of the circumstance, has added it in a note at the bottom of the page of some of the editions, printed either in England or in America; and the printers, after that, have placed it into the body of the work, and made me the author of it. If this has happened within such a short space of time, notwithstanding the aid of printing, which prevents the alteration of copies individually, what may not have happened in a much greater length of time, when there was no printing, and when any man who could write could make a written copy, and call it an original by Matthew, Mark, Luke or John?—*Author.*

said to have lived, several writings of the kind I am speaking of were scattered in the hands of divers individuals; and as the Church had begun to form itself into a hierarchy, or church government, with temporal powers, it set itself about collecting them into a code, as we now see them, called *The New Testament*. They decided by vote, as I have before said in the former part of "The Age of Reason," which of those writings, out of the collection they had made, should be the *Word of God,* and which should not. The rabbins of the Jews had decided, by vote, upon the books of the Bible before.

As the object of the Church, as is the case in all national establishments of churches, was power and revenue, and terror the means it used, it is consistent to suppose that the most miraculous and wonderful of the writings they had collected stood the best chance of being voted. And as to the authenticity of the books, the *vote stands in the place of it,* for it can be traced no higher.

Disputes, however, ran high among the people then calling themselves Christians; not only as to points of doctrine, but as to the authenticity of the books. In the contest between the persons called St. Augustine and Fauste, about the year 400, the latter says: "The books called the Evangelists have been composed long after the times of the apostles by some obscure men, who, fearing that the world would not give credit to their relation of matters of which they could not be informed, have published them under the names of the apostles, and which are so full of sottishness and discordant relations, that there is neither agreement nor connection between them."

And in another place, addressing himself to the advocate of those books, as being the Word of God, he says, "It is thus that your predecessors have inserted in the Scriptures of our Lord many things, which, though they carry his name agree not with his doctrine. This is not surprising, *since that we have often proved* that these things have not been written by himself, nor by his apostles, but that for the greater part they are founded upon *tales,* upon *vague reports,* and put together by I know not what, half-Jews, but with little agreement between them, and which they have nevertheless published under the names of the apostles of our Lord, and have thus attributed to them their own *errors and their lies.*" [19]

---

[19] I have these two extracts from Boulanger's "Life of Paul," written in French. Boulanger has quoted them from the writings of Augustine against Fauste, to which he refers.— *Author.*

The reader will see by these extracts, that the authenticity of the books of the New Testament was denied, and the books treated as tales, forgeries, and lies, at the time they were voted to be the Word of God.[20] But the interest of the Church, with the assistance of the fagot, bore down the opposition and at last suppressed all investigation.

Miracles followed upon miracles, if we will believe them, and men were taught to say they believed whether they believed or not. But (by way of throwing in a thought) the French Revolution has excommunicated the Church from the power of working miracles; she has not been able, with the assistance of all her saints, to work *one* miracle since the Revolution began; and as she never stood in greater need than now, we may, without the aid of divination, conclude that all her former miracles were tricks and lies.

When we consider the lapse of more than three hundred years intervening between the time that Christ is said to have lived and the time the New Testament was formed into a book, we must see, even without the assistance of historical evidence, the exceeding uncertainty there is of its authenticity. The authenticity of the book of Homer, so far as regards the authorship, is much better established than that of the New Testament, though Homer is a thousand years the most ancient.

It is only an exceedingly good poet that could have written the book of Homer, and therefore few men only could have attempted it; and a man capable of doing it would not have thrown away his own fame by

---

[20] Boulanger, in his "Life of Paul" has collected from the ecclesiastical histories, and from the writings of the fathers, as they are called, several matters which show the opinions that prevailed among the different sects of Christians at the time the *Testament*, as we now see it, was voted to be the Word of God. The following extracts are from the second chapter of that work.

The Marcionists (a Christian sect) assumed that the evangelists were filled with falsities. The Manicheans, who formed a very numerous sect at the commencement of Christianity, *rejected as false all the New Testament,* and showed other writings quite different that they gave for authentic. The Cerinthians, like the Marcionists, admitted not the Acts of the Apostles. The Encratites, and the Sévénians, adopted neither the Acts nor the Epistles of Paul. Chrysostom, in a homily which he made upon the Acts of the Apostles, says that in his time, about the year 400, many people knew nothing either of the author or of the book. St. Irene, who lived before that time, reports that the Valentinians, like several other sects of Christians, accused the Scriptures of being filled with imperfections, errors and contradictions. The Ebionites, or Nazarines, who were the first Christians, rejected all the Epistles of Paul and regarded him as an impostor. They report, among other things, that he was originally a pagan, that he came to Jerusalem, where he lived some time; and that having a mind to marry the daughter of the high priest, he caused himself to be circumcised; but that not being able to obtain her, he quarreled with the Jews and wrote against circumcision, and against the observance of the Sabbath, and against all the legal ordinances.—*Author.*

giving it to another. In like manner, there were but few that could have composed Euclid's "Elements," because none but an exceedingly good geometrician could have been the author of that work.

But with respect to the books of the New Testament, particularly such parts as tell us of the resurrection and ascension of Christ, any person who could tell a story of an apparition, or of a *man's walking,* could have made such books; for the story is most wretchedly told. The chance, therefore, of forgery in the Testament, is millions to one greater than in the case of Homer or Euclid.

Of the numerous priests or parsons of the present day, bishops and all, every one of them can make a sermon, or translate a scrap of Latin, especially if it has been translated a thousand times before; but is there any among them that can write poetry like Homer, or science like Euclid? The sum total of a person's learning, with very few exceptions, is *a b ab,* and *hic, hæc, hoc;* and their knowledge of science is three times one is *one;* and this is more than sufficient to have enabled them, had they lived at the time, to have written all the books of the New Testament.

As the opportunities of forgeries were greater, so also was the inducement. A man could gain no advantage by writing under the name of Homer or Euclid; if he could write equal to them, it would be better that he wrote under his own name; if inferior, he could not succeed. Pride would prevent the former, and impossibility the latter. But with respect to such books as compose the New Testament, all the inducements were on the side of the forgery. The best imagined history that could have been made, at the distance of two or three hundred years after the time, could not have passed for an original under the name of the real writer; the only chance of success lay in forgery, for the church wanted pretense for its new doctrine, and truth and talents were out of the question.

But as is not uncommon (as before observed) to relate stories of persons *walking* after they are dead, and of ghosts and apparitions of such as have fallen by some violent or extraordinary means; and as the people of that day were in the habit of believing such things, and of the appearance of angels and also of devils, and of their getting into people's insides and shaking them like a fit of an ague, and of their being cast out again as if by an emetic—(Mary Magdalene, the book of Mark tells us, had brought up, or been brought to bed of seven devils)— it was nothing extraordinary that some story of this kind should get abroad of the person called Jesus Christ, and become afterward the foundation of the four books ascribed to Matthew, Mark, Luke and John.

Each writer told the tale as he heard it, or thereabouts, and gave to his book the name of the saint or the apostle whom tradition had given as the eye-witness. It is only upon this ground that the contradiction in those books can be accounted for; and if this be not the case, they are downright impositions, lies and forgeries, without even the apology of credulity.

That they have been written by a sort of half Jews, as the foregoing quotations mention, is discernible enough. The frequent references made to that chief assassin and impostor, Moses, and to the men called prophets, establish this point; and, on the other hand, the church has complemented the fraud of admitting the Bible and the Testament to reply to each other.

Between the Christian Jew and the Christian Gentile, the thing called a prophecy and the thing prophesied, the type and the thing typified, the sign and the thing signified have been industriously rummaged up and fitted together like old locks and pick-lock keys.

The story foolishly enough told of Eve and the serpent, and naturally enough as to the enmity between men and serpents (for the serpent always bites about the *heel,* because it cannot reach higher; and the man always knocks the serpent about the *head,* as the most effectual way to prevent its biting),[21] this foolish story, I say, has been made into a prophecy, a type, and a promise to begin with; and the lying imposition of Isaiah to Ahaz, *That a virgin shall conceive and bear a son,* as a sign that Ahaz should conquer, when the event was that he was defeated (as already noticed in the observations on the book of Isaiah), has been perverted and made to serve as a winder-up.

Jonah and the whale are also made into a sign or a type. Jonah is Jesus, and the whale is the grave; for it is said (and they have made Christ to say it of himself), Matt. chap. xii, ver. 40, "For as Jonah was *three days* and *three nights* in the whale's belly, so shall the Son of Man be *three days* and *three nights* in the heart of the earth."

But it happens, awkwardly enough, that Christ, according to their account, was but one day and two nights in the grave; about 36 hours, instead of 72; that is, the Friday night, the Saturday, and the Saturday

---

[21] It shall bruise thy *head* and thou shalt bruise his *heel.* Genesis, chap. iii, verse 15.— *Author.*

night; for they say he was up on the Sunday morning by sunrise, or before. But as this fits quite as well as the *bite* and the *kick* in Genesis, or the *virgin* and her *son* in Isaiah, it will pass in the lump of *orthodox* things. Thus much for the historical part of the Testament and its evidences.

Epistles of Paul.—The epistles ascribed to Paul, being fourteen in number, almost fill up the remaining part of the Testament. Whether those epistles were written by the person to whom they are ascribed is a matter of no great importance, since the writer, whoever he was, attempts to prove his doctrine by argument. He does not pretend to have been witness to any of the scenes told of the resurrection and the ascension, and he declares that he had not believed them.

The story of his being struck to the ground as he was journeying to Damascus has nothing in it miraculous or extraordinary; he escaped with life, and that is more than many others have done who have been struck with lightning; and that he should lose his sight for three days, and be unable to eat or drink during that time, is nothing more than is common in such conditions. His companions that were with him appear not to have suffered in the same manner, for they were well enough to lead him the remainder of the journey; neither did they pretend to have seen any vision.

The character of the person called Paul, according to the accounts given of him, has in it a great deal of violence and fanaticism; he had persecuted with as much heat as he preached afterward; the stroke he had received had changed his thinking, without altering his constitution; and either as a Jew or a Christian, he was the same zealot. Such men are never good moral evidences of any doctrine they preach. They are always in extremes, as well of actions as of belief.

The doctrine he sets out to prove by argument is the resurrection of the same body, and he advances this as an evidence of immortality. But so much will men differ in their manner of thinking, and in the conclusions they draw from the same premises, that this doctrine of the resurrection of the same body, so far from being an evidence of immortality, appears to me to furnish an evidence against it; for if I have already died in this body, and am raised again in the same body in which I have lived, it is a presumptive evidence that I shall die again.

That resurrection no more secures me against the repetition of dying, than an ague-fit, when passed, secures me against another. To believe, therefore, in immortality, I must have a more elevated idea than is contained in the gloomy doctrine of the resurrection.

Besides, as a matter of choice, as well as of hope, I had rather have a better body and a more convenient form than the present. Every animal in the creation excels us in something. The winged insects, without mentioning doves or eagles, can pass over more space and with greater ease in a few minutes than man can in an hour. The glide of the smallest fish, in proportion to its bulk, exceeds us in motion almost beyond comparison, and without weariness.

Even the sluggish snail can ascend from the bottom of a dungeon, where a man, by the want of that ability, would perish; and a spider can launch itself from the top, as a playful amusement. The personal powers of man are so limited, and his heavy frame so little constructed to extensive enjoyment, that there is nothing to induce us to wish the opinion of Paul to be true. It is too little for the magnitude of the scene—too mean for the sublimity of the subject.

But all other arguments apart, the *consciousness of existence* is the only conceivable idea we have of another life, and the continuance of that consciousness is immortality. The consciousness of existence, or the knowing that we exist, is not necessarily confined to the same form, nor to the same matter, even in this life.

We have not in all cases the same form, nor in any case the same matter that composed our bodies twenty or thirty years ago; and yet we are conscious of being the same persons. Even legs and arms, which make up almost half the human frame, are not necessary to the consciousness of existence. These may be lost or taken away, and the full consciousness of existence remain; and were their place supplied by wings, or other appendages, we cannot conceive that it would alter our consciousness of existence.

In short, we know not how much, or rather how little, of our composition it is, and how exquisitely fine that little is, that creates in us this consciousness of existence; and all beyond that is like the pulp of a peach, distinct and separate from the vegetative speck in the kernel.

Who can say by what exceedingly fine action of fine matter it is that a thought is produced in what we call the mind? And yet that thought when produced, as I now produce the thought I am writing, is capable of becoming immortal, and is the only production of man that has that capacity.

Statues of marble or brass will perish; and statues made in imitation of them are not the same statues, nor the same workmanship, any more than the copy of a picture is the same picture. But print and reprint a thought a thousand times over, and that with materials of any kind —carve it into wood or engrave it in stone, the thought is eternally and identically the same thought in every case. It has a capacity of unimpaired existence, unaffected by change of matter, and is essentially distinct and of a nature different from everything else that we know or can conceive.

If, then, the thing produced has in itself a capacity of being immortal, it is more than a token that the power that produced it, which is the selfsame thing as consciousness of existence, can be immortal also; and that as independently of the matter it was first connected with, as the thought is of the printing or writing it first appeared in. The one idea is not more difficult to believe than the other, and we can see that one is true.

That the consciousness of existence is not dependent on the same form or the same matter is demonstrated to our senses in the works of the creation, as far as our senses are capable of receiving that demonstration. A very numerous part of the animal creation preaches to us, far better than Paul, the belief of a life hereafter. Their little life resembles an earth and a heaven—a present and a future state, and comprises, if it may be so expressed, immortality in miniature.

The most beautiful parts of the creation to our eye are the winged insects, and they are not so originally. They acquire that form and that inimitable brilliancy by progressive changes. The slow and creeping caterpillar-worm of to-day passes in a few days to a torpid figure and a state resembling death; and in the next change comes forth in all the miniature magnificence of life, a splendid butterfly.

No resemblance of the former creature remains; everything is changed; all his powers are new, and life is to him another thing. We cannot conceive that the consciousness of existence is not the same in this state of the animal as before; why then must I believe that the resurrection of the same body is necessary to continue to me the consciousness of existence hereafter?

In the former part of "The Age of Reason" I have called the Creation the only true and real Word of God; and this instance, or this text, in the Book of Creation, not only shows to us that this thing may be so, but that it is so; and that the belief of a future state is a rational belief, corroborated by facts visible in the Creation; for it is not more difficult to believe that we shall exist hereafter in a better state and form than at present, than that a worm should become a butterfly, and quit the dunghill for the atmosphere, if we did not know it as a fact.

As to the doubtful jargon ascribed to Paul in the 15th chapter of I. Corinthians, which makes part of the burial service of some Christian sectaries, it is as destitute of meaning as the tolling of the bell at the funeral; it explains nothing to the understanding—it illustrates nothing to the imagination, but leaves the reader to find any meaning if he can. "All flesh [says he] is not the same flesh. There is one flesh of men; another of beasts; another of fishes; and another of birds." And what then?—nothing. A cook could have said as much.

"There are also [says he] bodies celestial, and bodies terrestrial; the glory of the celestial is one, and the glory of the terrestrial is another." And what then?—nothing. And what is the difference? nothing that he has told. "There is [says he] one glory of the sun, and another glory of the moon, and another glory of the stars." And what then?—nothing; except that he says that *one star differeth from another star in glory,* instead of distance; and he might as well have told us that the moon did not shine so bright as the sun.

All this is nothing better than the jargon of a conjuror, who picks up phrases he does not understand, to confound the credulous people who have come to have their fortune told. Priests and conjurors are of the same trade.

Sometimes Paul affects to be a naturalist and to prove his system of resurrection from the principles of vegetation. "Thou fool [says he], that which thou sowest is not quickened, except it die." To which one might reply in his own language and say, "Thou fool, Paul, that which thou sowest is not quickened, except it die not; for the grain that dies in the ground never does, and cannot vegetate. It is only the living grains that produce the next crop." But the metaphor, in any point of view, is no simile. It is succession, and not resurrection.

The progress of an animal from one state of being to another, as from a worm to a butterfly, applies to the case; but this of the grain does not, and shows Paul to have been what he says of others, *a fool.*

Whether the fourteen epistles ascribed to Paul were written by him or not is a matter of indifference; they are either argumentative or dogmatical; and as the argument is defective and the dogmatical part is merely presumptive, it signifies not who wrote them.

And the same may be said for the remaining parts of the Testament. It is not upon the epistles, but upon what is called the Gospel, contained in the four books ascribed to Matthew, Mark, Luke and John, and upon the pretended prophecies, that the theory of the Church calling itself the Christian Church is founded. The epistles are dependent upon those, and must follow their fate; for if the story of Jesus Christ be fabulous, all reasoning founded upon it as a supposed truth must fall with it.

We know from history that one of the principal leaders of this Church, Athanasius, lived at the time the New Testament was formed; [22] and we know also, from the absurd jargon he left us under the name of a creed, the character of the men who formed the New Testament; and we know also from the same history that the authenticity of the books of which it is composed was denied at the time. It was upon the vote of such men as Athanasius, that the Testament was decreed to be the Word of God; and nothing can present to us a more strange idea than that of decreeing the word of God by vote.

Those who rest their faith upon such authority put man in the place of God, and have no true foundation for future happiness; credulity, however, is not a crime, but it becomes criminal by resisting conviction. It is strangling in the womb of the conscience the efforts it makes to ascertain truth. We should never force belief upon ourselves in anything.

I here close the subject of the Old Testament and the New. The evidence I have produced to prove them forgeries is extracted from the books themselves, and acts, like a two-edged sword, either way. If the evidence be denied, the authenticity of the scriptures is denied with it, for it is scripture evidence; and if the evidence be admitted, the authenticity of the books is disproved. The contradictory impossibilities contained in the Old Testament and the New put them in the case of a man who swears for and against. Either evidence convicts him of perjury, and equally destroys reputation.

Should the Bible and the New Testament hereafter fall, it is not I that have done it. I have done no more than extracted the evidence from the confused mass of matter with which it is mixed, and arranged that evidence in a point of light to be clearly seen and easily comprehended; and, having done this, I leave the reader to judge for himself, as I have judged for myself.

[22] Athanasius died, according to the Church chronology, in the year 371.—*Author.*

CHAPTER III

Conclusion

IN THE former part of "The Age of Reason" I have spoken of the three frauds, *mystery, miracle* and *prophecy;* and as I have seen nothing in any of the answers to that work that in the least affects what I have there said upon those subjects, I shall not encumber this Second Part with additions that are not necessary.

I have spoken also in the same work upon what is called *revelation,* and have shown the absurd misapplication of that term to the books of the Old Testament and the New; for certainly revelation is out of the question in reciting anything of which man has been the actor or the witness.

That which a man has done or seen needs no revelation to tell him he has done it or seen it, for he knows it already; nor to enable him to tell it or to write it. It is ignorance or imposition to apply the term revelation in such cases; yet the Bible and Testament are classed under this fraudulent description of being all *revelation.*

Revelation then, so far as the term has relation between God and man, can only be applied to something which God reveals of His *will* to man; but though the power of the Almighty to make such a communication is necessarily admitted, because to that power all things are possible, yet the thing so revealed (if anything ever was revealed, and which, by the bye, it is impossible to prove) is revelation to the person *only to whom it is made.*

His account of it to another person is not revelation; and whoever puts faith in that account, puts it in the man from whom the account comes; and that man may have been deceived, or may have dreamed it, or he may be an impostor and may lie.

There is no possible criterion whereby to judge of the truth of what he tells, for even the morality of it would be no proof of revelation. In all such cases the proper answer would be, *"When it is revealed to me, I will believe it to be a revelation; but it is not, and cannot be incumbent upon me to believe it to be revelation before; neither is it proper that I should take the word of man as the Word of God, and put man in the place of God."*

This is the manner in which I have spoken of revelation in the former part of "The Age of Reason"; and which, while it reverentially admits revelation as a possible thing, because, as before said, to the Almighty all things are possible, it prevents the imposition of one man upon another, and precludes the wicked use of pretended revelation.

But though, speaking for myself, I thus admit the possibility of revelation, I totally disbelieve that the Almighty ever did communicate anything to man, by any mode of speech, in any language, or by any kind of vision, or appearance, or by any means which our senses are capable of receiving, otherwise than by the universal display of Himself in the works of the creation, and by that repugnance we feel in ourselves to bad actions, and the disposition to do good ones.

The most detestable wickedness, the most horrid cruelties, and the greatest miseries that have afflicted the human race have had their origin in this thing called revelation, or revealed religion. It has been the most dishonorable belief against the character of the Divinity, the most destructive to morality and the peace and happiness of man that ever was propagated since man began to exist.

It is better, far better, that we admitted, if it were possible, a thousand devils to roam at large, and to preach publicly the doctrine of devils, if there were any such, than that we permitted one such impostor and monster as Moses, Joshua, Samuel and the Bible prophets, to come with the pretended world of God in his mouth and have credit among us.

Whence arose all the horrid assassinations of whole nations of men, women and infants, with which the Bible is filled, and the bloody persecutions and tortures unto death, and religious wars, that since that time have laid Europe in blood and ashes—whence rose they but from this impious thing called revealed religion, and this monstrous belief that God has spoken to man? The lies of the Bible have been the cause of the one, and the lies of the Testament of the other.

Some Christians pretend that Christianity was not established by the sword; but of what period of time do they speak? It was impossible that twelve men could begin with the sword; they had not the power; but no sooner were the professors of Christianity sufficiently powerful to employ the sword than they did so, and the stake and fagot, too; and Mahomet could not do it sooner. By the same spirit that Peter cut off the ear of the high priest's servant (if the story be true), he would have cut off his head, and the head of his master, had he been able.

Besides this, Christianity founds itself originally upon the Bible, and the Bible was established altogether by the sword, and that in the worst use of it—not to terrify, but to extirpate. The Jews made no converts; they butchered all. The Bible is the sire of the Testament, and both are called the *Word of God*. The Christians read both books; the ministers preach from both books; and this thing called Christianity is made up of both. It is then false to say that Christianity was not established by the sword.

The only sect that has not persecuted are the Quakers, and the only reason that can be given for it is that they are rather Deists than Christians. They do not believe much about Jesus Christ, and they call the Scriptures a dead letter.[23] Had they called them by a worse name, they had been nearer the truth.

It is incumbent on every man who reverences the character of the Creator, and who wishes to lessen the catalogue of artificial miseries, and remove the cause that has sown persecutions thick among mankind, to expel all ideas of revealed religion, as a dangerous heresy and an impious fraud.

What is that we have learned from this pretended thing called revealed religion? Nothing that is useful to man, and everything that is dishonorable to his Maker. What is it the Bible teaches us?—rapine, cruelty, and murder. What is it the Testament teaches us?—to believe that the Almighty committed debauchery with a woman engaged to be married, and the belief of this debauchery is called faith.

As to the fragments of morality that are irregularly and thinly scattered in these books, they make no part of this pretended thing, revealed religion. They are the natural dictates of conscience, and the bonds by which society is held together, and without which it cannot exist, and are nearly the same in all religions and in all societies.

The Testament teaches nothing new upon this subject, and where it attempts to exceed, it becomes mean and ridiculous. The doctrine of not retaliating injuries is much better expressed in Proverbs, which is a collection as well from the Gentiles as the Jews, than it is in the Testament. It is there said (Proverbs xxv, ver. 21), *"If thine enemy be hungry, give him bread to eat; and if he be thirsty, give him water to drink"*; [24] but

[23] Paine's acquaintance with the Quakers, it must be remembered, was with the sect to which his father belonged, and whose doctrines he correctly refers to.—*Editor.*

[24] According to what is called Christ's sermon on the mount, in the book of Matthew, where, among some other good things, a great deal of this feigned morality is introduced, it is there expressly said, that the doctrine of forbearance, or of not retaliating injuries, was not any part of the doctrine of the Jews; but as this doctrine is found in Proverbs it must, according to that statement, have been copied from the Gentiles, from

when it said, as in the Testament, *"If a man smite thee on the right cheek, turn to him the other also";* it is assassinating the dignity of forbearance, and sinking man into a spaniel.

Loving of enemies is another dogma of feigned morality, and has besides no meaning. It is incumbent on man, as a moralist, that he does not revenge an injury; and it is equally as good in a political sense, for there is no end to retaliation, each retaliates on the other, and calls it justice; but to love in proportion to the injury, if it could be done, would be to offer a premium for crime. Besides, the word *enemies* is too vague and general to be used in a moral maxim, which ought always to be clear and defined, like a proverb.

If a man be the enemy of another from mistake and prejudice, as in the case of religious opinions, and sometimes in politics, that man is different to an enemy at heart with a criminal intention; and it is incumbent upon us, and it contributes also to our own tranquillity, that we put the best construction upon a thing that it will bear. But even this erroneous motive in him makes no motive for love on the other part; and to say that we can love voluntarily, and without a motive, is morally and physically impossible.

Morality is injured by prescribing to it duties that, in the first place, are impossible to be performed; and, if they could be, would be productive of evil; or, as before said, be premiums for crime. The maxim *of doing as we would be done unto* does not include this strange doctrine of loving enemies; for no man expects to be loved himself for his crime or for his enmity.

Those who preach this doctrine of loving their enemies are in general the greatest persecutors, and they act consistently by so doing; for the doctrine is hypocritical, and it is natural that hypocrisy should act the reverse of what it preaches.

For my own part I disown the doctrine, and consider it as a feigned or fabulous morality; yet the man does not exist that can say I have persecuted him, or any man, or any set of men, either in the American Revolution or in the French Revolution; or that I have, in any case,

whom Christ had learned it. Those men, whom Jewish and Christian idolators have abusively called heathens, had much better and clearer ideas of justice and morality than are to be found in the Old Testament, so far as it is Jewish; or in the New. The answer of Solon on the question, Which is the most perfect popular government? has never been exceeded by any man since his time, as containing a maxim of political morality. "That," says he, *"where the least injury done to the meanest individual, is considered as an insult on the whole constitution."* Solon lived about 500 years before Christ.—*Author.*

returned evil for evil. But it is not incumbent on man to reward a bad action with a good one, or to return good for evil; and wherever it is done, it is a voluntary act and not a duty.

It is also absurd to suppose that such doctrine can make any part of a revealed religion. We imitate the moral character of the Creator by forbearing with each other, for He forbears with all; but this doctrine would imply that He loved man, not in proportion as he was good, but as he was bad.

If we consider the nature of our condition here, we must see there is no occasion for such a thing as *revealed religion*. What is it we want to know? Does not the creation, the universe we behold, preach to us the existence of an Almighty Power that governs and regulates the whole? And is not the evidence that this creation holds out to our senses infinitely stronger than anything we can read in a book that any impostor might make and call the Word of God? As for morality, the knowledge of it exists in every man's conscience.

Here we are. The existence of an Almighty Power is sufficiently demonstrated to us, though we cannot conceive, as it is impossible we should, the nature and manner of its existence. We cannot conceive how we came here ourselves, and yet we know for a fact that we are here.

We must know also that the Power that called us into being, can, if He pleases, and when He pleases, call us to account for the manner in which we have lived here; and, therefore, without seeking any other motive for the belief, it is rational to believe that He will, for we know beforehand that He can. The probability or even possibility of the thing is all that we ought to know; for if we knew it as a fact, we should be the mere slaves of terror; our belief would have no merit, and our best actions no virtue.

Deism, then, teaches us, without the possibility of being deceived, all that is necessary or proper to be known. The creation is the Bible of the Deist. He there reads, in the handwriting of the Creator himself, the certainty of His existence and the immutability of His power, and all other Bibles and Testaments are to him forgeries.

The probability that we may be called to account hereafter will, to a reflecting mind, have the influence of belief; for it is not our belief or our disbelief that can make or unmake the fact. As this is the state we are in, and which it is proper we should be in, as free agents, it is the fool only, and not the philosopher, or even the prudent man, that would live as if there were no God.

But the belief of a God is so weakened by being mixed with the strange fable of the Christian creed, and with the wild adventures related in the Bible, and of the obscurity and obscene nonsense of the Testament, that the mind of man is bewildered as in a fog. Viewing all these things in a confused mass, he confounds fact with fable; and as he cannot believe all, he feels a disposition to reject all.

But the belief of a God is a belief distinct from all other things, and ought not to be confounded with any. The notion of a Trinity of Gods has enfeebled the belief of one God. A multiplication of beliefs acts as a division of belief; and in proportion as anything is divided it is weakened.

Religion, by such means, becomes a thing of form, instead of fact—of notion, instead of principles; morality is banished to make room for an imaginary thing called faith, and this faith has its origin in a supposed debauchery; a man is preached instead of a God; an execution is an object for gratitude; the preachers daub themselves with blood, like a troop of assassins, and pretend to admire the brilliancy it gives them; they preach a humdrum sermon on the merits of the execution; then praise Jesus Christ for being executed, and condemn the Jews for doing it. A man, by hearing all this nonsense lumped and preached together, confounds the God of the Creation with the imagined God of the Christians, and lives as if there were none.

Of all the systems of religion that ever were invented, there is none more derogatory to the Almighty, more unedifying to man, more repugnant to reason, and more contradictory in itself, than this thing called Christianity. Too absurd for belief, too impossible to convince, and too inconsistent for practise, it renders the heart torpid, or produces only atheists and fanatics. As an engine of power, it serves the purpose of despotism; and as a means of wealth, the avarice of priests; but so far as respects the good of man in general, it leads to nothing here or hereafter.

The only religion that has not been invented, and that has in it every evidence of divine originality, is pure and simple Deism. It must have been the first, and will probably be the last, that man believes. But pure and simple Deism does not answer the purpose of despotic governments. They cannot lay hold of religion as an engine, but by mixing it with human inventions, and making their own authority a part; neither does it answer the avarice of priests, but by incorporating themselves and their functions with it, and becoming, like the government, a party in the system. It is this that forms the otherwise mysterious connection of Church and State; the Church humane, and the State tyrannic.

Were man impressed as fully and as strongly as he ought to be with the belief of a God, his moral life would be regulated by the force of that belief; he would stand in awe of God and of himself, and would not do the thing that could not be concealed from either. To give this belief the full opportunity of force, it is necessary that it acts alone. This is Deism. But when, according to the Christian Trinitarian scheme, one part of God is represented by a dying man, and another part, called the Holy Ghost, by a flying pigeon, it is impossible that belief can attach itself to such wild conceits.[25]

It has been the scheme of the Christian Church, and of all the other invented systems of religion, to hold man in ignorance of the Creator, as it is of Governments to hold man in ignorance of his rights. The systems of the one are as false as those of the other, and are calculated for mutual support.

The study of theology, as it stands in Christian churches, is the study of nothing; it is founded on nothing; it rests on no principles; it proceeds by no authorities; it has no data; it can demonstrate nothing; and it admits of no conclusion. Not any thing can be studied as a science, without our being in possession of the principles upon which it is founded; and as this is not the case with Christian theology, it is therefore the study of nothing.

Instead then of studying theology, as is now done out of the Bible and Testament, the meanings of which books are always controverted and the authenticity of which is disproved, it is necessary that we refer to the Bible of the Creation. The principles we discover there are eternal and of divine origin; they are the foundation of all the science that exists in the world, and must be the foundation of theology.

We can know God only through His works. We cannot have a conception of any one attribute but by following some principle that leads to it. We have only a confused idea of His power, if we have not the means of comprehending something of its immensity. We can have no idea of His wisdom, but by knowing the order and manner in which it

[25] The book called the book of Matthew says (chap. iii, verse 16), that *the Holy Ghost descended in the shape of a dove.* It might as well have said a goose; the creatures are equally harmless, and the one is as much of a nonsensical lie as the other. The second of Acts, ver. 2, 3, says that it descended in a mighty *rushing wind,* in the shape of *cloven tongues,* perhaps it was cloven feet. Such absurd stuff is only fit for tales of witches and wizards.—*Author.*

acts. The principles of science lead to this knowledge; for the Creator of man is the Creator of science, and it is through that medium that man can see God, as it were, face to face.

Could a man be placed in a situation, and endowed with the power of vision, to behold at one view, and to contemplate deliberately, the structure of the universe; to mark the movements of the several planets, the cause of their varying appearances, the unerring order in which they revolve, even to the remotest comet; their connection and dependence on each other, and to know the system of laws established by the Creator, that governs and regulates the whole, he would then conceive, far beyond what any church theology can teach him, the power, the wisdom, the vastness, the munificence of the Creator; he would then see, that all the knowledge man has of science, and that all mechanical arts by which he renders his situation comfortable here, are derived from that source; his mind, exalted by the scene, and convinced by the fact, would increase in gratitude as it increased in knowledge; his religion or his worship would become united with his improvement as a man; any employment he followed, that had any connection with the principles of the creation, as everything of agriculture, of science and of the mechanical arts has, would teach him more of God, and of the gratitude he owes to Him, than any theological Christian sermon he now hears.

Great objects inspire great thoughts; great munificence excites great gratitude; but the groveling tales and doctrines of the Bible and the Testament are fit only to excite contempt.

Though man cannot arrive, at least in this life, at the actual scene I have described, he can demonstrate it, because he has a knowledge of the principles upon which the creation is constructed.[26] We know that the

[26] The Bible-makers have undertaken to give us, in the first chapter of Genesis, an account of the Creation; and in doing this, they have demonstrated nothing but their ignorance. They make there to have been three days and three nights, evenings and mornings, before there was a sun; when it is the presence or absence of the sun that is the cause of day and night, and what is called his rising and setting that of morning and evening. Besides, it is a puerile and pitiful idea, to suppose the Almighty to say, Let there be light. It is the imperative manner of speaking that a conjuror uses when he says to his cups and balls, Presto, begone, and most probably has been taken from it; as Moses and his rod are a conjuror and his wand. Longinus calls this expression the sublime; and, by the same rule, the conjuror is sublime too, for the manner of speaking is expressively and grammatically the same. When authors and critics talk of the sublime, they see not how nearly it borders on the ridiculous. The sublime of the critics, like some parts of Edmund Burke's "Sublime and Beautiful," is like a wind-mill just visible in a fog, which imagination might distort into a flying mountain, or an archangel, or a flock of wild geese.—*Author.*

greatest works can be represented in model, and that the universe can be represented by the same means.

The same principles by which we measure an inch, or an acre of ground, will measure to millions in extent. A circle of an inch diameter has the same geometrical properties as a circle that would circumscribe the universe.

The same properties of a triangle that will demonstrate upon paper the course of a ship, will do it on the ocean; and when applied to what are called the heavenly bodies, will ascertain to a minute the time of an eclipse, though these bodies are millions of miles from us. This knowledge is of divine origin, and it is from the Bible of the Creation that man has learned it, and not from the stupid Bible of the Church, that teacheth man nothing.

All the knowledge man has of science and of machinery, by the aid of which his existence is rendered comfortable upon earth, and without which he would be scarcely distinguishable in appearance and condition from a common animal, comes from the great machine and structure of the universe.

The constant and unwearied observations of our ancestors upon the movements and revolutions of the heavenly bodies, in what are supposed to have been the early ages of the world, have brought this knowledge upon earth. It is not Moses and the prophets, nor Jesus Christ, nor his apostles, that have done it. The Almighty is the great mechanic of the creation; the first philosopher and original teacher of all science. Let us, then, learn to reverence our master, and let us not forget the labors of our ancestors.

Had we, at this day, no knowledge of machinery, and were it possible that man could have a view, as I have before described, of the structure and machinery of the universe, he would soon conceive the idea of constructing some at least of the mechanical works we now have; and the idea so conceived would progressively advance in practice. Or could a model of the universe, such as is called an orrery, be presented before him and put in motion, his mind would arrive at the same idea.

Such an object and such a subject would, while it improved him in knowledge useful to himself as a man and a member of society, as well as entertaining, afford far better matter for impressing him with a knowledge of, and a belief in, the Creator, and of the reverence and gratitude that man owes to Him, than the stupid texts of the Bible and of the Testament, from which, be the talents of the preacher what they may, only stupid sermons can be preached.

If man must preach, let him preach something that is edifying, and from texts that are known to be true.

The Bible of the Creation is inexhaustible in texts. Every part of science, whether connected with the geometry of the universe, with the systems of animal and vegetable life, or with the properties of inanimate matter, is a text as well for devotion as for philosophy—for gratitude as for human improvement. It will perhaps be said, that if such a revolution in the system of religion takes place, every preacher ought to be a philosopher. *Most certainly;* and every house of devotion a school of science.

It has been by wandering from the immutable laws of science, and the light of reason, and setting up an invented thing called revealed religion, that so many wild and blasphemous conceits have been formed of the Almighty.

The Jews have made Him the assassin of the human species to make room for the religion of the Jews. The Christians have made Him the murderer of Himself and the founder of a new religion, to supersede and expel the Jewish religion. And to find pretense and admission for these things, they must have supposed His power or His wisdom imperfect, or His will changeable; and the changeableness of the will is imperfection of the judgment.

The philosopher knows that the laws of the Creator have never changed with respect either to the principles of science or the properties of matter. Why, then, is it supposed they have changed with respect to man?

I here close the subject. I have shown in all the foregoing parts of this work that the Bible and the Testament are impositions and forgeries; and I leave the evidence I have produced in proof of it to be refuted, if any one can do it; and I leave the ideas that are suggested in the conclusion of the work to rest on the mind of the reader; certain, as I am, that when opinions are free, either in matters of government or religion, truth will finally and powerfully prevail.

AGRARIAN JUSTICE

In this work, his last great pamphlet, published in the winter of 1795–1796, Paine continued the discussion he began in Part II of the *Rights of Man* of the problem of the elimination of poverty and developed further his proposals for limiting the accumulation of property. The crux of the entire question of eliminating poverty, he points out, lay in the institution of private property, for this principle was the source of the evils of society. Landed property and private property, he argued, were made possible only by the operation of society since whatever property men accumulated beyond their own labor came from the fact that they lived in society. ". . . The accumulation of personal property," he wrote, "is, in many instances, the effect of paying too little for the labor that produced it; the consequence of which is, that the working hand perishes in old age, and the employer abounds in affluence." God had never opened a land office, he held, from which perpetual deeds to the earth should be issued. He spoke, he boldly declared, for "all those who have been thrown out of their natural inheritance by the introduction of the system of landed property." It is of some interest to note that Thomas Jefferson observed, in a letter to Rev. James Madison in February, 1787: "Whenever there are in a country uncultivated lands and unemployed poor, it is clear that the laws of property have been so far extended as to violate the natural right. The earth is given as a common stock for man to labor and live on. If for the encouragement of industry we allow it to be appropriated, we must take care that other employment be provided for those excluded from the appropriation. If we do not, the fundamental right to labor the earth returns to the unemployed. . . ." Philip S. Foner, ed., *Thomas Jefferson: Selections from His Writings,* pp. 56–57.

Since the operation of society had made possible the existence of private property, it followed that society was entitled to receive the surplus that men accumulated beyond their own labor back from them. Paine proposed a plan to deal with the problem of poverty by providing for the taxation of accumulated property to permit the state to give each man and woman reaching the age of twenty-one the sum of fifteen pounds, and every person fifty years of age or over ten pounds per year. His plan, which today would be called a system of social insurance, called for graduated inheritance taxes and ground rents.

Unlike many land reformers who preceded and followed him, Paine did not advocate the establishment of an agrarian society. For evidence that

Paine's proposal was too moderate for some contemporary Agrarians, see Thomas Spence's pamphlet published in 1797, *The Rights of Infants, with Scriptures on Paine's Agrarian Justice.—Editor.*

Author's Inscription

To the Legislature and the Executive Directory of the French Republic

THE plan contained in this work is not adapted for any particular country alone: the principle on which it is based is general. But as the rights of man are a new study in this world, and one needing protection from priestly imposture, and the insolence of oppressions too long established, I have thought it right to place this little work under your safeguard.

When we reflect on the long and dense night in which France and all Europe have remained plunged by their governments and their priests, we must feel less surprise than grief at the bewilderment caused by the first burst of light that dispels the darkness. The eye accustomed to darkness can hardly bear at first the broad daylight. It is by usage the eye learns to see, and it is the same in passing from any situation to its opposite.

As we have not at one instant renounced all our errors, we cannot at one stroke acquire knowledge of all our rights. France has had the honor of adding to the word *Liberty* that of *Equality;* and this word signifies essentially a principle that admits of no gradation in the things to which it applies. But equality is often misunderstood, often misapplied, and often violated.

Liberty and *Property* are words expressing all those of our possessions which are not of an intellectual nature. There are two kinds of property. Firstly, natural property, or that which comes to us from the Creator of the universe—such as the earth, air, water. Secondly, artificial or acquired property—the invention of men.

In the latter, equality is impossible; for to distribute it equally it would be necessary that all should have contributed in the same proportion, which can never be the case; and this being the case, every individual would hold on to his own property, as his right share. Equality of natural property is the subject of this little essay. Every individual in the world is born therein with legitimate claims on a certain kind of property, or its equivalent.

The right of voting for persons charged with the execution of the laws that govern society is inherent in the word liberty, and constitutes the equality of personal rights. But even if that right (of voting) were inherent in property, which I deny, the right of suffrage would still belong to all equally, because, as I have said, all individuals have legitimate birthrights in a certain species of property.

I have always considered the present Constitution of the French Republic [1] the *best organized system* the human mind has yet produced. But I hope my former colleagues will not be offended if I warn them of an error which has slipped into its principle. Equality of the right of suffrage is not maintained. This right is in it connected with a condition on which it ought not to depend; that is, with a proportion of a certain tax called "direct."

The dignity of suffrage is thus lowered; and, in placing it in the scale with an inferior thing, the enthusiasm that right is capable of inspiring is diminished. It is impossible to find any equivalent counterpoise for the right of suffrage, because it is alone worthy to be its own basis, and cannot thrive as a graft, or an appendage.

Since the Constitution was established we have seen two conspiracies stranded—that of Babeuf,[2] and that of some obscure personages who decorate themselves with the despicable name of "royalists." The defect in principle of the Constitution was the origin of Babeuf's conspiracy.

[1] Paine is referring to the Constitution of 1793. The clause Paine objected to granted citizenship to Frenchmen of twenty-one only if they paid a direct land or personal property tax and were enrolled upon their cantonal civic register. All citizens might vote in the primary or cantonal assemblies for electors. To be an elector, one had to be proprietor, usufructuary, or occupant of a habitation producing an income ranging from one hundred or two hundred days of labor.—*Editor.*

[2] Babeuf developed one of the earliest theories of communism. He headed the Secret Directory of Public Safety which organized the insurrection in May, 1796. Among the demands the Secret Directory raised at the time were: the abolition of the right of inheritance; the confiscation of the properties of those persons who neglected to cultivate their lands and of individuals who lived without working, and the establishment of public stores in each commune. The insurrection was crushed and Babeuf died on the guillotine on May 28, 1797.

It is significant to note that Paine supported the communistic aspects of Babeuf's theories, and that, although he decried the violent aspects of the Babeuf insurrection, he considered it as being correctly aimed at the removal of social inequalities in property.

For an excellent analysis of the Babeuf insurrection as well as the theories of Babouvism, see Samuel Bernstein, "Babeuf and Babouvism," *Science and Society,* Vol. II, pp. 29–57; 166–194.—*Editor.*

He availed himself of the resentment caused by this flaw, and instead of seeking a remedy by legitimate and constitutional means, or proposing some measure useful to society, the conspirators did their best to renew disorder and confusion, and constituted themselves personally into a Directory, which is formally destructive of election and representation. They were, in fine, extravagant enough to suppose that society, occupied with its domestic affairs, would blindly yield to them a directorship usurped by violence.

The conspiracy of Babeuf was followed in a few months by that of the royalists, who foolishly flattered themselves with the notion of doing great things by feeble or foul means. They counted on all the discontented, from whatever cause, and tried to rouse, in their turn, the class of people who had been following the others. But these new chiefs acted as if they thought society had nothing more at heart than to maintain courtiers, pensioners, and all their train, under the contemptible title of royalty. My little essay will disabuse them, by showing that society is aiming at a very different end—maintaining itself.

We all know or should know, that the time during which a revolution is proceeding is not the time when its resulting advantages can be enjoyed. But had Babeuf and his accomplices taken into consideration the condition of France under this Constitution, and compared it with what it was under the tragical revolutionary government, and during the execrable Reign of Terror, the rapidity of the alteration must have appeared to them very striking and astonishing. Famine has been replaced by abundance, and by the well-founded hope of a near and increasing prosperity.

As for the defect in the Constitution, I am fully convinced that it will be rectified constitutionally, and that this step is indispensable; for so long as it continues it will inspire the hopes and furnish the means of conspirators; and for the rest, it is regrettable that a Constitution so wisely organized should err so much in its principle. This fault exposes it to other dangers which will make themselves felt.

Intriguing candidates will go about among those who have not the means to pay the direct tax and pay it for them, on condition of receiving their votes. Let us maintain inviolably equality in the sacred right of suffrage: public security can never have a basis more solid. *Salut et Fraternité.*

Your former colleague,
THOMAS PAINE.

AUTHOR'S ENGLISH PREFACE

THE following little piece was written in the winter of 1795 and '96; and, as I had not determined whether to publish it during the present war, or to wait till the commencement of a peace, it has lain by me, without alteration or addition, from the time it was written.

What has determined me to publish it now is a sermon preached by Watson, Bishop of Llandaff. Some of my readers will recollect, that this Bishop wrote a book entitled "An Apology for the Bible," in answer to my second part of "The Age of Reason." I procured a copy of his book, and he may depend upon hearing from me on that subject.

At the end of the Bishop's book is a list of the works he has written. Among which is the sermon alluded to; it is entitled: "The Wisdom and Goodness of God, in having made both Rich and Poor; with an Appendix, containing Reflections on the Present State of England and France."

The error contained in this sermon determined me to publish my "Agrarian Justice." It is wrong to say God made *rich* and *poor;* He made only *male* and *female;* and He gave them the earth for their inheritance. . . .[3]

Instead of preaching to encourage one part of mankind in insolence . . . it would be better that priests employed their time to render the general condition of man less miserable than it is. Practical religion consists in doing good: and the only way of serving God is that of endeavoring to make His creation happy. All preaching that has not this for its object is nonsense and hypocrisy.

THOMAS PAINE.

AGRARIAN JUSTICE

TO PRESERVE the benefits of what is called civilized life, and to remedy at the same time the evil which it has produced, ought to be considered as one of the first objects of reformed legislation.

Whether that state that is proudly, perhaps erroneously, called civilization, has most promoted or most injured the general happiness of man,

[3] The omissions are noted in the London Edition of 1797, pp. V–VI.—*Editor.*

is a question that may be strongly contested. On one side, the spectator is dazzled by splendid appearances; on the other, he is shocked by extremes of wretchedness; both of which it has erected. The most affluent and the most miserable of the human race are to be found in the countries that are called civilized.

To understand what the state of society ought to be, it is necessary to have some idea of the natural and primitive state of man; such as it is at this day among the Indians of North America. There is not, in that' state, any of those spectacles of human misery which poverty and want present to our eyes in all the towns and streets in Europe.

Poverty, therefore, is a thing created by that which is called civilized life. It exists not in the natural state. On the other hand, the natural state is without those advantages which flow from agriculture, arts, science and manufactures.

The life of an Indian is a continual holiday, compared with the poor of Europe; and, on the other hand it appears to be abject when compared to the rich. Civilization, therefore, or that which is so called, has operated two ways: to make one part of society more affluent, and the other more wretched, than would have been the lot of either in a natural state.

It is always possible to go from the natural to the civilized state, but it is never possible to go from the civilized to the natural state. The reason is that man in a natural state, subsisting by hunting, requires ten times the quantity of land to range over to procure himself sustenance, than would support him in a civilized state, where the earth is cultivated.

When, therefore, a country becomes populous by the additional aids of cultivation, art and science, there is a necessity of preserving things in that state; because without it there cannot be sustenance for more, perhaps, than a tenth part of its inhabitants. The thing, therefore, now to be done is to remedy the evils and preserve the benefits that have arisen to society by passing from the natural to that which is called the civilized state.

In taking the matter upon this ground, the first principle of civilization ought to have been, and ought still to be, that the condition of every person born into the world, after a state of civilization commences, ought not to be worse than if he had been born before that period.

But the fact is that the condition of millions, in every country in Europe, is far worse than if they had been born before civilization began, or had been born among the Indians of North America at the present day. I will show how this fact has happened.

It is a position not to be controverted that the earth, in its natural, uncultivated state was, and ever would have continued to be, *the common property of the human race*. In that state every man would have been born to property. He would have been a joint life proprietor with the rest in the property of the soil, and in all its natural productions, vegetable and animal.

But the earth in its natural state, as before said, is capable of supporting but a small number of inhabitants compared with what it is capable of doing in a cultivated state. And as it is impossible to separate the improvement made by cultivation from the earth itself, upon which that improvement is made, the idea of landed property arose from that inseparable connection; but it is nevertheless true, that it is the value of the improvement, only, and not the earth itself, that is individual property.

Every proprietor, therefore, of cultivated lands, owes to the community a *ground-rent* (for I know of no better term to express the idea) for the land which he holds; and it is from this ground-rent that the fund proposed in this plan is to issue.

It is deducible, as well from the nature of the thing as from all the histories transmitted to us, that the idea of landed property commenced with cultivation, and that there was no such thing as landed property before that time. It could not exist in the first state of man, that of hunters. It did not exist in the second state, that of shepherds: neither Abraham, Isaac, Jacob, nor Job, so far as the history of the Bible may be credited in probable things, were owners of land.

Their property consisted, as is always enumerated in flocks and herds, and they traveled with them from place to place. The frequent contentions at that time about the use of a well in the dry country of Arabia, where those people lived, also show that there was no landed property. It was not admitted that land could be claimed as property.

There could be no such thing as landed property originally. Man did not make the earth, and, though he had a natural right to *occupy* it, he had no right to *locate as his property* in perpetuity any part of it; neither did the Creator of the earth open a land-office, from whence the first title-deeds should issue. Whence then, arose the idea of landed property? I answer as before, that when cultivation began the idea of landed property began with it, from the impossibility of separating the improvement made by cultivation from the earth itself, upon which that improvement was made.

The value of the improvement so far exceeded the value of the natural earth, at that time, as to absorb it; till, in the end, the common right of all became confounded into the cultivated right of the individual. But there are, nevertheless, distinct species of rights, and will continue to be, so long as the earth endures.

It is only by tracing things to their origin that we can gain rightful ideas of them, and it is by gaining such ideas that we discover the boundary that divides right from wrong, and teaches every man to know his own. I have entitled this tract "Agrarian Justice" to distinguish it from "Agrarian Law."

Nothing could be more unjust than agrarian law in a country improved by cultivation; for though every man, as an inhabitant of the earth, is a joint proprietor of it in its natural state, it does not follow that he is a joint proprietor of cultivated earth. The additional value made by cultivation, after the system was admitted, became the property of those who did it, or who inherited it from them, or who purchased it. It had originally no owner. While, therefore, I advocate the right, and interest myself in the hard case of all those who have been thrown out of their natural inheritance by the introduction of the system of landed property, I equally defend the right of the possessor to the part which is his.

Cultivation is at least one of the greatest natural improvements ever made by human invention. It has given to created earth a tenfold value. But the landed monopoly that began with it has produced the greatest evil. It has dispossessed more than half the inhabitants of every nation of their natural inheritance, without providing for them, as ought to have been done, an indemnification for that loss, and has thereby created a species of poverty and wretchedness that did not exist before.

In advocating the case of the persons thus dispossessed, it is a right, and not a charity, that I am pleading for. But it is that kind of right which, being neglected at first, could not be brought forward afterwards till heaven had opened the way by a revolution in the system of government. Let us then do honor to revolutions by justice, and give currency to their principles by blessings.

Having thus in a few words, opened the merits of the case, I shall now proceed to the plan I have to propose, which is,

To create a national fund, out of which there shall be paid to every person, when arrived at the age of twenty-one years, the sum of fifteen pounds sterling, as a compensation in part, for the loss of his or her natural inheritance, by the introduction of the system of landed property:

And also, the sum of ten pounds per annum, during life, to every person now living, of the age of fifty years, and to all others as they shall arrive at that age.

MEANS BY WHICH THE FUND IS TO BE CREATED

I have already established the principle, namely, that the earth, in its natural uncultivated state was, and ever would have continued to be, the *common property of the human race;* that in that state, every person would have been born to property; and that the system of landed property, by its inseparable connection with cultivation, and with what is called civilized life, has absorbed the property of all those whom it dispossessed, without providing, as ought to have been done, an indemnification for that loss.

The fault, however, is not in the present possessors. No complaint is intended, or ought to be alleged against them, unless they adopt the crime by opposing justice. The fault is in the system, and it has stolen imperceptibly upon the world, aided afterwards by the agrarian law of the sword. But the fault can be made to reform itself by successive generations; and without diminishing or deranging the property of any of the present possessors, the operation of the fund can yet commence, and be in full activity, the first year of its establishment, or soon after, as I shall show.

It is proposed that the payments, as already stated, be made to every person, rich or poor. It is best to make it so, to prevent invidious distinctions. It is also right it should be so, because it is in lieu of the natural inheritance, which, as a right, belongs to every man, over and above the property he may have created, or inherited from those who did. Such persons as do not choose to receive it can throw it into the common fund.

Taking it then for granted that no person ought to be in a worse condition when born under what is called a state of civilization, than he would have been had he been born in a state of nature, and that civilization ought to have made, and ought still to make, provision for that purpose, it can only be done by subtracting from property a portion equal in value to the natural inheritance it has absorbed.

Various methods may be proposed for this purpose, but that which appears to be the best (not only because it will operate without deranging any present possessors, or without interfering with the collection of taxes or *emprunts* necessary for the purposes of government and the Revolution, but because it will be the least troublesome and the most effectual, and also because the subtraction will be made at a time that best admits it) is at the moment that property is passing by the death of one person to the possession of another. In this case, the bequeather gives nothing: the receiver pays nothing. The only matter to him is that the monopoly of natural inheritance, to which there never was a right, begins to cease in his person. A generous man would not wish it to continue, and a just man will rejoice to see it abolished.

My state of health prevents my making sufficient inquiries with respect to the doctrine of probabilities, whereon to found calculations with such degrees of certainty as they are capable of. What, therefore, I offer on this head is more the result of observation and reflection than of received information; but I believe it will be found to agree sufficiently with fact. In the first place, taking twenty-one years as the epoch of maturity, all the property of a nation, real and personal, is always in the possession of persons above that age. It is then necessary to know, as a datum of calculation, the average of years which persons above that age will live. I take this average to be about thirty years, for though many persons will live forty, fifty, or sixty years, after the age of twenty-one years, others will die much sooner, and some in every year of that time.

Taking, then, thirty years as the average of time, it will give, without any material variation one way or other, the average of time in which the whole property or capital of a nation, or a sum equal thereto, will have passed through one entire revolution in descent, that is, will have gone by deaths to new possessors; for though, in many instances, some parts of this capital will remain forty, fifty, or sixty years in the possession of one person, other parts will have revolved two or three times before those thirty years expire, which will bring it to that average; for were one-half the capital of a nation to revolve twice in thirty years, it would produce the same fund as if the whole revolved once.

Taking, then, thirty years as the average of time in which the whole capital of a nation, or a sum equal thereto, will revolve once, the thirtieth part thereof will be the sum that will revolve every year, that is, will go by deaths to new possessors; and this last sum being thus known, and the ratio per cent to be subtracted from it determined, it will give the annual amount or income of the proposed fund, to be applied as already mentioned.

In looking over the discourse of the English Minister, Pitt, in his opening of what is called in England the budget (the scheme of finance for the year 1796), I find an estimate of the national capital of that country. As this estimate of a national capital is prepared ready to my hand, I take it as a datum to act upon. When a calculation is made upon the known capital of any nation, combined with its population, it will serve as a scale for any other nation, in proportion as its capital and population be more or less.

I am the more disposed to take this estimate of Mr. Pitt, for the purpose of showing to that minister, upon his own calculation, how much better money may be employed than in wasting it, as he has done, on the wild project of setting up Bourbon kings. What, in the name of heaven, are Bourbon kings to the people of England? It is better that the people have bread.

Mr. Pitt states the national capital of England, real and personal, to be one thousand three hundred millions sterling, which is about one-fourth part of the national capital of France, including Belgia. The event of the last harvest in each country proves that the soil of France is more productive than that of England, and that it can better support twenty-four or twenty-five millions of inhabitants than that of England can seven or seven and a half millions.

The thirtieth part of this capital of £1,300,000,000 is £43,333,333 which is the part that will revolve every year by deaths in that country to new possessors; and the sum that will annually revolve in France in the proportion of four to one, will be about one hundred and seventy-three millions sterling. From this sum of £43,333,333 annually revolving, is to be subtracted the value of the natural inheritance absorbed in it, which, perhaps, in fair justice, cannot be taken at less, and ought not to be taken for more, than a tenth part.

It will always happen that of the property thus revolving by deaths every year a part will descend in a direct line to sons and daughters, and the other part collaterally, and the proportion will be found to be about three to one; that is, about thirty millions of the above sum will descend to direct heirs, and the remaining sum of £13,333,333 to more distant relations, and in part to strangers.

Considering, then, that man is always related to society, that relationship will become comparatively greater in proportion as the next of kin is more distant; it is therefore consistent with civilization to say that where there are no direct heirs society shall be heir to a part over and above the tenth part *due* to society.

If this additional part be from five to ten or twelve per cent, in proportion as the next of kin be nearer or more remote, so as to average with the escheats that may fall, which ought always to go to society and not to the government (an addition of ten per cent more), the produce from the annual sum of £43,333,333 will be:

From £30,000,000 at ten per cent £3,000,000

From £13,333,333 at ten per cent with the addition of ⎫
ten per cent more. ⎭ 2,666,666

————————

£43,333,333   £5,666,666

Having thus arrived at the annual amount of the proposed fund, I come, in the next place, to speak of the population proportioned to this fund and to compare it with the uses to which the fund is to be applied.

The population (I mean that of England) does not exceed seven millions and a half, and the number of persons above the age of fifty will in that case be about four hundred thousand. There would not, however, be more than that number that would accept the proposed ten pounds sterling per annum, though they would be entitled to it. I have no idea it would be accepted by many persons who had a yearly income of two or three hundred pounds sterling. But as we often see instances of rich people falling into sudden poverty, even at the age of sixty, they would always have the right of drawing all the arrears due to them. Four millions, therefore, of the above annual sum of £5,666,666 will be required for four hundred thousand aged persons, at ten pounds sterling each.

I come now to speak of the persons annually arriving at twenty-one years of age. If all the persons who died were above the age of twenty-one years, the number of persons annually arriving at that age must be equal to the annual number of deaths, to keep the population stationary. But the greater part die under the age of twenty-one, and therefore the number of persons annually arriving at twenty-one will be less than half the number of deaths.

The whole number of deaths upon a population of seven millions and an half will be about 220,000 annually. The number arriving at twenty-one years of age will be about 100,000. The whole number of these will not receive the proposed fifteen pounds, for the reasons already mentioned, though, as in the former case, they would be entitled to it. Admitting then that a tenth part declined receiving it, the amount would stand thus:

Fund annually £5,666,666
To 400,000 aged persons at £10 each £4,000,000
To 90,000 persons of 21 yrs., £15 ster. each 1,350,000

5,350,000

Remains £ 316,666

There are, in every country, a number of blind and lame persons totally incapable of earning a livelihood. But as it will always happen that the greater number of blind persons will be among those who are above the age of fifty years, they will be provided for in that class. The remaining sum of £316,666 will provide for the lame and blind under that age, at the same rate of £10 annually for each person.

Having now gone through all the necessary calculations, and stated the particulars of the plan, I shall conclude with some observations.[4]

It is not charity but a right, not bounty but justice, that I am pleading for. The present state of civilization is as odious as it is unjust. It is absolutely the opposite of what it should be, and it is necessary that a revolution should be made in it. The contrast of affluence and wretchedness continually meeting and offending the eye, is like dead and living bodies chained together. Though I care as little about riches as any man, I am a friend to riches because they are capable of good.

I care not how affluent some may be, provided that none be miserable in consequence of it. But it is impossible to enjoy affluence with the felicity it is capable of being enjoyed, while so much misery is mingled in the scene. The sight of the misery, and the unpleasant sensations it suggests, which, though they may be suffocated cannot be extinguished, are a greater drawback upon the felicity of affluence than the proposed ten per cent upon property is worth. He that would not give the one to get rid of the other has no charity, even for himself.

There are, in every country, some magnificent charities established by individuals. It is, however, but little that any individual can do, when the whole extent of the misery to be relieved is considered. He may satisfy his conscience, but not his heart. He may give all that he has, and

[4] The following two sentences were omitted from the first English edition of 1797.— Editor.

that all will relieve but little. It is only by organizing civilization upon such principles as to act like a system of pulleys, that the whole weight of misery can be removed.

The plan here proposed will reach the whole. It will immediately relieve and take out of view three classes of wretchedness—the blind, the lame, and the aged poor; and it will furnish the rising generation with means to prevent their becoming poor; and it will do this without deranging or interfering with any national measures.

To show that this will be the case, it is sufficient to observe that the operation and effect of the plan will, in all cases, be the same as if every individual were *voluntarily* to make his will and dispose of his property in the manner here proposed.

But it is justice, and not charity, that is the principle of the plan. In all great cases it is necessary to have a principle more universally active than charity; and, with respect to justice, it ought not to be left to the choice of detached individuals whether they will do justice or not. Considering, then, the plan on the ground of justice, it ought to be the act of the whole growing spontaneously out of the principles of the revolution, and the reputation of it ought to be national and not individual.

A plan upon this principle would benefit the revolution by the energy that springs from the consciousness of justice. It would multiply also the national resources; for property, like vegetation, increases by offsets. When a young couple begin the world, the difference is exceedingly great whether they begin with nothing or with fifteen pounds apiece. With this aid they could buy a cow, and implements to cultivate a few acres of land; and instead of becoming burdens upon society, which is always the case where children are produced faster than they can be fed, would be put in the way of becoming useful and profitable citizens. The national domains also would sell the better if pecuniary aids were provided to cultivate them in small lots.

It is the practise of what has unjustly obtained the name of civilization (and the practise merits not to be called either charity or policy) to make some provision for persons becoming poor and wretched only at the time they become so. Would it not, even as a matter of economy, be far better to adopt means to prevent their becoming poor? This can best be done by making every person when arrived at the age of twenty-one years an inheritor of something to begin with.

The rugged face of society, checkered with the extremes of affluence and want, proves that some extraordinary violence has been committed upon it, and calls on justice for redress. The great mass of the poor in all countries are become an hereditary race, and it is next to impossible for them to get out of that state of themselves. It ought also to be observed that this mass increases in all countries that are called civilized. More persons fall annually into it than get out of it.

Though in a plan of which justice and humanity are the foundation-principles, interest ought not to be admitted into the calculation, yet it is always of advantage to the establishment of any plan to show that it is beneficial as a matter of interest. The success of any proposed plan submitted to public consideration must finally depend on the numbers interested in supporting it, united with the justice of its principles.

The plan here proposed will benefit all, without injuring any. It will consolidate the interest of the republic with that of the individual. To the numerous class dispossessed of their natural inheritance by the system of landed property it will be an act of national justice. To persons dying possessed of moderate fortunes it will operate as a tontine to their children, more beneficial than the sum of money paid into the fund: and it will give to the accumulation of riches a degree of security that none of the old governments of Europe, now tottering on their foundations, can give.

I do not suppose that more than one family in ten, in any of the countries of Europe, has, when the head of the family dies, a clear property left of five hundred pounds sterling. To all such the plan is advantageous. That property would pay fifty pounds into the fund, and if there were only two children under age they would receive fifteen pounds each (thirty pounds), on coming of age, and be entitled to ten pounds a year after fifty.

It is from the overgrown acquisition of property that the fund will support itself; and I know that the possessors of such property in England, though they would eventually be benefited by the protection of nine-tenths of it, will exclaim against the plan. But without entering into any inquiry how they came by that property, let them recollect that they have been the advocates of this war, and that Mr. Pitt has already laid on more new taxes to be raised annually upon the people of England, and that for supporting the despotism of Austria and the Bourbons against the liberties of France, than would pay annually all the sums proposed in this plan.

I have made the calculations stated in this plan, upon what is called personal, as well as upon landed property. The reason for making it upon land is already explained; and the reason for taking personal property into the calculation is equally well founded though on a different principle. Land, as before said, is the free gift of the Creator in common to the human race. Personal property is the *effect of society;* and it is as impossible for an individual to acquire personal property without the aid of society, as it is for him to make land originally.

Separate an individual from society, and give him an island or a continent to possess, and he cannot acquire personal property. He cannot be rich. So inseparably are the means connected with the end, in all cases, that where the former do not exist the latter cannot be obtained. All accumulation, therefore, of personal property, beyond what a man's own hands produce, is derived to him by living in society; and he owes on every principle of justice, of gratitude, and of civilization, a part of that accumulation back again to society from whence the whole came.

This is putting the matter on a general principle, and perhaps it is best to do so; for if we examine the case minutely it will be found that the accumulation of personal property is, in many instances, the effect of paying too little for the labor that produced it; the consequence of which is that the working hand perishes in old age, and the employer abounds in affluence.

It is, perhaps, impossible to proportion exactly the price of labor to the profits it produces; and it will also be said, as an apology for the injustice, that were a workman to receive an increase of wages daily he would not save it against old age, nor be much better for it in the interim. Make, then, society the treasurer to guard it for him in a common fund; for it is no reason that, because he might not make a good use of it for himself, another should take it.

The state of civilization that has prevailed throughout Europe, is as unjust in its principle, as it is horrid in its effects; and it is the consciousness of this, and the apprehension that such a state cannot continue when once investigation begins in any country, that makes the possessors of property dread every idea of a revolution. It is the hazard and not the principle of revolutions that retards their progress. This being the case, it is necessary as well for the protection of property as for the sake of justice and humanity, to form a system that, while it preserves one part of society from wretchedness, shall secure the other from depredation.

The superstitious awe, the enslaving reverence, that formerly surrounded affluence, is passing away in all countries, and leaving the possessor of property to the convulsion of accidents. When wealth and splendor, instead of fascinating the multitude, excite emotions of disgust; when, instead of drawing forth admiration, it is beheld as an insult upon wretchedness; when the ostentatious appearance it makes serves to call the right of it in question, the case of property becomes critical, and it is only in a system of justice that the possessor can contemplate security.

To remove the danger, it is necessary to remove the antipathies, and this can only be done by making property productive of a national blessing, extending to every individual. When the riches of one man above another shall increase the national fund in the same proportion; when it shall be seen that the prosperity of that fund depends on the prosperity of individuals; when the more riches a man acquires, the better it shall be for the general mass; it is then that antipathies will cease, and property be placed on the permanent basis of national interest and protection.

I have no property in France to become subject to the plan I propose. What I have, which is not much, is in the United States of America.[5] But I will pay one hundred pounds sterling toward this fund in France, the instant it shall be established; and I will pay the same sum in England, whenever a similar establishment shall take place in that country.

A revolution in the state of civilization is the necessary companion of revolutions in the system of government. If a revolution in any country be from bad to good, or from good to bad, the state of what is called civilization in that country, must be made conformable thereto, to give that revolution effect.

Despotic government supports itself by abject civilization, in which debasement of the human mind, and wretchedness in the mass of the people, are the chief criterions. Such governments consider man merely as an animal; that the exercise of intellectual faculty is not his privilege; *that he has nothing to do with the laws but to obey them;*[6] and they politically depend more upon breaking the spirit of the people by poverty, than they fear enraging it by desperation.

It is a revolution in the state of civilization that will give perfection to the Revolution of France. Already the conviction that government by representation is the true system of government is spreading itself fast in the world. The reasonableness of it can be seen by all. The justness of

[5] Late in 1802, Paine wrote that his property in America was "worth six thousands pounds sterling."—*Editor.*

[6] An expression used by Bishop Horsley in the Parliament of England.—*Author.*

it makes itself felt even by its opposers. But when a system of civilization, growing out of that system of government, shall be so organized that not a man or woman born in the Republic but shall inherit some means of beginning the world, and see before them the certainty of escaping the miseries that under other governments accompany old age, the Revolution of France will have an advocate and an ally in the heart of all nations.

An army of principles will penetrate where an army of soldiers cannot; it will succeed where diplomatic management would fail: it is neither the Rhine, the Channel, nor the ocean that can arrest its progress: it will march on the horizon of the world, and it will conquer.

Means for Carrying the Proposed Plan Into Execution, and to Render It at the Same Time Conducive to the Public Interest

I. Each canton shall elect in its primary assemblies, three persons, as commissioners for that canton, who shall take cognizance, and keep a register of all matters happening in that canton, conformable to the charter that shall be established by law for carrying this plan into execution.

II. The law shall fix the manner in which the property of deceased persons shall be ascertained.

III. When the amount of the property of any deceased persons shall be ascertained, the principal heir to that property, or the eldest of the co-heirs, if of lawful age, or if under age, the person authorized by the will of the deceased to represent him or them, shall give bond to the commissioners of the canton to pay the said tenth part thereof in four equal quarterly payments, within the space of one year or sooner, at the choice of the payers. One-half of the whole property shall remain as a security until the bond be paid off.

IV. The bond shall be registered in the office of the commissioners of the canton, and the original bonds shall be deposited in the national bank at Paris. The bank shall publish every quarter of a year the amount of the bonds in its possession, and also the bonds that shall have been paid off, or what parts thereof, since the last quarterly publication.

V. The national bank shall issue bank notes upon the security of the bonds in its possession. The notes so issued, shall be applied to pay the pensions of aged persons, and the compensations to persons arriving at twenty-one years of age. It is both reasonable and generous to suppose, that persons not under immediate necessity, will suspend their right of drawing on the fund, until it acquire, as it will do, a greater degree of ability. In this case, it is proposed, that an honorary register be kept, in each canton, of the names of the persons thus suspending that right, at least during the present war.

VI. As the inheritors of property must always take up their bonds in four quarterly payments, or sooner if they choose, there will always be *numéraire* [cash] arriving at the bank after the expiration of the first quarter, to exchange for the bank notes that shall be brought in.

VII. The bank notes being thus put in circulation, upon the best of all possible security, that of actual property, to more than four times the amount of the bonds upon which the notes are issued, and with *numéraire* continually arriving at the bank to exchange or pay them off whenever they shall be presented for that purpose, they will acquire a permanent value in all parts of the Republic. They can therefore be received in payment of taxes, or *emprunts* equal to *numéraire,* because the Government can always receive *numéraire* for them at the bank.

VIII. It will be necessary that the payments of the ten per cent be made in *numéraire* for the first year from the establishment of the plan. But after the expiration of the first year, the inheritors of property may pay ten per cent either in bank notes issued upon the fund, or in *numéraire*.

If the payments be in *numéraire,* it will lie as a deposit at the bank, to be exchanged for a quantity of notes equal to that amount; and if in notes issued upon the fund, it will cause a demand upon the fund equal thereto; and thus the operation of the plan will create means to carry itself into execution.

THOMAS PAINE.

INDEX